MW01221853

Netscape
Communicator 4
Professional Edition
BOOK

FOR WINDOWS

Netscape
Communicator 4
Professional Edition
BOOK

An imprint of
Ventana Communications Group

The Definitive Guide to Net-based
Business Communications

PHIL JAMES
TARA CALISHAIN

VENTANA

Official Netscape Communicator 4 Professional Edition Book
Copyright © 1997 by Phil James and Tara Calishain

Library of Congress Cataloging-in-Publication Data

James, Phil, and Tara Calishain
    Official Netscape Communicator 4 Professional Edition Book/Phil James and Tara Calishain
    ISBN 1-56604-739-0
Library of Congress Catalog Card Number: 97-060917

First Edition 9 8 7 6 5 4 3 2 1

Printed in the United States of America

Published and distributed to the trade by Ventana Communications Group
P.O. Box 13964, Research Triangle Park, NC 27709-3964
919.544.9404
FAX 919.544.9472
http://www.vmedia.com

Ventana Communications Group is a division of International Thomson Publishing.

Netscape Publishing Relations
Suzanne C. Anthony
Netscape Communications Corporation
501 E. Middlefield Rd.
Mountain View, CA 94043
http://home.netscape.com

Limits of Liability & Disclaimer of Warranty
The authors and publisher of this book have used their best efforts in preparing the book and the programs contained in it. These efforts include the development, research, and testing of the theories and programs to determine their effectiveness. The authors and publisher make no warranty of any kind, expressed or implied, with regard to these programs or the documentation contained in this book.

The authors and publisher shall not be liable in the event of incidental or consequential damages in connection with, or arising out of, the furnishing, performance or use of the programs, associated instructions and/or claims of productivity gains.

Trademarks
Trademarked names appear throughout this book and on the accompanying compact disk, if applicable. Rather than list the names and entities that own the trademarks or insert a trademark symbol with each mention of the trademarked name, the publisher states that it is using the names only for editorial purposes and to the benefit of the trademark owner with no intention of infringing upon that trademark.

Netscape and Netscape Navigator are registered trademarks of Netscape Communications Corporation in the United States and other countries. Netscape's logos and Netscape product and service names are also trademarks of Netscape Communications Corporation, which may be registered in other countries.

About the Authors

Phil James is a software design consultant, performance artist, part-time musician, and author of the best-selling *Official Netscape Navigator Books*, which have sold over 350,000 copies worldwide and have been translated into more than 10 languages. As a literary writer, his stories has appeared in a variety of print and electronic zines.

Tara Calishain owns CopperSky Writing and Research. An Internaut since 1991, she is the author of Ventana's *Official Netscape Guide to Internet Research* and *Official Netscape Messenger & Collabra Book*. She also writes for a variety of computer publications, including *boot* and cinet's *Gamecenter*.

Acknowledgments

I want to thank Tara Calishain, first of all, who added the Professional Edition chapters to this book. Tara proved to be an excellent co-author, and I am grateful to her for all the hard work.

A thank you to the people at Netscape who provided me the early information I needed, especially Edith Gong, Suzanne Anthony, and Sandy Cold Shapero.

I also want to thank Richard Jessup, who served as Technical Editor on the original version of this book, and Aaron Huslage, who tech edited the Professional Edition version.

Of course, it's the staff at Ventana who really make projects like this happen. I'd like to thank John Cotterman, JJ Hohn, Kristin Miller, Martin Minner, Marion Laird, Becky Steele, Amy Moyers, Patrick Berry, Lance Kozlowski, Caroline McKenzie, Jaimie Livingston, Christine Cleveland, and especially Rachel Anderson, for all their hard work on this book.

Lastly, thanks to my wife and kids, who still put up with me through the deadlines.

—P.J.

I want to express my sincere appreciation to Phil James, with whom it's been a blast to work. Also, many thanks to Rachel Anderson, JJ Hohn, Martin Minner, Kristin Miller, Becky Steele, and the other great folks at Ventana.

—T.C.

Dedication

This book is dedicated to my extended family:
    Irene (MomJ)
    Andrea (Artist)
    Sam (Computer Whiz)
Thanks for letting me be a part of your lives.

—T.C.

Contents

XXIIOFFICIAL NETSCAPE COMMUNICATOR 4 PROFESSIONAL EDITION BOOK

Foreword

While Netscape is without question one of the most visible software companies, we are also working hard to make our client-end products increasingly *invisible*. We don't believe software should dictate a user's experience, so we spend much of our time creating tools that enable content providers to present media-rich information in their own creative, innovative ways. Netscape software works quietly—but powerfully—behind the scenes, providing the needed foundation. We recognize that the emphasis in desktop computing has shifted from arcane procedures to content itself, and Netscape has taken a leadership role in reinforcing this shift.

Nowhere is this more apparent than in Netscape Communicator 4. Communicator gives content providers more flexibility than ever before in shaping and presenting information. Dynamic HTML and enhanced Java and JavaScript enable interactive user interfaces, limited only by a designer's imagination. And of course you can extend Communicator's multimedia power with a huge variety of plug-ins. Clearly, Communicator stretches way beyond the world of text links and Back and Forward buttons.

One of the most exciting components of Communicator is *Netcaster*. Netcaster takes this new content-based model a step further by letting you subscribe to information channels that may be updated at regular intervals. And because channel information is stored locally on your system rather than on a distant server, it may include large multimedia files that you access instantaneously. This feature has already inspired content providers to create forward-looking user interfaces that we wouldn't have dreamed of a few years ago.

But Communicator is not just about innovative approaches to presenting information—it's also about integrating online tasks. With Communicator, your computer becomes a communications center. Its components work together to provide a single seamless approach to communicating with your coworkers or with the world. You use the same tools to create HTML e-mail as you use to create a full-blown Web page; the same Address Book lets you initiate a conference call or fire off a quick message; and you no longer need separate applications to surf the Web and receive Web channels. Thanks to this integration, Communicator is much more than the sum of its parts.

Of course anyone in business knows that growth entails risk, and now that intranets and the Internet have become household words, the security of online communications is an important consideration. In its earlier Navigator products, Netscape took the lead in providing world-class SSL security. Now Communicator adds unprecedented *flexibility* in dealing with security issues. Object signing lets you know what entity is sending you a Java applet or JavaScript code; you can then choose to allow or disallow any actions, such as disk access, that may compromise the security of your system. S/MIME e-mail enables digitally-signed messages that assure you of the identity of your correspondent. And a new Security Advisor lets you tailor a broad range of security settings for your exact needs. Security has become as configurable as the rest of Communicator.

The *Official Netscape Communicator 4 Professional Edition Book* provides a broad, step-by-step introduction to the world's most innovative communications and collaboration product. As we enter a new era in desktop computing—an era in which *information* takes precedence over *procedure*—Communicator insures that you stay way ahead of the curve.

Marc Andreessen
Netscape Communications Corporation

Introduction

Each new release includes some new bells and whistles and perhaps even a change or two that really matters. But what *doesn't* change is your relation to the program. Familiar procedures result in familiar output.

Other applications, especially in the area of communications, evolve more quickly because they must keep pace with technological and social changes in the world at large. For example, as consumers started to shop electronically from home, software vendors had to come up with flexible new security protocols and schemes to protect online transactions.

Then there are programs that leap-frog themselves dramatically with each new version. Netscape Navigator was like that, jumping from a graphical Web browser to an integrated set of communications tools in just one upgrade. Now its successor—Netscape Communicator 4—moves us even further toward a new model of desktop computing.

In the new model I'm talking about, *information* takes precedence over *procedures*. It's really a very simple idea. Information is what you're interested in, so why not make it the program's central focus? Communicator supports a wealth of new capabilities that let content providers embed highly interactive elements or even entire user interfaces right into the information they send you. The information itself becomes your workspace, supported by simple software procedures and flexible configuration options.

What Is Communicator 4 Professional?

Communicator is more than the successor to Navigator 3. In fact, Navigator 4 is just one part of Communicator. Communicator is really a tightly integrated communications suite made up of the following components:

- **Navigator 4**—your window on the Web. Navigator 4 lets you experience and interact with a huge variety of multimedia documents on the Internet or on your office intranet. As you'll learn in this book, Navigator 4 includes many significant advances over previous Navigator versions.

- **Netcaster**—your desktop "channel tuner." With Netcaster you can subscribe to information channels that are updated on a regular basis, providing you with everything from up-to-the-minute stock quotes to weekly movie reviews to the latest paperwork from your HR department. Channels can even automatically update your software. And because channels are stored locally on your machine, you can access the media-rich information they provide instantaneously.

- **Messenger**—your e-mail link to the world. E-mail has rapidly become a commonplace means of getting in touch and staying in touch, and Communicator's Messenger component provides full-featured e-mail support. You can send and receive messages that look just like Web pages, with embedded links, graphics, animations, and even sound. In addition, Messenger supports the S/MIME standard for digitally signed messages, ensuring the security of information you send and receive.

- **Collabra Discussion Groups**—your key to specialized information and collaborative work. Communicator's Discussion Groups component lets you read and respond to messages in the thousands of specialized newsgroups on the Internet, forums for in-depth discussion of everything from astrophysics to zydeco. In addition, you can participate in private discussion groups on your own office intranet, bouncing ideas around with coworkers without leaving your desk.

- **Calendar**—the solution to your scheduling problems. With Netscape Calendar and the Netscape Calendar Server on your intranet, you can make changes to an online agenda, invite other people to meetings, check possible meeting times for conflicts, and even set up online reminders.

- **Composer**—your page creation workshop. With Communicator's Composer component, you can create your own HTML documents quickly and easily, even if you're a beginner. Specialized page templates make it easy, whether you're creating a simple home page for yourself or publicly accessible material promoting your company. A variety of *WYSIWYG* tools help you tailor your page to your exact needs, and you can even extend Composer's power with special Composer plug-ins.

- **Conference**—your Internet phone. Actually, the Conference component is much more than a phone. Yes, it lets you make long distance voice calls using the Internet, but it also lets you chat (type messages back and forth) or transfer files at the same time you talk. Using a unique whiteboard feature you can even share graphical information, marking up or changing each other's ideas, and a collaborative browsing feature lets Conference participants view the same Web sites simultaneously. Not only does Conference save on phone charges, it might save you from having to buy a couple of plane tickets!

- **IBM Host-On-Demand**—your key to accessing mainframe data. Though they're rapidly becoming outdated, many companies continue to use mainframes to house company information. IBM Host-On-Demand is a 3270 emulator that allows you to access mainframe data—from your Web browser!

- **AutoAdmin**—AutoAdmin is more a feature than an application. It allows your network administrator to update your Communicator software and add components from a central spot on the intranet.

But Communicator Professional is more than the sum of its parts. The components are integrated in such a way that you don't need to learn new commands or procedures for each new task. If you know how to use Messenger, you already know how to use the Discussion Groups component, and if you know how to find an e-mail address in the Address Book you already know how to place a Conference call.

Who Can Use This Book

This book is aimed at anyone who is reasonably familiar with some version of Windows and wants to get busy on the Net or on an office intranet. It's also aimed at anyone who's been communicating electronically for a while but wants to upgrade to Netscape Communicator. Here's what you need:

- A 486 or better PC with at least 16MB of RAM and Windows 95, Windows 3.1, or Windows NT installed.

- If you haven't already installed Communicator, about 30MB of space on your hard drive.

- A TCP/IP local area network (intranet) or a way to get on the Internet.

- For home access via an Internet access provider, a modem, preferably one that can run at 28.8 Kbps or greater.

The last two requirements need some explanation. First of all, you can gather from what I said earlier that Internet access is not really necessary in all cases. Thousands of people are using Netscape Communicator to share multimedia information within their own companies. This use relies not on the Internet but on intranets, enterprise-wide networks that a local system administrator sets up.

But let's say you're a home user who wants to get out into the big Internet ocean. Chances are that unless you're a very ambitious and wealthy computer nerd, you don't have a direct connection to the Net. That means you need a modem and an account with an Internet service provider. Neither is hard to get or very expensive any more. Of course, you should get the fastest modem you can afford, preferably one that can run at 28.8 Kbps, but a 14.4 Kbps modem will still do the job.

How This Book Is Organized

Chapter 1, "Your Intranet—How it Works," provides an overview of the technology we're dealing with: where it came from, some of its features, and where it's going. You'll learn what the difference really is between the Internet and the World Wide Web, and you'll learn enough about the technical underpinnings of the Net or your office intranet to understand any other technical discussions in the book.

In **Chapter 2, "Introducing Communicator,"** you will learn how this communications suite fits together. In addition, I will introduce you to all the Communicator-specific terminology you'll need. Once you read this chapter, you'll be ready to work through the step-by-step procedures for Communicator's individual components.

Chapter 3, "Browsing & Beyond," introduces you to the Navigator 4 component and the basics of browsing HTML and multimedia documents. In a few short minutes, you'll be cruising, surfing, or whatever the term is this year.

Web channels and "push" technology have garnered about as much media attention this year as Whitewater, and **Chapter 4, "Netcaster,"** shows you how to become part of an exciting trend. Follow the simple directions in this chapter and in moments you'll know how to subscribe to and configure a variety of information channels.

Electronic mail is one of the most important "meat and potatoes" Internet and intranet applications, and **Chapter 5, "Communication With the Office and the World: Messenger,"** covers it fully. Step-by-step tutorials guide you through all the procedures you need, and in no time you'll be zipping off messages as if you'd been doing it for years.

Chapter 6, "You Are Not Alone: Collabra & Discussion Groups," introduces you to one of the most fascinating services available on the Net or on your intranet. Discussion groups are forums where you can read or post about specialized information; they also let you work collaboratively with teams of coworkers. This chapter shows you how.

Of course the real *fun* of the new information technologies are their multimedia capabilities. **Chapter 7, "Media On the Move: Working With Sound & Video,"** explains how Communicator makes your computer screen look more and more like a TV screen. I show you some of what's available out there, and I walk you through configuring Communicator so that it uses your system optimally in dealing with these new types of information.

Chapter 8, "The Ancestors: FTP, Gopher, Telnet, and 3270 in Communicator," introduces you to four old Internet friends. These Internet services have been around for quite a while, but are still extremely useful tools. You'll learn how to explore file archives and download files via FTP, the standard file transfer protocol on the Net. You'll also learn how to use text-based systems to research highly specialized information.

Chapter 9, "Your Own Page (Using Composer)," covers Communicator's Composer component. This chapter leads you step-by-step through the process of designing and publishing a Web page, whether for your own use or for public access.

In **Chapter 10, "Advanced Communicator 4,"** we go beyond the basics and show you some of the more forward-looking extensions to a forward-looking piece of software. Don't be scared off by the word "advanced:" none of these features are difficult to use. In this chapter we explore VRML, Java, JavaScript, and plug-ins.

Chapter 11, "Netscape Conference," covers one of the most exciting Communicator components. Thanks to Conference you no longer have to watch the clock when making long distance calls—they don't need to cost any more than regular Net access. This chapter includes simple step-by-step procedures for Conference's many other features as well.

Chapter 12, "Netscape Calendar," shows you how you can get your schedule organized online. By using Netscape Calendar you can avoid schedule conflicts, get timely reminders for important meetings—even set up repeat meetings for a specified time period.

Want to do your banking on the Net? Before you do, you might want to read **Chapter 13, "Commerce & Security."** This chapter gives you the lowdown on Communicator's impressive security features, including encryption, digitally signed e-mail, and signed Java and JavaScript. After reading or working through this chapter you may worry less and sleep more soundly.

Chapter 14, "An Overview of Mission Control," introduces you network administrators out there to the wonders of Mission Control, a three application suite that makes customizing and administering Communicator Professional a lot easier. Mission Control is a separate program—it's not officially a part of Communicator Professional. But the program does so much to cover the AutoAdmin features of Professional that I felt compelled to cover them in this book.

Chapter 15, "Mission Control's Configuration Editor," teaches you to create customizations to Communicator Professional that you might not have considered possible. Want to change the meteor-shower animation? Want to add menu items specific to your intranet's resources? You can do it with the Configuration Editor.

In **Chapter 16, "JAR Archive & Install Builder,"** you'll learn how to package components and Communicator upgrades for distribution over your intranet. And with the Installation builder, you can build custom versions of Communicator to distribute to your patrons on the intranet.

And finally, in **Appendix A, "Installing Communicator 4 Professional & Setting Profiles,"** we'll walk through the processes of installing Communicator and creating a user profile.

Navigate!

To further enhance this book, we're providing a place to go for the latest information about this and other Netscape Press titles. Connect via the World Wide Web to http://www.netscapepress.com to access a complete catalog of Netscape Press titles, technical support, and updated information related to this book.

Netscapepress.com is also the home of *Navigate!*—the official electronic publication of Netscape Press and your best source for articles and reviews aimed at Netscape users. *Navigate!* features interviews with industry icons and experts as well as articles excerpted from upcoming Netscape Press titles. Netscape Press is a joint effort between Ventana and Netscape Communications Corporation and serves as the publishing arm of Netscape.

OK, enough introduction. Let's get busy exploring the vast new world of multimedia information!

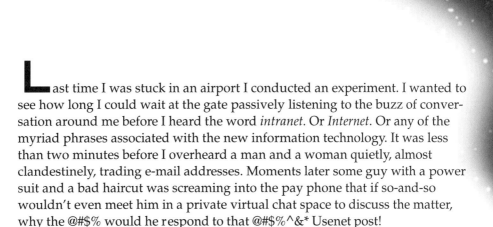

CHAPTER 1

Your Intranet— How It Works

Last time I was stuck in an airport I conducted an experiment. I wanted to see how long I could wait at the gate passively listening to the buzz of conversation around me before I heard the word *intranet*. Or *Internet*. Or any of the myriad phrases associated with the new information technology. It was less than two minutes before I overheard a man and a woman quietly, almost clandestinely, trading e-mail addresses. Moments later some guy with a power suit and a bad haircut was screaming into the pay phone that if so-and-so wouldn't even meet him in a private virtual chat space to discuss the matter, why the @#$% would he respond to that @#$%^&* Usenet post!

We're not in Kansas anymore.

Just about everywhere you go these days you hear these cyber-buzzwords. If you spend much time in airports or reading magazines, you'd think most people spend a significant portion of their time "cruising the Web" or "engaging in online transactions" or even "exploring virtual 3-D worlds." But as with most new technologies, jargon precedes popular understanding. New terminology makes it possible to share new ideas, but it also exacerbates the epidemic of Geek Answer Syndrome. There is no shortage of people who will blab on authoritatively but incorrectly about anything to do with information technology, flashing their vocabulary like bright plumage.

But fear not! After reading this chapter, you'll *really* understand what intranets are, what the Net and the Web are, and how you and your business can tap the power of these exciting new resources using Netscape Communicator Professional. In other words, you'll be well on your way to full cybergeek status! By the time you've finished this chapter, you may not have the technical knowledge of a Bill Gates, but you'll be able to answer the following questions and probably more:

- Just what *is* an intranet? What's the difference between an intranet and the Internet?

- What kinds of services and information are available on the Internet?

- How do Internet and intranet addressing work?

- What is the World Wide Web? How is it related to the Net?

- What is hypertext? How about hypermedia?

- What exactly can you do with Netscape Communicator?

- Are there any general guidelines for using intranets and the Internet?

What Are Intranets?

It's a lot simpler than you'd guess. A *network* is a collection of computers that are connected together so they can share information. If you've ever sat at your computer and accessed a spreadsheet that resided on Fred's computer, then you've used a network. An *intranet* is simply a network that lets people within an organization share the kind of information you can experience—and create—with Netscape Communicator Professional: pages full of text, graphics, sound, and video; fill-out forms; e-mail with pictures; specialized newsgroups and interactive conferences; directories full of files you can download; and a broad range of custom-tailored resources for research, education, or business.

Netscape Communicator may be the best piece of software you can use to access information on an intranet, but it's not the only one. In fact, the whole idea behind intranets is that they use standardized methods, or *protocols*, for moving information from one computer to another. That means an entire office, or even a corporation with many physically remote sites, can communicate using an intranet without worrying about specific hardware or software. Hot-shot programmers at a San José office can use their UNIX server machine to provide an animated demo program that a customer views in Sheboygan using a vintage Mac.

No two intranets are alike because the content varies—and varies extremely—from business to business. And yet, in a way, all are identical because the underlying protocols; the *ways* information is packaged and relayed from one machine to another, are always the same. Later in this chapter, in the sidebar called "Under the Hood: TCP/IP," you'll learn a little about some of these underlying protocols. But before that, I'd like to introduce you to the important concept of *clients* and *servers*.

Clients & Servers

In order to distribute information efficiently, intranets rely on two different kinds of software or hardware. When you are sitting at your desk looking at information that's out there on your company's intranet, the machine you're using is acting as a *client*. But where does this information really reside? You guessed it: on a *server*. A server is a computer or software program that "dishes up" information in a particular format. For instance, Netscape Calendar relies on a server program called the Netscape Calendar Server to access, organize, compare, and distribute schedule information to everyone on your corporate intranet that uses Netscape Calendar.

One machine on an intranet may house several different types of servers, and a computer can even act as a server and a client at the same time. You could run a small Web server on your desktop PC, letting people access multimedia pages you've created, while you're busy cruising around to other sites using a Web client like Netscape Communicator. In all but the smallest enterprises, however, servers are usually dedicated machines that do nothing but serve up information.

In Figure 1-1, you see a typical office intranet with several clients and servers.

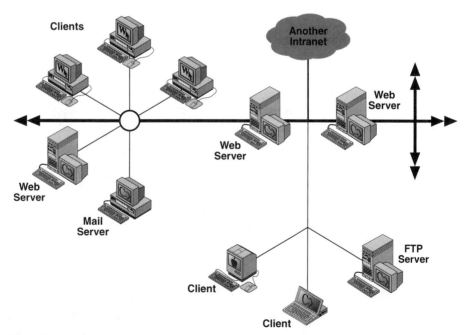

Figure 1-1: An intranet.

What Is the Internet?

The Internet is like an office intranet on steroids: it is a huge worldwide *public* network of networks. The Internet lets individuals on one network share information with users on another network that may be thousands of miles away. As with an intranet, the shared information can take many forms. For instance, you can use the Internet to send e-mail messages, download files, view video clips, or listen to music. You can even use the Net for banking and shopping. The Internet is just like an intranet in another way, too: it uses the same client-server model and the identical protocols! That's why intranets can extend outward and blend seamlessly with the Internet. At your office computer you may not even know when you're getting information from a local intranet server or when you're getting it from an Internet server halfway around the world.

The physical Internet looks like a vast net of wires. A few high-speed "backbone" cables branch out into other cables, which in turn radiate outward into finer strands. Most of the developed areas of the world have already been wired, so by routing your information or requests through this vast system you can reach other Internet users all over the world. Fortunately, the routing happens automatically, just as it does with telephone calls, so you don't need to know *how* data gets from your computer to a computer in Timbuktu.

And the system is democratic. Anyone can use it. You don't really need to have your own network in order to connect—you can communicate using the current infrastructure by plugging into somebody else's network. Maybe you're already doing this. If you have a *Serial Line Internet Protocol* (SLIP) or *Point-to-Point Protocol* (PPP) account, you simply connect via modem and phone line to your Internet Service Provider's network site (known as a "point of presence"). The actual transmission of data is free to you, but you or your company probably needs to pay the service provider for the time you spend accessing their equipment.

There are hundreds of thousands of users sitting at their PCs right now, gathering information from far-flung reaches of the globe. A very basic diagram of the Internet is shown in Figure 1-2.

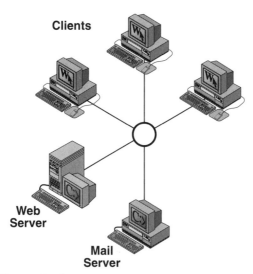

Clients

Web Server

Mail Server

Figure 1-2: The Internet.

Under the Hood: TCP/IP

You could probably get through life just fine without understanding the technical underpinnings of intranets and the Net. But if you like the nuts and bolts stuff, have I got a sidebar for you!

TCP/IP really means "the TCP/IP protocol suite." It is a group of protocols that allows data to be transmitted correctly from one machine to another over an intranet or the Net. And what exactly is a protocol? It's simply a set of standardized conventions for communication. In the human world, a typical protocol is saying "Your Honor" when you talk to a judge. In the world of data communications, a protocol might require that a sending machine include a special string of characters before and after every chunk of data so that the receiving machine can determine where that data begins and ends.

The TCP part of TCP/IP stands for Transmission Control Protocol. It divides any information you send into manageable blocks; conversely, it reconstructs received blocks into a stream of information. TCP does not require that all the blocks be received in the right sequence, since it attaches sequence numbers for reassembly. TCP also includes error checking; if blocks are missing or garbled, it requests that they be resent. When you run Internet applications, you remain blissfully unaware of all of this activity because the TCP software layer "sits

➡

below" the application software. Information is passed from the application software to TCP without any human intervention; at the other end, reassembled information is passed *from* TCP to the appropriate software program.

The IP part of TCP/IP stands for Internet Protocol. The Internet Protocol is the real workhorse of the Internet. When you send something over an intranet or the Internet, TCP passes its packets on to IP. This is roughly like dropping a letter off at the post office because IP repackages the data and makes sure that all of it gets delivered from point to point on the intranet or Internet on its way to the final destination: the specified IP or domain name address. Conversely, when IP receives packets, it "delivers" them up to TCP. There are other low-level Internet protocols, but these are the two most important ones, the basis of most intranet and Internet communication.

History of the Internet

We're going to go through this section quickly.

The Early 1970s
The U.S. Defense Department implements a network called ARPAnet that's cleverly designed so that even if part of its physical structure is destroyed, information can still be sent to any remaining destination. This *packet-switching* technology will become the foundation of the Internet.

The Early 1980s
Local area networks at a variety of research institutions start hooking into ARPAnet. Fast forward to a few years later: the National Science Foundation (NSF) establishes five supercomputer centers and connects them via their own network, NSFnet. This network-of-networks uses the same protocols as ARPAnet. Educational institutions and government agencies start plugging into NSFnet, and faster lines are installed all over the place. What is now known as the Internet opens its virtual doors to most of the academic and government community, who quickly come together to exchange research, ideas, and information.

The Early 1990s

Individuals can get on the Net, even from home, though it isn't easy. Gradually, thanks in part to improved software from the founders of Netscape, access becomes easier. People who enjoy communicating with others share all sorts of things—haikus and pictures of their pet cat. It's Internet as show-and-tell. Andy Warhol predicted a time when everyone would enjoy 15 minutes of fame. While that hasn't happened quite yet, at least everybody can enjoy 15 *kilobytes* of fame.

Now

Thousands of companies have started to promote and sell products over the Net, and we're all trying to figure out how to filter junk e-mail (also known as *spam*). At the same time, businesses are discovering that they can streamline operations and increase productivity by connecting their in-house networks to the Internet. Almost overnight, the Net grows from an academic resource into an ocean of Capitalist dreams.

And that's the history of the Internet so far.

TIP

> *In addition to* Internet *and* intranet, *you might hear or read the word* extranet *from time to time. What is an extranet? It's simply a TCP/IP network that links businesses to customers, suppliers, etc. You can also think of it as part of an enterprise intranet that is made available to the outside world for marketing or other specific purposes.*

What Is the Web?

There is a lot of confusion among non-netizens about what the World Wide Web really is, particularly about how it relates to the Internet as a whole. Let's clarify these issues right now.

The World Wide Web is, quite simply, a global hypermedia document that resides on and stretches across intranets and most of the Internet. Whoa! What does that mean in English?

Let's begin at the beginning. To understand the Web you really need to know what we mean by hypertext and hypermedia.

Hypertext & Hypermedia

Imagine you are reading this book on your computer screen instead of on the page. As you read along, you notice that some of the words are underlined and may appear in a different color or *font*, just like that. In this example, you try clicking your mouse on the word "font." Magically, a new document appears on your screen, explaining what fonts are. This new document also contains words and phrases that you can click on, taking you to yet other documents or to other places in the same document. That's what *hypertext* is all about: the nonlinear presentation of text, letting you jump from idea to idea following your own associative pathways. The clickable words and phrases are known as links, and the activity of moving around through these linked documents is known as *browsing*.

Now imagine that when you click on the *font* link you don't just get a text explaining fonts. Instead, a fancy picture pops up: a colorful depiction of fonts through the ages, from Guttenberg to Adobe. Perhaps you're even presented with a video clip, complete with a Charlton Heston narration. Congratulations! You've just learned what *hypermedia* is: the nonlinear presentation not just of text, but of a variety of other media including graphics and sound.

Hypermedia on the Net & on Intranets

So what does this have to do with intranets and the Internet? When you click on a link, the document that you get—whether it's text, graphics, sound, or full-motion video—does not have to be on the same machine as the original document. Thanks to a special protocol known as *HyperText Transfer Protocol (HTTP)*—the primary protocol for the World Wide Web—you can access documents from a server on your office intranet, or from any public World Wide Web server on the Internet! The basic Web page might be on your own computer or on a server run by your publications department; the video clip about fonts might reside on a machine in Hollywood or Timbuktu. Now here's the conceptual leap that makes this new technology so exciting: you can think of the collection of all the documents linked together as one big hypermedia document.

Let's go back to our original definition of the Web: a global hypermedia document that resides on and stretches across intranets and most of the Internet. Make sense now?

About Hypermedia

Suppose you're reading one of those wonderful but frustrating Russian novels in which 36 major characters are introduced during the first two chapters. If you're anything like me, you'll continually find yourself flipping back and forth trying to keep track of who's who. Was Natasha Galanskaya the one who ran away with the Count against her father's wishes, or was that Natalia Balanchina? Wouldn't it be great if you could just push a button on a character's name and instantaneously be transported to a full description of that character's relevant history? Well, you can't do that in a book or a magazine or even a regular computer document, but the magic of hypermedia makes it possible.

Let's look at another example of how hypermedia can improve the communication process, and even make learning more fun and interesting. Suppose you're a high school student studying astrophysics. One option is to open your textbooks and review the mathematics of planetary motion in the abstract. Even if you enjoy solving a few motion problems, it's still a fairly boring exercise. But what if your physics lab computer is linked to the Web and takes you to a virtual textbook with animations that show the orbits of the bodies, in full color and motion? Or plays back short lectures on the day's exercises, by the foremost authority in the field? Educators and trainers know the power of multimedia to speed learning and increase students' retention levels. This type of presentation has become popular in education and corporate training environments, as it presents information in an interesting and entertaining format.

When we click on the graphics, video, and sound objects embedded in a compound-document Web page, we are fulfilling prophesies made years ago for a global information system. When you're up and running with Netscape Communicator Professional, you'll see exactly what all the excitement's about.

Servers & Browsers

Remember how I said that both intranets and the Internet use what is called a client-server model? The Web is a great example of this. Special machines or software known as World Wide Web servers make the linked hypermedia documents available to the public or, in the case of intranets, to coworkers in your office. Individuals then move around through these documents using software known as Web clients or, more commonly, Web *browsers*. Obviously a Web browser has to be able to display or "play" a wide variety of hypermedia formats. The Web browser Netscape Navigator 4 is one component of Netscape Communicator Professional.

Because the World Wide Web uses a standardized protocol (HTTP) for transferring the information across intranets and the Internet, and because all Web software adheres to this protocol, any kind of Web browser will work with any kind of Web server. For instance, a site may decide to use one of the server packages developed by Netscape, but any World Wide Web browser will be able to access the information available at that site. Conversely, the browser we are discussing in this book can access hypermedia documents on any Web server anywhere in the world.

What's a Home Page?

Once you start exploring the World Wide Web, you'll encounter the term *home page* over and over again, and it won't always be used the same way. Here are some of the things it can mean:

- A home page is the document that's displayed by a Web browser such as Netscape Communicator when you first load the program. This document may be located on your local machine, on an office intranet machine, or at a remote site. In the case of Netscape Communicator, the default home page is a document located at Netscape's own Web site, but as with most other browsers, you can change this.

- A home page is the top-level document at a particular Web site. For instance, a typical small business's home page would contain a title, a logo, some introductory information, and a bunch of links to more detailed marketing information.

- A home page is a personal Web document created by an individual and made available to the public. Many access providers now let users copy Web documents to their public Web servers, and the Net sprouts hundreds of new personal home pages every day. You'd be surprised who's out there!

- In some contexts, a home page is simply any hypertext Web document, though strictly speaking this is not an accurate definition.

What You Can Do on the Internet or Intranets

What advantages do office intranets and the Internet offer you right now? What can you actually *do* with Netscape Communicator? Let's take a deeper look at a few of the services and resources that can have a real impact on your life.

Electronic Mail

Thanks to intranets and the Internet, you can send messages not only to your coworkers but to just about anybody who has a computer and a network connection, either directly or via a modem. If the individual you want to contact is not directly on your intranet or on the Net, you can use Netscape Communicator to send a message to him or her via one of the popular online services, such as CompuServe or America Online. The great thing about e-mail in Communicator is that you don't do anything different to send messages to your coworker two cubicles away or to your Congressperson in Washington.

There are a number of advantages to sending messages via e-mail instead of the U.S. Postal Service (known affectionately as "snail mail" by e-mail advocates). First of all, there's the speed. It may take only seconds for your message to reach somebody on the other side of the world. The recipient can read your text immediately on the screen, respond to it right away, save it for later, print it out, or quickly forward it to somebody else. You can create electronic mailing lists for sending notices to hundreds or even thousands of people at once. Messages you receive can be organized into convenient electronic folders and saved for as long as you want without taking up any office space. And with Netscape e-mail, you can format your e-mail message to look just like a Web page. Because of these advantages, and several others that you'll learn about in Chapter 5, e-mail has become my principal means of communicating with the world. I receive several dozen e-mail messages a day and send about as many. In just two weeks I generate more messages than all the old-fashioned paper letters I've written in my life!

On the Net, you send e-mail instead of snail mail. On an intranet, you use e-mail instead of routing paper memos or going down to your boss' office. E-mail can increase the efficiency of any office that employs more than three or four people.

Of course, it's a double-edged sword. I've known businesses where unbelievable amounts of time are wasted on e-mail gossip and "humor." Thanks to human nature, every new communications technology has the potential both for increased efficiency and for more creative ways of slacking off. Caveat e-mail!

Netscape Communicator Professional includes full-featured e-mail support, and Figure 1-3 shows what the main e-mail window looks like, whether you're on an intranet, the Net, or both. By the way, Communicator not only lets you include HTML code in your e-mail messages (see the sidebar below called "What's HTML"), it also lets you include pictures, sound, and even Java applets. (You'll learn more about Java in Chapter 10.)

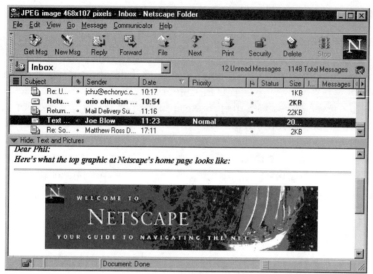

Figure 1-3: An e-mail message that includes text and a picture.

Enterprise-wide Documents

Netscape Communicator Professional provides organizations with a standardized front-end for viewing policies and procedures documents, company news, sales charts, and customer information. I know of several companies that put a new multimedia "Web page of the day" on their servers each morning. When employees fire up their desktop machines, they are greeted with an up-to-date office newsletter, complete with digital photos of top management that can be saved and manipulated in a graphics program!

Netscape Communicator Professional can help an office ensure that everyone is using the same paperwork; that in-house information is disseminated quickly and reliably; that meeting schedules remain conflict-free; and that data is presented as effectively as possible using the new technologies. Communicator can add impact to your job, making it a little flashier and more interesting. Imagine a monthly sales report appearing on your screen with animated 3-D graphs—or a division-wide layoff notice with soundtrack by Yanni!

Figure 1-4 shows an example of a colorful office newsletter that is viewed by the entire staff of an organization using Netscape Communicator.

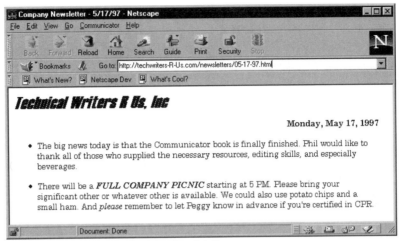

Figure 1-4: An office newsletter, updated daily.

Conferencing & Real-Time Collaboration

Netscape Communicator Professional lets you share ideas and plans with other individuals in specialized company-wide discussion groups—or in public Internet newsgroups. Instead of calling meeting after meeting, you can consult with a group of coworkers electronically. (If you *do* have to call a meeting, Netscape Calendar lets you schedule a group meeting and check for scheduling conflicts instantly.) You jot down an idea that everyone in your group sees and responds to; then you sift through their suggestions and post another message. The group conversation continues along these lines without requiring any kind of scheduling. Or, instead of tracking down expensive experts in a particular field, you can use Communicator to find knowledge-able people right on the Net, in online discussion groups that work exactly the same way. I'll cover these Communicator features in Chapter 6. Meanwhile, Figure 1-5 shows what this discussion group feature looks like.

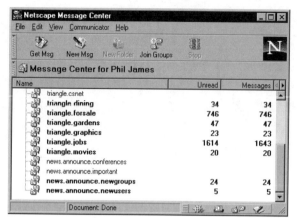

Figure 1-5: Some discussion groups in Netscape Communicator.

But Communicator also lets you collaborate in *real-time* with coworkers or friends. It means you can actually use your intranet or the Net to converse with people, either by voice or typed "chat"; it means you can send text or other files to each other as you speak; it means that as you cruise the Web, you can make the pages you view appear in a friend's browser at exactly the same time; and it means that no matter how far apart you are, you can add text, drawings, sketches, and other materials to a special shared workspace supplied by Communicator. Imagine collaborating with somebody in another country on the layout of a newsletter or the design of a jet engine. If you're less ambitious, imagine playing tic-tac-toe with your coworker down the hall. You'll learn more about these powerful collaboration tools in Chapter 10.

Research

Locating specific information used to be a tedious and time-consuming process. Remember digging through library card catalogs and then wandering through dusty stacks of books, only to discover that what you needed wasn't even at this library? Now finding references to topics can be as simple as typing in a keyword and clicking a button—from the privacy of your own home or office! The Internet includes entire libraries of specialized information, and thousands of these are accessible, free of charge, to the general public.

The Internet also supports a variety of research techniques and styles. Suppose you're trying to come up with a topic for a speech you have to deliver. At first you might want to browse a variety of materials to refine your subject area. This process is much like going to an area in a library and starting to pull books off the shelf, except that on the Internet you can leap from library to library, following associative links or trains of thought. Once you've determined the exact subject of your speech, you may need to track down some very specific information, such as statistics to back up a particular point. Once again there are Internet services that will help you; powerful search tools that will scurry around the Net and quickly find your needle in the information haystack. Netscape Communicator gives you access to these tools through the Net Search feature on the Netscape home page, shown in Figure 1-6.

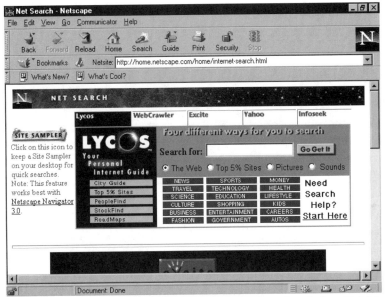

Figure 1-6: Net Search gives you access to a variety of search tools from the Netscape home page.

TIP

Many of your company's repositories of information may exist on mainframes, which in the past would make them difficult to access with personal computers. But Netscape Communicator Professional includes IBM Host-On-Demand, which allows your computer to communicate with a 3270-based mainframe system—from within Netscape's Web browser!

News & Information

This is the age of information, and in many fields success depends on getting the latest news as quickly as possible. The Internet provides numerous sources for specialized, up-to-date information. You may want to subscribe to an electronic mailing list, for instance, that keeps you posted on the latest developments in nanotechnology; you may want to get stock prices more current than those you can read in your local newspaper; or you may want to participate in a Usenet newsgroup where specialists in some arcane area of knowledge keep you abreast of what you need to know. Because of its scope and speed, the Internet is by far the most efficient way to make sure you maintain expert status in your little corner of the information universe. Netscape Communicator Professional gets you the information you need!

Software

One of the most astounding features of the Internet is the availability of thousands and thousands of software programs that you can download at no charge. In fact, until recently you couldn't even buy commercial Internet client programs for PCs that were anywhere near as good as the freeware and shareware available on the Net. (For more information about freeware and shareware, see Chapter 8.) That situation is starting to change, but there still are times when you need a program dedicated to a very specific task, such as playing a new kind of sound or video file.

Many of the sites that allow you to download programs are large, and most do not include descriptions of the files. Fortunately, Netscape Communicator helps you locate and download exactly what you need.

And, special new AutoInstall features in Communicator allow software to be updated automatically. Fall asleep struggling with version 2.1 and wake up in the morning to a brand new version 3.0! Further, you'll never have to wonder if you're working on the "company line" again—Netscape Communicator Professional includes AutoAdmin, which allows your company's intranet administrator to update your software automatically.

Figure 1-7 shows you some of the directories of files available at Netscape's own FTP site.

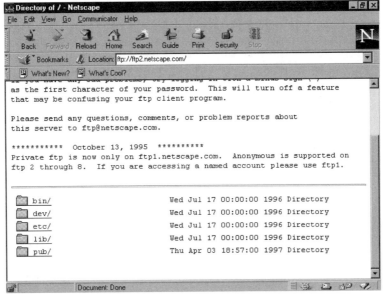

Figure 1-7: The Netscape FTP site.

Promotion, Shopping, & Online Transactions

For years the Internet was a commerce-free zone. It was funded and monitored by dedicated bureaucrats and academicians who instituted strict usage policies restricting anything that smelled vaguely of money. All that's changed. Now there are vast regions of cyberspace that look less like research libraries and more like your local mall, and most major corporations maintain Web sites where they promote their products and services. Figure 1-8 shows a portion of Yahoo's directory of companies (http://www.yahoo.com/Business_and_Economy/Companies/Directories/). From here you can browse to a wide variety of commercial Web sites.

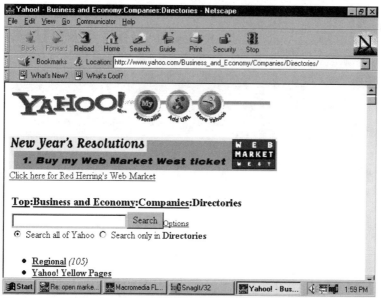

Figure 1-8: Yahoo's directory of companies.

Until recently, marketing types were up against a serious problem when it came to getting promotional information out to users: people had to know how to go out and find the stuff. That's changed. Netscape's Inbox Direct feature lets you subscribe to services that automatically send hypermedia information directly to you via e-mail. With Inbox Direct you can get graphs of your stock activity four times a day, charts of current weather conditions in your area, or a dazzling variety of carefully (and sometimes not so carefully) targeted electronic junk mail. In addition, Communicator supports *netcasting*, which allows a distant server to update areas in your browser window automatically. The commercial applications for this are obvious, but it's also a useful tool for keeping employees up to date in a corporate setting.

(This means that the game has changed when it comes to developing marketing materials. It's not just the race for the greatest four-color brochure or direct mailing piece—now it's also about the greatest HTML e-mail and best Web site.)

Lastly, Communicator includes a special "kiosk mode" for libraries, lobbies, and other publicly accessible areas. This special configuration is programmable with JavaScript (see Chapter 10), and displays the browser window without the usual toolbars and other "window dressing."

Recreation

Planning a vacation? The Internet can provide current travel information on just about any area of the globe. Considering taking up a new sport? Want to find out about the latest foreign movies? The Internet can point you to the resources you need.

But the Internet not only supplies information *about* recreational activities, it also provides its own diversions and amusements. If you like interactive online games, for instance, you may be in danger of staying glued to your keyboard and monitor well into the wee hours. Figure 1-9 shows one of the many games sites available to you via the Web.

Figure 1-9: The Games Domain site on the World Wide Web.

By the way, the accessibility of all these recreational sites is one of the reasons why your office intranet may not be connected to the Net!

OK, so there's all this great stuff out there and exciting things you can do with your computer. How do you get to it? Let's take a quick look at how information actually moves from one place to another on an intranet or the Net. A basic understanding of *addressing* will make it easier for you to find the servers or sites with information you're interested in.

Netcasting

One of the most exciting new ways of working with Internet and intranet information is known alternatively as *netcasting, webcasting,* or *push technology.* Netcaster is the Communicator component that gives you access to this new technology, and I cover it thoroughly in Chapter 4. But it may be helpful to get a brief overview in advance.

With netcasting, you subscribe to various *channels* that provide you with information. A channel is simply a collection of media-rich information stored on your computer and displayed on your desktop. You receive this information by *subscribing* to a channel. Once you subscribe, the information is downloaded to your machine. You may choose to have the material updated at regularly scheduled intervals. For instance, you can configure a weather channel to update itself a couple of times a day, or a stock ticker to update itself with new financial information every twenty minutes.

A channel may be full of text, graphics, and links, or it may be written in Java (see Chapter 10) and provide a completely novel user interface. Of course it can include sound, animation, video, and interactive elements that are limited only by the imagination of the content provider. And since these elements are stored locally, they display or play immediately. You avoid the "click-and-wait" procedure so common on today's crowded Internet.

What kinds of channels will you be able to access preview using Netcaster? Here are a few of the exciting possibilities:

- Online magazines delivered directly to your screen on a regular basis.

- Entertainment channels that include not only articles, listings, and multimedia previews, but interactive games and educational activities for children. Imagine a puzzle-of-the-day channel.

- Promotional channels that keep you updated on the latest product releases, add-ons, or technical information. You could even subscribe to a channel that automatically upgrades a piece of software as new versions become available. Fall asleep working with version 2.1 of a product and wake up to version 3.0!

- Informational channels that provide up-to-the-minute news in your area of interest, whether it's politics, finance, or sports.

In short, netcasting provides you with the same rich variety of information as the Web itself, but it's presented in a way that doesn't require you to explicitly seek it out. Once you subscribe to a channel, updated information comes directly to you at intervals you specify.

Internet & Intranet Addressing

Some of these messages are software commands, some are requests for data, and some include the human-readable data itself. Obviously there has to be a way for information to get to the proper recipient, and so the underlying suite of communications protocols includes an addressing scheme. At the heart of the addressing scheme is the concept of domains.

Domains & Domain Names

By *domain*, we simply mean where a computer resides. For instance, a specific computer at the University of Missouri is in the *missouri* domain, which in turn is within the top-level *edu* domain, the domain that includes all Internet-connected colleges and universities in the United States. The complete domain name of a machine called *bigcat* at the University of Missouri, for instance, would be *bigcat.missouri.edu*. No other machine anywhere on the Internet has the same domain name. Every name is registered with a special Internet organization to ensure that it is unique.

I have an e-mail account on echonyc.com. To reach my account, all you need to do is add my username to the domain name. My username is pjames, so my full e-mail address is *pjames@echonyc.com*. If you wanted to visit the Web pages at echonyc.com, however, you'd simply tell Netscape Communicator to get a document from the Web server machine at that site, www.echonyc.com.

But suppose you're on an intranet. It works the same way on a private network as it does on the public Net. Every server has a particular name. If I run a company called Geek Books R Us, for instance, my Web server machine might be called www.geekbooks.com. The only difference is that people from the world outside my company will not be able to reach this server—unless I connect my intranet to the Net.

At first these addresses may look impossible to pronounce, but pronunciation conventions have developed. Pjames@echonyc.com is pronounced "p-james at echo-n-y-c dot com," and ftp.vmedia.com is pronounced "f-t-p dot v-media dot com." Of course usernames don't have to be as simple as mine. If your LAN administrator Internet service provider lets you choose your own name, you might want to be zzzx_12_qwerty@serviceprovider.com. Then again you might not. Keep in mind that people who send you e-mail need to be able to remember your address.

Fortunately, the Internet almost never cares about case-sensitivity in e-mail addresses. In all cases the domain names are case-insensitive, and generally the actual e-mail IDs are as well. You can send a message to pJaMeS@EcHoNyC.cOm, and I will still get it. But most experienced Internet users stick with lowercase when typing addresses—it's just easier.

TIP

Even though Internet e-mail addresses usually aren't case-sensitive, remember that pathnames for URLs for Web pages and FTP directories are!

As I mentioned earlier, the last part of a domain name address is called the top-level domain. There are six standardized domain names currently in use, corresponding to types of organizations as shown in Table 1-1.

Domain	Type of Organization
com	Commercial entity
edu	Educational institution
gov	Government agency or department
mil	Military organization
net	Network resource
org	Other type of organization, usually a not-for-profit

Table 1-1: Top-level domains.

TIP

The IAHC, the committee in charge of these naming standards, recently added seven more top-level names to the list. These may also be used by anyone registering a new name:

Domain	Type of Organization
firm	businesses
store	online stores
web	Web-related organizations
arts	cultural and entertainment organizations
rec	organizations emphasizing recreational activities
info	organizations that provide information
nom	just individuals who want to be identified as such

In addition, Internet sites outside the United States are identified by a special two-letter, top-level domain name. For instance, a computer in Finland would have a top-level domain name of *fi*, and a computer in Germany would have a top-level domain name of *de* (for Deutschland). As you start using the Net, you will run into these foreign domain names on a daily basis. There is even a two-letter designation for the United States (you guessed it, *us*), but it is rarely used since the six "organization type" names are more descriptive.

IP Addresses

Domain name addresses are really easy-to-remember translations of the kind of addresses intranets and the Internet really use, numeric *IP addresses*. IP stands for "Internet Protocol." You may have read about IP in the earlier sidebar, "Under the Hood: TCP/IP." For now, it's only important to understand the difference between the two kinds of addresses.

If you're my age, you may remember when phone numbers always began with the name of the exchange, as in "Murray Hill Seven, Five Five Five Five." The Murray Hill Seven exchange, which you dialed as MU7, corresponded with a particular geographic area, in this case the Murray Hill neighborhood of Manhattan. But in fact your telephone didn't really care about Murray Hill, it simply transmitted down the line the fact that you had dialed the *numbers* 687. If you think of Murray Hill Seven as roughly equivalent to a top-level domain name, you can think of 687 as the top-level portion of the *IP address*.

Here's the point: an IP address is not only the numeric equivalent of a domain name, it's the form of address that really matters to the computers, routers, and other equipment that comprise an intranet or the Net. You could get by without all the friendly understandable domain names, but not without cold, hard, IP addresses. And so when you use a domain name address to attach to some resource such as a Web server, a special *Domain Name Service* (DNS) on your intranet or on the Net looks up the name and replaces it with an IP number. And as long as you're connected to an intranet or to the Net, you have your own IP address so that remote machines know how to send you the information you request.

IP addresses are structured very much like domain name addresses, but backwards. They consist of four numbers, each less than 256, separated by periods. The rightmost number specifies the actual machine, while those to the left identify the network and subnetwork. When I link to the Net via my PPP account with the service provider ThoughtPort, for instance, my IP address is 199.171.225.100. The "100" part of that address is my actual computer on the ThoughtPort network.

URLs

Besides e-mail addresses, domain names, and IP addresses, there's just one other kind of address you need to know about: the *Uniform Resource Locator*, or *URL*. URLs are like signs pointing to hypermedia documents on the Web. They provide the protocol and addressing information that Netscape Communicator or another browser uses to connect to the target document, whether it's on the Internet or your local intranet. The first part of a URL specifies the type of data or the protocol necessary to retrieve the data, the second part is the domain name that specifies the server where the information is located, and the optional third part specifies the pathname or directory where that data is stored. For instance, the URL http://www.vmedia.com/vvc/index.html tells Netscape Communicator to retrieve the file index.html from the vvc directory at www.vmedia.com (Ventana Online's Web server) using the HTTP protocol, the protocol for Web pages. (See Chapter 8 for information about accessing other kinds of resources available via other major Internet protocols, including FTP and Gopher.)

URLs are used in several different ways. First of all, they are part of the hidden information that tells your browser to jump to a remote document when you click on a link. In the middle of a Web document, for instance, the above URL might be used like this:

```
<a href="http://www.vmedia.com/vvc/index.html">Click here to go to the Ventana
Online home page!</a>
```

Only "Click here to go to the Ventana Online home page!" appears on the screen; all that other stuff is not visible, but Netscape Communicator Professional reads it out of the file and uses the information as directions to a target document. You can also type or paste URLs directly into the location field of Netscape Communicator to jump immediately to a remote document. And finally, you can add URLs to Netscape Communicator's configurable toolbar or as "bookmarks" for easy access at some later time.

What's HTML?

All Web pages that contain text are written in a language called HTML, which stands for HyperText Markup Language. HTML is simply ordinary ASCII text with embedded codes (usually referred to as *tags*) that represent instructions for displaying the text or for linking to other Web documents. For example, *<I>italic</I>* or *<B>bold</B>* in a Web document tells the browser to display the phrase "italic or bold" with the word "italic" in italics and the word "bold" in boldface. It is important to understand that HTML does *not* indicate exactly what the resulting text should look like—that is up to the browser software. On a system that can't display true italic or bold fonts the browser might just display the words in a different color. This makes HTML a universal language, ensuring that Web pages are displayable in one way or another on any machine or operating platform that can run a Web browser.

Figure 1-10 shows a typical Web page, and Figure 1-11 shows what some of the HTML source for it looks like.

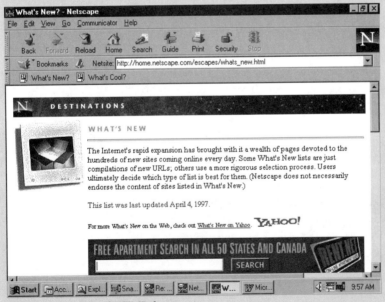

Figure 1-10: A typical HTML document.

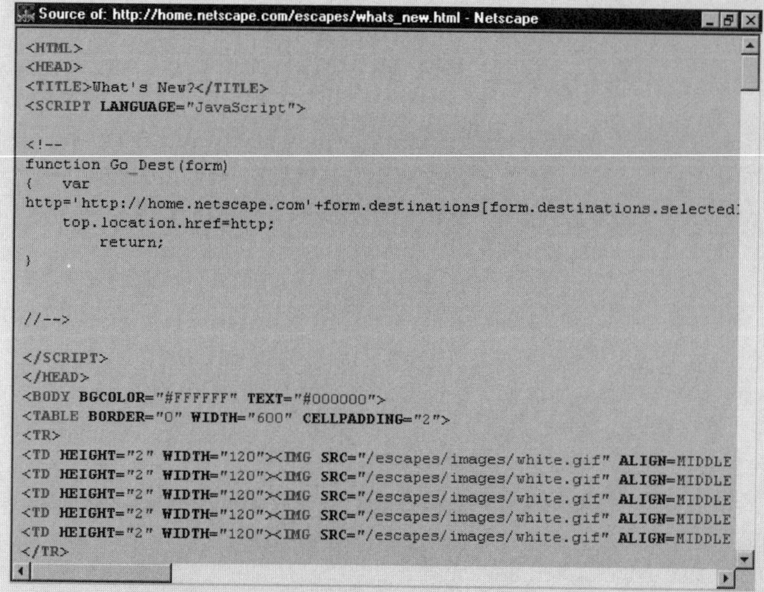

```
Source of: http://home.netscape.com/escapes/whats_new.html - Netscape
<HTML>
<HEAD>
<TITLE>What's New?</TITLE>
<SCRIPT LANGUAGE="JavaScript">

<!--
function Go_Dest(form)
{    var
http='http://home.netscape.com'+form.destinations[form.destinations.selected]
     top.location.href=http;
        return;
}


//-->

</SCRIPT>
</HEAD>
<BODY BGCOLOR="#FFFFFF" TEXT="#000000">
<TABLE BORDER="0" WIDTH="600" CELLPADDING="2">
<TR>
<TD HEIGHT="2" WIDTH="120"><IMG SRC="/escapes/images/white.gif" ALIGN=MIDDLE
<TD HEIGHT="2" WIDTH="120"><IMG SRC="/escapes/images/white.gif" ALIGN=MIDDLE
<TD HEIGHT="2" WIDTH="120"><IMG SRC="/escapes/images/white.gif" ALIGN=MIDDLE
<TD HEIGHT="2" WIDTH="120"><IMG SRC="/escapes/images/white.gif" ALIGN=MIDDLE
<TD HEIGHT="2" WIDTH="120"><IMG SRC="/escapes/images/white.gif" ALIGN=MIDDLE
</TR>
```

Figure 1-11: The HTML source, viewed using the Document Source command from Communicator's View menu.

HTML is an evolving language. No sooner had version 1 of the HTML specification been released than work began on a level 2 that would contain more advanced text-handling capabilities. HTML 2.0, completed and approved by a standards body known as the Internet Engineering Task Force (IETF), also includes support for interactive forms and image maps. Interactive forms let you enter data on the screen that is then sent to the host site, and image maps let you link to other documents by clicking on "hot spots" within an image.

The latest proposed upgrade to HTML is HTML 3.2. Netscape has been at the forefront of the collaborative design process in proposing and implementing new features for HTML 3.2. Many of these exciting new extensions are covered later in this book.

TIP

Files that contain HTML tags are known as HTML files, and they always have an extension of either .HTM or .HTML. On UNIX and other systems that support long filenames, the extension is .HTML; on DOS-based systems, it's .HTM. This extension tells the browser it is dealing with a hypertext document rather than some other type of hypermedia document, such as an image or audio file.

Some Pointers on Using the Net

We've talked about intranets, the Internet, the Web, and some of the technical underpinnings of all this new communications technology. We're going to end the chapter by focusing on something a little different: *you*.

The Internet is more than a collection of wires and computers; it's a culture. And like any culture it has its own unwritten rules of behavior, its own *should*s and *shouldn't*s and even outright taboos. But unless you're very young or come from a very geeky family, your mother never taught you any of this. But both you and your business need to be aware of these rules if you want to enjoy any success on the Internet.

There aren't many laws or cops on the Net, and the best way to keep it that way is with generosity, sensitivity, and common sense. The online culture has developed its own guidelines, and before actually exploring the Net it's a good idea to get familiar with some of these rules of the road. Here are just a few that will make your Internet travels more efficient and pleasant.

Avoid Traffic Jams

They stopped calling it a superhighway because sometimes it's more like driving through Bombay. Every day several thousand clueless newbies start exploring the Net. (Don't worry, you're not one of them: you bought this book!) Servers can support only a certain number of clients, and routers start to seem "sludgy" when they're called upon to transfer packets of data for thousands of users. Certain sites are practically impossible to reach, especially those distributing the latest free software.

To avoid traffic jams, and to avoid creating them, follow these simple rules of thumb:

- Connect during nonbusiness hours whenever possible. (Since this is a world-wide system, remember to compensate for different time zones!)

- If you're unable to connect with a particular server—for instance, if you get an "unable to connect with host" message when you try to access a Web page—wait a while before trying again. Bombarding the Net with unsuccessful connection attempts only adds to the problem.

- Use what are known as "mirror sites" for downloading files via FTP. Since some of the large anonymous FTP servers are so busy, a number of hosts sprinkled around the Net have been kind enough to "mirror" the exact contents, keeping their file lists completely up-to-date. The original site usually informs you about these mirror sites in its sign-on message. FTPing to a mirror is just like FTPing to the original host, except that you'll be out of the heaviest traffic.

■ Find the closest site that has what you need. Don't Telnet to Timbuktu if you can get the same information by FTPing to Peoria. When you access far-flung reaches of the globe, your packets of information must travel point-to-point through dozens of locations.

■ Don't create unnecessary message traffic. This is especially important in Usenet newsgroups (see Chapter 6). If you have something to say, by all means say it, but the Net provides a useful venue for practicing eloquent restraint. Don't post the entire text of your latest catalog to a Usenet newsgroup, and don't e-mail ten minute videos of your product in action just because you can.

■ Follow any instructions that are given to you for logging off a particular site. If you don't follow the proper procedures for logging off from a Telnet site, for instance, a connection may be left open, perhaps making it difficult for others to log in.

Understand Acceptable Use

Certain networks on the Internet, including the large backbones, have published standards for information that may be transmitted via their equipment and cabling. When you sign up with an access provider, you are mailed or e-mailed a document that outlines the acceptable use policies in effect for the networks used by that provider. You must adhere to these strictly! Besides the obvious prohibitions against using the network for trafficking in drugs and bombs, these policies usually make clear what kinds of commercial activities are permitted.

Here's a typical list of prohibitions from an acceptable use policy statement:

■ Users may not transmit any data or programs that cause disruption of service for others.

■ Users may not transmit any form of computer worm or virus.

■ Users must not use the network to violate intellectual property laws by distributing copyrighted or otherwise protected information, documents, or software programs.

■ Users may not distribute unsolicited advertising.

But the written policies are really only the beginning of acceptable use. Common sense and respect for others should be your guiding principles when communicating over the Net. The Internet is not a good place for personal attacks and threats, as they frequently escalate into full-blown "flame wars" that waste resources. It's not always a good place for challenging local community ethical standards, either, since various factions are looking for excuses to impose more stringent regulation. Make sure that you post your materials at the appropriate sites.

Respect & Protect Privacy

Privacy is the big hot topic on the Internet today. To what extent should government agencies have access to private Internet communications? Should the content of public sites be regulated? Should there be safeguards against commercial entities adding you to electronic mailing lists? It remains to be seen how all of these issues will be decided, but it is very clear that the Internet community expects its citizens to respect the privacy of other individuals. Nothing will get you in more trouble than trying to "hack" somebody else's account, trying to take advantage of technological loopholes to access private data, or publishing confidential information.

At the same time, you should realize that in a culture as large as the Internet there are going to be occasional problems with privacy, and you should do what you can to protect yourself and others by keeping your accounts secure:

- Always use good, specific passwords; your spouse's name or the name of a *Star Trek* character just won't cut it.

- Change your passwords often, especially in an office environment where someone might see you using your password. And don't leave your password sitting around on a piece of paper! If you must keep it written down somewhere, keep it at home or safely in your wallet.

- Always inform the appropriate network administrators when you think there may have been a security breach.

- If you're worried about particularly sensitive information, make sure that you're conducting communication with secure Web servers that support the SSL protocol built into Communicator (see Chapter 12).

- And just in case, don't make any information available on the Net that you wouldn't want to appear on the front page of *USA Today* or your company newsletter.

Be Willing to Ask for Help

In my experience, the most annoying Internet—and intranet—users are those who "know just enough to be dangerous." They go crashing around leaving a mess for others to clean up. Look, the Internet is full of *real* experts; if you don't know how to do something, just ask. You'll be amazed at how helpful and friendly the seasoned Net veterans can be. I've asked some pretty stupid questions on the Internet, but only rarely have I received a snooty response.

Of course, before asking questions of other users, you should look for available resources such as help files or appropriate technical documents. The Netscape site, which appears as soon as you load Netscape Communicator Pro if you're attached to the Net, is full of useful information. Many Usenet newsgroups even maintain files of frequently asked questions, called FAQs. But if you've exhausted other resources, there's nothing wrong with a plea for help.

Don't Be Afraid to Explore

On the other hand, one of the most valuable ways to learn how to use the Net is simply to explore. As long as you're not trying to do something too tricky or arcane, common sense will usually get you where you want to go. Half the fun of the Internet is wandering around, guided as much by your instincts as by a conscious plan. You can certainly do no harm by getting out there and seeing the world!

Moving On

What makes Netscape Communicator Professional the premier product for accessing both the Internet and office intranets is not its slick interface, or its availability on a variety of platforms, or its solid reliability, or even its early support of forward-looking Web features. What really sets this product apart is that it lets you do *everything you need to do* on the Net or on your intranet. In addition to browsing the Web, you can use Netscape Communicator to send and receive e-mail; to read and post newsgroup messages; to gather files; to collaborate with coworkers; to schedule meetings and manage tasks; and to explore a wide range of specialized Internet services. In the following chapters, we'll be exploring all aspects of this versatility using a hands-on approach, and pretty soon *you'll* be the one that answers your co-workers' Netscape questions.

We'll start in Chapter 2 with a quick overview of Communicator, and then in Chapter 3 we'll move on to Netscape Navigator 4, the Web browser itself.

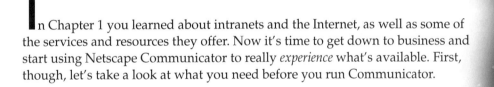

CHAPTER 2

Introducing Communicator 4 Professional

In Chapter 1 you learned about intranets and the Internet, as well as some of the services and resources they offer. Now it's time to get down to business and start using Netscape Communicator to really *experience* what's available. First, though, let's take a look at what you need before you run Communicator.

Requirements

Before you install Netscape Communicator Professional you should make sure you have the following:

- A 386sx or better PC with at least 16 Megabytes of RAM that runs Windows 3.1, Windows 95, or Windows NT.
- At least 20 Megabytes of free space on your hard drive.
- A CD-ROM drive to install the software from CD.
- If you want to use Communicator's Conference component, a 486 or better PC, a sound card, speakers, and a microphone. Though any sound card will work, one that offers full-duplex operation is preferable.
- A direct (hard-wired) connection to an intranet or to the Internet, or a dial-up SLIP or PPP connection to an intranet or the Internet.

If you're directly connected to an intranet or the Internet via an office network, that's probably all you need. Of course your network administrator may have to configure your system for proper access, but once that has been accomplished, you are ready to install and run Communicator.

> **TIP**
>
> *Two of Communicator Professional's components require something extra from your office intranet. Netscape Calendar requires that the Netscape Calendar Server be running on your company intranet, while Netscape AutoAdmin requires that your company be using the Netscape Admin Server. Before you attempt to use these components of Communicator Pro, check with your network administrator to make sure that the server components are in place. It'll save you a lot of headaches later.*

But if, for instance, you want to use a dial-up SLIP or PPP connection, this next section is for you.

Requirements for SLIP and PPP Connections to the Net

Obviously, if you want to connect to the Internet via a phone line, you need a phone line! There are a few additional requirements:

- A modem with a data rate of at least 14.4 kbps (known as a "14.4 modem"). A faster modem, with a rate of at least 28.8 kbps, is preferable, especially for browsing the World Wide Web. If you want to use ISDN, you need a special ISDN card or external ISDN adapter.

- A SLIP or PPP account with an ISP (Internet Service Provider). One of the best ways to find an ISP is through Netscape's ISP Select page at http://home.netscape.com/assist/isp_select/. Unfortunately, it's a chicken/egg situation—how do you access that page if you don't already have an ISP? Fortunately, these days you can often find a friend who is already on the Net and will help you get to the ISP Select page. If not, there are lots of national ISPs advertised in computer and Internet magazines, and your local yellow pages may list some ISPs in your area. If you purchased your computer recently, it may even have come with pre-installed startup packages from a few ISPs such as AT&T WorldNet.

> **TIP**
>
> *If you want to connect to the Net via ISDN, both your local phone company and your Internet Service Provider must support the technology. Often your phone company can help you find an ISP that supports ISDN. Make sure to research this carefully before buying any ISDN hardware!*

■ Dial-up software for connecting to your ISP. Windows 95 and Windows NT have this software built in, and your ISP will tell you how to configure it. If you're running Windows 3.1 you may need some supplemental software, but this is usually distributed by the ISP you choose, often fully configured. If your ISP seems unwilling or unable to help you get set up properly, find a new ISP!

Now that you know what you need, it's time for an overview of Communicator itself.

What *Is* Communicator 4?

Netscape Communicator is not really a single program; rather, it is a tightly integrated software *suite*. And what the heck does that mean? It means it's a group of programs, each with a specialized purpose, designed to work together cooperatively. For example, if the software component that browses the Web encounters a link that lets you send e-mail, it automatically launches the e-mail component. In Figure 2-1, the large circle is Communicator as a whole. The arrows that connect the individual components show how information may be shared cooperatively among the components so that you can move from task to task without ever needing to launch a separate application.

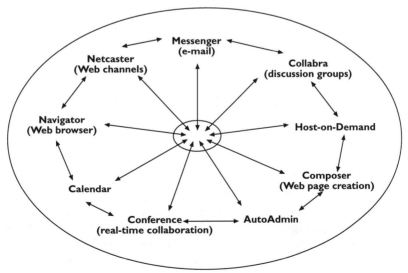

Figure 2-1: Communicator 4 and its components.

In subsequent chapters you'll learn about the various parts of the Communicator suite one at a time, working through step-by-step procedures that show you how to take advantage of highly specialized features. But to really harness Communicator's power, you need to get a clear picture of how it all fits together. There won't be many detailed procedures in this chapter; I'll just show you some features that affect operation of the suite as a whole, and introduce you to some terminology so that everything makes sense when we get down to the nitty-gritty. But first, let's fire up the program!

Startup Options

Technically, you cannot really launch Communicator—you can only launch one of its components. So when you double-click the Communicator icon, how does the program know which of its components you really want?

By default, Communicator launches its Web browser component, Navigator 4, when you click the Communicator icon. But you can change this behavior if you want. Once you are in any one of the component programs, select Preferences from the Edit menu. A Preferences dialog box appears. From the Category list at the left, select Appearance (if it's not already selected). The Appearance options on the right include four check boxes that let you choose to launch Navigator, Netcaster, Messenger, Collabra Discussions, or Page Composer at startup. You can select any combination of these four—Communicator has no problem with launching several of its components at once. Whatever you do, though, don't try *un*checking all four boxes—you may never get back to this dialog box again!

I'll include some more information on the Appearance preferences in Chapter 3.

Starting Communicator 4 the First Time

The first time you launch Communicator after installing it, it runs a Wizard that lets you enter some essential configuration information. In fact, it sets up what's known as a *user profile* for you—a set of configuration options that's specific to your individual use of the suite as a whole and its various components. For instance, you can enter your e-mail address, the address of your discussion groups server, etc. Most of this is information you've probably received from your network administrator already, but if you don't know all these details right now, don't worry about it. You can add or change any of the configuration options later on, and the chapters on the individual components will show you how.

But if you do want to enter everything correctly right away, here's the information you need:

- Your e-mail address.

- The username you use to access your e-mail server. If you use your ISP for e-mail, this is usually the same as your regular SLIP/PPP login name.

- Your e-mail password.

- The address of the server you use to send e-mail, which is also known as the outgoing mail server or SMTP server.

- The address of the server you use to receive e-mail (incoming mail server). This is usually the same as your outgoing mail server.

- Whether your incoming mail server uses POP3 or IMAP4 protocol (if you're using a commercial ISP, it's probably POP3).

- The address of your discussion groups server.

OK, let's get busy:

1. Double-click the Communicator icon on your desktop. The Profile Setup Wizard appears, as shown in Figure 2-12. To open the Profile Setup Wizard after you have run Communicator for the first time, double-click the Profile Manager. If you are already running Communicator you will be asked to exit in order for the Wizard to run.

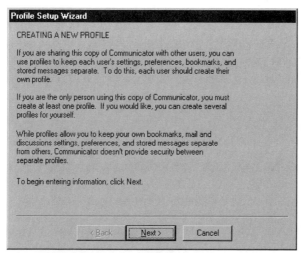

Figure 2-2: The Profile Setup Wizard.

2. Click Next. The second page of the Wizard appears, as shown in Figure 2-3.

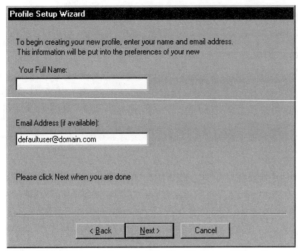

Figure 2-3: The second page of the Profile Setup Wizard.

3. Fill in your name. If you know your e-mail address, fill that in as well. Click Next again.

4. In the Profile Name field that appears on the next page, type in a name for your profile. Typically this will be your own name or a simple nickname (my user profile is "phil"). Don't bother changing the directory in the bottom edit box unless you plan to set up multiple user profiles and want a separate directory for each user. (See the section below called "Adding User Profiles to Communicator 4".)

5. Click Next. The Mail and Discussion Groups Wizard appears, as shown in Figure 2-4.

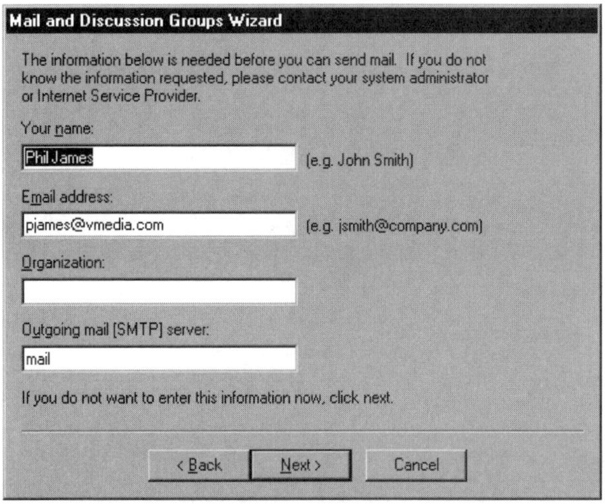

Figure 2-4: The Mail and Discussion Groups Wizard.

6. Enter your name, your e-mail address, and the domain name address of your outgoing e-mail (SMTP) server.

TIP

Don't worry if you don't know the address of your SMTP server—or even what one is! E-mail configuration is covered in depth in Chapter 5. The information is usually provided by your network administrator or Internet Service Provider, but if you don't have all the answers now you'll have the opportunity to enter the configuration information later. Just leave any fields blank and click Next.

7. After entering the information, click Next. The second page of the Mail and Discussion Groups Wizard appears, as shown in Figure 2-5.

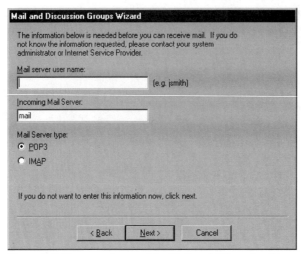

Figure 2-5: The second page of the Mail and Discussion Groups Wizard.

8. Enter your user name for your incoming mail server. Often, this is the same as your regular login name for your SLIP/PPP account. Then fill in the domain name address for your incoming mail server. (Typically, this will be the same address as your *outgoing* e-mail server.) Finally, select one of the option buttons depending on whether your e-mail server uses the POP3 protocol or the IMAP protocol for mail retrieval.

TIP

Again, ask your ISP or system administrator for this information. If you can't get it or simply don't understand, just click Next and wait for Chapter 5.

9. Click Next. On the final page of the Mail and Discussion Groups Wizard, enter the address of your discussion group server. If you're not planning on using Communicator's discussion groups feature or if you don't know the correct address, just leave the field alone.

TIP

For more information on discussion groups, please see Chapter 6.

10. When you have finished entering information in the Wizard, click Finish. Netscape Navigator 4, the Web browser component of Communicator, appears on your screen.

As I mentioned before, you can configure Communicator so that it displays other components instead of or in addition to Navigator 4 when you launch it. Once you are in any one of the component programs, select Preferences from the Edit menu. A Preferences dialog box appears. From the Category list at the left, select Appearance (if it's not already selected). The Appearance options on the right include five check boxes that let you choose to launch Navigator, Netcaster, Messenger, Collabra Discussions, or Page Composer at startup. You can select any combination of these five.

A Quick Look Around

Now that you've got the software up and running, let's take a quick look around. The next few sections of this chapter give a brief overview of some of Communicator's interface features that make it a fully integrated suite.

The Component Bar

Communicator integrates its components in a variety of interesting ways, but the most basic is via a special Component Bar, as shown below in Figure 2-6.

Figure 2-6: The Component Bar.

The Component Bar appears on your desktop whenever you launch one of Communicator's components. Let's say you want to send a quick e-mail message, so you start up Messenger by double-clicking the Netscape Messenger icon in your Netscape folder. When Netscape Messenger appears, the Component Bar appears right along with it.

And what can you do with the Component Bar? You can use it to launch any of the following Communicator components: the Navigator Browser, the Messenger e-mail Inbox, Collabra discussion groups, or Composer. Simply click the appropriate icon and the associated component appears immediately. Or if the component is already loaded, clicking its icon in the Component Bar will put the focus on its window, letting you continue your work without needing to search for the window you need.

TIP

Two Communicator components are not included in the Component Bar: Netcaster and Conference. To access either of these, simply double-click the appropriate icon in the Netscape Communicator folder. You can also select Netcaster or Conference from the Communicator menu item in any Communicator component.

By default, the Component Bar is what is known as a *floating* or unanchored control. That means you can move it anywhere on your desktop, just like a program window. Simply click and drag its title bar. And you can make it either horizontal or vertical too: just right–click on it and choose the orientation you want from the context menu that pops up.

But what happens if you click the Component Bar's Close button? If you're running the software now, give it a try. At first it might seem that the Component Bar has disappeared. But if you hunt around a little, you'll find that it has simply been transformed into a smaller *anchored* control, one that doesn't float but sits at the right hand side of the status line in any Communicator component that is currently running. Take a look at Figure 2-7.

Figure 2-7: The Component Bar as an anchored control within a Communicator program.

The Component Bar looks different when it's anchored in a status line, but it works exactly the same way. Click any one of the icons within it and you're transported to the associated component.

Once you've turned the Component Bar into an anchored control, it stays that way until you click the maximize icon (the left-most icon on the bar, which looks like a gray page with horizontal lines). It appears as an anchored control in every new Communicator component you launch, and it even persists in this form after you close down all Communicator components and re-launch. Similarly, once you click the maximize icon it maintains its "floating" form until you click its Close button.

> **TIP**
>
> *Why choose one or the other of the Component Bar's formats? A floating control is useful if you keep your Communicator components minimized, so that an anchored control would not always be available to you. An anchored control in the status line, on the other hand, saves you the trouble of finding a floating control on a busy screen if you're already working in a Communicator component.*

The Communicator 4 Menu

Netscape has provided another method of moving among the different Communicator components. Every Communicator component includes a Communicator item on its menu bar. When you click the Communicator item, you'll see something like the menu shown in Figure 2-8.

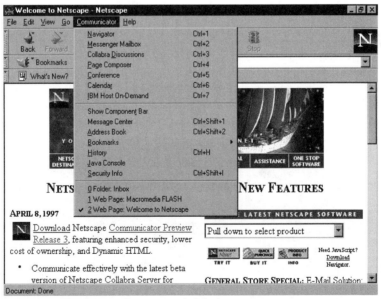

Figure 2-8: The Communicator menu in Navigator.

As you can see, the choices at the top of this menu let you access the other Communicator components with a simple click of the mouse. And if you prefer using the keyboard, Ctrl+1, Ctrl+2, Ctrl+3, etc., will move you around from component to component.

Shared Resources in Communicator 4

Remember how I called Communicator a *tightly integrated* software suite? Besides obvious interface elements such as the menus and the Component Bar, there are a number of other manifestations of this tight integration. Several important features, for instance, are used by more than one component.

The Address Book

Let's say you and your significant other have the same friends. (Unlikely, I know.) Do you really need two address books? No, you can each use a single one when you need to make a call or address a letter.

Similarly, Communicator components that require address information don't all need to have separate electronic address books. Instead, there is a single Communicator Address Book that may be accessed by all components when needed. That saves you from having to enter data more than once.

Figure 2-9 shows the Communicator Address Book.

TIP

You can access the Address Book by choosing Address Book from the Communicator menu, or simply by pressing Ctrl+Shift+2.

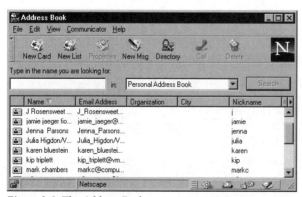

Figure 2-9: The Address Book.

Notice that there is a New Msg button *and* a Call button. Click the New Msg button and you can send an e-mail message to an individual using Messenger; click the Call button and you can initiate voice communications with the same individual using Conference. The Address Book even lets you enter supplemental information that is not required by any of the Communicator components, making it the only electronic rolodex you'll need. And on an intranet, you can import your company's address book right into your own Address Book.

The Message Center

Communicator's Message Center is another example of a shared resource; in this case one that's used by both Messenger and Collabra. Let's take a look at it in Figure 2-10.

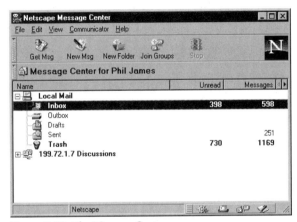

Figure 2-10: The Message Center.

TIP

You can access the Message Center by choosing Message Center from the Communicator menu, or simply by pressing Ctrl+Shift+1. You can also access it by clicking the Message Center button at the right side of the Messenger or Discussion Group window, just below the large Netscape icon.

The Message Center is a highly organized storage system for all your e-mail messages *and* all your discussion group (newsgroup) messages. At the top of the window you can see the mail category, and below it several folders in which e-mail messages are filed away. But below the last of the e-mail folders is the name of a discussion group server, secnews.netscape.com, and arranged hierarchically under that are several discussion groups available on that server.

Figure 2-11 shows what you get if you double-click one of the mail folders, in this case the Inbox.

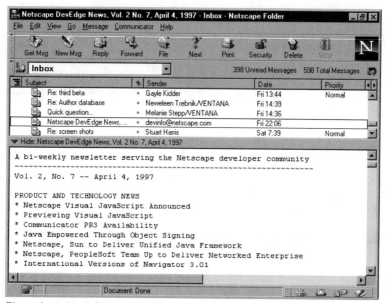

Figure 2-11: My Inbox e-mail folder, accessed from the Message Center.

As you can see, my Inbox folder contains a list of messages I've received via e-mail.

Now let's double-click one of the discussion groups, for instance netscape.devs-javascript. This time I get a list of messages that have been posted to that particular discussion group, as shown in Figure 2-12.

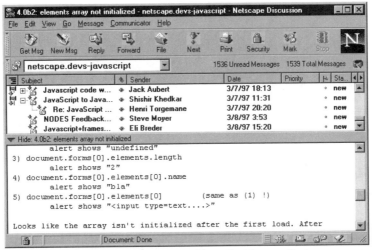

Figure 2-12: A discussion group accessed from the Message Center.

Thus the Message Center provides a sort of headquarters for all message-related activity in Communicator. Not only that, but as you can see from the last two illustrations, the user interface for accessing your e-mail is very similar to the user interface for accessing discussion groups. You don't have to learn a new set of keystrokes or mouse clicks to move from one Communicator component to another.

Security

Security is yet another area that is shared among the various Communicator components. Many of Communicator's windows include a Security Advisor button. Click it and Figure 2-13 shows what you get.

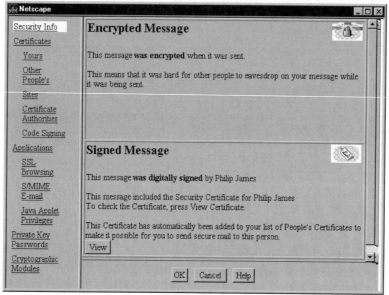

Figure 2-13: The Security Info window.

As you may be able to tell from the long list of security features on the left, this is a window that is shared by all the Communicator components, and that provides access to security features in Navigator and Netcaster as well as in e-mail and discussion groups. Again, there is no need to learn separate interfaces for the different components.

Preferences

Communicator is a very full-featured suite, and so there are many configuration options. Don't worry, most of these you never need to touch. The most important ones are set up for you automatically when you install the program, and other very specialized ones provide entertainment for the propeller-heads among us. Fortunately, Netscape has provided unified access to the preferences for all Communicator components, as shown in Figure 2-14. These are all available by choosing Preferences from the Edit menu of any Communicator component.

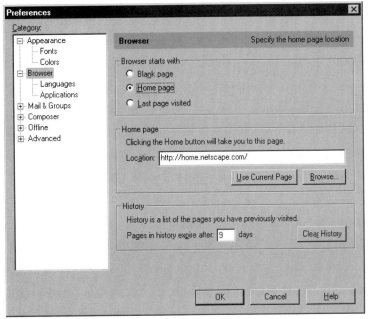

Figure 2-14: The Communicator preferences.

The designers at Netscape have grouped these settings very sensibly, but until you get used to this integrated way of working, some of the groupings may throw you off. The preferences are not divided up by component, but organized according to the *type* of option they affect. For instance, on one preferences page you might find a color setting that affects the backgrounds of both outgoing e-mail messages and new Web pages you create; on another page you might find an option that affects the network performance of several different components. You have to get used to thinking of Communicator as more than the sum of its parts.

I've been talking for a while about *integration*, and that is one of the features that sets Communicator apart from simple Web browsers, and even from other Internet suites. Now we'll move on to a concept that may seem alien at first and that affects the entire Communicator suite, not just individual components. You already know about user profiles, but did you know that Communicator lets you set up more than one of them?

Adding User Profiles to Communicator 4

When you use Communicator Professional at work, you may be using it while wearing a variety of "hats." For example, you might read discussion groups and monitor Web sites as a public relations firefighter. You may check different Web sites and keep up with product news as a vendor liaison. And you might read and respond to e-mail on a technical support basis.

Netscape programmers had your many job functions in mind when they designed Communicator. Communicator allows several different user profiles, each of which may have its own bookmarks (see Chapter 3), mail and discussion settings (see Chapter 5), preferences, and message folders that are completely separate from the others. It's almost like running the program on completely separate machines.

When you have several different user profiles configured for Communicator, Figure 2-15 shows what you'll see after launching any one of the components.

Figure 2-15: The Profile Manager dialog box.

At this point simply choose the correct profile and click Start Communicator.

As you saw earlier, when you first start Communicator it creates a single profile for you based on your responses to questions it asks; your name and e-mail address, for instance. So how do you create an additional profile in Communicator? Just follow the steps outlined below:

1. In the Netscape Communicator folder, double-click the Utilities sub-folder.

2. In the Utilities folder that opens up, double-click User Profile Manager. Then click New to create a new profile. The Profile Setup Wizard appears, just as it did when you first launched Communicator. If you are currently running Communicator you will be asked to exit in order for the Wizard to run.

3. Work through the questions in the Profile Setup Wizard, this time entering information that's appropriate to this new user.

TIP

If you are creating an alternate profile for your own use, make sure to fill in your actual name and e-mail address again, even if you have already configured these in your main user profile.

4. In the Profile Name that appears in the Wizard, type in a name for your alternate profile. If you want a separate directory for each user, change the name of the directory in the bottom edit box of this page.

5. When you have finished entering information in the Wizard, click Finish. Communicator returns you to the Select a Profile dialog box, which now contains two profiles: your original one and the new one. You can now select from the list and click OK to launch Communicator.

Once you fire up a Communicator component using a new user profile, you can make whatever changes you want to the preferences, bookmarks, etc., without fear of screwing up any other profiles that exist. For simplicity's sake, I'll assume throughout the rest of this book that you have a single user profile—in other words, I won't mention the Select a Profile dialog box every time I outline a procedure that includes launching the program. But now you know how to use this powerful Communicator feature to help keep your intranet or Internet wanderings more organized.

Working With Communicator 4 Online and Offline

Unless you are hard-wired into an office network, your computer is probably not on an intranet or the Net at all times. If you have a dial-up SLIP or PPP connection that you pay for on an hourly basis, you may want to cut costs by minimizing your online time. After you collect your latest e-mail messages, for instance, it is wasteful to leave your machine sitting on the Net while you read them all.

If you want to be online some of the time and off-line at other times, there are a couple of ways you can configure this: the first involves settings in your network dialer to control the amount of time your computer is idle before you are automatically disconnected. Note that your ISP may allow a maximum idle time before it initiates a disconnect. You cannot extend that time, of course, but you may wish to disconnect earlier.

■ If you are using Windows 95, the operating system can be configured so that your Dial-Up Networking connection is initiated whenever you launch Communicator or other Internet programs, and so that your connection hangs up if you are idle for a certain amount of time. To configure this, click Internet in Control Panel and check the Use AutoDial and Auto disconnect check boxes. You can also change the amount of idle time before Dial-Up Networking automatically terminates your connection.

■ If you are using Windows 3.1, the dialer provided by your ISP may include similar options for automatic connection and disconnection.

The second online and off-line control is in Communicator itself. Communicator has three modes for dealing with online and off-line operation in order to keep switching between them under your control. You'll learn more about them in Chapter 3, but see Figure 2-16 for a quick preview.

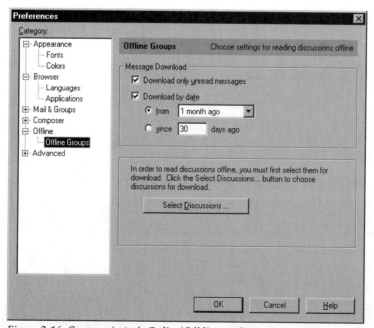

Figure 2-16: Communicator's Online/Off-line modes.

To get to this preferences tab, select Preferences from the Edit menu of any Communicator component, then click the Offline category. The choices here are fairly self-explanatory. If you select Online Work Mode, Communicator assumes you are connected to the Net or to an intranet at all times. When you send an e-mail message, for instance, Messenger will try to deliver your message to the specified address. If you are not currently connected, it will huff and puff and finally return an error message.

What happens if you choose Offline Work Mode and try to send a message when you're not connected? In this case Messenger simply stores your message in a special Outbox folder, queued for delivery when you eventually go online.

And how about clicking the "Ask Me" choice? In this mode Communicator will ask you if you want to go online when you first start one of its components. If you say you do, your Dial-Up Networking connection will be initialized (assuming you're using Windows 95 or Windows NT) and you will be connected to the Net.

TIP

If you have configured any Netcaster channels to update themselves on a regular basis (see Chapter 4), Communicator goes online automatically to download the new information unless you're in Offline mode. If you're in Online mode but not connected to the Net, Communicator attempts to establish a connection.

Moving On

In this chapter I've tried to give you a brief overview of Communicator as a whole, highlighting a few features and terms that could be confusing if they weren't explained before discussing the individual components.

But by now I'm sure you're ready to dive right in. In the following chapters we'll go through step-by-step procedures that will get you fluent with all aspects of using Communicator for browsing the Web, subscribing to Netcaster channels, sending and receiving e-mail, participating in discussion groups, creating your own Web pages, and talking or collaborating in real-time with other Communicator users. Let's start with the most popular of all Net and intranet activities, Web browsing.

CHAPTER 3

Browsing & Beyond

Now that you have a basic understanding of what Netscape Communicator as a whole is all about, it's time to take a look around your office intranet or the Net itself. In this chapter, you'll be using Netscape Navigator 4, which is the Web browser component of Netscape Communicator. You'll learn some of the best ways to use this tool to navigate effectively and efficiently. For instance, you'll learn:

- How to move around a Web document, and how to get from one document to another.

- How to work with forms and other unique Web documents.

- How to use navigation aids such as the configurable toolbar, bookmarks, and desktop shortcuts.

- How to take advantage of exciting Web resources like Yahoo!, where you can easily search for specific topics and keywords on pages all around the world.

- How to optimize the software so that it works exactly the way you want it to.

Netscape Navigator 4 is so simple to use that you could actually master the program by trial and error. Recently I taught our neighbor's son how to use it by saying, "When you see some words that are underlined and in another color, click on them. That takes you to other places." After an hour he was whizzing around the Web like a seasoned veteran. Of course, he is seven years old and learns this kind of stuff a lot faster than those of us who were born before PCs and Nintendo. By the end of this chapter, you may not quite be a Web-geek, but you'll know how to use the main features of Netscape Navigator 4 and how to find what you're looking for quickly and easily. Soon your co-workers will be asking you where you found those press releases and collections of industry information!

One quick note to avoid any confusion. Remember how I said that Netscape Navigator 4 is the Web browser component of Communicator? That means I'll be using the terms "browser window" and "Navigator 4 window" interchangeably. They're exactly the same thing.

OK, now let's get going.

The Browser Window

We'll start by taking a closer look at the Netscape Navigator 4 window:

1. Make sure you are connected to your intranet or the Internet, either directly or through a SLIP or PPP connection with your access provider.

   - In this tutorial I'll assume you're connected to the Internet itself, not just your corporate intranet. That way the text and illustrations will be correct for most readers. If you're not on the Internet, the principles discussed below will still be valid, but Navigator will not display the pages depicted in the illustrations. Your initial home page, for instance, will be the one set up by your network administrator rather than the Netscape home page shown below.

2. Double-click the Netscape Communicator icon to launch the program. If you have a SLIP or PPP account with an Internet Service Provider but are not currently connected, a dialog box may pop up asking you if you want to connect. Click Yes. The browser window appears, and the Netscape home page starts loading as shown in Figure 3-1.

TIP

Communicator can be configured so that instead of or in addition to the browser window, other Communicator components appear when you launch the program. You can make this change in the Appearance category, after selecting Preferences from the Edit menu.

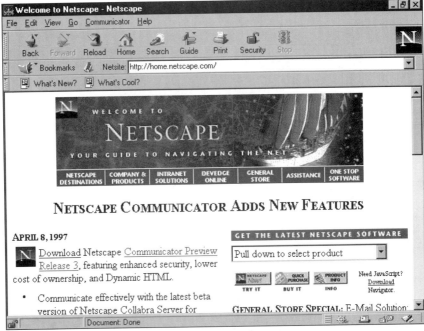

Figure 3-1: The browser window with the Netscape home page.

- By default, Netscape Navigator 4 uses the Netscape home page as your personal home page (in this context your *home page* is the document that loads automatically when you launch the program). Depending on the speed of your Internet connection and how busy the Netscape site is, this may take a few moments. Later in the chapter, you'll learn how you can select a different Web document as your home page in the sidebar "Changing Your Home Page." **Note:** If you are on an intranet, your network administrator may already have changed your home page.

- If you configured Communicator so that it requires a password, you will be asked to enter your password when you launch the program. For more about passwords, see Chapter 12.

Like any other Windows program, Navigator arranges many of its user-accessible features in a menu bar across the top of the window. I'll cover the commands available in the menus as they come up in using the program. But except for a few specialized commands, the menu bar is generally not the most efficient way to run the program. Let's take a look instead at the toolbars, the rows of buttons and icons just below the menu bar.

TIP

Your toolbars might not look exactly like the ones described below. That's because your network administrator has the option of changing the settings on your tool bars—adding buttons to it, removing buttons from it, and so on. Follow along with the instructions and if you run into a button that isn't explained in this chapter, ask your network administrator about it.

The Toolbars

I'm not talking about the floating gray thing at the top of your window with four icons on it. That's the Component Bar, and if you don't know what it does you haven't read Chapter 2. You can go back and check the section called "The Component Bar" if you want, but in brief: you click the icons in the floating gray thing to access Communicator's various modules such as your Mailbox, Collabra discussion groups, Composer, and of course, Navigator. You can move the Component Bar around your screen, and you can shrink it and anchor it to the Navigator status line (at the bottom of the window) by closing it. Clicking the left-most icon in the minimized Component Bar makes it expand and "float" again, but you can use all its icons to access other Communicator components even when it's minimized.

But right now we're in Navigator 4, and the bars full of icon buttons just under the menu are the toolbars I'm talking about. In a toolbar you click individual buttons or icons to control different program functions. Toolbars are so convenient that Netscape threw in three of them!

The Navigator toolbars are a little fancier than your average toolbar. For instance, you can move them around. Try this: click on the top toolbar, the one with the Back and Forward buttons, and drag it down the screen an inch. Notice how it changes places with the middle toolbar, as shown in Figure 3-2.

Not only can you move these toolbars around, you can roll them up and down like window shades. To the left of each toolbar there's a small tab with a down arrow in it. Just click one of these tabs and watch what happens. Yes, if you click all three you end up with something like Figure 3-3. To expand a minimized toolbar, simply click the up arrow.

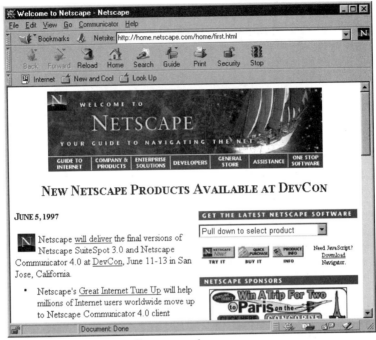

Figure 3-2: The top two toolbars reversed.

Figure 3-3: Navigator window with all three toolbars minimized.

TIP

Don't want any toolbars at all? You can choose which ones you want to hide right in the View menu. This is a good way to maximize the amount of screen space available for displaying large Web documents or graphics.

So that you can understand what I'm talking about in the next couple of pages, I'm going to give these three toolbars names. I'm going to call the large toolbar with all the icons in it the Command Toolbar. The Toolbar that contains the Bookmarks and Location/Netsite features I'll call the Location Toolbar, and the toolbar that's at the bottom I'll call the Personal Toolbar. Each of these toolbars has a very different function, so let's go over the components of each one individually.

The Command Toolbar

The Command Toolbar gives you access to all of the Navigator functions via standard icon buttons. And here's what all these buttons do, starting from the left:

- **The Back and Forward buttons**. Clicking these buttons allows you to cycle through the documents you have already viewed. You can revisit these documents in reverse order (relative to the order in which you originally viewed them) by pressing the Back button, and then you can retrace your path using the Forward button. If you simply place your mouse pointer on either button, a ToolTip shows you where the button will take you if you click it.

- **The Reload button**. When you click Reload, Navigator 4 reloads the current document from the Web or from its location on your intranet. What's the point? Please see the "Reloading & Refreshing" sidebar.

- **The Home button**. Clicking this button returns you to your home page.

- **The Search button**. Clicking this button takes you to Netscape's Net Search page, where you search the Web or Usenet newsgroups for particular information using a variety of search engines. I'll talk a lot more about searching later in the chapter, but Figure 3-4 shows what you get when you press the Search button.

Reloading & Refreshing

Navigator's Reload command makes the browser go out on your intranet or the Net and reload the Web document that's currently displayed.

Well, it's not *quite* that simple. First Navigator checks to see if the page has changed at all, and it only reloads it if it's different from the one stored in its cache from the last time you loaded it. This can be useful if you want the latest information from a site that changes daily, for instance. But since reloading means reconnecting with the remote site and possibly downloading files, it can also be slow, especially when the Net is particularly busy. If you want to redisplay a page in Netscape Navigator 4 but don't particularly care if it's the very latest version, you can use the Refresh command that's located in the View menu. This command loads the most recent version of the URL that has been saved to the program's cache.

You can also force a reload, in other words make Navigator go out and get a fresh copy of a page even if it hasn't changed. To do this, hold down the Shift key while clicking the Reload button.

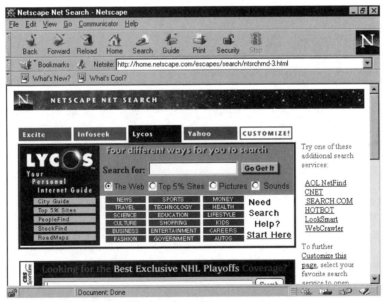

Figure 3-4: The Netscape Net Search page.

■ **The Images button.** This button isn't always present on the Command Toolbar. It only appears if you have configured Navigator 4 so that the program does not automatically display images it encounters in Web pages. This configuration can save you time on slow connections. The Images button becomes available so that you can *explicitly* request that graphics be displayed for the page you're currently viewing. Clicking the button won't change the program configuration; the next page you view will still display without images unless you click the button again.

To configure Navigator 4 so that it does not automatically display images, and so that the Images button appears on the Command Toolbar, please see the section below entitled "Advanced Preferences."

■ **The Guide button.** Click this button and a submenu appears, as shown in Figure 3-5.

Figure 3-5: The Guide submenu.

Just click one of the top three choices and you are transported to a specialized directory where you can browse for Web sites by category, search for individuals on the Net, or look for software that's available for free downloading. And the bottom two choices take you to special pages on the Netscape site that list some of the latest and greatest links.

- **The Print button**. This is pretty self-explanatory. Click this button to print the currently displayed document.

- **The Security button**. This button shows you the security status for any document you view in Navigator. If you are currently viewing a secure document, one that is protected by Netscape's SSL security protocol (see Chapter 13), the button displays a locked padlock; otherwise, it displays an unlocked padlock. If you click the button, you can view detailed security information about any secure document. Additionally, the Security button lets you change the security configuration for Navigator itself. Don't worry if this sounds alien to you at this point: I'll cover all you need to know about security in Chapter 13.

- **The Stop button**. If you are in the process of receiving a Web document, you can stop it from loading by pressing this button. Why would you want to do this? Often you don't really know what a document contains until you see some of it. Or perhaps you've already received the textual information you're interested in and simply want to stop the download of graphics, which can be quite slow in the case of large images.

- **The Netscape button**. The Netscape button appears at the far right of the Command Toolbar. When the icon becomes animated and shows a bunch of meteors whizzing by the big N, you know that the program is busy retrieving a document. While the meteors are falling, your Reload button changes to a Stop button as well. In fact if you click the Netscape button while a document is loading into the browser window, it works just like the Stop button; the document immediately stops loading. In addition, however, you are transported to Netscape's own home page. You can also use the Netscape button to get to the Netscape page when the program is *not* busy loading a document.

TIP

If you're on a corporate intranet, your system administrator may have changed the Netscape button to a different icon, perhaps your corporate logo. In this case clicking the button may take you to your own company's home page. Similarly, if your ISP supplied your copy of Communicator, the button may take you to that ISP's site. Click on it to see what happens—you can always click on the Back button to get back to where you were.

Now let's work our way down the screen to the next of the three toolbars.

The Location Toolbar

The program is called Navigator. It's about going places. And the Location Toolbar provides you with a few great tools for getting there:

- **Bookmarks.** At the left of the Location Toolbar you see the word "Bookmarks" and a book icon. This is called the Bookmarks QuickFile icon. When you click it, a menu appears that includes the items Add Bookmark, File Bookmark, and Edit Bookmarks. (If you already have a bookmarks file, for instance from an earlier version of Netscape Navigator, other items might appear in the menu as well.) At the bottom of the menu is a Personal Toolbar Folder item that lets you access the bookmarks you've added to the Personal Toolbar even if the Personal Toolbar is currently hidden. I'll be talking about bookmarks at length later in this chapter, but for now all you need to know is that they are shortcuts that let you navigate in one click to a location you've saved. Add Bookmarks stores the location of the currently displayed document for easy access right from this toolbar, and Edit Bookmarks lets you organize your bookmarks in convenient groupings. File Bookmark does the same thing as Add Bookmark, except that it lets you choose from several Bookmark folders if you have more than one. It also lets you add a bookmark to the Personal Toolbar Folder even if the Personal Toolbar is hidden.

- **The Netsite/Location box.** This text box has a label that changes according to how you use it. When Netscape Navigator 4 displays a Web document retrieved from a site that uses a Netscape Web server product, such as FastTrack or the Netscape Enterprise Server, the box is labeled Netsite; when it displays information retrieved from a non-Netscape server, the box is labeled Location. If you want to enter a URL manually, you can either type it or paste it directly into this field (the label changes to Go To while you're typing the new URL). Press Enter when you've finished entering the URL, and Netscape Navigator 4 jumps to that page.

TIP

*You'll notice an arrow button directly to the right of the Netsite box. You can click this button to display a drop-down list of the sites you've recently visited. Click any site in the list to return to it. (**Note:** This list only shows pages whose URLs you have entered in the Netsite/Location box and URLs you've opened using the Open Page command on the File menu. It does not display the URLs for sites you've visited by following links within Web documents.)*

Entering URLs the Easy Way

You learned in Chapter 1 that a URL, or the address of a particular resource such as a Web page, includes three parts: the protocol used to retrieve the resource (such as HTTP, Gopher, or FTP), the name of the server where the information you want is located, and optionally, a directory or file name. For instance, the URL for the Netscape home page is http://home.netscape.com, and the URL for one of its FTP sites is ftp://ftp.netscape.com. Both of these examples include a protocol specification and a server name.

Most often you get to a site by clicking a link within a Web page, but sometimes you need to type the URL itself into the Netsite or Location box. Wouldn't it be nice if you didn't always have to type that "http://" or "ftp://"?

Well, you don't! Netscape Navigator 4 is intelligent. You can leave off the protocol specification and the program will do its best to figure out what kind of resource you had in mind. For instance, if you type in **home.netscape.com**, Navigator 4 knows you really mean http://home.netscape.com. If you type in **gopher.well.com**, you are automatically transported to gopher://gopher.well.com. For names that start with the standard "www" you can even leave the www off. For instance, for the URL http://www.echonyc.com you can type as little as "echonyc.com!" It's a great time saver.

Throughout this book I'll tell you to type in complete URLs, including the protocol specification. I'm doing that so you get used to the format and to make very clear what kind of resource we're talking about. But after a while, you'll almost certainly want to take advantage of this handy shortcut.

■ **The Page icon.** The Page icon is a little picture of a page and a bookmark just to the left of the Netsite/Location box. This icon is really a shortcut representation of the current URL. You can drag the Page icon onto the Windows 95 desktop to create a shortcut to the URL, and you can drag it onto the Bookmarks QuickFile icon or onto the Personal Toolbar to create a new bookmark (see upcoming section on Bookmarks). You can even drag the Page icon into a Netscape Composer window to edit the document.

The Personal Toolbar

This is one of the nicest new features in Netscape Navigator 4. Notice that the Personal Toolbar contains three buttons: Internet, New and Cool, and Look Up. Clicking these buttons transports you to Netscape's own Netscape Guide What's New, What's Cool White pages and Yellow pages, where you will find links to a variety of interesting Web resources. But that's not what makes the Personal Toolbar exciting. Its real power is in its *customizability*. When you encounter a link in a document, you can drag it up to the Personal Toolbar to create a brand new icon button that sits next to the two default ones. Then all you need to do is click that icon button to access the link. Let's give it a try:

1. Make sure you're connected to the Internet.

2. Make sure your Personal Toolbar is open or maximized. If not, click the up arrow tab to its left.

3. If Navigator 4 is not currently displaying the Netscape home page, click the Home button and wait for the page to appear.

4. On the Netscape home page, scroll down and locate the link "Customer Service," as shown in Figure 3-6.

TIP

A link is simply some text or graphic element in a Web document which, when clicked, takes you to a different site. Text links, by default, are underlined and colored differently from the surrounding text. Graphics links are sometimes not as easy to differentiate from other components of the page, but when you place your cursor over either a text or graphics link, the cursor changes into a pointing hand.

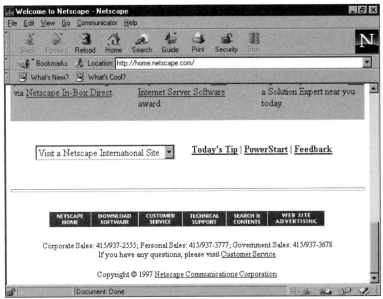

Figure 3-6: The Netscape home page, with Customer Service link.

If you were to click the link, Netscape's customer service page would appear. But you don't need customer service right now, so instead of navigating to the link, let's save it to the Personal Toolbar in case we need it later:

1. Click the Customer Service link and drag it up to the Personal Toolbar. Once you let go of the mouse button, the link appears there as a new button, as shown in Figure 3-7.

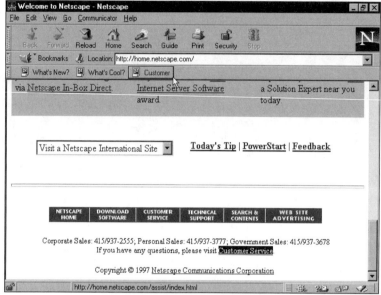

Figure 3-7: The Personal Toolbar with a new button.

2. Want to change the order of the icon buttons in the Personal Toolbar? Just click and drag them right or left.

Customizing the Personal Toolbar

Suppose you don't want the Internet, New and Cool, and Look Up buttons in your Personal Toolbar. Or suppose you want to change how a particular button reads, without changing the link itself. For instance, you might want the button that accesses the Netscape customer service simply to read "HELP!!!"

Here's the trick to remembering how to customize the Personal Toolbar: it's really just a Bookmarks folder that's presented in a different way, and the links in it are really just bookmarks. That means you customize the Personal Toolbar the same way you customize any other Navigator bookmarks.

Ah, but I haven't covered bookmarks yet. Well, let me give you just enough information to get started with your Personal Toolbar. This will help make bookmarks clearer to you, too, when you get to the Bookmarks section of this chapter:

1. Click the Bookmarks icon and then select Edit Bookmarks. The Bookmarks window appears, as shown in Figure 3-8.

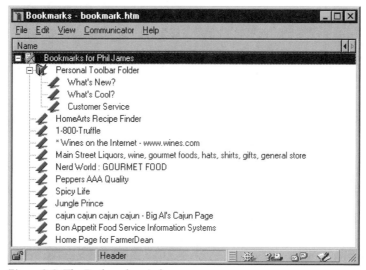

Figure 3-8: The Bookmarks window.

- ■ If no items appear under the Personal Toolbar Folder, double-click it to expand it, or simply click the "plus" icon.

2. Select one of the items under the Personal Toolbar Folder (What's New?, for instance), then right-click. A submenu appears, which includes the items Delete Bookmark and Bookmark Properties, among others.

3. To get rid of a bookmark from the Personal Toolbar, click Delete Bookmark.

4. To change the text that appears on the button, or to modify its URL or description, select Bookmark Properties and then edit the appropriate fields in the Bookmark Properties dialog box that appears, as shown in Figure 3-9.

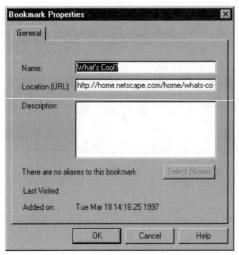

Figure 3-9: The Bookmark Properties dialog box for a Personal Toolbar button.

If you keep in mind that these convenient buttons are really bookmarks just like any other bookmarks, you'll never forget how to customize the Personal Toolbar.

Navigator's toolbars offer some extremely powerful tools for navigating to and viewing Web documents, either on the Net or on an office intranet. Now let's continue this overview by moving down the screen to the document display area itself.

The Display Window

The display window is the most important area within Netscape Navigator 4. This is where Navigator 4 displays the formatted text, links, hotspots, form fields, graphics, and other items that make up a Web page. Some of these fields and controls are "static," like a standard paragraph of text, while others are "active" and actually perform a function. Some controls may be immediately obvious, like a button, while others may be hidden. For example, the Netscape page in Figure 3-10 includes a Welcome to Netscape graphic with hotspots. When you click these hotspots, you are magically teleported to other Web pages, just as if you'd clicked a text link. You'll learn more about these components of a Web page later in this chapter. For now, though, just remember that if your mouse cursor turns into a hand with a pointing finger, you can click there to do something or go somewhere!

Figure 3-10: A graphic menu with hotspots.

TIP

Netscape Navigator 4 includes standard scroll bars along the right and bottom edges of the display window. If you resize the window (or if a Web page is longer than one screen length, which is usually the case), these controls let you scroll the display so that you can view the entire page.

Canvas Mode

Netscape Navigator is the perfect tool for displaying marketing or other information in a public setting such as on a public access terminal in a mall, library, or doctor's waiting room. But in settings like this, it looks a lot slicker if the actual information—perhaps a succession of static images or a video clip—takes up the entire screen, without any menu bars and window borders. And if the display is interactive, allowing viewers to click buttons to access new information, it is essential to eliminate or hide any user interface elements that will let them customize the display—for instance by scrolling an image out of view, or resizing the browser window, or even navigating to other Web sites!

➡

Navigator provides a special kiosk mode that Netscape also refers to as *Canvas mode.* When in Canvas mode, you cannot affect the display except through interface elements specifically programmed by the author of the Web page. For example, take a look at Figure 3-11:

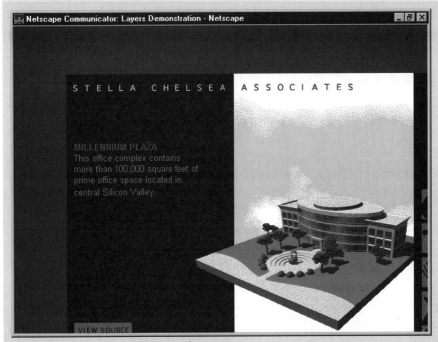

Figure 3-11: Navigator in Canvas mode.

A viewer can click any of the buttons or icons on the screen to access more detailed information but is effectively "locked out" of the Navigator software itself until he or she presses the Close Demo button (in an actual public setting this button would not exist). You won't suddenly find a competitor's Web site on the screen instead of your carefully crafted promotional material.

So how do you put Navigator into Canvas mode? That's easy: you don't do anything at all. The Web page *itself* includes specially programmed instructions to Navigator that tell it to "get out of the way." These instructions are written in an easy-to-use programming language called JavaScript that may be mixed in with regular HTML code. In Chapter 10 I'll show you how to create a page that puts any Navigator browsers that access it into canvas mode.

The Status Line

At the very bottom of the browser window lives the Navigator status line. What's it for? That's right, it displays current status information. For example, the padlock icon at the far left works the same way as the Security button on the Command Toolbar: it shows you the security status of the current document. If it is a locked padlock, you are viewing a secure document; if it's an unlocked padlock, you are viewing an ordinary document that's not protected by encryption (see Chapter 13). And if you click the padlock icon, you can see more detailed security information.

But the status line shows you lots more information as well, in the form of text messages. If you're currently receiving a picture from a Web site, for example, Navigator 4 fills in the status line with the name of the image file and a status bar that indicates the progress of the transfer. Or if you move your mouse pointer over a link, the status line shows its URL, as you can see in Figure 3-12.

Figure 3-12: The Navigator status line showing the URL of a link.

In addition, if you've closed your Component Bar, it appears in minimized form at the right side of the status line, as shown in Figure 3-13. You can click any of the icons to access other Communicator features such as e-mail or discussion groups, and you can re-expand the Component Bar by clicking the left-most icon.

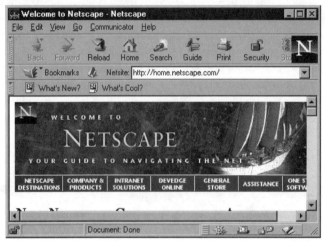

Figure 3-13: The Component Bar minimized on the status line.

Local Area URLs

As I mentioned in Chapter 1, you don't need the Internet to use Netscape Communicator effectively. In fact, you don't even need an intranet! If you're on a local area network (LAN), you can use the program to access documents within your own organization or your own computer. For instance, employees could call up the latest sales data or view a fancy multimedia demonstration of a new product or service. There are lots of things you *can't* do without an intranet and a real Web server, but in a very small office viewing stored documents may be all you need.

To access a document that is stored locally rather than at a remote site, press Ctrl+O or select Open Page from Navigator 4's File menu. An Open Page dialog box pops up. Now you can click Browse to look around your own computer or another computer on your LAN for the document you want. HTML documents appear with the Netscape logo, but you can also choose to view text or graphic files.

You can also access a locally stored document by clicking a link to it within another document. For instance, you may want to construct a home page that contains links to a variety of important files on your LAN. The URL for a locally stored file looks a little different from other URLs, and you should know how to construct one in case you ever need to enter one directly in the Netsite/Location box. A local file URL starts with **file:**. Next, as with all complete URLs, there are *two* forward slashes, then the exact path to the file. Got all that? Here's an example—an HTML file called PRODUCT.HTM that's located in the Public directory on the Q drive of your LAN: file://Q:/Public/PRODUCT.HTM. Of course if this file were on your own computer, you would specify one of your local drives, for instance C, instead of Q.

TIP

You can enter the path for the file using backslashes if you want; Navigator automatically converts them to forward slashes, which are the standard for Web browsers.

Netscape Communicator supports most of the same media on a LAN as it does on the Net or a true intranet. You can use the program to play sound files, run video clips, and even gather information from other employees using HTML forms (see "Forms on the Web" later in this chapter). And of course a document can contain a mix of links to Internet sites and to local files. This power and flexibility make Netscape Communicator an excellent tool for disseminating enterprise-wide information even without a Web server!

Links & Hotspots

Let's continue our discussion of Web navigation with the most common active control found within Web pages: the *link*. We've already discussed links a little bit, but now it's time to get into it a little deeper. OK, review time: a link is a special text string or image embedded within a document. It tells Navigator to jump to another document or to a different place in the current document. Linked documents may be physically stored at the same site or another site halfway across the world. As I explained in Chapter 1, this is the essence of hypertext.

Links are considered "followed" once you click them to display the new information. Navigator 4 changes the color of a followed link to indicate that you've used it before. This color coding can help you retrace your steps.

To use a link, simply move your mouse pointer over the link text and click. But how can you be sure you're on a link? You already know one visual cue, the pointing hand cursor, but there are others as well.

How Can I Tell I'm on a Link?

Navigator 4 provides a number of visual cues to indicate the presence of a link:

- By default, text links are underlined and appear in blue, while regular inactive text is not underlined and appears black. If you return to a page after using one of its links, the link then appears in red to indicate that you've been there. You can always click the same link again; it does not become inactive once you've clicked it. The change in color is only a helpful reminder.

- As I mentioned earlier, if you rest your mouse cursor on a link, the status line changes to indicate the link's URL. No URL in the status line, no link!

- As I also mentioned earlier, your mouse cursor changes to a pointing hand when it rests on a link.

Figure 3-14 shows a section of Netscape's own online handbook that contains a number of links.

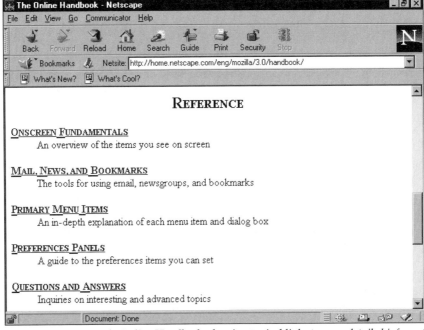

Figure 3-14: Netscape's Online Handbook, showing typical links to more detailed information.

TIP

Often the content of the text containing the link indicates what the link will do. For instance, "download PROGRAM.ZIP now" and "jump to the index" are self-explanatory.

Changing What Links Look Like

If you don't like blue or underlines, you can change the properties of link text. Click Preferences on the Edit menu and then choose Colors under the Appearance category at the left side of the window. (If you don't see the Colors item, double-click Appearance to expand the list.) In the Colors window, you can change the default colors for links you've used (Visited Links) and for those you haven't tried yet (Unvisited Links). You can also check a box to tell Navigator whether or not links should be underlined.

In this same dialog box you can also change the default background color for Web pages as well as the default color of regular (non-link) text. To change these settings, uncheck the Use Windows colors check box and then click the respective buttons. To force Navigator to display these colors no matter what a Web page specifies, check the check box at the very bottom of the dialog box.

Using Hotspots

Hotspots are just like links, except they are embedded within graphical information rather than text. Like links, hotspots perform an action when you click them. You might click one to jump to another page or to view an image or even to play a piece of music. Sometimes hotspots are smaller "thumbnail" versions of full-size images that you can download, or they may be beautifully designed arrows pointing to the next in a series of linked documents. Many sites also use hotspots as "menu items" within larger images that serve as menu systems. In the Netscape home page, for instance, you can click on various areas within the same graphic to jump to different documents. Let's give this a try:

1. Make sure you are connected to the Internet.

2. Double-click the Netscape Communicator or Navigator icon to launch the program. The main window appears, and the Netscape home page starts loading, as shown earlier in Figure 3-1.

3. In the large graphic near the top of the page, click the General Store section. The General Store appears, as shown in Figure 3-15.

Congratulations! You just used a hotspot to get from the Netscape home page to the General Store. Traveling sure is simple in cyberspace.

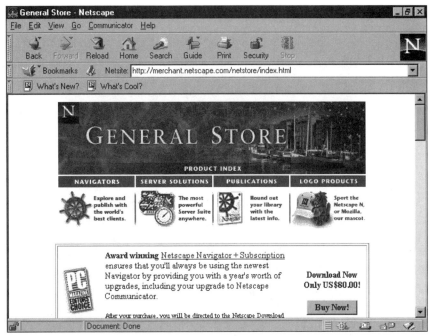

Figure 3-15: The General Store.

TIP

Usually, clicking a link causes the text and graphics currently displayed in the Navigator window to be replaced with new text and graphics. Sometimes, however, your current window will stay the same and an entire new window opens up to display the new information. The command to open a new window is part of the control information in the HTML file itself.

In this example, it was easy to find the hotspots in the graphic because they included text. But there are other ways to indicate hotspots as well. Sometimes they are displayed with a colored border, or the author of a Web page might refer to a hotspot in a line of text such as "Click the right arrow to move to the next page."

Right-Clicking Links & Images

Normally you click with your left mouse button on links and hotspots. But by clicking your *right* mouse button instead, you can access a wide range of ways to manipulate these interactive elements.

When you click a link with the right mouse button, a context menu appears that lets you:

- **Open in New Window**. This opens a new browser window that displays the document specified in the link. Your original window remains open. Navigator lets you keep multiple browser windows open, each displaying different Web documents or even the same document.

- **Open Link in Composer**. This opens the link in Netscape Composer, letting you modify the contents of the document.

- **Back**. Selecting this item is the same as clicking the Back button on the Command Toolbar.

- **Forward**. Selecting this item is the same as clicking the Forward button on the Command Toolbar.

- **Reload**. Selecting this item is the same as clicking the Reload button on the Command Toolbar.

- **Stop**. Selecting this item is the same as clicking the Bookmarks icon on the Location Toolbar. Not really, I just wanted to see if you're paying attention. Yes, it's the same as clicking the Stop button.

- **View source**. Want to see the actual HTML code for the current document? Click here.

- **View Info**. This option shows you lots of useful information about the current document, including the various graphic components it contains and when it was created.

- **Add Bookmark**. This lets you add the link to your Bookmarks without actually having to navigate to the target document.

- **Create Shortcut**. This lets you create a desktop shortcut to the link. It is equivalent to dragging the Link icon out to the desktop, except you do not currently need to be displaying the target document.

- **Send Page**. If you click this item a New Message window appears, letting you address an e-mail to any recipient you want. The message already includes the currently displayed document as an attachment (please see Chapter 5 if you don't understand this terminology).

- **Save Link as**. This lets you save the target HTML file on your hard drive or network drive.

- **Copy Link Location**. This copies the link to the Windows clipboard. It is the same as double-clicking the Page icon, except you do not need to be currently displaying the target document.

When you click a hotspot or graphic with the right mouse button, you see many of the same menu items, plus these additional specialized choices:

- **View Image**. This allows you to view the current image by itself, without the surrounding text or other graphics.

- **Set as Wallpaper**. This lets you use the current image as your Windows wallpaper.

- **Save Image as**. This lets you save the graphic to your hard drive or a network drive.

- **Copy Image Location**. This copies the URL of the image to the Windows clipboard.

- **Add Bookmark**. This lets you create a new bookmark for the graphic (see the later section on Bookmarks).

Using the Navigator 4 Controls

As I mentioned earlier, Navigator's topmost toolbar is the program's control center. You can use these buttons like the forward and reverse gears of a car, moving back and forth through Web documents. You can also use them to print the contents of any page or even to locate specific information on the Internet.

Of course, all these functions are also available from the menu bar, but most Internet surfers find that the graphical nature of the Web lends itself to mouse control, making the toolbar the easiest and most convenient method for harnessing the power of Netscape Navigator 4.

In this section, we'll discuss the buttons you'll use the most as we navigate through Netscape's own Web site.

TIP

Note that pages on the Netscape Web site may change from time to time, so the screens and links we use may not agree exactly with what you see on your screen. However, you should still be able to follow the steps in a general fashion.

The Forward & Back Buttons

You've already seen how easy it is to get to a new document by clicking a link or hotspot. But what if you need to return to a previously viewed page? Maybe you forgot to download a file, or you suddenly decide to back up and follow a different information trail. This is where the first two buttons on the toolbar come into play. Back and Forward allow you to retrace your steps to a previous page or, if you've already backtracked, to jump forward to the last page you accessed.

To see how this works, follow these steps:

1. Make sure you are connected to the Internet or intranet. If Navigator 4 is not currently running, launch it by double-clicking its icon or the Communicator icon.

2. In the Netscape home page, click the hotspot for the General Store. If you're already at the General Store because you're a good student who followed the last set of directions, just stay there!

3. Now click the Back button. We're back where we started, at the Netscape home page. Guess what the Forward button does? Go ahead and click it now. As you probably guessed, the General Store page pops up once more.

TIP

If you simply place your mouse cursor on either the Forward or Back button, a ToolTip shows you where the button will take you to when you click it. This can help you stay oriented when working with a page that has multiple frames (see the section called "Understanding Frames."

4. Now click a new link or hotspot. It doesn't really matter which one. Once the new document appears, click the Back button twice. As you probably expected, the Back button can lead sequentially back through all the pages you have visited. And of course Forward works the same way, in reverse.

Multiple Connections

You can display several Web documents at once with Netscape Navigator 4. Select New from the File menu, then Navigator Window from the submenu that appears. You can also simply press Ctrl+N. Another window pops up, and you can use it, like the first window, to navigate to any site. As I mentioned before, some sites automatically open new browser windows to display information, so you may have several windows open already.

And why would you want to connect to more than one site at a time?

- If you're researching a specific topic and you've found more than one page with pertinent information or links, it's a good idea to load each page in a separate window if you need to compare them. This can take up a lot of your system's memory, though, so be careful!

- Certain sites may be particularly slow, and opening an additional window allows you to continue exploring while you wait for the display of the first page to finish.

- Extra-large files like .MOV or .AVI animations may take several minutes to download. With a second window, you can continue surfing while you wait.

When you first open a new browser window, it "inherits" the history of the original window and displays the oldest page in that history, which is usually the Netscape home page. (The Back button won't work, though.) If you're wondering what I mean by *history*, it will all make sense after the section on "The History List & Bookmarks." Don't worry about it for now—all you need to know is that the new window is just like the old one, and you can use it to get anywhere you want on the Web.

The Reload Button

You already know about the Reload button, but here are some hints on when to use it:

- Use the Reload button to redisplay the current page if you originally pressed Stop while it was still loading. The Reload button will enable you to get the entire document.

- Use the Reload button to redisplay the current page if you originally displayed it in text-only mode and now want to see the graphics. *Note:* you may need to press Shift while clicking Reload in order to force Navigator to go back to the original source of the document rather than to a locally stored copy.

■ Use the Reload button to redisplay the current page if some of the text is garbled or there are other obvious display errors. Again, you may need to press Shift while clicking Reload in order to force Navigator to go back to the original source of the document.

The Home Button

You can click new links and dance around with the Forward and Back buttons as long as you want, but eventually you might get dizzy and long for home. To return to the Netscape home page, or to your corporate intranet's home page:

1. Click the Home button.

That's it. (I love one-step procedures.)

Your Home Page

Why do you even need a home page? There are several reasons:

■ A home page helps you stay oriented with a familiar starting point. Imagine what surfing would be like if you started without a home base—or, even worse, jumped to a random page every time you started the program!

■ Many seasoned Web surfers set their home pages to their favorite site, especially if the contents of the page change often. This way, you can check your favorite page each time you begin a Navigator session. If you have your own personal Web page, for example, you could set it as your home page.

■ Some pages are especially designed to offer as much as possible for new Web surfers, making them ideal launching pads for Web exploration. For example, the Netscape home page offers links to the newest and most popular pages, Web search tools, and a wealth of exciting Internet resources—all from one screen.

At some point, though, you may want to change your home page. Why? First, a purely practical reason: if your current home page is particularly busy or it's operated on a slower connection, it may take 30 seconds or so to load the page! Delays like that can get quite tiring after a few sessions, so you'd probably want to select a faster site (or perhaps even use a page you've created on your local hard disk). If you're really interested in saving time, you can even set your home page as "blank," so there's no load time at all.

Additionally, your interests are likely to change. You can save valuable Internet time by constructing a customized home page and including in it the sites you access the most. (To learn how to do this, see Chapter 9.)

➡

To change your home page, follow these steps:

1. Select Preferences from the Edit menu, then select Navigator from the Category list at the left of the window.

2. In the Home Page section, enter the URL of your new home page. Make sure you spell the address correctly! If you've saved or created a page on your local hard drive or a network drive, you can use the Browse button to find the HTML file you want to use. You can also click the Use Current Page button to set the document currently displayed as your new home page.

3. Click OK.

TIP

You may try to make changes to your home pages and other Netscape preferences only to find that you can't. Instead, you may find that the preferences have been "locked" by your system administrator and it's impossible to change them. If you want to change a setting in this case, you'll have to ask your system administrator.

I'm going to cover the Search and Guide buttons a little later in this chapter, when I talk about finding information on the Web—so for now, let's move ahead to the Print button.

The Print Button

Okay, so you've found the Secret to Life's Eternal Mystery on a particular Web page, and you'd like to save it for future reference. You could highlight the text with your mouse and copy the text to the Windows clipboard, but why not print out the whole thing? That way you can keep a hard copy of all of the contents of the page, including the images.

To print the contents of a page, click the Print button. Like most Windows applications, Navigator provides standard options that you can access from within the Print dialog box, and you can change the appearance of printed documents by selecting Page Setup from the File menu.

You can also display a preview image of the output before you print it by selecting the Print Preview option from the File menu. Figure 3-17 shows a print preview of the Netscape General Store.

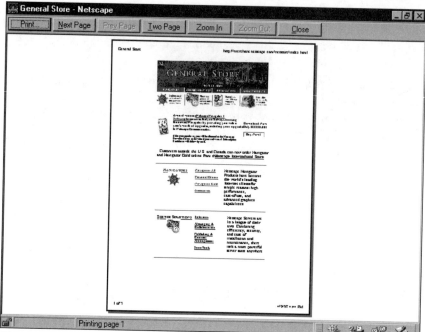

Figure 3-16: Print preview of the Netscape General Store.

The Security Button

When you click the Security button while displaying a regular non-encrypted Web document, you get something like Figure 3-17:

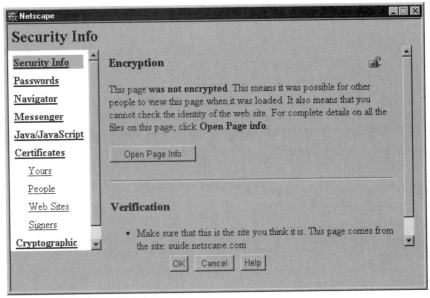

Figure 3-17: The Security Info page.

Basically, this page tells you that the current document is not a secure one. But when you connect to a secure site, one that's protected by encryption (see Chapter 13), all kinds of things change. First, a dialog box like the one in Figure 3-18 appears.

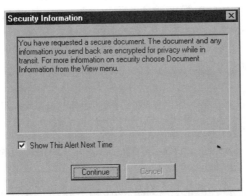

Figure 3-18: The Security Information alert.

By default, Navigator shows alerts like this both when you retrieve a secure document *and* when you return to a non-encrypted document after viewing a secure one. (To learn about changing these defaults, see Chapter 13.) Once you click continue, the secure document appears in the browser window and the Security button changes to depict a locked paddle lock. This indicates that you are currently viewing a secure page, as shown in Figure 3-19.

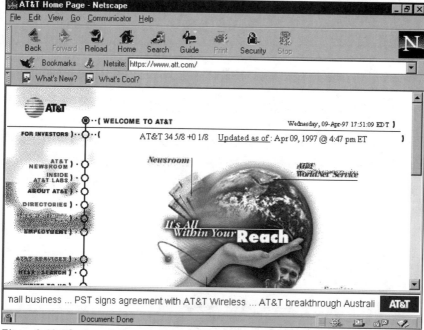

Figure 3-19: The Security button when viewing a Secure page.

TIP

The Security icon at the far left of the status line behaves just like the Security button, changing to a locked padlock when you access a secure site. You can also click this icon, just like the Security button, for additional information and settings.

What happens now when you click the Security button? Take a look at Figure 3-20.

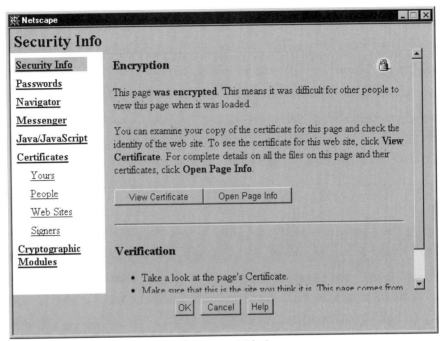

Figure 3-20: The Security Info page for a secure Web site.

As you can see, the Security button lets you display Security information for the current page. In addition, it lets you view and configure a wide variety of security settings. I'll cover those in Chapter 13, but for now let's move on to the final Command Toolbar button.

The Stop Button

OK, here are some hints on when to use the Stop button:

- Click the Stop button when you notice that the document you've requested is not the one you really want.
- Click the Stop button when a document seems to be taking too long to display—perhaps the remote Web server isn't operating properly.
- Click the Stop button when you're in the middle of retrieving that "Babes and Hunks on the Web" page and you suddenly realize your boss is standing right behind you.

I use the Stop button all the time to stop retrieving documents that are loading slowly. And why do some pages seem to take forever to load? Possible reasons for a long wait can include:

- **Heavy usage on the Web site you're calling**. Try calling during low-traffic hours—late at night or early in the morning.

- **Heavy usage on the system that provides your Internet connection**. Check with your access provider to see when the system is being used the least. Remember that the server where a particular page is located may be in another part of the world, so you may have to make allowances for time differences.

- **Extra-large graphics or files you're receiving**. (Remember, you can always keep track of where you are in the transfer process by watching the progress bar that appears in the Navigator status line.)

- **A slow data pipeline**. In plain English, this means that some sites are connected to the Web by leased modem lines or older networks, and these slower connections can be bottlenecks.

TIP

If Navigator is attempting to receive a Web page or a file and the transfer seems stuck, you can often retrieve the data successfully by aborting the current transfer with the Stop button and immediately trying the same link again.

Here's a good rule of thumb: the best time to surf the Net is when you and the rest of the country really should be sleeping. Of course, you can't do that in a job that requires "banker's hours." In that case, try to log on very early in the morning if possible, and avoid surfing at the business day's peak time of between 11AM and 1PM PST.

So far you've learned the basics of navigating a simple Web page. In most cases, it's as easy as clicking links and using the Forward, Back, and Home buttons. But besides plain old vanilla Web pages, there are a few different kinds of documents you'll encounter from time to time. First we'll take a look at fill-out forms and then at frames.

Forms on the Web

"Please fill in your name, address, and phone number." You've been doing it your whole life on paper, and now you can do it electronically too.

Forms are scattered all over the Web. Some let you fill in a search word and then find it for you in a collection of documents; some let you buy a CD or new software product; some even engage you in a real-time conversation.

Whatever their purpose, World Wide Web forms share a common look and feel when displayed in Netscape Navigator 4. Here's an example:

1. Make sure you are connected to the Internet.

2. In the Netsite/Location box enter **http://hoohoo.ncsa.uiuc.edu/ archie.html** and hit Enter. The Archie request form appears, as shown in Figure 3-21.

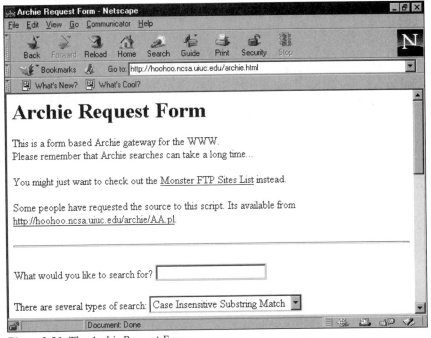

Figure 3-21: The Archie Request Form.

> **TIP**
>
> *Remember, you don't need to type in entire URLs. Entering* **hoohoo.ncsa.uiuc.edu/archie.html** *will do the trick.*

Archie is an Internet service that's been around much longer than the Web. It is a tool for finding files at FTP sites (see Chapter 8). But until the Web came along and provided convenient fill-out forms like this one, Archie was much more difficult to use.

Take a few minutes to scroll through this page and examine its various forms elements. There are boxes you can type text into, drop-down lists, and radio buttons. There is also a Submit button that lets you send your request once you have completed filling in the information. If you want, type something in the What would you like to search for? box and then click the Submit button. Let's say you typed the word test and left all the other fields alone. In a few seconds you'd be presented with something like Figure 3-22.

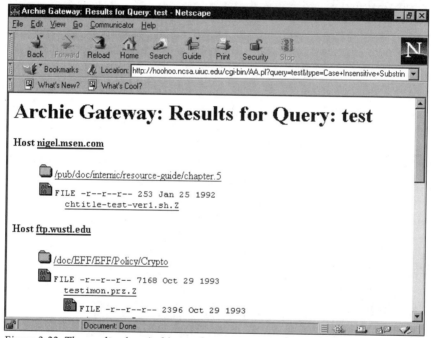

Figure 3-22: The results of an Archie search.

As the commercial uses of the Internet become more prominent, we'll see more and more forms for actual transactions. Already you can buy all kinds of products directly over the Net, and the Web's forms interface makes it easy. By the way, Netscape has been a leader in Internet security, and Netscape Navigator 4 indicates when a form is not secure by a special alert message. The message informs you that any information you submit is unencrypted and could be observed by a third party while it's in transit.

This may sound a bit frightening, but security is typically not a problem with the vast majority of forms you'll fill out online. As a rule, simply take the same precautions that you would if someone were asking similar questions over the telephone. If you feel uncomfortable providing a particular piece of private information, you'll probably want to follow Navigator's recommendation and cancel the form without submitting it. Chapter 13 discusses security issues in more detail.

As more and more companies start collecting data and even selling products via the Internet, online forms may become the bread-and-butter interface on the Web. But fortunately the Web is not all bread and butter, it's champagne and Jell-O, too. Let's take a look at something a bit more fun than forms: *frames*.

Understanding Frames

One of the coolest features of Netscape Navigator 4 is its support for frames. Frames are distinct areas within the Navigator display area. Special HTML commands in a Web document tell the program to partition the display. Each frame is a stand-alone environment that recognizes mouse clicks, has its own scroll bars, and can include all the features of any Web page. Each frame has its own distinct URL. In short, each frame is actually a window displaying its own Web page. Netscape Navigator 4 can actually "freeze" one of the frames so that it stays onscreen all the time while you interact with the links and hotspots in another frame. You may see logos, advertisements, or tables of contents handled in this fashion.

And not all frames look alike. Using Netscape Navigator 4 you may see frames with wide borders, narrow borders, or even no borders at all.

Let's take a look at an example of frames, as shown in Figure 3-23. This figure is the Netscape Web site at http://developer.netscape.com/. As you can guess from the URL, this is a more technical site. Home.netscape.com is where you hang your hat—developer.netscape.com is where you proudly display your pocket protector.

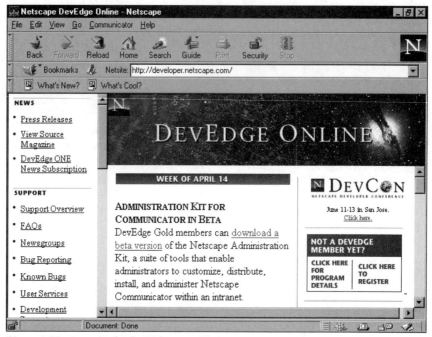

Figure 3-23: An example of a Web page with frames.

Because each frame is its own entity, make sure you select the appropriate frame (by clicking) when you decide to print something. Only the contents of the selected frame, and not the entire display window, print. In addition, you can reload the contents of individual frames by selecting Reload from the View menu, and you can even e-mail the contents of a frame by selecting Send Frame from the File menu.

The way developers use frames makes Web sites very flexible and dynamic for the user. At this Netscape site, notice how each of the two frames is used differently. The left-hand frame displays a clickable table of contents, while the larger right-hand frame displays the actual content. Also, notice how each frame has its own scroll bars.

Other sites use frames to display different types of elements. One frame, for instance, may contain text, while another contains graphics. As you click and read through the text, the graphics can change or rotate based on the text displayed. Frames are also used with multimedia or 3D objects. One pane may contain instructions or a story about how to navigate a VRML world with Cosmo or Live3D, while the other contains the actual VRML objects. (Don't know what Cosmo, VRML, and Live3D are? Please turn to Chapter 10.)

TIP

You can go back and forward in frames just as you do in the browser window as a whole. To go back to the information previously displayed in a frame, select that frame (by clicking in it) and click the Back button. To go forward, select the frame and click the Forward button. You can also right-click in the frame and choose the Forward or Back options from the context menu that appears.

Dynamic HTML

In Chapter 1 you learned a little bit about HTML, the language that's used to compose Web pages. But Navigator 4 supports some exciting new extensions to HTML that Netscape groups together as *Dynamic HTML*. Dynamic HTML gives Web designers more flexibility in making pages look exactly as they want them to look—and in making them more interactive. Here are a few of the features that comprise Dynamic HTML:

- **Dynamic Fonts.** Web pages can now specify exact fonts, font sizes, and font weights that Navigator will then display correctly in your browser window. If you don't already have the specified font on your system, it will be sent to you automatically along with the rest of the HTML information.

- **Style Sheets.** Web page developers can create style sheets that specify sets of design elements such as layout, fonts, bullet styles, etc. These style sheets can then be applied to multiple pages, allowing for a unified look and feel. This not only makes it faster to develop new pages, it means that you will be presented with a consistent user interface when navigating a particular site.

- **Dynamic Layers.** HTML developers may design pages that have multiple layers of information. Text may be overlayed on graphics, or vice versa. Layering also provides a simple way to enhance Web pages with animation.

With Dynamic HTML, various *HTML objects*—such as fonts—may be stored locally. When a Web page calls for the object, it doesn't have to be downloaded anew. Dynamic HTML also means that a Web page may quickly adapt aspects of its design to suit the needs of *your* system.

We've covered a lot of material so far. You should be pretty good at navigating Web documents at this point, either on the Internet or on an office intranet. You may be feeling a bit lost, however. As a technical writer I feel compelled to use clichéd automotive analogies—using clichéd automotive analogies is a lot of what we do for a living—so here goes: you now know how to operate the car, but do you know where you're going? Never fear, the next few sections of this chapter are focused on getting to places and finding things.

Finding Information in a Web Page

From time to time you'll encounter huge documents that are crowded with text and links. Scrolling slowly through a mountain of text line by line is one method of locating that link you remember, but Netscape Navigator 4 makes it much easier with the Find command.

Let's look for a specific string of text on Netscape's own home page:

1. Make sure you are connected to the Internet or intranet. If Netscape Navigator 4 is not currently running, launch it by double-clicking its icon or the Communicator icon.

2. If the Netscape home page is not currently displayed, click the Home button or enter **home.netscape.com** in the Netsite/Location box and hit Enter. In a few seconds, the Netscape page appears. Click the Company and Products link that's part of the large image at the top of the page. Netscape's Company and Products page appears.

3. Hit Ctrl+F or select Find in Page from the Edit menu. Navigator displays the Find dialog box, as shown in Figure 3-24.

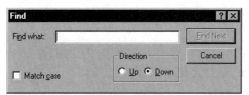

Figure 3-24: The Find dialog box.

4. Let's say you're sick of tech support and want a job as a Netscape programmer. OK, enter the word **work** in the Find what: field and click the Find Next button. In a flash, Navigator locates the "A Cool Place to Work" link, highlights it, and displays the surrounding section of the document, as shown in Figure 3-25. Simply click the link if you want more information about employment opportunities at Netscape.

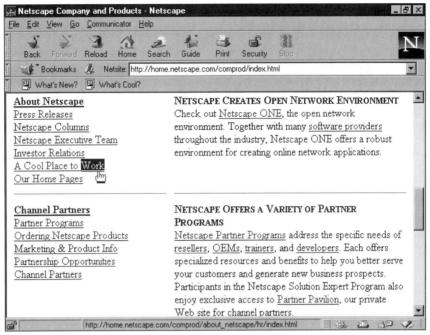

Figure 3-25: The results of a successful Find command.

- If you need a case-sensitive search, enable the Match case option; Navigator 4 will display only those instances in which the capitalization matches your entry. You can also specify in which direction the program should search—click the Up radio button to search upward through the document or on the Down radio button to move downward. The search begins at the current cursor position.

5. To search for more occurrences of the same string, click the Find Next button again.

TIP

Want to drive yourself crazy? Try using the Find command before the text of the page is completely loaded. The Find command can't find text on a page unless the page has been completely loaded!

Finding Information on the Web

Now you know how to find words or phrases in a single Web document. That's great, but don't set up shop as a research expert just yet. There are hundreds of thousands of people who know how to find information not just in a single document, but across all the publicly available documents on the Internet! That sounds impressive, but using Navigator 4 it's almost a no-brainer.

There are two different methods for finding specific information on the Web: *searching* and *browsing*. Searching means explicitly requesting documents containing specific words or phrases; browsing, in the sense we are using it here, means looking through subject indexes of documents as you refine your search. It's like looking for a needle in a haystack that gets smaller and smaller as you work your way down through categories of information. Let's try some searching first, using Navigator's Search button.

The Search Button

As I mentioned earlier, the sheer size of the World Wide Web makes it extremely difficult to locate a particular piece of information or a specific Web page by simply fishing for the right URL. For this reason, topical search engines have been around for as long as the Web itself.

Search engines usually look through an index of documents for a query string that you specify. Some search tools also allow you to add logical operators like "and," "either," and "or" so that you can perform more sophisticated searches.

Netscape Navigator 4 provides you with links to all the search engines you're likely to need. Clicking the Search button brings up the Net Search page, shown in Figure 3-26.

You can access a variety of search engines such as Infoseek, Lycos, Excite, and Yahoo! directly from this page. Simply click the appropriate tab near the top of the page.

The Fifth Tab

The Netscape Search page not only provides access to four of the most powerful search engines available, it also lets you add another! If you click the Customize tab, you can add AOL NetFind, HOTBOT, LookSmart SEARCH.COM, or WebCrawler. Not only that, Customize lets you determine which of these engines launch automatically whenever you click the Search button.

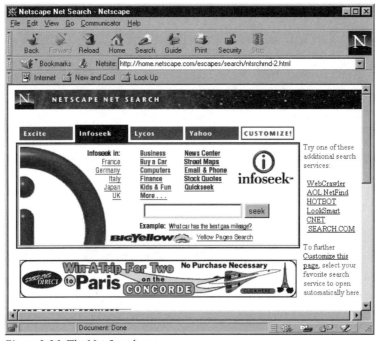

Figure 3-26: The Net Search page.

Navigator also provides a convenient shortcut to searching. If your search phrase consists of two or more words, just enter it in the Netsite/Location box and hit Enter. Navigator passes this phrase on to the current default search engine. You'll receive your result in seconds, without even needing to visit the Search page!

And why does your search phrase need two or more words in order for this convenient shortcut to work? Otherwise, Navigator thinks you are specifying a URL. If I enter **phil** in the Netsite/Location box, Navigator 4 tries to connect to phil.com or www.phil.com. But if I enter **"Phil James"**, it looks for my name on the Web using one of the search engines.

Let's search for a specific topic using Infoseek:

1. Click the Infoseek button.

2. Enter the string **Wittgenstein** in the search field and then click the seek now button. Infoseek returns the search results shown in Figure 3-27.

3. To jump directly to one of the pages, simply click the corresponding link.

A Net search is not guaranteed to locate every site on a particular topic, but if you're hunting for reference material or just surfing because you're interested in the subject, you'll probably find more than enough sites to keep you busy.

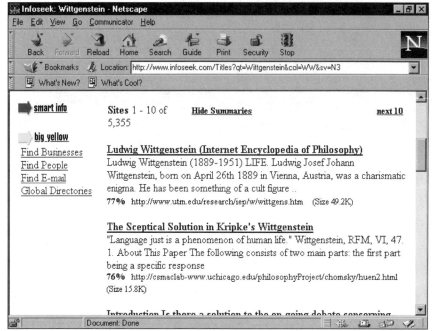

Figure 3-27: Search results from an Infoseek query.

Searching Newsgroups

In Chapter 6 you'll learn all about Usenet newsgroups, which are large discussion groups among Internet users who are often experts in a particular field. Newsgroups are especially useful for ferreting out very specific or very timely information. There are groups where you can get in-depth analysis of everything from Wittgenstein's philosophy to online marketing programs.

Several of the search engines available from the Net Search button let you find concepts, ideas, or phrases in this ever-changing morass of Usenet information. Once a week, for instance, I look up my own name to see what people are saying about my books—and I've even made some changes based on this information.

Let's try it. Press the Net Search button and then select Alta Vista from the list of search engines at the bottom of the page. Once the Alta Vista page appears, type in your request and select Usenet from the drop-down list to the right of the word "Search." Your browser window will look something like the one in Figure 3-28.

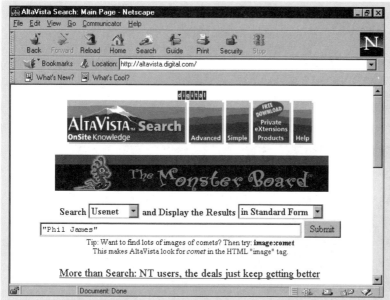

Figure 3-28: The author in search of himself. If you're looking for a phrase that includes spaces, put the whole phrase in quotes.

And Figure 3-29 shows what your window will look like after clicking Alta Vista's Submit button:

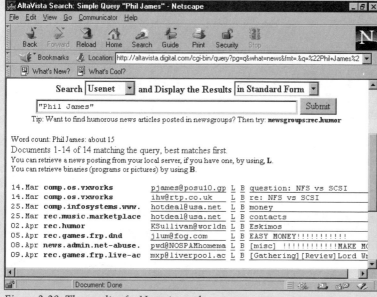

Figure 3-29: The results of a Usenet search.

Now let's move on to browsing for specific information using Navigator's Guide button.

The Guide Button

If you click the Guide button, a submenu appears, as shown below in Figure 3-30.

Figure 3-30: The expanded Guide button.

You've already seen the What's New? and What's Cool? links: they are bookmarks in your Personal Toolbar. The Internet item takes you to the Netscape Guide by Yahoo! which is a great front-end for searching out specific kinds of information on the Web; the People item is good for finding your long-lost Uncle Zelig; and the Yellow Pages item can provide you with the electronic and street addresses of businesses all around the world. You should take some time to explore these resources on your own, but for now let's take a quick look at two of them: Netscape Guide and People.

Exploring the Netscape Guide

For a taste of the limitless expanse of information available on the Web today, there's no better place to begin than the Netscape Guide, developed by Yahoo! Yahoo! started as a hobby project by Stanford University students David Filo and Jerry Yang in April 1994. Since then, Yahoo! has mushroomed into a profitable business that's become a career, but Filo and Yang still offer their original service free of charge to everyone, and their own site has become the home page for uncounted Web surfers. Their latest creative venture is this collaboration with Netscape on the Netscape Guide.

What are we waiting for? Let's start exploring! To access the Netscape Guide, make sure you are connected to the Net and then just click the Guide button. Next, select The Internet from the submenu that appears. The main Netscape Guide page appears, as shown in Figure 3-31.

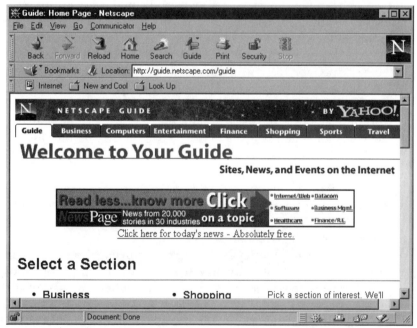

Figure 3-31: The Netscape Guide page.

You can see that the Guide is divided into several broad sections, accessible by clicking the tabs across the top of the page. For instance if you click the Business tab, you are taken to a page that includes several more subcategories such as Employment, Small Business, and Web Business. But Netscape Guide is much more than a simple hotlist of links. If you scroll down the top Business page, you'll discover daily news headlines related to business, a listing of Web events, an economic calendar, and even a facility for tracking FedEx letters and packages!

But the most interesting feature of the Netscape Guide is that you can customize it to display the information you're most interested in. To do this, simply click the Customize This Page link in any one of the categories.

TIP

Looking for a ton of business information all in one place? Try CEO Express at http://www.ceoexpress.com.

People

The Web is not just pages, it's also *people*. Behind every great URL, there's a living, breathing human being, or at least a Cro Magnon with some minor technical savvy.

How do you find people on the Net? There are a number of "Internet phone books," specialized listings, and search facilities available to anyone with a Web browser. Netscape's People facility gives you access to several of these. If you're looking for your long-lost Aunt Prudence and you know she likes to surf the Net, this is the place to start. And Netscape is committed to adding new directories and search tools to the page as they become available.

Figure 3-32 shows the "white pages" resources that are available through the People feature.

Some of these tools are good for finding a friend's e-mail address, others are good for finding a phone number or snail mail address. Most often I use them when I'm really bored and want some bittersweet what's-she-doing-now information on high school girlfriends.

So now you're an intrepid Net explorer, cruising through documents from around the world. You know how to search for obscure information, how to leap from idea to idea in great hypermedia bounds, and best of all, how to waste lots of time on the Web looking at groovy but useless sites. The rest of this chapter is devoted to *organizing* this huge mass of information. Using Navigator 4's history and bookmarks features, you can not only save the URLs of sites that you want to revisit, you can store them in categories and subcategories that make sense to you.

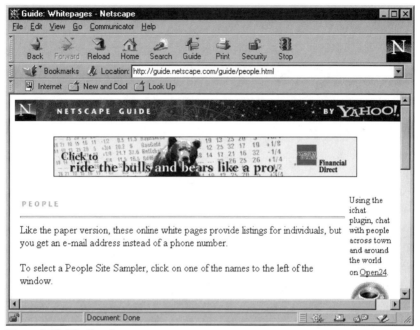

Figure 3-32: The People page.

The History List & Bookmarks

As you travel around the World Wide Web, you'll often find yourself jumping back to the same pages over and over again. From time to time you may also need a specific URL that you visited two or three sessions ago. And you're certain to find a number of Web pages that become your favorites, so you'll want to visit them often.

Netscape Navigator 4 provides several methods for keeping track of where you are on the Web—and where you've been. In this section, we'll discuss the two important features that help you maintain your own Web road map: the history list, which keeps track of where you've been in the current session, and bookmarks, which are permanent pointers to your favorite Web pages.

Using the History List

The history list is actually a collection of entries automatically maintained by Navigator 4. Each entry represents a single site you have visited. Each time you load a new Web page, the URL for that site is saved. This makes the history list an excellent tool for jumping among pages while you check references.

There are three ways to access a list of sites you've visited, and they each show slightly different information. First, the simplest:

1. After you have viewed several documents using Navigator 4, click the down arrow just to the right of the Netsite/Location box. A history list appears right there, as shown in Figure 3-33. Note that the list is scrollable, with only the most recent ten pages showing.

2. Click any entry in the list to return to that document.

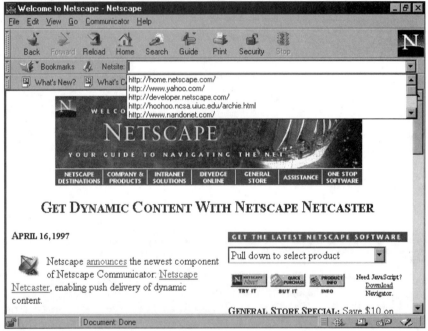

Figure 3-33: The drop-down history list.

This Netsite/Location box history list includes only URLs you've entered in the box itself or by using the Open Page command on the File menu; it does not include any sites you've visited by clicking a link.

You can also return to a previously viewed page by clicking Go on the menu bar. The menu that appears includes a history list at the bottom, as shown in Figure 3-34. Once again, you can simply select one of the entries to jump to it immediately.

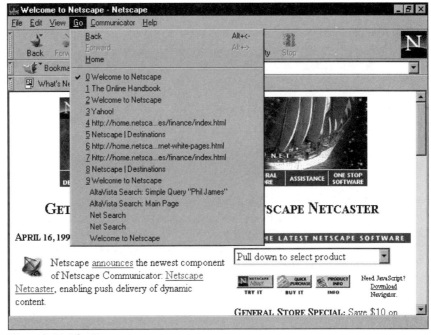

Figure 3-34: The Go menu.

The history list in the Go menu displays all the sites you've visited during this Navigator session. It includes pages that you've navigated to by clicking links as well as those you've visited by entering URLs in the Netsite/Location box. It does not, however, display any sites you've visited in previous Navigator sessions.

Lastly, you can display the history list within a dialog box, which allows for a neater and more complete presentation of each entry:

1. Select History from the Communicator menu, or simply press Ctrl+H.
   Navigator 4 displays the History dialog box, as shown in Figure 3-35.

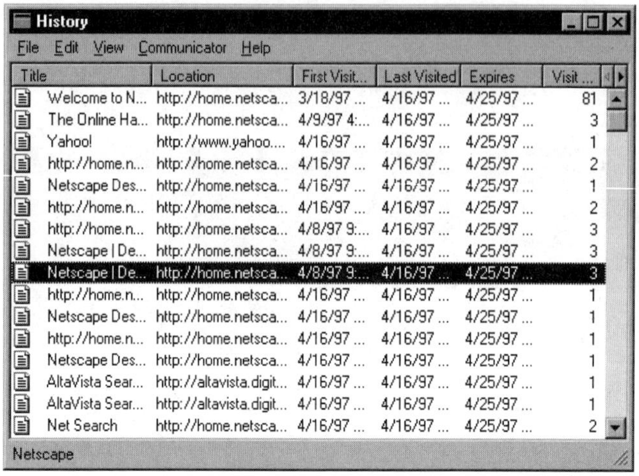

Figure 3-35: The History dialog box.

- Notice that each entry appears as a single line, complete with both the page title and its URL address as well as lots of other information you may or may not want. You can add or eliminate informational fields by clicking the arrow buttons to the right of the column labels, and you can adjust the size of the columns by placing your cursor on the edges of the labels and dragging right or left.

2. To jump to a particular page, simply double-click the entry.

3. To make a bookmark out of a link from this window, right-click the entry and select Add to Bookmarks from the context menu that appears. (I'll cover bookmarks in the next section.)

This very thorough view of your navigational history includes pages you've visited by clicking links and pages you've visited by entering URLs in the Netsite/Location box. But unlike the list at the bottom of the Go menu, it is persistent: it includes your history from previous Navigator sessions as well as your current session. In other words, quitting the program doesn't erase the list.

But how many previous sessions does it record? That depends on a setting that you can change. Read on.

Changing the History List Expiration Time

To configure how long the history list persists and accumulates new entries before it is cleared, follow these steps:

1. Select Preferences from the Edit menu, then click the Navigator category as shown in Figure 3-36.

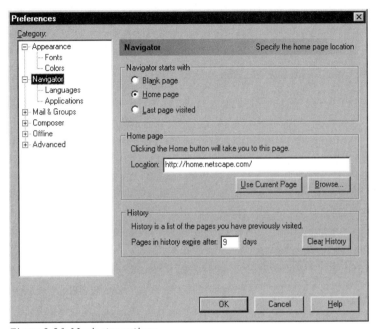

Figure 3-36: Navigator options.

2. In the History section of the right-hand dialog box, enter the number of days you want your history list to persist before it is cleared. If you are an active Web surfer, you may want to reduce the number.

3. To clear your history list immediately, click the Clear History button.

Bookmarks

Now that you're familiar with the history list, you may be saying to yourself, "Well, that's great for finding places I've been, but I want a more selective list of sites. And I don't want the entries to expire unless I erase them." Luckily, you don't have to resort to paper and pencil or try to maintain a text file of your favorite sites—Navigator 4 provides you with bookmarks, which are saved permanently in your own "Web page directory." You can also create a simple Web page of your own that includes your favorite sites; we'll discuss this in Chapter 9.

Adding & Using Bookmarks

The two actions you'll perform most often with bookmarks are (1) adding them and (2) using them to jump to a stored URL. There are four different ways to add a bookmark for the document that's currently displayed:

- Click the Bookmarks QuickFile icon and select Add Bookmarks from the menu.

- Right-click in the display window, then select Add Bookmark from the menu that appears.

- Drag the Page icon (the one just to the left of the Netsite/Location box) over to the Bookmarks QuickFile icon.

- Hit Ctrl+D.

TIP

When you drag the Page icon to the Bookmark icon, you can add the new bookmark directly to any subfolder of the Bookmarks file (see the section called "Organizing Your Bookmarks" to learn about Bookmark subfolders).

You can also add a bookmark for a link within a document by right-clicking the link and then choosing Add Bookmark from the context menu that appears.

Using bookmarks to jump to a document is just as easy:

- Click the Bookmarks QuickFile icon, then select one of the bookmarks that appears at the bottom (see Figure 3-37). You are immediately teleported to the selected URL.

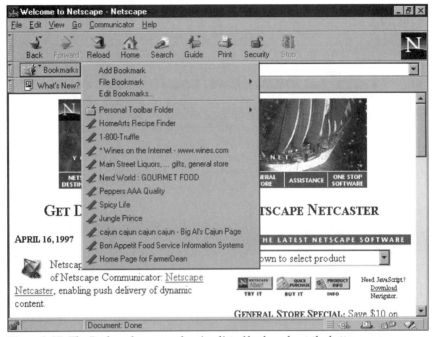

Figure 3-37: The Bookmarks menu, showing list of bookmarks at the bottom.

As with the history list, Netscape Navigator 4 also provides a fuller, alternative interface to your bookmarks: the Bookmarks window.

The Bookmarks Window

Now that you know how to use bookmarks at the simplest level, let's advance a bit. Just as history entries can be displayed in the History dialog box, you can also display a bookmark list that offers a lot more functionality than the Bookmarks menu. To open the Bookmarks window, click the Bookmarks QuickFile icon and then select Edit Bookmarks. The Bookmarks window appears, as shown in Figure 3-38.

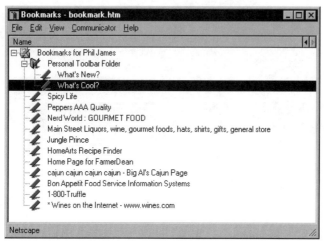

Figure 3-38: The Bookmarks window.

Depending on what sites you've already added to your bookmarks list, your window may look different from mine.

TIP

You can change the name of any bookmark folder, including the top-level one, by right-clicking it and selecting Properties from the context menu that appears. You can also change the name of individual bookmarks this way.

As you can see, Navigator 4 displays the contents of the current bookmark file in a tree format, with entries appearing under the folder icon. The Bookmarks window has its own menu bar, which we'll refer to as we explain the other bookmark functions. But to jump to the document represented by a bookmark entry you don't even need the menu. Simply double-click the entry itself.

TIP

Netscape Communicator lets you use more than one bookmark file and also makes it easy to switch between files. From the File menu in the Bookmarks window, you can choose Open to select a new file, or Save As to save the current file under a new name.

The Personal Toolbar Folder

You'll notice right away that one of the folders in the Bookmarks window is the Personal Toolbar folder. This includes all the bookmarks that you've placed on Navigator's Personal Toolbar, typically by dragging links onto it. Remember, the Personal Toolbar folder is just like any other Bookmarks folder. You modify any items within it exactly as you modify the items in any other folder, and the changes you make will be reflected automatically in the appearance of the Personal Toolbar.

Organizing Your Bookmarks

If you're familiar with the Windows drag-and-drop function and the tree structure common in Windows 95 applications like Explorer, you'll have no problem organizing your bookmarks any way you like.

For example, let's say you'd like to categorize your bookmarks by subject matter, with each subject represented by its own folder. For the purposes of this exercise, we'll add a new folder called Computers under the existing Main Bookmarks folder.

First, to create a new bookmark folder:

1. Select and then right-click the existing folder under which the new folder should be created. In this case, the existing folder is Phil James's Bookmarks.

2. Choose New Folder from the context menu. Navigator 4 displays the Bookmark Properties dialog box shown in Figure 3-39.

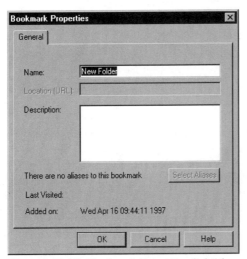

Figure 3-39: The Bookmark Properties dialog box.

3. Enter **Computers** in the Name field. If you like, you can add a simple text description that will display when you right-click the folder and select Properties.

4. Click OK to save the folder.

Now that you've added the Computers folder, you can either create new bookmark entries within it or move existing entries into it. To create a new bookmark:

1. Right-click the folder under which the new entry should be created. In this case, we'll click Computers.

2. Select New Bookmark from the context menu that appears. Navigator 4 displays the Bookmark Properties dialog box, shown before in Figure 3-39.

3. Enter the name for your new bookmark in the Name field. As an example, let's use **A nifty Computer URL**. If you like, you can add a simple text description that displays when you right-click the entry and select Properties.

4. Enter the URL into the Location (URL) field.

5. Click OK to save the entry. Your Bookmarks window should now look something like Figure 3-40.

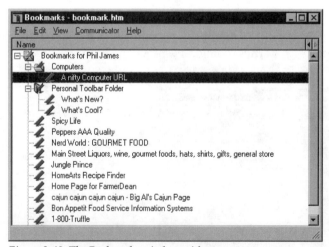

Figure 3-40: The Bookmarks window with new entry.

TIP

You can also insert folders and bookmarks by selecting the respective items from the File menu.

It's even easier to move an existing bookmark into a folder. Click and drag the entry icon (which looks like a sheet of paper with the edge folded down) and drop it on top of the desired folder. Notice that your cursor changes appearance to indicate you're dragging the entry to a new spot. The entry will now appear as a sub-branch under the folder.

When you add entries under a folder, Netscape Navigator 4 also displays the entries and folder hierarchy as part of the Bookmarks menu. Folders with entries in them appear with arrows on the right side of the menu; when you select the folder, the folder name expands to show the bookmark entries within it. And by dragging the Page icon over to the Bookmarks QuickFile icon, you can add the currently displayed page into any one of these folders!

If you'd like to separate your entries or folders on the Bookmarks menu, right-click the name in the Bookmarks window and select New Separator from the context menu. When you return to the Bookmarks QuickFile icon, you'll see a line separating that entry or folder from the others on the menu.

TIP

Once you've expanded your entries within several folders, it may be harder to find a particular entry. Of course, you can use the Find command in the Bookmarks window, but it also helps to close folders you're not using. Closing a folder hides all the bookmark entries under it. To close a folder, double-click its icon; to expand it and display the entries it contains, double-click its icon again. You can also single-click the plus or minus icon to the left of the folder icon. In addition, you can sort the display of your bookmarks in a variety of convenient ways by clicking the available choices on the View menu.

What's an Alias?

You'll notice that the context menu which pops up when you right-click a particular bookmark contains a *Make Alias* command. This command lets you create an alternate bookmark that links to the same URL as the original one. In addition, if you change the original bookmark in any way, the alias changes along with it.

What's the point? Using aliases, you can have the same bookmark in more than one folder. Simply move the aliases you create into whatever folder locations you want. If you simply *copy* the bookmark to a different folder, any changes in the original are not reflected in the copy. Aliases ensure that even multiple instances of the same bookmark remain up-to-date.

Changing Where New Bookmarks Get Added

There is another way to stay organized. You can configure Netscape Navigator 4 so that new bookmarks are always placed in a folder you specify. By default, when you click Add Bookmarks, the new bookmark is added to the end of the top-level bookmark folder. But let's say you want all new bookmarks to go into a subfolder called New. Here's how you do it:

1. In the Bookmarks window, select and right-click the folder you want to use for all newly added bookmarks.

2. Select Set as New Bookmarks Folder from the context menu. A page icon appears on top of the file icon for that folder, as shown in Figure 3-41.

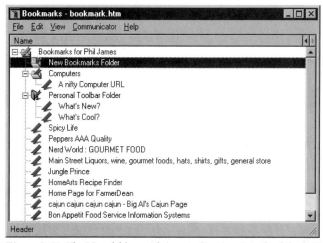

Figure 3-41: The New folder, with icon indicating it is the default New bookmarks folder.

There can be only one New bookmarks folder at a time, at least within the same bookmarks file. If you want to change it, simply select a different folder and repeat step 2. Remember, you can always return the program to its default mode of operation by selecting the top-level folder as the default New bookmarks folder.

Customizing the Bookmarks Menu Display

As you collect dozens or even hundreds of bookmarks, all neatly categorized within their folders, the Bookmarks menu starts looking pretty long. You probably don't need to see all these bookmarks every time you run the program, so why not limit what's displayed in the menu? Navigator 4 makes this easy:

1. In the Bookmarks window, select the folder that you want to have displayed on the Bookmarks menu, then right-click.

2. Select Set as Bookmark Menu from the context menu.

Now only the items in that folder (and any of its subfolders) will appear in the Bookmarks menu. You can always change back to the program's default display of all bookmarks by selecting the top-level folder and repeating step 2.

TIP

Want to be able to switch among several different Personal Toolbars, each containing different bookmarks? That's easy. You can make ANY bookmark folder your Personal Toolbar folder. Simply right-click the folder you want to use, then choose Set as Toolbar Folder from the context menu.

Importing & Exporting Bookmarks

As you build your collection of bookmarks, you may want to share your favorite Web sites with others. In fact, many Web surfers keep a "favorite sites" file or "hotlist" in HTML format that they can share with others through Internet mail. Navigator 4 makes it simple to import a bookmark file (bring new entries from some other HTML file into your bookmark file) or export your entries (create an HTML hotlist that others can use).

Remember, an HTML file is simply a text document that contains links to other Web documents. HTML documents are standardized so that all Web browsers can interpret them correctly. That's why importing and exporting allow you to trade files with any Web user, whether or not they have Netscape Communicator.

From the browser window, follow these steps to *import* a bookmark file:

1. Select Edit Bookmarks from the Bookmarks QuickFile icon menu. The Bookmarks window appears, as shown earlier in Figure 3-41.

2. From the Bookmarks window File menu, select Import. Navigator 4 displays a standard Windows or Windows 95 Import bookmarks file dialog, as shown in Figure 3-42.

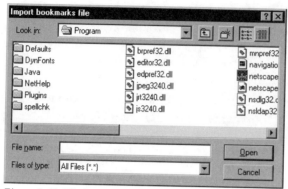

Figure 3-42: The Import bookmarks file dialog box.

3. Navigate to the directory where the HTML file is stored and then double-click it.

From the Navigator display window, follow these steps to *export* a bookmark file:

1. Select Edit Bookmarks from the Bookmarks menu. The Bookmarks window appears, as shown earlier in Figure 3-37.

2. Select the bookmark file you want to export.

3. From the Bookmarks window's File menu, select the Save As command. Navigator displays the standard Windows or Windows 95 save bookmarks file dialog box, as shown in Figure 3-43.

Figure 3-43: The Save bookmarks file dialog box.

4. Save the file in any location and under any name you want. Make sure the file type is set to HTML files.

Navigator 4 Shortcuts for Windows 95/NT

By far the easiest way to create convenient shortcuts to your favorite Web sites is to drag the Page icon into the Personal Toolbar, as explained earlier in the section called "The Personal Toolbar." But if you're running Netscape Navigator 4 under Windows 95 or Windows NT 4.0, you can also create iconized *desktop* shortcuts that will make connecting to your favorite Web page as easy as a click of your mouse—even when Communicator isn't running.

There are several ways to create desktop shortcuts:

- If you click and drag a link, the pointer will change to indicate that the link can now be dropped onto your desktop. A highlighted link is shown in Figure 3-44, while the new desktop shortcut should look something like Figure 3-45.

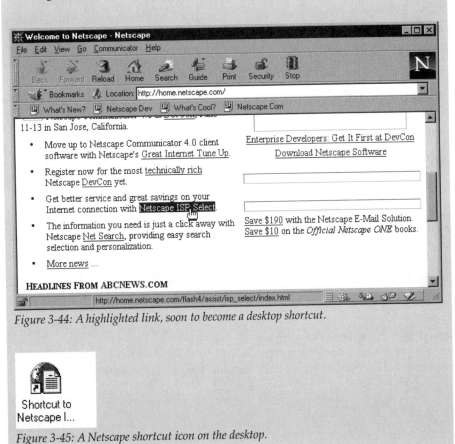

Figure 3-44: A highlighted link, soon to become a desktop shortcut.

Figure 3-45: A Netscape shortcut icon on the desktop.

- You can click your right mouse button on a link and then select Create Shortcut from the context menu that pops up.

- You can drag the Page icon (just to the left of the Netsite/Location box) out onto the desktop. This creates a desktop shortcut to the current URL, just as it would have created a Custom shortcut if you'd dragged it to the Personal Toolbar.

Once you've created a desktop shortcut, all you have to do is double-click it to access the site. Netscape Communicator doesn't even have to be running— clicking the shortcut will automatically launch Navigator 4 with the correct URL.

As you've seen, Netscape Communicator's browser window is pretty painless to use "right out of the box." You didn't have to spend hours configuring the software before you could start exploring, and in fact, you could just keep on Web-trucking without ever delving into the setup menus. But I know you too well—you're the kind of person who will never be satisfied with anything less than fully optimized software. In the final section of this chapter, you'll learn how to do a little bit of tweaking so that Navigator 4 works exactly as you want it to.

Tweaking Your Browser

If you select Preferences from the browser window's Edit menu, you'll see a Category list of six different Preference choices: Appearance, Navigator, Mail & Groups, Composer, Offline, and Advanced. The Composer Preferences are covered in Chapter 9, and Mail & Groups are covered in Chapters 5 and 6, so we won't bother looking at those right now. Let's start by glancing at the Appearance options. You'll quickly get a sense of what kind of customization is possible in Navigator 4.

Appearance Preferences

To access the Appearance preferences, simply select Appearance from the Categories list, as shown in Figure 3-46.

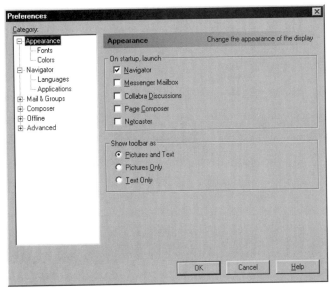

Figure 3-46: The Appearance options.

In the top section of this window, you can choose which Communicator components you want to launch automatically when you click the Communicator icon. If you select all five, for instance, you will have five different windows on your screen when you start Communicator, including an e-mail window, a Web page editing window, a Netcaster window, the Navigator browser window, and the Collabra discussion groups window. This can be hard on your system if you don't have a lot of free memory, so set this with caution!

In the bottom section of this page, you can choose how to display the buttons in the Command Toolbar. Until you get familiar with the program, Pictures and Text is probably the best choice.

There are two more Appearance windows: Fonts and Colors. To access these, the Appearance item in the Category list on the left must be expanded. If they are not in your list, double-click the Appearance item or simply click the plus icon. Fonts and Colors appear in the list, and you can click them to access the respective settings.

Fonts

Back in the Category list on the left, click the Fonts item. The window that appears lets you associate incoming data with particular display fonts, as shown in Figure 3-47.

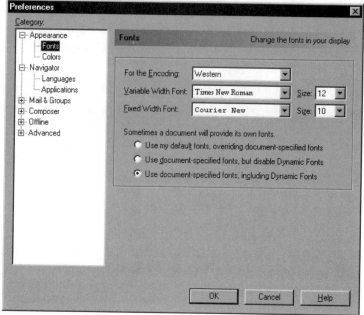

Figure 3-47: The Fonts options.

In the United States, just about all the Web information you receive will be in the Western, or ISO-Latin-1, character set, and this character set will be displayed using the default Times New Roman and Courier New fonts. However, you can change these fonts—and their sizes—if you want. Just click the appropriate drop-down list and make your choice.

If a Web page specifies a font that you don't currently have on your system, it may be downloaded to you automatically—without any intervention on your part—so that the document appears as intended in your browser window. Netscape calls this feature Dynamic Fonts. To take advantage of Dynamic Fonts, you must select the bottom option button; the top option button forces Navigator to use the fonts you have selected even if the Web page specifies a very different font, and the middle button lets Navigator display the special fonts specified in a document only if they're already on your system.

TIP

You can also change your font size right within the browser window. Simply select Increase Font or Decrease Font from the View menu. You can also hit Ctrl+] to increase the font size or Ctrl+[to decrease the size.

Colors

We already visited here earlier in the chapter. The Colors window lets you change the default colors for text and links that are displayed in Navigator 4 as well as in HTML information displayed in Messenger and other Communicator components. In addition, it lets you specify a new background color or even a .GIF file for the display background. You can also decide here whether or not you want Navigator 4 to always use these colors rather than responding to the special color requests in Web documents.

Now let's move on to the Navigator preferences.

Navigator 4 Preferences

In the Category list on the left, select Navigator. The Navigator options appear, as shown in Figure 3-48.

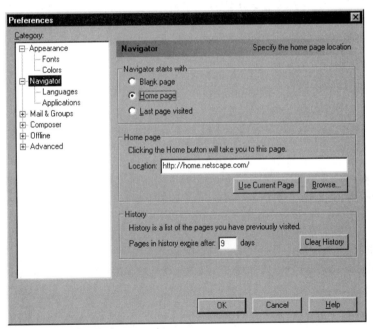

Figure 3-48: The Navigator options.

Here you can choose which Web document, if any, Navigator 4 displays when you launch the program. The default is the Netscape home page, located at the Netscape site. Earlier in the chapter we discussed why you may want to change this.

The top section of this page lets you elect to start Navigator with a blank page, with a specific home page, or with whatever the last page was that you visited before closing the program. This last option is a real convenience if you're doing research at a variety of specialized sites and want to continue where you left off.

In the middle section you specify what site Navigator will access when you click the Home button, or when you start the program if you chose Home page in the top section. Just type in the URL. You can also use the Browse button to find and specify a local HTML file you want to use, and you can use the Use Current Page button to use the currently displayed document as your home page.

In the bottom section you can set how long you want the URLs in your history list to stick around, and you can also click the Clear History button to delete all these saved URLs immediately. If you visit a lot of sites, your history list may get very long and too unwieldy to work with, so this button can really simplify your online life.

There is a Languages tab underneath the Navigator category on the left. If it is not displayed, double-click Navigator or simply click the plus icon.

Languages

In the Languages window you can specify which languages you want Navigator 4 to accept from a Web server. Just click the Add button and choose which languages you want to add. Let's say you access a site that includes separate versions of the lyrics to LL Cool J's "Doin' It" in Chinese, Dutch, and Swedish. You could view the Chinese lyrics properly only if you've added Chinese to the list. You can also use the up and down arrow buttons to prioritize the languages you add. If Chinese is first on your list, Navigator will attempt to display the page using Chinese characters first.

And now we move on to the Applications window.

Applications

Not all files that are placed on the Internet or on your office intranet are meant to be viewed in a Web browser. For instance, you wouldn't use Navigator 4 to view a Microsoft Word document or to uncompress a ZIP file (see Chapter 8 for more information on ZIP files). But Navigator *can* launch the correct program when it encounters a file that it is not designed to handle itself. For instance, you might click a link to a file called MORTGAGE.XLS. Because of the .XLS extension, Navigator knows it's an Excel file and launches the spreadsheet program (if it's available on your system) with the information correctly displayed. In this case, Excel is considered a *helper application.*

Let's take a closer look. Still in the Preferences window, select the Applications category under Navigator, as shown in Figure 3-49. If Applications is not displayed, double-click Navigator, or simply click the plus icon.

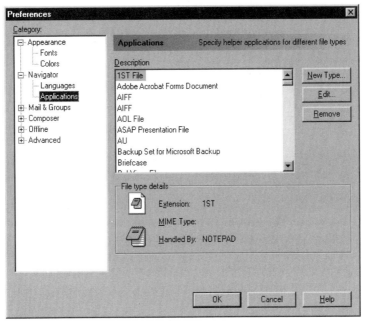

Figure 3-49: The Applications window.

TIP

When Navigator encounters a file type on the Net or on your office intranet that it doesn't "know about," it may pop up an "Unknown File Type" dialog box. This dialog box includes a button labeled Pick App. If you click the button, you are taken to the Applications window shown above in Figure 3-50. Follow the directions below to tell Navigator what helper application should be associated with this unfamiliar file.

This looks like a fairly complicated dialog box at first, but once you understand the concepts, it's really pretty simple. The large scrolling list includes the names of different kinds of files you might encounter as you cruise the Net or your office intranet with Navigator 4. As you click each file type from the list, the bottom section of the window changes to display details about the particular file type. For instance, Figure 3-50 shows the file type details for WRI (Microsoft Write) files.

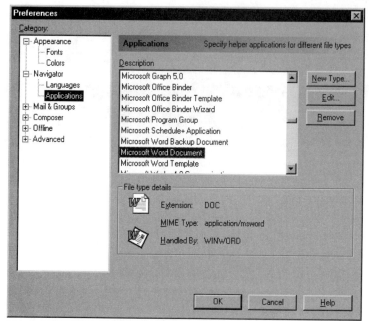

Figure 3-50: The Applications window, with file type details for Write files.

The bottom includes three fields:

- **Extension**. This is simply the extension for this kind of file. When Navigator encounters a file called CHAPTER3.DOC, for instance, it knows it's a Winword file because of the .DOC extension. An icon to the left of the field provides a graphical representation of the file type, just as it would appear on your Windows 95/NT desktop.

- **MIME Type**. MIME, or Multipurpose Internet Mail Extensions, is a universal standard for naming file types. Usually the MIME designations make sense, as in the case of Winword files, which are classified as application/msword.

- **Handled By**. This field specifies the helper application that will be launched when Navigator encounters a file of this type. An icon to the left represents the program. In this case, when Navigator encounters a file with the extension .WRI, it launches the program Write, which then displays the file correctly.

But what if you don't want Microsoft Word to start up every time Navigator encounters a .WRI file? What if you want to view the contents of the file in some other application such as WordPad or WordView—or what if you simply want to save it to disk?

No problem. Just click the Edit button. The Edit Type dialog box appears, as shown in Figure 3-51.

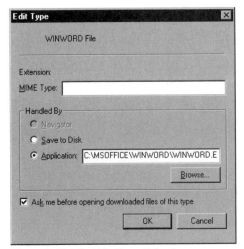

Figure 3-51: The Edit Type dialog box.

In the Handled By section, select Save to Disk if you simply want files of this type saved rather than displayed or otherwise processed. Or if you want them handled by a different application, make sure the Application option button is selected and then click the Browse button to select a different program.

TIP

If you want Navigator to ask you before it automatically opens files of this type in a helper application, check the check box at the bottom of this Window. This is useful, for example, if you sometimes want to view Winword files immediately and sometimes simply want to save them to disk.

What about the top option button, the one labeled Navigator? In this case it's grayed out (made unavailable) because Navigator itself cannot display Winword files—it must call upon the services of a helper application such as Microsoft Word. But take a look at Figure 3-52, which shows the Edit Type dialog box for GIF Image files.

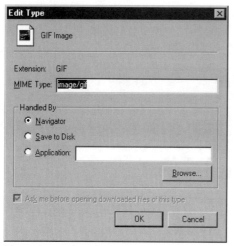

Figure 3-52: The Edit Type dialog box for GIF Image files.

Since Navigator *can* display GIF files without any outside help, the Navigator option button is available—and selected by default. If you click a link to a GIF file, it will be displayed using the browser window. But you may want a different program, such as a full-featured graphics program, to display any GIF files you encounter. In that case, simply select the Application option button and browse for the program you want to use. In any case, click OK when you're finished editing this file type.

TIP

Settings in the Applications window affect every Communicator component, not just Navigator 4. For instance, they affect the way attached files are handled in Netscape Messenger (see Chapter 5).

If you want to get fancy, you can even add new file types and subtypes to Communicator's default list. However, this is truly a propeller-head option: you should not even be thinking about it except to add a new standardized MIME type, and unless you really know what you're doing. Assuming you have the proper geek credentials, though, it's pretty easy. In the Applications window, click New Type. Then just fill in the blanks.

And yes, you can even delete file types by clicking the Remove button. I do not recommend this. There is no harm in having extra file types listed, even ones you'll never encounter, but unless you're pretty technical it may be hard to add back a type you've deleted.

Now let's move on to the Offline category.

Offline Preferences

Still in the Preferences window, select the Offline category, as shown in Figure 3-53.

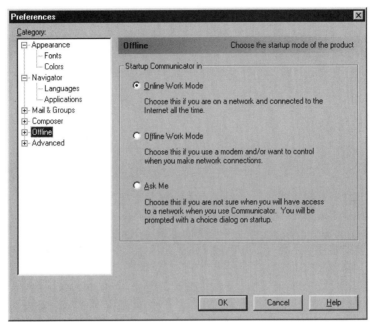

Figure 3-53: The Offline Preferences.

The choices here are fairly self-explanatory. If you select Online Work Mode, Communicator assumes you are connected to the Net or to an intranet at all times. If you choose Offline Work Mode, Communicator assumes you are not always connected. These choices affect the behavior of Messenger and Discussion Groups more than Navigator (see Chapters 5 and 6).

And how about clicking the "Ask Me" choice? In this mode Communicator will ask you if you want to go online when you first start one of its components. If you say you do, your Dial-Up Networking connection will be initialized (assuming you're using Windows 95 or Windows NT) and you will be connected to the Net.

Now let's advance to the last of the Preference categories, Advanced Preferences.

TIP

You may have noticed that I'm skipping the Download category under Offline. That's because the settings that appear there only relate to e-mail and discussion groups, and they are covered fully in Chapters 5 and 6.

Advanced Preferences

Don't worry, this is not a geeks-only zone by any means. The folks at Netscape throw in the word Advanced so you can feel good about yourself, but it's really pretty easy.

Go ahead and click Advanced in the Category list on the left of the Preferences window. The Advanced preferences window appears, as shown in Figure 3-54.

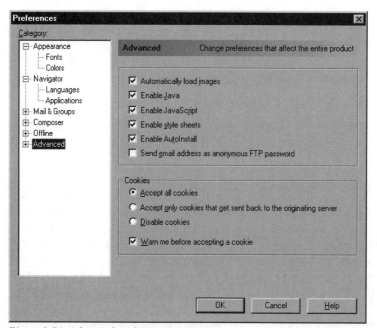

Figure 3-54: Advanced preferences.

Let's cover the options in the top section one at a time:

- **Automatically load images**. If you leave this checked, Navigator will automatically load all the images that are part of the Web page you are currently visiting. On very slow connections this may be tedious, and you may want to uncheck this box to experience the Web in much faster "text only" mode. If this box is unchecked, a Show Images button becomes available on the Control Toolbar. Using Show Images, you can force Navigator to display the graphics at particular sites, on a case-by-case basis, even though *automatic* display is disabled.

- **Enable Java**. You'll learn about Java in Chapters 4 and 10, but for now, all you need to know is that it's a programming language that extends the abilities of Navigator and makes your computer do amazing things. Java programs, or "applets," that are included in a Web page are downloaded by Navigator and then run locally on your machine. Because you are in effect running a new program that you know nothing about, Java may in rare cases create havoc on your system or pose security risks. If you are worried about this, uncheck this box and read Chapter 13, where I discuss security in detail.

- **Enable JavaScript**. Same idea here. JavaScript is a simpler language than Java, though, and it has more built-in security. It is used for lots of small "special effects" within the browser window, things like scrolling marquees and kiosk mode. Go ahead and uncheck this box if you want, but you will be missing out on some of the graphical niceties of the Web pages you visit.

- **Enable style sheets**. I mentioned style sheets earlier. They are collections of formatting and layout information that may be stored for reuse by multiple Web pages. In most cases you should leave this item checked.

- **Enable AutoInstall**. Communicator includes an exciting new feature whereby new plug-ins (see Chapters 7 and 10), upgrades, or other extensions to the program may be installed automatically. You don't need to request or install the software yourself. Once you've approved an electronic security certificate that appears on your screen identifying the source of the software, the files simply download, unpack their virtual bags, and makes themselves at home on your computer. A typical example: Navigator encounters a multimedia file that requires a special plug-in in order to display properly. You are asked to approve the installation of the new plug-in, which then installs itself automatically on your system. Within minutes or even seconds, the multimedia file is displayed correctly in the browser window. In rare cases where this imposes a security risk, you may want to uncheck this check box.

■ **Send e-mail address as anonymous FTP password**. When you log onto anonymous FTP sites to browse and download files (see Chapter 8), the convention is to send your e-mail address as the password. In most cases you should not check this box; Navigator will generate one for you.

The bottom section of this window deals with *cookies*, and whether or not you want Navigator to accept them. Cookies, in this case, are bits of information that a Web site stores on your own hard drive. This enables the site to "remember," from session to session, information that's specific to your use of the site. For instance, you may have chosen a particular color configuration on the site, or a category of information that you want to access each time. Cookies enable Web page designers to do things that would be very clumsy otherwise, but not everybody likes the idea of them. They may be used, for instance, to provide advertisers and other collectors of demographics with information about the trail of pages at their site you have visited.

This dialog box lets you deal with cookies in one of three ways. You can accept them; you can accept them only if the information they contain is sent back to the originating Web site, not to some other URL; or you can reject them. My personal advice: unless you have a specific reason to worry about cookies, let Navigator accept them and don't lose any sleep.

If you expand the Advanced category in the list on the left, you'll see that there are two other subcategories: Cache, Proxies, and Disk Space. The last of these items is covered in Chapters 5 and 6, but let's take a look at the first two now.

Cache Settings

Bear with me for a few minutes, we're going to get a little bit technical. Don't worry, it won't hurt much. If you're not too concerned about performance right now, you can just skip the rest of this chapter and come back here later. But if you want to make sure Navigator 4 is operating as efficiently as possible—and this can be important when you're paying for Internet access on an hourly basis—read on.

A *cache* (pronounced just like the green stuff) is a reserve area (a file) on your computer that houses information downloaded from the Internet as you navigate. You can think of it as a temporary holding cell that Navigator uses to store data between the time it is downloaded and the time it is displayed. If your cache is large enough, it can store entire Web pages and even graphics. That way, when you return to a previously visited site, Navigator doesn't have to download the information all over again; it can simply grab it from the cache.

There are actually two caches, a memory cache and a hard disk cache. The memory cache holds text and graphics only as long as you run any component of Communicator. The hard disk cache, on the other hand, is persistent: it holds information even after you exit the program. That way you can retrieve large documents quickly, without having to re-download them from the original site on the Net.

TIP

The Navigator 4 Refresh command (available from the View menu) redisplays the current document using information stored in the cache. The Reload button, on the other hand, actually goes back to the original document site, checks to see if it has changed since the last time you accessed it, and then reloads it from the Internet if there are any changes. So, if you think that a document may have changed since the last time you visited it during the current session, you should use the Reload button to view any updates.

There are advantages and disadvantages in setting high cache sizes for both types of caches. Even though memory caches are much quicker than disk caches, devoting more RAM to this type of cache can slow down your computer's overall performance. On the other hand, higher disk cache settings eat up your hard disk space.

Follow these steps to change your settings for cache sizes:

1. Click the Cache category under Advanced to display the Cache settings window, shown in Figure 3-55.

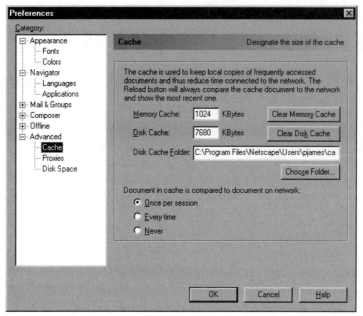

Figure 3-55: The Cache settings.

2. You can set the size of the memory cache in the Memory Cache field. The default setting is 1024K of RAM. Unless you have a large amount of memory on your system, such as 32MB or more, you may want to keep this setting where it is. Otherwise, you can try setting it at 1200K to see if your browsing speeds increase.

3. Set the amount of hard disk space that you want to reserve for a disk cache. This value is entered in the Disk Cache field; its default is set to 7680K (7M) of hard disk space. On most newer computers that come with hard disks of 450MB or more, you should have no problem reserving even more for this cache if you want.

TIP

Experiment with both the memory cache and hard disk cache sizes to determine the best settings for your system. If you tend to use Communicator without other applications running at the same time, such as a word processor or spreadsheet, you can set the memory cache much higher to make Netscape Navigator 4 run quicker. If you generally run Netscape Communicator with other applications that need large amounts of memory, keep the memory cache low, around 600K. This ensures that each application has ample RAM to run properly.

4. To clear the current content from your disk or memory caches, click Clear Memory Cache or Clear Disk Cache. When you click either of these buttons, a confirmation box pops up, asking if you are sure you want to clear the selected cache. Click OK to confirm that you do; click Cancel if you change your mind.

Why Would I Want to Clear a Cache?

Depending on how much navigating you do or how often you visit a site, you may want to periodically clear a cache setting. Having a cache decreases the time it takes to access sites that you've recently visited, but it does increase the strain on your local computer. When your memory cache is set to a high value, the amount of memory devoted to Communicator cannot be used by other resources. This slows down your machine when you run these other applications. Also, you may want to clear the memory cache if you've been online for several hours and you feel your machine responding sluggishly to Navigator 4. After you clear the cache, you should notice an improvement in your PC's performance.

---

5. Click one of the radio buttons toward the bottom of the page. If a document stored in cache has been revised, you'll want to see the revision instead of the old document. These buttons specify how Netscape Navigator 4 checks the Web for document revisions:

   - **Once per session.** Checks for page revisions only once during the time you start and quit Communicator. This is the default setting, and you will probably find it adequate unless you are trying to keep up with late-breaking news on CNN.

   - **Every time.** Checks for changes each time you request a Web document rather than relying on data stored in the cache. Because Navigator 4 is constantly checking the cached item against the Web page, you encounter a little performance degradation when you use this option.

   - **Never.** Performs no verifications; a page available in cache is always brought from cache. Not a good selection if you want to see the latest-and-greatest offerings at a particular Web site.

Proxies

The next category under Advanced is Proxies. Let's take a quick look at the Proxies settings page shown in Figure 3-56.

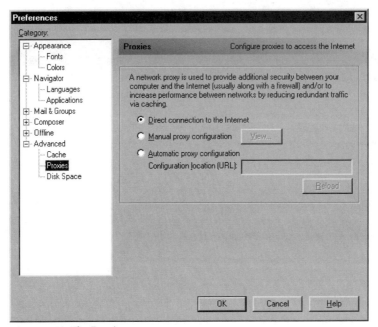

Figure 3-56: The Proxies page.

Some corporate networks do not let you access Internet resources directly. Instead, you send your requests for information to a special *proxy server*, which then relays your request on to its intended site—if you have the right permissions. Similarly, incoming information is collected by the proxy, and you access it from there. Some networks have different proxy server addresses for different types of Internet resources. If your Proxies page is set up correctly, however, all this buck-passing is completely transparent to you. When you try to access home.netscape.com, for instance, it looks to you like you're accessing it directly, even though all the information goes through an intermediary address that keeps track of everything you do.

If you don't think you have a proxy server, leave the top option button selected. If you think you *do* have a proxy server, ask your network administrator how to fill in this page. The Manual proxy configuration choice lets you set up a different network address for each type of Internet resource, and the

Automatic proxy configuration choice lets you specify the URL for a special configuration file on your network that includes all the necessary proxy information.

The last category under Advanced is Disk Space. The options in this window only apply to e-mail and discussion group messages, however, and so I will cover them in Chapters 5 and 6. When you are done with the other categories in the Preferences window, simply click OK to return to Navigator 4.

Moving On

In this chapter, you learned the basics of navigating Web pages, as well as how to operate the major features of Communicator's browser component, Netscape Navigator 4. You now know how to search for a particular site, as well as where you can find the newest and coolest pages on the Web. You also know how to change some of the program's settings so that it operates exactly the way you want it to.

Now let's move on to something everybody's talking about: Netscape Netcaster and what's commonly known as *push technology*. In the next chapter you'll learn how to subscribe to information *channels* that give you quick access to media-rich information that updates itself automatically!

CHAPTER 4

Netcaster

Without a doubt, Netcaster is the Communicator component that has received the most media attention. With its new flexible approach to multimedia information, it has stirred the imaginations of content providers, Information Systems (IS) managers, and end users.

Netcaster is so new, in fact, that content providers are constantly coming up with new ways to exploit its power. This chapter shows you how to use Netcaster and introduces you to some of the exciting possibilities it inspires.

What is Netcaster?

In a nutshell, Netcaster is the Communicator component that delivers information to you automatically—you don't need to search the Web or your office intranet for what you want. With Netcaster, the information comes to *you*. (Yes, this is the "push" technology that you may have heard about.)

In addition, Netcaster lets you download and then later browse Web sites offline, without being connected to the Net or your intranet. Not only does this save you money in online charges, it saves you time as well. Instead of waiting for a large image to display, for example, you see it immediately when you click its link.

To really understand Netcaster, though, you need to understand the concept of channels.

What is a Channel?

In the context of Netcaster, a channel is a Web site that is delivered automatically to your desktop. Or, you can think of it as a collection of media-rich information in a particular area of interest. You *subscribe* to a channel, which is then downloaded to your machine and stored locally so that you can access it quickly. Netcaster can also update your channels automatically, going online and collecting the latest information at regular intervals that you specify.

What Kind of Channels are Available?

Back in the early and mid 1980's, the number and variety of cable channels on television was dazzling. There was the Weather Channel, the Golf Channel, and of course millions of different shopping channels.

The Web makes the variety available on cable seem dull by comparison. Since any Web site can be a channel, the possibilities of Netcasting are almost endless. You can have channels on press releases, industry news, stock quotes—the list goes on and on!

But trying to consider that amount of variety might blow your mind. So, in the interest of saving a few neurons, let's look at some of the channels that are set up specifically for Netcasting:

- **ABCNEWS.com**. Instead of waiting for the ABC news to come on in the evening, let the news come to you. The ABCNEWS.com channel dishes up stories and updates around the clock, as you can see in Figure 4-1.

- **The Sporting News**. Do you want sporting news, statistics, and scores? The Sporting News channel pushes it your way, as shown in Figure 4-2.

- **Lycos Direct**. With a more Internet-centric content, Lycos Direct offers you not only news and updates, but also site reviews and coverage of what's best on the Internet (see Figure 4-3).

Figure 4-1: ABCNEWS.com means you don't have to wait for the news.

Figure 4-2: Did the Cubs win the World Series? Find out here.

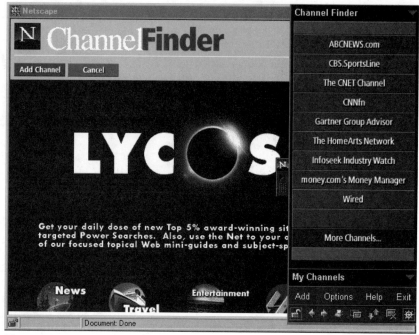

Figure 4-3: Lycos cuts down your surf time by bringing you the best of the Internet.

What is a Webtop?

A *webtop* is a channel that appears full-screen and is anchored to your desktop. In other words, a webtop remains on your screen all the time. You may work in other windows or open other channels on top of the webtop. It actually serves as a temporary replacement for your Windows desktop.

A webtop may be updated automatically at regular intervals, just like any other channel. That means it can provide you with late-breaking news as you work in other applications. This ability to update automatically can be a great help in a corporate intranet, to ensure that everyone is on "the same page." Figure 4-4 shows a typical corporate webtop.

Sounds great, doesn't it?

So, how do you actually get into Netcaster?

I thought you'd never ask.

TIP

You network administrators out there might want to consider implementing webtops across your intranet. It's an easy, powerful way to institute a common interface.

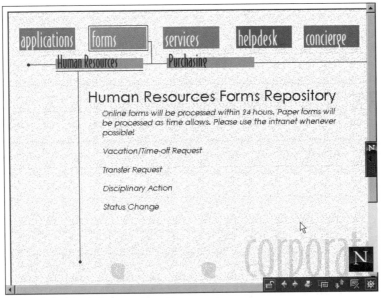

Figure 4-4: A typical corporate webtop.

Starting Netcaster

To start Netcaster, either choose the Netcaster icon from the Communicator program group, or choose Netcaster from any component's Communicator menu. You'll get the Netcaster drawer, which looks like Figure 4-5.

Figure 4-5: The Netcaster drawer.

TIP

At the time of this printing, Netcaster is available for download from the Netscape Home Page. Once you have downloaded it from the Netscape Home Page and installed it, Netcaster will automatically integrate itself into your Communicator software.

Java Security

When you first start Netcaster, a Java Security alert pops up like the one shown in Figure 4-6.

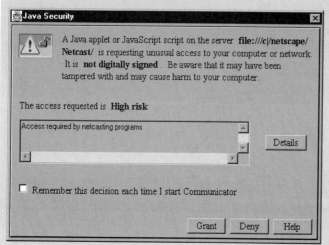

Figure 4-6: The Java Security alert.

The text here sounds pretty threatening, but not to worry. All it means is that Netcaster is what is known as a *signed Java* application—an application written in the Java programming language that needs your explicit approval before it is allowed to perform certain tasks, such as accessing your hard drive.

As a language, Java includes a variety of safeguards. Typically, it *cannot* access your hard drive without special permission. JavaScript, a simpler but related language, is even more secure. And that's where *signed* Java and JavaScript comes in. With signed Java or JavaScript, an application presents you with a special *security certificate* that positively identifies its creator or distributor. You can approve or reject the certificate. If you reject it, the application will not run at all. You are also given the option of allowing or disallowing specific types of access to your system that may compromise security. These types of access are outside the usual security restrictions of regular unsigned Java and JavaScript. In other words, in accepting a certificate you are agreeing to loosen security.

In the alert shown above, you can accept the certificate (grant full access to the application) by clicking Grant, or you can reject it (deny the necessary access) by clicking Deny. Be warned, though, that if you click Deny, Netcaster won't run. You may as well just move along to Chapter 5! If you check the Remember this Decision check box you will never have to see this alert again.

Before choosing Grant or Deny, you can view in detail what types of access to your system Netcaster is requesting. Go ahead and click the Details button. The Java Security's Target Details window appears, as shown in Figure 4-7.

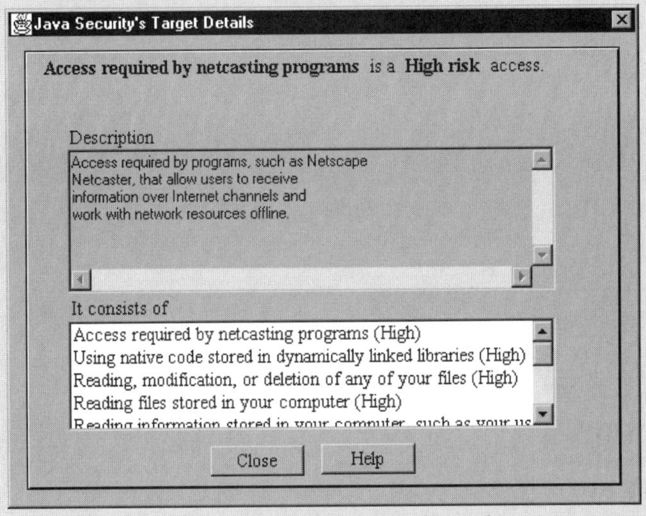

Figure 4-7: The Java Security's Target Details window.

Since you probably got this copy of Netcaster from a trusted source, you don't have to worry too much about granting "high risk access" to the program. After all, other Communicator components have been accessing your hard disk already. But in the case of *other* signed Java or JavaScript objects that you might encounter in cruising the Web, you should weigh the pros and cons of granting high risk access very carefully.

You can learn more about Java and JavaScript in Chapter 10, and about dealing with Java and JavaScript security issues in Chapter 13.

Looking at the Netcaster Drawer

The Netcaster drawer is a separate entity from the channels that display beside it. The Netcaster drawer remains available all the time, even when you're moving between channels or choosing a new channel.

> **TIP**
>
> *In this book I'll be using the terms Netcaster drawer and Netcaster window interchangeably, depending on context. They are the same thing.*

Sometimes, however, you might want to hide the drawer in order to allow a channel—or even another program—more screen real estate. The next section tells you how.

Hiding the Netcaster Drawer

About halfway down the Netcaster window there's a small textured tab on its left side. You can see a picture of it in Figure 4-8.

Figure 4-8: The tab on the Netcaster drawer.

To hide the Netcaster drawer, just click the tab. All of the Netcaster drawer will vanish except for the small tab, as you can see in Figure 4-9. To retrieve the Netcaster drawer, simply click the tab again. The Netcaster drawer reappears complete with tab.

As you explore the Netcaster drawer you might find yourself somewhat confused because of the two lists that are presented in the drawer; the Channel Finder and the My Channels lists. Here's how they work.

Figure 4-9: The Netcaster drawer hidden except for the tab.

The Channel Finder & My Channels Lists

Netcaster's Channel Finder lists a number of interesting channels that are available and lets you preview them to see if you want to subscribe to them. The Channel Finder is somewhat similar to the "preview channels" that cable companies use to interest you in subscribing to HBO or a sports network, for instance.

Once you've actually subscribed to a channel, it appears in another Netcaster list, the one called *My Channels*. These are channels that have already been stored on your hard drive and that you can access immediately.

Let's take a closer look at these two different lists.

The Channel Finder

The Channel Finder is an integral part of the Netcaster drawer, as you can see in Figure 4-10.

Figure 4-10: The Channel Finder listing.

As I mentioned earlier, the Channel Finder listing is sort of like a preview channel. It includes several of the channels available through Netcaster, with an option to see more by clicking on the "More Channels" button. If you click a channel in the Channel Finder, you can see some sample content for that channel. You are then given the opportunity to subscribe to it.

But although your cable provider may offer the "People Who Chew With Their Mouths Open Channel," that doesn't mean you want to watch it. Your cable guide doesn't have any way to customize a list by showing only the channels you want to watch, but Netcaster does. It's called My Channels.

My Channels

To access the My Channels list—that is, the list of channels to which you've actually subscribed—click the black box towards the bottom of the screen that says My Channels. The My Channels list pops up, looking like what you see in Figure 4-11.

Figure 4-11: The My Channels listing.

Initially the only channel on your list is the Netscape Channel. As we continue through this chapter you'll learn how to add channels and configure them to update when you want. Soon you too will have "57 channels and nothing on!" (By the way, if you want to get back to the Channel Finder list, just click the Channel Finder button above the My Channels button.)

TIP

The channels listed on Channel Finder are there only to let you know about the major channels available. They will not update automatically—only those channels you've added to your "My Channel" list will update.

Now that you know how to start Netcaster and how to tell the difference between the My Channels and Channel Finder lists, let's talk about what you can do with Netcaster itself.

There are two toolbars on the Netcaster drawer. The top one is a text toolbar and the bottom one is an icon toolbar. In the next section I'll cover the text tool bar only. The icon toolbar is for moving around webtops and will be covered later in this chapter.

The Text Toolbar

To use any of the commands on the text toolbar, just click it. The tools are Add, Options, Help, and Exit.

Add

Click Add to add a channel to your My Channels list. (More about that shortly.)

Options

The Options command lets you set your options for individual Netcaster channels that you've subscribed to, as well as for the program as a whole. When you click the Options button you'll see a box like the one in Figure 4-12.

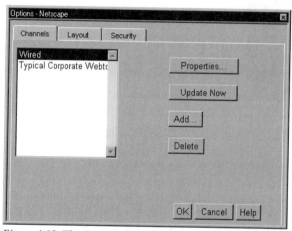

Figure 4-12: The Options dialog box.

The Options dialog box has three tabs: Channels, Layout, and Security. The first tab, Channels, lets you:

- Set the properties for individual channels in the My Channels list. To do this, select a channel from the list and click the Properties button.

- Manually update individual channels so that any new information is automatically downloaded to your hard drive. To do this, click the Update Now button.

- Add a new channel (by clicking the Add button). Later in this chapter we'll walk through the process of adding a channel this way.

- Delete a channel. To do this, select a channel and click Delete.

We'll talk more about adding channels and setting channel properties later in the chapter.

Now, click the layout tab to set the layout options for the program as a whole. You'll see a screen like that in Figure 4-13.

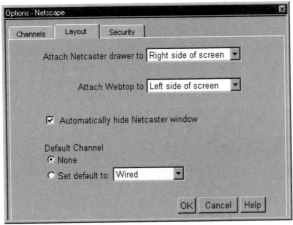

Figure 4-13: The layout options in Netcaster.

The first two options in this tab let you decide where you want the Netcaster drawer and actual channel information—or the webtop—to appear on your screen. Netcaster's default setting is for the Netcaster drawer to appear on the right side of the screen and the actual channel information to appear on the left. But by using the pull-down menu beside "Attach Netcaster drawer to" and "Attach Webtop to," you can change the placement of the Netcaster drawer and the webtop.

Below these two pull-down menus is a check box labeled "Automatically hide Netcaster window." When this box is checked, the Netcaster drawer will hide itself automatically every time you choose a channel. (The drawer tab will remain, however, so you can click on it and cause the drawer to reappear.)

The last option in this tab is the default channel selector. The default channel is the channel that automatically appears when you first launch Netcaster; it's kind of like the home page preference you set when you use Netscape Navigator. The default channel for Netcaster is no channel at all. If you want to keep it that way, just leave the "None" button under this option checked. If you want to have a default channel, however, click on the "Set default to" radio button and use the pull-down menu to choose any of the channels in the My Channels listing as your default channel.

Help

Help brings up the help file for Netcaster.

Exit

Exit quits the Netcaster program.

By now the Netcaster drawer is probably feeling more familiar to you. Let's get down to business and add some channels to your My Channels list. You've already seen two ways to add new channels:

- You can click the Add button in the text toolbar.
- You can click the Add button in the Channels tab of Options.

But perhaps the most convenient way to add new channels is through the Channel Finder. That's where we're going next.

Using the Channel Finder

As I mentioned at the beginning of this chapter, *any* Web site can be a Netcaster channel. However, not all Web sites are suited to this form of presentation. Fortunately, the Channel Finder can get you started examining a few choice sites that were specifically designed as Netcaster channels.

Let's walk through the process of previewing and adding a channel from the Channel Finder list.

Adding a Channel

Look at the Channel Finder list and find a channel that you think might be interesting. In this example we'll use the CNNfn channel. When you click on the button that says CNNfn, a *descriptor card* pops up with a logo for CNNfn, as you can see in Figure 4-14.

Click the Add Channel button in this descriptor card, or just double-click the card itself. A Navigator window appears with preview information on the CNNfn channel. You can see it in Figure 4-15.

Figure 4-14: The CNNfn descriptor card in the Channel Finder list.

Figure 4-15: The preview window for CNNfn.

Look over the information in the preview window. If you decide you want to subscribe to it, click the Add Channel button in the upper left hand corner of the preview window. A dialog box pops up so you can set the properties for this channel.

Setting Channel Properties

In the Name box, make sure the name of the channel is as you want it to appear in the My Channels list—CNNfn, perhaps, or CNN Financial. Below that, in the Location field, the URL should already be filled in. (If you're adding a channel manually, you'll have to type it in yourself. Just type in the URL as you would type it to go to a Web page.) Below the name and location field, there's a pull-down menu to specify how often you want this channel to be updated with new information from the Web. You have several choices, ranging from every 30 minutes to every week. For this example, choose every day.

Now that you've got all the basic information down, you need to establish how you want this channel to look on your screen. Click the Display tab to bring up the Display properties dialog box, as shown in Figure 4-16.

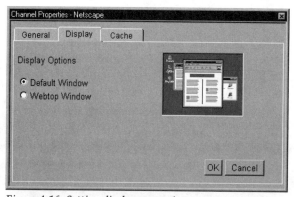

Figure 4-16: Setting display properties.

The only thing you have to decide within this tab is whether you want the channel to appear as a default window (a standard Navigator window), or as a webtop, which takes up the whole screen. For the sake of this example, let's set the channel to appear in a default window.

The final setting you'll want to establish is the size of the channel's cache. The cache is the amount of space the channel will take up on your hard drive to store its text, pictures, and other multimedia. Obviously if you have a small hard drive, you'll want to be conservative in assigning cache space to your channels. On the other hand, assigning too little cache space to a channel means that you won't be able to download the entire channel for offline browsing. (We'll go over offline browsing at the end of the chapter.)

To access the cache settings, click the cache tab. You'll get a screen that looks like the one in Figure 4-17.

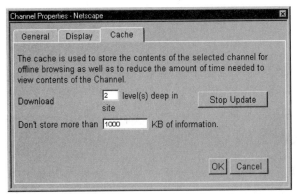

Figure 4-17: Setting the cache properties for a channel.

First, decide how many informational *levels* of the channel you want to download and store. What do I mean by levels? Here's how it works:

- The first level is the first page of the channel, including any graphics or other multimedia files it contains.

- The second level consists of all the pages to which the first page links.

- The third level consists of all the pages to which the second page links, and so on.

If the first level has five links, while all the pages in the second level have ten links, and the third level has twenty links—well, you can see that going deeper than just two or three levels can take up a lot of space on your hard drive. For the sake of this example, click the field next to the word level(s) and enter the number 2. This indicates that you want to download and store two levels of the CNNfn site.

Finally, you're going to have to indicate the maximum amount of space you want to give this channel on your hard drive. The option here reads "Don't store more than ____ KB of information." Click the KB field and type in the amount of space you want to devote to this channel's cache. Bear in mind that 1000KB of space equals a full megabyte, while 2KB of space is hardly enough for the average text file. For this example, enter 1000 in the KB field. That'll devote 1MB of your hard drive space to the CNNfn channel.

TIP

Once you indicate the number of levels you want to download and the amount of diskspace you want to reserve, Netcaster begins to download the channel to your hard drive. To stop this process, click the Stop Update button in the cache tab.

Once you've set the options in the cache tab, click the OK button. CNNfn now appears on your My Channels list, as you can see in Figure 4-18.

Figure 4-18: CNNfn in the My Channels list.

TIP

You can hide the CNNfn description box in the Channel Finder listing simply by clicking it.

Now that you know how to add a channel, let's talk some more about working with channels—specifically, how to add them manually and adjust their properties. After that, we'll discuss how to move around in webtops.

Manually Adding a Channel

We've walked through adding a channel in the Channel Finder, but eventually you're going to want to add a channel that isn't listed in the Channel Finder. Why? Because as was mentioned in the beginning of this chapter, any Web site can be a channel. Of course, there's no way that the Channel Finder can list every Web site in existence—heck, not even the search engines can do that.

Now let's manually add a channel and set its properties. It's almost as simple as doing it with the Channel Finder. The channel properties you set, by the way, are the same ones that you see when you add a channel through the Channel Finder and when you adjust settings using the Options button, so you are already familiar with much of this process.

To begin adding a channel manually, click Add in the Netcaster drawer. The Add channel dialog box appears, as shown in Figure 4-19.

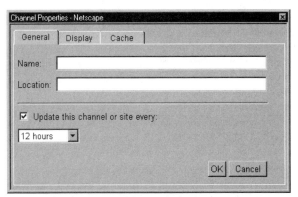

Figure 4-19: Manually adding a channel.

From here, you set the properties just like you did when you added a channel in Channel Finder. The only difference is that you'll have to specify the name and the URL of the channel. Remember, any URL will work!

But what if you decide you want to change a channel's properties, or if you want to delete a channel altogether?

Changing Channel Properties & Deleting Channels

Eventually you're going to change your mind about a channel. You may want to change how much space you want to devote to it, or how often you want it to update. You may even decide to delete it, freeing up valuable hard drive space for other information.

OFFICIAL NETSCAPE COMMUNICATOR 4 PROFESSIONAL EDITION BOOK

Changing channel properties or deleting channels is easy. Click Options in the Netcaster drawer. You'll see the Options dialog box we discussed earlier in the chapter, as shown in Figure 4-20.

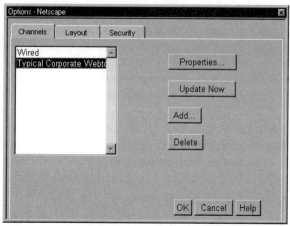

Figure 4-20: The Options dialog box.

To remove a channel, follow these steps:

1. Scroll through the list of channels in the dialog box until you find the channel you want to delete.

2. Click it to highlight it.

3. Click the Delete button.

To change the properties of a channel, do the following:

1. Scroll through the list of channels in the dialog box until you find the channel you want.

2. Click it to highlight it.

3. Click Properties. The Properties dialog box appears, as shown in Figure 4-21.

4. Modify any of the properties and click OK.

Figure 4-21: The Properties dialog box.

You now know how to add channels, change channel properties, and even delete channels you no longer want to use. So you're a great administrator of your desktop system, but we've left something out. How do you actually *access* a channel once you've added it to your My Channels list?

Accessing Channels

To access a channel, click the My Channels button in the Netcaster drawer. A list of the channels available to you pops up. Find the channel in which you're interested and click it. The channel appears on your screen, and depending on how you've set your options, your Netcaster drawer may vanish.

A channel works a lot like a Navigator page. There are hypertext links and hot spots—places on the channel that link to other pages in the channel when they're clicked. However, sometimes moving around in the anchored full-screen channels—what we've been calling webtops—can get confusing. To alleviate that confusion, Netcaster offers an icon bar for moving around on the webtop.

Moving Around in a Webtop

At the beginning of the chapter we discussed webtops. Since webtops take up the entire screen, and since they act as a temporary replacement for the Windows desktop, navigating within one can be confusing. You do not have the usual Navigator toolbars available as navigational aids. To solve this problem, Netcaster provides a special icon bar at the bottom corner of the screen. It contains icons that are very similar to the ones you're used to in Navigator 4 (see Chapter 3).

> **TIP**
>
> *Webtops have hyperlinks just like other Web pages do. You can click these hyperlinks to move around within a channel, just as you would use hyperlinks to move around in a Web page.*

If you're using the Webtop mode to display a channel and you've got your options set so that the Netcaster drawer disappears when you open a channel, you might find yourself with the webtop, the drawer tab, and an icon bar in the lower corner of the screen, as shown in Figure 4-22.

Figure 4-22: The icon bar.

Using the Icon Bar

The webtop may contain links, buttons, and other navigational objects, but the icon bar provides a convenient external interface. Here's what the icons in the bar represent, from left to right:

Security. This is an icon of a lock. If the lock is in an unlocked position, it means that this webtop (or any channel) is "insecure," and any information sent between your computer and this webtop is unencrypted (see Chapter 12). On the other hand, if the icon is in a locked position, this channel is "secure," and suitable for sensitive communications like commerce and online purchasing. Please see Chapter 12 for more information on security issues.

Back arrow. Goes to the previous page on the webtop.

Forward arrow. Goes to the next page on the webtop.

Printer. Prints the webtop.

Webtops. Hides or displays the webtop. Click once on this icon to hide the webtop; click it again to display it. This is convenient for switching between viewing the current channel and getting some other work done.

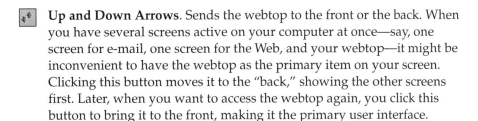 **Up and Down Arrows**. Sends the webtop to the front or the back. When you have several screens active on your computer at once—say, one screen for e-mail, one screen for the Web, and your webtop—it might be inconvenient to have the webtop as the primary item on your screen. Clicking this button moves it to the "back," showing the other screens first. Later, when you want to access the webtop again, you click this button to bring it to the front, making it the primary user interface.

Screen and X. Closes the webtop.

Navigator logo. Opens a new Netscape Navigator window.

Using Netcaster Offline

In the last 20 or so pages, you have learned the basics of using Netscape Netcaster. Now let's see how you can leverage its features to save time and connection fees.

You don't have to be connected to the Internet all the time to take advantage of Netcaster. Once you've updated the channels you're interested in, you can disconnect from the Internet and browse them just as if you were still online.

But how do you tell if your channels are updated, and how do you update your channels manually? Read on.

Manually Updating Channels

Make sure you're connected to the Internet or your office intranet and then launch Netcaster. Open the My Channels list. Under some of your channels you may see a red and gray animated progress bar.

Figure 4-23: The progress bar.

This progress bar shows that new material is still being "pushed" to your channel from the Internet or your intranet. Until this bar disappears, the download is still in progress, and any effort to browse this channel offline won't be completely successful.

Sometimes you'll want to force an update to a particular channel. For example, you may have a site that you want to update only weekly, but before you browse it offline you want to make sure it contains all the latest information. To manually update a channel, follow these steps:

1. Click the Options button in the Netcaster drawer. The Options dialog box appears as shown in Figure 4-24.

Figure 4-24: The Options dialog box.

2. Scroll through the list of channels in the box and highlight the channel you want to update.

3. Click the Update Now button. Assuming you're connected to the Net or your office intranet, the channel begins to update immediately.

4. Click OK to dismiss the Options box.

Again, wait until the progress bar vanishes to make sure the entire channel has been updated.

Offline Browsing

Once the progress bar has disappeared, how do you browse offline? Simply disconnect your Internet or intranet connection, click the My Channels button, and choose a channel from the list. You'll be able to browse a channel just like you would online—only a lot faster since the information is already on your hard drive.

TIP

If you've imposed small cache sizes on your channels, then you might not be able to completely browse a downloaded channel. The channels will download updates only until their allotted space on your hard drive has been filled. If you repeatedly try to browse channels offline but find that the channels have not been completely downloaded, try increasing the cache size for your channels.

And remember, you can do this any time with any Web page you wish. If there's a Web page that you like to check regularly for updates, it's a real time-saver to download the information in advance and browse it at your leisure. For example, say you checked in on the Netscape Press site every Monday, poking around to see what new books are on the horizon. With Netcaster, you could set up the Netscape Press What's New page as a channel that updates weekly. Once a week Netcaster would grab any new material, ensuring that you don't miss out on any book announcements. This can save you a lot of time. You don't have to surf to the site or wait for the page to load; instead, it's sent to you.

Moving On

As you can see, Netcaster is one of the most exciting and flexible communications facilities available, whether you're connected to a corporate intranet or the Net as a whole. And since it's a brand new feature, you can expect the software to evolve and grow as information providers stretch its limits.

Now let's look at one of the oldest and best known bread-and-butter communications applications: e-mail. The next chapter is a complete tutorial on using Netscape Messenger to send and receive electronic messages that can even look like complete Web pages!

CHAPTER 5

Communication With the Office and the World: Messenger

Netscape isn't content with just making the world's best Web browser. In Netscape Communicator, Netscape has created a multipurpose software product that can do much more than just display Web documents.

The most basic of all Internet tools is electronic mail, or *e-mail*. E-mail is the most widely used software tool of any kind, and Netscape Communicator provides a separate interface called *Messenger* just to handle this service. In this chapter, we'll show you how to use the Netscape Messenger window to send, receive, read, and store e-mail. This window, shown in Figure 5-1, is accessed by clicking the Mailbox icon in the Component Bar, by clicking the Messenger icon on your desktop, or by selecting Messenger Mailbox from any component's Communicator menu.

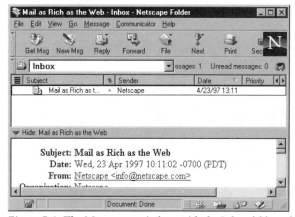

Figure 5-1: The Messenger window, with the Inbox folder selected.

Before we get into that, however, let's begin with a few words about e-mail itself.

What Is E-mail & How Does It Work?

E-mail, as you probably know, is the electronic messaging service of intranets and of the Net. When you send a message to a friend via e-mail, that message travels from your machine over your office intranet or the Internet itself until it arrives at your friend's machine, or to a special electronic post office on a machine he or she can access. The message is then kept there until your friend retrieves and reads it.

How does the intranet or Internet know how to get a piece of e-mail from your machine to your friend's post office account? It works just about like regular old-fashioned snail mail: all the necessary delivery information is contained in your friend's e-mail address.

When you write a piece of e-mail, it's essential to get the address right. There's no friendly Mr. Postman to figure out that you really meant the house down the block from the address you indicated. Every character counts. If there is a mistake in the address you enter—even one wrong letter—the mail will simply be returned to you as undeliverable.

The standard form for an address is *user@domain*. This address is in two parts, separated by an @ sign (press Shift+2 on your keyboard). The part before the @ is the username, and the part after the @ is the domain name—the name of the machine where that user has an e-mail account. It is important that e-mail addresses not have any spaces in them.

Usernames are how individual users are identified on systems that may be accessed by many people. For instance, the username part of Count Dracula's e-mail address, dracula@transylvania.com, is *dracula*. Domain names are the names of the machines themselves. The domain name in the address, transylvania.com, identifies the name of a machine, *transylvania*. The *.com* at the end of the domain name means that this is a commercial service. There are also *.gov* services, which are governmental institutions; *.edu* services, which are educational institutions; and so on. We touched on some of this in Chapter 1. Sometimes addresses will end with information about a country or network instead of or in addition to a type of service. For example, addresses ending in *.ca* are in Canada, and addresses ending in *.uk* are in the United Kingdom.

What's My E-mail Address?

Your e-mail address is your identity in the online world; you were probably given your e-mail address by the people who provide you with Internet access. If you are on an office intranet, your e-mail address may be your network login name followed by an @ sign and the domain name of your company. Then again, it may not—you really need to check with your system administrator.

If you get on the Net using a SLIP or PPP account, you can usually figure out your e-mail address. If your login name is *frank* and your Internet access provider is *graveyard.com*, then your e-mail address is probably frank@graveyard.com. If this isn't correct, then you will have to check with your network administrator to see what your password is.

> **TIP**
>
> *If your Internet service provider doesn't provide you with an e-mail account, you should seriously consider switching service providers!*

Exchanging Messages With Online Services

What if you have friends who are not connected directly to the Internet via a LAN or a SLIP or PPP account, but are users of some online service such as America Online (AOL) or CompuServe? Can you exchange e-mail messages with them?

Sure! Users of CompuServe, MCI Mail, AT&T Mail, Prodigy, or AOL can send you e-mail using your regular Internet address. Typically, the procedure is no more complex than sending a message to another user of the service. You can also send e-mail to a user on any of these services, using Netscape Navigator 4 in the same way you would when communicating with another individual on the Net. The only difference is the addressing. If an online service user gives you his or her ID, you have to know how to turn it into a valid Internet address so that any message you send can be delivered. The method for translating addresses varies from service to service.

CompuServe

User IDs on CompuServe take the form of two numbers separated by a comma, as in *71234,5678*. To send e-mail to a CompuServe subscriber, you address it to that ID number at (@) the domain *compuserve.com*. The only trick is that the comma between the two numbers must be replaced by a period. Thus the Internet e-mail address for the user whose ID is 71234,5678 would be:

```
71234.5678@compuserve.com
```

That's all there is to it; you send the message just like any other e-mail.

MCI Mail

MCI Mail users really have three IDs: a number; a "handle," or abbreviated name; and a normal full name. For instance, the user Jake Barns might have the following set of IDs:

```
123-4567
jbarns
Jake Barns
```

To send e-mail to Jake, you could use any of the following Internet e-mail addresses:

```
1234567@mcimail.com
jbarns@mcimail.com
jake_barns@mcimail.com
```

Please note that in the user number you drop the hyphen, and in the full name you have to add an underscore (_) character between the first and last names.

America Online

All you need to know is the AOL user's "screen name;" you just add the at sign (@) and the domain *aol.com*. A valid Internet e-mail address for an AOL user might be, for instance:

```
aoluser@aol.com
```

Note that even if the AOL user has a space in his or her AOL name—John Doe, for instance—you can ignore that space and simply address your e-mail to johndoe@aol.com.

Prodigy

This is just like America Online. You send e-mail to a particular user ID at *prodigy.com*. Here's an example:

```
abc123@prodigy.com
```

AT&T Mail

As with AOL and Prodigy, each AT&T Mail user has a unique username. To address a message, you simply append *@attmail.com* to the username. A valid address might be as follows:

```
dialtone@attmail.com
```

OK, you've learned a little about e-mail addressing and how e-mail works. Now it's time to look at Netscape Messenger itself. We'll start by getting a brief overview of the program, examining the features of the Messenger window, and then by actually working through the common e-mail tasks: sending and receiving messages, organizing folders, and keeping track of addresses.

Getting Started

Make sure that you are connected to the Net or to your office intranet. Now go ahead and double-click the Messenger icon on your desktop, or select the Mailbox icon from the Component Bar. As soon as the component starts running, a Password Entry dialog box appears asking for your e-mail password, as shown in Figure 5-2.

Figure 5-2: The Password Entry dialog box.

Your e-mail password is the password your incoming e-mail server requires in order for you to retrieve new messages. If you're not currently connected to your office intranet or the Net, you can still use Messenger offline. In this case, click Cancel when asked for your password. You should also click Cancel if you don't know what your current password is.

Your E-mail Password

Once you type in your password, Messenger remembers it for as long as any of the Communicator components is running. If you quit Communicator altogether, you will have to enter your password again the next time Messenger tries to access your incoming mail server. If you're on a relatively secure computer and want Messenger to always remember your e-mail password, even after you've quit and restarted the program, select Preferences from the Messenger's Edit menu and then select the Mail Server category on the left side of the dialog box that appears. On the right, in the Mail Server window, click the More Options button and then check the "Remember my mail password" check box. Click OK to save your changes.

Once you click OK after entering your e-mail password, Messenger logs into your incoming mail server and checks for any new messages. You are left in the Messenger window, with your Inbox folder (a folder for storing new e-mail) selected, as shown in Figure 5-3.

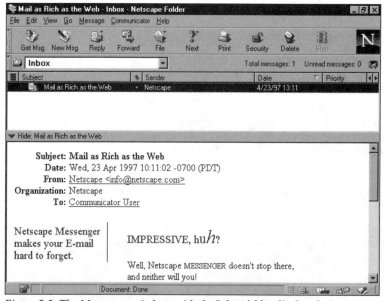

Figure 5-3: The Messenger window, with the Inbox folder displayed.

We'll examine this window in detail in a few minutes, but first a section for those of you who didn't enter your e-mail account information the first time you ran Communicator (see the section in Chapter 2 called "Starting Communicator the First Time"). If you need to add or modify e-mail account information such as your e-mail address or the address of your server, read on. Otherwise, jump to the section called "The Messenger Window."

Adding or Modifying Account Information

Before getting started, you need to have the following information handy:

- Your e-mail address.
- The username you use to access your e-mail server. If you use your ISP for e-mail, this is usually the same as your regular SLIP/PPP login name.
- Your e-mail password.
- The address of the server you use to send e-mail, which is also known as the outgoing mail server or SMTP server.
- The address of the server you use to receive e-mail (incoming mail server). This is usually the same as your outgoing mail server.
- Whether your incoming mail server uses POP3 or IMAP4 protocol. (If you're using a commercial ISP it's probably POP3. If you're using Communicator Professional and are on an intranet or LAN, you might be using IMAP4 as your network administrator.)

Once you have all this information on hand, click Preferences in the Messenger's Edit menu and then select Identity from the category list on the left. The Identity dialog box appears, as shown in Figure 5-4.

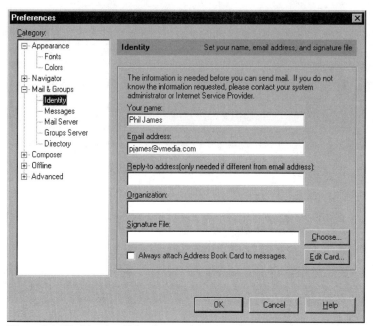

Figure 5-4: The Identity dialog box.

Enter your actual name and e-mail address in the appropriate fields. You may also enter a reply-to address if it is different from your e-mail address, as well as an optional organization name.

TIP

> *You may want to use a different reply-to address if you have several e-mail accounts, for instance one at home and one at work.*

Don't worry about the Signature File and Address Book Card options—those will be explained later in this chapter.

Once you have completed the Identity dialog box, click the Mail Server category on the left. The Mail Server dialog box appears, as shown in Figure 5-5.

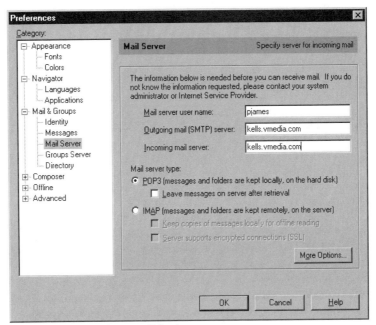

Figure 5-5: The Mail Server dialog box.

In this dialog box, enter your e-mail account name (often the same as your login name on your intranet or for your SLIP/PPP account), the address of your outgoing mail (SMTP) server, and the address of your incoming mail server. In most cases, these two addresses will be the same. In the bottom section of the dialog box, select whether your incoming e-mail server is of the POP3 or IMAP variety.

SMTP, POP3 & IMAP

Like all Internet and intranet programs, Netscape Communicator, relies on established protocols to send and receive data. As explained earlier in this book, protocols are simply conventions that allow one piece of software to exchange data with another. For instance, a client program might expect a particular kind of acknowledgment after it sends a packet of data. Both sender and receiver need to play by the same rules.

Internet mail programs use SMTP (Simple Mail Transport Protocol) to *send* messages. The client, Netscape Messenger, first establishes a connection with the remote SMTP server, the machine that acts as host for the recipient's e-mail account. Once the link is established, Messenger sends the recipient's name. If the server can accept mail for that user, it responds with an OK. If there are several intended recipients, this negotiation continues for each of them. Finally Messenger sends the actual body of the e-mail message.

To *retrieve* messages from your e-mail server, Netscape Messenger uses one of two different protocols, depending on how the server is configured. The more common and older protocol is called POP3 (Post Office Protocol, version 3). Recently, IMAP (Internet Message Access Protocol) has become very popular. IMAP stores all your messages, in their correct folders, on the mail server. This means that if you access your mail from several different machines, you will always see exactly the same thing. (You may also keep local copies of your messages for offline reading, though.) I won't go into the details of POP3 and IMAP because they're somewhat complex, but it's important to make sure that your e-mail account is on a server that supports one of these protocols (most do). And if you have a choice between POP3 and IMAP, choose IMAP.

If you are using a POP3 server, notice that you can elect to leave your messages on the server after you retrieve them. That way you can retrieve them again, perhaps from a different computer. This option is useful if you travel, or if you sometimes work from home.

And if you are using an IMAP server, notice that you have a couple of extra options:

■ **Keep copies of messages locally for offline reading**. As I mentioned in the sidebar above, IMAP servers store all your messages so that you can re-access them at any time, and from any computer. However, you can also keep copies of these messages on your local machine in case you want to read them when you're not connected to your IMAP server. To do so, check this check box.

■ **Server supports encrypted connections (SSL)**. Some IMAP servers support special encryption that assures the privacy of your messages. If the IMAP server on your intranet supports encrypted connections, check this check box.

Now click the More Options button. The More Mail Server Preferences dialog box appears, as shown in Figure 5-6.

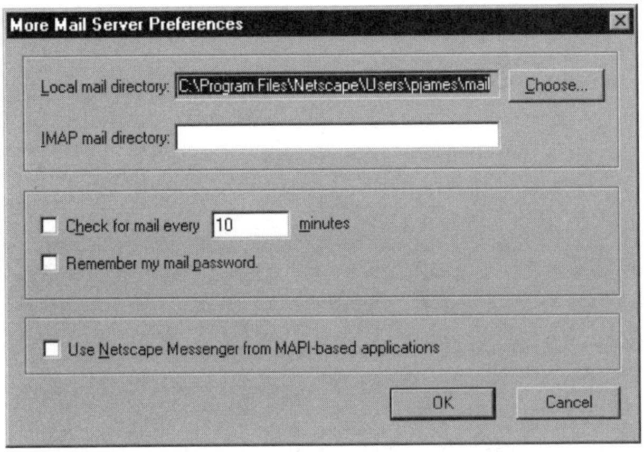

Figure 5-6: The More Mail Server Preferences dialog box.

The top two edit fields let you specify directories for local storage of your e-mail messages. If you're using POP3, you should probably leave the top field alone unless you have a very specific reason for changing the directory; if you're using IMAP and have specified that you want to store messages locally, you need to complete the second field.

You'll learn more about how Messenger checks for new mail messages later in the chapter, so for now you can ignore the second set of options. As for the bottom check box, check it if you want IMAP-enabled Windows applications to always use Netscape Messenger when they let you send an e-mail message.

Once you have completed the Mail Server preferences, click OK to return to the main Messenger window.

The Messenger Window

The top pane of the Messenger window shows a summary list of the messages you've received, while the bottom pane shows the actual contents of any message that you select in the top pane. Right away you can see that you've already received one e-mail, an introductory message from Netscape. (This message wasn't actually delivered to you via your e-mail server, it was "built into" the program.) Let's examine the top pane, the message list pane, first.

If you see only one pane, click the blue up-arrow at the bottom left of the window. This will make the message content pane appear. You can hide it again by clicking the down-arrow marked Hide between the two panes. You can also resize the panes by placing your cursor in the area between them and then clicking and dragging up or down.

> **TIP**
>
> *You can create a desktop shortcut to your Inbox folder—or to any e-mail folder or discussion group in the drop-down list—by clicking and dragging the icon to the left of the list out onto the Windows 95/NT desktop.*

The Changing Mailbox Icon

The Mailbox icon in the Component Bar will not always look the same. Before you send or retrieve any messages, it may look like an envelope next to an empty inbox. This form of the Mailbox icon indicates that Messenger has not accessed your e-mail server to retrieve new messages. Either you are not connected to the Net or your office intranet, or you have not yet entered your e-mail password. Once Messenger has your password and can access your server to check for mail, and once you actually have some messages in your Inbox, the icon changes to an inbox with an envelope *inside* it.

The Mailbox icon in the Component Bar changes in another way, too. Messenger periodically checks your mail server to see if new messages have arrived there. If there *are* any new messages, the Mailbox icon contains a green down arrow. You can then retrieve your new messages if you wish.

The Message List Pane

Notice the envelope icon to the left of each message. It changes according to the status of the message:

- When you first receive a message, before you select it for viewing the icon depicts a vertical envelope with a green arrow next to it. This is the "unopened" icon.

- Once you've viewed the contents of a message, the icon changes to depict an opened letter next to its horizontal envelope. This is the "opened and read" icon.

■ Even after you've viewed the contents of a message, Messenger lets you "flag" it as unread (see the sidebar below called "Flagging Messages as Unread"). If you flag a previously read message as unread, the icon changes to a simple horizontal envelope. There is no separate letter to indicate "opened" or green arrow to indicate "unopened."

Notice that there are several informational fields for any messages you've received, including the pre-installed message from Netscape:

TIP

For now, ignore the button to the left of the Subject label. I'll talk about that later in the chapter, in the section called "Threading."

■ **Subject**. This shows the subject of the message, as specified by the individual who sent the message.

■ **Sender**. Typically this will be an e-mail address or the name of the sender.

■ **Date**.This is when the message was sent to you. If it was sent today, this field contains the *time* it was sent. If it was sent between one and six days ago, this field contains the day of the week and the time the message was sent. If it was sent more than a week ago, this field contains the *date* it was sent. Thus you can see at a glance which messages are very recent.

■ **Priority**. The author of a message you receive may have marked it as urgent, normal, or as low-priority. Not all messages contain this information.

In addition, there is a green diamond between the Subject and Sender fields. When you see a green diamond next to a particular message, it means that the message hasn't been read yet. Typically, you will have more than one message in the top pane. When new messages arrive, they will always have the green diamond next to them. Once you select a particular message from the list, however, the contents appear in the lower pane and the green diamond disappears, indicating that the message has been read. In addition, the Subject, Sender, and Date information no longer appear in bold font.

Flagging Messages as Unread

Even after you read a message, you can mark it as unread by clicking in the "green diamond" field. The green diamond reappears and the Subject, Sender, and Date become bold again. This is a useful reminder if you want to reread a particular message later. Besides marking messages as unread, there are also a variety of marking options available in the Mark submenu of the Message menu:

- **Thread read.** Select this option to mark an entire subject *thread* as read (see the section below called "Threading").

- **All Read.** Select this option to mark all the messages in your Inbox as read.

- **by Date.** This option lets you specify a date before which all messages will be marked as read. In other words, it will make Messenger display only newer messages as unread.

- **for Later.** This option marks a message or set of messages as read for the duration of the current Messenger session. After that, they return to un-read status.

To mark or unmark multiple messages, select them using Ctrl+click, then choose the appropriate action from the Mark submenu. You can select just your flagged messages to mark or unmark, or even all your messages, by clicking the appropriate choice in the Select submenu of the Edit menu.

There are several other informational fields for every message you receive, but they do not show up automatically. You can access them by clicking the left arrow that's just to the right of the Date label. Try it now:

1. Click the arrow just to the right of the Priority label. As you click repeatedly, new informational fields appear, squeezing into the window as shown in Figure 5-7. Each click adds one new field.

2. Now click the right arrow. The fields disappear one by one as you click, and the original fields stretch to fill the window.

3. Using the left and right arrows, adjust the label bar until it appears as it did initially, with the Date field as the right-most field.

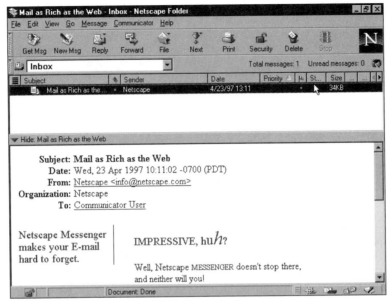

Figure 5-7: New informational fields for received messages.

And what are these additional informational fields? They are:

- **Status**. This field may contain a variety of information about the message. If you haven't read the message yet, it contains the word "New." It also tells you whether or not you've replied to a message. If you've replied, it contains the word "replied." As I get older and more forgetful, I grow more and more fond of the Status field.

- **Size**. This is the actual number of bytes in the message.

- **Unread**. This field is useful only when you are viewing messages in *threaded* order. It indicates how many messages in a particular thread are still unread. For instance, if you reply to a message that you receive and then the original sender responds to your reply, you'll have a thread containing two messages in your Inbox. This field indicates how many of them are unread. Don't worry if you don't completely understand this right now, there's a whole section on threading later.

- **Total**. This is the total number of messages in a particular thread.

Now look at Figure 5-7 again. That's right, I left something out of my description. There's a "red flag" field between Priority and Status. The red flag works pretty much like the green diamond: if you click the red flag column to the right of a message, the flag appears; click again and it's gone. Figure 5-8 shows a message that has been red-flagged.

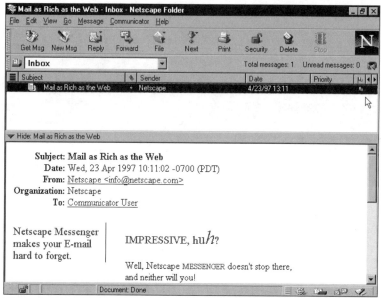

Figure 5-8: A red-flagged message.

What's the point? The red flag is exclusively for your own purposes. You can use it as a reminder, for instance, to read a message more thoroughly later, or to forward it to another recipient.

TIP

You can change the order of the informational fields by dragging the labels (Subject, Sender, Date, etc.) to the right or left. On my own system at home, I have moved the red flag field to the left, next to the green diamond, since I use it often and don't want to scroll to the right to find it.

That's the Message List pane in a nutshell. I'll go over the buttons and commands that are useful here when we actually get into sending and receiving e-mail, but for now, let's take a quick look at the bottom pane of the window, the Message Content Pane.

The Message Content Pane

The bottom section of the Messenger window is where all the excitement happens. This pane contains the actual content of any message you select from the Message List Pane. As soon as you click *any* informational field for a message at the top, you have in effect opened its envelope and the contents are revealed below.

Using the scroll bar to the right of the Message Content Pane, take a few moments to scroll down through the sample message from Netscape. Probably the first thing you notice is that four headers near the top indicate the subject of the message, its date, who it's from, and who it's intended for, as shown in Figure 5-9.

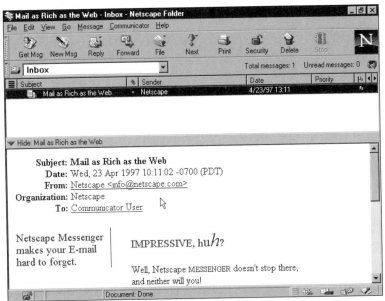

Figure 5-9: The informational headers at the top of a received message.

TIP

If you want, you can configure Messenger so that it displays more informational headers as part of each message. The additional headers provide technical details about the message's addressing, content type, etc. To make this change, select Headers from the View menu and then click All in the submenu that appears. Or if you prefer the lean clean look, click Brief.

Notice that the To and From headers are blue and underlined, just like links in a Web page. In fact, they *are* links. If you click either one, the name and e-mail address is added to a personal Address Book Card, which you can use later to automate the process of addressing new messages. I'll cover that in depth later, in the section called "The Address Book," but for now scroll a little further down in the Message Content Pane.

Take a look at Figure 5-10, which depicts more of the contents of the sample message from Netscape.

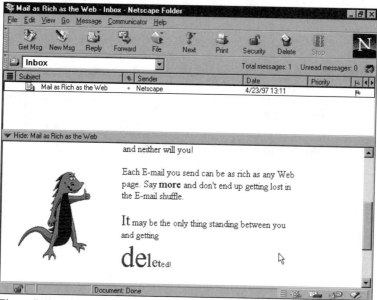

Figure 5-10: A little further down in the sample message.

As you can see, this doesn't look like a regular old-fashioned e-mail message at all, it looks like a Web page! That's right, Messenger supports formatted text, graphics, links, and other HTML features just like a Web browser. If you click a link in the message, Messenger launches Netscape Navigator 4 with the appropriate URL. And you can even replay the animation included in this message by clicking the Replay button!

TIP

As you can see in the above example, Messenger displays images and HTML files as part of the message itself, or inline. But if you don't like this behavior and just want to deal with the enhanced material as separate attachments to any messages you receive, select Attachments from the Messenger's View menu and then click As Links from the submenu that appears. You'll learn more about attachments in the section called "Dealing With Attached Files You Receive."

One last thing about the Message Content Pane: you can make it disappear. To do this just click the down arrow in the area between the two panes, just to the left of the word Hide. As expected, the beautifully formatted message vanishes, and all you are left with is your message list. To display the message now, double-click one of its informational fields. It appears in a separate window, as shown in Figure 5-11.

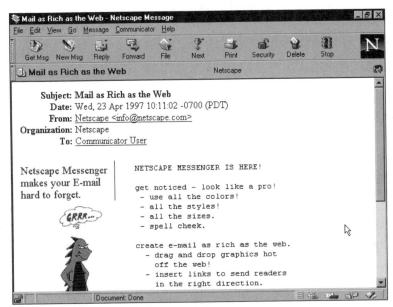

Figure 5-11: The message in its own window.

Why would you want Messenger to display only the message list instead of the message contents as well? There are several possibilities:

- It may be easier to get an overview of messages you've received, or to organize them into folders and threads, if you display as much of the list as possible.

- Messages that contain a lot of graphics may take time to display. You can often work more quickly with your message list by foregoing the actual message contents.

- Your boss often wanders by your desk, and you don't necessarily want him or her to see the contents of all your messages.

To display both panes again, simply click the up arrow at the bottom left of the window.

Now that you've configured your account information and gotten the lay of the land, or at least the lay of the main window, you're ready to start sending and receiving e-mail with Netscape Messenger. Of course there are a number of options that could dramatically enhance your use of the program, but I'll cover most of these as they come up in the context of actual tasks, and then I'll talk about a few advanced options near the end of the chapter. But for now let's get busy with the nitty-gritty of sending and receiving e-mail messages. This is where it gets fun.

Creating & Sending an E-mail Message

In the next few sections you will actually compose an e-mail message to your-self, send it, and retrieve it from your mail server. Why send a message to yourself? It's not just because you're such a fan of yourself, it's also because this is the easiest way to learn and test Messenger's capabilities. But first, there's something I need to explain. Messenger lets you send two different kinds of messages: Plain Text and HTML.

Plain Text and HTML Messages

As you saw in Figure 5-10 above, formatting and graphics can greatly enhance e-mail messages, giving them more impact and letting them convey information more flexibly. Netscape calls messages that include HTML formatting and other typical features of a Web page *HTML Messages*. Unfortunately, though, not all e-mail programs are created equal, and so there are quite a few people out there who will not be able to fully appreciate the careful creative work you've put into an HTML message. In fact, it will look like a bunch of confusing HTML code on their screen.

If you know the recipient of your message uses Messenger or some other browser that supports HTML messages, feel free to get creative. But of course Messenger also lets you send Plain Text e-mail, messages that do not include all the multimedia bells and whistles. Messenger even lets you specify in your Address Book (see the section below called "The Address Book") which recipients can receive HTML messages and which can only receive Plain Text. If you try to send an HTML message to somebody who is configured as unable to view it properly, Messenger will give you the option of sending your message as Plain Text. You can even send the same message to multiple recipients in different formats: HTML for those who can handle it, Plain Text for those who can't. Again, this will be covered in more depth in the section called "The Address Book."

Messenger has two different windows for composing new messages, one that's suited to Plain Text messages and another that includes features which help you create HTML. By default, Messenger presents you with the more universal Plain Text menu. But if you think you will generally be sending HTML messages, you can configure Messenger so that it brings up the HTML window for new messages by default. To do this:

1. Select Preferences from the Messenger's Edit menu, then click the Messages category.

2. In the Messages dialog box that appears, check the top check box, labeled "By default, send HTML messages."

But Messenger allows even more flexibility in dealing with HTML/Plain Text messages. In the same dialog box, click the More Options button. The More Messages Preferences dialog box appears, as shown in Figure 5-12.

➡

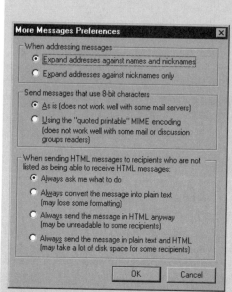

Figure 5-12: The More Messages Preferences dialog box.

Take a look at the bottom section of this dialog box, which deals with the HTML/Plain Text issue. Carefully read all the choices. Obviously, the first choice is the most flexible, allowing you to choose "on the fly" whether to send an HTML or Plain Text message to a particular recipient. (Remember, this option will only work if your *default* is to send HTML messages.)

In the next few sections all the screenshots will show the HTML window for creating new e-mail messages, but the principles discussed in the text will be the same if you're sending Plain Text.

OK, let's send a message:

TIP

You do not need to be connected to the Internet (or your office intranet) right now. You can compose your message without being connected, then connect some time before you actually send it.

1. Start Messenger, if it's not already running. Remember, you can do this by double-clicking the Netscape Messenger icon on your desktop or by clicking the Mailbox icon in the Component Bar. If Navigator or some other component is already running, you can also select Messenger Mailbox from the Communicator menu.

2. In the Inbox window, click the New Msg button. The Message Composition window appears, as shown in Figure 5-13.

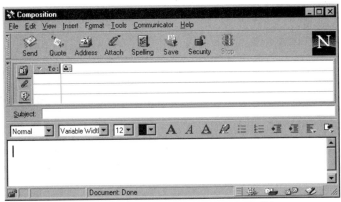

Figure 5-13: The Message Composition window (HTML).

As you can see, this window is divided into two parts. The top part contains the addressing and other header information for your message; the text that will appear at the very beginning of the message when it is received. Netscape calls this the Addressing Area. The bottom part is the pane where you actually create your message.

In the top line of the Addressing Area, there's a To button and a bunch of blank space to the right of a little "person" icon. That blank space is where you type in the name of your message recipient. In this case, type in your own e-mail address. You'll end up with something like Figure 5-14.

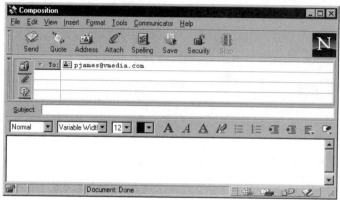

Figure 5-14: The To field filled in.

TIP

You don't have to compose your message in any particular order. If you want to create the body of your message in the bottom pane before you address it, that's fine. It's just the same as snail mail: you can address an envelope either before or after you write your letter.

Suppose you want your message to go to more than one person? Well, you can include as many addresses as you want on the same line, separating them with commas. Messenger will automatically add new To fields to accommodate the new recipients. But there are other ways you can send your message to more than one person. Try this:

1. Click the space just below your original To button. A new To button appears, as well as a new person icon.

2. Click the new To button. A drop-down list appears with six different options. If you click Cc, for instance, the To button becomes a Cc button, as shown in Figure 5-15.

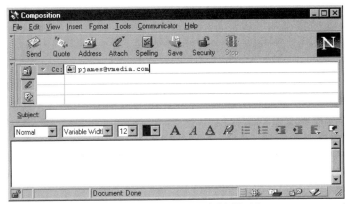

Figure 5-15: Mail message with a new Cc field filled in.

And what do these various addressing options mean? Each of the headers in the top pane has a specific function. The To field you already know about, so here are the others:

- **Cc**. The Cc field works like carbon copies in the old-fashioned world of paper and typewriter—a copy of your message is sent to everyone listed on the Cc line. Typically, the message is sent to these recipients for their information, and they don't need to reply. Note that the designated recipient or recipients of the mail will see who has been Cc'ed.

TIP

Instead of typing in e-mail addresses, click the Address button to select addresses from your Address Book. You can read about setting up your Address Book later, in the section called, unsurprisingly, "The Address Book."

- **Bcc**. Bcc, for *Blind Cc*, is used when you want to send a copy of a letter to someone but do not want that person's name to appear in the Cc line. The recipient or recipients of the mail who are listed on the To and Cc lines will not know who has been Bcc'ed.

- **Groups**. In this field, you can list the names of any Usenet newsgroups or Collabra discussion groups you'd like your epistle posted to. You will learn more about newsgroups and discussion groups in Chapter 6.

- **Reply-To**. The Reply-To line is where you can put the e-mail address of another account where you want responses sent. This is useful if you want to receive replies at a different mail account from the one you are currently using.

- **Followup-To**. This field is also for use with Usenet newsgroups and Collabra discussion groups. For more information, please see Chapter 6.

Now it's time to fill in the Subject line. The Subject is whatever you want it to be—it tells the recipient what your message is about. Try to keep your Subject lines, which are optional, short and informative. In this case, just enter **Letter from me**.

Now let's move down the window and create the actual body of your message:

1. Place your cursor in the large bottom pane of the Message Composition window and click.

2. Start typing. For the purpose of this tutorial, simply type in the phrase **I'm reading this like totally awesome book about Netscape Communicator**, as shown below in Figure 5-16.

Figure 5-16: A message to yourself.

- If you need to edit your message, use the cursor, backspace, and delete keys just as with any text editor. You can also drag with your mouse to select portions of the text that you want to cut, copy, or paste. These operations use the default Windows key combinations, or you can select the commands from the Edit menu.

TIP

You can give yourself more room to create your message by hiding the Addressing Area and even the toolbar. To do this, click the arrow icons just to the left of these areas. You can re-expand (or unhide) them later by clicking the "closed" icons. This works just like the toolbars in Navigator 4.

You could send this test message just as it is, but remember that Netscape Messenger lets you make your message look like a Web page! Using the toolbar that's just above the message content area, you can control the formatting and color of your text and even insert links, horizontal lines, tables, and graphics. Let's try some of this.

TIP

The next section is about editing your message using HTML features. If you don't think you'll be sending any HTML messages in the near future, feel free to skip ahead to the section called "Sending Your Message." You might want to catch the sidebar called "Check Your Spelling," though. The spelling checker works for both HTML and Plain Text messages.

Beautifying Your Message

OK, your message is nice and honest, but it's kind of plain. In Chapter 9 you'll learn many ways to add graphical (and sonic) interest not only to e-mail messages but to entire Web pages you create yourself, but for now I'll just work across the toolbar and show you a few interesting tricks.

TIP

In creating HTML messages, Messenger uses the services of another Communicator component, Netscape Composer. That means that some of the interface for creating HTML messages may be affected by your Composer preferences (see Chapter 9).

Select a Style

The first control on the message composition toolbar is a drop-down list of *HTML styles*. Styles are tags that tell a Web browser or e-mail viewer to display text in a particular way. For instance, a Heading 1 style tells the client program to display the corresponding text as a large header, usually surrounded on the top and bottom by some empty space. Let's add a header to the test message:

1. Place your cursor at the beginning of the phrase you typed, click, and hit Enter. You now have a blank line above your original text.

2. Move your cursor up to the blank line and click. Enter the words **News Flash**.

3. Click the arrow to the right of the drop-down style box (which now contains the Normal style tag) and select the Heading 1 item. Your Message Composition window should now look like Figure 5-17.

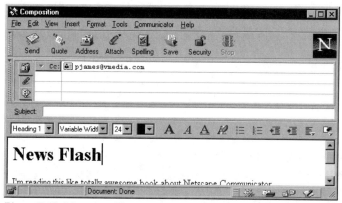

Figure 5-17: Message with a Heading 1 style added.

Change Fonts

You can also change the fonts that are used in your message. To do this, you select a new item from the Font list, the second control on the toolbar.

1. Click and drag your mouse across the words News Flash so that the entire phrase is selected (appears in reverse).

2. Click the arrow to the right of the Font list and select Fixed Width. Your Message will now look something like Figure 5-18.

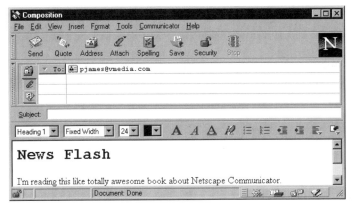

Figure 5-18: A new font for the heading.

Change Font Size

The next control lets you manipulate very precisely the relative or absolute size of text in your message. Depending on how you've configured Composer (see Chapter 9), the font sizes that appear in this list may be:

- Relative HTML sizes—with 0 as normal, positive (plus) values as increasingly larger, and negative values as progressively smaller.

- Absolute point sizes, such as 10 or 12 points.

- A combination of relative and absolute units. In this case, the list will be divided into two clear sections.

Experiment a little with custom font sizes to get the feel of how this control works. You can even select individual letters to create dramatic effects. In the following illustration, Figure 5-19, I've selected individual letters of the word awesome. I've given the "a" a value of +2, the next letter a +3, and so on.

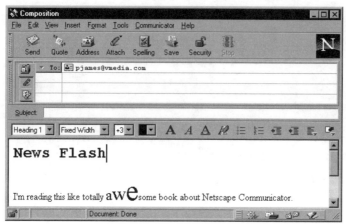

Figure 5-19: Fun with font sizes.

Change Font Color

If this book were printed in color, you could see what the next control does. Try it on your own. Select some text from your message and then drop down the list of colors, as shown in Figure 5-20.

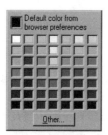

Figure 5-20: The color list.

Now simply choose a new color for the text you've selected. You can have your message looking like an ad from the 1960s in no time.

Add Bold, Italic, & Underline

Messenger makes it easy to add bold, italic, and underline text to your message. You do it with the three "A" buttons to the right of the color list. Here we go:

1. Click and drag your mouse to select the word awesome once again.

2. Click the first two A buttons (bold and italic). Your window will now look something like Figure 5-21.

Figure 5-21: The word awesome in bold and italic.

Character Styles

Besides bold, italic, and underline, Messenger supports a number of other character styles such as subscript, superscript, and blinking text. To format text with these special attributes:

1. Select the text.

2. Select Style from the Format menu.

3. Choose the character style you wish to apply.

Don't like some of the character style changes you've made? You can always remove any styles you've added. Simply select the text you wish to "unstyle" and click the Remove All Styles button, just to the right of the Underline button. This feature not only removes character styles, it also removes any HTML links in the selected text.

Make a Bulleted or Numbered List

Now let's add some more text to our message:

1. In your message, place your cursor after the word Communicator and click. Enter the phrase **Here's why:**

2. Press Enter and add three new very brief paragraphs like the ones shown in Figure 5-22.

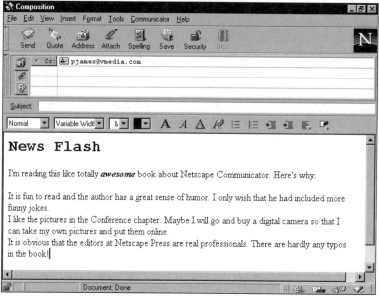

Figure 5-22: Some new text.

3. Click and drag to select all three of the new paragraphs.

4. Click the Bullet button. You'll get something resembling Figure 5-23.

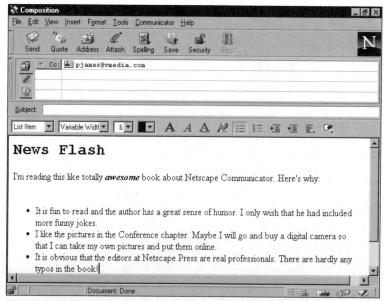

Figure 5-23: A bulleted list.

Want a numbered list instead? Reselect the three new lines and click the Numbered List button, just to the right of the Bullet button. Voilà! Instant high-impact presentations for that quarterly sales meeting.

Adjust Indents

Communicator lets you adjust how far a paragraph is indented. This is especially useful if you want to create multi-level lists. Check it out:

1. Select the numbered list you just created and make it a bulleted list again. (Click the Bullet button.)

2. Go to the end of the It is fun to read line, click, and press Enter.

3. Enter **Humor** and press Enter.

4. Enter **Light-hearted**.

5. Using your mouse, select these last two lines you typed.

6. Click the second of the two Indent buttons, the one with the *right* arrow indicating more indent. Figure 5-24 shows what you get.

Figure 5-24: A multi-level list.

You can use the leftmost Indent button to return the new items to the same level as the original three bulleted phrases if you want, or you can create yet deeper levels for your list. Feel free to experiment.

Change Alignment

The second to last button on the toolbar lets you specify the alignment for particular paragraphs. For example:

1. Scroll back up to the beginning of your message and click your cursor anywhere in the phrase News Flash.

2. Click the Alignment button, then select the bottom of the three new buttons that appear, the Right Alignment button. The beginning of your message now looks like Figure 5-25.

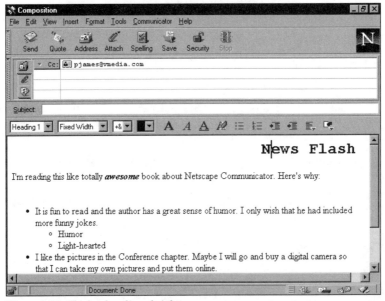

Figure 5-25: The header aligned right.

Netscape Messenger lets you choose Left Alignment, Center Alignment, and Right Alignment. HTML does not currently support full or block justification, in which both the right and left edges of text are perfectly lined up.

Check Your Spelling

Speling chalenjed? No problum!

See that button with the ABC and the checkmark on it? That's your personal spelling assistant. Click it and you can make all your e-mail messages read like they've been thoroughly worked over by Netscape Press' crack editorial team.

Figure 5-26 shows a message with a few problem words in it.

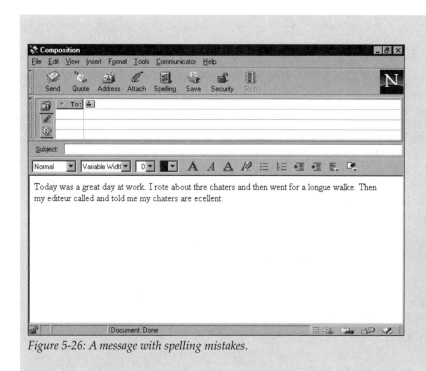

Figure 5-26: A message with spelling mistakes.

Click the Spelling button and you see something like Figure 5-27.

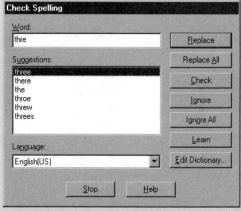

Figure 5-27: The spelling checker at work.

The spelling checker has found the first of the errors. If you've used Microsoft Word or any other major word processing program, this dialog box should look pretty familiar to you. It offers you an alternate spelling for the word, or in some cases a list of possible spellings. If you don't like the choice or choices it offers you, type in the correct spelling in the Change To box yourself. Here's what the various buttons do:

- **Replace.** The spelling checker changes the currently selected word to the spelling that is highlighted in the Suggestions box. Highlight the spelling you want to use before clicking the Replace button. You can also type a new spelling directly into the Word box before clicking the Replace button.

- **Replace All.** The spelling checker changes every instance of this particular misspelling within your message.

- **Ignore**. If you click this button, the spelling checker doesn't bother correcting the selected word and instead goes on to the next misspelling it finds, if any.

- **Ignore All.** If you click this button, the spelling checker won't stop at any further words in your message that are spelled this way.

- **Stop.** Click this button to exit the spelling checker. It will not look for any further errors in your message unless you press the Check Spelling button again.

- **Learn.** If you click this button, the spelling checker adds the selected word, as it is currently spelled in your message, to a custom dictionary. Once it is added to the dictionary, the spelling checker will no longer consider it a misspelling when it encounters this word in *any* message you write. This can be useful for company names and specialized technical words that you use frequently.

- **Edit Dictionary.** This button lets you edit your custom dictionary directly, adding words that the spell checker will not flag as errors when it encounters them. For instance, if you often spell check messages that include your own e-mail address as a signature, you might want to add that address to the dictionary, as shown in Figure 5-28.

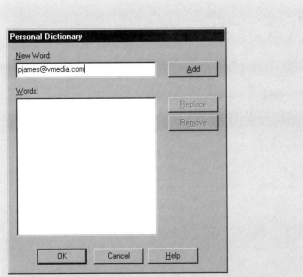

Figure 5-28: Adding your e-mail address to the Personal Dictionary.

You can also use this feature to *delete* words from your dictionary.

Figure 5-29 shows the e-mail message after Communicator's spelling checker has done its job:

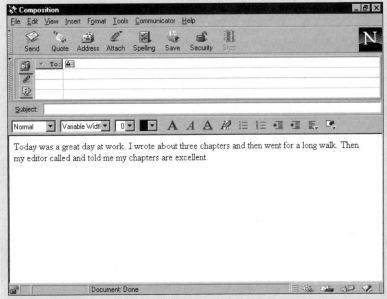

Figure 5-29: The message after spell checking.

Add a Link

Now scroll back down to the bottom of the message. Hit Enter a couple of times, but make sure the Bullet button is not depressed or all your blank spaces will be bulleted! At the very bottom of your message you'll add a link to the electronic version of this book. Here's how:

1. Click the rightmost button on the toolbar. A vertical row of five new buttons drops down, as shown in Figure 5-30.

Figure 5-30: The Insert Object buttons.

2. Click the Link button, the one with a chain link on it. A Character Properties dialog box appears, as shown in Figure 5-31.

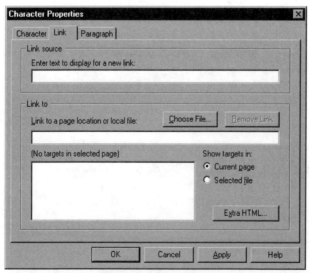

Figure 5-31: The Link Properties dialog box.

3. In the Link source field enter the words **Ad for a Great Book**.

4. In the Link to field enter **http://www.vmedia.com/communicator**.

5. Ignore the other options. They will make more sense to you after you read Chapter 9. For now, just click OK. You are returned to your message, which now contains a link as shown in Figure 5-32.

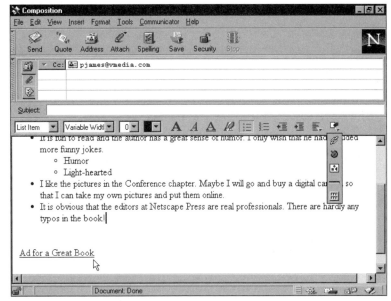

Figure 5-32: A new link in your message.

I love this feature. Whoever receives your message (you, in this case) can simply click this link to travel to a Web site, either on your corporate intranet or on the Net itself. You can give it a try later, after you send and receive your new e-mail.

Add a Target

Targets (sometimes called *anchors*) are a different kind of link. Instead of referring to a different HTML document, they refer to a particular location within the current document. This can be useful in very long e-mail messages. Your recipient clicks on a link and is transported to the concluding remarks at the end of your message or back to the executive summary at the beginning.

Chapter 9 covers targets in depth, so I'm not going to get into that here. But when you're ready to use this feature, just press the second of the Insert Object buttons, the one with the arrow and target.

Add a Picture

If you click the third of the Insert Object buttons, a pretty threatening dialog box pops up as shown in Figure 5-33.

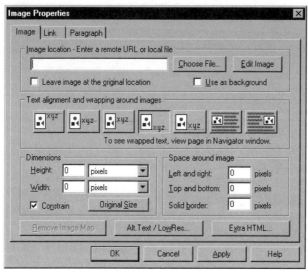

Figure 5-33: The Image Properties dialog box.

Don't worry, it's not as bad as it looks. In the Image location field you simply enter or paste the URL of a remote picture you want to include in your message, or you can click the Choose File button and select a graphics file from your own hard drive or a network drive. Then select one of the Text alignment buttons in the middle of the dialog box. Each button provides a different option for how the graphics will be integrated with surrounding text. I'm not going to go into any more detail right now since it's all covered in Chapter 9, but an example of what you can do with graphics in an e-mail message is shown in Figure 5-34.

TIP

There's an even easier way to add pictures to your messages: just drag them in. That's right, you can click any image on your desktop or in a folder and drag it right into the Composition window. If the original is in a format other than GIF or JPEG, Messenger will even convert it to one of these Net-friendly formats.

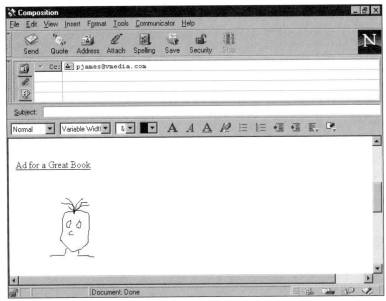

Figure 5-34: The message with an image.

Add a Horizontal Line

Your message is starting to get that *all fluff, no substance* look that's so familiar in this Age of the Image. Hey, that's *good*! You're on your way to becoming a typical Web designer. But let's add just a little more fluff for good measure:

1. Scroll back up to the top of your message.

2. Put your cursor at the end of the News Flash line and press Enter.

3. In the Insert Object button list, click the second to last button, which depicts a horizontal line. What you get is shown in Figure 5-35.

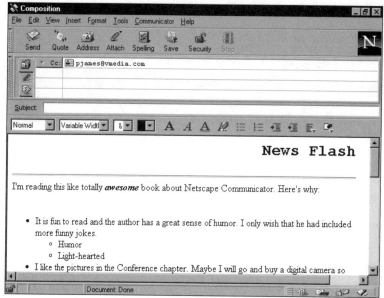

Figure 5-35: The message with a horizontal line.

Don't like the way that horizontal line looks? You can change it! Right-click the horizontal line and select Horizontal Line Properties from the context menu that appears. Then play around with the settings until you get something you like. You can save these settings as your default for horizontal lines by checking the "Save settings as default" check box.

Add a Table

Yes, you can even add tables to your e-mail messages. I'll cover tables in Chapter 9 (you knew that), but if you're a die-hard HTML geek and want to start experimenting right away, just press the last of the Insert Object buttons and get busy.

By the way, here's an interesting use of tables in e-mail. Figure 5-36 shows a report I get a couple of times a day from the Mercury Mail service called Closing Bell. It is formatted as a table showing the ups and downs of various stocks I'm interested in. (Is it something your company could use to distribute information to clients and prospects via e-mail?)

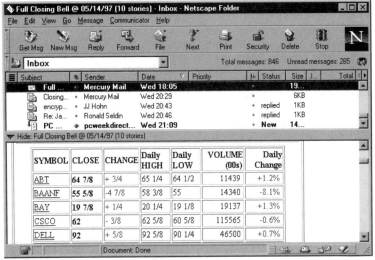

Figure 5-36: An example of tables in e-mail.

Page Colors and Properties

We're not quite done tweaking the message yet. This next set of configuration options, accessible only through the menus, affects various characteristics of the message as a whole, not just individual elements within it. Let's take a look:

1. Still in the Message Composition window, select Page Colors and Properties from the bottom of the Format menu. The Colors and Background tab appears, as shown in Figure 5-37.

2. To change the overall color scheme of your message, select from the drop-down Color Schemes list. The Use custom colors option button is automatically selected, and you are shown a sample of your new colors.

3. To change individual elements within the chosen color scheme, click any of the buttons for Normal text, Link text, etc., and then select a new color from the palette that appears. Note that you can also change the background color of your message.

4. If you want to return to eliminate these changes, click the option button at the top labeled "Use viewer's browser colors." With this option selected, colors you add to your e-mail will not be saved; when your recipient displays your message, it will appear with his or her default browser colors.

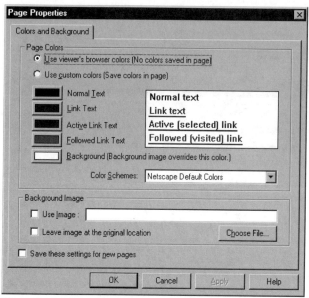

Figure 5-37: The Colors and Background tab.

You can also specify an image, rather than a solid color, to use as the background for your message. To do this:

1. Check the Use Image check box in the Background Image section.

2. Enter the URL of the image you want to use, or click the Choose File button. A Choose Image File dialog box appears, as shown in Figure 5-38.

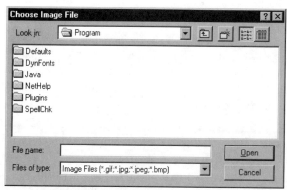

Figure 5-38: The Choose Image File dialog box.

3. Choose a GIF or JPEG file from your local hard drive or network drive and click Open.

TIP

If you check the "Leave image at the original location" check box, the message you send will download the image from the location you specified each time your recipient views the message. That means it should be located at an accessible Web site.

As you work with these appearance changes, you can click Apply at any time to see what they look like in your actual message. Remember, reverting to your original look is as simple as choosing an option button, so there's no real danger. If you like what you've done, though, and want to use your customized color scheme as a default in future rich text messages, check the check box labeled "Save these settings for new pages."

When you're done with the Colors and Background settings, click OK to return to your message.

MAILTO: Tags

Besides calling up the Message Composition window, Netscape Communicator offers another way to send mail. Web pages can include special HTML tags called MAILTO: tags. They look just like ordinary links, although often they appear in italics. When you click one of these, Netscape Communicator automatically pops up the Message Composition window, allowing you to send a message to the recipient indicated in the MAILTO: tag.

MAILTO: tags provide a convenient way to solicit feedback or comments in a Web document.

Sending Your Message

This is where the virtual rubber finally hits the virtual road. For this exercise, you'll need to be connected either to your office intranet or to the Net. If you connect to the Net via a dial-up SLIP or PPP connection, go ahead and establish that link now. Once you're connected, return to the Netscape Messenger window and the message you just composed.

Actually putting your message "in the mail" is very simple:

1. Make sure you're connected to the Net or to your office intranet.

2. Click the Send button. Depending how you configured Messenger for handling HTML vs. Plain Text recipients, a dialog box may appear asking you which format you want to use, as shown in Figure 5-39.

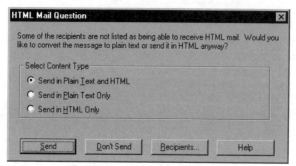

Figure 5-39: The HTML Mail Question dialog box.

TIP

The dialog box won't appear if you've already entered yourself in the Address Book as a recipient who prefers HTML e-mail (see the section below called "The Address Book").

- Most of the options in this dialog box are pretty obvious. The first one tells Messenger to send two copies of the message, one in Plain Text and one in HTML, to each recipient; the second one tells Messenger to send the message in Plain Text only; and the third tells Messenger to send the message in HTML format only.

3. Once you've selected an option, click the Send button. Or, if you want even more flexibility, click the Recipients button. A dialog box appears letting you specify different formats for different recipients of the same message, as shown in Figure 5-40.

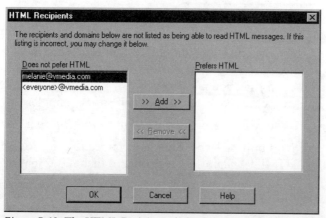

Figure 5-40: The HTML Recipients dialog box.

TIP

Messenger automatically creates the entry <everyone> followed by the domain address of your recipient(s). If you move this over to the Prefers HTML box, Messenger will assume that every e-mail ID on that server prefers receiving HTML. In the example shown above in Figure 5-40, let's say I add <everyone>@echonyc.com to the Prefers HTML list. Since my e-mail address includes echonyc.com, I am assured of receiving all the formatting and graphics in this HTML message I send to myself. But if I had cc'd Joe_Blow@echonyc.com, he would get the message in HTML format too, even though I didn't explicitly add him to the list.

4. Once you've indicated in this dialog box which of your recipients should receive your message in HTML format and which should receive it in Plain Text, click OK.

5. Back in the HTML Mail Question dialog box, click Send.

Please realize that there won't always be this many steps to sending a message. In many cases, as soon as you click Send in the New Message window your message is on its way. That's the way it works if you create a message without any HTML formatting, or if you have already specified in the Address Book that your recipients prefer HTML e-mail.

Sending Options

The US Postal Service lets you send letters in a variety of ways. You can send packages third class and save money, or you can pay a little extra to insure a valuable gift, or you can send your Dear John letters by certified mail so you're absolutely certain that someone-who-used-to-be-special knows you're ditching him. Similarly, Netscape Messenger offers a variety of sending options.

In the Message Composition window, there are three small tabs at the left of the Addressing Area. The top one depicts an address book with a stylized human figure on it, the middle one depicts a paper clip, and the bottom one depicts a checklist. This bottom one is what we're interested in right now, because it lets you access the sending options. Click it and what you get is shown in Figure 5-41.

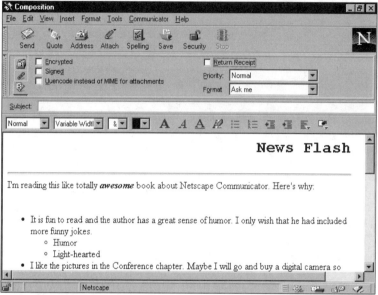

Figure 5-41: The Sending Options tab.

You can check any or all of the check boxes prior to clicking the Send button. Your message will receive the "special handling" you specify:

- **Encrypted**. If you check this, your message is sent in a form that is unreadable until it is decrypted at the other end by the recipient's copy of Messenger. This privacy feature only works if you already have a copy of your recipient's Security Certificate, which includes the key used to encrypt the message. Please see the section on "E-mail Security" later in this chapter.

- **Signed**. If you check this, Messenger will automatically "sign" your message with the special unique digital signature that's part of your Personal Security Certificate. That means the recipient of the message knows it's really you who sent it, or at least that it was sent using your computer. It also means that your recipient can now send you encrypted messages, since your signature includes your encryption key. Again, you must have a Personal Security Certificate to use this feature. Please see the section on "E-Mail Security" later in this chapter.

■ **Unencode instead of MIME for attachments**. Unencoding and MIME are two different standards for transferring binary (non-text) data across networks or the Internet. Typically, if you want to attach a non-text file such as a spreadsheet, graphic, or program to your message, it is automatically MIME-encoded (please see the section below called "Attaching Files to Messages"). But if a particular recipient does not have a MIME-enabled e-mail program that can decode the information correctly, try checking this box. Unencoding is a less flexible but more universal older standard.

■ **Return Receipt**. If you check this, you will automatically receive (via e-mail, of course) a confirmation that your message has arrived at its destination.

In addition to the check boxes, there are two drop-down lists:

■ Use the **Priority** list to indicate just how important you think your message is. If you select Highest, for instance, the message will include that designation in its headers, letting your recipient know that this is no idle chit chat. Some e-mail client programs will graphically flag messages that are given specific priorities; as you've already seen, Messenger has a special Priority field that indicates any special priority for incoming messages.

■ The **Format** list is available only if Messenger is configured so that you send HTML messages by default. In this case, you can select *Plain Text* from the list, overriding the HTML formatting, or you can choose *Ask me*, so that when you send the message you are presented with the HTML Mail Question dialog box shown earlier in Figure 5-39.

Signatures & Sig Files

Many Internet users attach special *signatures* to the end of each message. A signature is really just a line or two of text, typically something you might put on a business card. *Phil James, Bon Vivant and General Man-About-Town*. Stuff like that. You don't want to type in this same information each time you create a message, though, so Messenger lets you create a text file that automatically gets appended to every e-mail you create. Seasoned Internet users call this a *sig file*.

How do you create a sig file? It's no different from creating any other text file. Just start typing in Notepad or some other editor and then save your work with a file name like SIG.TXT. Select Preferences from Messenger's Edit menu and click the Identity tab. In the Signature File field, specify the exact location and name of your sig file. (You can use the Browse button to find it and fill in the field for you.) Now whenever you send a message, the contents of your sig file are appended at the end.

If you want to move quickly and come back later to some of the niceties of sending e-mail, as well as some of Messenger's advanced features, you can jump ahead for now to the section called "Retrieving Your E-mail."

Saving Copies of Sent E-mail

By default, a copy of every message you send is stored in a folder called Sent. In the Messenger window, click the down arrow to the right of the word Inbox. You'll see a list of available folders. Select Sent to see the contents of that folder. The message you just e-mailed should appear in the Messenger window.

If you want to store your sent messages in a different folder, if you want to e-mail them to yourself as well as to your recipient, or if you don't want to bother storing them at all, select Preferences from the Edit menu, then click the Messages category under Mail & Groups. Let's go over the options available in the Copies of outgoing messages section of this dialog box, as shown below in Figure 5-42.

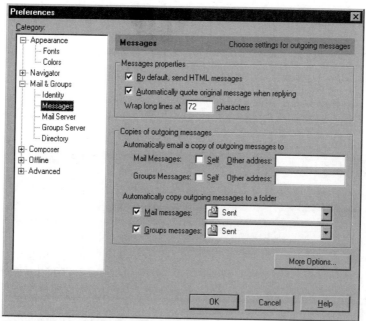

Figure 5-42: The Messages preferences, showing options for copies of outgoing mail.

TIP

Note that there is a setting here for discussion group messages as well. I'll tell you all about discussion groups in Chapter 6.

- **Automatically e-mail a copy of outgoing messages to**. One way to keep copies of your outgoing messages is to actually send yourself the same message. If you click the Self box, all outgoing e-mail will be sent not only to your recipient, but back to you as well. If you have several different e-mail accounts, you may want to e-mail a copy of your outgoing correspondence to a different address. In this case, simply fill in the Other address box.

- **Automatically copy outgoing messages to a folder**. Instead of actually e-mailing outgoing messages back to yourself, you can simply copy them to a Messenger folder (see the section "Working With Folders" later in the chapter). As I mentioned earlier, you'd normally use the Sent folder for this purpose, but you may want to select a custom folder you've created. And to keep Messenger from saving any sent messages, just uncheck the box.

Drafts

Let's say you don't want to send your message right away but want to keep working on it in subsequent Messenger sessions. In the Message Composition window, just click the Save button. Your work-in-progress is moved to a folder called Drafts that you can select from the drop-down folder list at any time. Then simply click your message in the Drafts folder, work on it some more, and click the Send button when you're finally ready to send it.

8-bit Encoding and Long Lines

There are two more rather technical options for e-mail messages you send. You can leave these options alone unless you get complaints that your messages aren't arriving properly, or that portions of them are unreadable.

Some recipients of your messages may claim that they cannot read the end of the lines of text of messages you send, or that lines of quoted text are wrapping before a new quote character (>) appears. (Please see the section below called "Replying to E-mail" if you don't know what I'm talking about.) If this is the case, select Preferences from the Edit menu, then the Messages category under Mail & Groups. Change the value in the "Wrap long lines. . ." field.

In addition, for some mail servers it may be necessary to encode your messages with a special encoding called "8-bit MIME." This will only be the case if your message text contains "high bit" characters such as symbols and if these are not displayed properly by your recipient's mail reader. You can make this change by going to the same Messages dialog box and then clicking the More Options button. In the center section of the dialog box that appears, select the second option button.

Retrieving Your E-mail

Remember, e-mail is a little different from snail mail in that it doesn't come right to your house. When somebody sends you a message, it is stored on a mail server until Messenger goes out and grabs it. That means the message you just sent to yourself doesn't appear automatically in your Inbox—you have to click the Get Msg button.

Let's give it a try:

1. Make sure you're still connected to the Internet or to your office intranet. Back in the Messenger window, click the Get Msg button.

2. If you have quit Messenger since you sent your message, you may encounter the Password Entry dialog box again. Simply enter your e-mail password.

Once you enter your password, Netscape Messenger logs you in to your post office account to retrieve your mail. Your Messenger window now looks something like Figure 5-43.

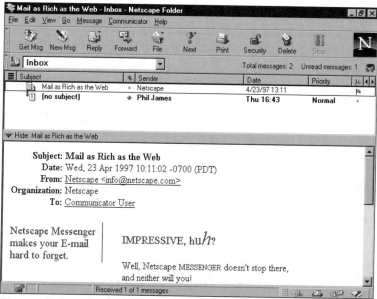

Figure 5-43: The Messenger window with your newly received e-mail message.

Mail Retrieval Options

If your incoming e-mail account is on a POP3 server, you can choose to handle retrieved messages in one of two different ways. Once you've retrieved your messages, they may be deleted from the server or they may be stored there indefinitely. If they are not deleted, you can access the same messages again. This is useful if you access your e-mail account using two different computers, for instance one at home and one at work.

To select whether or not messages will be deleted from your POP3 server once they are retrieved, select Preferences from Messenger's Edit menu and then click the Mail Server category. If you want your messages left on the server after retrieval, check the "Leave mail on server after retrieval" check box.

What if you're accessing your e-mail via an IMAP server? With IMAP, messages are *always* kept on the server. You *re*-access them every time you go online. But you can elect to store copies of your messages locally as well, so that you can view them even when you're not online. To configure the program this way, select Preferences from Messenger's Edit menu and then click the Mail Server category. Check the "Keep copies of messages locally for offline reading" check box.

If you are new to e-mail, your test message is probably the only one that will be retrieved. But if you have already been using this e-mail account, Messenger will get the rest of your e-mail stored at that address as well.

Replying to E-mail

Replying to a piece of e-mail differs from sending new mail in several important ways. First of all, when you reply, Netscape Messenger fills in the To field automatically, since the intended recipient is usually the sender of the original message. The program also fills in the Subject field with "Re:" and the subject of the mail you are replying to.

There is another important difference: the program lets you use a special quote feature to include the text of the e-mail you are responding to right in the body of your reply.

Let's try it. In the Messenger window, select a received message and click the Reply button, then choose either Reply to Sender or Reply to Sender and All Recipients from the submenu that appears.

TIP

If you want to respond only to the individual who sent the message, click Reply to Sender; if you want your response to go to any people who were Cc'd on the message, select Reply to Sender and All Recipients. If you choose this second option, the To field will be filled in automatically with the address of the sender and the Cc field will be filled in automatically with the names of any individuals who were Cc'd.

Once you click either Reply to Sender or Reply to Sender and All Recipients, the Message Composition window appears with the correct fields filled in. In addition, the original message is included in the content area. Notice that every line of the original message text begins with a vertical blue bar, indicating that this is quoted material.

TIP

If you have configured Messenger so that you send Plain Text messages by default, the quote character that begins each line of quoted text will be ">" instead of a blue bar. This is the Internet standard for indicating quoted material in Plain Text messages.

To Quote or Not to Quote

Maybe you don't want the quoted original message to appear in the Composition window *every* time you create a response. To change this, select Preferences from Messenger's Edit menu and then click the Messages tab. Uncheck the check box labeled "Automatically quote original message when replying."

This doesn't mean that you can never include original messages in your replies, just that you have to tell Messenger to do so explicitly. That's a piece of cake. In the Composition window, simply click the Quote button. I find it more convenient to use the program this way. It just takes a second to click the Quote button, but it's tedious to edit out automatically quoted messages when you *don't* want to include them.

At this point, you can add whatever text you like below—or above—the quoted text. You can also add other people to the To or Cc fields if you like. If the message you have quoted is long, or if you want to respond to only one or two sentences of a letter, it is considered polite to delete the portions not relevant to your reply, although it is bad etiquette to delete or alter quoted text without indicating removals by inserting [...] or (snip) or some other indication that you edited the quoted material.

Following these steps for replying to your test message, you should end up with a Composition window like the one shown in Figure 5-44.

Once you've completed your reply, sending it is just like sending a new message: simply click the Send button. The status line will display messages telling you about the status of your message transmission.

TIP

To reply quickly to a message, right-click it and select Reply to Sender or Reply to Sender and All Recipients from the context menu that appears.

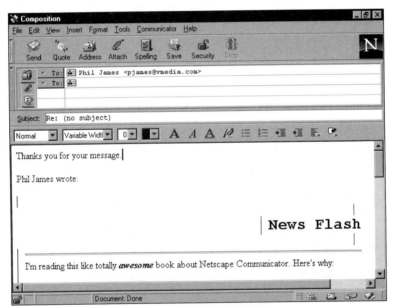

Figure 5-44: A reply including a quote of the original message.

Forwarding Messages

You use the Forward button when you want to send a letter along to someone other than the people listed in the From or Cc fields. Forward is similar to Reply, with a couple of differences. The Subject line is filled in with the subject line of the letter labeled Fwd instead of Re (with the entire field enclosed in square brackets), and the To field is not filled in. It's up to you to fill in the To field with a new recipient for the message.

The message being forwarded is automatically included as an attachment to the mail rather than as text in your actual message. (You'll learn more about attachments in the section called "Attaching Files to Messages.") Clicking the Quote button will include the text of the forwarded letter, bracketed by the quote character, but if you use this feature to annotate the forwarded letter, remember to delete the attachment so that you don't send two copies of the same text. To forward a message quickly, right-click it and select Forward or Forward Quoted from the context menu that appears.

Mail Checking & Notification

Wouldn't it be nice if you didn't have to click the Get Msg button periodically to check for new messages? Well, Messenger can even handle this task for you. All you really have to do is tell Messenger how often you want it to check the server. Here's how:

1. Select Preferences From Messenger's Edit menu.

2. Click the Mail Server category.

3. Click the More Options button near the bottom of the dialog box. A new dialog box appears, as shown in Figure 5-45.

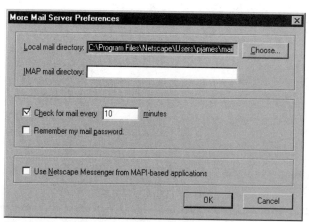

Figure 5-45: The More Mail Server Preferences dialog box.

4. Make sure the "Check for mail every" check box is checked, and enter the number of minutes for how often you want Messenger to log onto the mail server to check for new messages.

You may also want to check the "Remember my mail password" check box—as long as you're not worried about other people using your computer to send gag e-mail on your behalf! (This is probably not a box you want to leave checked if you're using Communicator Professional in a corporate environment. There are just too many people with access to your computer.) With this box checked, Messenger will no longer ask for your password the first time you send an e-mail or retrieve new messages. This can be a real convenience if you're letting Messenger check for mail automatically.

When you're done with this dialog box, click OK. Click OK once more in the Preferences dialog box to return to the main Messenger window.

So how do you know that new e-mail has arrived at your server? As long as your machine can connect to your mail server, Messenger gives you three different signals that new mail has arrived there:

- It makes a "ding" sound in your PC's speakers.

TIP

If you don't like dings, you can turn this feature off by selecting Preferences from the Edit menu of any other Communicator component, clicking the Mail & Groups category, and unchecking the "Enable sound alert when messages arrive" option.

- It puts a green down-arrow next to the Messenger icon in the Component Bar.
- It puts an envelope icon in your Windows 95 or NT 4.0 taskbar tray.

To retrieve your new messages, you can simply click either of these icons. Within moments, the new mail appears in your Inbox. The envelope icon disappears from the taskbar tray and the green arrow disappears from the Component Bar icon.

But what if you don't want to keep Communicator running all the time just to see if you have new mail? With Communicator, Netscape provides a special supplemental program that can tap you on the virtual shoulder when you have new mail on your server—without even running Communicator. In fact, this special Mail Notification program does more than tap you on the shoulder. If you want, it can play selections from your favorite Broadway show when you get a message. On a more practical level, it can also launch Messenger if there's a message. Check it out:

1. Make sure you are connected to your office intranet or to the Net itself.

2. In the Netscape Communicator folder on your desktop, double-click the Utilities subfolder. Then, click the Netscape Mail Notification icon. A small envelope icon appears in your Windows 95 or Windows NT taskbar tray.

- If Notification cannot automatically check your server—for instance, if you're not connected to an intranet or the Net, or if you have not told Messenger to remember your password following the instructions above—you will see a red X through the icon until you remedy the problem.

3. Place your cursor on the tray icon. A tool tip pops up indicating that "There are no new messages waiting."

    - If the program is currently checking for new mail, the icon looks like a spinning blue disc.

4. Now right-click the icon. A context menu appears with the following choices:

    - **Check Now**. Typically, you set Notification to check your server for new mail at regular intervals (you'll find out how in a minute). But if you want the program to go out and look for new mail right now, click this command.

    - **Run Mail**. Click this to start Messenger if it's not currently running, or to switch to it if it's already loaded.

    - **New Message**. Click this to create a new e-mail message in Messenger.

    - **Exit**. Click this to shut down Mail Notification.

You can also check or uncheck the Enabled item to enable or disable e-mail notification.

Oops, I left one description out: Options. I left it out because that's where we're going right now, and we're going to look at it in some detail. To configure Mail Notification:

1. Click the Options item on the Mail Notification context menu. The Netscape Mail Properties dialog box appears, as shown in Figure 5-46.

2. In the Notification tab, enter a number of minutes for the frequency with which the program will check for new mail on your server.

3. Click one of the "Notification When Mail Arrives" options. (Yes, this is where you can enter PHANTOM_OF_THE_OPERA.WAV or the name of any other sound file.)

    - If you elect not to have Notification holler at you when it discovers new mail on your server, you'll still find out pretty quickly. The icon in your Windows taskbar tray sports a bright red flag that waves back and forth when you have new mail. I have Notification check my server every couple of minutes, so leaving the sound on would drive me batty.

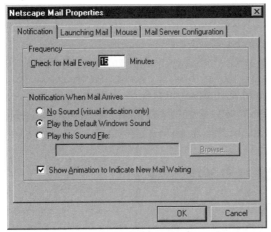

Figure 5-46: Netscape Mail Properties.

4. Click the Launching Mail tab, as shown below in Figure 5-47.

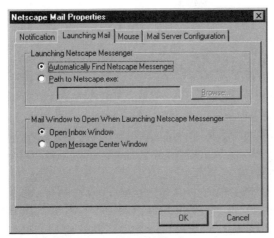

Figure 5-47: The Launching Mail tab.

- In the top half of this dialog box, you can tell Notification how to find Messenger—obviously it needs to find the program in order to launch it. You should do fine leaving the top option button selected.

- In the bottom half of this dialog box, you can tell Notification to launch Messenger with the Inbox window displayed or the Folder window displayed. So far in this chapter we've only looked at the Inbox window, which is the one that makes the most sense in this option unless you're automatically routing certain incoming messages to particular custom folders (see the section on "Working with Folders" below). For now, leave this set to Open Inbox Window.

5. Click the Mouse tab, as shown in Figure 5-48.

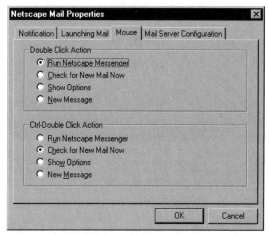

Figure 5-48: The Mouse tab.

- This is pretty self-explanatory: simply decide what action you want to initiate by double-clicking (or Ctrl+double-clicking) the Mail Notification icon.

6. You can ignore the Mail Server Configuration tab at this point—it is only useful for trouble-shooting if Notification doesn't seem to be working. Just click OK. The Properties dialog box disappears and you are ready to use Notification.

That's all there is to it. Now you simply wait for Notification to do its job. Periodically, at the interval you've configured, it goes out and checks for new messages on your mail server. If it finds any, you may hear a sound, and the icon in your taskbar tray suddenly looks like the one in Figure 5-49.

Figure 5-49: The Notification icon indicating that there is a new message on the mail server.

When you place your cursor over the icon it indicates exactly how many messages it found. To launch or return to Messenger and retrieve those messages, simply double-click the Notification icon (assuming that's the way you've configured the Mouse tab).

With Mail Notification loaded, you'll know right away when you receive new mail. And since you know right away, you'll be able to respond quickly. The next section shows you how.

The Address Book

So far we've been addressing messages manually, by typing actual e-mail addresses into the To and Cc fields. But that's a tedious process, and you're bound to incorporate some mail-stopping typos from time to time. Wouldn't it be great if instead of entering dracula@transylvania.com you could pick the address from a list, or even just type in drac? Well, both of these shortcuts are available thanks to Messenger's Address Book facility.

The Address Book is actually a collection of informational "cards" about individuals. It's like a giant electronic Rolodex. The Address Book has two options—it allows you to enter single addresses and groups of addresses, or custom mailing lists. And there are several ways to enter new individuals into the Address Book. Let's start with the simplest first:

1. Select any message in the Message List pane. Once its content appears in the Message Content pane, click the blue underlined link in the To, From, or Cc header at the top of the message. A window like the one in Figure 5-50 pops up.

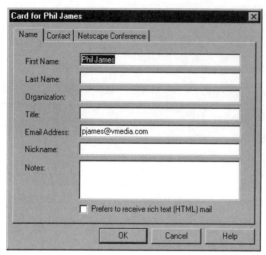

Figure 5-50: A new card.

The Address Book is also used by Netscape Conference, which I cover in Chapter 11. That's what the Netscape Conference tab is for. You can ignore it for now.

2. Fill in any fields you want. You may want to edit the First Name and Last Name fields, but the Email Address field is already correct. It doesn't matter what you enter in the Nickname field as long as it's easy for you to remember and to associate with this entry. This is the shortcut name (like drac) that you'll be able to enter in the To field when you create a new message. The completed Name tab should look something like Figure 5-51.

   ■ If you check the Prefers to receive HTML check box, any HTML messages you send to this individual will automatically be sent in HTML format—Messenger will not ask you if you want to convert it to Plain Text.

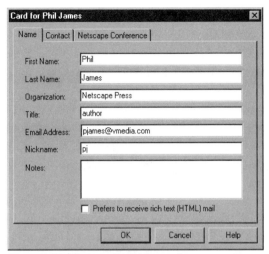

Figure 5-51: The completed Name tab.

3. Click the Contact tab and fill in as many of the fields as you wish. This information is optional, but if you complete it, the Address Book becomes a handy reference as well as an e-mail addressing tool.

4. Click OK. Your Address Book now contains a new entry.

Let's see how it works:

1. Back in the Messenger window, click New Msg. The Composition window appears.

2. In the To field, enter **drac**. Notice that as you start to type, Messenger completes the word for you. You only need to type the first few letters of long nicknames.

TIP

*By default, Messenger expands not only nicknames you type in, but also actual names. In other words, typing **drac** and typing **Count** will both result in the e-mail address dracula@transylvania.net. But you can configure the program so that only nicknames get expanded into e-mail addresses, not names. To make this change, select Preferences from Messenger's Edit menu and click the Messages category. Then click the More Options button. In the top section of the More Messages Preferences dialog box that appears, select the option "Expand addresses against nicknames only."*

Now you can simply complete the actual text of your message and click Send. But that's only one way to do it. There is an alternate and equally convenient approach to addressing your e-mail using the Address Book:

1. From the Messenger window, click New Msg. The Composition window appears.

2. Click the Address button. The Select Addresses window appears, as shown in Figure 5-52.

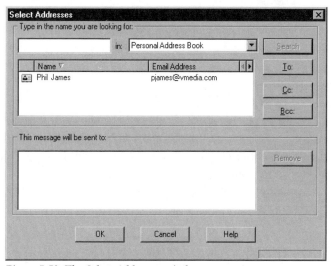

Figure 5-52: The Select Addresses window.

3. Select a name from the list in the top pane and click the To button. The address is added to the bottom pane.

   ▪ You can keep adding addresses to the bottom pane by selecting them and pressing the To, Cc, or Bcc buttons. You can also remove recipients for your message by selecting them in the bottom pane and clicking Remove.

TIP

To find names quickly in a long Address Book, start typing the name in the top left box. Messenger will take you right to it.

4. When you're done adding recipients for your message, click OK. You are returned to the Composition window, with the To, Cc, and Bcc fields correctly filled in.

Address Lists

You can also add lists of recipients to the Address Book. That way, a single nickname can represent as many addresses as you want. For instance, you could create an Address Book entry called Congress Critters that lets you automatically send the same message to Jesse Helms, Al D'Amato, and Dick Armey. To create a list, you need to access the Address Book window.

1. Select Address Book from the Communicator menu, or simply press Ctrl+Shift+2. The Address Book window appears, as shown in Figure 5-53.

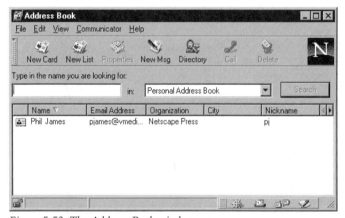

Figure 5-53: The Address Book window.

TIP

Notice that you can add individuals from this window as well: simply click the New Card button. Remember, too, that the Address is used by Netscape Conference (see Chapter 11). That's what the Call button is for.

2. Click the New List button. A dialog box like the one in Figure 5-54 appears.

Figure 5-54: The Mailing List dialog box.

3. Fill in the List Name field with the "official" name of this list, **Congress Critters**.

4. Fill in the List Nickname field with an easy-to-type nickname like **con**.

5. Optionally, fill in the Description field. This field is just for your reference.

6. Now start adding nicknames from your Address Book to the bottom pane. They will be expanded automatically into full names. You can also type in actual e-mail addresses that are *not* already in your Address Book, and you can remove names by selecting them and clicking the Remove button.

7. When you are finished adding names to your address list, click OK. Your Address Book window now contains a new list, as shown in Figure 5-55. Lists are designated with a "two person" icon to distinguish them from regular individual entries.

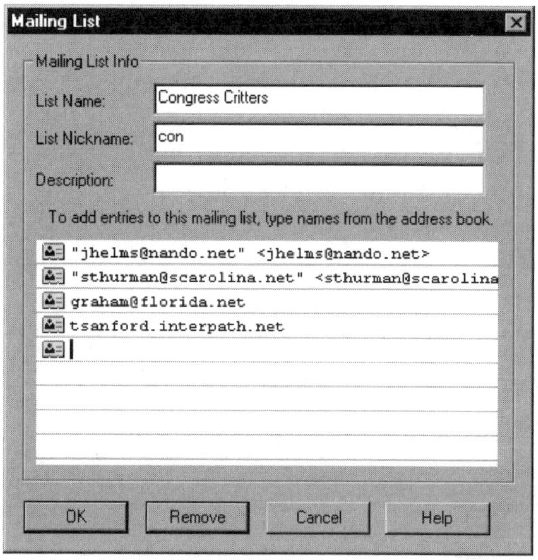

Figure 5-55: The Address Book with a new mailing list.

You use lists exactly the same way you use other Address Book entries. You can either type the list's nickname in the To field of the Message Composition window, or you can click the Address button and select it. In either case, your message will go out to every member of the list.

I've shown you how to click the Address button from the Composition window in order to address a new message. But you can do it the other way around, too. You can go to the Address Book window without ever calling up the Composition window. Then, select an individual or list name and click Compose. You'll be taken to the Composition window with the To field already filled in.

TIP

You can save your Address Book as a file, and you can import other people's Address Book files into your personal Address Book. These Save As and Import options are both available in the Address Book's File menu.

Adding Your Address Card to Messages

Earlier in the chapter I showed you how you can add a special signature to all your outgoing e-mail messages. But there's an even cooler feature. You can automatically add your own Address Book Card to every message you send. As you know, this card includes information such as your home or business address and your phone number. When other Messenger users receive a message which includes this information, Figure 5-56 shows you what they see.

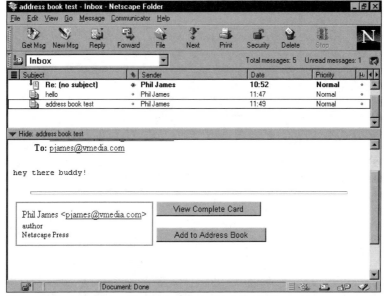

Figure 5-56: A message with added Address Book Card information.

If recipients click the View Complete Card button, they see lots more information about you, as shown in Figure 5-57.

TIP

Obviously the amount of information that appears depends on how much information you've entered in your own Address Card.

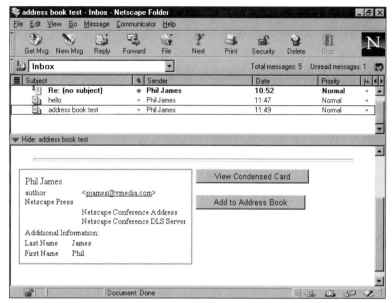

Figure 5-57: A message with complete Address Book Card information.

But here's where it gets interesting. When the recipient of your message clicks the Add to Address Book button, all of the information about you is copied to a new Address Card on that user's system. In effect you're giving your recipient an electronic rolodex card that can be used to automate any e-mail he or she wants to send you.

Creating or editing your own Address Card, the one you include with outgoing e-mail messages, is the same as creating or editing anyone else's card. You can access it from the Address Book window, or click your name in the To field of any message you receive. Then just fill in whatever fields you want. But how do you tell Messenger to include this information in outgoing e-mail messages? That's easy:

1. From Messenger's Edit menu, select Preferences, then select the Identity tab.

2. Check the "Always attach Address Book Card to outgoing messages" check box.

3. If you want to create a new card or edit your current one, click the Edit Card button.

TIP

Checking the "Always attach. . ." box means that your Address Book Card will be appended to every message you send. You may not want the program to behave this way. To publish your Address Book Card selectively, adding it to some messages but not to others, leave this box unchecked. Then you can use the Attach command to add it to particular e-mail messages. For information on how to do this, see the section called "Attaching Files to Messages" below.

Searching Directories for E-mail Addresses

The Address Book is a great way to organize and access information that you already know. But let's say you want to send a message to your Uncle Waldo in Minnesota and you don't remember his e-mail address. Fortunately, the Address Book contains a facility that lets you search special "lookup" directories located on the Net or on your corporate intranet. Straight out of the box (or rather straight off the CD) Communicator supports Bigfoot, Four11, InfoSpace, WhoWhere, and Switchboard, all excellent address search databases. It even supports the FedEx package tracking system—instead of searching for an individual, just type in a tracking number!

There are two ways to search for individual e-mail addresses:

1. Select Address Book from the Communicator menu of any component.

2. Once you're in the Address Book, enter the name you are looking for (or part of it) in the field in the upper left corner of the window.

3. Click the down arrow next to the field that now contains the phrase "Personal Address Book." From the list that appears, select a different database or lookup service such as Bigfoot.

TIP

To use the listed directories, you must be connected to the Net. Your list, however, may contain additional intranet databases configured by your network administrator.

4. Click Search. In a few seconds Communicator retrieves a list of names that contain the string you specified. For instance, Figure 5-58 shows a bunch of Phil Jameses listed on Bigfoot.

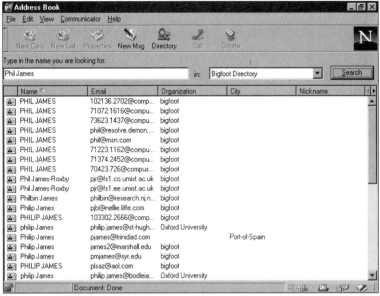

Figure 5-58: And all these years I thought I was unique!

Want to send a message to one of these Phil James impostors? Select the name, right-click, and select New Message from the context menu that appears. You will be transported immediately to the Message Composition window, with the appropriate e-mail address already filled in. This is a major convenience and one of my favorite Messenger features.

In the second and more robust method of searching for e-mail addresses, you still start from the Address Book window. This time, however, click the Directory button. A Search dialog box appears, as shown in Figure 5-59.

Figure 5-59: The Search dialog box.

TIP

You can also access this search facility by clicking the Directory button in the Message Composition window.

Here's how to use this facility:

1. Drop down the "Search for items" list and select a database such as Four11 or Bigfoot.

TIP

You can reorder the directories in this list. To do so, select Preferences from the Edit menu, then the Directory category under Mail & Groups. Use the up and down arrows to change the positioning of directories in the list.

2. Using the three boxes in the middle of the dialog box, restrict your search based on what you know about the individual you are looking for.

Hmm, this may need some explaining. Let's pretend you're looking for a friend named Bill Clinton who unfortunately is not *the* Bill Clinton. (Or fortunately. You decide.) Since you know the exact name, just drop down the middle list (which now reads "contains") and select "is" instead. Then simply enter Bill Clinton in the rightmost edit box.

But wait a second: you know of at least one other Bill Clinton, and there may be many more. You should restrict your search further so that you don't get the addresses of thousands of these guys. Click the More button and you are given some extra fields to narrow down your search, as shown in Figure 5-60.

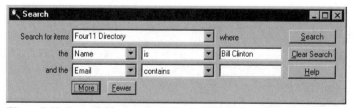

Figure 5-60: Extra fields to narrow the search.

You can keep adding fields to restrict your search until you're comfortable that the results will be useful. Then hit Search. After a few minutes of huffing and puffing, you should get something that looks like Figure 5-61.

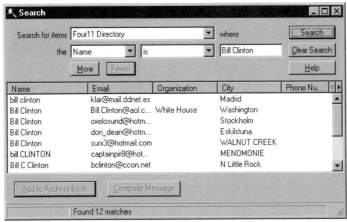

Figure 5-61: The search results.

TIP

Want your search results to display last name first? Select Preferences from Messenger's Edit menu, then click the Directory category. Select the last option button on the page and click OK.

Notice the buttons along the bottom of the window. From right here you can select an individual and add him or her to your Address Book. You can even pop an address right into the Message Composition window by clicking the Compose Message button.

TIP

Can't find somebody using Messenger's Search utility? Try using Navigator 4 to access some other large search services on the Web. Just click Navigator's Places button and select People from the submenu that appears.

Adding Search Directories

Warning: You have just entered a geeks-only zone. If acronyms make you queasy and you'd rather read a good novel than track down obscure technical information, get out of this sidebar quickly and proceed to the section called "Working with Folders."

By default, Messenger includes your Address Book, the Four11 Directory, the Bigfoot Directory, InfoSpace, Switchboard, and WhoWhere in its list of searchable databases. These are all excellent services. But you—or your intranet administrator—can add other services to the list as well. These databases may be located on your local intranet or out in some faraway corner of the Net, it doesn't matter. There is only one rule: they must be configured as *Lightweight Directory Access Protocol (LDAP) servers*.

LDAP is a special protocol that lets Messenger, as a client, "talk" to one of these database servers. Using established conventions, it can post queries like the ones we've looked at. Using the same LDAP protocol, the server returns the information to Messenger via the Net or an office intranet.

To add an LDAP server to Messenger's list, you need to know its domain name, its port number, and whether or not it requires a password. If you're fairly technical and can get this information (and if you have a password if it's on a secure server), here's how you configure Messenger:

1. Select Preferences from Messenger's Edit menu.

2. Click the Directory category under Mail & Groups.

3. In the Directory category, click the New button. An Add Directory Server dialog box appears.

4. In the Description field, enter a name for the server that will appear in Messenger's list.

5. In the LDAP Server field, fill in the domain name address of the LDAP server.

6. In the Search Root field, fill in the search root, if any, given to you by the LDAP administrator.

7. Fill in the Port Number field with the correct port number for the server.

8. In the Maximum Number of Hits field, enter the maximum number of results you'd like to receive in response to your query.

9. If this is a secure server, check the Secure box. You can also check the Save Password box if you don't want to enter your password each time to initiate a search.

10. When you've completed the LDAP Server Properties dialog box, click OK. The new server will appear in Messenger's list.

Searching Your E-mail

As you start to receive more e-mail messages, you may lose track of what each one is about. Subject lines are often vague or misleading, and it can take hours to look through dozens or even hundreds of messages for the one piece of information you really need. Fortunately Messenger provides a powerful search feature. To use it, select Search Messages from Messenger's Edit menu. A Search dialog box appears, as shown in Figure 5-62.

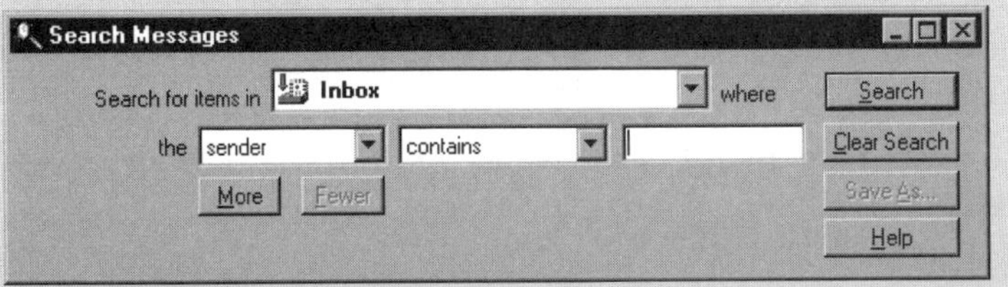

Figure 5-62: The Search Messages dialog box.

To use this tool, press the down arrow to the right of the first box and select where you want to search. To search your e-mail rather than newsgroup articles (see Chapter 6), you'd select either in Inbox or in All mail folders. (You'll learn more about folders in the section below called "Working with Folders.")

Next, construct a search criterion by completing the three boxes in the middle of the dialog. In the first box, select from the list which part of the messages you want to search. Perhaps you want to search the From field for a particular name or the body of the message for a particular word. Next select an item from the second box. Does the area of the message you've chosen contain the word? Or does it begin or end with the word? Lastly, type in the word (or partial word) you're interested in. If you need to make your search more precise by specifying more search criteria, press the More button and keep working. This lets you develop very complex searches. You could look, for instance, for a message that contains the word Windows but *wasn't* sent by Microsoft.

When you've completed your search criteria, simply click the Search button. If it exists, Messenger finds what you're looking for.

Messenger also supports a much simpler kind of search for text within individual messages. With a message selected, simply hit Ctrl+F or select Find in Message from the Edit menu. To find subsequent occurrences of the same word, simply press Ctrl+G or select Find Again from the Edit menu.

Attaching Files to Messages

Besides including HTML tags and inline images in messages, you can also include entire HTML files or attach any kind of file, whether it's text or binary. There are no restrictions on the type of material you can include with your message. You can send spreadsheets, graphics, sounds, word processor files, programs, you name it. You can even attach files that are not on your own computer by sending the URLs for the files as attachments to your message!

To attach a file to an e-mail message:

1. Follow all the steps outlined earlier for creating a new e-mail message or replying to one.

2. Before sending the message, click the Attach button. A submenu pops up with several choices:

   ■ **File**. Select this to attach a file.

   ■ **WEB Page**. Select this to attach the URL for a remote Web page.

   ■ **My address book card**. You can select this on its own or in addition to either of the other choices. With this item checked, your own Address Card will be appended to the message, as explained earlier in the section called "The Address Book."

3. For the purposes of this exercise, click File. An Enter file to attach dialog box appears, as shown in Figure 5-63.

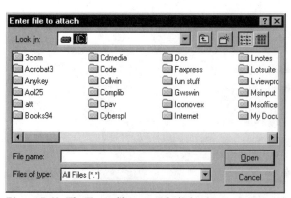

Figure 5-63: The Enter file to attach dialog box.

4. Select a file from your computer (or your network) and then click Open. You are returned to the Messenger window, with the Attachment tab selected in the Addressing Area and a file listed as an attachment, as shown in Figure 5-64.

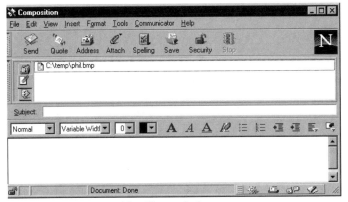

Figure 5-64: Message with a file attached.

5. To add more files, click the Attach button again. Or, as a shortcut, you can simply click within the area that displays the attached files.

6. Once you have attached all the files you want, you send the message like any other, by clicking the Send button.

TIP

When your message includes attachments, the paper clip icon on the Attachments tab is red rather than blue.

Pretty simple, isn't it? But there's an even easier way to attach files to your e-mail messages:

1. Again, follow all the steps outlined earlier for creating a new e-mail message or replying to one.

2. At the left side of the top pane, click the Attachments tab, the one that depicts a paper clip. You should now see a big empty Attachments area in the top pane, as shown in Figure 5-65.

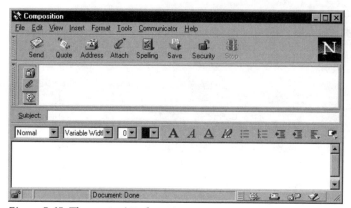

Figure 5-65: The empty Attachments area.

3. Now click and drag the icon for any file on your system into this area. You can select files from your desktop, from any folder on your system, or from Windows Explorer, for example. Once you've dragged the file into the area, it appears in the Attachments list, as shown above in Figure 5-65. You can even drag multiple files into the Attachments area all at once. Don't worry, the files aren't deleted from your system—only *copies* are sent with your e-mail.

TIP

Before you start sending tons of attachments with your e-mail messages, you should be aware of a couple of things:

1. *Don't be fooled by how you're sending the attachment. If you're sending a 1MB sound file via e-mail, it will take just as long—or longer—to download it via e-mail as it would to download it via Web pages. Don't send huge attachments unless you absolutely have to!*

2. *Plain text messages cannot contain viruses. However, attachments* can. *For that reason it's bad nettiquite to send unsolicited attachments to someone, especially to several people like a mailing list.*

Be cautious when using attachments. They're very handy, but the capacity to send them is easily abused.

Attaching Web Pages

Instead of attaching a locally stored file to your message, you can attach the URL for a Web page or other multimedia file that's located somewhere else. To do this, click the Attach button and then select Web Page instead of File from the submenu that appears. A dialog box like the one in Figure 5-66 appears.

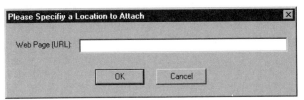

Figure 5-66: The Please Specify a Location to Attach dialog box.

Just enter a URL and click OK, then complete and send your message. Assuming your recipient is using Messenger or another HTML-enabled e-mail program, he or she will see the Web page right within the message. And by the way, just as with files you can drag Internet shortcuts right into the Attachments area.

TIP

You can send messages with attached URLs right from the Navigator window, too. Let's say you're viewing an awesome graphic and you want to send it to a friend. Just click Send Page from Navigator's File menu. A new message Composition window pops up with the URL for the file already attached. Once again assuming your friend is using Messenger or another HTML-enabled e-mail program, he or she will see the graphic immediately in the message.

Making Sure Your Attached Files Arrive Safely

E-mail is a system designed primarily for exchanging text messages, and attached files require special handling by Internet and intranet software. Netscape Communicator's default settings will work fine in most cases, but if somebody complains that a binary file you attached to a message was corrupt or wouldn't run, click the Sending Options tab before sending your message (the tab with the checklist on it, just under the Attachments tab) and select "Uuencode instead of MIME for attachments." This makes Netscape Messenger use an older alternate method of encoding for the attachments to this message.

Dealing With Attached Files You Receive

Not only does Netscape Messenger let you attach all kinds of files to e-mail messages, it also includes special options for dealing with attached files that you receive. For instance, as I mentioned before, when you receive an image file, it is automatically displayed as an image, and attached HTML files are automatically displayed just like Web pages. If you don't want images and HTML formatting displayed inline (as part of the message), select Attachments from Messenger's View menu and then click As Links from the submenu that appears.

TIP

Every message that includes at least one attachment also contains a paper clip icon near the top. If you click this icon, a new frame opens up that includes icons for each of the attachments. Clicking the attachment icons displays them in separate windows, or, in the case of a binary file, opens it or saves it to disk. More about attached binary files coming right up!

What if you receive an attachment that cannot be displayed automatically in the Message Contents pane, for instance a spreadsheet file or Word document? Figure 5-67 shows what you'll see at the bottom of the message:

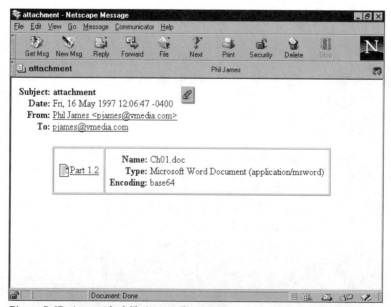

Figure 5-67: An attached file in a mail message.

As you can see, the fields on the right inform you of the name of the file, what MIME type it is (more about MIME in a moment), and what method was used to encode it. At the left, there is a clickable link. In most cases, if you click on this link Messenger will automatically launch the correct application on your system for viewing or otherwise processing the attached file. For instance, if the attached file is a Word document, Messenger will launch Microsoft Word. Within seconds, you'll see the attached file displayed right within Word. In some cases, the file may be saved to disk instead of displayed within another program. Don't worry, you'll be asked where you want to save it!

MIME Types

MIME, or Multipurpose Internet Mail Extensions, includes a universal standard for naming file types. Usually the MIME designations make sense, as in the case of Winword files, which are classified as application/msword. The first part of the designation lets you know that the file is associated with an application, the second part specifies the exact application. By knowing the MIME type of a file it encounters, a program such as Communicator can know what application to launch.

Messenger cannot automatically handle every type of file you might receive. Obviously, there are thousands of different file formats, and new ones come along every day. Figure 5-68 shows the dialog box that appears when you click an attached file that Messenger doesn't know how to handle.

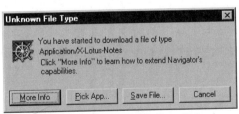

Figure 5-68: The Unknown File Type dialog box.

Let's go over each of these buttons:

- **More Info**. If you're connected to the Net, clicking this button takes you to Netscape's Plug-In Finder page. There you can download a special plug-in application that will extend Communicator's capabilities so that it can handle this type of file properly (please see Chapter 10).

- **Pick App**. If you click this button, a new dialog box appears, as shown in Figure 5-69.

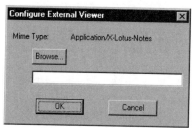

Figure 5-69: The Configure External Viewer dialog box.

If you have an application on your system that can deal with this type of file, enter its path and name here. You can use the browse button to find the helper application if you want.

- **Save File**. This button lets you save the file to disk so that you can deal with it later in another application.

- **Cancel**. Even if you click cancel, the file will still be available to you later whenever you view the e-mail message it's attached to.

You can also use a special configuration facility for customizing the way Netscape Communicator associates particular types of files with different helper applications, but that topic is beyond the scope of this chapter. For a full discussion, turn back to the section called "Applications" in Chapter 3. All of the information there applies to Messenger as well as to Navigator 4 and other Communicator components.

Working With Folders

You've been using e-mail for a week and your Messenger window is clogged with thousands of messages. These include pep talks from the CEO, dire warnings from the people in Accounting, and some *very* interesting gossip about your immediate supervisor. Do these messages really all belong together in the same Inbox?! *It's TIME TO GET ORGANIZED!*

Let's take another look at the Messenger window, as shown below in Figure 5-70.

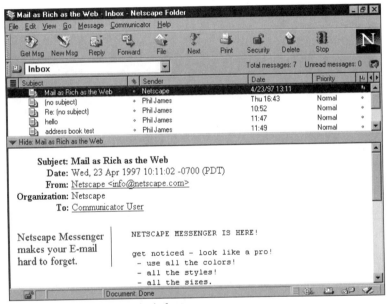

Figure 5-70: The Messenger window.

The drop-down folder list at the left of the window displays the word Inbox. This is because the Inbox is the default folder where all new mail is stored. Now press the down arrow to the right of the listbox. You'll see something like Figure 5-71.

There are five default mail folders in addition to one or more news folders. Don't worry about the news folders for now; I'll cover those in the next chapter. The five mail folders are:

- **Inbox**. You already know all about this one.

- **Unsent Messenges**. If you are working offline, this is where messages are stored before they are actually sent. Please see the sidebar ahead on "Working Offline."

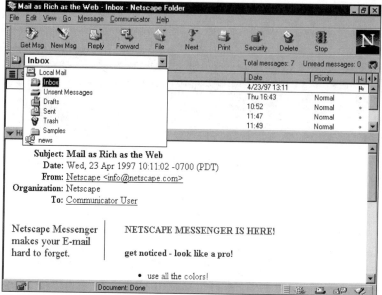

Figure 5-71: Some more Messenger folders.

- **Drafts**. As I mentioned earlier, this is a folder in which you can store messages that you are still working on. From the Message Composition window, you click the Draft button and your current message is moved to the Drafts folder. From there, you can work on your message some more and simply click the Send button when you're finally satisfied with your work.

- **Sent**. This folder, by default, stores a copy of all messages that you send.

- **Trash**. When you delete a message using the Delete button, it's not gone forever. It's simply moved to the Trash folder. That way you can recover messages you've deleted accidentally. Messages are only really gone when you delete them from the Trash folder. By the way, you can empty your Trash folder quickly by selecting Empty Trash from the Message Center's File menu.

TIP

Not all of these folders may exist when you run Messenger the very first time. Some of them are created the first time they're needed, for instance when you send or delete your first message.

You can move to a particular folder simply by clicking it in the drop-down list. Then only the messages in that particular folder are displayed.

Working Offline

If you think of your messages as *belles-lettres* and like to polish your prose until it sparkles with wit and wisdom, you need this sidebar—especially if you're a SLIP or PPP user paying for all that time connected to the Net. Messenger lets you create as many messages as you want without being connected. Later, you can send them in a batch all at once.

How does this work? Well, you create a message offline—without being connected to the Net. Then, instead of clicking the Send button, you select Send Later from the File menu. The Composition window disappears. Your message has been copied to the Outbox folder, a temporary storage area for messages waiting to be shipped off on their journey across the Internet.

So some time later you connect to the Net and want to send whatever messages you've stored in the Outbox. From Messenger's File menu, simply click Send Unsent Messages. Messages in your Outbox are also sent when you retrieve new messages.

Of course you can use the Send Later option even if you're permanently connected to an intranet, but it becomes especially valuable for dial-up Internet connections when you're paying by the minute.

This is also a good time to talk about Messenger's configuration options for working online or offline. Select Preferences from Messenger's Edit menu and then click the Offline category. What appears is shown in Figure 5-72.

➡

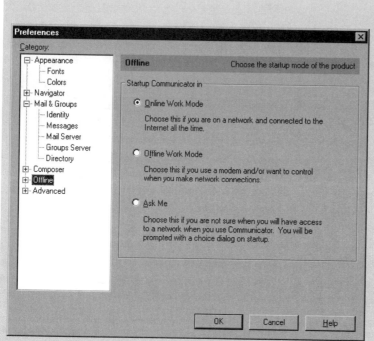

Figure 5-72: The Offline dialog box.

The choices here are fairly self-explanatory. If you select Online Work Mode, Messenger assumes you are connected to the Net at all times. When you click the Send button, for instance, it will try to send your message to the specified address. If you are not currently connected, it will huff and puff and finally return an error message.

What happens if you choose Offline Work Mode and try to send a message when you're not connected? Messenger simply places your message in the Outbox folder, queued for delivery when you eventually go online. By the way, when you're in Offline mode, the Send button automatically becomes a Send Later button.

Messenger behaves the same way when you have selected Ask Me and are not connected, placing outgoing messages in the Outbox and ignoring requests to retrieve new mail. The difference here is that in Ask Me mode Communicator will ask you if you want to go online when you first start the program.

Moving Messages Between Folders

The whole idea of folders is that they help you organize your messages, sort of like files in a file cabinet. That means you have to be able to move messages from one folder to another. It's easy in Netscape Messenger:

1. Select a message in your Inbox (or any other folder). Optionally, select several messages using Ctrl+click.

2. Click the File button. A submenu appears with the names of all your folders, as shown in Figure 5-73.

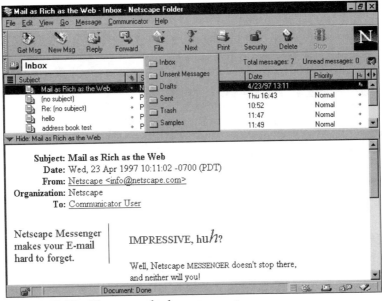

Figure 5-73: The File command submenu.

3. Click the folder to which you want to move your selected message(s).

You can also copy (rather than move) selected messages by selecting the Copy Message command from the Message menu.

TIP

When you want to move a message to a folder quickly, just right-click it and select File Message from the context menu that appears.

Of course you can also simply *delete* messages by selecting them and clicking the delete button. As a safety precaution, they are stored in your Trash folder until you explicitly delete them from there.

Creating New Folders

It's great to know how to move messages from folder to folder, but there's not much to be gained in moving them around among Messenger's default folders. To really get organized, you need to create new folders. Let's create one called Office Gossip:

1. In the Messenger window, with any folder displayed, click the small button at the far right on the toolbar, just underneath the Netscape logo. This is the Message Center button. The Message Center window appears, as shown below in Figure 5-74.

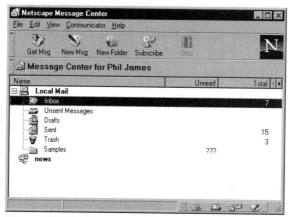

Figure 5-74: The Message Center window.

- The Message Center window displays a hierarchical view of all your folders, including discussions you've subscribed to (see Chapter 6).

2. Select the top level folder, called simply Local Mail. Right-click and select New Folder from the context menu that appears. A dialog box pops up asking you to enter a name for the new folder.

TIP

If you don't want to make this a top-level mail folder but instead a sub-folder of some already existing folder, select from the list at the bottom of this dialog box.

3. Enter **Office Gossip** and click OK.

Voilà! Look at the Message Center window now, as shown in Figure 5-75.

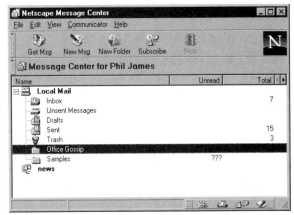

Figure 5-75: The Message Center window with a new folder.

Your new folder will appear in the regular Messenger window folder list. You can now move individual messages from your Inbox into this new folder, following the instructions in the previous section "Moving Messages Between Folders."

By the way, you can create sub-folders of folders, too. For instance, if you select the Office Gossip folder in the Message Center window and then click New Folder in the File menu, you can create a sub-folder called Really Hot Office Gossip. You can hide or reveal sub-folders in the Message Center window by clicking the plus and minus signs to the left of the parent folder. Only the hierarchical location of a sub-folder differentiates it from any other folder—otherwise it's exactly the same.

TIP

The Message Center window is a great place to empty your Trash folder in one fell swoop. Simply select Empty Trash Folder from the File menu. And there's one other small housekeeping chore you should do periodically. From the same file menu, select Compress Folders. This gets rid of any extra disk space that's being used up unnecessarily as a result of deleting messages from folders.

Mail Filtering

What if a friend of yours at work *only* sends you gossipy messages? No work-related stuff, no weather reports, just hard-core who's-doing-what-with-whom. Maybe you get so many of these messages that it becomes a pain to move them to your Office Gossip folder. Hey, no problem. Messenger can do the work for you!

Yes, Messenger includes a special filtering feature that automatically moves incoming mail into particular folders—instead of the Inbox—based on certain criteria such as the sender, the subject, or even a word that appears in the body of the message! If you don't want any messages with the word broccoli in them, you can get Messenger to move them into the Trash folder as soon as they come in.

Here's how it works:

1. From Messenger's Edit menu, select Mail Filters. The Mail Filters window pops up, as shown in Figure 5-76.

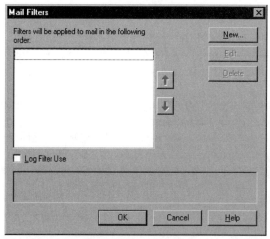

Figure 5-76: The Mail Filters window.

2. Since you don't have any filters yet, click the New button. A new Filter Rules dialog box appears, as shown in Figure 5-77.

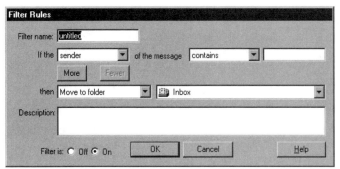

Figure 5-77: The Filter Rules dialog box.

3. Fill in a name for your filter, replacing the word Untitled in the first edit box. For instance, you might call it Broccoli.

4. Now start filling in your filter rules. For this example, drop down the first list box and select the item body. You can leave the word "contains" in the next box, but in the last box to the right enter **broccoli**. This means that the filter will be triggered whenever it encounters the word "broccoli" in the body of a message.

TIP

If you want to make your rule more precise, you can click the More button and add further criteria. For instance, you might want the filter to be triggered only if it encounters the word broccoli AND the date is after next week some time. I don't know why you might want that, but you might.

5. Next, tell Messenger what action to take when it encounters the criteria you've specified. For this example, leave the Move to folder command, but in the right-hand box select the Trash folder.

   ■ Instead of moving these messages to the Trash folder, you could simply select delete from the drop-down list on the left. The effect would be the same.

   ■ Two of the actions available in the drop-down list are Ignore Thread and Watch Thread. You'll understand what these mean after reading the section below, "Sorting and Threading Messages."

6. Fill in a description for your filter so that you can see at a glance what it's all about. Your completed Filter Rules dialog box should look something like Figure 5-78.

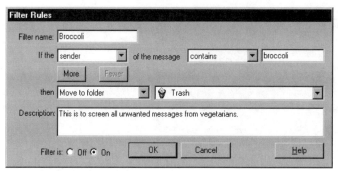

Figure 5-78: A completed Filter Rules dialog box.

7. Click OK. You are returned to the Mail Filters dialog box with your new rule displayed, as shown in Figure 5-79.

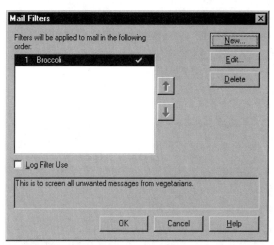

Figure 5-79: A new rule.

- As you can see, the Mail Filters dialog box lets you edit or delete any filter you've created. But more importantly, it lets you toggle filters on and off. To turn any filter off without deleting it, simply click in the On column. The checkmark changes to a dot, and the filter becomes inactive. To turn it back on, click again.

- If you have several filters, you may need to experiment with the order in which they're activated. You can do this by using the arrows at the left side of the dialog box. For instance, you have a filter that deletes all incoming messages that contain broccoli and another one that moves messages from your coworker Jack into the Gossip folder. Jack sends you some gossip about your boss and some broccoli—should it be deleted or moved to the Gossip folder? This is where the order of the filters becomes important.

- You can create a log file of filter use by checking the Log Filter Use check box. Messenger will create a file that details every time a filter was "fired." This can be useful for debugging your filters—or for figuring out why you have all those messages in your Trash folder.

In this section you've learned how to organize your e-mail messages by filing them away in folders. But Messenger also provides several features that help you organize your messages *within* individual folders, and that's what we'll examine next.

Hiding Old Messages

Messenger provides a convenient trick that will make you *look* organized even if you're not. Let's say you have lots and lots of messages in your Inbox folder, some read and some unread. You can force Messenger to display only the unread, or new, messages in the message list pane. To do this, simply select Messages from the View menu, then New from the submenu that appears. Messenger now only displays messages that you haven't yet read, or that you've marked as unread. To switch back to viewing all your messages, select All from the same submenu.

You'll notice that the submenu also includes several other choices related to *threads*. You'll learn all about threads and threading in just a few minutes.

Sorting & Threading Messages

Take a quick look at my actual real life Inbox folder shown in Figure 5-80:

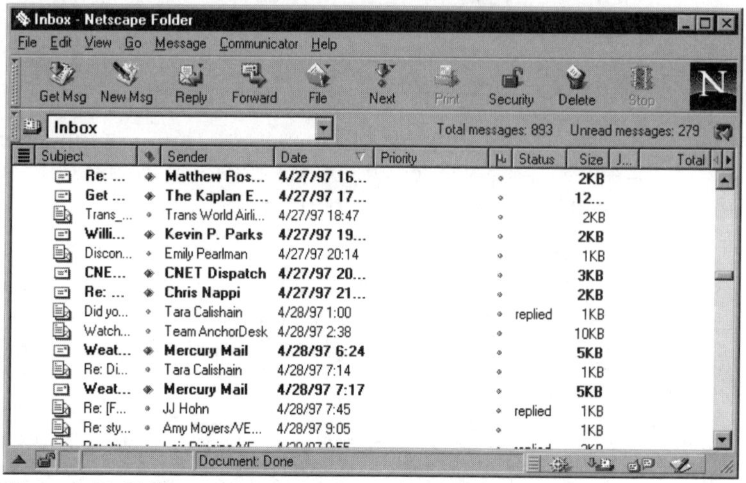

Figure 5-80: Phil's actual real life Inbox folder.

You can probably tell from the subject fields that there are all kinds of messages: personal notes, business correspondence, weather, and stock reports, etc. Yes, I'll admit it: I'm an e-mail slob. I'm just not very good about creating tidy folders and efficient filters. And because my Inbox gets so crowded, I rely heavily on Messenger's sorting and threading features. Sorting and threading affect the order and hierarchy of messages within individual folders. Instead of wandering through a huge random list of e-mail you've received, you can move efficiently through a list you've unrandomized in useful ways.

TIP

The Next button is an effective way to navigate large lists of messages. The Next button takes you to the next unread message.

Sorting

By default, mail in a folder is sorted in chronological order, with the earliest mail at the top of the folder and the latest mail at the bottom. To sort alphabetically by subject, click the Subject bar (column label), as shown in Figure 5-81. Note that Messenger places a small arrow in the Subject bar indicating that this is the current sort criterion.

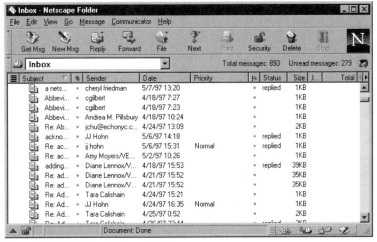

Figure 5-81: Mail sorted by subject.

You can also sort by sender name, as shown in Figure 5-82. To do this, simply click the Sender bar.

In fact, you can sort by *any* of the informational fields available.

Let's go back to sorting by date for a moment. Suppose you want the most recent messages at the top of the list rather than at the bottom? You can reverse the order of any sort tools by selecting Ascending in the Sort menu under View. This makes date sorting run from most recent to earliest, and alphabetical sorting run from Z to A, as shown in Figure 5-83.

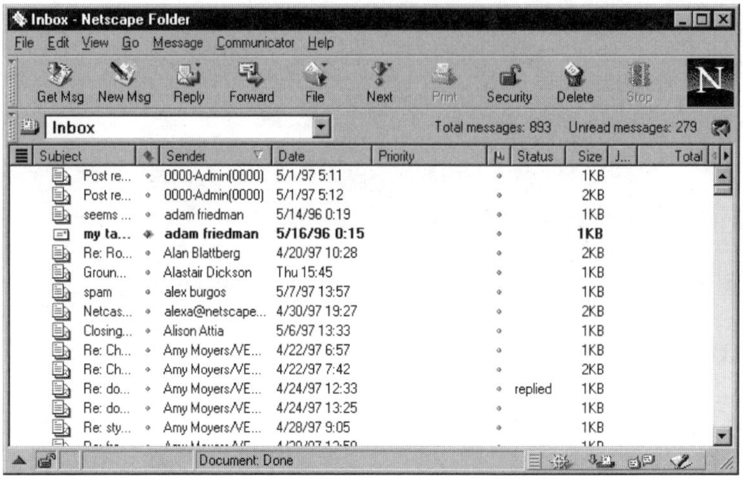

Figure 5-82: Mail sorted by sender.

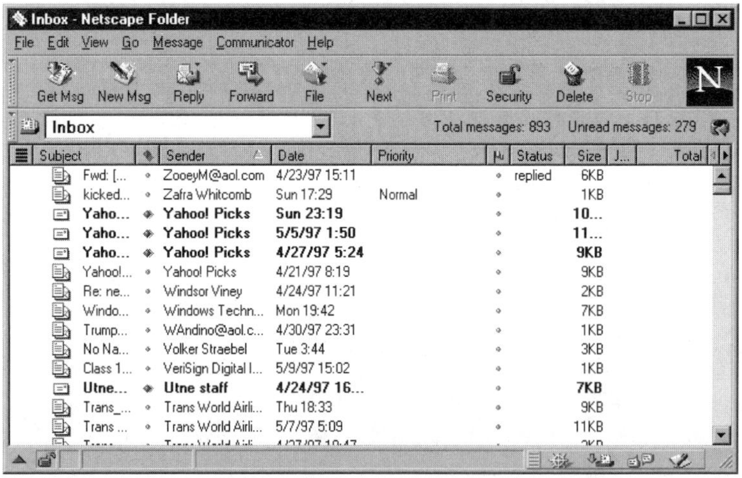

Figure 5-83: Mail sorted by sender in reverse order.

Threading

I bet you're wondering, "What's that button with the lines on it to the left of the Subject, Sender, and Date bars? And when is this @#$%^&* book going to explain it?"

Then there are the Curious George types among you who've already clicked the button. The lines on the button became indented when you clicked it, but unless you've collected a bit of e-mail already you didn't notice any other change.

This is the *Thread* button. When you click it, your messages are sorted in thread order. That means any messages which have the same subject line are grouped together, and then each of those *groups* is placed in the list in order by date.

Confused?

Let's say that on January 1 you get a message from your mother. On January 2 you get a message with the subject line "Make Big Bucks on the Internet." On January 3 you get a message from your father. On January 4 you get another message labeled "Make Big Bucks on the Internet." If you are currently sorting by date but don't press the Thread button, here's the order of messages:

- Jan 1 - letter from Mom
- Jan 2 - "Make Big Bucks on the Internet"
- Jan 3 - letter from Dad
- Jan 4 - "Make Big Bucks on the Internet"

But after you press the Thread button, here's the order of messages:

- Jan 1 - letter from Mom
- Jan 2 - "Make Big Bucks on the Internet"
-     Jan 4 - "Make Big Bucks on the Internet"
- Jan 3 - letter from Dad

Notice that I indented the second "Make Big Bucks" message. That's the way Messenger does it, too. The January 2 message is the initial message in the thread; subsequent messages with the same subject are grouped *underneath* it, not only spatially but hierarchically as well.

Let's see what this looks like in the Messenger window. Figure 5-84 shows a portion of my Inbox with Threading turned on.

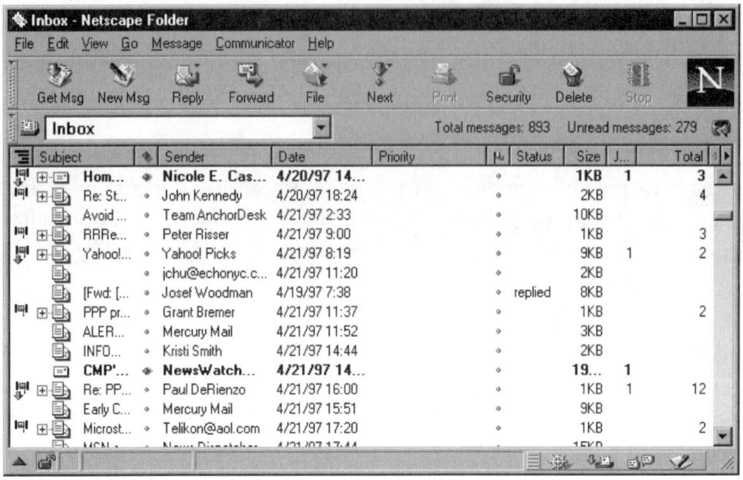

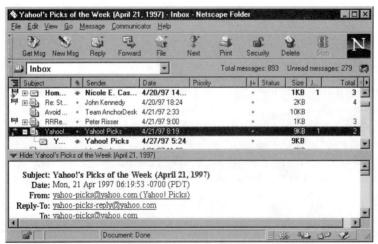

Figure 5-84: My Inbox after clicking the Thread button.

Notice the item Yahoo!'s Picks of the Week. That's the initial message of a thread. To see all the messages in that particular thread, simply click the plus sign to the left of the initial message, as shown below in Figure 5-85.

Figure 5-85: The expanded view of the Yahoo!'s Picks thread, showing all the messages I've received with the same subject.

One of the best things about threading is that the subject lines don't always have to be *exactly* the same for two messages to be considered part of the same thread. *Replies* to messages are automatically put in the same thread with the original message. Let me explain:

You get a message from the accounting department with the subject "Invoice from Vendor #5." You respond, and your messages is automatically titled, "Re: Invoice from Vendor #5." The account department reads your mail but returns a few more questions. Their response will also be titled "Re: Invoice from Vendor #5" or perhaps even "Re: Re: Invoice from Vendor #5." Even though the subject lines are not exactly the same, Messenger knows to stick them together in the same thread.

TIP

To exit "thread mode" and return to a different sorting order for your messages, simply click one of the label bars such as Sender or Date.

Selecting Threads

Often it is useful to select all the messages in a particular thread, for instance if you want to move them to a different folder. Of course you can click the plus sign to expand a thread, then individually select each message using Ctrl+click, but Messenger provides a much simpler technique:

1. Scroll down the message list to the initial message of the thread you want to select.

2. Click the small blue icon to the very left of the message. This is the thread selection control. The entire thread is selected, as shown in Figure 5-86.

You do not need to expand the thread (by pressing the plus sign) before clicking the thread selection control.

TIP

Messenger puts a blue-green down arrow next to the icon of any thread that contains messages you haven't read yet. This is a convenient way to find newly retrieved messages when you are sorting by thread rather than by date.

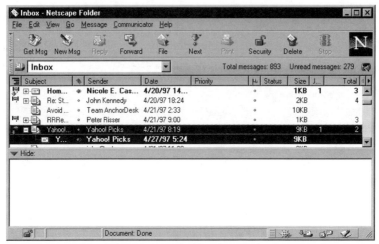

Figure 5-86: A thread after pressing the blue thread selection control.

Watching & Ignoring Threads

Maybe not all threads are equally important to you. You'd better stay pretty aware of messages from the boss about a project you're working on, but you can probably live without some of that juicy office gossip. Fortunately, Messenger lets you mark individual threads as *watched* or *ignored*. Watched threads are ones you really care about. You can choose to view *only* watched threads if you want, thus filtering out anything you don't want to see right now. Ignored threads are the opposite. When new messages arrive in ignored threads, Messenger doesn't even alert you by putting the green arrow next to the thread icon.

To mark a thread as watched:

1. Make sure your messages are currently sorted by thread. If they are not, click the Thread button.

2. Select the initial message of the thread you want to mark as watched. Or, mark a "lone" message if you want to see if responses to it come in.

3. From the Message menu, select Watch Thread. Optionally, you can just type **W**.

To view just the new messages in your watched thread(s):

1. Select Messages from the View menu, then Watched Threads with New from the submenu that appears.

2. To return to viewing all your messages, select All from the same menu.

   ▪ Note that you can also choose to view *all* threads with new messages.

And to *ignore* threads:

1. Make sure your messages are currently sorted by thread. If they are not, click the Thread button.

2. Select the initial message of the thread you want to mark as ignore. Or, mark a "lone" message if you want to ignore any future responses to it.

3. From the Message menu, select Ignore Thread. Optionally, you can just type **K**.

That's all there is to it. Now you won't be alerted by the green arrow icon when new messages arrive in the thread. You can, however, choose to see messages in ignored threads by selecting Messages from the View menu and then Ignored from the submenu that appears.

Mailing Lists

By now you're pretty good at using Netscape Messenger. In fact if you've tried everything I've suggested so far in this chapter, you probably qualify as a power user. Wear that pocket protector with pride! But now I'd like to move away from the technical aspects of e-mail and back into the realm of *content*. This is a section about how to get more mail, for those of you who don't get enough.

TIP

This section is only useful if you can send and receive Internet e-mail. If you're on an intranet that doesn't allow you to exchange messages outside your own company domain, skip ahead to the section on "E-mail Security."

Internet e-mail is not just for exchanging private messages. It can also be used for gigantic group conversations among Internet users via an Internet service known as *mailing lists*.

A mailing list is simply a list of the e-mail addresses of everyone who wants to send and receive mail about a certain topic. There are mailing lists for discussing bonsai trees, rap music, adoption, cars, computer software, folk dancing, and on and on. There are thousands of lists, with new ones being created every week.

Adding your e-mail address to a mailing list is a way of joining these conversations. This is called *subscribing*, and removing your e-mail address from such a list is called *unsubscribing*. Once you've subscribed to a list, any mail you send to the list address gets sent back out to all the other e-mail addresses included on the list, and any mail from any of the other subscribers also gets sent to you.

When you subscribe to a mailing list, you immediately begin receiving mail from the other subscribers. If, after reading what other people on the list are talking about for a few days, you have something to add, you can send mail back to the list address, and everyone else on the list sees your message.

So how do you find out what mailing lists are out there, and how to subscribe to them? The closest thing the Net has to an official list is Stephanie da Silva's list of *Publicly Accessible Mailing Lists*, originally created by Chuq Von Rospach. This list is an impressive compendium of mailing lists with a name, a short description, and information on how to subscribe for each one. The list itself is currently in 22 parts, arranged alphabetically and stored on a machine at MIT.

How do you retrieve this list of lists? Simple, you use Netscape Messenger:

1. In the Messenger window, click the Compose button. The Message Composition window appears.

2. Enter **mail-server@rtfm.mit.edu** in the To field.

3. Enter **Mailing Lists** in the Subject field. (Do this for your own information. The MIT mail-server doesn't care what's in the Subject field.)

4. Type only one line in the body of the message:

```
send pub/usenet/news.answers/mail/mailing-lists/part01
```

Your completed message should look like the one in Figure 5-87.

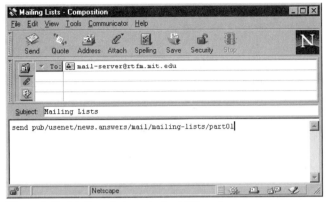

Figure 5-87: Mail ready to go to the MIT mail server.

This message instructs the MIT mail server, a kind of electronic file clerk, to send you Part 1 of the list. The list is large, and Part 1 is only the beginning! If you want to see more of the list, send another piece of mail to mail-server@rtfm.mit.edu with just this line:

```
send pub/usenet/news.answers/mail/mailing-lists/part*
```

You need to replace the asterisk shown above with the number for the part of the list you're interested in. To get to Part 7, for instance, enter **part07** after the final slash.

TIP

> *A little leery about going through such huge lists? If you've got Web access, try Liszt at http://www.liszt.com. It's a searchable database of mailing lists, with over 50,000 lists. It's all here, from Ants to Zimbabwe!*

Using Mailing Lists

There are a few differences between sending and receiving mail from a mailing list and sending and receiving personal mail, because mailing lists are a public forum. When you send a message to a mailing list, you don't even know how many people are reading it, much less who all of them are. This changes the way people read and write e-mail. Mailing lists are famous for long-running, voluminous, and often quite heated exchanges of e-mail, and because they are public forums, there are different rules of conduct there.

Mailing List Etiquette

- **Read before you write.** This is Rule #1. Before you send e-mail to a mailing list, remember that you are writing for a particular audience, and make sure that what you have to say is relevant. The rule of thumb when dealing with mailing lists is to read what other people are saying for about a week before sending any mail yourself, to make sure that any questions or comments you may have are pertinent. (Reading a list without posting is called *lurking*.)

- **Don't waste people's time.** This advice seems self-evident, but you will often see people posting mail that adds nothing to the discussion. Don't jump into a conversation just to tell everyone you agree with what someone else has said. If you are quoting another person's message, only quote what is relevant to your point. Nothing wastes people's time more than scrolling through screen after screen of a message they have already read once, only to read "I think you are completely correct" at the end.

- **Use private e-mail when appropriate.** When you read something posted to a mailing list, you have a choice between replying to the writer in private or sending your reply to the entire list. If you merely want to say you agree, or ask where you can get a copy of something mentioned in the post, send e-mail to the writer instead of to the list.

- **Use the Subject line carefully.** As with private e-mail, the Subject line is the first thing anyone sees in mail from you, and it tells people whether they are interested in what you have to say. Use the Subject line to describe, as succinctly as possible, the contents of your mail.

- **Don't send attachments to mailing lists.** If you send a 20K attachment to a list that has 100 people, you've added 2MB to the Internet mail traffic. Doesn't sound too bad? Consider that most mailing lists have far more than 100 people—and most of them don't want your attachment. Don't ever send unsolicited attachments to a mailing list.

- If you are no longer interested in a particular mailing list, use the proper procedure for unsubscribing. When you signed up for the list, you were probably sent a message that included thorough instructions. Now's the time to follow them! In most cases, you send your *unsubscribe* command to an address that's different from the one where you send regular messages. Nothing annoys mailing list recipients more than getting *unsubscribe* messages along with the usual information.

One of the main differences between mailing list mail and personal mail is that when you want to reply to a message, you have a choice between replying only to the author of the article or sending the reply out to the whole list. If you have something to add to the debate, you should send your mail to the list, but if you just want to say that you agree with what someone has said, send it to the author only. The best way to tell what's appropriate is to read what other people are posting to the list to see what kinds of things are being discussed in public.

When replying to something you have read on a mailing list, make sure to examine the To field of your outgoing mail. Different mailing lists handle the return address differently. On some lists, when you use the Reply function, the To field is set up assuming that you want to send mail out to the whole mailing list, while on others it is set up assuming that you want to reply only to the author of the original post. If you want to reply to the whole group, you would select Reply to All.

TIP

Checking the To line of your mail before you reply will prevent you from sending mail you meant to be private to everyone on the list, or from sending mail you meant to be public only to one other person.

One concept that you will sometimes hear discussed on mailing lists is the *signal-to-noise ratio*. This is an engineering term that has been pressed into service to describe the percentage of messages sent to any given mailing list that are useful or interesting. Lists where there is generally an engaged and articulate discussion going on are said to have a high signal-to-noise ratio, while lists where the subscribers are posting messages needlessly are said to have a low signal-to-noise ratio. Good mailing list etiquette helps create a high signal-to-noise ratio.

Inbox Direct

Netscape Messenger also supports a very different kind of mailing list called *Inbox Direct*. With Inbox Direct you still subscribe to services that send you specialized messages, but typically these are not messages you'd respond to. For instance, my Inbox Direct subscriptions include a local weather report and stock quotes that I receive several times a day.

But the main difference between Inbox Direct messages and regular old mailing list messages is that they are all HTML-enhanced, with colorful graphics and even sound. In fact, when you subscribe to an Inbox Direct service, you are really asking for specialized Web pages to be delivered directly to your Messenger Inbox on a regular basis, just as paper magazines are delivered to your house via snail mail. You can think of Inbox Direct as the e-mail version of Netcaster. In fact, services like Inbox Direct are often referred to as *mailcasting*.

To subscribe to Inbox Direct services, use Navigator 4 to go to the Netscape home page (http://home.netscape.com) and click the Inbox Direct link.

TIP

If you subscribe to many mailing lists, your Messenger folders will get pretty crowded pretty quickly. Not only that, you might start using up more hard drive space than you want to! Netscape Messenger lets you control the "runaway Inbox" problem not only through the filtering options covered earlier in the chapter, but also by restricting the size of messages you can receive.

If you don't want to receive e-mail larger than a particular size (which may often be junk e-mail anyway), select Preferences from the Edit menu of any Communicator component, then expand the Advanced category by double-clicking it or by clicking the plus sign. Select Disk Space from the new categories that appear. Now check the first check box and in the edit field type the upper size limit of messages you want to receive.

In this same dialog box, you can also require Messenger to ask you if you want to compact your folders when it will save a certain amount of disk space. Just check the second check box and set the minimum space saved.

Lastly, you can save disk space by configuring Messenger so that it deletes the bodies of old messages, saving just the headers. This is especially useful if you're saving messages on your mail server as well as locally. To access this feature, click the More Options button in the Disk Space dialog box. Check the check box in the dialog box that appears and set the minimum age for deleting the bodies of messages.

E-mail Security (S/MIME)

I'll end this chapter with a very brief discussion of one of the hottest topics in the online world: e-mail security. As we start using e-mail for financial transactions and other sensitive communications, the privacy of our messages becomes increasingly important. There's a whole chapter later in the book on security (Chapter 13), so we're not going to get into too much detail here. But it's important to understand the basics.

Messenger supports a standard known as S/MIME (Secure MIME) for digitally signed and encrypted e-mail messages. S/MIME can assure you that messages you send and receive are authentic and have not been read anywhere between their point of origin and their final destination. In this section I'll cover the basic features of S/MIME as implemented in Messenger.

TIP

If your incoming e-mail server is an IMAP server (rather than POP3), it may support encrypted connections, automatically encrypting information it sends you. If your network administrator has told you that this is the case, select Preferences from Messenger's Edit menu and then click the Mail Server category. Check the very last check box, "Server supports encrypted connections," in the Mail Server dialog box.

Let's start with sending signed and encrypted messages.

Sending Signed and Encrypted Messages

Messenger lets you send *signed messages* that include a digital security certificate assuring the recipient that the message did in fact come from you, or at least from somebody sitting at your computer. Digital security certificates are issued by special certifying organizations. Getting a personal security certificate can be compared with getting a passport from the Post Office, except this is a "cyber-passport" and you can obtain one electronically, using Netscape Communicator of course. In Chapter 13, I show you how to get a new personal security certificate, but for now let's assume you already have one. Let's see how you attach it to your e-mail:

1. Follow the steps outlined earlier in this chapter for creating a new e-mail message.

2. In the Composition window, click the Sending Options tab, as shown in Figure 5-88.

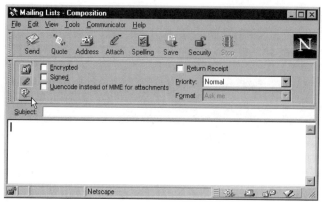

Figure 5-88: The Sending Options tab.

3. Check the check box labeled "Signed."

4. Send your message by clicking the Send button.

TIP

After you check the Signed check box, a signature tag appears as part of the icon on the Security button.

That's it! And what does the recipient see when they look at a signed message? I'll cover that in the section below called "Receiving Signed and Encrypted Messages," but for now let's move on to sending encrypted messages.

Encrypted messages are ones that are scrambled using a special *algorithm*, or formula, so that they cannot be read at any point between your computer and your recipient's computer. In encrypting your message, Messenger uses a key that's part of your recipient's digital security certificate—that's how your recipient can *de*crypt it at the other end. Yes, you have to have received a signed message from an individual before you can send that individual an encrypted message. Or you have to have received the individual's certificate some other way, perhaps from a directory server. You do not necessarily need your *own* digital certificate in order to send encrypted e-mail, but without one nobody will be able to send *you* encrypted messages.

To send an encrypted message:

1. Follow the steps outlined earlier in this chapter for creating a new e-mail message.

2. In the Composition window, click the Sending Options tab, as shown earlier in Figure 5-88.

3. Check the check box labeled "Encrypted."

4. Send your message by clicking the Send button.

TIP

After you check the Encrypted check box, the padlock icon on the Security button appears locked rather than open.

Receiving Signed and Encrypted Messages

What happens when you receive a signed and/or encrypted message? Check out Figure 5-89.

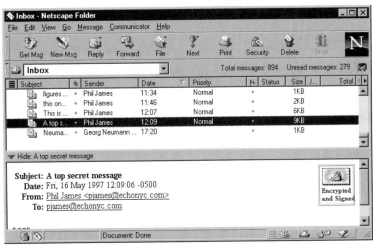

Figure 5-89: A signed and encrypted message selected in Messenger.

The Messenger window looks different in several ways:

■ The Security button now depicts a locked padlock (indicating an encrypted message) with a tag hanging from it (indicating that it's also a signed message).

■ The status line padlock is now locked, and the "signed" icon appears to its right.

■ Just to the right of the usual headers, the message itself contains a special "Encrypted and Signed" icon.

TIP

Remember, signing and encryption are related but independent S/MIME features. You may receive messages that are just encrypted, or just signed. In these cases the icon will of course be slightly different.

The whole idea of signed messages is that you can verify the identity of the sender. Obviously the mere presence of these new icons doesn't necessarily give you the assurance you need. When Immigration agents ask you to verify your identity, they usually want to see a bit more than your passport's blue and gold cover. Well, go ahead and click the new icon within the message, or the Security button, or the padlock icon on the status line. Any one of these actions has the same result: it opens up the message sender's electronic passport. A new Security Info window appears, providing detailed security information as shown in Figure 5-90.

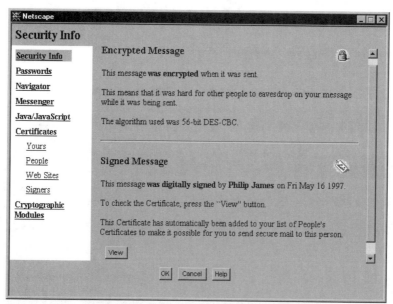

Figure 5-90: Security Info for a signed and encrypted e-mail message.

To see more identifying information about the message sender, simply click the View button. The details of the individual's security certificate appear in a new window, as shown in Figure 5-91.

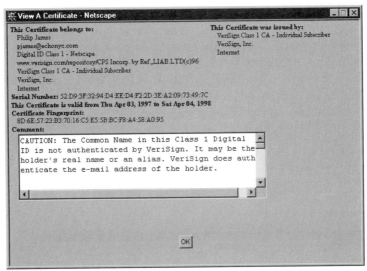

Figure 5-91: The View A Certificate window.

TIP

> *Much of the information in this window will make more sense after reading Chapter 13, but in a glance you can at least ascertain who really sent the message—or at least whose computer it was sent from.*

Click OK when you've finished viewing the sender's security certificate.

Messenger Security Options

Back in the Security Info window shown in Figure 5-90, notice that there are a variety of configuration categories in the left-hand frame. To reconfigure any Messenger security options, you would click the Messenger category. But that is beyond the scope of this chapter. If you want to get busy with e-mail security settings now, please turn to Chapter 13 for very thorough information.

Moving On

E-mail is a big subject, and at some point in this chapter you were probably wondering if it would ever end. But the perseverance was worth it, wasn't it? I mean, now you can go around saying things like "just e-mail me, babe."

In the next chapter, you'll learn another way to communicate with others on your office intranet or on the Net: discussion groups. Like Messenger, the discussion groups feature is a tool for sending and receiving messages. But where mail is usually private, discussion groups provide shared or even fully public forums where you can bandy about ideas or work on projects collaboratively. Collabra uses much of the same user interface as Messenger, so this next chapter is going to be an easy one.

CHAPTER 6

You Are Not Alone: Collabra & Discussion Groups

Only a few human urges are stronger than the urge to "put in your two cents," and you'll find few better correctives to narrow thinking than encouraging the expression of varied opinions. Of all the new communications technologies, discussion groups are perhaps the clearest example of a tool that enhances participation in decision making, learning, and even in focused entertaining chit-chat.

> **TIP**
>
> *Many of the techniques you'll use in working with discussion groups are identical with procedures you're already familiar with from Communicator's e-mail facilities. Chapter 5 contains large chunks of material that I could repeat here, but in the interest of keeping this book under 20 pounds and sparing a few trees, I'll instead assume that you're already familiar with the basics of Messenger. At times I may steer you toward the appropriate sections in Chapter 5.*

What Are Discussion Groups?

Discussion groups share some basic features with e-mail. In fact, both facilities are based around sending and receiving messages. There's a big difference, though. When you send messages to a discussion group rather than to an individual e-mail recipient, those messages are read by several people, potentially by every member of the group. And when you receive discussion group messages, you aren't the only one reading them. Again, every member of the group gets the same messages. Ten people might respond to one message, and you will see not only the original message but all ten responses. You can respond to the original message yourself, or to any one of the responses, and everyone will see your message too.

So a discussion group is really a group of people engaged in an electronic conversation. The conversation may be fast- or slow-paced. A controversial message may elicit dozens of immediate responses, or an informational message may elicit no response at all. And the conversation may be more or less focused depending on the goals of the group. For instance, you might have a small discussion group within your company dedicated to reworking personnel policy. But you can also find very large discussion groups that feature endless debates about TV shows or the latest supermodel—which brings up the whole issue of *public* versus *private* discussion groups.

Private Discussion Groups

Private discussion groups are, unsurprisingly, groups that the general public can't access. Earlier, I used the example of a discussion group dedicated to reworking personnel policy. That would be a private group within the company, open only to certain employees.

On intranets, private discussion groups are often established and configured using Netscape's Collabra server. This special program handles the message traffic. All messages are actually sent to the Collabra server, which acts as a central clearing house. Individual members of a particular discussion group use Communicator to "grab" any new messages from the Collabra server as well as to send any responses or new messages.

A single Collabra server may service many different discussion groups. But when your copy of Communicator logs on to a Collabra server to grab new messages, it accesses messages only from the groups you belong to. The Collabra server may be set up to allow you to join new groups, however, and you may even have permission to create new discussion groups.

TIP

If you're on an intranet and interact with several people to exchange ideas and information, consider the addition of private discussion groups to your array of intranet tools.

Private discussion groups via Collabra are much more manageable than mailing lists. They are easily moderated and their organization into threads makes conversations hard to track. Furthermore, information can be kept for a long time for referral without having to go through an archive process.

Discussion Group Terminology

Although discussion groups have some similarities with e-mail, experienced users generally use slightly different terminology. Instead of *sending* a message, for example, you *post it to the group*, or simply *post* it. And the message itself is often referred to as a *posting* or a *post*.

The large public discussion groups that comprise Usenet (see the sidebar called "What Is Usenet?" below) are almost always referred to as *newsgroups*, and the entire system that makes these public groups available is known as *Usenet, Netnews,* or *network news.* Client programs (like Communicator) that let you access discussion groups are often called *news readers.* When you join a discussion group or newsgroup, you *subscribe* to it, and when you quit the group, you *unsubscribe* from it. Subscribing to a discussion group simply means that Communicator will "remember" the group from session to session so that you may click on its name to open it rather that having to rejoin each time.

You need to know one other important term: *threads.* You may remember this word from Chapter 5. In the context of discussion groups, threads are individual trains of conversation posted to a particular group. I post a message. You post a response. Ten people respond to your response, and so on. Generally speaking, threads share a common theme, so you could refer, for instance, to "the Whitewater thread" in a newsgroup dedicated to Bill Clinton. Large public discussion groups sometimes have several simultaneous threads.

Public Discussion Groups

Public discussion groups are groups that anyone can join. Generally, they are slightly less focused than private discussion groups. You won't find a public discussion group about your company's personnel policy (unless you work for the government), but you can probably find a newsgroup devoted to personnel policy in general—or even personnel policy within a particular industry. Some public newsgroups cover broad areas like photography, aviation, and alternative health practices. Public discussion groups provide a public town square where you can get together with people of like interests to say what's on your minds.

No single server exists for all public discussion groups. Instead, the messages are duplicated among many servers. A discussion group server *subscribes* to various public groups from what is called a news feed, which is simply a computer on the Net that distributes discussion group messages to other servers. Then you, in turn, subscribe to particular discussion groups from your server. (See the sidebar called "What Is Usenet?" below.) When you read messages from the rec.arts.photography public discussion group, for instance, you are downloading the messages from your discussion group server, but they are the same messages people are downloading from different servers all around the world. Conversely, when you respond to a message in a public discussion group, you are actually uploading the message to your discussion group server, but from there it travels across the Net and is distributed to thousands of other discussion group servers.

What Is Usenet?

The most prominent system of public discussion groups is *Usenet*, also known as *Netnews*. Usenet is simply a huge collection of discussion group servers that make their groups available to other servers and to the general public. Public discussion groups disseminated via Usenet are known as *Usenet newsgroups*.

Usenet was originally developed for UNIX systems in 1979. It has become a worldwide network of thousands of Usenet sites (discussion group servers) running many operating systems such as UNIX, MS-DOS, and Windows NT, on various types of computers. Millions of people share messages electronically over these Usenet sites. The messages are sent from server to server using the UNIX-to-UNIX Copy Protocol (UUCP).

Usenet servers don't have to be connected to the Internet, since UUCP doesn't require the Internet for the transport of messages. But because thousands of Usenet sites *do* have access to the Internet, it has become the most commonly used electronic postal route for public discussion groups. The total number of distinct newsgroups on the Internet is in the thousands and growing daily. Consequently, millions of people who may have started using the Internet to gain access to the World Wide Web or to e-mail find that they can participate in Usenet newsgroups as well, provided they have Netscape Communicator or other client software.

Although UUCP is used to transfer discussion group messages from server to server, the servers use a different protocol to communicate with client programs such as Communicator. When your computer logs on to a discussion group server to read messages or post responses, it uses the Network News Transfer Protocol (NNTP) to communicate with the server.

In Netscape Collabra, Communicator's discussion group component, private and public groups look alike. You don't need to learn different interfaces for the two types of groups. Figure 6-1 shows the Message Center window (one of the two main discussion group windows) with a combination of public and private groups. The groups listed under the server news.computerland.net are all public groups that I have subscribed to, and the groups listed under secnews.netscape.com are private groups. Remember, private groups exist only on the server itself, whereas public groups "live" on many servers at once.

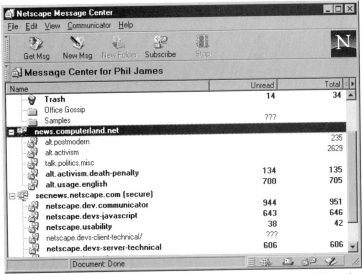

Figure 6-1: The Message Center window with a combination of public and private discussion groups.

TIP

Notice that the public discussion groups (newsgroups) are named according to a convention that looks a little like that for domain names, with descriptive words separated by dots. (You'll learn more about this convention in the section called "How Many Public Groups Can I Get?") The private discussion groups, on the other hand, do not necessarily adhere to this format because Netscape's Collabra server, the server for these private groups, allows for "friendlier" names.

Discussion groups are differentiated in one more way. Both types, public and private, may be either *moderated* or *unmoderated*.

Moderated & Unmoderated Discussion Groups

You've probably heard the term "signal to noise ratio." It's an engineering term used to describe how much of the data that's being communicated is usable information. For instance, if you have a very bad phone connection, you're getting lots of data in the form of hiss but very little usable information in the form of spoken words.

The term applies to discussion groups as well. Because of the human "two cents" urge I mentioned at the beginning of this chapter, people sometimes talk (or type) when they really have nothing much to contribute. This scenario is especially true in large public newsgroups.

To help improve the signal to noise ratio, some discussion groups (whether public or private) are *moderated*. In this case, the discussion group server does not automatically and immediately make all postings available to the group as a whole. If you post a new message or a response to a moderated group, somebody—yes, an actual human—reads what you wrote and determines whether your message is germane to the ongoing discussion. Send a message about Johnny Depp's hair to a moderated newsgroup on particle physics and nobody but the moderator will ever see your words. (Well, maybe some of the moderator's friends.)

How Many Public Groups Can I Get?

How many angels can dance on the head of a pin? Nobody knows, and the same is true regarding the total number of Usenet newsgroups available at any time via the Internet. To impose some order on the basically anarchic structure of Usenet, newsgroups have a fairly strict hierarchical naming convention. Newsgroup names look similar to Internet addresses; they are a series of words or abbreviations separated by dots, as in this example:

```
rec.arts.movies.reviews
```

The first word in the name denotes the major category to which the newsgroup belongs. A few of the major, hierarchical categories of Usenet newsgroups are:

■ **alt.** *Alternative* newsgroups contain articles that are often very interesting but can be on the controversial side, if not downright disgusting. Reader beware! This major category alone accounts for thousands of Usenet newsgroups.

■ **comp.** *Computer* newsgroups discuss computer-related issues.

■ **misc.** The *miscellaneous* newsgroups category (as you no doubt have guessed) is a catchall category for discussions that don't fit into one of the other categories.

■ **news.** The *news* category is for newsgroups discussing Usenet network news itself. These newsgroups are great sources of information about Usenet.

■ **rec.** *Recreation* newsgroups discuss recreation, sports, and the arts.

■ **sci.** *Science* newsgroups cover scientific topics.

■ **soc.** *Social* newsgroups focus on issues of perceived social importance.

■ **talk.** If you like good arguments, *talk* newsgroups are the place for you.

Newsgroups in these categories are usually distributed worldwide. Other major categories that may be distributed throughout the world include *bionet* (biology newsgroups), *biz* (business newsgroups), and *vmsnet* (discussions about the VMS computer operating system). Geographical, organizational, and commercial newsgroups are usually distributed only within their areas of interest.

Newsgroups in the *bit* major category are actually an alternative distribution method for Bitnet listserv mailing lists. Conversely, many newsgroups also distribute articles via mailing lists to users who don't have access to a news server. In effect, the pertinent messages are mailed to the user's electronic mailbox, enabling the user to get network news via a simple dial-up Internet e-mail account.

Because of the sheer volume of Usenet traffic, and due to the timely nature of much of the newsgroup content, most newsgroup servers put a limit on the number of days an article will be available for reading. Past the time limit, an article is said to have expired and is removed from the server. The time limit varies from server to server, but many long-standing newsgroups keep archives of expired articles.

TIP

There are special newsgroup search services that let you search for information in newsgroup archives. The most popular of these is DejaNews, which you can access via Navigator 4 at http://www.dejanews.com. For a source that can automatically check Usenet postings for information you specify and send the results to you via e-mail, check out Reference.Com at http://www.reference.com.

Do you have access to all the newsgroups on the Internet? Maybe, maybe not, depending on your server. Later in this chapter, we'll see how to get a list of all the newsgroups available through your server.

The best way to gain an understanding of Usenet newsgroups is to browse through several of them, reading the messages but not responding. This practice is affectionately known as *lurking*. In this case, lurking for a while makes a lot of sense. Before you know it, you'll feel compelled to jump in there and participate in the conversation.

Usenet Pictures

One of the more popular pastimes unique to the Internet is the trading of digital pictures of all kinds—pictures of animals, cartoons, heavenly bodies of various sorts, you name it. Whereas digital pictures can be made available on FTP sites or attached to electronic mail, Usenet has become a widely used method of sharing favorite electronic images. Most such files are posted in the newsgroups that have names beginning with *alt.binaries.pictures;* however, they may appear in postings in any newsgroup.

Because of its high resolution and the relatively high data compression, the Joint Photographic Experts Group (JPEG) file format is the current favorite for storing high resolution digital pictures for transmission over the Internet.

If a discussion group message contains either a GIF file or a JPEG file, Communicator displays the image, along with the rest of the article, in the message content pane.

You can even save the images to disk in a viewable form. Simply right-click on the graphic and select Save Image as... from the context menu that appears.

Specifying Your Discussion Group Server

You're probably eager to try your hand at reading discussion groups right away, but we still need to take care of a little housekeeping. Before the Collabra discussion group component of Communicator can access messages, you have to give it the name of your discussion group server.

TIP

Most ISPs provide access to a news server along with their e-mail and HTTP servers. Often, the name of the news server will take the form news.myserviceprovider.com.

You can give the name in two different ways. You may have already entered the address of your discussion group server when you installed Communicator, or when you created a new profile. Or you may have entered the information when editing your profile using the Profile Manager. But if not, you can access this configuration option from any Communicator window.

> **TIP**
>
> *Before you can use discussion groups effectively in Communicator, you also need an e-mail account. If you have not configured Netscape Messenger to send and receive e-mail, please read Chapter 5.*

To configure a discussion group server in Communicator:

1. From any Communicator component, select Preferences from the Edit menu. Then click the Mail & Groups category to expand it, as shown in Figure 6-2.

2. Click the Groups Server category, as shown in Figure 6-3.

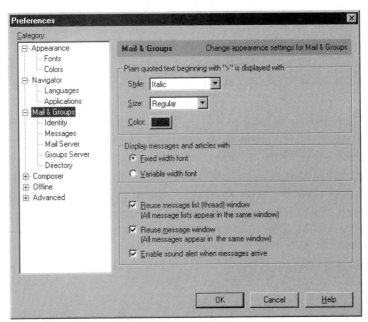

Figure 6-2: The expanded Mail & Groups category.

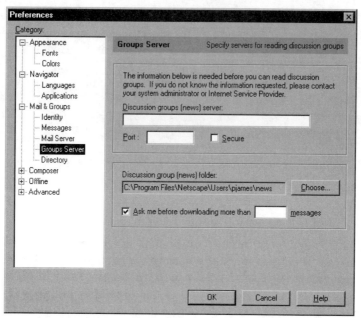

Figure 6-3: The Groups Server dialog box.

3. Enter the address of your Discussion groups (news) server. You should get this information from your network administrator if you're on an intranet or from your ISP if you're connecting to the Net by modem.

4. Leave the Discussion group folder field alone unless you want to change the location on your system where discussion group messages will be stored.

Perhaps I need to explain the last option in this dialog box. The more popular Usenet newsgroups are very busy, and it is not unusual for several hundred new messages to appear each day. When you tell a client program you want to get all new messages for a particular group from the server, you might not know what you're asking for! Thousands of messages may have accumulated since the last time you checked. Fortunately, Communicator lets you know when there are a high number of new messages. As long as you keep this option checked, the program will not only inform you when you're about to download more than 500 new messages, it will also give you the option of *limiting* the download to 500. And in the box to the right of the check box, you can change that limit of 500 to any number you want.

Figure 6-4 shows a completed Groups Server dialog box. Simply click OK to return to save your changes and return to Communicator.

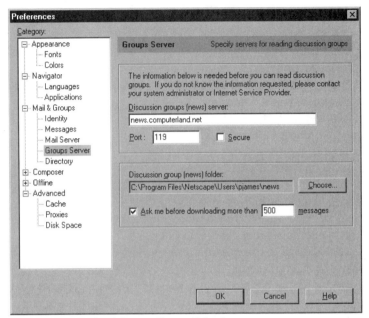

Figure 6-4: Completed Groups Server dialog box.

Getting Started: the Message Center

In Communicator, discussion groups are accessed via a window called the Message Center. You can make that window appear in three different ways:

- Click the Discussion Groups icon in the Communicator Component bar.
- Click the Discussion Groups icon in the Communicator folder on your desktop.
- From Messenger (see Chapter 5), click the Message Center button, which is at the far right, just underneath the large Netscape icon as shown in Figure 6-5.

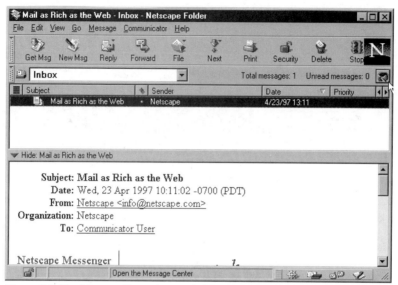

Figure 6-5: The Message Center button in Messenger.

TIP

You can also access a specific discussion group directly from the Navigator 4 window, either by clicking a link to that group or by entering its URL in the Location/Netsite box. URLs for newsgroups always begin with the prefix news://. For instance, to access the public discussion group alt.activism on the Computerland server, I would type news://news.computerland.net/alt.activism. This would bypass the Message Center window. Instead, I'd be taken directly to the discussion group window for alt.activism, showing the messages in that group.

No matter which of these methods you use, the results are the same. The Message Center window appears, as shown in Figure 6-6.

You may remember this window from the discussion of e-mail folders in Chapter 5. Notice that it contains not only your e-mail folders (Inbox, Drafts, Sent, and so on) but also the name of your discussion group server. You can see that I use four different discussion servers: secnews.netscape.com, news.computerland.net, edda.vmedia.com, and localhost (this last one is on my own machine and is just for testing). Using this number of servers is somewhat unusual—chances are, you use just one server for all your discussion group needs, but in the sidebar called "Adding Servers," I'll show you how you can access several different servers.

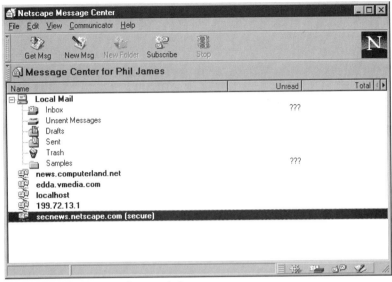

Figure 6-6: The Message Center window.

Discussion Host Properties

If you right-click a discussion group server in the Message Center window and then select Discussion Group Server Properties from the context menu, a dialog box appears giving you some added information about the server, as shown in Figure 6-7.

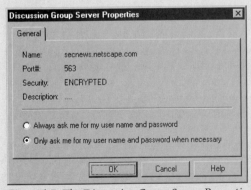

Figure 6-7: The Discussion Group Server Properties dialog box.

In this example, information from the discussion group server is encrypted, meaning that it is a special secure server (see Chapter 13). Additionally, it uses a different port from the standard 119 that is used by most public servers.

Notice the options at the bottom of the dialog box. If you are using a publicly accessible server that permits anonymous login, you would select the bottom option; otherwise, select the top option to transmit your username and password each time you log on to send or retrieve messages.

Why do some of the discussion group servers I use have plus signs to their left? The plus signs indicate that I have subscribed to one or more discussion groups on those servers. To expand the list, showing the actual discussion groups I've subscribed to, I simply click the plus signs (or double-click the server names). Figure 6-8 shows the expanded view of the servers, in which the discussion groups are listed.

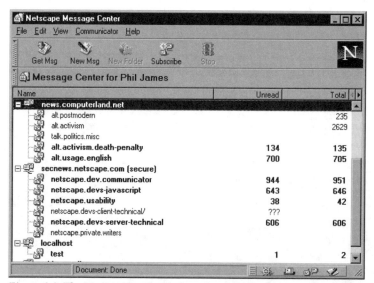

Figure 6-8: The Message Center window, showing discussion groups I've subscribed to.

To collapse this view, hiding the names of the actual discussion groups, click the minus signs or double-click the server names.

And, of course, this action brings up the next topic: how do you subscribe to discussion groups?

Subscribing to Discussion Groups

Communicator provides two different ways to subscribe to new discussion groups. If you know the name of the group, you can simply specify it. If, on the other hand, you don't know exactly which group or groups you want to join, you can browse a list of all available discussion groups on the server and make your choice from the list.

To specify a discussion group to join, follow these steps:

1. Make sure you are connected to your intranet or to the Net.

2. Using any of the methods outlined in the preceding section, open the Message Center window, as shown earlier in Figure 6-6.

3. Select your discussion group server by clicking its name.

4. Click the Subscribe button. The Subscribe to Discussion Groups window appears, as shown in Figure 6-9.

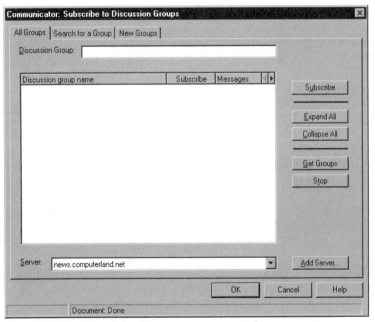

Figure 6-9: The Subscribe to Discussion Groups window.

You can also access this window by selecting the discussion server in the Message Center window, right-clicking, and selecting Subscribe to Discussion Groups from the context menu that appears.

TIP

Each of the tabs in the Subscribe to Discussion Groups window includes a drop-down Server list that lets you select a different discussion group server if you've configured more than one. You can even add a new server from here by clicking the Add Server button. See the sidebar called "Adding Servers."

After a few minutes, the window starts to fill with the list of all the discussion groups available on this server. If the list is long, this process might take a while. Finally, it looks something like the one in Figure 6-10.

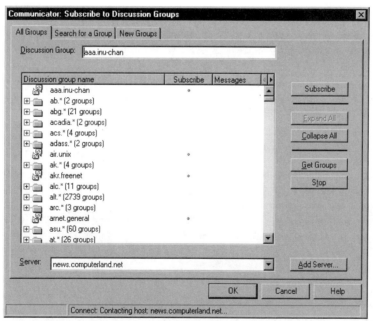

Figure 6-10: A complete list of discussion groups available on this server.

TIP

As Communicator retrieves the list of available groups, it immediately displays them. If the group or groups you're interested in have already appeared in the window, you can halt the retrieval of additional groups by clicking the Stop button. If you want to retrieve a more complete list some time later, simply click the Get Groups button.

Notice that some of the groups contain a wildcard character and may be expanded by clicking the plus sign to the left of the name. You can't subscribe to alt.*, for instance, but you could subscribe to any of the 2,632 *alt* groups that become available when you expand the hierarchy.

Let's give it a try:

1. Click the plus sign next to alt.*, or simply double-click the item itself. An expanded list appears, as shown in Figure 6-11.

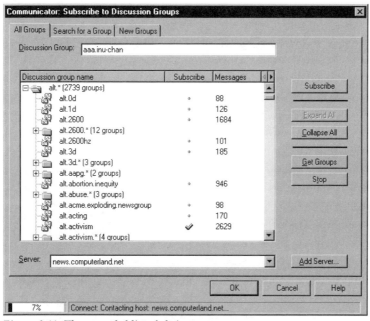

Figure 6-11: The expanded list of alt. groups.*

- Notice that some of the *alt* groups may be expanded to yet another level.

- You can also expand and collapse the display of groups using the Expand All and Collapse All buttons. Expand All, however, expands the display to include *all* levels underneath the selected level, not just the next level. Once you click Expand All, you won't need to click any more plus signs. Conversely, Collapse All shrinks the display of the discussion groups so that only the selected level appears.

2. When you find a discussion group you want to subscribe to, select it and click the Subscribe button. Or just click the dot in the Subscribe column next to any groups you want to subscribe to. In either case, a checkmark appears in the Subscribe column. Figure 6-12 shows the list of *alt* groups with several checked for subscription.

- To *un*subscribe from a group, simply click the checkmark.

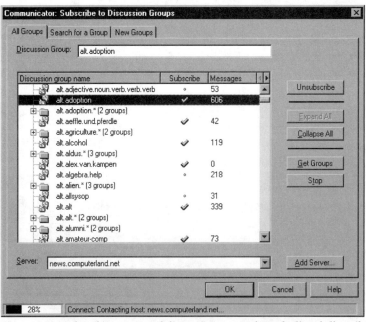

Figure 6-12: Subscribing to several discussion groups from the list of all available groups.

Searching for Groups

Maybe you don't know the exact name of a discussion group you want to subscribe to, but browsing through a long list of available groups could be very tedious. Communicator provides a search utility to help you find a group you're interested in.

To find a discussion group in a particular area of interest, follow these steps:

1. Still in the Subscribe to Discussion Groups window, select the Search for a Group tab, as shown in Figure 6-13.

2. Enter a word to search for and click the Search Now button. Figure 6-14 shows the results of searching for any groups that contain the word "aviation."

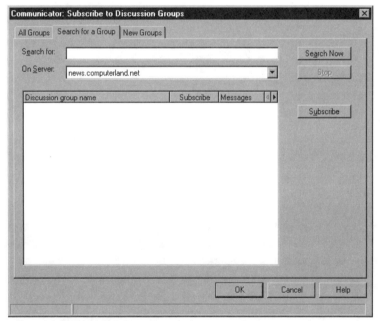

Figure 6-13: The Search for a Group tab.

TIP

Looking for business newsgroups? Try these: misc.business.consulting, misc.business.marketing.moderated, misc.business.records-mgmt, and misc.entrepreneurs.moderated.

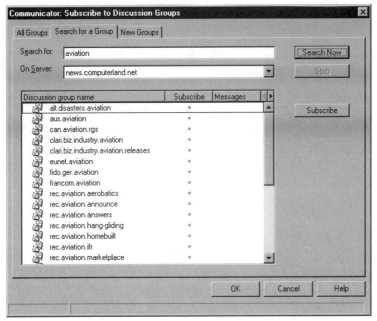

Figure 6-14: Aviation-related groups available on the server.

You can subscribe to groups right in this search window by selecting them and clicking Subscribe. Alternatively, you can just click the Subscribe column for any groups you're interested in. And remember, you can *un*subscribe from any group by clicking the checkmark in the Subscribe column.

Other Ways to Find Public Discussion Groups

There are a number of lists of public discussion groups available online. One of the best is at http://home.netscape.com/escapes/newsgroups/index.html. This list is organized by category and includes brief descriptions of each group. If you're using Navigator 4 to view this site, clicking a group name automatically opens a discussion group window and displays current messages in the group. Another such service with descriptions and a search feature is provided by http://tile.net/news/.

Some sites, including Netscape's own, host discussion groups about their products. At the Netscape site (http://home.netscape.com) for example, click Assistance and then User Groups. This will take you to http://help.netscape.com/nuggies/, where you can click on a discussion group of interest and not only open the group but also add its server.

Displaying New Discussion Groups

Periodically, most discussion group servers add new groups. They may be private groups that somebody in your company has created, or they may be new Usenet newsgroups that have become available on the Net. Communicator provides a separate view of any discussion groups that have been added since the last time you clicked the Clear New button. Let's take a look:

1. Still in the Subscribe to Discussion Groups window, click the New Groups tab, as shown in Figure 6-15.

2. Subscribe to any new groups following the procedures outlined in the preceding two sections.

3. To clear the list of new groups, click Clear New.

If no new discussion groups are listed, you may not have retrieved a list since the last time you clicked the Clear New button. Try clicking Get New and see what appears.

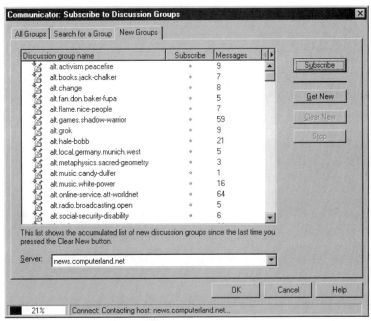

Figure 6-15: The New Groups tab.

Adding Servers

As I mentioned earlier, Communicator lets you participate in discussion groups on more than one server. And adding a server is simple:

1. In the Message Center's File menu, click New Discussion Group Server. Or, in the Subscribe to Discussion Groups window discussed in the preceding sections, click the Add Server button. In either case, the New Discussion Groups Server dialog box appears, as shown in Figure 6-16.

Figure 6-16: The New Discussion Groups Server dialog box.

2. Enter the domain name of the server in the Server field.

3. Unless your network administrator or ISP has given you specific instructions, leave the Port field set to 119.

4. If your network administrator has told you this server is secure, check the Secure check box.

5. If this server requires a name and password for access, check the Always use name and password check box. Most servers maintained by ISPs do not require this option to be checked.

After you have completed the dialog box, click Add. Your new server now appears in the Message Center window as well as in the drop-down list of servers in the Subscribe to Discussion Groups window.

Retrieving Discussion Group Messages

Now we're up to the fun part.

OK, you've subscribed to a discussion group or two and are ready to see what people are talking—or typing—about. Here goes:

1. Make sure you're connected to your intranet or to the Net.

2. Launch Collabra Discussion Groups by clicking its icon on the desktop, by clicking the Discussion Groups button on the Component bar, or by clicking the Message Center button in Messenger. The Message Center appears (as shown earlier in Figure 6-6).

3. Click the plus sign to the left of the discussion server you want to use. The display now includes a list of all the discussion groups you've subscribed to on that server, as shown in Figure 6-17.

4. Double-click the name of the discussion group you want to retrieve.

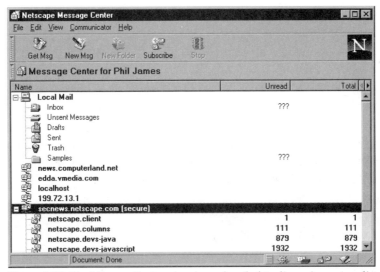

Figure 6-17: The Message Center, showing subscribed-to discussion groups listed under the server name.

Right-clicking a Discussion Group

As in most areas of Communicator, right-clicking the name of a discussion group from the list brings up a context menu that provides access to a variety of commands and features. In this case, Figure 6-18 shows what you get:

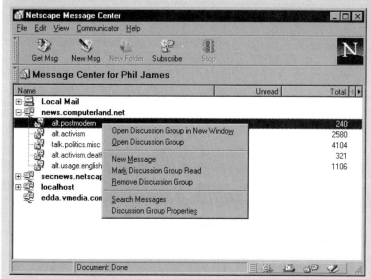

Figure 6-18: The context menu for a discussion group.

Most of these options are self-explanatory. You can open the group (the same as double-clicking it), remove the group (unsubscribe from it), create a new message, or mark all the messages in the group as read. You can also view the properties of the particular group and search for text within its messages. See the section called "Searching Your Discussion Group Messages" later in this chapter.

As soon as you double-click the name of a discussion group, a couple of different windows may pop up:

■ You may be presented with a dialog box that indicates more than a certain number of new message headers appear in the group, as shown in Figure 6-19.

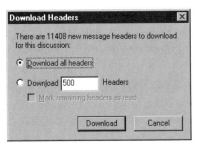

Figure 6-19: The Download Headers dialog box.

■ If you want *all* the new messages to appear in the message list pane, simply click Download. If you want to download only a certain number, select the second option button; you also can change the number. If you select the second option button and specify 100, for instance, Communicator will display only the 100 newest messages in the discussion group.

■ The bottom check box lets you automatically mark all the remaining messages—the ones you don't download—as read. They therefore will not be downloaded the next time you click Get Msg or double-click the discussion group. After you have decided how you want to limit incoming messages, if at all, just click Download.

■ And why message *headers?* Communicator's Discussion Groups component does not immediately download actual message content, but only the information to include in the message list pane. When you select a message, the actual content is immediately downloaded. Obviously, this feature conserves disk space.

TIP

You can prevent the Download Headers dialog box from appearing by changing the default limit (500 messages) that triggers it or by disabling this feature altogether. To make these changes, select Preferences from the Edit menu of any Communicator component. If the Mail & Discussion Groups category is not expanded to show its subcategories, double-click it or click the plus sign. Next, click the Groups Server category. You'll find the options I'm talking about at the bottom of the right-hand dialog box. Simply select the Ask me. . . check box to remove the checkmark or change the number to its right.

■ If you're connecting to a private discussion group that requires a username and password, dialog boxes requesting these elements may appear. Simply enter the information and click OK for each of the dialog boxes.

Once you have responded to any of these message limit or security dialog boxes, you're in the main discussion group window, as shown in Figure 6-20.

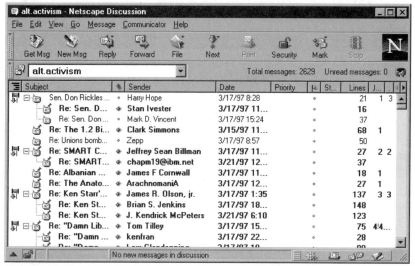

Figure 6-20: The main discussion group window displaying message headers from the alt.activism newsgroup.

TIP

You can create a desktop shortcut to a particular discussion group. In the discussion group window, click the small icon to the left of the discussion group name. Then simply drag the icon onto your desktop.

Downloading all the message headers might take a while. A progress bar on the status line indicates the progress of the download. You can halt the download at any time by clicking the Stop button.

The new window looks almost exactly like your e-mail Inbox window, but a few significant differences are apparent:

■ The Delete button has been replaced with a Mark button. That's because marking messages in various ways is a very important function when you're dealing with discussion groups, since the volume of messages may be much greater than it is with personal e-mail. You may want to select large batches of messages to mark as read, for example.

■ Message size is indicated as a number of lines rather than a number of bytes.

■ The messages are automatically sorted in thread order. Of all the different ways you can sort messages in Communicator, thread order makes the most sense for discussion groups. Especially in large groups, many different conversations may be going on at once, and you need to be able to isolate these threads so that you can work with them effectively. Remember, the initial message of each thread is indicated by a plus sign and a special icon to its left. If you click the plus sign, it expands the thread, revealing all the subsequent messages; if you click the icon, it selects the entire thread.

TIP

Don't know what I'm talking about with this thread stuff? If not, go back and read the section called "Threading" in Chapter 5.

Marking Discussion Group Messages

Due to the volume of messages in public discussion groups, marking them may be your key to staying organized. Clicking the Mark button lets you mark messages or groups of messages in a variety of ways:

■ **Read:** This option marks the selected message or messages as read.

■ **Unread:** This option lets you return a message marked as read to its original unread status.

■ **Thread Read:** This option lets you mark an entire thread as read, even though you have selected only the initial message of the thread.

■ **Category Read:** Categories are subfolders within a discussion group. They are supported by Collabra servers. For example, a Human Resources discussion group on your intranet may include a Personnel Policies category. This option lets you mark an entire category as read.

■ **All Read:** This option lets you mark all the messages in the discussion group as read.

■ **by Date:** This option lets you mark as read all messages before a particular date so that you don't have to read through old material. When you select this option, a dialog box appears asking you to specify the cut-off date.

■ **for Later:** This option marks selected messages as read for this session only. In subsequent sessions, they will appear as unread.

Reading Messages

The process of reading messages works just like e-mail. To read a message, simply select it by clicking. Communicator immediately downloads the message content and displays it in the bottom pane of the window. Clicking the Next button always takes you to the next *unread* message.

Just as with e-mail, you can hide the content pane by clicking the arrow between the two panes, and you can display a message in its own window by double-clicking it. And just like e-mail messages, discussion group postings may include links to Web pages or to other discussion groups. In fact, every discussion group message includes a header with clickable links to all the different groups to which this particular message has been posted. You can see an example of these links in Figure 6-21.

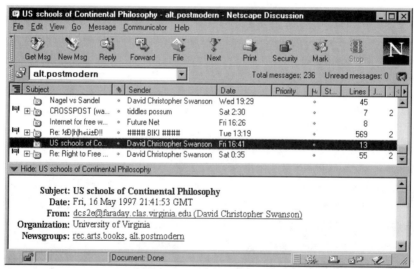

Figure 6-21: The Newsgroups header in a discussion group message, showing all the groups to which this message has been posted.

Click one of these links and you are transported to the new discussion group—as long as it's available on your server. As for the numbers in the References header, they are simply links to other messages in the same discussion thread. The numeral 1 denotes the original message in the thread; the numeral 2 denotes the second message; and so on. You can go directly to the referenced message by clicking the numeral.

> **TIP**
>
> *Just as with e-mail messages, you can choose to see more or less of this header information. Click Headers in the View menu and then select All, Normal, or Brief, from the submenu that appears.*

From the discussion group window, you can collect new messages from the server at any time by clicking the Get Msg button.

Saving Disk Space

Since discussion groups may include hundreds or even thousands of active messages, Communicator provides a number of options for storing them.

Select Preferences from the Edit menu of any Communicator component, then expand the Advanced category and select Disk Space, as shown in Figure 6-22.

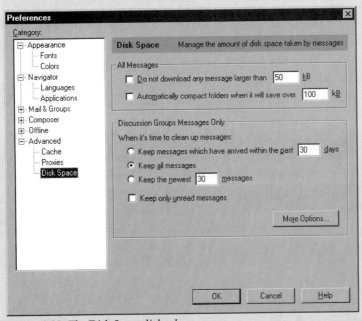

Figure 6-22: The Disk Space dialog box.

- To restrict the retrieval of messages to those smaller than a certain size, check the first check box and specify a size.

- Communicator includes a facility for compacting folders (eliminating wasted space from deleted messages). You use this facility by choosing Compact Folders from the File menu, but you can also configure the program so that it prompts you to compact folders when the resulting savings in disk space would be greater than a specified amount. To activate this prompting feature, check the second check box and enter an amount in kilobytes.

- To limit the time that messages are stored, select the first option button in the Discussion Groups Messages Only section of this dialog box, and then specify the maximum time that messages should stay on your system.

- To keep all messages until you explicitly delete them, select the Keep all messages option button.

  To keep only a certain number of new messages for each discussion group, click the next option button and specify a number.

- If you want to keep only unread messages and automatically discard all read messages whenever you leave the discussion group window, check the bottom check box. **Note:** If you check this check box, the previous three options affect only unread messages.

- Now click the More Options button for more disk space choices, as shown in Figure 6-23.

Figure 6-23: The More Disk Space Options dialog box.

Remember that when you select a message in the message list pane, it is downloaded to your computer. But if you check the check box here, Communicator will automatically delete the contents of all discussion group messages older than a specified number of days. The message description remains in the message list pane, but the contents are re-downloaded if you select the message. **Caution:** Obviously, discussion group servers don't keep messages forever— they are periodically removed or "scrolled off." If you configure Communicator so that it automatically deletes the contents of old messages, you might not be able to retrieve those messages later from the server even though they still appear in the message list. Of course, old messages may still be accessible via a newsgroup search service which has its own archive database. For example, see DejaNews at http://www.dejanews.com/forms/dnq.html.

Replying to Messages

Again, the process of replying to messages works almost exactly like e-mail. Select a message you want to respond to, and then follow these steps:

1. Click the Reply button. A submenu appears with several reply options, as shown in Figure 6-24.

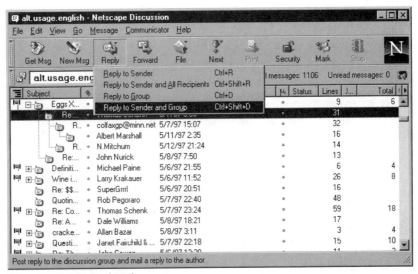

Figure 6-24: The Reply submenu.

2. Select one of the options:

- To send a private "offline" e-mail response to the author of the original message, click Reply to Sender. In this case, your message will *not* be available to other members of the discussion group.

- To send a private "offline" e-mail response to the author of the original message *and* to all of his or her intended recipients, click Reply to Sender and All Recipients.

- To reply to the discussion group as a whole (in other words, to make your response available to everyone in the group), click Reply to Group.

- To make your response available to this group as a whole *and* to send it privately to the message originator, click Reply to Sender and Group. This option assures that the message originator reads your response in a timely fashion.

After you've selected an option, the Message Composition window appears, as shown in Figure 6-25.

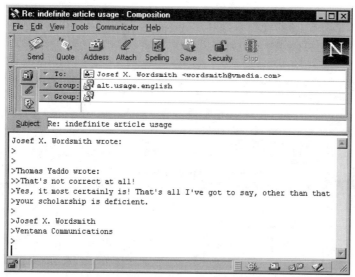

Figure 6-25: The Message Composition window after clicking Reply to Sender and Group.

TIP

Notice that the address fields include all the groups to which the original message was posted. If you leave these fields alone, you will be continuing the same thread in each of these discussion groups. If you do not think your response is appropriate to any of the groups, simply delete that address.

3. Enter your response just as you would enter an e-mail message. Although Communicator lets you beautify your message with all kinds of HTML formatting, I recommend avoiding this in messages intended for public Usenet groups. Many readers will have client software that cannot interpret the HTML commands correctly. However, you should have no problem with attaching images to your messages. In fact, thousands of JPEG images are distributed in public newsgroups every day.

TIP

You may want to edit the quoted message in your response, saving only those portions that you are responding to directly. Discussion group messages are often composed of original text interspersed with brief quoted sections of the original posting.

4. When you finish addressing and writing your message, click Send. Your message is delivered to your discussion group server. If you're responding to a public Usenet group, your message then makes its way to thousands of other discussion group servers.

Initiating a New Thread

In addition to responding to messages that already exist in discussion groups, you can start a new thread yourself. Doing so is as simple as sending an e-mail message.

1. In Communicator's Message Center, click a discussion group. Alternatively, if you're already in Messenger, you can simply select the discussion group from the drop-down list of mail folders and discussion groups.

2. Once the discussion group window is displayed, click the New Msg button. A blank Message Composition window appears, as shown in Figure 6-26.

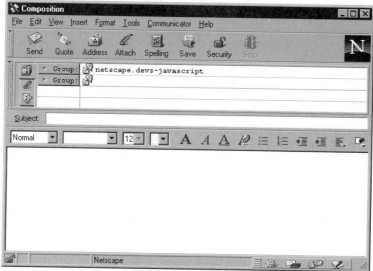

Figure 6-26: A new Message Composition window.

Notice that the first address field is automatically filled in with the name of this group. You can add other groups for your message as well, or you can click the Group button and then select To or CC to send your message simultaneously to an individual via e-mail.

3. Using any of the procedures you learned in Chapter 5, create a new message.

4. Once you have completed your message, click the Send button.

That's all there is to it! Your new message is transferred to your discussion server as well as to any e-mail recipients you've specified. If you're posting your message to a public Usenet group, within hours it will start appearing on servers all around the world. The next time you get new messages you might have several responses in your thread.

Searching Your Discussion Group Messages

As you start to receive more discussion group messages, you may lose track of what each one is about. Fortunately, Communicator provides a powerful search feature. To use it, select Message Search from the Edit menu. A Search Messages dialog box appears, as shown in Figure 6-27.

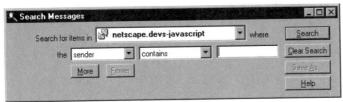

Figure 6-27: The Search Messages dialog box.

Notice that the Search for items in field already contains the name of the current discussion group. To broaden the scope of the search, click the down arrow to the right of the field. From the submenu that appears, you can choose to search any group you want.

Next, construct a search criterion by completing the three boxes in the middle of the dialog. In the first box, choose whether you want to search the sender field or the subject header of the message. Next, select an item from the second box. Does the area of the message you've chosen contain the word? Or does it begin or end with the word? Finally, type in the word (or partial word) you're interested in. If you need to make your search more precise by specifying more search criteria, click the More button and keep working. Clicking this button lets you develop very complex searches.

After you've completed your search criteria, simply click the Search button. If the item you're searching for exists, Communicator finds what you're looking for.

The software also supports a much simpler kind of search for text within individual messages. With a message selected, simply press Ctrl+F or select Find in Message from the Edit menu. To find subsequent occurrences of the same word, simply press Ctrl+G or select Find Again from the Edit menu.

Going Offline

Communicator lets you go offline—i.e., disconnect from your intranet or the Net—simply by clicking Go Offline in the File menu. But you may want to finish some discussion group business before actually disconnecting. Luckily, when you click the Go Offline item a Download dialog box appears, as shown in Figure 6-28.

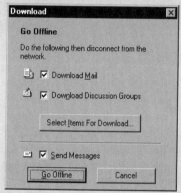

Figure 6-28: The Download dialog box appears before going offline.

As you can see, this dialog box lets you retrieve new mail and send any messages in your Outbox before actually disconnecting. It also lets you get the latest discussion group messages from any groups you specify using the Select Discussion Groups button. Simply check or uncheck the Choose field in the list that appears.

Moving On

Discussion groups are one of the most flexible new communications tools. You can use them to collaborate on projects at work, to ferret out arcane information, to confer with experts in particular areas of interest, and to participate in giant slow-motion conversations. Discussion groups provide both increased efficiency and virtually endless opportunities for sharing ideas and information.

In the next chapter, you'll learn more about what makes Communicator a real multimedia program, as we cover the basics of graphics, sound, and video.

CHAPTER 7

Media on the Move: Working With Sound & Video

By now you have some idea what Netscape Communicator has to offer. Unlike simple browser programs, you can use Communicator not only to gather information, but also to subscribe to Web channels, exchange e-mail, read discussion groups, and collaborate with coworkers. That's great, but when we talk about it in the abstract it doesn't sound all that exciting, does it? To understand why the Web and related resources have generated so much excitement, you really have to take a look—and a listen! It's the multimedia aspects of the new communications technology that have insured its acceptance beyond the world of government offices and college labs. We all like pictures; we all like sound. Pictures and sound are how we amuse ourselves—and how people sell us stuff.

Netscape Communicator offers fuller support for multimedia than any other communications program to date. As a Communicator user, you now have at your fingertips a vast assortment of multimedia documents that virtually come to life when you view them.

Multimedia Mail

In this chapter I'll generally depict multimedia documents in Navigator 4, Communicator's browser window. But Messenger, Netcaster, and Collabra discussion groups support the same kinds of graphics, video, and sound. I've viewed some amazing video clips out on the Web, but I've also received a couple of pretty surprising singing telegrams in my e-mail! The only difference is what window they appear in.

Graphics on the Web

Pictures play an important role in our lives: we hang them on our walls; we pay money to stand and look at them in museums; we take snapshots of our loved ones and favorite places. Pictures are perhaps the most common form of communication in our society, and that is becoming true for online communications as well. In fact, much of the growth and popularity of the Web and of intranets is a result of people like you and me having a new way to gather and disseminate information in a colorful and creative way.

In the following sections, you'll read about the types of graphics that are available on the Internet or your office intranet. And of course you'll learn how you can view and download them with Netscape Communicator.

What Kinds of Images Are Available?

Each month, thousands of new Web pages are created and placed online. Almost all of them contain some sort of graphic. Graphics can be small or large, colorful or black and white, tasteful or tasteless. You can probably find the exact image you're looking for on the Web, if you look long enough. It may not be legally posted there, but it will be there (I discuss copyright infringement later in this chapter).

So what kinds of images can you expect to find on the Web? Almost anything. There are:

- Paintings by Renoir, Van Gogh, and little Jimmy from Ms. Wharton's first grade class.

- Publicity shots of your favorite movie and television stars, including Moe Howard, Jim Carrey, and Wynona Rider.

- Detailed weather maps.

- More *Star Trek* and *Deep Space Nine* photos than we care to know about.

- Colorful advertisements from IBM and Microsoft and Absolut and Ford and...

- Cartoons and animations.

- And yes, even pictures of naked people, if you look in the right places.

Graphics in Netscape Communicator 4: an Overview

Fortunately for all you picture lovers, Communicator includes features that let you view the vast majority of graphics on the Web. Graphics appear in a variety of sizes, shapes, and formats. In one way or another, Netscape Communicator can either display them or provide an easy way for you to view them in another application. The best way to understand the types of graphics and how they display is to link to a fairly typical site.

TIP

In this chapter I'll be using examples from the Internet, but the principles and procedures are the same on an office intranet. In other words, you should probably go ahead and read this chapter, even if you're not connected to the Net.

To view a graphic in Netscape Communicator:

1. Make sure you are connected to the Internet.

2. Double-click the Netscape Navigator 4 or Communicator icon to launch the program. The Navigator 4 window appears, and the Netscape home page starts loading.

3. Click your mouse inside the Netsite/Location field at the top of the window to select the URL http://home.netscape.com/.

4. Replace the URL with the one for the Ventana Online page by entering **http://www.vmedia.com** (or simply **vmedia**). Then press Enter. Navigator 4 retrieves the Ventana Online page, as shown in Figure 7-1.

Figure 7-1: The Ventana Online page.

Notice that Navigator displays text first, then fills in the graphics. Sometimes you see a description of the graphics before it starts loading, in the top left corner of its frame. On the Ventana page, the big "Ventana" is really a graphic image. In fact, although there are plenty of words, there is very little actual text on this page: almost everything is done with graphics. Notice also the animated gears. Simple animation like this has become a common special effect in Web pages.

TIP

Animations add life to a Web page, but they can also slow down the display of other information. Navigator 4 makes it easy to disable animations. Simply select Stop Animations from the View menu.

Have I Got the Entire Document?

Many Web pages take some time to download to your computer. How can you be sure you've received the whole thing? Navigator 4 provides several clues.

First, you can look at the status line at the bottom of the browser window. This area indicates the transfer progress of the Web document. Toward the left side of the status line, just to the right of the paddle lock icon, a gray bar moves horizontally whenever Navigator is in the process of downloading information. And to the right of the progress bar, in the central portion of the status line, a readout displays the size, percentage downloaded, and the rate at which Navigator 4 is retrieving the document or components it references. You may have a difficult time reading this line because it's constantly changing as different graphics or other elements of the page start to download, but it will give some idea of how fast things are going. When the document has completely transferred, the gray bar disappears and the status line laconically reads Document: Done.

Another way to see if a document is still transferring is to watch the animated Netscape logo in the top right corner of the window. As the document transfers, a meteor shower streams across the big Netscape *N*. When the shower ends, the document has finished downloading and all the graphics are displayed.

On a Web page like the one shown in Figure 7-1, you may see several different graphics and notice that they're used in a variety of ways. By far the most prevalent type of image you encounter in Web pages is an *inline graphic*. Inline graphics are part of the Web document itself; they appear alongside the text.

Inline graphics can include photos, buttons, icons, cartoons, and many other types of pictures. They are used for the following purposes:

- Logos
- Decorations
- Bullet points
- Illustrations
- Separators

Sometimes graphics are not inline, but exist only as a separate image file that you can download to your hard disk for later viewing, or one that you need to view in a separate application from Netscape Communicator. One common external viewer is LView Pro, which was used to display the graphic shown in Figure 7-2. You'll learn more about these types of images and how to view them in the section entitled "Graphics on Demand," later in this chapter.

Figure 7-2: A graphic displayed in LView Pro.

When you connect to a site, such as http://www.vmedia.com (Ventana's Web site), the Web document begins to transfer to your computer and appears in the browser window. As the document displays, you usually see some text first, and then the graphics begin to appear. Depending on the speed of your connection, images may seem to flow in line by line or pop right up along with the text. It all has to do with the amount of data that your modem or dedicated line can transmit to your computer monitor. For example, high-speed connections, such as ISDN or T1 lines, can transmit more data per second than modem connections.

TIP

Tired of waiting for a document's images to display? Click the Stop button on the Navigator 4 Control Toolbar to stop the transfer. If you want to re-initiate the transfer later, click Reload.

Or turn off the automatic display of graphics entirely, as described later in this chapter under "Text-Only Mode."

To accommodate users with all kinds of connections, some sites offer two different versions of the same page. One page usually includes a lot of graphics, that a typical modem user will not want to wait to download to his or her computer. The other usually has very few images and mostly text. When you link to a site that has these options, such as the Internet Underground Music Archive (IUMA), you must make a choice to view the page with a lot of images, or one that has been toned down a little to avoid unnecessary waiting.

Figure 7-3 shows you the site when you choose to see the graphics-intensive pages. Figure 7-4 shows what you'll see if you choose the same pages with fewer graphics. Running with a 14.4 Kbps modem, the graphics-intensive page took more than 2 minutes to display. The "lite" version took only 12 seconds!

Figure 7-3: The IUMA site with lots of graphics.

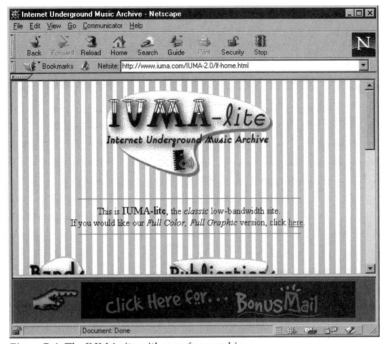

Figure 7-4: The IUMA site with very few graphics.

TIP

Most sites include the same textual information in both their graphics version and their text-only pages—the only thing you'll miss are the images themselves.

Later you'll learn how to optimize the display of graphics in Netscape Communicator, but first, let's discuss a couple of special-purpose graphics often used in Web pages: background images and icons.

Background Images

Background images do just what their name implies—they provide the background to the text and other graphics in a Web document. Background images typically are very small images that are repeated again and again over the entire background. (This technique is sometimes referred to as *texture mapping* in graphics design programs.) The images can be solid colors, textures, patterns, or whatever the Web author comes up with. For example, the Graphion home page pictured in Figure 7-5 shows a gray granite background. Some other backgrounds that you may encounter include marble, wood grain, and metallic, but occasionally you'll even see some company's logo repeated a hundred times across your screen. *Blech!!*

Figure 7-5: Graphion's home page, showing a gray granite background.

When you create a Web page with Composer or some other HTML editor, you can specify an image to be used as the background. (As you saw in Chapter 5, you can even add an image background to your e-mail!) Not all Web sites use backgrounds, but it's fast becoming the norm. Backgrounds offer the Web author a way to set a standard color, texture, or image for the entire Web site.

Icons

Icons are another type of graphic you'll encounter on almost all Web pages. Icons are small images or buttons, sometimes miniatures of larger images you can find at that site. Icons are used to highlight certain points on the page, lead you to another Web page or site, or let you view or download a larger image. Let's look at each of these uses.

In Figure 7-6, you see a set of icons to the left of some text on the Web page. These icons serve the same purpose that bullets do in a book or business document: to distinguish key points. Icons can also be used to highlight special text on a page.

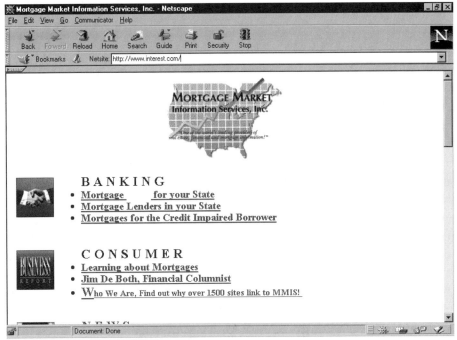

Figure 7-6: Icons emphasize important text on the page (© Mortgage Market Information Services, Inc.).

The second type of icon is actually a hotspot that links to another page or another site, sometimes to graphics of products or announcements. This type of icon works the same as linked text on a page—when you click it, you connect to that other site or page. Icons of this type sometimes have a small blue border around them to indicate that they are links. Figure 7-7 shows examples of icons that you click to advance to another related site.

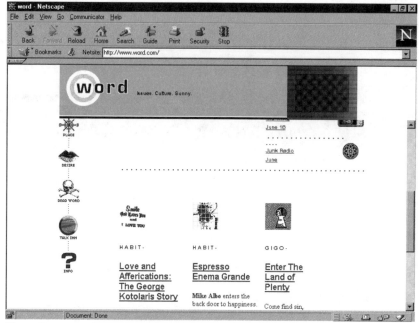

Figure 7-7: Icons that provide links.

Icons are also used as small "try-before-you-download" versions of larger graphics. When you click this kind of icon, often called a *thumbnail*, the larger image begins to transfer. The advantage of this approach is obvious: the smaller thumbnails transfer to your machine much more quickly than full images you may not even be interested in.

For example, the Web page in Figure 7-8 shows small icons of Renoir paintings (http://sunsite.unc.edu/wm/paint/auth/renoir/). You can scroll down the page and click the painting you'd like to see in full size. Now a larger painting displays in Navigator 4, as shown in Figure 7-9.

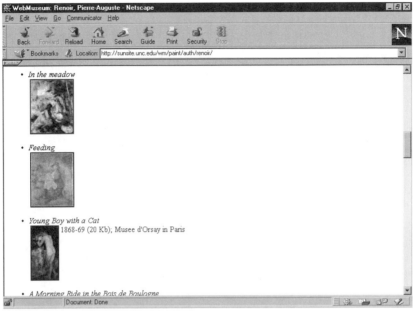

Figure 7-8: Thumbnail of a painting.

Figure 7-9: Full view of the same painting.

TIP

Some conscientious Web page authors include file sizes and estimated transfer times next to icons or thumbnails. Use these estimates to determine if the wait is going to be worth it. When I am on these sites, I find the smallest file and download it first. If I don't like the quality, I probably will not download another one.

Graphics Formats Supported by Netscape Communicator 4

The graphics in Web documents typically come in standard file formats that most Web browsers, such as Navigator 4, can understand and display on your computer. The standard file formats include Graphics Interchange Format (GIF), Joint Photographic Experts Group (JPEG), and XBM. GIF and JPEG are the most common graphics you'll encounter in Web pages. XBM is a UNIX graphics format and is more likely to be found at university or research areas that generally work with high-speed computing applications. Navigator 4 natively supports these three graphics formats. That means that when the program encounters a GIF, JPEG, or XBM file, it displays it automatically in the browser window.

Though GIF and JPEG are the most common, many other types of graphics formats appear occasionally on the Web, including Macintosh PICT, BMP, PCX, TIFF, and encapsulated PostScript (EPS) formats. A brand new standard called PNG (Portable Network Graphics) is starting to become prominent as well. Later in this chapter in the section on plug-ins, you'll learn how to extend Communicator's multimedia powers so that it supports some of the less-common image formats. With plug-ins, you don't have to run another program to view these graphics—they are displayed right within the Navigator window.

Both GIF and JPEG as well as other image files are compressed to save transmission time and to limit their storage size. It is beyond the scope of this book to get into the technical differences between JPEGs and GIFs, but the two formats excel in different areas. JPEG compression is often used for ultra-realistic photographic images, while GIF is used for colorful graphics. GIF images may also be *transparent*. Transparent GIFs are graphic files that have been customized to eliminate the background color of the image. Thus they appear to "float" on top of the Web page instead of being stuck inside a rectangular prison. There are even animated GIFs, files which contain a set of images that are automatically and repeatedly "flipped through" like a card deck to provide a simple simulation of motion.

TIP

JPEG files generally have an extension of .JPG; GIF files always have an extension of .GIF.

PNG Graphics

JPEG and GIF files have been *the* Web standard for a long time, but it may not last forever. The new PNG (Portable Network Graphics) standard offers some significant advantages:

- More colors—PNG images may contain literally trillions of colors.

- Smaller file size—due to new compression techniques, PNG images may be up to 30% smaller than equivalent GIF images.

- Enhanced transparency—PNG graphics may contain several layers or levels of transparency.

- Searchable content—PNG images may contain special embedded "meta" information about content or authorship. A viewer can search for this information just like text.

Graphics on Demand

Some Web sites offer images you can download to your computer for subsequent viewing. These differ from inline graphics because they are not part of the text of the Web page display, but are only *linked to* the document. You can still view many of these files in Navigator 4, using it simply as a file viewer instead of a Web browser. Or, if you want to edit the file or save it in a different format, you can view it in a stand-alone graphics application such as Paint Shop Pro.

At the Saturn Web site shown in Figure 7-10, for example, you can download a picture of one of the auto maker's new models and then view it in the Navigator 4 window.

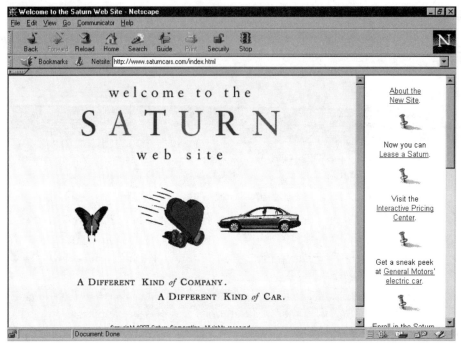

Figure 7-10: The Saturn Web site.

To download a picture:

1. Make sure you are connected to the Internet. If Netscape Navigator 4 is not currently running, launch it by double-clicking its icon or the Communicator icon.

2. In the Netsite/Location box at the top of the window, select the currently displayed URL and replace it with the following address on the Saturn Web site: **http://www.saturncars.com/car/97-Models/SL/index.html**. Press Enter.

TIP

Remember, you can abbreviate URLs. Leave off the http:// if you want.

3. After the Web document transfers to your computer and displays, you'll see that the right-hand frame contains small pictures of the Saturn SL/SL1 taken from various angles. Click on any one of these photos to view a full-size picture. Now Navigator displays the larger picture in the left-hand frame, as shown in Figure 7-11.

Figure 7-11: The Saturn SL/SL1: thumbnail picture to the right, full-size picture to the left.

TIP

Want to see the image on its own, without the frames? Right-click it and select View Image from the context menu that appears. The image is now displayed in the browser window on its own. To return to the frames, simply click the Back button.

Who Owns the Image?

The easy answer to this question is "probably not you." Almost every image on the World Wide Web and the Internet is owned by someone or by a legal corporation. Don't think that just because you can download an image to your computer's hard disk you own the rights to the file. In most cases, you do not. In fact, some images have been placed on the Web illegally, without permission from their owners. By downloading these images, you may also be breaking the law.

Fortunately, most sites comply with international copyright laws and make available only those images they own or have legally licensed from another party. These images are provided for you to view but typically are not for reuse in any form.

Some sites legally allow you to download graphics for use in commercial or noncommercial ways. Clip-art images, for example, fall into this category. Many sites offer downloadable images that you can incorporate in business documents, Web documents, and other sources. But remember, you are still responsible for making sure that the images you download are indeed owned or licensed by the person providing them.

Other sites require that you first pay a fee to acquire the rights to view and download images. Sites such as MTV, Sony, and Playboy, offer repositories like this. Again, copyright laws restrict you from reselling these images as your own. You can only look at them; you can't plaster them all over Usenet newsgroups.

Now that the full-size image is onscreen, what can you do with it? Not much, since Netscape Communicator is designed only as a *viewer* of certain graphics types, not as a full-featured graphics editor. But what you *can* do is save the image to your hard disk for later viewing, editing, or other processing. If you enjoy a particular image and you've waited several minutes for it to transfer to your machine, you owe it to yourself to save it to disk.

To save an image to disk:

1. Right-click the image and then select Save Image As from Navigator 4's File menu. The Save As dialog box appears, as shown in Figure 7-12.

Figure 7-12: The Save As dialog box.

2. Choose a location for the file and then click the Save button. The Saving Location dialog box appears, showing the progress of the file transfer.

   ■ Because the file has already been downloaded to your computer, it takes only a few seconds to save it to the appropriate location on your disk.

3. Click the Back button to return to the previous Web page.

Redecorating Your Desktop

Not only can you save any image you encounter on the Web, you can even set it as your Windows wallpaper. Netscape Communicator makes this so easy that you may end up with all kinds of wacked-out designs on your screen. You should see my "At Home with Dom DeLuise" wallpaper.

To save an image as your Windows wallpaper:

1. Place your cursor over the image.

2. Click the right mouse button.

3. Select Set As Wallpaper from the context menu that appears.

Once you have set your new wallpaper, you may want to configure your system so that the image is tiled instead of centered. To make this change, click the Display icon in Control Panel, select the Background tab, and set the Netscape Wallpaper to Tile rather than Center.

Text-Only Mode

They say a picture is worth a thousand words, but we writers have never bought that. In spite of all the dire warnings of bow-tied professors, we have not degenerated into an illiterate society that worships only images. In fact as technology gets better and better at surrounding us with imagery, more and more *words* get published! Just look at how thick this book is. I use the Macintosh version of the book as a platform for my monitor.

You really see how important words are when you have a modem connection to the Net. If you have a slow modem and have been following the various links in this chapter, you're probably growing tired of waiting for some of the documents to transfer. In fact, if you have a modem that operates at less than 28.8 Kbps, you may already be working on next year's letter to Santa. But besides speeding up your Internet connection, there is another approach: you can bypass graphics altogether.

Navigator 4 gives you the option of turning off the automatic display of graphics by deselecting the "Automatically load images" option in Advanced settings. When this option is turned off, a small icon appears as a placeholder wherever an image is supposed to display. Figure 7-13 shows a Web document in text-only mode, with several placeholders for graphics.

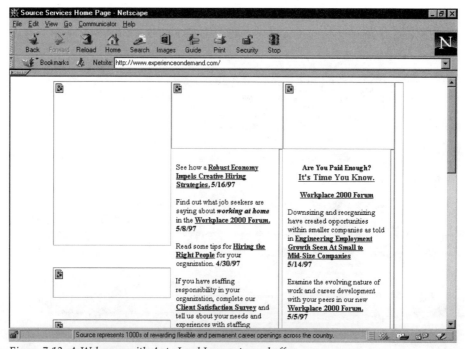

Figure 7-13: A Web page with Auto Load Images turned off.

And how exactly do you turn off the automatic loading of images? Easy:

1. Select Preferences from Navigator's Edit menu. The Preferences window appears.

2. From the list on the left, select Advanced. The Advanced preferences appear in the right section of the window, as shown in Figure 7-14.

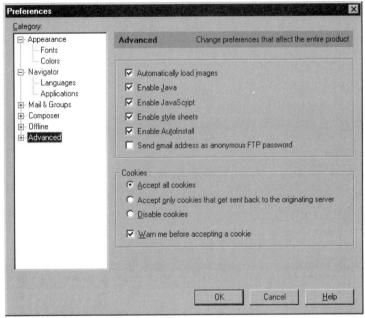

Figure 7-14: The Advanced preferences.

3. Uncheck the "Automatically load images" check box and click OK.

Even with this change to Communicator's image-viewing default, you can still view graphics on particular pages on a case-by-case basis. If you come across a particular document whose graphics you want to view, just click the Images button. This reloads the document with graphics displayed. Graphics are turned on for that page only; the Images button does not affect the "Automatically load" option.

> **TIP**
>
> **Important note:** *The Images button is available on the Navigator 4 Command Toolbar only when "Automatically load images" is deselected in Advanced preferences.*

As I mentioned earlier, though, Netscape Communicator cannot display every kind of graphic file that might exist out there on the Net. The programmers at Netscape work hard to support all of the most common types of graphics, but every day independent computer scientists are working on new file formats, some with better compression, some with more precise rendering of colors. If you want to display graphics other than those supported directly by Netscape Communicator, there are two ways to extend its power: plug-ins and helper applications.

Plug-ins

I'm not going to say a whole lot about plug-ins here, because they're covered more completely in Chapter 10. Basically, a plug-in is a special piece of software that extends Communicator's power. It seamlessly adds new features to the program. Plug-ins designed to display particular types of graphics make it look as though the features were built right in to Communicator—in most cases the graphics display within the browser window, just like ordinary GIF or JPEG files. You'd never know that Communicator is calling on any other software to do the work.

Plug-ins don't just display graphics. There are plug-ins that display particular word processor files as well as spreadsheets and databases. There are even plug-ins that play sound and animation files and a variety of full-motion video formats. Just about anything that extends Communicator's multimedia features can be implemented as a plug-in, and dozens of new ones appear every month.

Let's say that in the process of browsing the Web or your office intranet, you come upon a link to a graphics file that Communicator doesn't support out of the box. What happens? There are a variety of different scenarios, depending on the programming of the Web page containing the link and on whether or not the file type is one that has been registered with Netscape. (Registration with Netscape allows a new plug-in for the file type to be installed automatically, via a special "SmartUpdate" feature.) If it *is* a file type that has been registered with Netscape:

- You may be asked to agree to a license and approve the installation of a particular plug-in. Once you approve the installation, the plug-in may be installed on your system automatically.

TIP

Some plug-ins include a special digital security certificate that you can view before the plug-in is installed on your system. This certificate assures you that you are getting the plug-in from its rightful vendor. Plug-ins that include a digital certificate are known as signed *plug-ins. For more information on digital certificates, please see Chapter 13.*

- The plug-in may be installed automatically right away, if you previously approved a digital security certificate (see Chapter 13) from the plug-in vendor. As soon as the plug-in is installed, you can see the Web page with the multimedia information rendered correctly.

- You might be transported to Netscape's Plug-in Finder page with the appropriate plug-in selected from Netscape's list. Just follow the directions that appear, which will vary from plug-in to plug-in.

If the file type is *not* one that has been registered with Netscape, Figure 7-15 shows what you'll get. For the purposes of this example I've chosen a TIFF file, a fairly common older graphics format that you might encounter on an intranet.

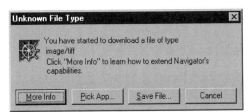

Figure 7-15: The Unknown File Type dialog box.

TIP

What's that Pick App button? That's for setting up helper applications, not plug-ins. For more information on helper applications, see the section below, cleverly titled "Setting Up Helper Applications."

There's still a good chance you can get a plug-in that will let you view this file type. Simply click More Info. Netscape's Plug-in Finder page appears, as shown in Figure 7-16.

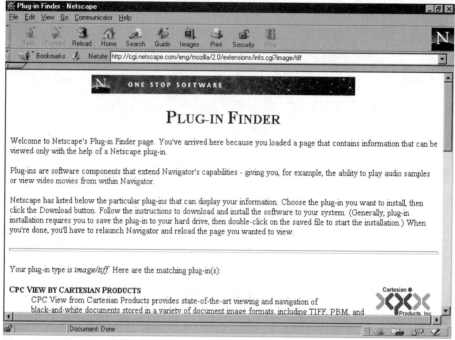

Figure 7-16: The Plug-in Finder page.

Make sure to read the text at the top of the Plug-in Finder page, then scroll down for a list of appropriate plug-ins, as shown in Figure 7-17. Note that the Plug-in Finder page lists only those plug-ins that will display TIFF files. It's easy to find an appropriate plug-in when you don't have to search through a huge list of plug-ins you're not interested in.

When you read about the various plug-ins that are designed to display TIFF files, they all sound pretty good. So how do you choose one? Well, perhaps one of them supports more graphics types than the others, and lets you view encapsulated postscript files, for instance, as well as TIFFs. Or perhaps one was written by a company with a reputation for quality products. Choosing a particular plug-in doesn't mean you have to stick with it for the rest of your life. You can try one out and see how it works. If you don't like it, you can download and install a different plug-in to display TIFF files at any time.

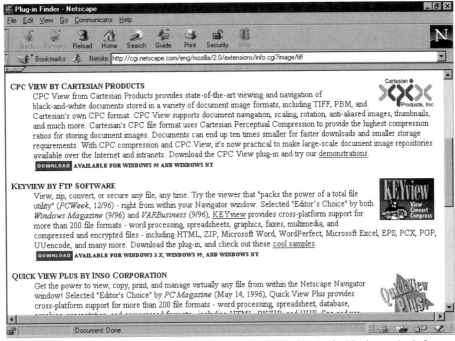

Figure 7-17: Some of the plug-ins available for viewing TIFF files in the Navigator 4 window.

TIP

For a complete list of all *kinds of available plug-ins, check out Netscape's Plug-in page at http://home.netscape.com/comprod/mirror/navcomponents_download.html. You can also get to this page by selecting About Plug-ins from Navigator's Help menu and then clicking the* click here *link near the top of the Help page.*

To download one of the plug-ins, simply click the Download button next to the text description. A new page appears. Follow all the directions. The process varies quite a bit from plug-in to plug-in, so I'll leave you on your own here. Some plug-ins are free, others are available in special try-before-you-buy versions, and for some, you'll have to get out your credit card right away. But if you follow the directions carefully for installing a particular plug-in, you'll end up with what's almost like a new version of Communicator, one that's now able to automatically display TIFF files, as shown below in Figure 7-18.

Figure 7-18: The browser window, now able to display TIFF files.

TIP

*After you've downloaded a new plug-in, make sure to read any readme files very carefully. The installation process may require that you exit Netscape Communicator while the new software updates your system. Even if the instructions just tell you to exit Navigator, make sure to close down **all** Communicator windows!*

In a perfect cyberworld, there would be built-in support or a plug-in for every type of graphic available on the Internet. We're almost there, but not quite. If Netscape doesn't automatically support a particular graphic type, and if there is no plug-in available, you may need to set up what is known as a Helper application.

Setting Up Helper Applications

You read earlier in this chapter about how you can download images to view in another application, such as LView or Paint Shop Pro. When configured to work with Netscape Communicator, these applications are called *helper applications*. Virtually *any* program that can run on your system can be used as a helper application in Communicator. For instance, you could make any files with a .DOC extension appear in Microsoft Word, or any XLS files appear in Excel. But to make applications like these work with Communicator, you may need to set them up manually using the Applications category (under Browser) in the Communicator Preferences window.

Helpers vs. Plug-ins

Let's say there's a plug-in available to display a particular type of file. Is there any good reason to set up a helper application instead? Sure! Although plug-ins are ultra-convenient and ultra-cool, helper applications have their own advantages:

- You may already have an appropriate application for dealing with a particular kind of media file. Why crowd your hard drive with a plug-in— particularly one that isn't free—if you already have what you need?

- You may not want the file to display within the Navigator 4 window, but in a separate application with controls and commands that you're used to.

- Often a helper application offers more features than a plug-in. Obviously you can do a lot more with a spreadsheet in Excel than you can in a plug-in designed simply to display the data.

First, obtain a helper application and install it on your system—or decide on one that you already have. Applications that let you view or edit graphics are available from various sources, including third-party books, software stores, FTP and Gopher sites, and World Wide Web sites. Some of the applications that you may want to obtain are listed in Table 7-1.

Viewer Name	Supports File Types
LView Pro	GIF, JPEG/JPG, TIFF, BMP
Paint Shop Pro	GIF, JPEG/JPG, TIFF, BMP
GhostView	PostScript

Table 7-1: Some graphics viewers that can be used as helper applications.

Since Netscape Communicator automatically displays GIF and JPEG files, unless you're interested in editing or format conversion, you won't gain much with a helper application that supports only these formats. You need one that offers the capabilities to read those formats and others, such as TIFF and BMP. These file types are fairly common, and some Web sites may include them in their documents or file archives.

Once you acquire and install a helper application on your system, use the following steps to configure it to work with Netscape Communicator to display any TIFF files you encounter:

1. Select Preferences from Navigator's Edit menu.

2. Select the Applications category under Navigator, as shown in Figure 7-19. If Applications is not displayed, double-click Navigator, or simply click the plus icon.

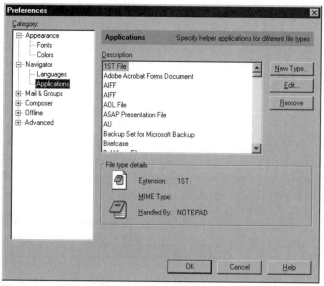

Figure 7-19: The Applications window.

TIP

You can access this same window by clicking the Pick App button in the Unknown File Type dialog box shown earlier in Figure 7-15.

This looks like a fairly complicated dialog box at first, but once you understand the concepts, it's really pretty simple. The large scrolling list includes the names of different kinds of files you might encounter as you cruise the Net or your office intranet with Navigator 4. As you click each file type from the list, the bottom section of the window changes to display details about the particular file type. For instance, Figure 7-20 shows the file type details for GIF files.

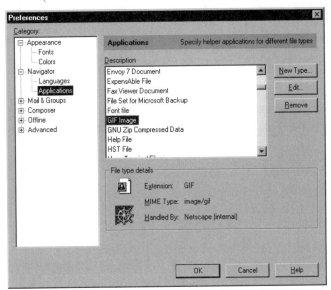

Figure 7-20: The Applications window, with file type details for GIF files.

The bottom box includes three fields:

- **Extension**. This is simply the extension for this kind of file. When Navigator encounters a file called SOMETHING.GIF, for instance, it knows it's a GIF file because of the .GIF extension. An icon to the left of the field provides a graphical representation of the file type, just as it would appear on your Windows 95/NT desktop.

- **MIME Type**. MIME, or Multipurpose Internet Mail Extensions, is a universal standard for naming file types. Usually the MIME designations make sense, as in the case of GIF files, which are classified as image/msword.

- **Handled By**. This field specifies the helper application that will be launched when Navigator encounters a file of this type—or, it simply reads "Netscape (internal)" if it's a file type that Netscape can display without a plug-in or helper application.

Now scroll down the list of file types and select TIFF Image. Unless you've already configured a helper application or plug-in for TIFF files, your window will look something like Figure 7-21.

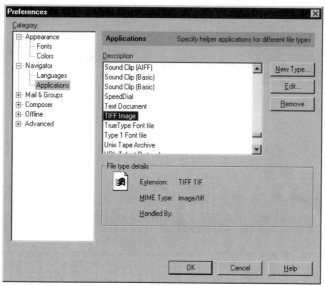

Figure 7-21: The Applications window, with file type details for TIFF files.

Notice that the "Handled by" field is blank; no application has been configured to view TIFF files, and when Navigator encounters one it will present you with the Unknown File Type dialog box shown earlier in Figure 7-15. Here's how to add a particular application that will be launched automatically whenever Navigator encounters a TIFF file:

1. Still in the Applications window with TIFF Image selected, click the Edit button. The Edit Type dialog box appears, as shown in Figure 7-22.

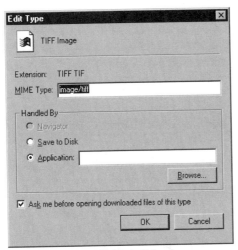

Figure 7-22: The Edit Type dialog box.

2. In the Handled By section, notice that the Navigator option button is unavailable, since Navigator cannot handle this file type on its own. Make sure the Application option button is selected and then click the Browse button to select a program on your system that can display TIFF files. For instance, you might choose the program **C:\LVIEW\LVIEWPRO.EXE** as the helper application for TIFF files. Optionally, select Save to Disk if you simply want files of this type saved rather than displayed or otherwise processed.

TIP

If you want Navigator to ask you before it automatically opens files of this type in a helper application, check the check box at the bottom of this Window. This is useful, for example, if you sometimes want to view TIFF files immediately and sometimes simply want to save them to disk.

The subject of graphics on the Internet is a very large one, and we've covered only the basics in this chapter. Chapter 10 will go into more advanced uses of graphics through VRML and advanced plug-ins as well as Java and JavaScript, but for now let's see—or rather, hear—what's up with sound in Netscape Communicator.

Simple Animation: Server Push & Layering

Most Web pages require that you interact with them in some way. They usually include links to other pages, graphics to click, animations to view, or sound objects to download and listen to. All of these items are initiated in some way by the user, the person using the client application (Netscape Communicator, in this case).

Another type of HTML instruction enables Web authors to design pages that deliver an updated version of the page without interaction from the user. This technology is called *server push*. Using server push, the server transmits Web page instructions and information to your browser window. As you navigate to various Web sites that support server-push technology, the connection between you and the server on the other end remains open. The server can continue to "push" updated information and data to your computer continuously. By pushing several different images into the same location on a Web page, for instance, a server can give the impression of a single animated image. The connection between you and the server closes when you leave the site.

An example of a Web site that supports server push is the Word site at http://www.word.com. It uses server push in a variety of ways, often to display advertisements during the time you are moving from one page to another. The advertisement appears, gives you a few moments to read it, and then disappears so that you can continue on to the item that you originally selected.

Throughout Word, there are clever icons that rely on server push for animation. But there are all kinds of uses for server push. A sports site, for instance, can use server push to keep a scoreboard updated with the latest scores and team highlights.

Starting with the current version, Navigator also supports a new HTML feature called *Dynamic Layers*, or simply *layering*. Layering lets HTML developers design pages that have multiple layers of information. Text may be overlayed on graphics, or vice versa. Layering provides yet another way to enhance Web pages with animation.

Sound on the Web

Many computers you purchase today come with sound cards and speakers. This has fueled the growth of sound capabilities on the Net as well as on office intranets. Thousands of Web sites now include sound files that offer a new way to experience online content. Radio stations, public television stations, and network news shows are providing sites that feature sound recordings.

Some sites even include *live* performances of rock bands or the play-by-play of weekly football games. As the Web matures, you'll be able to sit back and listen as you work on that marketing proposal or college term paper. The history of technology is a history of distractions, and the good folks at Netscape are doing their best to distract you by enabling Communicator to play the sounds of the Net.

Why Can't I Use My PC's Speaker?

You can, but you'll be disappointed with the results. Every PC comes equipped with a tiny speaker in it that you may hear beep every once in awhile. You'll hear it beep a few times, for instance, when you start up your computer. You can make this speaker play some of the sound files you find on the Internet by acquiring a speaker driver from Microsoft (called SPEAKE.EXE) and loading it on your system. You also need to acquire an application that plays different sound files. For many users, the reigning champion during the past year or so has been WPLANY.EXE, which is short for "We Play Anything." You can download WPLANY.EXE from ftp://ftp.cam.org/systems/ms-windows/slip-ppp/viewers/wplny09b.zip.

SPEAKE.EXE is part of Microsoft's Windows Driver Library, an archive file that includes other drivers as well. The URL is ftp://ftp.microsoft.com/Softlib/softlib.exe.

Supported Sound Files in Netscape Communicator 4

Netscape Communicator includes built-in support for the following sound file formats: AU, SND, AIF, AIFF, AIFC, MIDI, and WAV. It's not important to know what all these acronyms mean, but you *should* know that the three most popular sound types on the Web are AU, SND, and WAV. MIDI (Musical Instrument Digital Interface) files are really music files rather than sound files, digital "scores" that can be played correctly on any electronic musical instrument that supports the General MIDI standard. And that probably includes your sound card.

Listening to Sound in Netscape Communicator 4

When you connect to a Web site that contains sound files, you will generally see a speaker icon or some similar icon indicating that it is a sound file. If the sound file is of a type that Netscape Communicator supports, you can click the icon and Communicator automatically plays the file. Or if a sound file is embedded directly into an HTML page, you may not even have to click a link.

Now let's look at a typical example of a sound file on the Web. We'll return to the IUMA site to check out the experimental/spoken word band Asbestos Removal Crew.

TIP

We're using the browser window for this tutorial, but remember that sound files can be included in e-mail or discussion group messages as well.

1. Make sure you are connected to the Internet. If Netscape Navigator 4 is not currently running, launch it by double-clicking its icon or the Netscape Communicator icon.

2. In the Netsite/Location box at the top of the window, select the currently displayed URL and replace it with **http://www.iuma.com/IUMA-2.0/ftp/ volume3/Asbestos_Removal_Crew/**. Press Enter. After a few moments, the page appears, as shown in Figure 7-23.

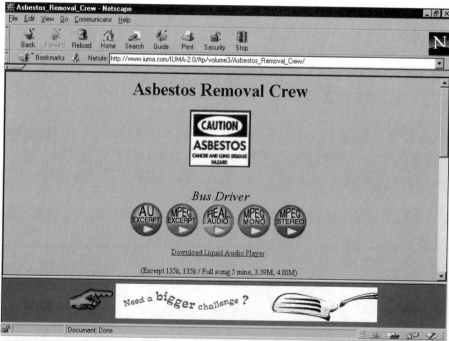

Figure 7-23: The Asbestos Removal Crew page on IUMA.

Since Navigator supports AU sound files right out of the box, scroll down and click the icon labeled "AU Excerpt." A sound control panel pops up. The controls are pretty much like those on any electronic device: click the arrow button to start playing, click the other button to stop. You can adjust the volume of the selection by dragging the slider to the right or left.

TIP

The sound controls will not display until the entire sound file has been downloaded. If it's a large file, or if you are on a slow connection, the sound control panel may be empty and gray for a while.

When the sound file ends, it stops automatically and you can do one of two things: play it over and over again or get a life.

Using RealAudio With Netscape Communicator 4

As I'm sure you just discovered, sound files can take a while to download to your machine. But fortunately, there are some new *streaming* standards that speed up the process. What do I mean by streaming? Suppose the sound file starts playing over your computer's speakers before it's completely downloaded. That's streaming. Instead of clicking a link and twiddling your thumbs, you can click a link and start hearing business news, press conferences, and more. Not quite instant gratification, but close.

By far the most prominent streaming sound format on the Web is RealAudio. Using the RealAudio plug-in, which is available from the RealAudio Web site at http://www.realaudio.com, you can hear news, sporting events, music, and much more. The RealAudio format almost makes you feel as though you're listening to the radio, right on the Net. In fact, some traditional radio stations have started to supplement their broadcasts with RealAudio files on the Web.

The complete RealAudio system consists of two pieces. The first piece is one you'll probably never have to use unless you become a Web site administrator. The *RealAudio Server* is the software that enables Web sites to offer RealAudio files.

The other piece of the RealAudio puzzle is the client software that enables users like you to listen to RealAudio recordings. In this case, it's a plug-in that works seamlessly with Netscape Communicator, just as if it were a built-in feature.

Obtaining RealAudio

The RealAudio plug-in, which is what you want to install on your system, is currently free of charge. To get a copy of RealAudio, connect to RealAudio's Web site (http://www.realaudio.com/) and download the software to your computer. You will be asked to fill out a short form before downloading it.

TIP

Currently the RealAudio people are distributing two different plug-ins that will play RealAudio files: the plain old RealAudio plug-in, and a new one called RealPlayer. What makes RealPlayer different is that it also lets Communicator display a new kind of streaming video file called RealVideo (more about this in the section on video, later in the chapter). If you think you might want to experiment with RealVideo as well as RealAudio, you should download RealPlayer.

Make sure to read the list of system requirements to run the program. The requirements include 2MB of free disk space and a sound card with a Windows Sound driver. (The RealAudio Player and RealPlayer are not compatible with the PC Speaker program or other software programs that emulate a sound card.)

Installing & Configuring RealAudio

So you've completed the forms, chosen the correct version of RealAudio or RealPlayer, and downloaded it to your computer. It's sitting on your computer and ready to install. To install RealAudio or RealPlayer, run the file you just downloaded by double-clicking it in the Windows Explorer (or in the File Manager, if you are using Windows 3.1). The installation program starts doing its thing. Simply follow the instructions that appear on your screen. When asked, make sure to indicate that you want to install the plug-in version of the program. At the conclusion of the setup process, the RealAudio player or RealPlayer launches and plays a welcome message. If the message sounds distorted, see the "Sound" section of the RealAudio Release Notes, which are stored on your system where you installed RealAudio or RealPlayer.

Can I Create My Own RealAudio Files?

Yes, you can, but you'll need some extra software. Specifically, you must download a copy of the RealAudio Encoder from the Progressive Networks Web site. Using Encoder, you start with a WAV or AU audio file and convert it to the RealAudio file format, with the extension .RA. Within the RealAudio file you can insert a name of the file, author, and copyright information. This information is displayed on the user's machine when he or she is playing it back. Of course, the file you've created doesn't do you much good unless you have a way to distribute it to the public. You must copy it to a site that has the RealAudio server software. For more information on RealAudio servers, see the RealAudio Web site at http://www.realaudio.com/.

Trying Out RealAudio

When you connect to sites that contain RealAudio links, you can listen to a link by clicking it. It's that easy. The RealAudio player or RealPlayer first contacts the host computer that contains the audio file. After a few moments during which it downloads the initial section of the file, it starts to play it over your system speakers. You can adjust the volume of the playback by using the slider control on the right side of the player.

TIP

RealAudio links are often indicated with an icon of a radio or boom box, sometimes with the letters "RA" on it. Take a look at C-Span (http://www.c-span.org) for a typical use of iconized links like this, and for an example of RealAudio used effectively in conjunction with articles and stories.

So that you can try out RealAudio, Table 7-2 lists some sites that include RealAudio files. In the future, look for events such as football games, rock concerts, speeches, and the like to be simulcast as RealAudio events that you can listen to live.

Site Name	Address
National Public Radio	http://www.npr.org/
ABC Radio Network	http://www.abcradionet.com/
Delta Dream Vacations	http://pwr.com/LEISURE/DELTA.html
Advanced Digital Services	http://206.65.169.39/
Grace Hour	http://www. ggwo.org
Nightstand	http://www.nightstand.com/
Tabernacle Baptist Church	http://www.tabernacle.org/~tbc/
Toyota Motor	http://www.toyota.co.jp/
North Carolina News Network	http://www.capitolnet.com/ncnn/
Tech Talk Radio Network	http://ttn.nai.net/
BBC Radio 3: Facing the Radio	http://www.bbc.co.uk/ftr/
Black Cat Radio	http://www.memphiscat.com/
MusicNet	http://www.man.net/~musicnet/
OneWorld	http://www.oneworld.org/realaudio/index.html

Table 7-2: Some sites that have RealAudio files.

The RealAudio President

Politicians of every stripe are clamoring over the new telecommunications technologies, though they frequently misunderstand them. It is no surprise that several of President Clinton's speeches are available on the Web via RealAudio. Just point Navigator 4 to http://www.whitehouse.gov/WH/EOP/OP/html/OP_Speeches.html and start looking around—or listening around. If you have a good sound card and listen carefully enough, you might even hear Bill inhale.

Netscape's Own Streaming Sound

RealAudio may be the most prominent streaming sound protocol, but it's not the only game in town. Netscape has developed its own Media Server and Media Player to play sounds across the Net in real time, and best of all the player is included right within Communicator. Let's give it a try:

1. For the sake of this exercise, make sure you're on the Net.

2. Replace the current URL in the Netsite/Location box with **http://207.24.196.98/default.htm**. This is the main demo page for *elemedia*, a telephony and media project under development by Bell Labs (R&D folks who used to be with AT&T but are now part of Lucent Technologies). Take a look at Figure 7-24.

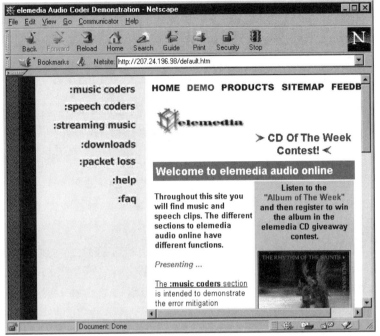

Figure 7-24: The elemedia page.

3. In the left-hand frame, click :streaming music. The frame on the right now contains some instructions that you don't need. Scroll to the bottom and click the "On to the Music" link. Now if you scroll down the right-hand frame you'll see a choice of musical selections.

4. Click anything except Hootie and the Blowfish. Being a classical kind of guy, I go for Bach's Brandenburg Concertos, so this is what I see next in the right-hand frame shown in Figure 7-25.

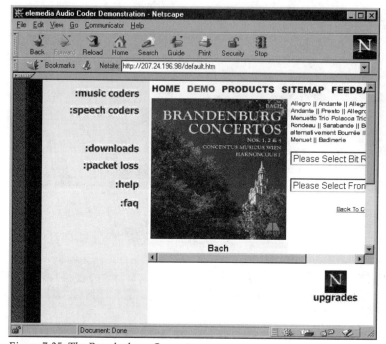

Figure 7-25: The Brandenburg Concertos.

5. There are two drop-down lists. From the top one choose a mono or stereo bit rate and from the bottom one choose the actual selection you want to hear. The bit rate you choose should be close to the maximum that is possible for your computer. For instance, if you're connected to the Net via a 28.8 Kbps modem, choose a bit rate of about 28800 bps; if you're on a fast hard-wired connection, choose a faster rate. Immediately, a sound control appears in the right-hand frame, as shown in Figure 7-26.

6. Again, this is just like a standard tape or CD player. Click the Play button to play your selection. You'll see some flashing dots on the button as the Media Player initiates the download of the file. Then you should start hearing music. The Play button becomes a Pause button.

7. Adjust the volume with the plus and minus buttons. When you want to stop listening, click the Stop button.

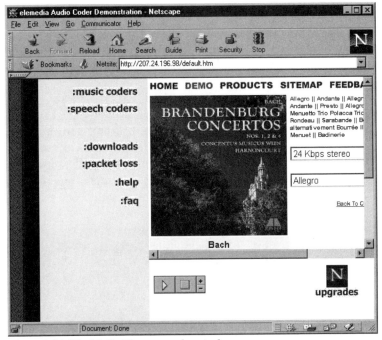

Figure 7-26: The Media Player sound control.

Media Player Settings

If you right-click the Media Player control and then select Properties from the context menu that appears, what you get is shown in Figure 7-27.

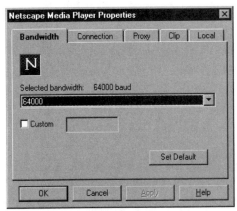

Figure 7-27: Netscape Media Player Properties.

> **TIP**
>
> *You can also access the Media Player Properties dialog box by double-clicking the Configure Media Player icon in the Utilities subfolder of the Communicator folder.*

It is beyond the scope of this book to get into all the settings; many of them only apply if you're on an intranet that uses the Netscape Media Server, and you should consult with your network administrator before changing them. But in the bandwidth tab, it's a good idea to set the maximum bandwidth for any audio streams you receive. If you're using a 28.8 Kbps modem with a PPP connection, for instance, you should select 28800 from the drop-down list. On the other hand, if you're on a fast T1 or T3 hard-wired connection, select the fastest speed available from the list. If there are pauses in the audio as you listen, you may need to try a different rate. Once you have selected your rate, you can set it as the default by clicking the Set Default button. The Media Player will use this bit rate every time Communicator accesses a streaming sound file on a Netscape Media Server.

Video in Netscape Communicator 4

Some of us spend so much time on the Web that sometimes we forget what real life is. Real life is an operating environment that includes mountains, oceans, trees, crying babies, barking dogs, Big Macs, and the Menendez brothers. It's not the greatest user interface, but it sure beats anything Bill Gates could come up with. And one of the most interesting features of real life is that things move! We do not experience life as a succession of still images such as those you usually encounter on the Net, but as a constant ebb and flow of matter through space.

Now you can come a little closer to real life on the Web. One of Netscape Communicator's most exciting new features is LiveVideo, the technology that lets you view video clips, often called movies, right within the browser window.

Let's give it a try:

1. Make sure you are connected to the Internet. If Navigator 4 is not currently running, launch it by double-clicking its icon or the Netscape Communicator icon.

2. In the Netsite/Location box at the top of the window, select the currently displayed URL and replace it with **http://home.netscape.com/comprod/ products/navigator/version_3.0/multimedia/video/index.html**. Press Enter. After a few moments, the Netscape LiveVideo page appears.

3. Scroll about a third of the way down the page and you'll see a video clip in progress at the left side of the page. It depicts various international flags superimposed over scenes of the various countries, as shown below in Figure 7-28.

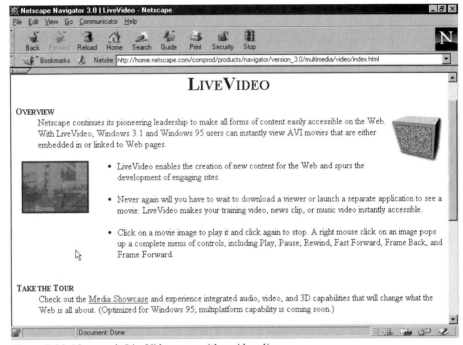

Figure 7-28: Netscape's LiveVideo page with a video clip.

4. To stop the motion of the images, simply click the small video window; to start the clip up again, click once more.

5. Now click your right mouse button on the video. A context menu appears letting you pause, rewind, or fast forward the video, as shown in Figure 7-29. It also lets you step through the movie frame-by-frame using the Frame Forward and Frame Back commands.

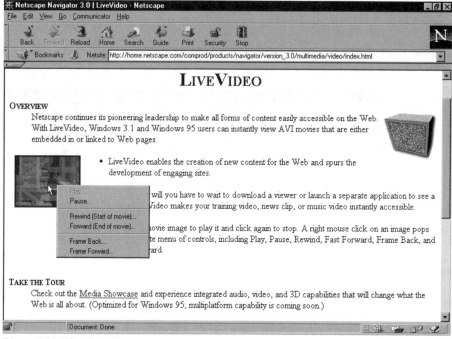

Figure 7-29: The LiveVideo context menu.

How does this work? When Netscape Navigator encounters what is known as an AVI file (AVI is Microsoft's format for video files), LiveVideo automatically kicks in and lets you view the image the way it was meant to be viewed. No need for external programs or helper applications—just sit back and enjoy.

Video With Sound

Wait a minute! Something is very wrong. Here we are using the slickest newest technology, and all we're getting is silent movies. Weren't talkies invented around 1928?

Not to worry: LiveVideo supports soundtracks as well as moving images. Not all AVI files include sound, but when you click on one that does, Netscape Communicator will make you feel like you're sitting at Loewe's Cineplex staring up at the big screen. Just add popcorn.

Here's a nice example of an AVI clip that includes sound, put out by the government of Newfoundland and Labrador. Of course, in order to hear the soundtrack, you'll need a sound card supported by your version of Windows:

1. Make sure you are connected to the Internet. If Navigator 4 is not currently running, launch it by double-clicking its icon or the Netscape
   Communicator icon.

2. In the Netsite/Location box at the top of the window, select the currently
   displayed URL and replace it with **http://www.gov.nf.ca/itt/business/
   people.avi**. Press Enter. After a few moments, the first image of an AVI
   file appears in your browser window, as shown in Figure 7-30.

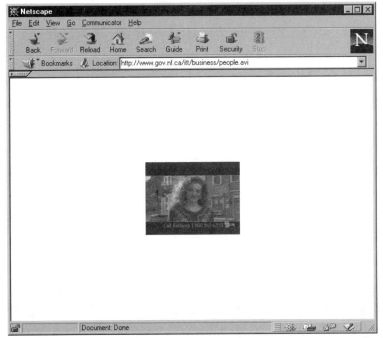

Figure 7-30: An AVI video clip by the government of Newfoundland and Labrador.

TIP

*Large AVI files and AVI files that include sound may take a while to download.
And I mean quite a while. If you have some filing in your in-box, now would be a
good time to get it done.*

3. Click the image. Immediately it begins playing, complete with music and
   voice-over.

Other Video Formats

AVI is one of the most common video formats on the Web, but it's not the only one. As you venture into the far reaches of cyberspace you may encounter:

- QuickTime movies (with the extension .MOV, .MOOV, or .QT)
- MPEG movies (with the extension .MEPG, .MPG, .MPE, or .MP2)
- Flick files (with the extension .FLI or .FLC)
- IFF/ILBM files (with the extension .IFF)

The current version of Communicator only plays AVI and QuickTime files automatically, but the Netscape developers were smart enough to make the program extensible. If you want Communicator to play other animation formats right in the browser window, all you have to do is find a plug-in for that particular media type. We've talked about plug-ins earlier in the sections on graphics and on RealAudio, and we'll come back to them in Chapter 10.

TIP

To play QuickTime movies on your system, you need to have the latest version of Apple QuickTime for Windows installed. The software is available at http://quicktime.apple.com/qt/sw/sw.html. Make sure to follow all instructions for installing it. Once QuickTime is on your system, you're ready to go. Try QuickTime out at http://www.wandering.com, which makes excellent use of video clips in presenting information about Italy.

Streaming Video

One of the most exciting new developments in multimedia on the Web is streaming video. This works pretty much like streaming audio: instead of waiting for an entire file to arrive at your computer, you start viewing the moving images on your screen as the stream of information is downloaded. Earlier in the chapter in the section on RealAudio, I mentioned RealPlayer, a plug-in that handles not only RealAudio but also the RealVideo streaming standard. RealPlayer is available at **http://www.realaudio.com**. That same site offers many links to RealVideo sites so that you can try out your new multimedia toy once you've installed it.

Moving On

In this chapter, you've learned the basics of viewing graphics and listening to sound in Netscape Communicator. You've also learned how to play video clips or movies, right in the browser window. By now you should have a sense of how vast the possibilities are when it comes to incorporating new media into Web pages. Advertising executives are jumping up and down with excitement, scheming all kinds of ways to inundate you with the latest multimedia innovations.

But in the next chapter we go back to basics again, to some of the ancestral text-based protocols that enrich intranets and the Internet as much as all this flashy stuff. If you do any kind of thorough research using Communicator, you're bound to bump into three old friends of the cyber-traveler: FTP, Gopher, and Telnet.

CHAPTER 8

The Ancestors: FTP, Gopher, Telnet & 3270 in Communicator

I hope by now you have found a few ways that Netscape Communicator can simplify and enrich your life. Through its many easy-to-use features, you can access the Internet or your office intranet for sending and receiving multi-media e-mail; for viewing a wide variety of information maintained not only from your own workplace but by educational and government institutions around the world; for reading the subject-specific information contained in local or Usenet newsgroups; and perhaps simply for relaxing and having some fun.

The advanced features of Netscape Communicator plunge you into an electronic world full of bright images and sounds, and they let you jump around from link to link, blazing new information trails. Communicator's hypermedia browsing facilities provide a whole new approach to research, an approach that's very different from the plodding linear methods we grew up with. Some say that hypermedia browsing more closely models the way our brain really works, encouraging us to integrate knowledge by associative leaps rather than by carefully planned logical stitching.

However, there are some research tasks that call for a more traditional approach to the great volume of data available on the Net; there are also some wonderful repositories of knowledge that were put on the Internet before the WWW and have not been converted or are not even candidates for the Web. Fortunately, Communicator supports the older Internet services that are still very useful tools. The most important of these are *FTP*, *Gopher*, and *Telnet*.

TIP

What about the Professional-Only 3270 emulator, IBM Host on Demand? We'll cover that in a sidebar later in the chapter.

FTP

FTP is one of the simplest and most obvious acronyms you'll come across on the Net: it simply stands for File Transfer Protocol. That sounds pretty generic, but every implementation of FTP follows the same very specific rules for sending and receiving data. The file must be broken up into pieces at one end and reassembled properly at the other; the data has to be checked for errors and stamped with the correct filename and date; and the FTP software has to enable users to navigate through the host system's directories to find the right file.

Throughout the Internet are scattered literally thousands of servers that provide files to users via FTP, and they all do their job in much the same way. Many of these sites are known as *anonymous* FTP sites, which means they allow any Internet user to log on specifically for the purpose of retrieving files. You don't need to be a registered user on the system. Typically, when logging in to anonymous sites, you specify *anonymous* as your username and your e-mail address as the password (see the sidebar, "Your Anonymous Password"). Netscape Communicator takes care of the login process automatically; you don't even see any prompts from the remote system.

Your Anonymous Password

When you log on to an anonymous FTP site, the server asks your software for a name and password. Communicator sends the username "anonymous" and automatically generates a password. Some FTP servers, however, require that you use your e-mail address as the password when you log on anonymously, and it used to be considered "good form" to do this even when it wasn't required. As more and more direct e-mail marketeers scour server logs for potential new customers, however, it may be wise not to spread your e-mail address around too widely.

To configure Communicator so that it sends your e-mail address as your password when you log on to anonymous FTP sites, select Preferences from the Edit menu and then click the Advanced category. Simply check the check box labeled "Send e-mail address as anonymous FTP password" and click OK.

➡

Of course Communicator needs to *know* your e-mail address before it can use it. If you followed the instructions in Chapter 5, you're all set. But if for some reason you decided not to use Netscape Messenger, you can still enter your e-mail address into the program. From the Edit menu, select Mail and Discussion Preferences. Then go to the Identity tab, fill in the informational fields, and click OK. Now Navigator's FTP feature can send your e-mail address to anonymous FTP sites.

Are there FTP sites that are not anonymous? Sure! Many corporations, for instance, maintain non-anonymous FTP sites so that employees can trade work-related files while on the road. Of course, you need an account and a real password to access files on these FTP servers. But for the sake of keeping our examples general in this chapter, we'll be dealing primarily with anonymous sites. If you think you need FTP access to your office intranet, please talk to your system administrator—and see the sidebar later in the chapter called "Non-Anonymous FTP."

What is Out There?

So what kinds of files are available at these anonymous FTP sites? You name it! There are:

- Fully functional software programs, including spreadsheets, text editors, modem programs, databases, and a dazzling variety of utilities.

- Updates and patches to most major retail software programs.

- Electronic texts ranging from Shakespeare's complete works to David Letterman's latest Top Ten list.

- Thousands of images, sounds, video clips, and animations.

- Technical reports, journals, electronic magazines, news summaries, and archives of user messages.

- Books and tutorials like this one that will help you get started with just about any software task.

Figure 8-1 shows some of the directories at a well-known FTP site, the University of North Carolina SunSITE. We'll explore this site more thoroughly later in the chapter.

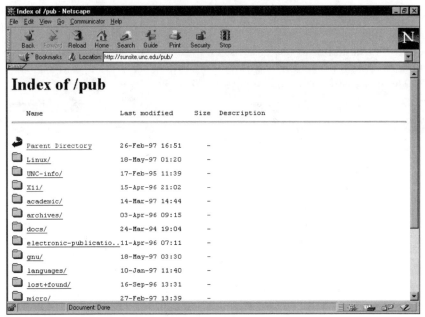

Figure 8-1: Some of the directories of files at SunSITE.

"And I can do whatever I want with all this stuff?" I hear you asking. Well, yes and no. To understand why I'm waffling on this question, you need to understand that there are three broad categories of files on the Internet, and each of these categories has different rules and guidelines for usage.

Public Domain

Public domain files are files that have no copyright, and there are no restrictions whatsoever on their usage. For instance, you can do whatever you want with Shakespeare's *Hamlet* or *A Winter's Tale*. Modern texts are sometimes released into the public domain as well, by authors who care more about wide distribution than about collecting any royalties or other fees. Many political polemics, for instance, are public domain.

But what about software? Sure, there's lots of public domain software on the Net. These have often been created by altruistic developers as a resource for the good of the community. The old adage "you get what you pay for" doesn't always hold true on the Net. For instance, until recently, some of the very best Internet client software was public domain. Of course, there are developers who release unfinished or buggy programs into the public domain to collect feedback, as part of their development process or simply because they don't want to go through the process of refining their work. But programs like these are usually clearly marked, and in some situations they can provide a cost-effective way of dealing with very specific software tasks. And some public domain software is a true group effort: perhaps a programmer started a project years ago, and then somebody downloaded it and worked with it a bit more, then somebody else added new features, and so on. Since there are no restrictions on the redistribution or modification of public domain software, a program may evolve over the course of many years, forged as much by public scrutiny and feedback as by the work of any single designer.

Freeware

Freeware files are copyrighted, but there are no charges for using them. Let's say you write a program that you are very proud of, but you want to make sure anybody can use it for free. You place it on the Internet with a copyright notice and perhaps a text file explaining any restrictions on its use. For instance, you may want to make sure the software is always distributed in its original form, unmodified, and bearing your name as the sole author. You may want to make it clear that nobody else may sell the software, but may only distribute it freely as you have.

Many people misunderstand freeware, confusing it with public domain files. No, they are very different. Freeware is free, but you have to play by the rules.

Shareware

Shareware is a great marketing innovation that came into being almost concurrently with PCs. Shareware files or programs are distributed on a trial basis: you can download them and use them for free, but only for a short evaluation period. If you like the resource and want to keep using it, you must pay a fee (usually small) to the author or delete it from your machine. Generally it's OK to make copies for your friends to evaluate, but you, of course, can't charge for the software.

Shareware files and programs are copyrighted. You must not copy them except as specifically allowed by the author, and you must abide by any restrictions detailed in the license or accompanying documentation. There has been plenty of litigation over misuse of shareware materials!

The advantages of shareware for the user are obvious: you get to try something without spending a penny. But there are advantages for shareware authors as well. Distribution costs are kept to a minimum, and there are no middlemen to eat profits. The author also enjoys a direct relationship with the customer and often refines the product based on individual feedback rather than distributors' charts and graphs.

What About Viruses?

In spite of all the hype it gets, the Net is no utopia—it is more like a microcosm. Just as there is a slight chance you could get mugged on your way to the corner store, there is a slight chance that you will someday download a file that "crashes your hard drive" or otherwise messes with your system, causing you that peculiarly modern form of grief known as "restoring everything from backups." (That's assuming you bothered to keep an up-to-date backup like everyone told you to!)

How common are viruses? Certainly much less than sensationalistic mass media stories would have you believe, but there are some out there. The best defense, of course, is making sure that at any given moment you could restore everything you need from backup tape or disks. If this is not the case at your house, I suggest you put this book down and get busy backing up files.

There are other precautions you can take as well. Virus-checking programs such as McAfee Associates' SCAN are available at most major FTP sites, and there are a number of excellent commercial products as well, such as Norton Anti-Virus. It's a good idea to check your entire system once in a while using one of these programs. If you do discover a problem, delete all infected files from your hard drive, or follow any instructions that came with your antivirus software. You will probably also need to completely restore your hard drive from backup.

Yes, this can be a serious inconvenience. But in the interest of alleviating some of the techno-paranoia that flares up whenever the news weeklies don't have a juicy-enough scandal, let's debunk a few myths:

- You cannot get viruses from pure ASCII text files or e-mail messages that contain only text. Generally speaking, something has to be *run* on your computer to infect it. Of course, this includes macros such as those that are sometimes included with Word documents or Excel spreadsheets.

- Most viruses do not destroy hardware, they just mess up your software so badly that it seems as though your hardware is faulty. Getting rid of all infected software and then completely restoring your system from backup will usually solve the problem.

- Viruses do not jump from disk to disk across your office.

- You won't catch any viruses by hanging around in particular Usenet newsgroups, though at times it *can* feel like you're coming down with something nasty!

For more information about viruses, here are a few Web sites to check out:

- The Frequently Asked Questions (FAQ) file for the VIRUS-L/comp.virus mailing list (http://www.cis.ohio-state.edu/hypertext/faq/usenet/computer-virus-faq/faq.html).This FAQ contains a lot of basic information about viruses, including common symptoms and how to proceed if your system is infected.

- Virus Information (http://csrc.ncsl.nist.gov/virus/). This page contains a comprehensive set of links to additional virus-oriented sites, as well as reviews of antivirus software.

How to Know What You're Getting

FTP sites are really just directories full of files, much like the directories on your own computer. The FTP protocol itself includes no provisions for describing the files or providing additional information, although it does let you view file details such as size, time, and date. So how do you know what all the files in an FTP directory really are? There are two ways:

- Many of the larger FTP sites have Web "front ends." In other words, you initially access them via a Web document that explains a little about the site and what it contains. When you're ready to download a file, you click on a link that fires up the actual FTP protocol, showing you lists of files and directories or going right ahead and transferring the file you want. Figure 8-2 shows an example of a Web front end to an FTP site, on the Netscape server itself.

- Most well-established FTP sites include informational files that describe the rest of the available files. These informational files are often named README or INDEX (sometimes in lowercase), or sometimes they have names that begin with a dot, as in .INDEX. You may also encounter informational files called something like WELCOME.TXT.

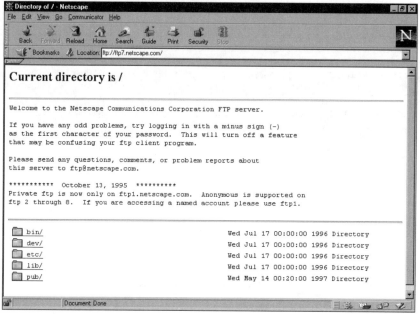

Figure 8-2: Web front end to the Netscape FTP server.

TIP

> *By default, Navigator 4 displays text files at FTP sites rather than automatically saving them to your hard drive. But what if you want to save a text file after viewing it? No problem. Just press Ctrl+S or select Save As from the File menu.*

Now let's click the WELCOME.TXT file link at Ventana's own FTP site to view its contents, shown in Figure 8-3.

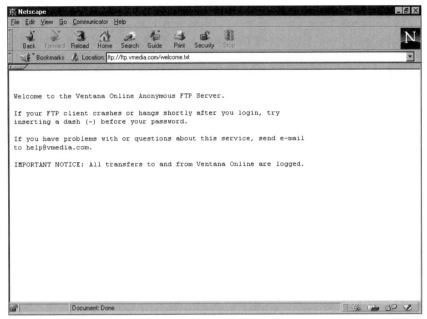

Figure 8-3: The contents of Ventana's WELCOME.TXT file.

As you can see, the WELCOME.TXT contains important information about the system itself.

Common Filename Extensions

Knowing somebody's last name won't necessarily tell you anything about the person, but the few characters that compose the extension to a filename are packed with information. For instance, if a file ends with .TXT, you can be pretty sure it's an ASCII text file, readable on virtually any system by using a simple text viewing program. But not all extensions are so obvious, so I've compiled a table of some of the most common ones you'll come across. Table 8-1 is by no means complete, but it's a good reference to keep handy as you start exploring FTP sites.

Extension	Type of File
.TXT	Simple text file, readable using Notepad, WordPad, or even the DOS type command.
.ASC	Probably a simple ASCII text file as well.
.DOC	May be a text file or a Microsoft Word document.
.EXE	An executable file (DOS or Windows program) that can be run from the command line or from the Windows Run command (or by double-clicking the file's icon in Windows 95). Often it is a *self-extracting archive* file; when you run it, it is decompressed into several files.
.ZIP	An archive file that has been compressed using the PKZIP compression program. You can use PKUNZIP or WinZip to extract the separate files that are part of the archive (see "Understanding Compression" later in this chapter).
.HQX	A file that has been archived using the BinHex compression program; you must use BinHex to decompress it. This compression standard is more common in the Macintosh world, and chances are good that an .HQX file is really intended for Mac use.
.SIT	A compressed, or "stuffed," Macintosh file. Probably not useful on your PC, although if you need one of these files, several good PC unstuffers are available on the Net.
.ARJ	Another type of compressed file. Several compression and decompression programs such as WinZip and DRAG AND ZIP can handle these files.
.LHA	See note on .ARJ above.
.ARC	See note on .ARJ above.
.ZOO	See note on .ARJ above.
.Z	A file compressed using the UNIX Zip. You can use the program GZIP, or a general purpose utility such as WinZip or DRAG AND ZIP, to decompress it.
.GZ	A file compressed using the GNU Zip program for UNIX. See note on .Z above.
.TAR	An archive file that has been compressed using the UNIX tar facility. It may be decompressed using a PC version of tar or a general purpose utility such as WinZip or DRAG AND ZIP.

Table 8-1: Common filename extensions on FTP sites.

Understanding Compression

You no doubt noticed that many of the notes in Table 8-1 refer to compression. When you look at the staggering number of files on the Internet (or, if you have Windows 95 or NT, at the staggering number of files on your hard drive!), it is clear that it's important to shrink files so that they are as small as you can possibly make them. And of course the smaller the file, the quicker it travels from one machine on the Internet to another, reducing overall transfer time and network traffic. But what exactly is file compression?

Think about the number 20,000,000,000,000,000,000,000. Now imagine trying to read this number to another person so that he or she can write it down. You *could* say "two zero zero zero zero zero zero zero zero zero zero zero zero zero zero zero zero zero zero zero zero zero zero," but that's the stupid way to do it. If you want to maintain your friend's respect, you'll probably say "two followed by 22 zeros." You have effectively compressed the information into fewer words, and your friend can decompress it by actually writing out the 22 zeros.

There are 256 different characters that may appear in a computer file in any order, or just half that number in the case of ASCII text files. In some files, there are no repeated characters and no repeated patterns of characters, but most are full of repetitions even if the repetitions are accidental. This means that most files can be compressed. Think of a database, for instance, in which there are lots of spaces that fill out fixed-length fields. It's easy to see how you can compress a file like this by indicating the space character and the number of times it should be repeated.

Of course, I'm oversimplifying. Compression techniques have become very sophisticated and use a variety of subtle approaches, or *algorithms*, that go far beyond merely tallying repeated characters. Some try to maximize the amount of saved disk space; others try to speed up the process of compressing and decompressing files. Most try for some sort of balance between these two aspects of the process.

You have to decompress most compressed files before they can be used; compressed files are good only for transferring and storing the information. The exceptions to this are compressed graphics and sound files, which you can view or listen to directly, without running any decompression software. In this case, Netscape Communicator (or some other viewing program) is automatically decompressing the file for you.

Clearly, you really need a compression program to deal with all the files you collect from the Net. In the next section, you'll kill two birds with one virtual stone: you'll learn how to use Netscape Communicator's FTP features as you download a copy of WinZip 6, one of the best compression/decompression programs available.

Smaller + Smaller = Bigger

As you travel around to different FTP sites, you'll notice that even large graphics files such as GIFs are rarely "zipped up" into archives; they're often left just as they are, with their original extension. Why?

Well, GIF files are *already* compressed. The graphics standard includes an algorithm for storing these files in as few bytes as possible. Images are obvious candidates for compression, since so many pixels are repeated. Think of the background, for instance, or large patches of color. If a graphics file contained position and color information for each individual pixel that appeared onscreen, it would be gigantic!

OK, so a GIF file is already compressed. But couldn't you make it even smaller by compressing it again? Nope. Curiously, by running a GIF file through a compression program such as PKZIP or WinZip, you actually make it *bigger*!

Kind of strange, huh? Well think about it: assuming that GIF compression is pretty tight (which it is), you're only going to eke out a few more bytes of space savings. But this added compression actually costs more space than it saves, for PKZIP has to add to the file the information about how to decompress it. In other words, it has to announce "this file has been compressed using PKZIP version *x*" as well as a bunch of other technical information. For this reason, it may not always be worth compressing small files that are known to contain lots of nonrepeating information. However, sometimes it may be worth it.

Downloading Your First File

In this example, you'll access a Web page that serves as a front end for an FTP site. You will be able to download the WinZip 6 file simply by clicking a link on the Web page, without wading through the actual directories on the FTP server itself. Later in the chapter, you'll see how Netscape Communicator displays this more "raw" FTP information.

To download WinZip 6 using Netscape Communicator's built-in FTP:

1. Make sure you are connected to the Internet.

2. Double-click the Netscape Communicator icon to launch the program. If it's already running, make sure you're in the browser window (Navigator 4). If you're not, click the browser icon on the Component Bar. The browser window appears, and the Netscape home page starts loading as shown in Figure 8-4.

    - If Navigator 4 is already running and is displaying a different document, you may need to click the Home button or the Netscape icon.

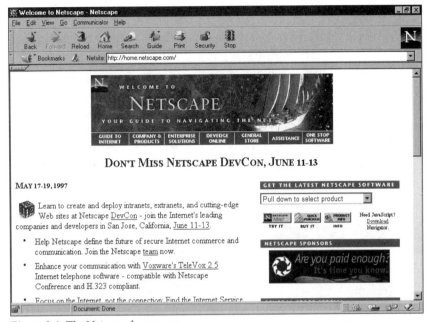

Figure 8-4: The Netscape home page.

3. Click your mouse inside the Netsite field at the top of the window to select the URL http://home.netscape.com/.

TIP

> *Remember, you don't always have to type in entire URLs; in many cases you can leave off the two slashes and everything that comes before them. If you simply enter home.netscape.com, Communicator is smart enough to figure out that you mean a Web site and will automatically use the HTTP protocol. Similarly, if you enter ftp.vmedia.com, Communicator knows you are trying to connect to an FTP site and will use FTP.*

4. Replace this URL with the one for the WinZip home page by entering **http://www.winzip.com/** or just **winzip** . Once you have typed in the new URL, press Enter. Navigator 4 retrieves the WinZip home page, as shown in Figure 8-5.

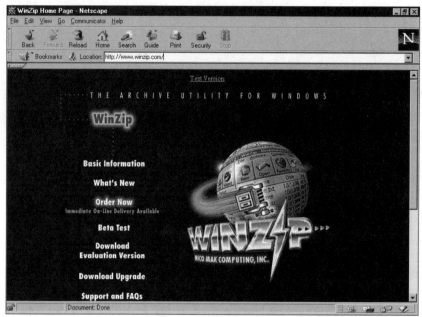

Figure 8-5: The WinZip home page.

5. You may want to take some time to look around the WinZip home page. When you are ready, scroll down the page and click the Download Evaluation Version link. The WinZip: Download Page appears, as shown in Figure 8-6.

TIP

You can save FTP sites as bookmarks just like any Web document. Select Add Bookmark from the menu that appears when you select the Bookmarks Quickfile button, or drag the Page icon over the Bookmarks Quickfile icon. You can also simply type Ctrl+D. This is convenient if you don't have time to download a long file immediately but want to be able to find it easily later on.

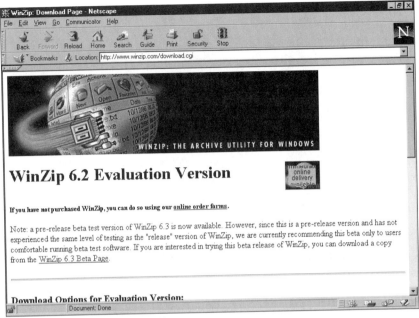

Figure 8-6: The Download WinZip page.

6. Now scroll down to the link that actually lets you download the correct file for your system—Windows 95/NT or Windows 3.1 (don't click just yet). Notice that the status line indicates the URL pointed to by the link, for instance ftp://ftp2.winzip.com/winzip/winzip95.exe. The *ftp* at the beginning of the URL tells Netscape Communicator to use the FTP protocol to connect with the site ftp2.winzip.com, switch to the *winzip* directory, and download the file *winzip95.exe*.

7. Click the appropriate link, depending on whether you are using Windows 95/NT or Windows 3.1.

Depending on various Communicator settings that will be discussed later in the section called "Helper Applications," there are a couple of different messages you might get at this point when you attempt to download a file. A warning box might pop up, like the one shown in Figure 8-7.

Read the text carefully. This dialog box appears if the type of file you're downloading is configured in Communicator as a type that should be opened or run automatically as soon as it is downloaded, *and* if Communicator is configured to ask you before opening this kind of file. As you'll find out in the "Helper Applications" section, it's easy to change this option.

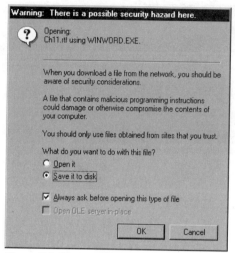

Figure 8-7: The possible security hazard warning box.

But sometimes when you attempt to download a file you may get a message like the one shown in Figure 8-8.

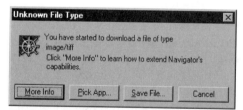

Figure 8-8: The Unknown File Type dialog box.

This simply means that no special action, helper application (viewer), or *plug-in* has been configured for this kind of file, and you can choose what to do with it. Netscape Communicator can automatically run a file like this as soon as it has been received, or it can automatically pop up a Save As dialog box that lets you save the file to disk for later viewing or processing. To learn how to make these configuration changes, see "Helper Applications" later in this chapter.

As you learned in Chapter 7, Communicator also supports special programs known as plug-ins. Plug-ins, like helper applications, may be associated with particular kinds of files you find on FTP sites. But unlike helper applications, which are really separate applications from Communicator, plug-ins let you view or otherwise act on files right within the browser window. By clicking the More Info button in the dialog box shown above in Figure 8-8, you are taken to Netscape's Plug-In Finder page, and you may decide to install a plug-in designed specifically for the "unknown file type" you are trying to download.

If you *don't* get one of the two dialog boxes shown in the previous illustrations, one of two things will happen:

- The file will be downloaded and automatically run. This means it may be executed on its own or it may appear in an associated application that Communicator launches automatically. For example, the type of compressed executable file you're downloading may simply run, whereas a Word document may appear in a Word window.

- A typical Windows Save As dialog box may appear. In this case, choose a location (such as your C:\TEMP or C:\Download directory) for the file, and then click the Save button. The Saving Location dialog box appears, showing you the progress of the file transfer. Once Netscape Communicator has finished downloading the file, the Saving Location dialog box disappears.

Congratulations! You've just downloaded your first file via FTP, and you now have an important tool for dealing with files you will download in the future. To install WinZip 6, simply run the executable file that you saved on your hard drive (unless Communicator has already launched it automatically). You can run it from the DOS command line or using the Windows Run command. You can also double-click it in Windows Explorer or File Manager. Be sure to read any informational files included with the program, and please remember that WinZip 6 is shareware: if you continue to use it, you must register it. The WinZip package contains complete information on how to do this.

Now let's visit an anonymous FTP site the more traditional way, without relying on a Web page as the front end.

TIP

Once an FTP transfer has started, you can go back to browsing in the browser window. The file will keep downloading as you work. You can even start another FTP transfer and download several files at once.

Smart Resume

The new communications technologies are pretty amazing, but they're not perfect. You can expect occasional minor glitches. Here's something that has happened to me many times: I'm downloading a huge file via FTP when suddenly my Internet connection is dropped. The download stops, and I am left with a file that is absolutely useless.

But thanks to Communicator's Smart Resume feature, you don't need to start the download all over again. When you're back online, click on the link or file once more. Communicator determines that you already have part of the file and resumes the download right at the point it was cut short. In other words, it appends the rest of the data to the end of the partial file that you've already received. This can be a huge time saver!

Navigating FTP Sites

For this tutorial, we'll look at the very large anonymous Oak site at Oakland University in Rochester, Michigan. Primarily a mirror of the Simtel collection of files, this site houses literally thousands of programs of interest to the Internet community, from casual Net surfers to seasoned experts. I use Oakland as an example because it is fairly typical of some of the large public FTP sites scattered around the Net—and because you usually don't run into too much of a traffic jam trying to get on.

1. Make sure you are connected to the Internet and displaying Communicator's browser window (Navigator 4).

2. In the Location box at the top of the window, select the currently displayed URL and replace it with **ftp://oak.oakland.edu/**. Press Enter. After a few moments, the top-level directory at the Oak site appears, as shown in Figure 8-9.

3. If there is any information at the top of the page, read it. Then scroll down. You can now see a list of several subdirectories of this top-level directory. Notice that Navigator 4 indicates directories with a Folder icon.

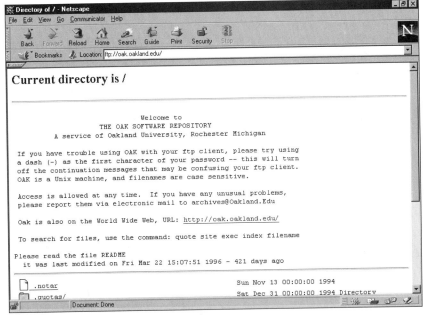

Figure 8-9: The top-level directory at Oak.

4. Most of the good stuff on Oak is under the /pub directory, so let's go there. (Pub directories often contain files that are useful to the general public.) Scroll down and click the /pub link. The /pub directory appears, as shown in Figure 8-10.

From here you can cruise around on your own for a while—Communicator makes it so easy that you don't need me to hold your virtual hand any more. If you're interested in ham radio files, click the link to the hamradio/ directory; if you're a Macintosh person, click macintosh/. You can always back up a level using the Back button, or you can return to any level you've already seen via the Go menu.

TIP

*If you know where you want to go on an FTP server, you can include the directory right in the URL. For instance, you could enter **ftp://oak.oakland.edu/pub/** right in the Location box in Netscape Navigator 4. And if you know what file you want to retrieve, you can even include the filename in the URL!*

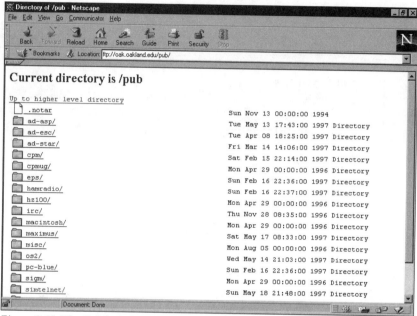

Figure 8-10: The Oak /pub directory.

FTP Traffic Jams

FTP sites are among the busiest resources on the Net. They may not get as many users as the most popular Web pages, but because of the way FTP works, there is a built-in traffic problem.

When you access a Web page, you quickly download the document and are off. Click a link on the page, and you bop back to the site, or to a different site. You flit from site to site, never staying longer than it takes to get the requested information. But with FTP, you remain logged in to the server while cruising and perusing its directories at your own pace, and of course you remain logged in as you download files which typically are much larger than Web pages. The Web is like a fast-food joint, or like the old-fashioned automats where you walked around grabbing the dishes you wanted; FTP is like a real restaurant, with its share of customers who just never seem to stop eating!

Because of this inherent traffic problem, you may sometimes get a message telling you that too many users are already logged on when you connect with an FTP site. Sometimes, however, you will simply be unable to connect at all, and the browser window will just seem to be spinning its wheels. The solution to either of these problems is simple: try again later. In fact, try again *much* later, at a time when there are likely to be fewer info-junkies cruising the Net (3 A.M. works pretty well).

You say you like to sleep at night? Fortunately, there is another solution. For many of the larger public FTP servers, there are also *mirror sites*, FTP servers that contain the exact same files and directory structure but may experience less traffic. These mirror sites are kept in sync with the original: anything you can get at the original you can get at its mirror, and you can be sure that you're downloading the same version. Often the "sorry, we're too busy" message you get when trying to log on to an FTP server includes a list of mirror sites.

Some of the most useful files on Oak are the Windows 95 utilities contained in the pub/simtelnet/win95/util/ directory. You already know that you can get there by clicking your way down, level by level. But since you already know how to navigate this way, let's accelerate the process by taking a shortcut:

1. In the Location box near the top of the browser window, change the currently displayed URL so that it reads **ftp://oak.oakland.edu/pub/simtelnet/win95/util/**.

    ■ A long URL like this is an excellent candidate for a bookmark. I, for one, don't want to type it again!

2. Press Enter. Navigator 4 automatically takes you to the correct directory, as shown in Figure 8-11.

Notice the 00_index.txt file at the top of the directory list. You should read this file for capsule descriptions of all the files in this directory.

Now take a few moments to scroll down the list of files. Notice that Netscape Navigator 4 labels each one with a special blank file icon that has a bunch of 0s and 1s on it. This means that Navigator knows it's a binary (non-text) file but doesn't recognize the .ZIP extension. When you click on one of these filenames, the program will pop up the Unknown File Type dialog box mentioned above. If you want, though, you can have WinZip automatically extract .ZIP files. See "Helper Applications" later in this chapter.

You can also send, or upload, files to some anonymous FTP servers, though this is unusual on public sites. To upload a file to the FTP directory currently displayed in the browser window, select Upload File from Navigator's File menu. An Upload File dialog box appears. Simply select from your system the file you want to upload, then click the Open button. Assuming you have permission to upload files to the site, your file is transferred.

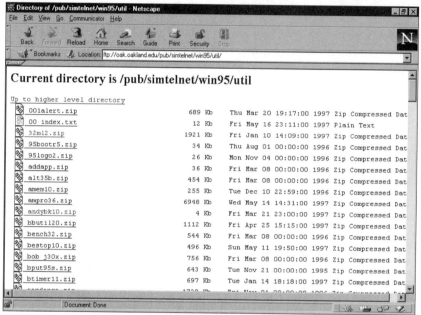

Figure 8-11: The ftp://oak.oakland.edu/pub/simtelnet/win95/util/ directory at Oak.

What Are Symbolic Links?

As you look around FTP sites, you'll notice that in any given directory there are files, subdirectories, and something called "symbolic links." What exactly are they?

A symbolic link is really just a nickname or, more exactly, a pointer to another directory or file. Imagine you are the administrator of an FTP site, and you just put a brand new evaluation version of Netscape Communicator in the directory */pub/pc/windows/win95/www/apps/netscape*. That's buried pretty far down in the directory structure, and people are going to take quite a while navigating down to that level. In addition, if they type in the entire URL, they are likely to make mistakes, taking even more time and further adding to the traffic problem. You want to make sure that users get to the new Netscape file quickly and efficiently. What to do? Create a symbolic link in the top-level directory, and call it, for instance, new_netscape. When a user clicks new_netscape, he or she is automatically transported to the directory where the file *really* lives.

The administrators of FTP sites can create symbolic links to directories or to files. If you click a link that's associated with a directory, you "teleport" to that directory; if you click a link to a file, Navigator 4 views the file or begins the download process. Symbolic links make it quicker, and much more pleasant, to navigate FTP sites that have complex directory structures.

Searching for Files

FTP is great if you know what you're looking for and where to find it. But what if all you know is that you need a particular kind of program, and you have no idea where to start looking? Or what if you can only remember part of the name of a file you want? Fortunately, the Net offers a wide variety of services for locating files in the FTP haystack. One of the old standbys, and still one of the most useful tools on the Net, is a service known as Archie.

Archie

Archie is an Internet service that lets you search indexes of most of the files available at anonymous FTP sites. These indexes are maintained on special Archie servers located around the world. To use Archie effectively, you need to know part of a file's name, or at least be able to make a reasonable guess about what characters might be in its name. For instance, let's say you want to find WinZip 6 but don't remember the exact name of its self-extracting archive file. Archie lets you specify a string of characters that appear anywhere in the name. It would be safe to guess that the string "winzip6" appears somewhere in the filename, so you can use that as your Archie search criterion and find the correct file even if its name is "latestwinzip600z.exe."

For advanced users interested in specifying very precise search parameters, Archie even supports the full set of regular expressions that let you search for all kinds of patterns within filenames. For instance, you could look for a file that begins with a lowercase letter, followed by any number of digits, followed by the string "zsa-zsa," followed by a number greater than five, followed by an extension of either .TAR or .SH, followed by another extension of . . . well, you get the idea. It is beyond the scope of this book to provide a tutorial on regular expressions, but I like to think of them as wildcards on steroids. If you want more information, why not use some of the Internet search tools you've learned about so far?

OK, let's give Archie a try:

1. Make sure you are connected to the Internet. If Netscape Navigator 4 is not currently running, launch it by double-clicking its icon or the Netscape Communicator icon.

2. In the Netsite/Location box at the top of the Navigator 4 window, replace the currently displayed URL with **http://www-ns.rutgers.edu/ htbin/archie** and press Enter. In a few moments, the Rutgers University Archie Request Form page appears, as shown in Figure 8-12.

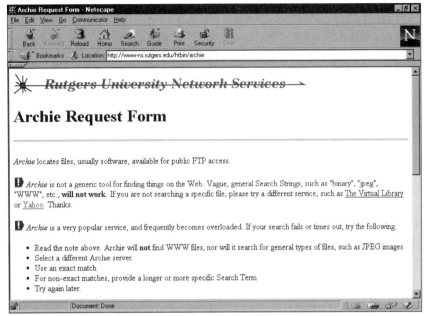

Figure 8-12: The Archie Request Form page.

3. Scroll down the page until you get to the search form itself. Fill it out as follows:

  ▪ In the Search By section, click the top radio button, Looking for Search Term in File Names (Ignore UPPER/lowercase).

  ▪ In the Search Term box, enter **winzip**.

  ▪ Leave the other settings alone.

  ▪ Your completed search form should look like Figure 8-13.

4. Now click the Start Search button. In a few moments, the Archie Search Results page appears, as shown in Figure 8-14, providing you with links to a few different FTP sites where you can get WinZip.

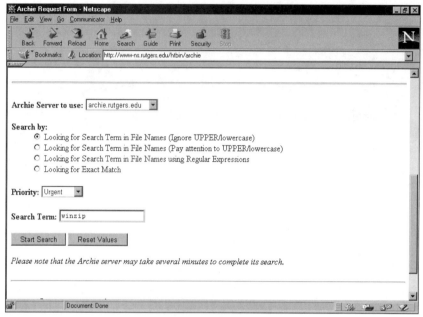

Figure 8-13: The completed Archie search request.

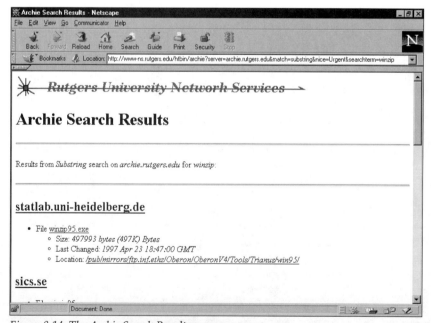

Figure 8-14: The Archie Search Results page.

As you can see, Archie is great if you know something—*anything*—about the name of the file you are looking for. But what if you're looking for a particular *kind* of file—a mortgage calculator, for instance—that could have any name at all? Luckily, the Internet provides other search utilities for this situation as well. One of the best is the c | net shareware page.

The clnet Shareware Page

To get to the c | net Shareware Page:

1. Make sure you are connected to the Internet. If Netscape Navigator 4 is not currently running, launch it by double-clicking its icon.

2. In the Netsite/Location box at the top of the Navigator 4 window, replace the currently displayed URL with **http://www.shareware.com/** (or just **shareware**) and press Enter. In a few moments, the shareware.com page appears, as shown in Figure 8-15.

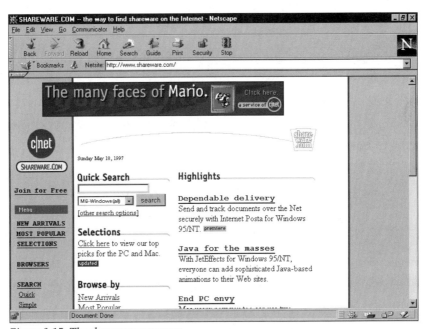

Figure 8-15: The shareware.com page.

3. After reading the introductory information on this page, scroll down to the search form.

4. Since we are interested in mortgage calculators for Windows, leave the drop-down list of file categories set to MS-Windows (all). In the search word box, enter **mortgage**. Your completed search form should look like Figure 8-16.

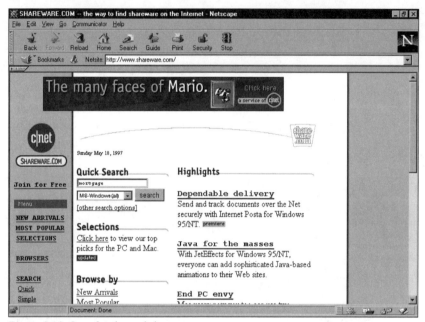

Figure 8-16: Completed search form.

5. Click the search button. In a few moments, the Search Results page appears as shown in Figure 8-17, with links to several different mortgage programs for Windows. You can click any one of these to retrieve the file from its FTP site.

The shareware.com page provides such a powerful search tool that you'll probably want to add it to your bookmarks, or maybe even to the Custom Toolbar.

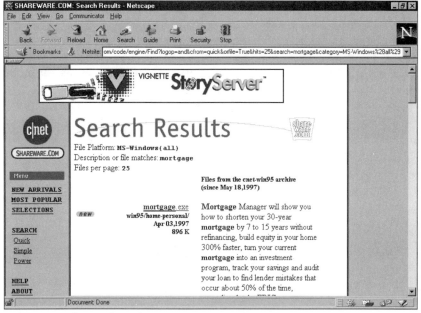

Figure 8-17: The search results.

Using Web Tools to Find Files

While there are other specialized tools for finding files on FTP sites, you may not actually need them. The World Wide Web is becoming more and more prominent as a front end for FTP servers. This means that you can find many files without specialized FTP search services; you simply use the same search engines you use for locating other types of information on the Web itself. The best of these utilities are available by clicking the Navigator 4 Search button. While an Infoseek search, for instance, may not get you directly to a particular file, it will probably take you to a Web page with a link to the file you're interested in. And of course, you can find lots of files by browsing through the dozens of categories that appear when you click the Places button and choose Destinations.

As I mentioned earlier, Netscape Communicator does more than just go out and retrieve files for you—it can actually help you start working with them right away. In the next section, you'll learn how to take advantage of this powerful feature.

What Are RFCs?

Just when you thought we were done with acronyms!

RFC stands for Request for Comment, and that's exactly what it is: a document put out on a public FTP site so that other Net users can read it and comment on the content. But an RFC contains very specialized information, technical information about the Internet itself. In fact, many of the Internet standards that have developed over the years are the result of this RFC process.

Most RFC files are slow, tedious reading, and nobody's turned them into a musical yet. But they are invaluable to anybody wanting to learn more about the Net, and a few of them are even fun. RFC 1208, for example, is a large glossary of networking terminology, and RFC 1325 has lots of tips for new Internet users.

How do you know what the different RFC files cover? Here are two URLs:

- ftp://isi.edu/in-notes/rfc-retrieval.txt

- ftp://isi.edu/in-notes/rfc-index.txt

The first file provides instructions on locating and downloading RFCs, and the second contains short descriptions of all the RFCs that currently exist.

Helper Applications

You've already seen that when you click on a text file at an FTP site, Navigator 4 automatically displays the contents rather than simply downloading the file to your hard drive. But that's only a small example of the automation that's possible. To understand how all of this works, let's go back to an FTP site we looked at earlier and associate WinZip with files that have the .ZIP extension.

1. Make sure you are connected to the Net.

2. In Navigator's Netsite/Location box, enter **ftp://oak.oakland.edu/pub/ simtelnet/win95/util/** and press Enter. (If you're on a Windows 3.1 machine, go instead to **ftp://oak.oakland.edu/pub/simtelnet/win3/**.)

3. Navigate down to a directory that interests you, then click a ZIP file to download. The Unknown File Type dialog box appears, as shown earlier in Figure 8-8. This time, click the Pick App button. A Configure External Viewer dialog box pops up.

4. If you want all ZIP files to be handled automatically by WinZip 6 as soon as they are retrieved, click the Browse button and find the WinZip program on your hard drive. For instance, if you are using Windows 95 or NT 4, you'd navigate to C:\Program Files\WinZip, select Winzip32.exe, and click the Open button.

5. Back in the Configure External Viewer dialog box, click OK. Now Communicator will download the file you've chosen and immediately launch WinZip 6 when the entire file has been saved to your hard drive.

Communicator also provides a separate and more powerful interface for associating particular types of files with appropriate actions or applications. Select Preferences from the Edit menu, then select the Applications category under Navigator, as shown in Figure 8-18. If Applications is not displayed, double-click Navigator, or simply click the plus icon.

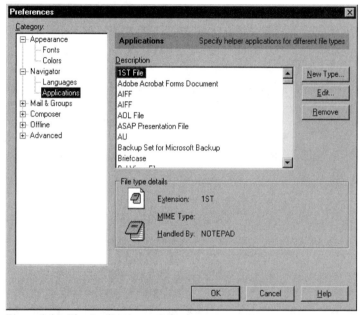

Figure 8-18: The Applications window.

This looks like a fairly complicated dialog box at first, but once you understand the concepts, it's really pretty simple. The large scrolling list includes the names of different kinds of files you might encounter as you cruise the Net or your office intranet. As you click each file type from the list, the bottom section of the window changes to display details about the particular file type. For instance, Figure 8-19 shows the file type details for Winword (Microsoft Word) files.

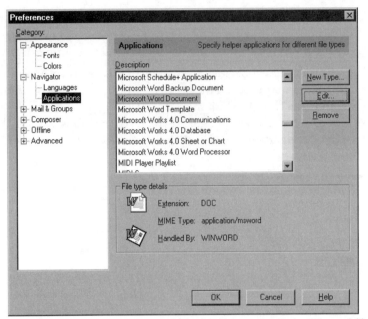

Figure 8-19: The Applications window, with file type details for Winword files.

The bottom includes three fields:

- **Extension**. This is simply the extension for this kind of file. When Navigator encounters a file called CHAPTER3.DOC, for instance, it knows it's a Windword file because of the .DOC extension. An icon to the left of the field provides a graphical representation of the file type, just as it would appear on your Windows 95/NT desktop.

- **MIME Type**. MIME, or Multipurpose Internet Mail Extensions, is a universal standard for naming file types. Usually the MIME designations make sense, as in the case of Winword files, which are classified as application/msword.

- **Handled By**. This field specifies the helper application that will be launched when Navigator encounters a file of this type. An icon to the left represents the program. In this case, when Navigator encounters a file with the extension .DOC or the MIME designation application/ msword, it launches the program Winword, which then displays the file correctly.

But what if you don't want Microsoft Word to start up every time Navigator encounters a .DOC file? What if you want to view the contents of the file in some other application such as WordPad or WordView—or what if you simply want to save it to disk after retrieving it via FTP?

No problem. Just click the Edit button. The Edit Type dialog box appears, as shown in Figure 8-20.

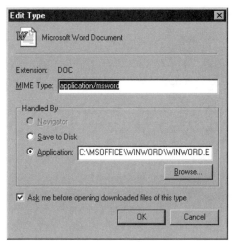

Figure 8-20: The Edit Type dialog box.

In the Handled By section, select Save to Disk if you simply want files of this type saved rather than displayed or otherwise processed. Or if you want them handled by a different application, make sure the Application option button is selected and then click the Browse button to select a different program.

TIP

If you want Communicator to ask you before it automatically opens files of this type in a helper application, check the check box at the bottom of this Window. This is useful, for example, if you sometimes want to view Winword files immediately and sometimes simply want to save them to disk. When Communicator encounters this file type, it will pop up a dialog box like the one shown earlier in Figure 8-6.

What about the top option button, the one labeled Navigator? In this case it's grayed out (made unavailable) because Navigator itself cannot display Winword files—it must call upon the services of a helper application such as Microsoft Word. But take a look at Figure 8-21, which shows the Edit Type dialog box for GIF Image files.

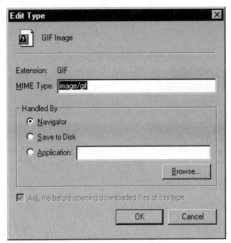

Figure 8-21: The Edit Type dialog box for GIF Image files.

Since Navigator *can* display GIF files without any outside help, the Navigator option button is available—and selected by default. If you click a link to a GIF file, it will be displayed using the browser window. But you may want a different program, such as a full-featured graphics program, to display any GIF files you encounter or download via FTP. In that case, simply select the Application option button and browse for the program you want to use. In any case, click OK when you're finished editing this file type.

TIP

Settings in the Applications window affect every Communicator component, not just Navigator 4. For instance, they affect the way attached files are handled in Netscape Messenger (see Chapter 5).

If you want to get fancy, you can even add new file types and subtypes to Communicator's default list. However, this is truly a propeller-head option: you should not even be thinking about it except to add a new standardized MIME type, and unless you really know what you're doing. Assuming you have the proper geek credentials, though, it's pretty easy. In the Applications window, click New Type. Then just fill in the blanks.

TIP

And yes, you can even delete file types by clicking the Remove button. I do not recommend this. There is no harm in having extra file types listed, even ones you'll never encounter, but unless you're pretty technical it may be hard to add back a type you've deleted.

Netscape Communicator's Applications facility lets you deal efficiently with just about any file on any Internet FTP site. And if you want to further automate the program with new viewers, sound players, editors, or any kind of helper application, guess how you get these programs? By FTP, of course!

Non-Anonymous FTP

Grabbing files from anonymous FTP sites may be the most entertaining use of Netscape Communicator's built-in FTP facility, but there are other practical applications as well. For instance, when I finish writing this chapter, I will FTP it to Netscape Press, where an editor will edit the text and then place it back on the FTP server so I can look over her changes. To do this, I have to log onto an FTP site which requires that I enter a login name and a password.

Here's how to log onto a non-anonymous FTP site to exchange files:

In Navigator's Netsite/Location box, enter the URL for the site you want to connect to via FTP, but include your login name as part of the URL. For instance, when I want to log onto the WELL for the purposes of anonymous FTP, I type **ftp://pjames@well.com** and hit Enter. Immediately a dialog box appears asking me for a login password. Once you enter it, your home directory appears—or the directory you've been given access to by the system administrator. You navigate around the site just as you would navigate around a public (anonymous) FTP site, and the procedure for downloading files is identical. To send a file, select File Upload from Navigator's File menu. Using the Upload File dialog box that appears, choose a file from your local system to upload.

Some systems even let you include your password as part of the URL for a non-anonymous FTP connection. Simply type a colon after your login name, and then your password for the account. Using the example we looked at earlier, I would enter **ftp://pjames:mypassword@well.com**.

Now you've got the basic scoop on navigating FTP sites and downloading files. You've also learned some strategies for finding files on the Net by name or by subject area, and you've seen how Netscape Communicator can be customized to help you deal with your new files more efficiently. Now all you need is a bigger hard drive!

But before heading off to the computer store, why not take a few minutes to learn about two of the other ancestral tools that can still help make your online life easier and more rewarding? The first of these is Gopher.

Gopher

What if you don't know exactly what you're looking for on the Net and want to refine your search carefully as you explore? What if you want to delve deeply into a particular area of interest, for instance constitutional law? Typical Web sites may not help you, for often the links to other information are as arbitrary, whimsical, and wild as the imagination of the page's author.

Gopher servers, on the other hand, serve up information in tidy hierarchical menus and submenus, sticking to a subject and presenting it in top-down, outline format. Using World Wide Web documents, you leap rapidly from peak to peak. Using Gopher, you follow logically related information trails.

How Do They Come Up With These Names?

Most of the Internet services were developed not by commercial software companies, but by individuals in academia, often graduate students. This evolution is reflected in some of the jargon. If the marketing division of a software company had been involved, we'd probably be talking about Super UltraSearch Max Plus instead of Gopher. But the Golden Gopher is the mascot of the University of Minnesota where this powerful tool was developed, and there were no people in suits around calling the shots.

Once you name something "Gopher," you have to extend the metaphor. If you visit many Gopher sites, you'll discover that they are sometimes called Gopher *holes*. And avid Gopher users often talk about *burrowing* to other sites. It's all kind of quaint in this age of cyber this and surf that.

In addition to extending metaphors, computer people have a compulsive need to mix them, and so it is very common on the Net to talk about *GopherSpace*. (You can put yourself into an altered state trying to visualize that one.) GopherSpace is simply the total collection of hierarchically organized resources available to you via Gopher.

In the old days (about three years ago), Gopher servers were usually accessed with specialized Gopher client programs, but Web browsers like Netscape Navigator 4 make extra software unnecessary. The Navigator component of Communicator can log you on to a Gopher server and then present you with the information so that it looks very much like any Web page. Menu items are colored like other Web links, and clicking on them brings up the appropriate submenus. Let's give it a try using the *WELL Gopher* as an example.

Using Gopher

The WELL is a large information service known for the variety of its online forums and the lively interactions of its users. It also maintains a very interesting Gopher site that's accessible to anyone on the Net. To begin exploring it:

1. Make sure you are connected to the Internet.

2. Double-click the Navigator 4 or Netscape Communicator icon to launch the program. The browser window appears, and the Netscape home page starts loading, as shown in Figure 8-22.

Figure 8-22: The Netscape home page.

3. Click your mouse inside the Netsite/Location field at the top of the window to select the URL http://home.netscape.com/.

4. Replace this URL with the one for the WELL Gopher site by entering **gopher://gopher.well.com/**. Then press Enter. Navigator 4 retrieves the top-level WELL Gopher menu, as shown in Figure 8-23.

   - Notice that when you connect to a Gopher server, virtually all the text in the browser window is composed of links. In the top level of the WELL Gopher, these are links to submenus rather than files, as indicated by the folder icons. The exception is the Search All Menus on the WELL Gopher item, which brings up a searchable index of the entire Gopher server.

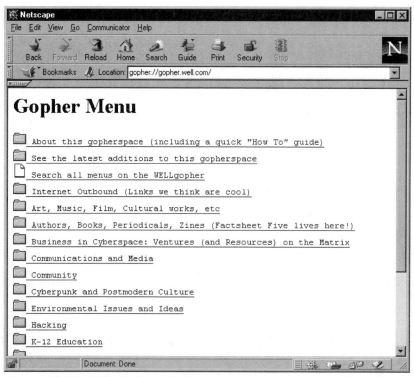

Figure 8-23: The WELL Gopher.

TIP

*Remember that you can type in partial URLs—Netscape Navigator 4 is smart enough to figure them out. Instead of entering **gopher://gopher.well.com/**, for instance, you could simply enter **gopher.well.com**. Because your abbreviated URL has the word "gopher" in it, Navigator assumes this is a Gopher site.*

5. Click the top menu item, About This Gopherspace. A new submenu appears, as shown in Figure 8-24.

   ▪ Notice that most of the links are to actual text files now, as indicated by the icons.

6. Click on the top item, What is this place? (The basic story). This time a text file appears, as shown in Figure 8-25.

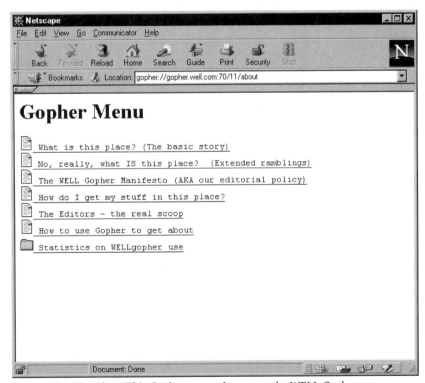

Figure 8-24: The About This Gopherspace submenu on the WELL Gopher.

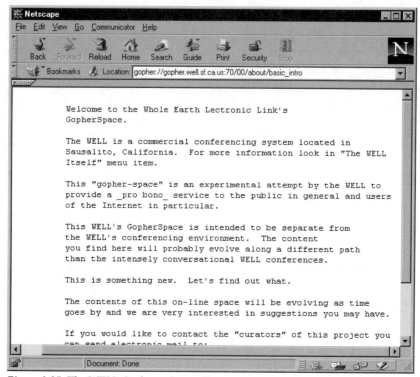

Figure 8-25: The WELL Gopher welcome file.

7. After reading the file, click Navigator 4's Back button to return to the About This GopherSpace menu. You may want to read some of the other articles here, such as "How to use Gopher to get about," or the "extended ramblings" version of the "What is this place?" file. (The WELL is famous for its extended ramblings.)

8. When you're done reading, click Back again to return to the top-level WELL Gopher menu. From there you can begin to explore many different areas. Feel free to browse. The WELL Gopher is especially known for its information on media, communications, cyberpunk literature, and music.

`TIP`

> *Gopher menus can be saved, printed, copied, or made into bookmarks and shortcuts just like any other kinds of pages. In most cases, you needn't pay attention to whether you're at a Web, Gopher, or File Transfer Protocol (FTP) site. If you can see it in the browser window, you can work with it using any of the techniques you learned in Chapter 3.*

Although the hierarchy of all Gopher sites is similar, their content varies greatly. There are Gopher sites that specialize in just about any academic field you can think of, from art to astrophysics. In addition, there are Gopher sites that are just plain fun.

But the great thing about Gopher is that it allows a site to include links to other sites on its menus as well. In other words, you are not restricted to the information available only on that particular server. Gopher is really the precursor of the Web in letting sites link to one another in a vast information net.

As you start burrowing from one site to another, you are actually creating a customized hierarchical pathway for yourself, and you can move backward and forward along it to find the information you need. Let's see how this works.

Stretching Gopherspace

To demonstrate how you can "stretch" GopherSpace, let's use the WELL Gopher site again as a starting point (if the WELL Gopher is already displayed in your browser window, skip ahead to step 3 below):

1. Make sure you are connected to the Internet. If Navigator 4 is not currently running, launch it by double-clicking its icon or the Communicator icon.

2. In the Netsite/Location box at the top of the window, select the currently displayed URL and replace it with **gopher://gopher.well.com/**. Press Enter. After a few moments, the top-level menu at the WELL Gopher site appears, as shown earlier in Figure 8-24.

3. This time, click the Internet Outbound (Links We Think Are Cool) link. The Internet Outbound Gopher menu appears, as shown in Figure 8-26.

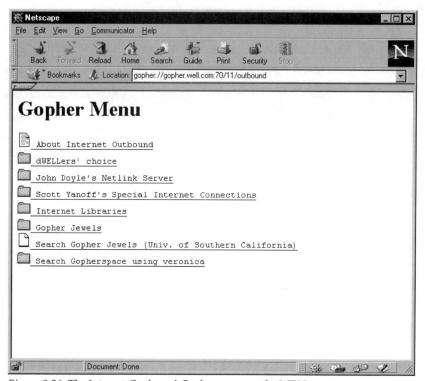

Figure 8-26: The Internet Outbound Gopher menu on the WELL.

4. All of the links on this menu provide useful starting points for Gopher burrowing. For this tutorial, click Scott Yanoff's Special Internet Connections. The Special Internet Connections Gopher menu appears, as shown in Figure 8-27.

   ■ Notice the icons depicting a computer terminal next to some of the links. This is how Navigator 4 indicates a Telnet connection. If you click on one of these links, Navigator launches a Telnet session with the host site. (More about Telnet later in this chapter.)

The Yanoff List, as it is sometimes known, offers you a wide variety of new jumping off points—or digging down points—for further Gopher burrowing. You should feel free to explore, and you may want to save this menu as a bookmark.

But before you descend into the Gopher tunnels, note that the Location box contains the URL gopher://gopher.well.sf.ca.us:70/11/outbound/Yanoff. *WELL* is still part of the site address because you've never really left the

WELL. No matter how far or deep you burrow through the menus, *WELL* will still form the initial part of the URL. The URL provides a map of the path you took to get to the target information.

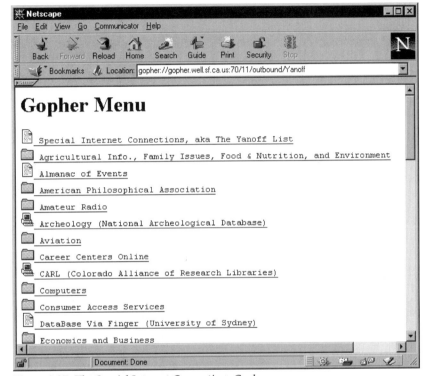

Figure 8-27: The Special Internet Connections Gopher menu.

There are many ways to get to The Yanoff List, but you have constructed a tunnel that begins at the WELL and passes through the Internet Outbound menu. What this means is that you have a complete record of your travels, and in saving a particular URL as a bookmark, you are actually saving a map of your entire journey. With this kind of hierarchical structure, there is really no way to get lost.

This is what I mean by stretching GopherSpace. With each new link you click, you are further extending a *customized* information pathway. You can see why Gopher is a useful research tool when you're trying to refine your quest for particular information.

The WELL is only one of many tunnel entrances. In the next section, I'll list some interesting Gopher sites to begin your explorations.

Great Gopher Holes I Have Known

Table 8-2 lists a few of the best-known Gopher sites.

URL	Description
gopher://gopher.uis.itd.umich.edu/	University of Michigan archive
gopher://ashpool.micro.umn.edu/	University of Minnesota archive
gopher://wx.atmos.uiuc.edu/	Weather maps
gopher://gopher.eff.org/	Electronic Frontier Foundation archive
gopher://gopher.well.sf.ca.us/	Whole Earth 'Lectronic Link (WELL) archive
gopher://wiretap.spies.com/	The Internet Wiretap
gopher://siggraph.org/	Conference proceedings and materials from the graphics special interest group (SIGGRAPH) of the Association for Computing Machinery
gopher://gopher.cpsr.org:70/11/cpsr	Computer Professionals for Social Responsibility archive
gopher://akasha.tic.com/	Sample issues of John Quarterman's Matrix News Internet newsletter; several works from Bruce Sterling
gopher://gopher.echonyc.com	Interesting information about New York City and media

Table 8-2: Some well-known Gopher sites.

Now that you know something about Gopher, let's take a brief look at another faithful old workhorse of the Internet, Telnet.

Telnet

The World Wide Web is the showroom of the Net. It's where you'll find information in all the latest styles and colors. If you want to show a newbie what the Net is all about, you'll almost certainly start with the Web.

But a fancy new car right off the showroom floor isn't always the best way to travel. Sometimes you need an all-terrain vehicle, a rugged tool that will take you places you can't access using the newer Web protocols. Telnet dates back to the days when the information superhighway was just a two-lane blacktop, and fortunately, you can still take advantage of its raw power through Netscape Communicator. And please slap me if I use another driving metaphor.

Using Telnet, you log in to other computers on the Net interactively. Once you log in, the Telnet host presents you with a command line or with text-based menus; you type menu choices or commands. Typical public Telnet sites include library card catalogs, weather information services, and a variety of specialized databases. You can also Telnet to text-based online services such as the WELL or Echo. And if you have a UNIX account on another computer on the Net, you can use Telnet to log in and run any UNIX program available on the host machine.

MUDs & MOOs

It's great to be able to access vast libraries of esoteric information via the Internet, but at some point we have to step back and take stock again of what computers are really for: playing games!

Some of the most interesting games spawned by modern information technology are MUDs and MOOs. MUDs are *Multiple-User Dimensions*, real-time, interactive role-playing games. MOOs are the object-oriented version, in which users can create their own objects, such as new rooms or features of the landscape. There are also variants of MUDs known as MUCKs, MUSHes, and MUSEs.

What all these games have in common is that several players at a time use the Internet to interact with one another as characters in a fictional world. Some of these text-based virtual worlds are full of magic and dragons, others are more like discussion forums, and some are meeting places for playing out group fantasies. Here are a couple of Web pages to get you started:

■ MUDs, MOOs, and Other Virtual Hangouts: (http://jefferson.village.virginia.edu/iath/treport/mud.html). Lots of information about MUDs and MOOs, and links to several sites.

■ MUDs, MOOs, and MUSHes, "Hip-Waders in the CMC Swamp": (http://www.oise.on.ca/~jnolan/mud.html). Links to information and games.

Also check out the Usenet newsgroups under rec.games.mud. It's important to read the FAQs and whatever other information you can get before trying these games, as each has its own culture and rules of etiquette.

How does this remote login process work? Telnet is really a *terminal emulation* protocol. That means it makes your PC behave like a terminal that's directly connected to the host computer. What is a terminal? A terminal is a device that can't really do anything on its own, but when it is attached to a computer it provides users with a display screen and a keyboard. In other words, a terminal provides the user interface to a host computer. Normally, terminals are attached to the host by means of cable, but terminal emulation programs allow you to connect remotely using a PC and phone lines. With terminal emulation programs like PROCOMM PLUS and Hyperterm, you dial directly into a host; with Telnet, you connect via the Internet or a corporate intranet.

Figure 8-28 shows a typical Telnet session. In this example, I am logged in to the Echo online service, and you can clearly see the interactive nature of this kind of connection.

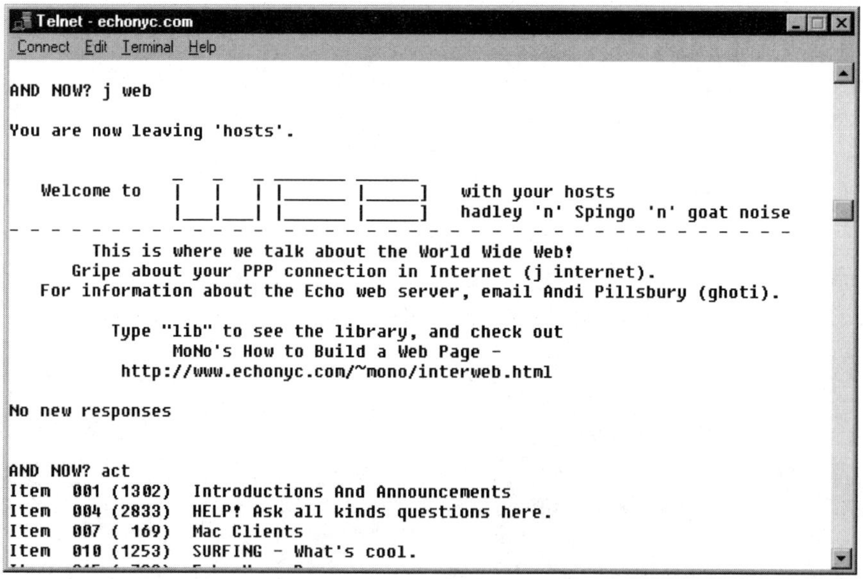

Figure 8-28: A Telnet session with Echo.

Telnet & Netscape Communicator 4

Let's see how observant you are: what's wrong with Figure 8-28?

That's right, it depicts some other software instead of Netscape Communicator. Instead of the usual toolbar and Netscape logo, you see a much simpler window. Did the author make a mistake? Did the editors miss it?

No. The fact is that Netscape Communicator does not actually include built-in Telnet. In fact, Web browsers almost *never* include built-in Telnet. Let me explain.

Terminal emulation programs and Web browsers are two very different kinds of software. Terminal emulation programs concentrate on providing direct access to the host computer operating system and its applications, while Web browsers concentrate on displaying multimedia documents.

Since these two functions are not a good fit, the authors of most World Wide Web programs have decided to support Telnet by launching an external helper application when necessary. If you click a link that represents the URL for a Telnet connection, Navigator 4 launches your Telnet session by executing a separate program, passing to it the address of the site. As soon as you're finished with the Telnet session, you can return to the browser window and to whatever document was last displayed in it. In fact, you don't even have to wait. If you're the kind of person who likes to do several things at once, you can go back and forth between active Telnet sessions and Navigator 4.

In order for Telnet to work, you have to have a program available on your system called **telnet.exe**. Fortunately, Windows 95 and NT come with this Telnet application, so Communicator can launch it automatically when necessary.

TN3270

Almost all public Telnet sites whose host computer is running the UNIX operating system these days support the standard version of the protocol that uses the VT100 terminal emulation. However, if the host is an IBM mainframe running an IBM operating system you may need a variant of Telnet known as *TN3270*. TN3270 sites require that you use a program that makes your PC act like an IBM 3270 terminal instead of a DEC VT100.

You're in luck. The Professional version of Netscape Communicator—and the Professional version only—contains a 3270 emulator called IBM Host On Demand. It temporarily turns your PC into a "dumb terminal," capable of communicating with a mainframe computer.

You launch the application by choosing Communicator IIBM Host On Demand. When you do, you'll get a screen that looks like Figure 8-29.

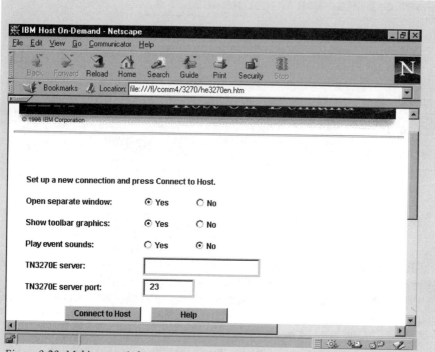

Figure 8-29: Making a mainframe connection.

You'll have the radio button options to: open the connection in a separate window (you can either open it in a separate window or open it in the Web browser itself), show the toolbar graphics (there are additional buttons a dumb terminal has that your keyboard doesn't have—Host on Demand gives you the option of putting those buttons onscreen), and play event sounds. When you make these three yes/no decisions, you'll have to fill out the name of the server to which you're connecting and the server port. Ask your network administrator if you're not sure about these.

When you're connected, you'll get a screen that looks a lot like Figure 8-30.

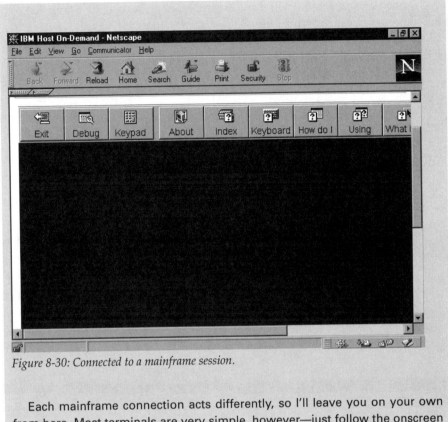

Figure 8-30: Connected to a mainframe session.

Each mainframe connection acts differently, so I'll leave you on your own from here. Most terminals are very simple, however—just follow the onscreen instructions and you should be fine.

Using Telnet

As with any other Internet service supported by Netscape Communicator, you can get to a Telnet site by any one of several methods. You can:

- Click a Telnet link in a Web document or at a Gopher site.
- Type a URL in Navigator 4's Netsite/Location box.
- Select a Telnet link from Bookmarks.
- Select a Telnet site from your Personal toolbar.
- Double-click a desktop shortcut to a Telnet site.

Any one of these actions will have the same result: Navigator 4 launches your Telnet application, which then logs you in to the site specified in the URL.

Let's give it a try by going back to a Telnet link you may have noticed earlier in a Gopher menu, the National Archeological Database. You may not be the slightest bit interested in archeology, but I have chosen this site because it is very typical of research sites that are publicly accessible via Telnet.

For the sake of this tutorial, I'm assuming you're using the Windows 95 Telnet application. The basic instructions should be close to accurate even if you're using a different program:

1. Make sure you are connected to the Internet. If Netscape Navigator 4 is not currently running, launch it.

2. In the Netsite/Location box at the top of the window, select the currently displayed URL and replace it with **gopher://gopher.well.sf.ca.us:70/11/ outbound/Yanoff**. Press Enter. (Hey, if you'd saved the Yanoff menu as a bookmark, you wouldn't have to type in the URL again.)

3. Click the Archeology (National Archeological Database) link. After a few seconds, the Telnet application appears with a login prompt from the remote site, as shown in Figure 8-31.

   - In addition, a small message box pops up telling you to log in to this site as "nadb," as shown in Figure 8-32.

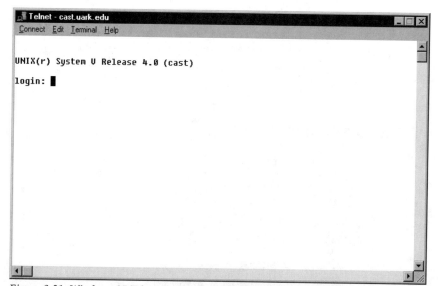

Figure 8-31: Windows 95 Telnet program with login prompt from the National Archeological Database.

Figure 8-32: Login information message box.

TIP

Not all sites supply you with login instructions like this, but many do. Depending on the exact timing of data received from the remote site, the Telnet window might cover the informational message box so that it is invisible to you. Before experimenting with different logins to see what will work, move or temporarily minimize the Telnet window to make sure you didn't miss an important message.

*If the remote system presents you with a login prompt but no information about what to enter, try entering **guest** and pressing Enter.*

4. Click on OK in the message box. It disappears.

5. At the login prompt in the main Telnet window, enter **nadb**. You are now logged in to the National Archeological Database, as shown in Figure 8-33.

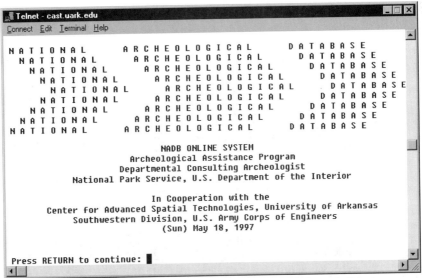

Figure 8-33: You're logged in to the National Archeological Database via Telnet.

6. As directed by the remote system, press Return (Enter) to continue. The NADB Connection Menu appears. Since you are connected via the Internet, select item 4, Internet to NADB, and press Return.

7. Continue following any directions that appear in the Telnet window. As is typical with research sites like this, you are asked to enter some information about yourself and to choose an ID number. Once you've gotten through this process, the NADB Main Menu appears, as shown in Figure 8-34.

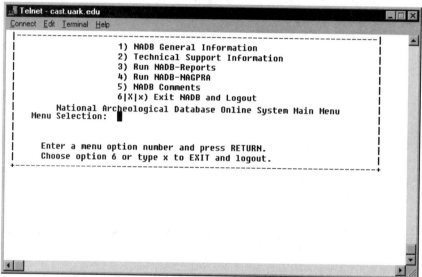

Figure 8-34: The NADB Main Menu.

TIP

Most Telnet programs let you copy text directly from the terminal window so that you can save it or paste it into other applications.

8. At this point, you can choose an item from the menu to get more information about the NADB or to access its search tools immediately. If you're interested in archeology, feel free to return to this site later, but for now let's select menu option 6 (or enter the letter **x**), Exit NADB, and log out. If you are using the Windows 95 Telnet program, a message box pops up explaining that your connection to the host has been lost, as shown in Figure 8-35.

Figure 8-35: The Connection to host lost message.

9. Once you are disconnected from the remote host, you can simply quit your Telnet program.

That's all there is to it. At first it may seem awkward that Navigator 4 needs to launch a separate helper application for Telnet access, but there are several advantages to this system. The most significant bonus is that you can use any Telnet application you want, including ones that are much more configurable and full-featured than the program included with Windows 95.

Speaking of configuration, let's take a quick look at some ways to tailor your Telnet application so that it works most efficiently for you.

Logging Off Remote Systems

Your Telnet program probably provides a way to disconnect from a remote site at any point, without even telling the remote host that you are leaving. In the Windows 95 Telnet program, you simply choose the Disconnect option from the Connect menu.

Whenever possible, however, you should end your session cleanly by logging out from the remote Telnet site, choosing the appropriate menu options or following instructions for quitting. Otherwise, the software at the remote Telnet site may not immediately realize you are gone and may keep the connection open for several minutes, exacerbating Net traffic jams.

Unless you're having technical problems with the connection, disconnecting without logging out is considered poor online etiquette.

Customizing Your Telnet Application

Most Telnet applications offer a variety of options to make your online life easier and more productive. Since the Windows 95 Telnet program is typical of the simple applications that are available, we'll use it as an example. If you're using a different program, you may have to look around a little for the configuration options we're examining, but they should be there somewhere.

1. Launch Telnet by clicking its icon on the desktop or by using the Windows 95 Run command. The main Telnet window appears, as shown in Figure 8-36.

   ■ Most Telnet applications don't require you to be connected to the Net to change preferences or configuration options.

Figure 8-36: The Windows 95 Telnet application.

2. Select Preferences from the Terminal menu. The Terminal Preferences dialog box appears, as shown in Figure 8-37.

Figure 8-37: The Terminal Preferences dialog box.

The options in this dialog box are pretty typical of what's available in Telnet programs. Here are some tips for configuring these settings:

- **Local Echo**. Most remote Telnet sites echo back to you all the characters you type so that you can see what you are doing. Generally you should leave this check box unchecked; check it only if your typing is invisible to you.

- **Blinking Cursor**. Check this box if you want your cursor to blink while you are in Telnet. This can help you find the cursor on remote systems that include lots of lines or underscores in their screens.

- **Block Cursor**. Check this option if you want a block cursor instead of the usual cursor. This may be much easier to see on some systems.

- **VT100 Arrows**. The VT100 terminal emulation includes two different sets of character sequences ("mappings") that can be sent to the remote Telnet host when you press the arrow keys. Unless your arrow keys don't seem to be working properly at a particular site, leave this box unchecked. (For the propeller heads out there, unchecked means Keypad Application Mode, and checked means Keypad Cursor Mode. The remote site may send sequences that temporarily change your default setting.)

- **Buffer Size**. This option lets you specify how many lines you can scroll back to see text that has scrolled out of the Telnet window. Since the VT100 terminal displays 25 lines of text at one time, this option should be set to 25 or greater.

- **Emulation**. Unless a remote Telnet host explicitly requires VT52 emulation, you should keep this set to VT100/ANSI. Other Telnet programs may let you choose from a wider variety of terminal emulations, but VT100 is the most commonly supported one on publicly accessible sites.

- **Fonts**. Click this button to change the font of the text that appears in your Telnet window.

- **Background Color**. Click this button to change the background color of your Telnet window.

Once you have made your configuration changes, click OK to return to the main Telnet window.

Moving On

This has been a "back to the basics" chapter—a quick look at some of the older workhorse Net services available through Netscape Communicator. In its support of FTP, Gopher, and Telnet, Communicator provides you with some of the most dependable tools available for gathering information. But enough of looking into the past. In the next chapter, we explore the future—or at least *your* future as a designer of your own Web pages! This may sound daunting at first, but not to worry. Netscape Composer makes it very, very easy.

CHAPTER 9

Your Own Page (Using Composer)

So far in this book, I've covered lots of ways to gather information from your intranet or from the Net itself. With Communicator, you can experience everything from plain-vanilla office memos to videos of John Travolta doing that sort of twist thing he does. But gathering information—or even sitting back and receiving it in e-mail—is only one side of the Communicator coin. Communicator includes a special module called Netscape Composer that lets you create your own beautifully formatted multimedia documents that others can then access.

Why Your Own Page?

I'm glad you asked. You might want to create your own Web pages for several reasons:

- **Presentations for work.** Instead of carrying those ubiquitous PowerPoint transparencies into your next meeting, why not create fully formatted and illustrated documents that co-workers can access right from their own computers? An example of a typical business document in HTML format is shown in Figure 9-1.

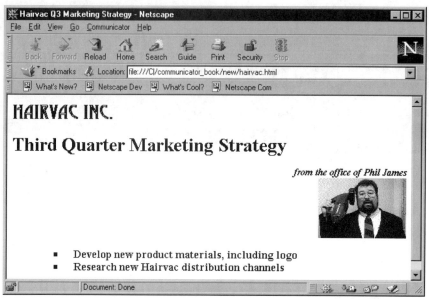

Figure 9-1: A business presentation in HTML format.

- **Slicker e-mail.** When you use the HTML editing window to create e-mail in Netscape Messenger (see Chapter 5), you are actually accessing Netscape Composer. That's why you can make your messages look like Web pages: they really *are* Web pages. But you can also work separately in Composer and then add the results later to your e-mail messages. For example, you may want to include some fancy letterhead in every message or a page that includes pictures of your kids.

- **A home base.** Remember how Navigator lets you choose a home page, the page that displays initially when you load the program? Well, you can make that home page your *own* home page, a special document that includes links to your favorite sites, formatted to your own exact specifications, as shown in Figure 9-2. You can store this special starter page on a Web server or simply on your own machine.

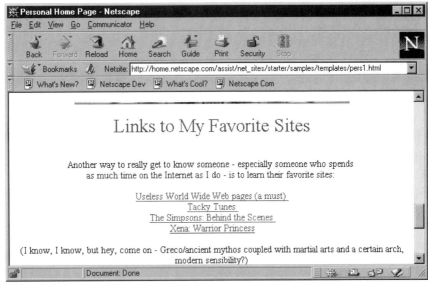

Figure 9-2: A personal home base.

PowerStart

In this chapter, you'll learn several different ways of creating Web pages, but I *don't* cover one very useful tool: Netscape's *PowerStart* facility. PowerStart uses a Wizard very similar to the Page Wizard described later in this chapter. However, it helps you create a slightly different kind of Web page, a sort of home base that includes not only your most-used links, but also a personal notepad and access to various services that automatically update the information in your browser window. For example, without even a mouse click, your PowerStart page can display the latest technology news, stock quotes, or weather reports for your area.

So why don't I cover PowerStart in this chapter? Because configuring PowerStart is almost identical with using the Page Wizard described later in the chapter, and Netscape includes very thorough instructions as well. To access PowerStart, simply click the PowerStart link on Netscape's home page at http://home.netscape.com. Just follow the directions to create your PowerStart page. Once it's created, you access it the same way—by clicking the PowerStart link. Of course, you'll probably want to set it as your startup home page or create a link to it on your Personal toolbar.

Note: PowerStart requires an Internet connection—it will not work on an intranet alone.

- **Setting up shop.** Do you have something to sell? Thousands of Internet users each day are setting up commercial sites that advertise products and services, and that even allow customers to make purchases. With pages created in Netscape Composer, you can tap into a whole new market.

- **Self-publishing.** Maybe instead of something to sell, you have something to *say*. Sure, you can publish the company newsletter on your intranet, but the Web also makes it possible for individuals to publish their own artwork, literary pieces, and even music. If Doubleday won't give you that half-million dollar advance you deserve, why not put your Great American Cyber-Novel up on a Web server?

- **Coordinating and organizing.** Thousands of organizations, large and small, keep members informed of activities through Web pages. Whether you're planning a Little League picnic or a march on Washington, you can disseminate the necessary information and work out the logistics through a well-designed Web site. Figure 9-3 shows the Web site maintained by the American Civil Liberties Union. It is a good example of well-planned HTML.

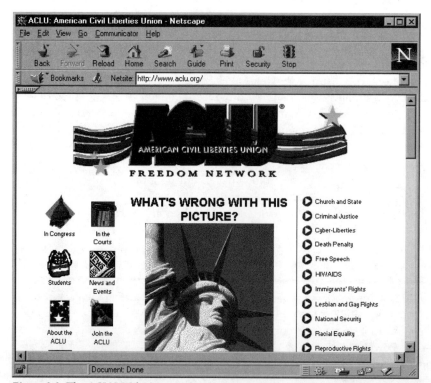

Figure 9-3: The ACLU Web site.

There are many more uses for Web pages—perhaps you can use Composer to develop some for your own company.

What You Need

If you're creating a Web page that only you will see—for example, a special "hot list" composed of links to your favorite sites—all you really need is Netscape Communicator and a little bit of space on your hard drive or on a network drive. You create the file using Composer and then save it locally, in any directory you want. You can then view it in Navigator 4 by pressing Ctrl+O or selecting Open Page from the File menu. Alternatively, you can register it as your default home page (the page that is displayed when you start Navigator 4 or when you click the Home button) by selecting Preferences from the Edit menu, clicking the Navigator category, and then customizing the fields as shown in Figure 9-4.

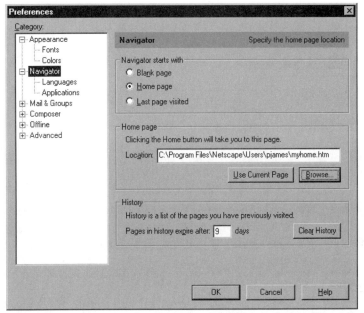

Figure 9-4: The Navigator configuration window with a local home page specified.

Notice the unusual format of the URL for a local file (as opposed to one that resides on an actual Web server). The URL for a local file starts with the word *file*. Next, as with all complete URLs, there is a colon and two forward slashes, then the exact path to the file. Got all that? Here's an example—an HTML file called PRODUCT.HTM that's located in the Public directory on the Q drive of your LAN: file://Q:/Public/PRODUCT.HTM. Of course if this file were on your own computer, you would specify one of your local drives, for instance C, instead of Q.

You can enter the path for the file using backslashes if you want; Communicator automatically converts them to forward slashes, which are the standard for Web browsers.

Even if you want others to be able to view your home Web page, you may not need to do any more than copy it to a directory on your intranet where your audience has read permission. They would then simply go through the same steps as above to view the document, but instead of specifying a drive on their machine, they'd specify the correct network drive. This method is the simplest way of publishing a Web page. But it's not necessarily the best way. Many features, such as built-in security, forms, streaming multimedia, and Java, only become available to you as an HTML author if you put your work up on an actual Web server. In addition, publishing your page via a Web server is the only way to make it available to those people who can't access directories on your local area network.

Your Web Server

So do you need to run out and buy a Web server if you want to publish Web pages? *Absolutely not!* In fact, unless you're at least as much of a geek as I am, you shouldn't even consider getting your own server.

Why? You can find Web servers all over the place just waiting to provide a home for your latest creation. Maybe there's one on your intranet right now. If not, try convincing your network administrator to get one. Or if you log on to the Internet from home, your ISP (Internet Service Provider) may maintain a Web server that customers can use at no extra charge. If all else fails, plenty of commercial entities will be happy to house your pages for a small monthly fee.

In choosing a Web server for your pages, you should think about these few basic considerations:

■ **Are you charged for using extra disk space?** HTML files are generally pretty small, but if your Web page includes many graphics, sound, or video files, you may go beyond the free storage limit. Check with the administrator of your Web server to make sure you won't receive unexpected bills.

Of course, being as efficient as possible in your use of graphics and other large media files is always wise. This way, you not only reduce storage charges, but you also assure that clients can load your pages quickly, even on slow connections.

■ **Can you easily update your files?** Information is as relative and dynamic as anything else. Yesterday's truth is today's theory and tomorrow's superstition. If the Web server you use doesn't make updating your files easy—for example, if you have to get permission from the administrator every time you make a change—you need to find a new Web server.

■ **Does the Web server provide the features you need?** Don't assume that just any Web server will support all the services you need. For example, if you want to collect information via HTML forms, make sure that your Web server can do this job for you. It will probably take some extra work on the part of the server administrator to set up this service for you. Or, if you need SSL security, make sure that you're placing your pages on a machine running one of Netscape's security-enhanced server applications. Starting a Web radio station? You'll need to put your sound files on a Netscape Media Server or a RealAudio server. In short, think about what kinds of bells and whistles you may want to add to your Web page in the next year or so, and then make sure your Web server supports them.

■ **Is the server reliable?** As the Net grows, Web servers sometimes have a hard time keeping up with the traffic. Your local ISP may have been the most reliable one in the world until somebody posted those insider stock tips. Now, with two hundred thousand hits a day tying up the lines, sometimes nobody can get through to your modest little numismatics page. If the administrators of your Web server are not committed to upgrading hardware as necessitated by traffic, or if they are unable to maintain their equipment and software in top-notch condition, it's time to look elsewhere.

OK, you've chosen a Web server that will store and make available the documents you create. Later, in the section called "Publishing Your Page," I'll show you how to put these documents up on the server. But first you have to *create* a document or two. And before you do that, you have to configure Composer so that it works exactly the way you want it to.

TIP

Looking for some space to put up your Web pages? Try Geocities at http://www.geocities.com and Tripod at http://www.tripod.com.

Configuring Composer

Let's breeze through this configuration so we can get to the fun stuff:

1. Click the Netscape Composer icon on your desktop. Alternatively, from any other Communicator module, click the Composer button in the Component bar. The Composer window appears, as shown in Figure 9-5.

Figure 9-5: The Composer window.

2. From the Edit menu, select Preferences and then, if necessary, click the Composer category in the left-hand pane. The Composer preferences dialog box appears, as shown in Figure 9-6.

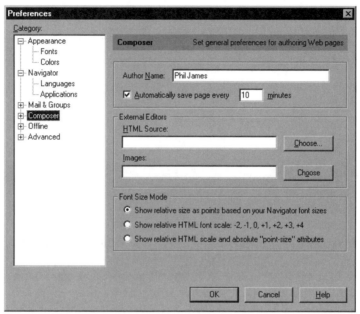

Figure 9-6: The Composer preferences dialog box.

3. In the Author Name box, fill in your name.

4. While you're working through this chapter, you may want to *un*check the Auto save check box. That way, you can always revert to the original file you're working on if you make a big mess of it while editing. But once you've worked through this chapter and are actually creating your own Web pages, you should probably come back and check the Auto save check box. If Composer automatically saves your work every 10 minutes or so, you can't lose *too* much of your hard work in the event your computer crashes.

5. In the next two fields, enter the full path and program names of any external editors you want to use for editing HTML code or graphics images directly. You can use the Choose buttons to locate these programs on your system.

External Editors??

Wait a second: Composer is supposed to be an HTML editor. Why do you need to specify additional external editors here?

Netscape Composer is known as a *WYSIWYG* editor—What You See Is What You Get. That means you can manipulate text and graphics directly on the screen, and you see pretty much what your page will look like at all times. As you adjust the size of fonts or move graphics around on your page, Composer is busy behind the scenes generating the actual HTML source code that will tell other people's browsers how to display your page. For example, when you select some text and click the Bold button, you see bold text on your screen. But Composer, behind the scenes, has changed the actual HTML file you're generating so that the text you selected is now surrounded by the standard HTML bold on and bold off tags, like this:

<B>your selected text here</B>

You are insulated from these programming details by the graphical interface Composer provides.

Sometimes, however, you may want to manipulate the HTML source directly. For example, you may want to add some advanced or specialized HTML commands that are not available through the Composer interface. (If Composer covered *every* tag and option available in the HTML specification, your screen would be covered with dozens of buttons and toolbars!) Or you may want to tweak the spacing of some elements on your page very precisely, which is sometimes easier to do by changing a value than by moving a mouse around.

Remember, the actual HTML files generated by Composer, like all HTML files, are text files. So to edit HTML code directly, you need a text editor. Chances are you already have one you like. Rather than making you learn a new program, the Netscape programmers decided to let you specify your *own* editor for working directly with HTML code. Then to edit your HTML source code using an external editor, you simply choose HTML Source from Composer's Edit menu. You'll learn more about this topic in the section called "Editing Your HTML Source."

TIP

Composer also lets you specify your own program for editing graphics files. Composer launches this application when you click the Edit Image button in the Image Properties dialog box that you access by right-clicking an existing image or by clicking the Insert Image button on Composer's toolbar (see the section called "Adding a Picture").

The next three options relate to how Composer expresses the relative sizes of text within the document you create. As you may have noticed, the main Composer window includes a drop-down list from which you can choose the font size for new text you type in or change the font size for selected text. (See the section called "Changing Font Size.") The numbers in this list will vary depending on which option button you select in the Composer preferences dialog box:

- **Show relative size as points.** The numbers in the drop-down list indicate the actual point size of the text. The point sizes available will vary depending on the font style you've selected.

- **Show relative HTML font scale.** The numbers in the drop-down list express the *relative* size of the font using a standard scale. In this scale, 0 is the size of text in the Normal style; negative values are progressively smaller, and positive values are progressively larger than the Normal font.

- **Show relative HTML scale and absolute "point-size" attributes.** This option allows both point sizes and HTML scale sizes to be displayed in the drop-down list. In other words, it combines the two options outlined above. The list shows the relative HTML scale first. If you scroll down the list, you can access the absolute point sizes.

Now on to Composer's Publishing options. In the left-hand category list, click the Publishing subcategory under Composer. (You might have to expand the Composer category by double-clicking it or clicking the plus sign.) The Publishing preferences dialog box appears, as shown in Figure 9-7.

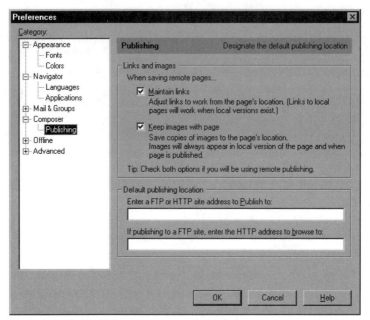

Figure 9-7: The Publishing preferences dialog box.

If you intend to place your Web pages on a remote server, or even a server on your own intranet, you need to fill this dialog box out very carefully. Some of the concepts may be new to you, so I'm going to go through each option in detail:

■ **Maintain links.** Typically, you create your Web pages on your own machine before publishing them on a remote server. You may create a main HTML file that includes links to *other* HTML files on your own machine. What happens when you upload all this stuff to your server? How does the main HTML file know how to find the other HTML files now that they're no longer on your local machine?

Well, if you leave this check box checked, Composer will automatically adjust the links in your files when it uploads them to the server.

Showing how this process works is easier than explaining it abstractly. Let's say you have a file called main.html in a folder or directory called C:\home_page. And let's say that main.html contains a link to another file called pictures.html that is located in a subdirectory of C:\home_page called Pictures. In other words, you have two files: C:\home_page\main.html and C:\home_page\Pictures\pictures.html.

OK, now pay attention here. When you publish your page, let's assume you upload your files to a Web server whose URL is http://www.server.com. The directory they've given you is user1, so the URL to your main HTML file, once you upload it, is http://www.server.com/user1/main.html, and the URL to your pictures file is http://www.server.com/user1/Pictures/pictures.html. Originally, your main.html file included a link to C:/home_page/Pictures/pictures.html, but since the Maintain links box is checked, Composer automatically adjusts this link to http://www.server.com/user1/Pictures/pictures.html. Your main file always knows where the pictures file is, and browsers won't get "File not found" errors.

TIP

While the Maintain links feature is very convenient for intermediate and advanced users, if you're a Web publishing beginner, you should keep all your HTML and associated files in a single directory and upload them all to a single directory on the Web server. Keeping things simple is the best way to avoid "File not found" errors in your pages.

- **Keep images with page.** If you keep this option checked, Composer uploads copies of your images to the server along with your HTML files. The images therefore will appear when somebody browses to your site as well as when you view your document locally. Again, if you're publishing on a remote Web server, keeping this box checked is usually essential.

- **Enter a FTP or HTTP site address to Publish to.** Typically, you upload your pages to a Web server using Composer's built-in FTP protocol. However, Composer also supports HTTP uploads. In either case, type in the URL for your publishing location, including the full path to your publishing directory. For example, your publishing location might be ftp://www.server.com/user1/public_html/.

- **If publishing to a FTP site, enter the HTTP address to browse to.** This address is the actual location of your Web pages, for example http://www.server.com/user1/public_html/. Filling in this information is essential if you have entered an FTP address in the previous field, which is usual.

When you are finished making changes, click OK to return to the main Composer window. Now let's get busy with the creative process itself. Netscape Communicator provides two convenient tools that make it easy to get started—the Page Wizard and page templates.

Creating Your Page Using Page Wizard

Our first order of business is to fire up Netscape Composer:

1. For this exercise, make sure you are connected to the Net, either through a direct connection or a SLIP/PPP connection with your Internet Service Provider.

TIP

The Page Wizard actually "lives" on Netscape's own Web site. If you are on an office intranet but are not currently connected to the Net itself, you will not be able to use this convenient feature. You should skip ahead to the section called "Creating Your Page Using a Page Template."

2. Click the Netscape Composer icon on your desktop. Alternatively, from any other Communicator module, click the Composer button in the Component bar. The Composer window appears, as shown in Figure 9-8.

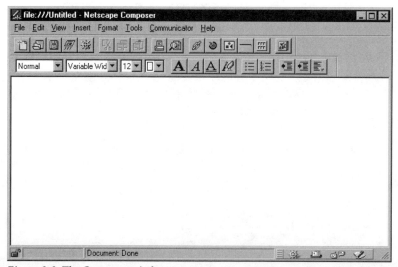

Figure 9-8: The Composer window.

Now you're ready to start composing your page using the Wizard:

1. In Netscape Composer, click the New Page button, the one at the far left of the special Composer taskbar. A dialog box composed of five buttons appears, as shown in Figure 9-9.

Figure 9-9: The Create New Page dialog box.

2. Click the From Page Wizard button. Composer launches Navigator 4 and takes you to Netscape's Page Wizard site, as shown in Figure 9-10.

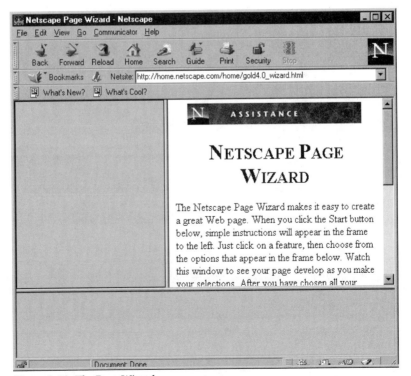

Figure 9-10: The Page Wizard.

3. Scroll down the frame that contains text, and read the description of the Page Wizard feature. When you're done reading, click the Start button. Now some instructions appear in the left-hand frame, as shown in Figure 9-11, and the right-hand frame contains a preview of the page you are building.

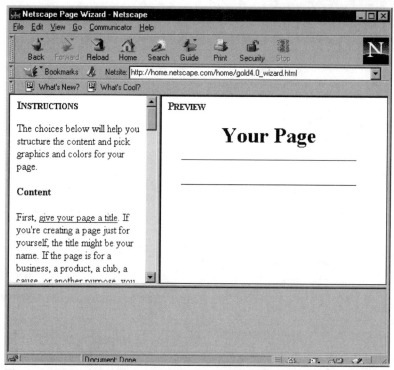

Figure 9-11: Two frames activated in the Page Wizard.

Scroll down the left-hand frame. As you can see, it contains several links that are actually options for customizing your document. Here's the rundown on how the three frames in the browser window will operate as you start to create your page:

- In the left-hand frame, you choose particular options you want to configure. We'll call this the *Options frame*.

- Once you click one of these links, the bottom frame will display various choices. For example, if you click a link labeled Background Color, various background color choices appear in the bottom frame. We'll call this bottom frame the *Selection frame*.

- The right-hand frame, where we started this whole process, shows you a preview of your Web page. As you choose new elements in the Option and Selection frames, this *Preview frame* is automatically updated to reflect your latest changes.

The left-hand Options frame always contains the same information. Therefore, if you don't like a change you've made, you can always go back and click that option again.

Let's go through the various options offered by the Page Wizard.

Titling Your Page

Everything's got to have a name, right?

1. In the Options frame, click the "give your page a title" link. The Choices: Title edit field appears in the Selection frame.

2. Enter a title for your page; then click the Apply button. As you can see in Figure 9-12, the Preview frame is automatically updated.

   - If you make a mistake or want to change your title, simply edit what you typed in the Choices: Title box, and click Apply again.

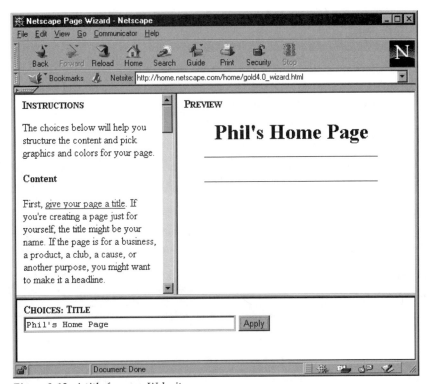

Figure 9-12: A title for your Web site.

Creating an Introduction

An introduction is the place where you tell people what your page is about. If you're just creating a page for your own use, the introduction is the place where you remind yourself of who you are.

1. In the Options frame, scroll down to the link "type an introduction" and click it. A new edit box appears, as shown in Figure 9-13.

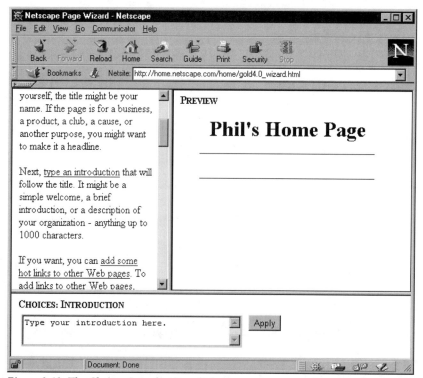

Figure 9-13: The Choices: Introduction edit box.

2. Start typing. When you are satisfied with your introduction, click Apply. Once again, the Preview frame is updated with the new information.

Now comes the fun part: adding some links to other sites.

Adding Links

You probably already know what's in your own home page, so why not explore beyond your own little world by adding some links?

1. Scroll down the Options frame to the "add some hot links to other Web pages." Click it.

2. In the Selection frame, type a site name in the Name field and its URL in the URL field. In Figure 9-14, for example, you can see that I've entered a link to the Ventana Web site.

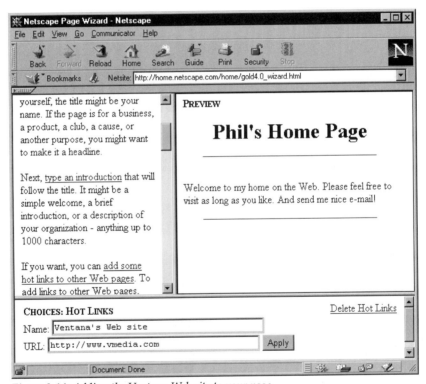

Figure 9-14: Adding the Ventana Web site to your page.

3. Click Apply. The link is added to your page.

4. You can enter as many new links as you want, clicking the Apply button each time. All these links are added automatically to your page.

OK, you've got your links. Now maybe you want to add some concluding remarks to your page.

Adding a Conclusion

To add some more text after your links, follow these steps:

1. In the Options frame, scroll down to the "type a paragraph of text to serve as a conclusion" link.

2. In the Choices: Conclusion box, enter up to 1,000 words.

3. As before, click Apply. The preview frame is automatically updated.

Let's add one last touch to this very basic page: a clickable e-mail address so people can contact you or so that you can send yourself the kind of messages I know you love.

Adding Your E-mail Address

If you've been cruising the Web for a while, you've probably noticed that many pages include a link that lets you send e-mail to the creator of the page or to a site administrator. Click the link, and you're automatically transported to Netscape Messenger, where you can simply type a message and click the Send To field that is already filled in with the correct recipient. This special kind of link is called a *Mail to link*, and you can add one to your own page as well.

1. Scroll down the Options frame to "add an e-mail link," and click it.

2. In the Selection frame, type in your full e-mail address, and click Apply. Your page now contains a new Mail to link.

Now that you've added some basic information to your Web page, you're ready to configure what it looks like.

Configuring Visual Elements

When you're ready to configure visual elements, your work gets fun:

1. Scroll down the Options frame to the "preset color combination" link, and click it. A number of color schemes appear in the Selection frame, as shown in Figure 9-15.

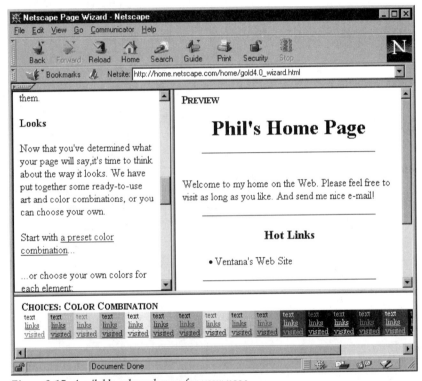

Figure 9-15: Available color schemes for your page.

2. Select one of the color combinations. As usual, the Preview frame immediately reflects your choice. You can see in Figure 9-16 that I chose a combination that includes a gray background.

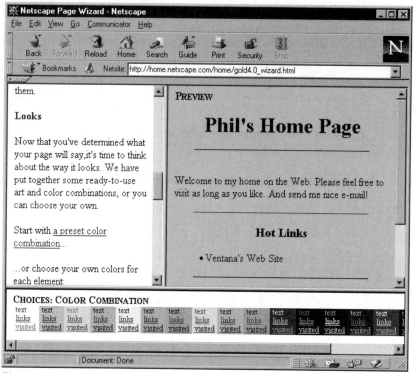

Figure 9-16: The page with new colors.

What if you don't like the color combinations available, or what if you want to add a background texture to your Personal Workspace? No problem. As you can see in the Options frame, the Wizard lets you choose custom colors for many display elements, including background color, background pattern, text color, link color, and visited link color. Simply click the appropriate option, and make your choices from the Selection frame.

Now scroll down and click the next link in the Options frame, the one that lets you choose a bullet style. As you can see in the Selection frame, several of the choices are actually animated GIFs. Instead of basic square or round bullets, you can use one of these graphics in your page for any bulleted lists you add.

Finally, the Wizard lets you choose a horizontal rule style. You know the drill: scroll down to the "choose a horizontal rule style" link, and click it. Now several choices for a horizontal rule appear in the Selection window, as shown in Figure 9-17. As with the bullets, several of them are animated.

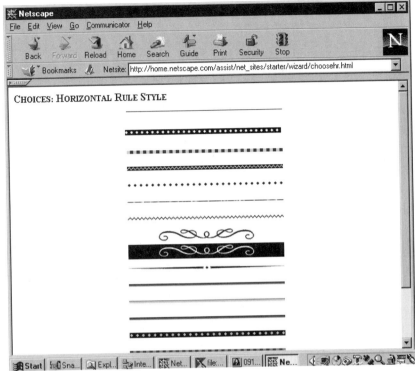

Figure 9-17: The horizontal rule option.

The horizontal rule you choose is the line that will separate the various areas of your page.

OK, you've added some information and some graphical interest to your page. Now comes the most important step: saving your work.

Saving Your Page

Saving is easy. When you've customized your page to your satisfaction, click the Build button at the very bottom of the left-hand Options frame. Immediately, the Navigator 4 browser window displays your new page, as shown in Figure 9-18.

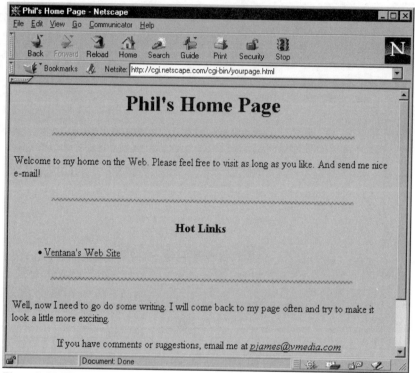

Figure 9-18: The Navigator window after clicking Build in the Page Wizard.

To save your page, simply press Ctrl+S or select Save As from the File menu. A Save As dialog box appears, letting you save your new file in any directory you want, either on your local hard drive or on a network drive. You may also change its name in the File name edit box. To edit your file some more, simply select Edit Page from the File menu. You are returned to Composer, with the current page available for more editing.

Naming Your Files

If you are planning to publish your pages on a Web server and want to make them accessible to the general public, you should name the top-level file (the one that people are supposed to see first, before clicking any links) **index.html** or **index.htm.** (Check with your system administrator or ISP about which extension to use.) Files with these names are treated a little differently by the Web server: they are displayed automatically when a user browses to your site. In other words, if you store your HTML files at http://friendly_server.com/~joe_blow/, users will see your index.html file just by entering that URL in their browser programs, without any filename explicitly specified. But if no index.html or index.htm file exists, the users will probably get a "File not found" error.

Creating Your Page Using a Page Template

Page templates are sample documents designed for specific purposes, such as a company newsletter or advertising for a small business. The idea is that you modify them for your own use, keeping elements of the original design and thus saving time over creating a page completely from scratch. You may be familiar with the concept of templates from your word processor.

Any Web page can serve as a page template; there is nothing really unique to them. However, using templates that are designed for that particular purpose is helpful. They will contain less nitty-gritty specific information and more broad design features that you can easily adapt to your own needs.

Netscape provides a number of page templates on its own Web site, and we will work with one of them now. However, the techniques discussed in this section apply to using any page template, whether it's one supplied by your MIS department and located on your office intranet or one you've developed yourself and are storing on your hard drive. Of course, to work with the templates located at Netscape's site, you have to be connected to the Net. Once you've established your connection, you can just follow these steps:

1. Run Composer by clicking its icon on your desktop or in the Component bar.

2. In the Composer window, click the far left New Page button. The Create New Page dialog box appears, as shown earlier in Figure 9-9.

3. Click From Template. The New Page From Template dialog box appears, as shown in Figure 9-19.

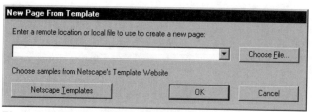

Figure 9-19: The New Page From Template dialog box.

4. As you can see, this dialog box lets you choose a local file to use as a template, or in fact a file located at any URL you specify. Since we're going to use one from Netscape's Web site, though, click the Netscape Templates button. In a few seconds, the Templates Page appears in a Navigator 4 window, as shown in Figure 9-20.

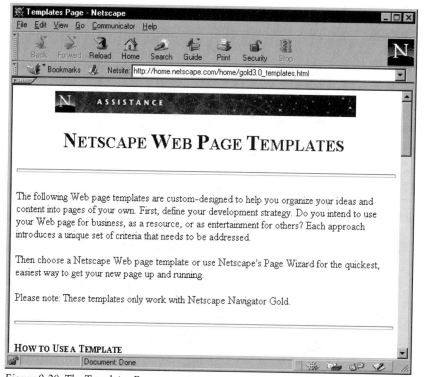

Figure 9-20: The Templates Page.

5. Read the text in the page; then scroll down and click the "My Home Page" link. Netscape then provides you with a template for a simple home page.

As you look over the template you've chosen, you can see that it includes some formatting and graphics elements that may be useful to you in your own page. Obviously, though, it needs a lot of modification. In the next section, we'll play around with the page in Composer, learning the most important of Composer's many commands.

To start editing the template in Composer, select Edit Page from Navigator's File menu. Composer appears, displaying the template as shown in Figure 9-21. Now would be a good time to press that Save button and save the file locally under whatever name you want to give it.

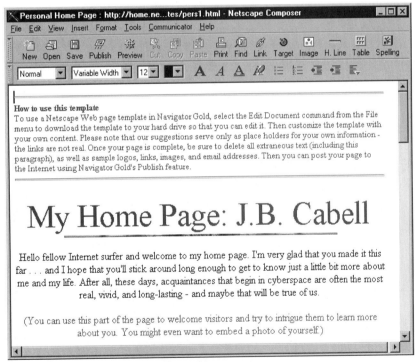

Figure 9-21: The Home Page template in Composer.

Rolling Your Own

The next section is about modifying a template, a Web document supplied by Netscape that can serve as a starting point for creating your own page. But if you are not starting with a template, you can also create a page from scratch. Just click the New Page icon in Composer, choose Blank Page, and either start typing or paste text in from any other Windows program. Once you have some material to work with, even just a word or two, the skills and commands covered in the next section will work for you just as well as they do for somebody starting from a template. The only difference between editing a template and editing a new blank document is how much material you start with. And, of course, something doesn't really have to be *called* a template to be used as one. A time-honored approach to creating Web pages is to take an existing one you like—from anywhere on the Web—and modify it sufficiently to call it your own. This approach is also an excellent way to hone your Web authoring skills.

One word of advice, though: as soon as you start working in your own document, save it right away to your hard drive (or a network drive) so you don't lose any of your work. To do so, click Composer's Save button or simply press Ctrl+S. Then select a location for your new file. Typically, you save all the documents that make up a particular Web page (text, graphics, sound files, and so on) together in a directory or folder. For example, you may want to save your first home page to the directory C:\home_page. This way, you can easily find your work if you want to modify it later. (You open Web files that already exist on your machine by clicking Composer's Open File button, the second from the left on the top toolbar.) In addition, this approach makes it easy to publish your work on a remote Web server. I'll cover this information later in the section "Publishing Your Page."

Modifying Your Page

Way back in Chapter 5, I showed you how to edit your e-mail messages so that they look just like Web pages. In this section, we'll cover many of the same Composer features in more detail, modifying your document until it looks exactly like you want it to. For the purposes of this exercise, we'll edit the template document we looked at earlier, but even if you're building a Web page completely from scratch, you'll use the same Composer features and commands. OK, let's get busy.

Editing Text

You're in the Composer window shown earlier in Figure 9-21. You've saved Netscape's home page template under a new filename and you're ready to start editing the content so that it's suited to your particular needs.

Composer supports the navigation keys that are typical in any Windows text editor, as shown in Table 9-1:

Navigation Key	Action
Left arrow	Moves the cursor left one character
Ctrl+left arrow	Moves the cursor left one word
Right arrow	Moves the cursor right one character
Ctrl+right arrow	Moves the cursor right one word
Up arrow	Moves the cursor up one line
Down arrow	Moves the cursor down one line
PgUp	Moves the cursor up one screen
PgDn	Moves the cursor down one screen
Home	Moves the cursor to the beginning of the line
Ctrl+Home	Moves the cursor to the beginning of the document
End	Moves the cursor to the end of the line
Ctrl+End	Moves the cursor to the end of the document

Table 9-1: Navigation keys in Composer.

TIP

The keys in Table 9-2 can help you edit a document faster, but if you forget them, you can access all the most important editing commands from the menus. And Communicator includes buttons for Cut, Copy, and Paste commands, just like common word processors. There's even a Find button for locating text within a document you're working on.

In addition, Composer supports a full range of keys or key combinations you can use to actually modify text, as shown in Table 9-2:

Key	Action
Backspace	Deletes the character to the left of the cursor
Del	Deletes the character at the current cursor position, or deletes selected text
Enter	Adds a line break, with a blank line below it
Shift+Enter	Adds a new line break, with no blank line below it
Ctrl+A	Selects the entire document
Ctrl+B	Changes selected text to boldface
Ctrl+C	Copies selected text
Ctrl+I	Changes selected text to italic font
Ctrl+Shift+L	Inserts a link at the cursor location
Ctrl+M	Increases the indent
Ctrl+Shift+M	Decreases the indent
Ctrl+S	Saves the file
Ctrl+V	Pastes the contents of the clipboard to the current cursor location
Ctrl+X	Cuts selected text
Ctrl+Z	Undoes the last editing change
Shift+Ctrl+Z	Redoes the last undone change
Shift+Ctrl+End	Selects text from the cursor position to the end of the document
Shift+Spacebar	Adds a nonbreaking space (a space that will not cause a line break)

Table 9-2: Text editing keys in Composer.

Now let's try out some of these keys. Using your mouse, move your cursor to the beginning of the line that reads My Home Page and click the left button. Now press the End key. Your cursor moves to the end of the line. Again using your mouse, click and drag over the name J.B. Cabell until it is selected (appears in reverse colors), as shown in Figure 9-22.

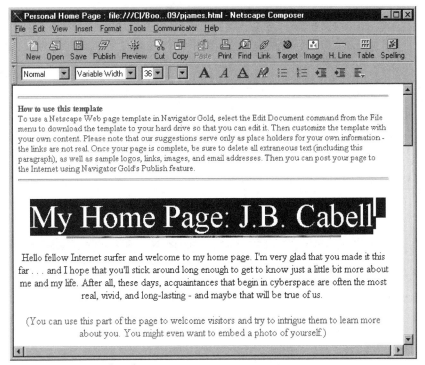

Figure 9-22: Some selected text.

At this point, you could delete the text you don't want, but replacing it is simpler. With the name still selected, just start typing your own name. The selected text is automatically replaced, as shown in Figure 9-23.

Using the keys listed in Tables 9-1 and 9-2, the Cut, Copy, Paste, and Find buttons, and commands on the Edit menu, you can modify all the text you want in the template document. But suppose after modifying the contents, you still don't like the way things *look*? Netscape Composer offers a full range of features for modifying the way text appears in a Web document.

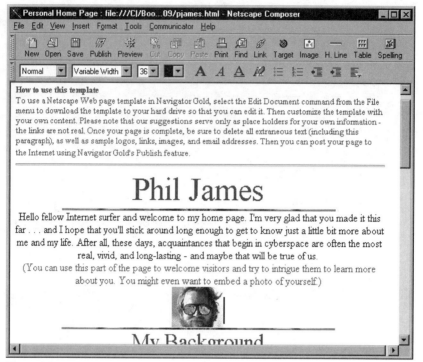

Figure 9-23: A new name.

Selecting a Style

The first control on the bottom of the two Composer toolbars is a drop-down list of *HTML styles*. Styles are tags that tell a Web browser or e-mail viewer to display text in a particular way. For example, a Heading 1 style tells the client program to display the corresponding text as a large header, usually surrounded on the top and bottom by some empty space. Let's change the style of the text we just edited:

1. Place your cursor anywhere in the line that reads Home Page: Phil James (or your own name). Since styles apply to an entire paragraph, you don't have to click and drag to select the line in order to change its style.

2. Click the arrow to the right of the drop-down style box (which now contains the Normal+ style tag), and select the Heading 1 item. Your Composer window should now look something like Figure 9-24.

- Note that the text is now bold. This type face is a characteristic of the Heading 1 style, at least when it's displayed in Navigator 4. Composer shows you what the text in your page will look like in a Netscape browser, but it may look different in a different (non-Netscape) program because it is up to the client program to interpret HTML tags in a way that is appropriate to the system. A text-only browser, for example, will not be able to display a large bold font and may display all Heading 1 information set apart from other text and surrounded by asterisks, for example. These days, however, you're pretty safe assuming that for most people the page you're creating will look pretty much as it does to you in Composer.

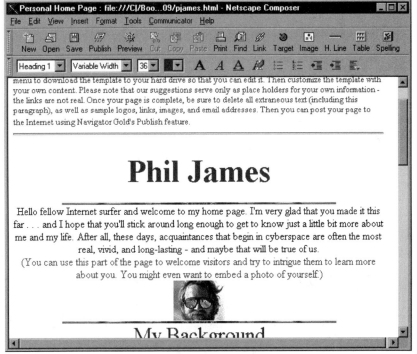

Figure 9-24: A new Heading 1 style added for the edited text.

Changing Fonts

Styles are a composite of different text display information, including relative size and positioning. But once you've chosen a style for a particular piece of text, you can tweak its appearance further, modifying font, size, color, and other characteristics. Let's change the display font for your name:

1. Click and drag your mouse across the words Phil James (or your own name) so that the entire phrase is selected (appears in reverse).

2. Click the arrow to the right of the Font list, and select Fixed Width. Your name will now look something like Figure 9-25.

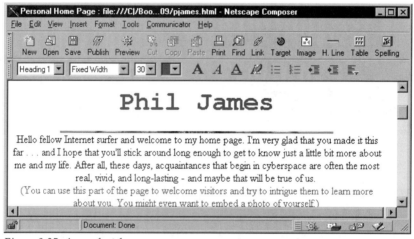

Figure 9-25: A new font for your name.

Changing Font Size

The next control lets you manipulate very precisely the relative size of your text. You can even select individual letters to create dramatic effects. In Figure 9-26, I've selected individual letters of my name. I've given the P a value of +1, the next letter a +2, and so on.

TIP

The drop-down list of font sizes may be configured to display relative HTML sizes, absolute point sizes, or both. See the section called "Configuring Composer" earlier in the chapter for a discussion of these options.

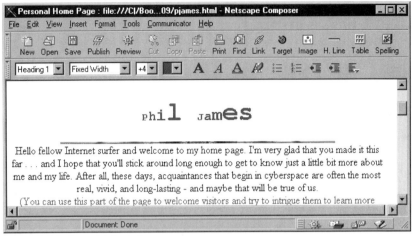

Figure 9-26: Fun with font sizes.

Play around a little on your own with custom font sizes.

Changing Font Color

I wish this book were printed in color so you could see what the next control does. Instead, you'll have to try it on your own. Select some text from your page, and then drop down the list of colors, as shown in Figure 9-27.

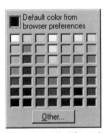

Figure 9-27: The color list.

Now simply choose a new color for the text you've selected. Changing the font color is easier than painting your nails.

Adding Bold, Italic, & Underline

Messenger makes it easy to add bold, italic, and underline text to your message. You do it with the three "A" buttons to the right of the color list. Here we go:

1. Click and drag your mouse to select your name once again.

2. Click the first two A buttons (bold and italic). Your window will now look something like Figure 9-28:

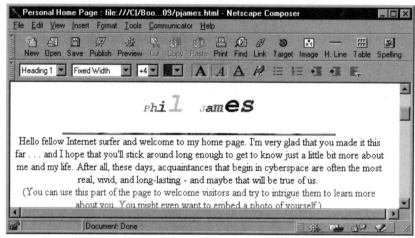

Figure 9-28: Your name in bold and italic as well as different sizes and colors.

Character Styles

Besides bold, italic, and underline, Messenger supports a number of other character styles such as subscript, superscript, and blinking text. To format text with these special attributes:

1. Select the text.

2. Select Style from the Format menu.

3. Choose the character style you wish to apply.

Don't like some of the character style changes you've made? You can always remove any styles you've added. Simply select the text you wish to "unstyle" and click the Remove All Styles button, just to the right of the Underline button. This feature not only removes character styles, it also removes any HTML links in the selected text.

Making a Bulleted or Numbered List

Let's make some more dramatic changes:

1. Place your cursor at the end of your name and press Enter.

2. On the new line, enter the phrase **A few things about me:** and press Enter.

3. On the next line, enter **Incredibly intelligent** and press Enter.

4. Enter **Warm and winning personality** and press Enter again.

5. Enter **Amazing Sales Savvy**. Your page now looks something like Figure 9-29.

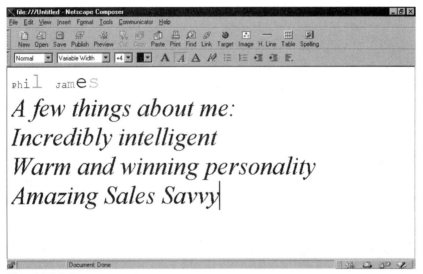

Figure 9-29: Some new text.

6. Click and drag to select the last three new paragraphs.

7. Click the Bullet List button. You'll see something like Figure 9-30.

Want a numbered list instead? Reselect the three new lines, and click the Numbered List button, just to the right of the Bullet List button. Voilà!

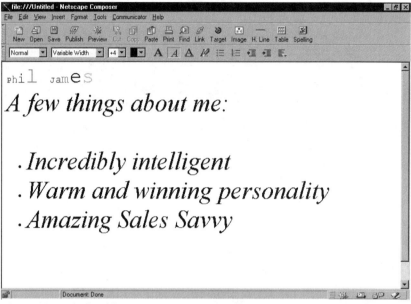

Figure 9-30: A bulleted list.

List Styles

Composer includes some advanced options that let you adjust the appearance of your lists. To access these features, select all the items in your list by clicking and dragging. Then right-click, and choose Paragraph/List Properties from the context menu that pops up.

A dialog box appears with a List section in the center. In this List section, you can choose from a variety of styles, both for the list itself and for the bullets. You should experiment with these settings to see what looks best on your page.

If you've specified a numbered list rather than a bulleted list, you can also change the starting number of the first item in your selection.

Adjusting Indents

Composer lets you adjust how far a paragraph is indented. This feature is especially useful if you want to create multi-level lists. Check it out:

1. Select the numbered list you just created, and make it a bulleted list again. (Click the Bullet List button.)

2. Go to the end of the sales savvy line, and then click your mouse and press Enter.

3. Enter **Networkin' fool** and press Enter.

4. Enter **Harvey MacKay fan**.

5. Using your mouse, select these last two lines you typed.

6. Click the second of the two Indent buttons, the one with the *right* arrow indicating more indent. Figure 9-31 shows what you get:

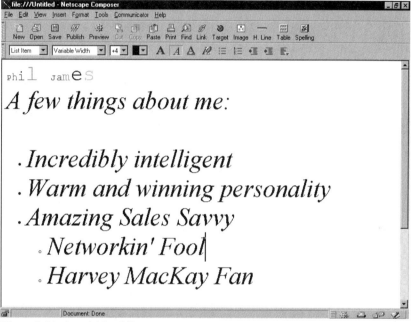

Figure 9-31: A multi-level list.

You can use the left most Indent button to return the new items to the same level as the original three bulleted phrases if you want, or you can create yet deeper levels for your list. Feel free to experiment.

TIP

You can also change the indentation by pressing the Ctrl+M and Ctrl+Shift+M keys.

Changing Alignment

The last button on the bottom toolbar lets you specify the alignment for particular paragraphs. For example:

1. Scroll down the template document, and click your cursor anywhere in the paragraph under the "My Background" header, the paragraph that begins "I was born in a small town...."

2. Click the Alignment button, and then select the bottom of the three new buttons that appear, the Right Alignment button. The paragraph now looks like Figure 9-32.

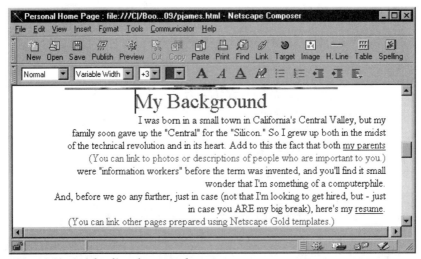

Figure 9-32: A right-aligned paragraph.

Netscape Composer lets you choose Left Alignment, Center Alignment, and Right Alignment. HTML does not currently support full or block justification, in which both the right and left edges of text are perfectly aligned.

The Preview in Navigator Button

Composer gives you a good "layout view" of your document, but it does not show you *exactly* what people will get when they surf to your page. Most significantly, in this special Netscape editing mode, you cannot click a link to jump to a new document—clicking in Composer is for editing the current file, not for hurtling yourself across the vast expanses of the Web.

In the next few sections, we'll work with adding links. To test these links, you'll have to leave the normal Composer window momentarily and view your document-in-progress in browser mode, just as any other client would view it. To do so, you click the Preview in Navigator button on the top Composer toolbar, the fifth button from the left. Once you've tested your links in the browser view, you can simply return to Composer for further editing.

Editing & Adding Links

The Web is about links, and of course you can use Composer to edit any links in the template document or to add new links of your own. In the "My Background" paragraph you just realigned, right-click the "my parents" link, and then select Link Properties from the context menu that pops up. A Link tab appears on the Character Properties dialog box appears, as shown in Figure 9-33.

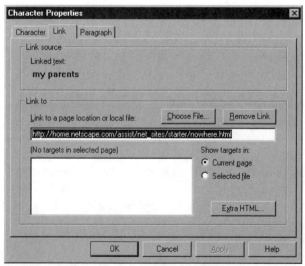

Figure 9-33: The Link tab on the Character Properties dialog box.

As you can see, the location of the linked file (a local file in this case) is already selected, so to change it, all you need to do is start typing. Alternatively, you can click the Choose File button to select a different HTML file from your own computer.

Linked Files & Relative Links

If you're like most Web authors, you've got more to say than you can fit in one HTML file. Typically, a Web site consists of several linked files. When people click a link in your main file, they are transported to a different file that gives more specific or detailed information about a particular topic. They can get back to the main file by clicking another "return" link.

So how do you keep these linked files organized as you're developing your Web site? The easiest approach is to keep them all in the same folder or directory on your hard drive, or in the same directory on a network drive. That way, you don't have to specify paths in the Character Properties dialog box shown in Figure 9-33. There is an added advantage to this approach: if you publish your pages on a remote Web server, Composer can automatically upload all these linked files to the same directory on the server. When a user clicks a link, the linked file will be in the riht place. If your link had specified a particular location on your hard drive, the file might not beaccessible to remote users—although Composer can be configured to adjust links during the uplad process so that they're always valid.

You can also place linked files, including graphics, in subfolders or subdirectories of the main directory. For example, if your main HTML file is in your C:\home_page directory, you may want to store graphics in C:\home_page\graphics and other linked files in C:\home_page\more_html. When you specify these locations in the Character Properties dialog box, however, you should leave off the drive designator and just enter, for example, \home_page\graphics. That way, Composer can upload all the files to the same directory structure on a server. If your main HTML file is uploaded to the user1/home_page/ directory on a remote UNIX machine, the supplemental files can be uploaded automatically to user1/home_page/graphics/ and user1/home_page/more_html/, assuming those directories exist. Your linked files are located in the same place, *relative to each other*, no matter where you create or publish your site. By not specifying exact locations but only relative link locations, you're making sure that your Web site is portable to different servers, even if you don't use Composer to upload the files.

Of course, you can also create links to documents on completely different Web servers. To do so, you'd specify entire URLs, as in http://remote_server.com/directory/file.html.

But what about creating new links? That's just as easy:

1. Scroll down to the very bottom of the template document and press Enter a couple of times.

2. Click the Insert/Make Link button on the top Composer toolbar, the one with a chain link on it. Again, the Character Properties dialog box appears, as shown in Figure 9-34.

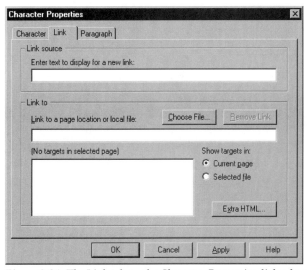

Figure 9-34: The Link tab on the Character Properties dialog box.

- Notice that this time no Link source or Link to text appears, since you are not editing an existing link.

3. In the Link source field, enter the words **Netscape Press Web Site**.

4. In the Link to field, type **http://www.netscapepress.com.**

5. Click OK. You are returned to your Web page, which now contains a link, as shown in Figure 9-35.

- If you're an advanced user of HTML, you can add supplemental HTML commands to any link by clicking the Extra HTML button in the Link Properties dialog box. For example, you could add HTML attributes or JavaScript code right into the HREF tag that Composer creates.

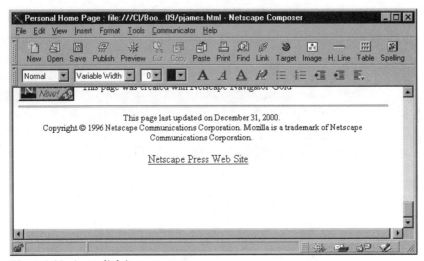

Figure 9-35: A new link in your page.

TIP

Composer includes a shortcut for turning text into links. Simply click and drag to select some text. Then right-click and choose Create Link Using Selected from the context menu that appears.

Drag & Drop Links

You can add links to your Web document in one other way: just drag them in!

Let's say you're cruising the Web with Navigator 4, and you find a site you like. You want to add a link to the site into your own page. All you have to do is drag Navigator 4's link icon, just to the left of the Netsite/Location box, into the Composer window. The link is copied directly into your page.

Instead of dragging the link icon, you can also simply drag a link from another page into the one you're working on. In addition, you can drag in links from the Bookmarks window and even from mail messages. If it's a link, Composer will take it!

Lastly, you can click the name of any HTML file on your desktop or in Explorer and drag it into the page you're working on. A link to that file is created automatically.

Adding Targets

Targets (also known as *anchors*) are different kinds of links. Instead of referring to a different HTML document, they refer to a particular location right within the current page. This capability can be useful when you're organizing a long document. Your reader clicks a link and is transported to the concluding remarks at the end of your page, for example, or back to the executive summary at the beginning. Let's add a target to the template page you've been working on:

1. Scroll to the section of the page titled "My Interests." Place your cursor just to the left of that heading.

2. Click the Insert Target button, just to the right of the Link button. A dialog box like the one in Figure 9-36 pops up.

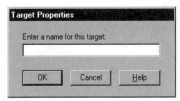

Figure 9-36: The Target Properties dialog box.

3. Enter **interests** and press OK. You are returned to your page, which now includes a target icon next to the "My Interests" header.

   - This icon will *not* appear in your actual Web page. It appears only when your page is loaded in Composer to indicate to you the location of any anchors. You can also right-click the icon to change the properties, just as you right-click a regular link.

4. Place your cursor at the very top of the page, and click the Insert/Make Link button. The Link tab on the Character Properties dialog box appears, this time with your new anchor listed in the bottom text box as shown in Figure 9-37.

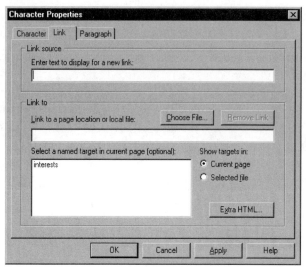

Figure 9-37: The Link tab on the Character Properties dialog box, showing your new anchor.

5. In the Link source box, enter **Interests**.

6. Leave the Link to box blank.

7. Select the word interests in the bottom box. The link #interests is automatically entered into the Link to box.

   ■ The # character followed by the anchor name is the standard code for specifying a specific anchor location in an HTML file. Anchor locations may be included in URLs, too. For example, entering the URL http://www.phil.com/home_page/homepage1.html#interests in Navigator 4 would take you directly to the Interests section of the specified HTML file, assuming that anchor existed.

8. Click OK. You are returned to your page, which contains a new link as shown in Figure 9-38.

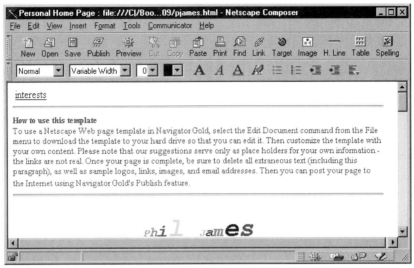

Figure 9-38: A new Interests link.

Clicking this new link in a browser window takes you down to the My Interests section of the document.

TIP

> *Remember, you can test any of these new links by clicking the View in Browser button.*

Adding a Picture

Just to the right of the Insert Target button is the Insert Image button. By now you've probably got this figured out: place your cursor where you want a picture in your document, and then click the Insert Image button. The button itself is pretty unassuming, but once you click it, you're faced with a pretty threatening dialog box, as shown in Figure 9-39.

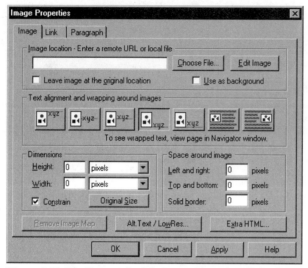

Figure 9-39: The Image tab of the Image Properites dialog box.

TIP

In this section, I'll show you how to add a new image to your page. But you use the same dialog box to change any of the properties of an image that's already in your page. To access this dialog box for editing your image properties, simply right-click the image and select Image Properties from the context menu that appears.

Don't worry, this dialog box is not as bad as it looks. Here we go:

- **Image location.** In the Image location field, you simply enter the URL of a remote picture you want to include in your message, or you can click the Choose File button and select a graphics file from your own hard drive or a network drive.

- **Edit Image button.** Once you've selected an image file, you can edit it with a graphics editor by clicking the Edit Image button. (To learn how to specify an external graphics editor that will be launched when you click this button, see the section called "Configuring Composer" earlier in this chapter.)

- **Text alignment buttons.** The buttons in the middle of the dialog box are fairly self-explanatory. They control the spatial relationship between an image and the text that surrounds it. A number of configurations are available, and after pressing one of these buttons, you'll need to view your page in a browser window (click Composer's View in Browser button) to see how your choice looks.

- **Dimensions.** Composer lets you adjust the size of an image you place in your page. You can set the dimensions either in pixels or in percentage of the window—you switch between these two units of measurement by selecting from the list box to the right of the actual dimensions. To return an image to its original size, click the Original Size button; to maintain the aspect ratio of an image—in other words to ensure that when you increase or decrease one dimension, the other dimension is adjusted proportionately—make sure the Lock width/height check box is checked.

- **Space around image.** These settings are fairly self-explanatory. To add blank space around the image, set the top two boxes to a positive value. To add a solid border around your image, set the bottom box to a positive value.

- **Remove Image Map button.** I'm sure you've already discovered that when you click a particular area in some images, you are transported to a different URL than if you'd clicked on a different area. The graphic at the very top of the Netscape home page is an example of this: click one part of the image and you get product information; click another and you are transported to the General Store. This movement is done through what is called an *image map*. An image map is a special supplemental file that associates areas of an image with corresponding actions. It is beyond the scope of this book to teach you how to create image maps in your own pages, but if you *do* know how to do it, the Remove Image Map button may be useful to you at times.

- **Alt. Text/LowRes button.** Not all browsers are created equal. Some, such as Lynx, emphasize universality and portability over advanced features and display only text—no graphics at all. Lynx users will not see any of the pictures you add to your page. Fortunately, though, HTML lets you add a special *alt tag*. With the alt tag, you can specify some text that will display in place of the image on text-only systems. Let's say you're adding a picture of yourself to your page. Click this button and you can enter the words "picture of me" in the Alternate text box that appears. When text-only users view your page, they will know exactly what they are missing, and may even run out and buy a new browser. **Note:** This feature also makes your pages user-friendly for those people who have turned "Show Images" off in Navigator. Based on your *alt* descriptions, they can decide whether to display images for this particular page.

You access another helpful feature with this same button. You can specify an additional low resolution image that will load right away, while the main higher resolution image is still being transferred from Web server to browser. That way, your users won't have to wait too long before they see *something* on the screen. Typically, you'd specify a low resolution version of the same image.

■ **Extra HTML button.** This button is for advanced users. It lets you add additional HTML tags or JavaScript for your image.

OK, let's add a picture. As you can see in Figure 9-40, I've specified a new image to appear at the current cursor location in my page. I have left all the other settings at their default values.

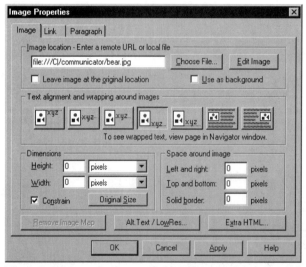

Figure 9-40: A new image specified in the Image Properties dialog box.

TIP

Remember, you can specify either a local file location or a remote URL.

Click Apply now, and the image appears in your page at the current cursor location, as shown in Figure 9-41.

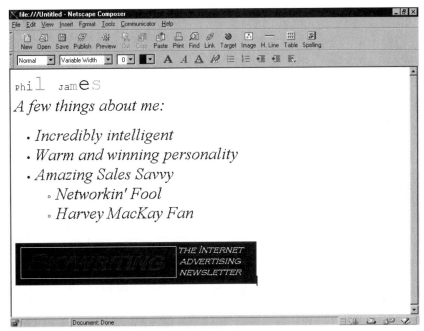

Figure 9-41: The Web page with a new image.

Pretty simple, isn't it? Actually, we can make it even easier. Read on!

After you drag a new image into the Web page you're working on in Composer, you will probably want to edit some of its attributes, such as size and exact position on the page. Simply right-click the image, and select Image Properties from the context menu. Additionally, you may want to save the image to your hard drive or a network drive under a new name. Again, right-click and select Save Image As from the menu that appears.

But what if you want to make the picture a link, so that when users click it, they are transported to a different URL? With Composer, you can assign a URL to any image on your page. In the next section, you'll learn how to turn your images into clickable links.

Drag-and-Drop Images

Earlier you learned how you can drag links from other Web pages right into the Composer window. Well, you can do the same thing with images.

If you're cruising the Web with Navigator 4 and find a picture you like, click and drag it right into the Composer window. The image is immediately copied into your own Web page. **Note:** Make sure you're not violating any copyright restrictions!

In addition, you can click the name or icon of an image file on your desktop or in Explorer and drag it into the page you're working on. The image is immediately copied into your page.

But here's an even cooler feature: if you attempt to drag in an image that's not in GIF or JPEG format (common standards for the Internet and intranets), Composer may even convert it for you!

Let's say you have a BMP file you want to use in your page. But a BMP file may not display properly in some browser programs, and since it is larger it will transfer more slowly than a JPEG. When you drag a BMP file into your page in Composer, a dialog box appears that lets you choose a new name and a location to store the JPEG version of the file. Once you have selected a name and location, Composer then lets you choose what image quality you want. Make your choice, click OK, and your Web page now includes a brand new JPEG that's been converted from the bitmap you initially dragged in.

Making Your Picture a Link

Making your picture a link is a very quick procedure. Don't blink or you might miss it:

1. While you're still in the Image Properties dialog box shown in Figure 9-40, click the Link tab. The Link dialog box appears with your image specified in the Link source section, as shown in Figure 9-42.

2. In the Link to section, type in a URL or choose a local file that will be accessed when users click the image.

3. Click Apply. Your new image is now a clickable link!

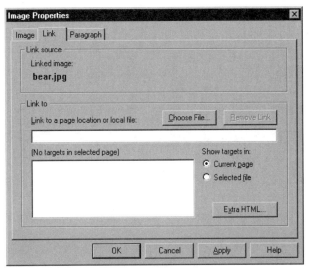

Figure 9-42: The Link tab with image file specified.

TIP

There's a quick way to turn an image that's already in your page into a clickable link, or to modify the URL linked to an existing image. In Composer, simply place your cursor on the image and right-click your mouse. Then select Create Link Using Selected from the context menu that appears.

We have only one more detail to deal with: positioning or *aligning* the image on the page.

Aligning the Image

OK, we're still in the Image Properties dialog box shown in Figure 9-40. Click the Paragraph tab this time. You see the tab shown in Figure 9-43.

Proceed directly to the Alignment section, and click one of the three option buttons, depending on whether you want your image to be centered on your page or aligned to the left or right margin. For the sake of this exercise, let's choose Right. Now click OK and you are returned to your Web page in the main Composer window, with a new image aligned to the right margin, as shown in Figure 9-44.

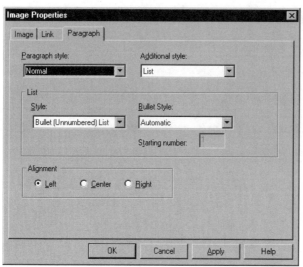

Figure 9-43: The Paragraph tab.

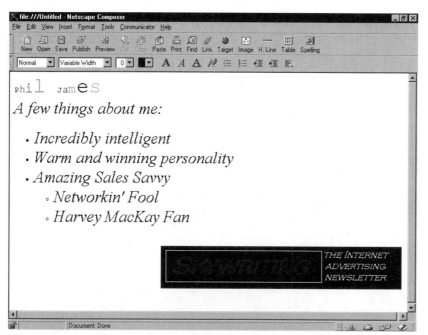

Figure 9-44: The Web page with a new image, aligned to the right.

You may want to add just a few more special elements to your Web page: *horizontal lines* and *tables*.

Adding a Horizontal Line

With all these fonts and pictures, your Web page is starting to look like—well, like a Web page. But what would a Web page be without those horizontal lines you see all over the place?

1. Place your cursor right after your name near the top of the page and press Enter.

2. In the top toolbar, click the Insert Horizontal Line button. You then see the page shown in Figure 9-45.

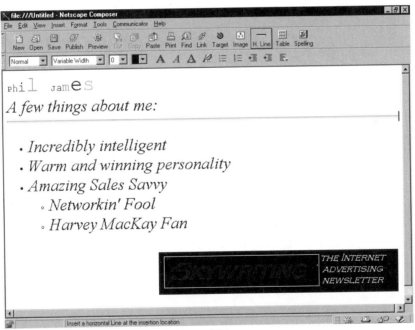

Figure 9-45: The page with a new horizontal line.

Don't like that line? Right-click it and choose Horizontal Line Properties from the context menu that pops up. The Horizontal Line Properties dialog box appears, as shown in Figure 9-46.

It's time to experiment again. Try different heights and widths. If you set your width to less than the width of your page, try different alignments. Or try losing the 3D shading effect that's become ubiquitous on the Web. If you like what you come up with and want to set it as your default horizontal line, make sure the Save settings as default box is checked before you click OK.

Now we move on to one of HTML's most powerful features: tables.

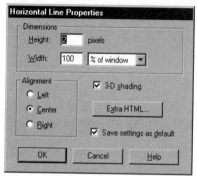

Figure 9-46: The Horizontal Line Properties dialog box.

Adding a Table

We all know what tables are: things with rows and columns in them. You can easily spot a table in a Web page, so I'm not going to get into a lot of introductory fluff here. This section is going to be a learn-by-doing section. Here we go:

1. In Composer, with your Web template displayed, position your cursor just below the horizontal line we added.

2. Click the Insert Table button, the one at the far right of the top toolbar. The New Table Properties dialog box appears, as shown in Figure 9-47.

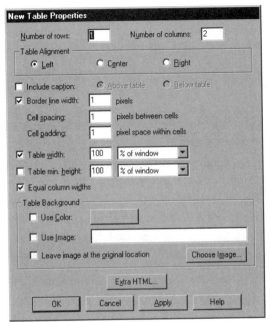

Figure 9-47: The New Table Properties dialog box.

3. Fill in the properties for your new table:

- Enter the number of rows and columns. For the purposes of this exercise, leave it at two each.

- In the table alignment section, click the Left option button if it is not already selected. Clicking this button will place your new table at the left edge of the page.

- For the purposes of this exercise, check the Include caption check box, and click the option button labeled "above." This feature will let you add a caption directly above your table.

- Enter a width for the table border. (Again, the default is fine.)

- Leave the cell spacing at 1 pixel as well.

- Cell padding refers to the minimum amount of space between any item within a cell (text, graphics, links, and so on) and the edge of the cell. You may want to adjust this setting occasionally to make your table look less busy, but for now the default is OK.

- The table width setting is just its initial width—you can stretch or shrink it once it's placed on your page. For the purpose of this tutorial, set the Table width value to 15% of the window.

- Table min. Height is what it sounds like: the minimum height for the table, no matter how little you add into its cells. Again, let's not mess with this setting.

- If you want your initial column widths to be identical, leave the Equal column widths option checked.

- If you want a new background color for the table, check the Use Color option and then click the button to the right. Select a new color from the palette that appears.

- The last two options let you choose an image instead of a solid color as the background for your table, and to specify whether the image file is left at its current location or sent along with the HTML file.

4. Click OK. You are returned to your page, which now includes a new table as shown in Figure 9-48.

Notice that your cursor is within the outlined area above the table. In this area, you add a caption, so start typing. How about entering the words **My new table**, as shown in Figure 9-49.

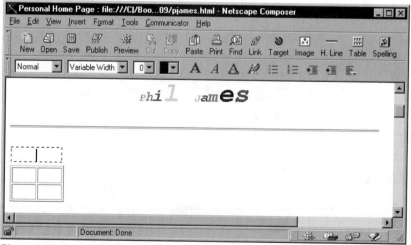

Figure 9-48: A new table.

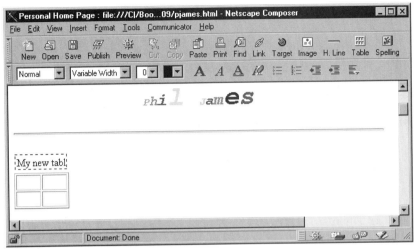

Figure 9-49: Adding a caption.

Hmm, doesn't look very good. The words don't fit very well in the box, do they? No problem. Place your mouse cursor on the right edge of the table; then click and drag to the right. You widen your table this way, as shown in Figure 9-50.

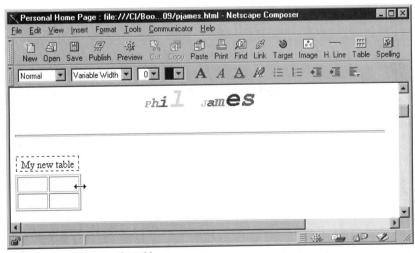

Figure 9-50: Widening the table.

This method is not the only way to widen the table, though. Individual columns widen to accommodate material (text, graphics, links, and so on) placed within them. Let's try widening these columns:

1. Make the table very narrow again by clicking and dragging the right edge leftward.

2. Place your cursor in the top left cell, and enter **Wideningthecolumn.** The column grows as you type, as shown in Figure 9-51.

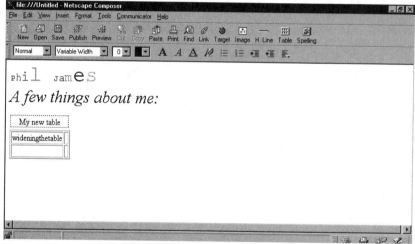

Figure 9-51: A column growing to accommodate new text.

Of course, you can also change the attributes of text in a table the same way you change the attributes of text *anywhere* in your Web page: just select it and start playing with the style, size, and font buttons. Again, your table will resize itself to accommodate your modified text.

TIP

To align text within a cell, simply select it and click the regular Composer Alignment button. You can then center the text or align it to the left or right of the cell.

Adding Images & Links to a Table

As I mentioned, text is not the only thing you can put into a table. Any element you can place in your Web page you can place just as easily in a table cell. Let's move an image from the main body of our Web page into a table cell:

1. Click and drag to select the image we recently added to the Web page, shown earlier in Figure 9-44.

2. Press Ctrl+X to cut the image. Alternatively, you can click the Cut button in the toolbar.

3. Place your cursor in the top right cell of the new table, and press Ctrl+V to paste the image. (You could also select Paste from the toolbar.) Your table now contains the image, as shown in Figure 9-52.

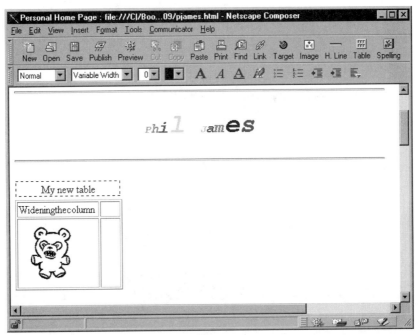

Figure 9-52: The table with an image in it.

What about links? You create them in tables the same way you create them in the rest of your page. For example, to make the new image a link, you follow these steps:

1. Right-click the image in the table.

2. From the context menu that pops up, select Create Link Using Selected.

3. In the Link tab that appears, fill in the Link to field as you would for any other link.

Row & Cell Properties

We've already set a variety of properties for the table as a whole. You can change them, by the way, by placing your mouse anywhere in the table, right-clicking, and selecting Table Properties from the context menu. Then select the Table tab, which looks just like the New Table Properties dialog box we saw earlier. You may want to change the number of rows or columns, for example.

But Composer also lets you change the configuration of individual rows and cells. For example, you can make every row a different color if you want, or even every cell! Let's take a closer look at these options:

1. Place your cursor inside a cell of the table and right-click.

2. When the context menu appears, select Table Properties. The Table Properties dialog box appears, as shown in Figure 9-53. Notice that this time it has three separate tabs: Table, Row, and Cell.

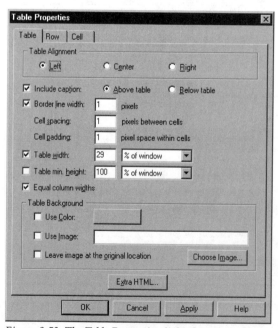

Figure 9-53: The Table Properties dialog box.

3. Unless you want to change the configuration of the table as a whole, click the Row tab, as shown in Figure 9-54.

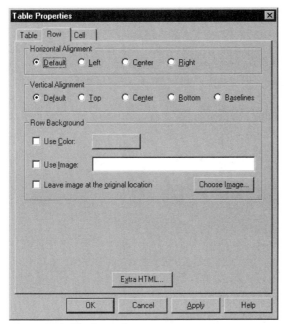

Figure 9-54: The Row tab.

In this tab, you can choose a variety of options for the entire row where your cursor is currently positioned. For example, you can adjust the text alignment so that all text within the row is aligned at the right edge, or you can adjust vertical alignment so that all text within the row sits on the bottom of the cells rather than hovering in the middle. If you choose Default for either of the alignment options, the row will simply "inherit" the alignment properties already established in the Table tab.

You can also choose a color for the row. Simply select the Use Color option, click the button to its right, and select from the palette that appears. As with the table as a whole, you can also specify a background image. When you've configured the row to your satisfaction, click the Apply button.

Now, you can change the properties for the individual cell at the current cursor position:

1. Click the Cell tab, as shown in Figure 9-55.

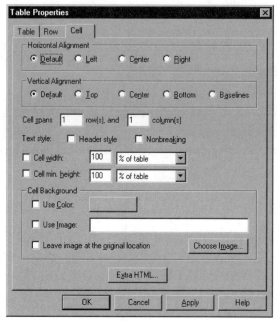

Figure 9-55: The Cell tab.

2. Select attributes for the individual cell:

- You're already familiar with the text alignment options, so let's leave them alone. "Default," in this case, means that the cell will inherit the text alignment attributes of its row; if the corresponding text alignment attribute in the Row tab is also set to Default, the cell will inherit the attribute of the table as a whole.

- Enter the size of your cell in the next two boxes. As you can see, a single cell may span multiple rows and columns. To see what this looks like, enter **2** in the right-hand columns box.

- In the next line, you can choose to apply a Header style to the text in your cell. You can also determine whether the text will wrap to another line when you reach the right edge of the cell.

- The rest of the options—cell width, height, and background color—are ones you've already seen in the Row and Table tabs. If you want to adjust the size or color of an individual cell, this is the place to do it. And again, you can even add separate images to individual cells.

3. After you've finished adjusting the properties of an individual cell, click OK to return to your page.

Figure 9-56 shows a table whose cells have been customized using the procedures outlined above.

Figure 9-56: A table with customized cells.

We've been buried in some pretty technical nitty-gritty for a while, and we're almost done modifying the home page template. But before putting it out into the world, you better check your spelling.

Checking Your Spelling

Cant spel? With Communicator, it's not an issue.

See that button with the ABC and the checkmark on it? That's your personal spelling assistant. Click it and you can make your Web page read like it's been thoroughly worked over by Netscape Press' editorial team.

Figure 9-57 shows a section of the page with a few problem words in it.

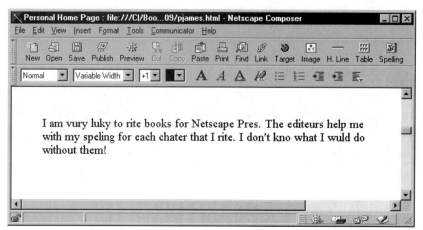

Figure 9-57: A section of the page with spelling mistakes.

Click the Check Spelling button and you see something like Figure 9-58.

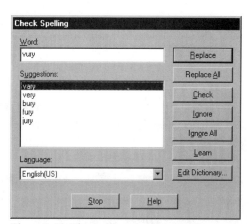

Figure 9-58: The spelling checker at work.

The spelling checker has found the first of the errors. If you've used Microsoft Word or any other major word processing program, this dialog box should look pretty familiar to you. It offers you an alternate spelling for the word, or in some cases a list of possible spellings. If you don't like the choice or choices it offers you, type in the correct spelling in the Change To box yourself. Here's what the various buttons do:

- **Replace.** The spelling checker changes the currently selected word to the spelling that is highlighted in the Suggestions box. Highlight the spelling you want to use before clicking the Replace button. You can also type a new spelling directly into the Word before clicking the Replace button.

- **Replace All.** The spelling checker changes every instance of this particular misspelling within your page.

- **Ignore.** If you click this button, the spelling checker doesn't bother correcting the selected word and instead goes on to the next misspelling it finds, if any.

- **Ignore All.** If you click this button, the spelling checker won't stop at any further words in your message that are spelled this way.

- **Stop.** Click this button to exit the spelling checker. It will not look for any further errors in your page unless you press the Check Spelling button again.

- **Learn.** If you click this button, the spelling checker adds the selected word, as it is currently spelled in your message, to a custom dictionary. Once it is added to the dictionary, the spelling checker will no longer consider it a misspelling when it encounters this word in *any* page (or e-mail message) you create. This can be useful for unusual proper nouns and specialized technical words that you use frequently.

- **Edit Dictionary.** This button lets you edit your custom dictionary directly, adding words that the spell checker will not flag as errors when it encounters them. For instance, if you often spell check Web pages that include your own e-mail address, you might want to add that address to the dictionary, as shown in Figure 9-59.

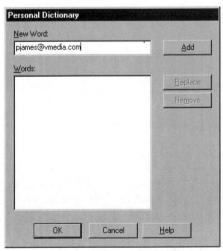

Figure 9-59: Adding your e-mail address to the Personal Dictionary.

You can also use this feature to *delete* words from your dictionary.

Figure 9-60 shows the section of the page after Communicator's spelling checker has done its job:

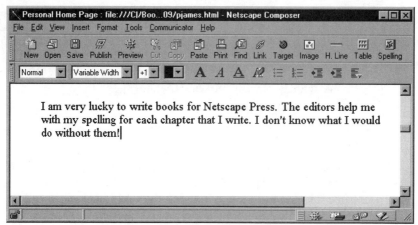

Figure 9-60: The section of the Web page after spell checking.

OK, we're in the home stretch now. You're almost ready to release your page on the unsuspecting public. But first, we must address a few broad, general options that affect various characteristics of the page as a whole, not just individual elements within it.

Page Colors & Properties

Let's do some more beautifying:

1. Still in the Composer window with the page we're working on displayed, select Page Colors and Properties from the bottom of the Format menu. The Page Properties dialog box appears, with the General tab selected as shown in Figure 9-61.

2. In the top part of the General tab, fill in a title for your page. If your own name doesn't appear as the author, modify that information as well.

3. You can enter a short description of your page, as well as some keywords and a classification. All these information fields will appear as special "Meta Name" tags within your document and may be used by browsers and by search engines such as Yahoo to help users find and classify the page.

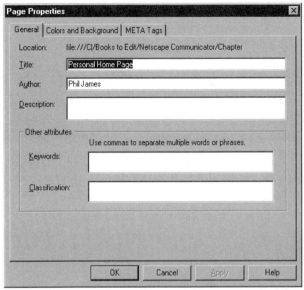

Figure 9-61: The Page Properties dialog box with the General tab selected.

Now let's move on to Colors and Backgrounds for your page:

1. Click the Colors and Background tab, as shown in Figure 9-62.

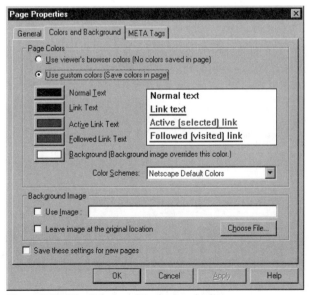

Figure 9-62: The Colors and Background tab.

2. To change the overall color scheme of your message, select from the drop-down Color schemes list. The "Use custom colors" option button is automatically selected, and you are shown a sample of your new colors.

3. To change individual elements within the chosen color scheme, click any of the buttons for Normal Text, Link Text, and so on, and then select a new color from the palette that appears. Note that you can also change the background color of your page.

4. If you want to return to the default colors, click the option button at the top labeled "Use viewer's browser colors."

You can also specify an image, rather than a solid color, to use as the background for your message. To do so, follow these steps:

1. Check the Use Image check box in the Background Image section.

2. Click the Choose File button. A Choose Image File dialog box appears, as shown in Figure 9-63.

Figure 9-63: The Choose Image File dialog box.

3. Choose a GIF or JPEG file from your local hard drive or network drive and click Open.

TIP

To make your Web page reference the image file in its current location, check the "Leave image at the original location" check box.

As you work with these appearance changes, you can click Apply at any time to see what they look like in your actual page. Remember, reverting to your original look is as simple as choosing an option button, so you're in no real danger of messing up your page. If you like what you've done, though, and want to use your customized color scheme as a default in future pages you create, check the check box labeled "Save these settings for new pages."

When you're done with the Colors and Background settings, click the META Tags tab. It is beyond the scope of this book to cover advanced HTML commands, but on this tab you enter META tags and user variables. If you don't know what I'm talking about, take a look at Netscape Press' excellent book *HTML Publishing for Netscape*.

Click OK to accept all your Page Property changes and return to the main Composer window.

Saving Your File

Ow, just look at that page! I've demonstrated how you can turn a perfectly good template into a useless mess. But, hey, you can't learn to create Web pages if you don't get your virtual hands dirty. You've learned to manipulate text and graphics elements so well by now that you can continue working on the file on your own, adding and deleting and moving things around until you've got something you'll be proud to show the whole world. Well, to show your mother, anyway. But before you show it to her, make sure to save it. Just click the Save button, select a location for your file, and type in a filename.

Once you've saved your page the way you want it, you're ready to publish it. I'll show you how in just a minute. But before that, here's a short section for my geek readers on how to manipulate HTML code directly. Non-geeks may skip ahead to the section called "Publishing Your Page."

Editing Your HTML Source

As I mentioned earlier in the chapter, sometimes you may want to leave the comfortable Composer interface and plunge into the details of actual HTML code. You may want to tweak a value so that graphical elements line up exactly the way you want them to, or you may want to add some frames, JavaScript, or advanced HTML tags that are not available through Composer.

Fortunately, Composer makes it easy to jump back and forth between a text editor and its own interface. Using the same template file, let's see how this works:

1. In Composer, with the template file we've been working on open, select HTML Source from the Edit menu. You will be asked whether you want to save your changes to the file. Click OK.

   If you haven't specified an external HTML editor in the Composer preferences, you will be asked to specify one now. See the "Configuring Composer" section near the beginning of this chapter.

2. Follow any instructions that appear for specifying an HTML editor. Composer will launch your external editor with the HTML source for your page loaded. Figure 9-64 shows the HTML source in WordPad.

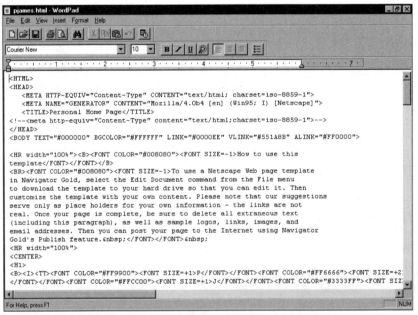

Figure 9-64: HTML source file in WordPad.

3. Make any changes you want to the HTML code, and then click your text editor's Save command. For now, do not close the file or your text editor.

TIP

If your editor can save files in a variety of word processor formats, make sure to save your HTML file as ASCII text.

4. Go back into Composer. As soon as you select the Composer window on your desktop, a Reload File dialog box pops up.

5. To see the effects of the changes you made directly to the HTML code, click Yes. Composer reloads the page with your changes.

6. If you want to make more changes to the HTML code, return to your text editor and repeat steps 3 through 5. You can bop back and forth *ad nauseum* between your text editor window and the Composer window.

7. When you've made all the changes you want, close your text editor.

And now that you've tweaked your page to your satisfaction, it's time to go public!

Composer Plug-ins

Directly editing HTML code is only one option for tweaking your page and adding niceties that aren't available through the Composer interface. Netscape has actually provided a mechanism for incorporating new capabilities right into Composer: Composer plug-ins.

You already know about regular plug-ins and how they can be used to enhance the multimedia powers of Navigator. Composer plug-ins are very similar. They are special add-on programs that you can download from Netscape and other Web sites. Once a Composer plug-in is installed, the new feature it provides is listed right in Composer's Tools menu. For example, a plug-in might allow you to change selected text to small caps or some other special font. The command to do this will appear on the Tools menu along with the other Composer features. And, of course, you can have as many plug-ins as you want.

It is beyond the scope of this book to discuss Composer plug-ins in depth, but for more information check out Netscape's Home Page.

Publishing Your Page

You've been working for hours on your page, adding text and graphics, adjusting the relative position of various elements, and creating tables. At a certain point, you realize that the law of diminishing returns has taken effect, and you need to let go and let *other* people be dazzled by your creativity.

Of course, you can simply put your HTML files on a network drive where they will be accessible to others. That is the simplest way to publish your work, but as I mentioned earlier, it's not always the best. To really exploit the power of Web publishing, you need to publish your files on an actual Web server. And to do that, you use Composer's Publish button, the fourth button from the left on the top toolbar. Let's try it:

1. Make sure you are connected to your intranet or to the Net itself.

2. In Composer, and with a Web file loaded, click the Publish button. The Publish Files dialog box appears, as shown in Figure 9-65.

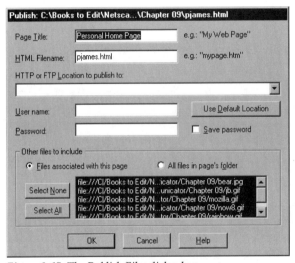

Figure 9-65: The Publish Files dialog box.

If you've followed the instructions up until now, the top section of this dialog box should already contain the title of your page as well as its actual filename. And if you've already chosen a default publishing site for your Web pages, the correct HTTP or FTP location field may be filled in as well. If it is not, you can click the Use Default Location button or even type in the correct address now. And if you have already uploaded files to various Web servers, you may be able to select the correct URL from the drop-down list.

Once you have entered the correct address to send your files, fill in any User name and Password information that's necessary to complete the upload. You can get this information from your system administrator or your ISP. If you're using an ISP's Web server, in many cases this information will be the same as for your regular SLIP/PPP account. Notice that Composer can also "remember" your password so that you don't have to type it in each time you upload files to your Web server.

In the bottom section of this dialog box, you can construct a list of *all* the files you wish to upload to your Web server. If your page contains images, you can choose to upload just the image files by selecting the left-hand option button. If you want to upload HTML or other files, click the right-hand option button. The window now displays all the files in the current directory or folder, and they are all selected for upload. You can click any individual file to *de*-select it, or click again to re-select it. In addition, you can use the Select All and Select None buttons to speed up the process of selecting files for upload. Remember, you must upload any local files you've created that are linked to your main file, as well as any image files that appear in your page.

When you're ready to send your files to the Web server, just click OK. That's all there is to it!

Moving On

In this chapter, you've learned how to use Composer to create and publish your own Web pages. Congratulations! You have joined the vanguard of modern electronic publishing!

Of course, I only scratched the surface of this very large topic. There are thousands of different ways to enhance Web pages with innovative design, multimedia, JavaScript, and other little tricks. In the next chapter, I cover some of the powerful multimedia features available in Communicator, but mainly from the viewpoint of the browser rather than the Web author. If you want more in-depth information about Web authoring, dozens of books—maybe even hundreds—are available. Be sure to select one published by my friends at Ventana.

OK, on to some of the most exciting features of Communicator. By the end of the next chapter, you will indeed be a Web power user.

CHAPTER 10

Advanced Communicator 4

As you learned in the last chapter, Communicator is one of the most robust tools available for displaying a wide range of multimedia content. But the story doesn't end there. As new technologies develop, Netscape is quick to incorporate them. And Communicator even includes methods by which developers can tack new modules onto the program, seamlessly integrating powerful new multimedia features. This open architecture ensures that Communicator will stay current as the world at large comes up with ever more exciting ways to package information.

In this chapter we'll look at four ways in which Communicator is keeping up with all the changes in multimedia presentation:

- VRML 2.0 support, letting you navigate the three-dimensional virtual worlds that are starting to crop up around the Net. VRML 2.0 is the best legal way to get dizzy without leaving your desk chair.

- Plug-ins, which allow developers to extend Communicator's power in all kinds of imaginative ways. Plug-ins are software components you can add to Navigator as needed to process multimedia and other non-HTML files. Thanks to a couple of plug-ins, my computer is now playing MIDI music files off the Net while it displays 3D models of agricultural chemicals.

- Support for the hundreds of Java applets available on the Web, as well as the thousands waiting to be written. Java is a full-featured, general-purpose programming language, and Communicator is designed to execute Java programs referenced in Web pages. This means that the ways to extend Communicator are virtually limitless. In addition, many Netcaster channels (see Chapter 4) are implemented in Java.

■ JavaScript is a much simpler language whose statements can be incorporated directly in Web pages to extend Navigator's capabilities. JavaScript can make sure you've entered a valid zip code in a Web form, make text scroll across your screen, or even replace the status information at the bottom of the browser window with a joke. I think of JavaScript as the tool of choice for "stupid Navigator tricks" (as well as some pretty clever Navigator tricks).

TIP

This chapter emphasizes the use of advanced presentation features in Navigator 4. But all the same multimedia power is available in Netcaster as well. For instance, the same kinds of plug-ins that extend Navigator's capabilities also extend the power of Netcaster, and the Java and JavaScript features mentioned here apply to Netcaster as well. For more information on Netcaster, please see Chapter 4.

Feeling adventurous? Let's start right in with VRML.

VRML

First, how do you say it? Some people say V-R-M-L, carefully articulating each letter, but they're not the cool people. The cool people say *VER-MUHL*, with the stress on the first syllable just like in *thermal*.

And what exactly does it stand for? *V*irtual *R*eality *M*odeling *L*anguage. It's really a pretty simple concept. Just as HTML is a markup language that tells a Web browser to display various elements such as headings, italic text, and links, VRML is an extension (a special plug-in), which tells a Web browser to display various components of three-dimensional *virtual worlds*. These include objects that rotate or otherwise move through space in a "realistic" way, as well as graphical backgrounds that make you feel as if *you're* moving as you manipulate your mouse. To get technical, VRML is a standard for encoding computer-generated graphics into a file format for transmission across the Net or an intranet; it is also the standard a Web browser uses to interpret and display these graphics so that you can interact with them. Some people see VRML as an eventual replacement for HTML itself, offering a more intuitive and lifelike way of navigating the Web.

Moving Worlds? Live3D? Cosmo?

Here's some more terminology you may encounter, but first a little history.

Originally, Silicon Graphics (SGI) came up with Open Inventor, a file format that became the basis for VRML; they also developed QvLib, which was the software component responsible for "understanding" and interpreting the file. Gavin Bell of SGI then wrote the proposal for the VRML 1.0 standard. The standard was adopted, and developers began implementing it.

Of course as soon as version 1 of any standard is accepted by the technology community, somebody starts working on version 2. There have been several rival proposals, but the one that really caught on is called *Moving Worlds*. Developed and supported by a broad consortium of software and hardware vendors, it provides many new features including full motion, live content and animation, enhanced audio, and the ability to connect with databases. Most importantly, it has strong support for multiuser interactivity. You won't have to get dizzy alone any more.

Just as the HTML standard doesn't specify exactly what a heading or footnote should look like in every Web browser, VRML doesn't specify exactly how to display graphical objects such as wire-frame models. Virtual worlds may look and feel a bit different from one VRML browser to another. *Live3D* is simply Netscape's own particular implementations of VRML 2.0; Cosmo is the implementation for 32-bit systems (Windows 95 and NT).

Let's go ahead and try some VRML navigation.

VRML Navigation

There are VRML sites you can get to right from the Netscape home page, but first we're going to try something even simpler. Netscape includes a sample VRML file with the program, so you can try your hand at exploring virtual worlds without even being connected to the Net. Let's try it:

1. From the Navigator File menu, select Open Page. Optionally, you can simply press Ctrl+O. The Open dialog box appears.

2. In the Files of type drop-down list at the bottom of the dialog box, select VRML Worlds.

3. Now navigate to the following directory: Program Files\Netscape\ Communicator\Program\Plugins\Cosmo\ui\.

TIP

If you are using Windows 3.1, or if you specified a different location for Communicator when you installed it, this path might be slightly different. In any case, the folder we want is called ui and it's under the Live3D directory.

4. Once you are in the correct folder, double-click on the file vrml.wrl, and once in the dialog box, click Open. After a few seconds, a three-dimensional page appears, as shown in Figure 10-1.

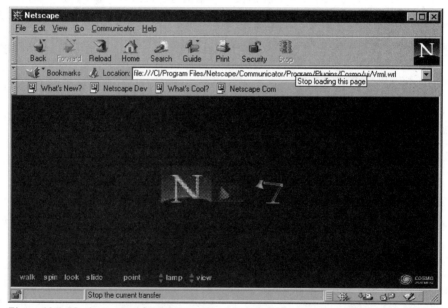

Figure 10-1: Navigator 4 with VRML page.

Let's take a few minutes to get oriented. There are seven clickable labels along the bottom of the window: walk, spin, look, slide, point, lamp, and view. Each of these labels represents a different operational mode for your controls. In other words, if you click slide, your mouse and keyboard might act differently in the window than they do when you click walk.

And since you've got to walk before you can slide, let's start there:

1. Make sure the walk mode is selected. (Modes are yellow when selected.)

2. Move your mouse around the window. Notice whenever your pointer rests on the large N, the words *Live3D Home Page* appear, as shown in Figure 10-2.

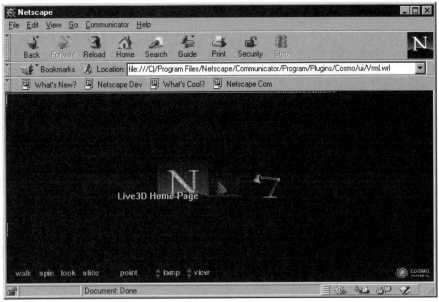

Figure 10-2: Link to Netscape's Live3D site in the sample VRML page.

This is a simple link to the Netscape Live3D home page. Links in VRML do not appear as underlined text, but as a temporary element in the graphic.

3. If you are currently connected to the Net, try double-clicking your left mouse button while the link is displayed. You are transported to the Live 3D site. Click the Back button to return to the VRML page. If you are running Windows 95 or NT, you can also click the Cosmo logo at the bottom right corner of the window to access the Cosmo home page.

TIP

At some VRML sites, you need to be in point mode in order to see links to other URLs. For point mode, simply click the point label.

4. Now click your left mouse button and while holding it down, drag your mouse slowly around the window. Notice that you seem to move in relation to the images, as shown in Figure 10-3.

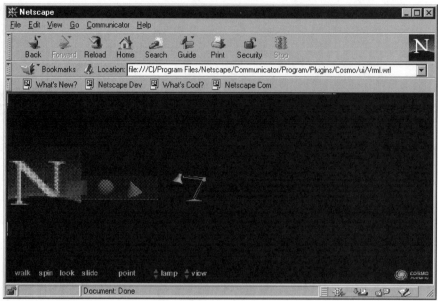

Figure 10-3: Moving around the sample VRML image.

- As you drag to the right or left, you seem to move right or left in relation to the object.
- As you drag up, you seem to move toward the object.
- As you drag down, you seem to move away from the object.

TIP

You can also use your arrow keys to move left, right, forward, and back.

5. Ready for some fun? Try dragging with your *right* mouse button instead of the left. Immediately you see the power of VRML: you are now moving around the object as if it's three-dimensional (see Figure 10-4).

6. One more move: hold down the Alt key while dragging with the left mouse button. The object "slides" in the window in a two-dimensional manner. In other words, the up-and-down component of your mouse movement does not change your apparent distance from the object.

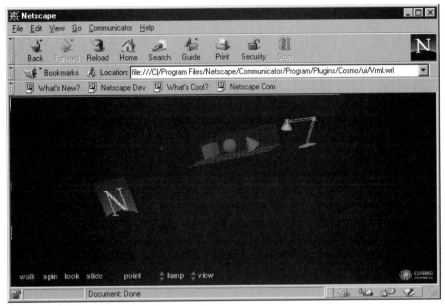

Figure 10-4: Three-dimensional movement.

TIP

In walk mode, the A and Z keys slide you up and down.

7. There's still one more move I want to show you. Click the view label. The VRML window returns to its original state, as shown in Figure 10-1.

Lost in Cyberspace

I sure love that view label. I was born in the early fifties and never saw a video game until I was an adult. My idea of fast-paced action was when the Lone Ranger and Tonto discovered a hideout, one that looked suspiciously like the hideout they found in the previous episode. Now drop me into a VRML page, and in a matter of seconds I'm hopelessly lost, wandering the far reaches of space looking for something—*anything*—recognizable.

My kids, on the other hand, seem to find virtual worlds utterly familiar, warm, and homey. So if you were born before the Kennedy assassination, here's my big hint for exploring VRML effectively: bring a kid along, and if you can't bring a kid, just keep clicking that view button.

Now let's check out some animation. Click your right mouse button and drag to the right until you see the image as three distinct objects: the Netscape logo, the set of geometric shapes, and the lamp. OK, let go of that right mouse button before everything slides off your screen! Now put your cursor over the lamp until the word "Headlight" appears. Click it and what happens is shown in Figure 10-5.

That's right, simply by clicking you have adjusted and turned on the lamp. It casts its light on the other objects, changing their appearance appropriately. In fact, if you move the objects around so that the lamp casts its light behind the Netscape logo, it lights it up like a rear-projection screen. This demonstrates some of the power of Navigator. Want to turn the lamp off? You guessed it, just click Headlight again.

Now, do you want to see something really spectacular?

1. Click the look label.

2. Start looking around by dragging with the left mouse button. As you discover immediately, you are now moving through space very quickly.

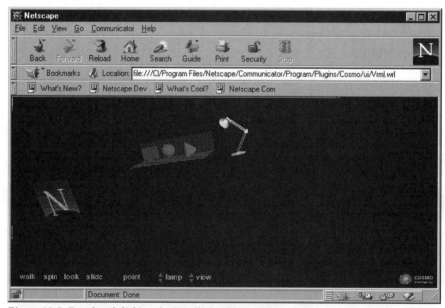

Figure 10-5: Results of clicking the Headlight object.

The way the labels work in different VRML worlds varies a bit. For example, try turning the lamp on again, clicking the Lamp label, and then playing with the up and down arrows just to the left of it. In this particular 3D world, the arrows act like a dimmer switch, and you can make the objects blaze with light or glow softly. That's how it works in *this* virtual world, but in another the lamp label might simply turn underlining on and off! The only way to know what's going to happen is to click.

TIP

> *Notice that each of the geometric shapes is also a control that affects the way you navigate this world. The red cube puts you into walk mode, the green sphere puts you into fly mode, and the blue cone puts you into point mode. This use of custom objects as navigational controls is typical of Live3D worlds.*

The VRML Context Menu

One of the most powerful features of VRML is that it lets *you* control the way the graphic information appears on your screen. You can do this by clicking your right mouse button anywhere within the browser window. A Context menu pops up, as shown in Figure 10-6.

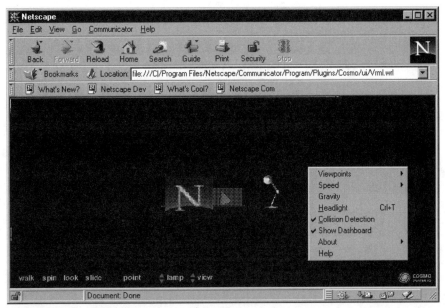

Figure 10-6: The Context menu.

From the Context menu there are a number of ways to reconfigure your navigation environment. I'm not going to cover all of these, mainly because they're a lot harder to describe than they are to explore. You can have some fun checking them out on your own, but here are a few things to try:

- Want to make your travels really wild? Select Bank when Flying from the Navigation submenu. Your imaginary craft will tilt in the direction of your turns.

- Getting too dizzy or confused? Select Stay on Ground when Walking from the Navigation submenu.

- Want to turn off the buttons at the bottom of the window for a better view of your virtual world? Uncheck the Navigation Bar item on the Options submenu.

If you want to preserve the changes you have made, simply click Save Current Settings As Default in the Options submenu.

What's the Point?

So far, VRML applications have concentrated on pretty, imaginative pictures. You can see some great examples of individual images at http://www.tcp.ca/gsb/VRML/vrml-modelshop.html. (Don't miss the rotating zebra head!) But what about more serious applications?

Well, just about everything you can do with ordinary HTML you can do with VRML as well. VRML pages can include links to other documents, enhance sites with sound and video, and even collect user information for online transactions. You can think of the added dimension as providing yet more ways to organize information.

In addition, VRML provides a visual analog for the "real" world. Imagine an online real estate company providing three-dimensional models of houses. You could check out the front yard, then the back yard, then go inside and wander through the rooms. You could click various appliances to find out what brand they are or how old they are. And think of the educational possibilities: kids in school wandering through three-dimensional depictions of the human body, clicking to get more information on their favorite organs.

No, you're not going to see that in 1997, but it's quite likely in 1998. VRML is just emerging from its "proof of concept" stage, and real-world applications haven't caught up with the technology yet. In addition, VRML pages are still pretty slow to load over modem connections. But for a taste of things to come, check out Netscape's own showcase site at http://home.netscape.com/comprod/products/communicator/multimedia/live3d/cool_worlds/index.html.

Plug-ins

Right out of the box (or the CD sleeve), Netscape Communicator lets you experience most of what is available on the Net. But as the Web becomes more popular and the technology improves, more sophisticated multimedia content is becoming available all the time. You just saw, for instance, how VRML is adding new dimensions to Web content—literally. Movies, desktop-published documents, and video conferencing are slowly making their way onto the Web as well. Not only are these new types of data putting strains on the infrastructure of the Internet, they are also forcing Web browsers to evolve from text and graphics displayers to real-time, interactive multimedia viewers.

Not to worry. Your investment in Netscape Communicator is a good one. The Netscape developers have come up with an open-extendible architecture that lets the program evolve as technology itself evolves. Through plug-in applications developed by independent software vendors, Navigator 4 and Netcaster enable you to experience most of what is currently available online.

Plug-ins extend Communicator's capabilities so that it can display or play a wide variety of documents and file types, such as Adobe Acrobat PDF (Portable Document Format) files, Macromedia Director movies, and MIDI music files. It uses what's known as its *Live Objects* technology to enable developers to create rich multimedia content for the Internet or office intranets.

Up until Netscape Navigator 2.0, Web users were required to configure separate helper applications that worked independently of their Web browsers to view and control most multimedia documents. Now when you download and configure plug-ins to work with Netscape Navigator 2.0 or later, the plug-ins effectively become part of the browser itself. Movies, sound events, presentation graphics, and more display directly in the Navigator 4 window. In fact, plug-ins are so well integrated with the program that you'll quickly forget you're using them.

How Plug-ins Display in Navigator 4

When you use a plug-in with Netscape Communicator, it may not always be apparent that the plug-in is a separate application. With helper applications, you always know when a graphics program or a media player starts because you see it display in a separate window. Plug-ins, however, can interact with Navigator 4 in one of three modes of operation:

- **Full-screen plug-ins.** Full-screen plug-ins are just that—plug-ins that take up an entire browser window. They are referenced in an HTML document with a link which the user must click in order for the results to be seen or heard. These are less common than embedded plug-ins.

OFFICIAL NETSCAPE COMMUNICATOR 4 PROFESSIONAL EDITION BOOK

■ **Embedded plug-ins.** Embedded plug-ins are referenced in HTML documents so that when a document is loaded, the plug-in activates and displays the object or plays the sound. Figure 10-7 shows a typical embedded plug-in, an interactive Shockwave tic-tac-toe game.

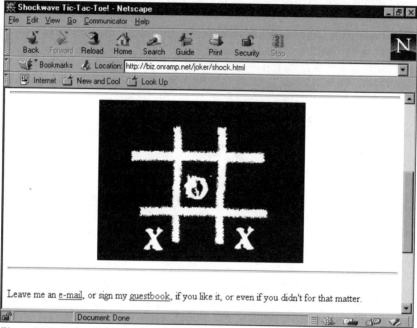

Figure 10-7: A plug-in tic-tac-toe game.

TIP

If you navigate to a site that contains an embedded image or animation for which you do not have the correct plug-in, you'll see a blank area with an icon that looks like a blue jigsaw puzzle piece in the middle.

As a Web author, you specify embedded plug-ins by using the <EMBED> HTML tag, as shown in the following syntax:

```
<EMBED SRC="movie.mpg", WIDTH=150, HEIGHT=250 AUTOSTART=TRUE>
```

In this example, when the user clicks on the plug-in reference on the Web page, an MPEG player activates automatically and plays a film clip named "movie.mpg."

■ **Hidden plug-ins.** Hidden plug-ins are ones that users cannot see or otherwise control, such as a plug-in that plays a music file in the background.

There are dozens of excellent plug-ins available for Netscape Communicator, and many of them are available in shareware or beta versions right on the Net.

Just to show you how easy it is to work with plug-ins, here's some more detailed information on one of the most exciting—the Macromedia Shockwave plug-in.

Shockwave & Netscape Communicator

The Shockwave plug-in lets you view Macromedia Director movies as well as FreeHand and Authorware multimedia files in Netscape Communicator. Developers can include this media in HTML documents by using the <EMBED> tag. Documents can even include more than one movie per HTML page.

When you access a site that includes a Director file, you can scroll through the Web page even while the movie is playing. You can interact with the movie by clicking on it, and you can enter text from the keyboard into text fields within the movie. And the movie itself can access information from the Internet and open URLs.

To download a copy of Shockwave, enter: **http://www. macromedia.com/ shockwave/download/plugin.cgi** in Navigator's Netsite/Location field and press Enter. Next, click the link Get the Shockwave Plug-in for Your Browser. On the next page, click the link for your appropriate operating system, such as Windows 95. You now can download the file by clicking one of the links provided.

After you download the Shockwave plug-in file, exit Netscape Communicator. This is very important. *Plug-ins may not install properly if any Communicator component is running!* Now double-click the downloaded file. This decompresses it and installs Shockwave on your system.

TIP

Macromedia currently offers two different Shockwave packages: Shockwave Flash, which is useful for viewing smaller animations on the Web, and Shockwave Director, which is used by Communicator to play larger multimedia documents, interactive games, etc. You can also get both versions in one package by downloading Shockwave Essentials.

Once Shockwave is installed, you can start Netscape Communicator and test its new capabilities. One page that uses a multimedia image to enhance its appeal, unsurprisingly, is Macromedia's own Welcome page. The URL is: http://www.macromedia.com/shockwave/welcome.html, and what it looks like is shown in Figure 10-8, if you've installed Shockwave properly.

As you can see—and hear—Shockwave enhances Web pages not only with animation but also with sound and embedded HTML links. You can see other uses of Shockwave at the Macromedia's Shockwave Gallery, http://www.macromedia.com/shockwave/epicenter/, but Shockwave presentations are also sprinkled all around the Web.

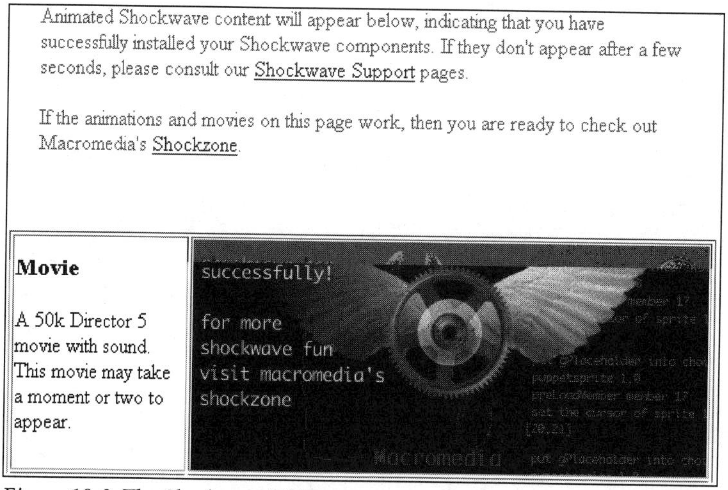

Figure 10-8: The Shockwave Welcome page.

AutoInstall

What if you're browsing the Web and suddenly Navigator 4 encounters a file that it cannot display or play for you because you don't have the associated plug-in installed? There are a variety of different scenarios, depending on the programming of the Web page containing the link and on whether or not the file type is one that has been registered with Netscape. (Registration with Netscape allows a new plug-in for the file type to be installed automatically, via a special *AutoInstall* feature.) If it *is* a file type that has been registered with Netscape:

- You may be asked to agree to a license and approve the installation of a particular plug-in. Once you approve the installation, the plug-in may be installed on your system automatically.

- The plug-in may be installed automatically right away, if you previously approved a digital security certificate (see Chapter 13) from the plug-in vendor. As soon as the plug-in is installed, you can see the Web page with the multimedia information rendered correctly.
- You might be transported to Netscape's Plug-in Finder page, with the appropriate plug-in selected from Netscape's list. Just follow the directions that appear, which will vary from plug-in to plug-in.

Non-automatic Installation

If the file type is *not* one that has been registered with Netscape, Figure 10-9 shows what you'll get.

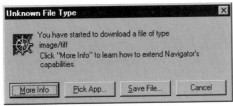

Figure 10-9: The Unknown File Type dialog box.

In this case, click More Info. Once again, you'll be transported to the Plug-in Finder Page, as shown in Figure 10-10.

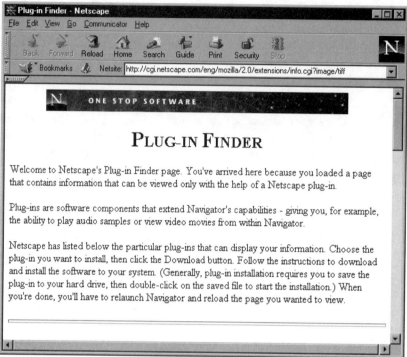

Figure 10-10: The Plug-in Finder page.

Of course you can always access the Plug-in Finder *before* you encounter a new kind of file, selecting whatever plug-ins may be useful or interesting to you. Simply click the Navigator Plug-ins link on Netscape's home page (http://home.netscape.com). Or, you can select About Plug-ins from the Navigator Help menu and then click the "click here" link near the top of the page.

If you scroll down the Plug-in Finder page, you'll see a graphical index of third-party plug-ins loosely arranged by function, as shown in Figure 10-11. Start exploring from here and you'll find some pretty fascinating ways to extend Communicator's power!

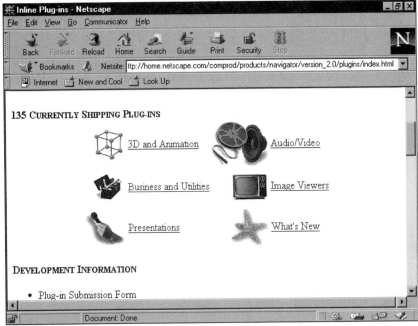

Figure 10-11: Netscape's Plug-in Finder page, showing the index of third-party plug-ins.

Finding Out Which Plug-ins You Already Have

Plug-ins are such an exciting feature that you may become a "plug-in fool" like me, downloading add-ons that make Communicator do everything except do your taxes. And, if you're like me, you won't remember what you've already installed and may download the same plug-in several times!

Fortunately, Netscape takes care of people like you and me. To see what plug-ins are currently installed, select About Plug-ins from the Help menu of any one of the Communicator components, or enter **about:plugins** (no space after the colon) in Navigator's Netsite/Location field. The Installed plug-ins information page appears, as shown in Figure 10-12.

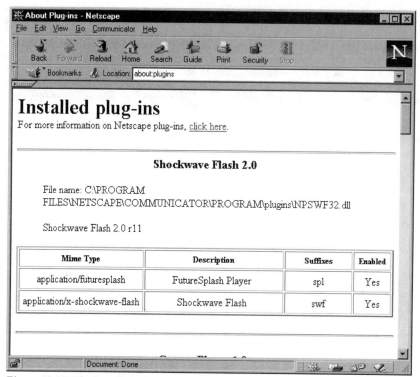

Figure 10-12: The Installed Plug-ins information page.

As you can see by scrolling down the page, it includes the name of each installed plug-in, what kind of files it operates on (listed by MIME type as well as by file extension or suffix), and whether or not it's currently enabled. This is a good place to determine what version of a particular plug-in you have, too. There may be a newer version available that *does* do your taxes.

TIP

> *You can also get to Netscape's Plug-in Finder from here, by clicking the "click here" link near the top of the page.*

Java

When you get older and your grandchildren ask you about the good old days of the World Wide Web, you'll tell them about Java. You'll tell them that Java was the technology that got us one step closer to bringing real-time interaction between people on the Internet. Java not only enhances Web pages with impressive graphics, it enables software developers to create secure two-way Web applications in a straightforward fashion. These applications are called *Java applets*. Figure 10-13 shows an example of what a Java applet can do.

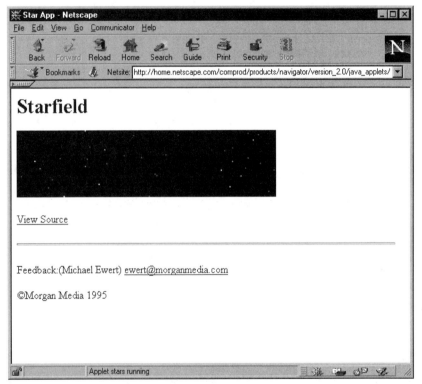

Figure 10-13: A Java applet in Navigator 4.

Many Netcaster channels (see Chapter 4) are also implemented in Java. Because they are written in a separate programming language rather than in HTML, they are able to provide a complete interactive interface.

So What Are Applets?

Java applets are the hottest new eye-candy on the Web. But what exactly are they? They are simply small applications written in the Java programming language. Yes, Java is an entire programming language developed by Sun Microsystems, Inc. (For the propeller-heads reading this, it's similar to C++ but without pointers.) Java lets developers create platform-independent multimedia applications for distribution on the Web. With Navigator 4, you can visit sites that include Java applets (or even full-blown applications) and actually run them.

Since Java applets are cross-platform, you run the same code on a Mac as you do on a Windows 3.1 or Windows NT machine. When you get to a Web page that includes Java applets, you don't have to choose which version to link to. And since Netscape was in the technological vanguard in supporting Java, you don't need a special helper application to interpret the Java code—Communicator does it all.

With traditional Internet and World Wide Web content, the focus is mainly one-way—from the server to the user. It's similar to the cable television that comes into your house. You can receive data from this cable, but you cannot transmit data back through it. We've seen that format allow for some two-way interactivity, but Java really opens up the possibilities. When Java applets are integrated with a Web browser, such as Navigator 4, you can experience live information updating, interaction with other users, and instant interaction with Internet servers.

References to Java applets are included in Web pages with the <APPLET> tag. Each applet is a separate software component that is downloaded with the page. A Java run-time application included in Navigator 4 executes the Java applet and enables you to interact with the applet.

As more and more developers acquire Java programming skills, and more and more people start using browsers like Navigator 4 that support Java, Web sites will begin to include them. In fact, they may become as plentiful as graphics and other files you encounter on the Web now. For this reason, you need to know how to interact with Java applets when you encounter them.

Interacting With Java Applets

When you arrive at a site that includes a Java applet, you really don't have to do anything special. Netscape Communicator does all the work. Information that Navigator needs for running the Java applet is embedded in the HTML documents using the <APPLET> tag. Netscape Communicator automatically downloads and interprets the applet. A complete download may take up to several minutes. Once the applet arrives on your machine, you interact with it per the individual applet's instructions.

Figure 10-14 shows a Java crossword puzzle that lets you actually enter words.

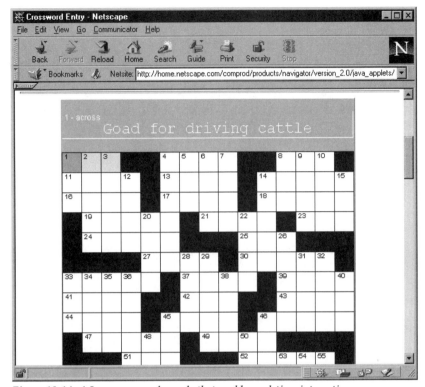

Figure 10-14: A Java crossword puzzle that enables real-time interaction.

If you scroll up the window you'll see that this Java applet, like many others, includes a list of instructions (shown in Figure 10-15):

```
How to play:
    1) The current word you are working on is highlighted in yellow.
    2) The current letter is highlighted in cyan.
    3) Click any letter to move to that word.
    4) <spacebar> switches between across and down. It pivots around the
       current letter.
    5) <back space> erases the current letter.
    6) Incorrect letters are drawn in red.
```

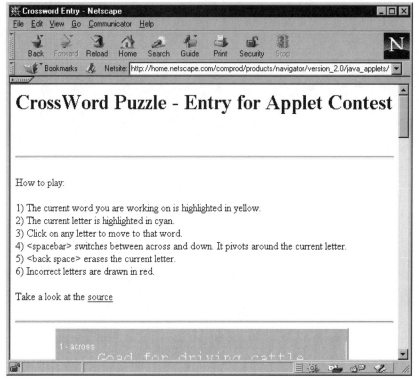

Figure 10-15: Instructions for the Crossword Puzzle applet.

As you can see, you fill out the crossword puzzle while it's actually displayed in Navigator 4. You can type in letters, delete letters, and move from one box to another using your mouse and keyboard. The main difference between this type of application and a crossword puzzle that may have appeared earlier on the Internet is that the Java applet lets you interact with it directly in Navigator 4. Previously you would have had to download a file that runs separately from Navigator 4.

If you're interested in taking a look at some more Java applets, you can do so by visiting one of the sites listed in Table 10-1. These sites include one or more applets that automatically display in the Navigator 4 window. Remember that most Java applets are interactive, so get in there with your mouse.

TIP

As you know, the exact locations of files on the Web often change. If you have trouble with any of the links listed in the table above, simply navigate to http://www.javasoft.com:80/applets/applets.html and select from there.

Applet	Where You Find It
Blinking Text	http://www.javasoft.com/applets/Blink/example1.html
Curve	http://fas.sfu.ca:80/1/cs/people/GradStudents/heinrica/personal/curve.html
Crossword	http://home.netscape.com/comprod/products/navigator/version_2.0/java_applets/Crossword/index.html
Imagemap	http://www.javasoft.com/applets/applets/ImageMap/example1.html
Modern Clock	http://www.wsrn.com/southern/java/DateClock.html
Pythagoras	http://home.netscape.com/comprod/products/navigator/version_2.0/java_applets/Pythagoras/index.html
Simple 3D Viewer	http://www.javasoft.com/applets/applets/WireFrame/example1.html
StarField	http://home.netscape.com/comprod/products/navigator/version_2.0/java_applets/StarField/index.html
Traditional Clock	http://www.javasoft.com/applets/Clock/index.html

Table 10-1: Some Java applets and where to find them.

Another great site can be found at the Gamelan Java Directory, at http://www.gamelan.com/. This Web site is full of links and resources to Java sites and development news. If you're serious about Java, either as a developer or end user, you need to check out this site every so often to see what's new on the Java front.

Signed Java

Typically, applets are written in a Java language subset that includes several security precautions. For instance, applets can't perform most file system access or file I/O routines.

There may be times, though, when you *want* to grant a Java applet more access to your system. For instance, you may want a Java applet at work to be able to update certain data files stored on your hard drive.

For both tightening and loosening security, Communicator supports what are known as *signed Java applets*. A signed Java applet is one that will not be downloaded to your system until you approve a special digital security certificate (see Chapter 13) that positively identifies the sender. If the Java applet performs any unusual function that could compromise security, you will be asked to approve this action as well. If you have run Communicator's Netcaster component (see Chapter 4), you may have already seen an alert like this. A Java Security alert informs you of what level of risk is involved in the access that is being requested, and it lets you click a button to grant or deny access. You can grant access for this Communicator session or for all subsequent Communicator sessions. If you decide to grant access to the holder of the certificate for subsequent sessions, Communicator keeps a copy of the digital certificate. In addition, you can view detailed information about the requested access privileges by clicking a Details button.

What if you want to change these access privileges later? You can adjust the privileges allowed to Java applets on a certificate-by-certificate basis at any time. To adjust the Java privileges for a particular certificate you've already received:

1. Click the Security button or the Security icon at the left of the status line in any Communicator component.

2. In the left hand frame of the Security page, click Java/JavaScript, as shown in Figure 10-16.

The scrolling list includes all the security certificates that you've already approved, presumably when launching a new signed Java applet. If you select a certificate from the list, you can then use the buttons on the right to:

■ **View Certificate.** Click this button for a detailed view of the certificate.

Remove. Click this button to remove the certificate from the list. Java applets from this point of origin will no longer be downloaded and executed automatically on your computer. Instead, you will be presented again with the option of approving a digital certificate.

■ **Edit Privileges.** Click this button for the Edit Privileges page. In the Edit Privileges page you can choose which privileges you want to grant for this session only or for any future sessions; it also may let you choose privileges that are specifically denied. For more information, please see Chapter 13.

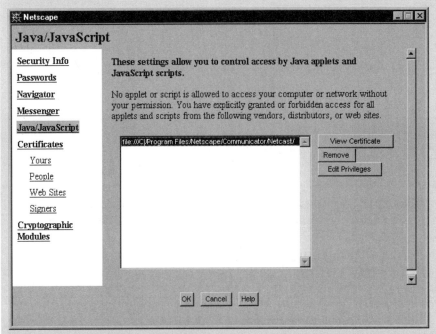

Figure 10-16: Java/JavaScript security options.

If you want, you can even disable Java completely in Netscape Communicator. To do this, select Preferences from the Edit menu of any component and then click the Advanced category. In the window that appears, uncheck the "Enable Java check box. You can disable JavaScript here as well. Please refer to the upcoming section on JavaScript.

Creating Your Own Applets

For those interested in developing Java applets, you can obtain Sun's official documentation and the Java API (application programming interface) from http://java.sun.com/java.sun.com/aboutJava/index.html. Remember, this is a serious programming language. If you don't have any previous experience with C++ or a similar object-oriented language, now's the time to go out and buy a book about programming in Java.

Java is what's known in the computer industry as a "cool new feature." It's not just something that's needed to perform a particular task—it also looks toward the future and has a strong element of fun to it. What you can do with Java is limited only by your imagination.

> **TIP**
>
> *For detailed technical information on a particular Java applet, click the Java Console item in the Communicator menu.*

JavaScript

As you travel around the Web, you may notice some user interface niceties that don't seem part of regular old HTML. For instance, there might be some text in your Navigator 4 status bar that ties in with the Web page you're viewing. Or words may scroll across the browser window. Or when you type a bogus area code into a form, a message pops up telling you your entry isn't valid. Some of the following material may be of interest to you only if you are planning to create your own Web pages (see Chapter 9). Once you have a basic understanding of what JavaScript is, feel free to skip over the technical stuff!

If you wonder how the author of the Web page is pulling off these tricks, a good guess would be JavaScript. You can think of JavaScript as "Java Lite:" a language that's less powerful than Java but easier to use. While Java programs are independent binary files compiled using special Java programming tools, entire JavaScript programs may be entered directly into an HTML page with a simple text editor. Communicator simply interprets the new commands along with the HTML. Table 10-2 points out some of the differences between Java and JavaScript.

Whoa! In case you're not a programmer, let me put that in plain English: Java is for the big stuff, JavaScript is for smaller effects. Java requires special development tools and a solid understanding of object-oriented programming concepts, while you can probably add some simple JavaScript to your own Web pages after a few hours of playing around, or even minutes if you cut and paste existing examples.

JavaScript	Java
Code is human-readable and embedded right in HTML file.	Java applets are separate from HTML pages.
Interpreted by Communicator—not compiled.	Applets are compiled before being placed on server.
Uses objects but does not support classes or inheritance.	Completely object-oriented. Applets are made up of object classes that support inheritance.
No need to declare data type of variables.	Strong typing: data types need to be declared.
References to objects checked dynamically at run-time.	Static binding at compile time.

Table 10-2: Differences between Java and JavaScript.

LiveConnect

LiveConnect is the Netscape technology that lets plug-ins, JavaScripts, and Java applets interact with each other. For example, thanks to LiveConnect, clicking a button in a Web page could start up separate video and audio plug-in files that are perfectly synchronized. Or it might start a brief movie, which could then trigger a sound file. In other words, LiveConnect allows for real-time integration of various separate media files and interactive JavaScripts or applets.

JavaScript Nuts & Bolts

There are two ways that JavaScript can be embedded in HTML scripts. First, a Web author can use the <SCRIPT> tag. Here's a simple example:

```
<HTML>
<HEAD>
</HEAD>
<BODY>
<SCRIPT LANGUAGE="JavaScript">
document.write("Everybody loves Communicator! (And the <I>Official Netscape
Communicator 4 Professional Edition Book</I>, of course.)")
</SCRIPT>
</BODY>
</HTML>
```

Yep, you guessed it: what appears on your screen is the phrase "Everybody loves Communicator!. . .". OK, you would never really *do* it that way, but at least this gives you an idea of how it works. As you can see, the SCRIPT tag is inside the BODY area of the document. Now just imagine that instead of using the predefined *document.write* function, we had used something more interesting. How about a function that scrolls the words across your browser window in rainbow colors?

Or here's a more practical example using a square function you define yourself:

```
<HTML>
<HEAD>
<SCRIPT LANGUAGE="JavaScript">
function square(i) {
   document.write("The number to be squared: ", i,"<BR>")
    return i * i
    }

</SCRIPT>
</HEAD>
<BODY>
<SCRIPT LANGUAGE="JAVASCRIPT">
x = prompt("What number is to be squared? ", "number, please")
document.write("The result of this calculation is: ", square(x), ".")
</SCRIPT>
<BR>
The script is all finished calculating the square.
</BODY>
</HTML>
```

The result?

```
JavaScript Prompt: What is the number to be squared?
The number to be squared: 2
The result of this calculation is 4.
The script is all finished calculating the square.
```

If you study the code a little, you can see that it defines the square function as one that will print the phrase "The number to be squared:" after accepting a number from the user via the built-in prompt method which asks "What is the number to be squared?", then multiplies that number by itself and returns the result. Once defined like this, the function may be used anywhere later in the document.

The <SCRIPT> tag is pretty convenient, but there is also an even more powerful way of working with the language: *event handlers*. This sounds pretty techie, but it's actually quite simple. Netscape Communicator obviously recognizes when a user performs some action such as clicking on a word or phrase. With JavaScript, you can associate chunks of code with actions (or events). In other words, when a user clicks on a word, JavaScript knows to do something. Take a look at this example:

```
<INPUT TYPE="button" VALUE="Add It Up Now" onClick="AddItUp(this.form)">
```

This snippet of code executes a user defined function called AddItUp whenever you click the button labeled "Add It Up Now." It could be used as the last button in a form to add all the numbers you'd previously entered.

JavaScript can use *properties* such as "visible" and "color" to return your specified response. You might, for example, design a Web page that includes listings and descriptions of your products. Let's say you sell countertops, and each model of countertop comes in various styles, textures, and colors. Customers to your site may want to design a virtual kitchen by mixing and matching colors and textures with different countertops and other fixtures. With JavaScript, you can include a selector that enables users to adjust the colors and textures of specific countertops. You could create the entire site as a Java applet, but why not use Java only where necessary (such as for creating the virtual kitchen and countertop and the selector)? Then use JavaScript to change the colors and textures of the countertop in the applet.

There's no end to the kinds of fun things you can do with JavaScript. For instance, JavaScript can detect whether or not a plug-in is available and adjust the Web page accordingly. Suppose a page includes a fancy 3D-animated image that requires a plug-in you don't have. JavaScript could figure this out and substitute a plain old GIF or JPEG. JavaScript can even change JPEG and GIF images "on the fly." Imagine staring at a picture of Alan Greenspan that suddenly turns into Tom Peters. Graphics can change automatically at a particular interval or when the viewer clicks a button or icon.

TIP

For a more comprehensive and up-to-date user reference on JavaScript, see the JavaScript Authoring Guide at http://home.netscape.com/eng/mozilla/3.0/handbook/javascript/index.html.

Kiosk (Canvas) Mode

As I mentioned way back in Chapter 3, Navigator 4 supports a special "kiosk" mode (called *Canvas mode* by Netscape). When in Canvas mode, you as a Navigator user cannot affect the display except through interface elements specifically programmed by the author of the Web page—in JavaScript. For example, take a look at Figure 10-17:

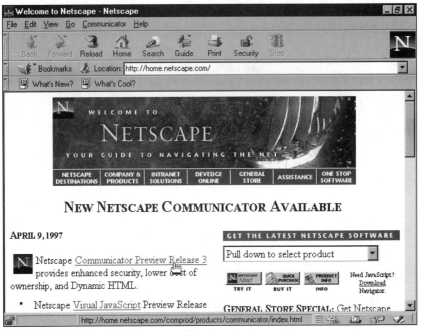

Figure 10-17: Navigator in Canvas mode.

A viewer can click any of the buttons or icons on the screen to access more detailed information but is effectively "locked out" of the Navigator software itself until he or she presses the Close Demo button (in an actual public setting this button would not exist).

And what are the JavaScript commands that you can put in a page in order to force Navigator into Canvas mode? That's easy:

```
window.open('pageURL',
'windowName','titlebar=no,left=-1,top=-1,
width=screenWidth,
height=screenHeight,alwaysRaised=yes');
```

The above lines of JavaScript create a full-screen window without browser menus, scroll bars, toolbars, or other visual "chrome." Another *very* useful JavaScript trick.

Moving On

In this chapter we've looked at some of the advanced capabilities of Netscape Communicator; forward-looking extensions such as VRML that put you at the cutting edge of Web browsing. We've also seen how plug-ins and Java can extend the power of Communicator in ways that are hard even to imagine.

All this multimedia muscle is pretty impressive, but there's another area that Web browsers haven't touched until recently: real-time interaction with other Internet (or intranet) users. Imagine placing long distance phone calls over the Internet, talking to somebody in Tibet with no costs beyond what you normally pay for Net access. Imagine clarifying your conversation by typing messages to each other while you talk, or even sending each other text files. Imagine working together long distance by means of an electronic drawing board that lets you mark up each other's ideas.

On second thought, don't bother imagining any of this: it's already available to you! In the next chapter, you'll learn how to take advantage of the interactive power of Communicator's Conference component.

CHAPTER 11

Netscape Conference

Some software is not only useful, but also genuinely fun to use. For decades now, we've been playing with variations on the old tin-cans-and-string phone that intrigued us as kids, and Netscape Conference has to be one of the coolest variations yet. Here are some of the things you can do with this exciting Communicator component:

- Talk to friends or business associates without ever paying a phone bill.
- Examine complete information on a caller before "picking up the phone."
- Type real-time messages back and forth with an individual halfway around the world.
- Place graphical information on a virtual whiteboard that both you and a remote Internet or intranet user can mark up and edit as you talk.
- Transfer files to remote users quickly and efficiently.
- Browse the Web collaboratively with a remote user, leading each other from link to link.

And as a bonus, many of these features are tightly integrated with other Communicator components.

What Is Conference?

Conference is a program that sends and receives voice and other data in real time over the Net or over an intranet. If you're not familiar with the term *real time*, here's what it means: when you talk, another user hears your voice right away, just as if you were using a telephone. You don't need to play a sound file. Conference also sends and receives text and graphical information in real time. For example, if you wanted to work on a sales brochure with a peer who has an office in another state, you could discuss it over the Internet. You could even show the thumbnails of the draft and mark up possible changes. Perhaps the best way to think about Conference is as a multimedia phone service.

Most of the services you've learned about in this book—e-mail, newsgroups, the Web itself—are client-server based. You use a client program such as Netscape Communicator to access information that's stored on a server. But Conference is different. It's a *peer-to-peer* service. You communicate directly with other individuals, not with servers storing the information they've created. Of course intranet or Internet servers are still involved in the process, but only to pass the information along transparently from user to user. You are immediately in touch with millions of people all around the world.

Pretty amazing, isn't it? And remember, this whole process is accomplished using the Internet or an intranet. That means no phone bills. Go ahead, ring up your marketing department in Peoria, and then turn around and send a spreadsheet to Baton Rouge.

There is one slight catch, though: anyone you communicate with using Conference has to be running Conference as well. That's because the program uses special proprietary protocols to send and receive multimedia data as efficiently as possible. But since Conference is part of Netscape Communicator, this exciting new technology is rapidly becoming commonplace. Not too long from now you might hear some self-satisfied young businessman say, "Have your avatar e-mail my droid, we'll do Conference."

Hardware Requirements

In addition to the requirements for running the rest of Netscape Communicator, Conference has a few specific requirements of its own. Of course, you can use Communicator without it, but here's what you need to run Conference:

- A 486 or better machine running at a CPU speed of at least 50 MHz.

- For SLIP and PPP connections, a modem with a speed of *at least* 14,400 kbps; I highly recommend a faster modem for this feature.

■ If you plan to use the voice features (in addition to the Chat, Whiteboard, and collaborative Web browsing features), a Windows-compatible sound card with speakers and a microphone.

TIP

For full-duplex audio conferencing (letting both parties speak at the same time), you need a full-duplex sound card and a driver that supports full-duplex operation. Most sound card manufacturers keep updated drivers at their Web or FTP sites, available for free download.

OK, let's get busy and actually run Conference.

Running Conference the First Time

You can start Conference by double-clicking its icon in the Communicator folder or program group, or you can simply choose Conference from the Communicator menu of any Communicator component. Either way, if this is the first time you've run Conference, the Setup Wizard appears, as shown in Figure 11-1.

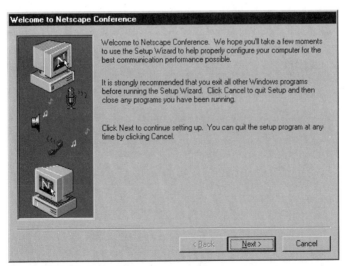

Figure 11-1: The Setup Wizard.

TIP

Notice also that as soon as you fire up Conference, a telephone icon appears in the tray area of your Windows 95 or Windows NT 4.0 taskbar. When you're connected to or are attempting to reach another Conference user, the handset turns red to indicate "call active." And if you right-click the icon, you can access the Conference window itself or Conference preferences. You can even select Do Not Disturb from the icon's right-click context menu to block any incoming calls.

The first screen of the Wizard is a typical Welcome message; read it and click Next. Now you are presented with a list of hardware requirements for running Conference, but you already know them. Click Next again.

At last, you get to a dialog box in which you need to do some real work, the Business Card dialog box. It's shown in Figure 11-2.

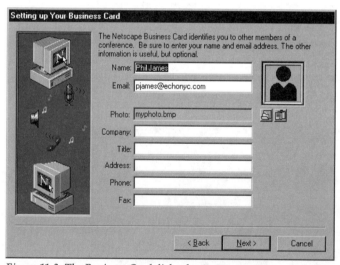

Figure 11-2: The Business Card dialog box.

Filling Out Your Business Card

Want other users to know something about you when you call them? Sharing that information is easy with Conference. Now you can set up Conference's business card feature, which is kind of like caller ID on steroids.

In the Name field, type your—wait a minute, how many times have you filled out a form like this? You can probably figure out what to do here just fine without me. After you've completed the form, it should look something like the one shown in Figure 11-3.

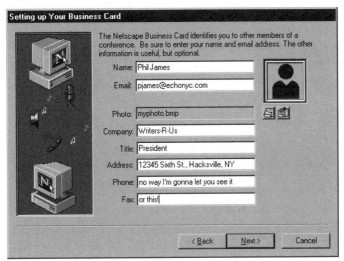

Figure 11-3: A completed business card.

But wait, there's more! Don't you want the world to know what you look like? Yes, you can actually add a picture to your business card. Here's how:

- To add a picture from a file, click the button just to the right of the Photo field. A standard file selection dialog box appears, letting you choose a picture from anywhere on your system.

- To add a picture that's already saved in the clipboard, click the button to the far right of the Photo field. The picture will be pasted in immediately.

In either case, your picture is plugged into your business card, and your completed form should now look something like Figure 11-4.

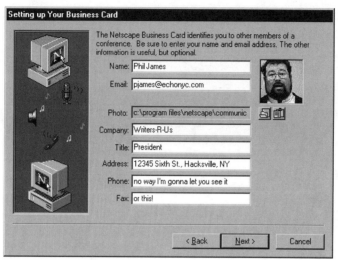

Figure 11-4: A Conference business card with my picture.

TIP

> *You probably already thought of this idea: it doesn't have to be a picture of you. It could be your company logo or even a favorite painting or cartoon. (Make sure you're not violating any copyrights, though.)*

OK, you've completed your business card. Click Next and the Wizard pops up a Directory Preferences dialog box. Let's take a closer look.

Setting Up Directory Preferences

Figure 11-5 shows the Directory Preferences dialog box.

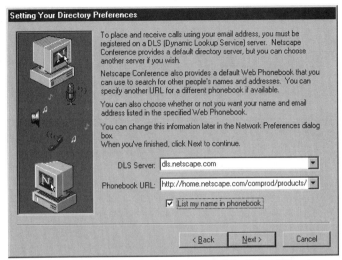

Figure 11-5: The Directory Preferences page of the Setup Wizard.

Notice that this page has two different fields for entering information. The first one is for the Dynamic Lookup Service (DLS) server you want to use. In Conference, you can initiate calls to an individual simply by entering his or her e-mail address. Conference then logs on to the DLS server and finds an actual Internet IP address that's associated with that e-mail address. For instance, if I tell Conference I want to call joe@some_company.com, the DLS server may send Conference the address 123.456.789.123, the actual IP address of Joe's computer. As long as Joe is currently running his own copy of Conference, the connection is established.

The default DLS server is dls.four11.com. You should probably leave this field unchanged unless you're on an intranet and your network administrator has given you a different server address to enter.

The other field on this page lets you specify a Phonebook URL. It is the Web page that appears when you click the Web Phonebook button in Conference. It lets you choose from among users all around the Net who are currently running Conference. Simply click a name and you're connected to that individual, ready to talk or to use any of Conference's collaborative features. This method is a lot easier than using an old-fashioned paper phone book. You'll learn more about the Web Phonebook later, but here's a sneak preview in Figure 11-6.

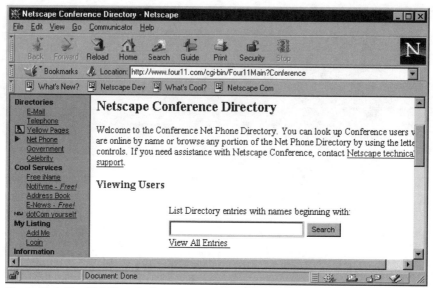

Figure 11-6: The Web Phonebook.

You should leave the Phonebook URL setting alone unless you know of a different Web Phonebook you can access.

How do all these people get into the Web Phonebook? They are all people who left the List my name in phone book option checked, as shown earlier in Figure 11-5. If you leave it checked, you too will be listed in the default Web Phonebook whenever you're connected to the Net and start Conference. Don't worry, you can change this option at any time later if you want an "unlisted number."

OK, click Next and we're on to the Specify Your Network Type dialog box.

Specifying Your Network Type

For Conference to operate at optimum speed and with the best sound quality possible, it needs to know the data rate of your Internet or intranet connection. Conference uses different types of audio compression—known as *CODECs*—depending on your connection type. As you can see in Figure 11-7, the Wizard lets you choose anything from a 14,400 kbps modem connection up to a hard-wired LAN connection.

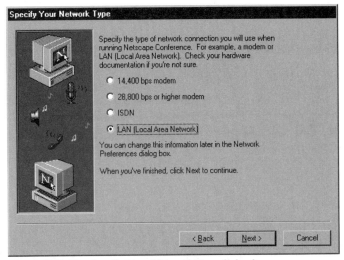

Figure 11-7: The Specify Your Network Type dialog box.

After you have selected the appropriate option button, click Next for some questions about your sound card.

TIP

If you have specified a LAN connection, the Wizard will pop up an extra screen that gives you some information about running Conference behind a firewall on an office intranet. If your office uses a firewall (see Chapter 13 if you don't know what I'm talking about), read this screen carefully.

Detecting Your Sound Card

Figure 11-8 shows the Detecting Your Sound Card dialog box.

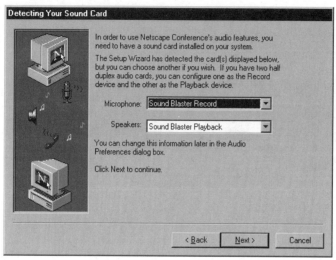

Figure 11-8: The Detecting Your Sound Card dialog box.

If your sound card is properly installed on your system, chances are that Conference has already found it and correctly identified it. Its name should appear in both the Microphone and Speakers fields. If you have more than one sound card in your computer, you may be able to choose from the drop-down lists. If no sound card at all appears on either list, your computer does not have a sound card, it is not properly installed, or it is not supported by Conference. You can still use Conference's non-audio features, but you will not be able to actually talk across the Net or your intranet.

TIP

If you have more than one half-duplex sound card installed on your system, you can use different ones for Microphone and Speakers. That way, you can realize full-duplex operation—while you're "talking out" one card, you can be listening to a voice "coming in" on the other card. Of course, it's simpler and more economical to use a full-duplex card and make sure you have a full-duplex driver for it.

Now click Next again. A dialog box labeled Testing the Audio Levels (Screen 1 of 2) appears. Read the text carefully. If you don't currently have a microphone attached to your system, click Skip. Otherwise, click Next to test and set your audio levels. Screen 2 of the audio testing portion of the Wizard appears, as shown in Figure 11-9.

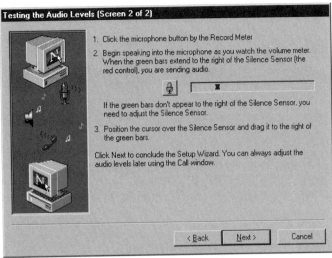

Figure 11-9: Testing the Audio Levels (Screen 2 of 2).

You should read the instructions on the screen, but to understand what's going on, also read the following sidebar.

Dealing with Half-Duplex Sound Cards: The Silence Sensor

As I explained earlier, you can use two kinds of sound cards: half-duplex and full-duplex. With a full-duplex card, you and the person you're talking to via Conference can both speak at the same time, just as you can with a telephone. If either of you has a half-duplex card, however, you'll have to take turns, as with a CB radio. Netscape Conference handles half-duplex communication in two different ways:

1. You can simply click a Microphone button whenever you want to speak and then a Speakers button whenever you want to listen.

or

2. You can configure Conference so that it automatically switches between your voice and your friend's voice, without any intervention on your part.

Take my word for it, the second scenario is much easier! But a potential problem exists. Suppose your office is noisy. How does Conference know when it's you talking and not just the sound of your computer? Since Conference goes out of "listen" mode whenever it hears sound at your end, your friend might *never* get a word in edgewise.

➡

The Sound Sensor comes in at this point. See that red dot inside the microphone meter shown in Figure 11-9? That dot lets you set the minimum level of sound at which Conference assumes you are speaking; everything less than that level is ignored as silence. To set the level higher (in other words, if your environment is noisy and you want to make Conference ignore more ambient noise rather than interpreting it as speech), drag the red dot to the right.

OK, let's follow the instructions on the screen:

1. Click the small microphone button to the left of the upper panel. This way, you can check sound levels without actually being connected.

2. Try talking into the mike. You'll see green bars move to the right across the panel. The dark green indicates sound that is really too soft for a clear conversation; the maroon bars indicate the ideal volume for talking; and if you see red bars, you should get a job in a rock band.

3. If no green at all is showing when you're not talking, you can leave the blue Silence Sensor control exactly where it is. But if some green appears in the window, indicating significant ambient noise, you should drag the dot to the right until it is just above that level, as shown in Figure 11-10. That way, Conference starts to send audio immediately when you begin speaking.

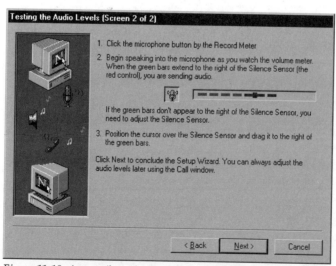

Figure 11-10: A new silence level.

Once you have set the Silence Sensor, click Next and then click Finish on the last page of the Wizard. By the way, you can access the Setup Wizard at any time to change any of the options you've just set. In Conference, simply select Setup Wizard from the Help menu.

TIP

You can change the Silence Sensor setting at any time later without running the Wizard again. The blue dot control is right within the main Conference window.

The Conference Window

As soon as you click the Wizard's Finish button, the Conference window appears on your desktop, as shown in Figure 11-11.

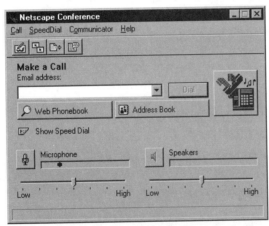

Figure 11-11: The Conference window.

Let's take a quick look around and get familiar with this new communications tool before we actually initiate a call. The Conference window is divided into three main areas, which I'll call the addressing area, the business card button, and the Microphone and Speakers controls.

The Addressing Area

Near the top of the Conference window is the addressing area, which is composed of a drop-down list box, a Dial button, a Web phone book button, and an Address Book button. We'll work with all these elements in depth in the section called "Initiating a Call" later in this chapter. These controls let you find and dial remote Conference users.

Can I Use Conference to Call People Who Use Different Conferencing Software?

The short answer is: "Yes, you can!" Netscape Conference utilizes a recently adopted real-time conferencing standard known as H.323, and many of its features will be compatible with products from other vendors that follow the same H.323 standard.

The slightly longer answer is: "Your mileage may vary." Since this standard is new, not every conferencing or Internet phone package uses it yet, and others may implement H.323 only for some basic features. Trying to connect to somebody who uses a different software package is certainly worthwhile, though. If it doesn't work, tell that person to get Communicator!

The Conference Button

Now click the big colorful square button at the right side of the Conference window. You see something like Figure 11-12.

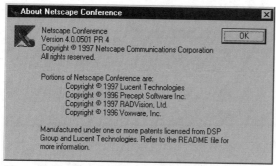

Figure 11-12: About Netscape Conference.

Hmm, why would the Netscape engineers devote such a big button to the mundane task of displaying this very ordinary About information? As you'll discover in a few minutes, everything changes when you actually place a call.

If the person on the other end has a picture as part of his or her business card, the button displays that picture. And when you click the button, you see the business card itself, as shown in Figure 11-13.

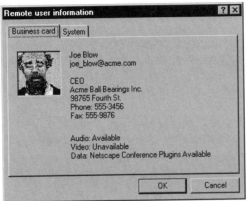

Remote user information

Business card | System

Joe Blow
joe_blow@acme.com

CEO
Acme Ball Bearings Inc.
98765 Fourth St.
Phone: 555-3456
Fax: 555-9876

Audio: Available
Video: Unavailable
Data: Netscape Conference Plugins Available

OK   Cancel

Figure 11-13: The results of clicking the Conference button while connected to another user.

Thus the Conference button is the key to knowing when you're connected and when you're offline. But the Conference button also conveys a variety of other information:

- By default, Conference prompts you when a call comes in, asking whether you want to answer it or not. The Conference button indicates this "prompt me" mode by displaying a phone that looks like it's being taken off the hook.

- If you change this setting so that Conference automatically answers all calls, the button depicts a phone that is clearly off the hook.

- If you elect to put Conference in "Do Not Disturb" mode so that it answers no incoming calls, the image on the button becomes a "not" sign over the telephone.

TIP

The Conference icon in your Windows 95 or Windows NT 4.0 taskbar tray changes just like the Conference button, indicating these various states even when Conference is minimized. When you are connected to another Conference user, the Taskbar icon depicts two connected telephone handsets.

And how do you switch between these three answering modes in Conference? From the Call menu, simply select Always Prompt, Auto Answer, or Do Not Disturb. You'll learn more about these features later, in the section called "Answering Calls."

The Microphone & Speakers Controls

Back in the main Conference window, notice the two horizontal black areas just below center. These two controls indicate where you'll see the volume level for your own voice and for the voice of the person you're talking to. Your voice is depicted in the Microphone meter; the person you're talking to is in the Speakers meter. You can adjust the mike sensitivity for your own voice by dragging the slider just below the Microphone meter, and you can adjust the volume of the "incoming" voice by dragging the slider just below the Speakers meter.

The buttons to the left of each meter are on/off switches. Click them to enable or mute either your outgoing sound or the sound of the person you're talking to. You know that Microphone or Speakers sound is on if you see a green display of the sound level in the respective meter. You can turn Microphone sound on even when you're not connected—this is a good way to set your sound level. (I'll talk more about sound level when I actually show you how to place a call.)

I told you about the Sound Sensor earlier. Although you may have adjusted it properly in the Setup Wizard, you can readjust it right here if you want. Simply use your mouse to drag the blue dot in the Microphone meter to the right or left.

TIP

If you have a half-duplex sound card, make sure that autoswitching is enabled. To enable autoswitching, select Preferences from Conference's Call menu; then click the Audio tab. Near the top of the tab, make sure the Recording/Playback autoswitch check box is checked. As long as this option is selected, Conference senses when you're done talking and automatically switches to "listen" mode so your friend can get a word or two in before you start up again. No need to click the Microphone button when you want to speak or the Speakers button when you want to listen.

Initiating a Call

When you initiate a connection to a remote user, you have to tell Conference how to reach that individual—or more specifically, that individual's computer. Conference needs the numeric IP address of the computer you're trying to connect to. (Remember, numeric IP addresses are the unique strings of numbers that positively identify every computer currently connected to the Internet or an intranet.) Of course, you're not likely to know your friends' numeric IP addresses, especially if they have SLIP or PPP accounts that assign them a new IP number each time they connect to the Net! So how does this process work?

Fortunately, Netscape Conference can look up IP addresses automatically by means of special directory servers. All you do is enter somebody's e-mail address. Conference logs on to a directory server and requests the current IP address that's associated with that e-mail address. If the person you're trying to reach has Conference running, the server can find his or her current numeric IP address, since Conference reports this information to the server when the program is launched.

So "dialing" an individual across the Net is as simple as entering an e-mail address, right?

Actually, it's even simpler. Conference provides three different methods that further automate the process: The Web Phonebook, the Address Book, and Speed Dial buttons.

The Web Phone Book

Let's get right down to business. The phone book I am using in this example is located out on the Net, so make sure you are currently connected. Launch Conference by double-clicking its icon on your desktop or by selecting it from the Communicator menu of any Communicator component. The main Conference window appears, as shown in Figure 11-11. Now follow these steps:

1. Click the Web phone book button. Navigator 4 is launched automatically, and within a few seconds the Conference Directory page appears, as shown in Figure 11-14.

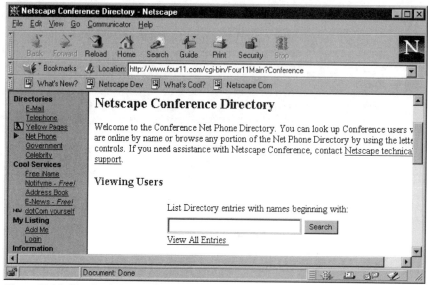

Figure 11-14: The Conference Directory page.

2. Scroll down to the Viewing Users section of the page and type the beginning of your name in the edit box, as shown in Figure 11-15.

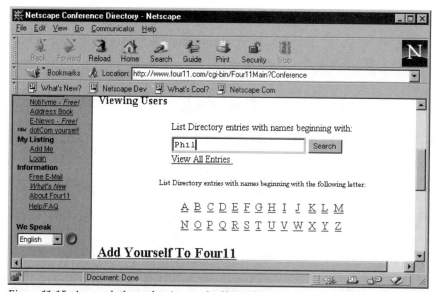

Figure 11-15: As usual, the author in search of himself.

- The default Web phone book will generally include your own name. This is because when you start Conference, it automatically reports your addressing information to this server. You can choose *not* to have your name listed in the phone book, or you can specify a different phone book and DLS server to store your information. For instance, your office intranet may have its own server. To change either of these settings, select Preferences from the Call menu and then click the Network tab if it is not already selected.

TIP

You can also get a complete list of Conference users by clicking View All Entries, or you can click one of the letters of the alphabet to list all names beginning with that letter.

3. Click the Search button. In a few seconds your search results appear, as shown in Figure 11-16.

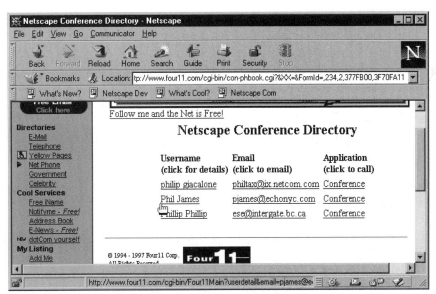

Figure 11-16: The search results.

4. If the list has several entries, scroll down until you find the individual you're interested in.

Notice that each Web phone book entry contains three fields, Username, E-mail, and Application. Let's examine each one separately:

- **Username**. If you click the individual's name, you will be presented with detailed information. Not only can you view the information, you can add it directly into your Communicator Address Book. (Why would you want to do this? See the section below called "The Address Book.") To add this individual to your Address Book, click the "get vCard" link. On the next page that appears, click the Add to Address Book button. The individual is added automatically to your Address Book.

- **Email**. If you click the individual's e-mail address, a Message Composition window appears (see Chapter 5) with the correct address already filled in. Just type your message and click Send!

- **Application**. In most cases, this field will contain the word "Conference." Just click it to initiate a Netscape Conference call to the individual.

Conference doesn't let you call yourself, so to try its communications features, you'll have to select a different name from the phone book. Use Navigator's Back button to return to the previous display. You can then choose a different initial letter for the names you want to show, or you can select View All Entries to see everyone who is currently using Conference. When you've found the name of an individual you want to call, simply type the word "Conference" in the Application field.

What happens when you click Conference? For that answer, you'll have to wait for the section called "Establishing the Connection." Right now, I want to show you how the Address Book provides another convenient way to initiate calls.

The Address Book

The Address Book is one of Communicator's shared resources. You've probably used it in Messenger for sending an e-mail message or for creating a new list of recipients. Conference uses the exact same Address Book for initiating calls. Let's take a look:

1. Launch Conference by double-clicking its icon on the desktop or by selecting it from the Communicator menu of any Communicator component.

2. Click the Address Book button. The Communicator Address Book appears, as shown in Figure 11-17.

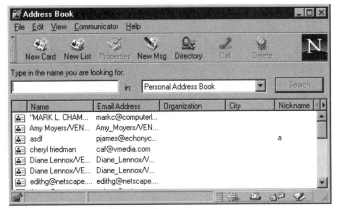

Figure 11-17: The Address Book.

3. Select a name from your list and click the Call button. That's all there is to it! Conference automatically initiates the call to this individual.

   ■ OK, it may not always be *quite* that simple. This will work just fine as long as the individual you're trying to contact uses the default Netscape Conference DLS server, the one you've already specified (generally netdls.four11.com). If you think you are more likely to find this individual on a different DLS server, you need to reconfigure the Address Book entry as described in step 4.

4. Double-click the Address Book entry you want to reconfigure. The card for that individual appears, as shown in Figure 11-18.

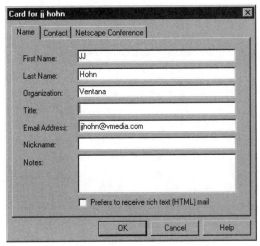

Figure 11-18: The card for an Address Book entry.

TIP

If you don't have any entries in your Address Book yet, click the New Card button and start filling in the information. For more detailed instructions, see the section called "The Address Book" in Chapter 5.

5. Select the Netscape Conference tab, as shown in Figure 11-19.

Figure 11-19: The Netscape Conference tab.

6. From the drop-down list, select either Specific DLS Server or Hostname or IP Address.

7. In the second field, enter the address of the DLS server, the domain name for the individual's machine, or the numeric IP address of the individual's machine.

A reconfigured Netscape Conference tab should look something like Figure 11-20.

Now just click OK. The Address Book entry you selected can now be used by Conference. Just select it and click the Call button. To see what happens next, move ahead to the section "Establishing the Connection."

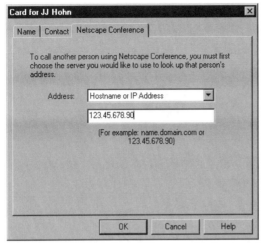

Figure 11-20: A reconfigured Netscape Conference tab.

Entering Addresses Directly

The Web Phone book and the Address Book make it easy to "dial" individuals across the Net, but sometimes you may want to enter an e-mail address—or even a domain name or numeric IP address—directly. You can simply type an e-mail address right into Conference's Email address field. Then just click the Dial button to complete your call.

If you want to type in a direct IP address, you need to put it in parentheses, as shown in Figure 11-21. This way, Conference knows you're not specifying an e-mail address and won't try to go contact a DLS server to translate it.

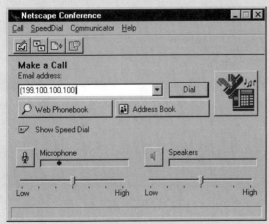

Figure 11-21: Conference with a direct IP address entered.

To avoid typing the parentheses, select Direct Call from the Call menu and then just type in the IP address.

If you don't know the numeric IP address of the machine you want to connect to, but you know its fully qualified domain name, you can also enter this information directly in either the Email address field or the Direct Call dialog box. If you enter it in the Email address field, you need to surround it with parentheses, just like the numeric IP address.

Speed Dial Buttons

In addition to the Web Phone book and the Address Book, Conference provides a third and even more convenient way to initiate calls: Speed Dial buttons. They are exactly like the speed dial buttons you may have on your telephone: just press one and the next thing you know you're talking to your PR, accounting, and marketing department. (Don't start talking until you know you've hit the right button.)

OK, let's get busy:

1. In Conference, click Show Speed Dial. The Speed Dial buttons appear, as shown in Figure 11-22.

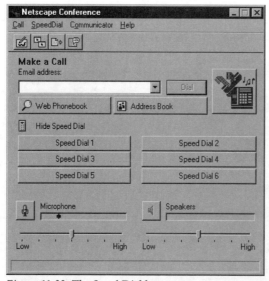

Figure 11-22: The Speed Dial buttons.

2. Right-click the Speed Dial 1 button. The Speed Dial Edit dialog box appears, as shown in Figure 11-23.

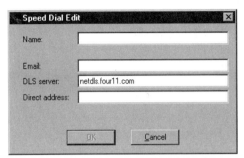

Figure 11-23: The Speed Dial Edit dialog box.

3. Complete the dialog box:

- Fill in the name of a person you call frequently. This name will actually appear on the Speed Dial button.

- Fill in his or her e-mail address.

- Leave the DLS server field alone unless you know the name of a different DLS server that stores the addressing information for this individual.

- If you want to use the Speed Dial button to connect directly to a specific machine rather than look up the individual via a DLS server, type in the numeric IP address or fully qualified domain name address for the machine. You do not need to surround this address with parentheses. (See the sidebar called "Entering Addresses Directly.")

4. After you've completed the dialog box, click OK. You are returned to the Conference window, which now includes a newly labeled Speed Dial button, as shown in Figure 11-24.

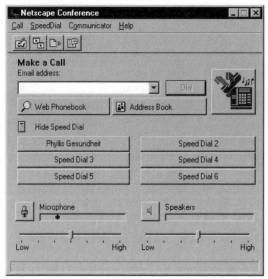

Figure 11-24: The Conference window with a new Speed Dial button.

To initiate a call, simply click the Speed Dial button you have just created.

TIP

To clear a Speed Dial button, select the name of the button from the Speed Dial menu; then click Clear from the submenu that appears. You will be asked if you really want to clear the contents of the button. Click OK. You can also edit the contents of a button at any time by right-clicking it.

Establishing the Connection

OK, you've just clicked a name in the Web phone book. Or you've selected a name from your Address Book and clicked the Call button. Or you've clicked one of your Speed Dial buttons. Or you've entered an address for a direct call. What happens next?

In Figure 11-25, you see the Pending Invitation that appears while you're waiting for somebody to accept your call.

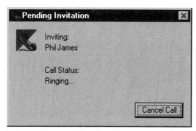

Figure 11-25: The Pending Invitation message.

If you want to cancel the call, simply click the Cancel Call button. The remote user you're trying to reach may cancel the call as well, in which case you'll get a Call Status message like the one shown in Figure 11-26.

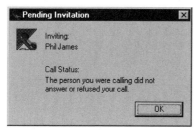

Figure 11-26: A Call Status message indicating that the remote user refused the call or simply did not answer.

But what happens when the remote user accepts your call? It's very, very simple: no messages, no dialog boxes, just the ability to communicate. Figure 11-27 shows what your screen looks like now.

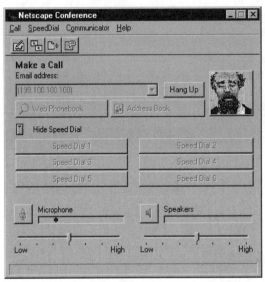

Figure 11-27: Conference after a connection has been established.

The Business card button may show a picture of the remote Conference user, and clicking it displays that individual's card, as shown in Figure 11-28. You can even learn about the remote user's hardware and software configuration by selecting the System tab.

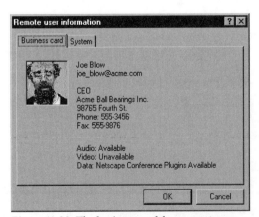

Figure 11-28: The business card for a remote user.

Of course, the remote user has your card too. You have just exchanged business cards without even knowing it. More importantly, though, you can now talk to each other. To learn how to do that, read on!

TIP

If either you or the remote Conference user does not have a sound card properly set up, you will still get a window that looks like Figure 11-27 when you connect, and you can still view each other's business cards. The Conference status line, however, will indicate that audio communication is not possible. Of course, you can use Conference's non-audio features: chat, the whiteboard, file transfer, and collaborative Web browsing.

Leaving Voice Mail

If the individual you're trying to reach is not currently available—perhaps because he or she is not currently running Conference or is already connected to another Conference user—Figure 11-29 shows what you'll get:

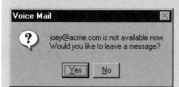

Figure 11-29: The Voice Mail dialog box.

If you click No in this dialog box, you are simply returned to the Conference window. But if you click Yes, a voice mail recorder pops up, as shown in Figure 11-30. This utility lets you record a sound file that will be sent to the individual via e-mail.

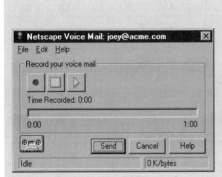

Figure 11-30: The voice mail recorder.

To record your message, click the red-dotted Record button and start talking. Click the Stop button when you are finished. To listen to your message before you send it, click the Play button. If you don't like what you hear, click Record again and talk some more. When you've created a message you're satisfied with, simply click Send.

Once you click Send, a new Message Composition window appears, as shown in Figure 11-31.

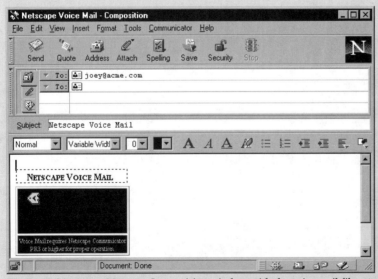

Figure 11-31: A new Message Composition window with the voice mail file attached.

Notice that the To field already contains the address of the person you were trying to reach. (If you weren't using a valid e-mail address, you can edit the To field now.) Your voice mail file is already embedded in the message. You can add some text if you like, or simply click the Send button.

Figure 11-32 shows what your recipient sees, assuming he or she is using Messenger.

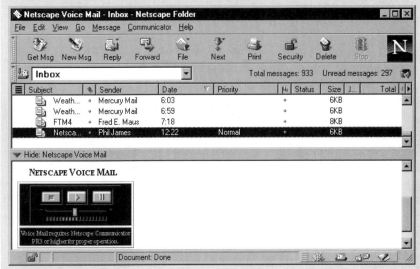

Figure 11-32: A received e-mail message containing voice mail.

To listen to the message, your recipient simply clicks the Play button. The special voice mail control also includes a Stop button, a Pause button, and a slider to adjust the volume.

This is what is known in the industry as a VCF (Very Cool Feature).

Once You're Connected

After you're connected to another user, follow these steps carefully:

1. Talk.

2. Listen.

3. Repeat steps 1 and 2 until you're tired of the conversation.

OFFICIAL NETSCAPE COMMUNICATOR 4 PROFESSIONAL EDITION BOOK

Pretty technical stuff, huh? As you talk, watch the green level indicators for a while. If either voice is too loud or too soft, you can adjust the microphone sensitivity and audio volume while you're conversing. And if somebody fires up the vacuum cleaner, you can tweak the Silence Sensor as well, moving that blue dot further to the right.

Audio Settings

If you're having problems with the audio in Conference—for instance, if you can't hear your colleague well even after adjusting the Speakers level—take a look at Conference's Audio settings. You get there by selecting Preferences from the Call menu and then clicking the Audio tab. A button in this tab lets you access Advanced audio settings. **Note:** You must hang up any active Conference session before you can modify most of the Audio preferences.

Getting into the nitty-gritty of all the available adjustments to your audio is beyond the scope of this book, and most of them are very dependent on what kind of connection you have. Fortunately, the program itself includes some good detailed information that you can read by clicking the Help button. You should be able to find the answer to any concerns right there.

All good things must end. So what about hanging up? Either participant can do it. All you do is click the Hang Up button.

Now you know all about initiating calls to remote Conference users. But what about answering calls?

Answering Calls

As you might guess, answering calls is *really* easy. Remember, though, that to answer calls you must have Conference running—or a smaller supplemental program called Conference Attendant that I'll talk about in a minute, in the section aptly called "Conference Attendant."

Figure 11-33 shows what you see onscreen when somebody calls you via Conference:

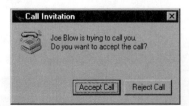

Figure 11-33: The Call Invitation dialog box.

Of course, your speakers ring like a phone at the same time this dialog box appears.

Notice that the Call Invitation dialog box specifies the name of the person calling you, and separate buttons let you accept or reject the call. If you reject it, you're back in the idle state. If you accept the call, your window will look just like it did when you initiated a call. You're ready to start talking.

Suppose you're the gregarious type and want to answer all incoming calls without even clicking the Accept button? That's easy. From the Call menu select Auto Answer.

But now suppose you're busy writing a book about Netscape Communicator and don't want to be bothered by incoming calls. For that, there's Do Not Disturb, one of my favorite Conference features.

Do Not Disturb

To activate the Do Not Disturb feature, simply select Do Not Disturb from Conference's Call menu. Selecting this option makes you unavailable for incoming calls until you switch back to Always Prompt or Auto Answer. When the Do Not Disturb feature is activated, the Business card button includes a big "not" sign, as shown in Figure 11-34.

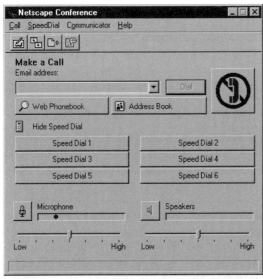

Figure 11-34: The Conference window with Do Not Disturb activated.

The phone icon in the taskbar tray is overlaid with a red "not" sign as well.

Conference Attendant

You may not want Netscape Conference sitting on your desktop at all times, simply waiting for calls to come in. Of course you can minimize the program, but Netscape provides a neater way to save screen real estate: Conference Attendant.

Netscape Conference Attendant is a supplemental feature that acts as a sort of watch dog, waiting for Conference calls. Once one comes in, the usual Conference interface appears on your screen.

To start Conference Attendant, double-click the Netscape Conference Attendant icon in the Utilities subfolder of the Communicator folder. A small Conference icon appears in your taskbar tray, but that is the only sign that Conference is running. But don't worry, unless you've selected Do Not Disturb, the Attendant won't miss your calls.

If you right-click the Conference Attendant icon in your taskbar tray, a context menu appears. From this menu you can:

- Launch one of the other Conference features (Whiteboard, Collaborative Browsing, File Exchange, or Chat). I'll cover these features in the next few sections of this chapter.

- Select your answering preference (Always Prompt, Auto Answer, or Do Not Disturb).

- Change your Conference Preferences.

- Show the normal Conference window.

- Exit Conference completely (including Attendant).

TIP

Once Conference Attendant is running, closing the normal Conference window does not shut it down. It remains loaded, ready to answer your calls and to provide you this alternative access to Conference features. To unload Attendant, you must select Exit Conference from the context menu.

So far I've shown you how to get connected with Conference and how to use the software as a long-distance voice phone across the Net. But Conference offers much, much more. In the next few sections, I'll cover the whiteboard feature, collaborative browsing, file exchange, and chat. Rather than follow the order of the buttons on the Conference toolbar, we'll work through these features in an order that makes it easier to understand the concepts behind them. Let's start with Chat.

Chat

In cyberspace, chatting doesn't mean talking. It means typing messages back and forth in real time. America Online, for instance, has specialized chat rooms where you can have typed conversations with people of like interests. (And if you can't find a chat room for some of your stranger interests on AOL, your interests are very strange indeed.) Chatting is very different from leaving messages on a newsgroup or some online service. The "real-timeness" of chatting gives it a quality of immediacy and vibrancy much like voice conversation. And obviously, it's a great means of communication for people with hearing or speech disabilities.

The Conference Chat feature even lets you send entire text files. You can be conferencing with somebody about a particular legal document and send the text itself as you speak!

TIP

Even if you don't have a sound card, you can communicate with other Conference users using its Chat and whiteboard features. In fact, you may find it a better option than audio chat if you're using a slow modem.

Let's give it a try:

1. Connect with a Conference user following the step-by-step instructions in the section "Initiating a Call" earlier in this chapter.

2. Click the Chat button, the one that depicts a document and a conversational "balloon." The Chat window appears, as shown in Figure 11-35.

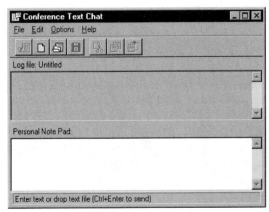

Figure 11-35: The Chat window.

By default, Conference is configured so that the Chat window pops up as soon as the Conference user at the other end tries to chat with you. If you do not like this behavior (in other words, if you don't want to feel "pushed" into a chat without explicitly requesting it yourself or agreeing to it by voice), select Options from the Chat menu and select Pop Up On Receive to remove the checkmark.

3. Type a word or sentence in the white Personal Note Pad pane. After you've completed it, send it by pressing Ctrl+Enter or clicking the Send button at the far left in the toolbar.

   ■ Notice that as soon as you send your text, it appears in the upper Log panel, prefaced by the label **local user>**. Text you receive from the individual you're connected to also appears, prefaced by the label **remote user>**. The Log panel keeps a running record of your entire chat, including what you type and what the other Conference user types.

The Conference user at the other end of the connection doesn't see anything you type until you press Ctrl+Enter or click the Send button. This feature gives you time to think about what you're saying. That's good, since both parties can keep a log of the entire chat!

The two of you can keep chatting indefinitely, and you can keep *talking* at the same time. You can facilitate communications by cutting, copying, and pasting text in the Personal Note Pad, and you can even copy text from the Log and paste it into the Note Pad. What a great way to remind people of what they said a few minutes ago! All these editing tools are available via the usual editing buttons at the top of the Chat Tool window.

Including Text Files

This Chat feature gets its own section because it's one of my favorites. Including text files while you're chatting is really very simple: you can paste entire text files into the Personal Note Pad by clicking the Include button (the third from the left) and selecting the file you want to include. Figure 11-36 shows you the result.

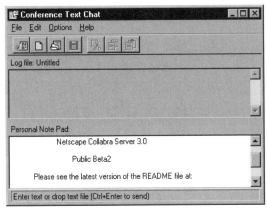

Figure 11-36: The Personal Note Pad with an included text file.

You don't need to follow any special procedure for sending included files: pressing Ctrl+Enter will do the trick.

Log Files

At any point while the Chat window is displayed, you can save the contents of the Log to a file by clicking the Save button. You might want to name your log file with the date of the chat session and the name of the other chatter, as in 4-1Joe. You can also start an entire new log file by clicking the New button.

> **TIP**
>
> *Unless you save your current log file, the information in the Log panel will be lost when you select a new file.*

Leaving Chat

When you're finished chatting with your fellow Conference user, simply close the Chat window. This action does not break your connection; you can keep talking as long as you want, and you can start chatting again simply by clicking the Chat button in the Conference window.

And now, on to the whiteboard.

The Whiteboard

You can think of Conference's Whiteboard as Chat on steroids. It lets you share not only text messages, but also graphics and even screen captures of whatever's on your monitor right now. Or you can think of it as a paint program that two people work in at once, collaboratively creating rich, colorful content even though they might be thousands of miles apart.

If you've ever used any paint program, such as Microsoft Paint (which comes with Windows), you'll have no trouble figuring out the Whiteboard. Covering every detail of its operation is beyond the scope of this book. I'll just hit the important points as well as some interesting features that aren't immediately obvious. After that, I think you'll find it's the kind of feature that's a lot more fun to learn by using.

Starting the Whiteboard

To start the Whiteboard, follow these steps:

1. Connect with a Conference user following the step-by-step instructions in the section "Initiating a Call" earlier in this chapter.

2. Click the Whiteboard button, which looks like an artist's palette. The Whiteboard window appears, as shown in Figure 11-37.

TIP

By default, your whiteboard also pops up as soon as the individual you're connected with starts working with his or her Whiteboard. If you don't like this behavior, uncheck the Pop Up On Receive option from the Whiteboard's Options menu.

Now you can start adding elements to your Whiteboard using the various tools and the width, fill, and color options at the left-hand side of the window. You can also add text by selecting the Text tool (the button with a big "T" on it) and choosing your font size and style at the top of the window. For example, Figure 11-38 shows my Whiteboard with a few simple geometric shapes and some text.

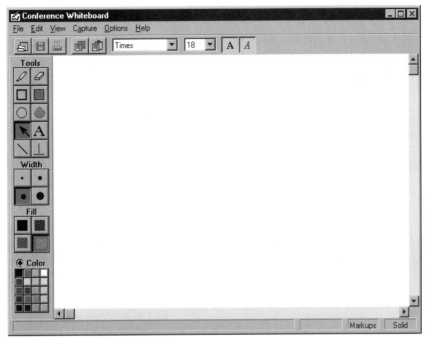

Figure 11-37: The Whiteboard window.

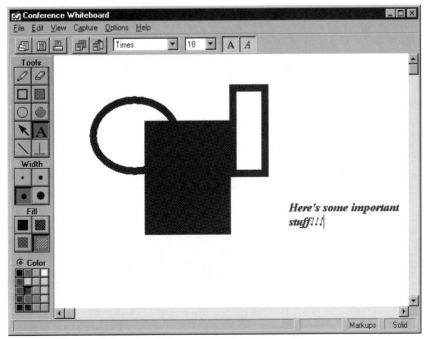

Figure 11-38: My Whiteboard with some important stuff on it.

Notice the Whiteboard's scroll bars. You are not limited to what you can fit within the window. This virtual Whiteboard is less like the kind of whiteboard you buy at an office supply store than it is like an endless roll of drawing paper.

You might be wondering what's going on at the other end of the Conference connection. Here's the scoop:

- Everything you draw or paint appears on the remote Whiteboard exactly as it appears on yours. Not only that, it gets there right away. If your Conferencing friend starts unleashing his or her artistic talents, you'll see that artwork right away too.

- Text that's added to the Whiteboard using the Text tool, on the other hand, is sent after you press Enter. This feature allows for a combination of collaboration and effective written conversation. The Whiteboard is a truly collaborative feature that adds a new dimension to the phrase "it's almost like being there."

And, of course, the two of you can keep yacking away into your microphones as you create your collaborative masterpiece. Kids could entertain themselves for hours with this feature. So could I.

Don't like what's on your Whiteboard? Of course you can delete parts of the window using the Erase tool, but you might want to get rid of the whole thing. Simply select Clear Whiteboard from the Edit menu. Remember, though, that you're erasing it for your fellow Conference user as well!

And what if you're convinced your collaborative masterpiece will some day sell for millions at Sotheby's? Just click the File Save button.

Pasting Images Onto the Whiteboard

One of the most interesting uses of the Whiteboard is to share graphical material that's already been created. Imagine talking to somebody a thousand miles away and suddenly saying, "Here, let me show you a picture of my kids!" Or your sales materials or your projected profits for the next quarter.

To paste an image onto the Whiteboard, follow these steps:

1. Click the File open button at the top left of the Whiteboard window.

2. Using the standard Open dialog box that appears, select a file from your hard drive or a network drive. Notice that you can choose files from among seven different graphics formats.

3. Click the Open button. The dialog box disappears, and you are returned to the Whiteboard window.

4. Your Whiteboard cursor is now a crosshairs, and an outline shows the size of the graphics you selected. Move the outline to the location on the Whiteboard where you want to place it.

5. Once you have decided the location for your graphic, click the left mouse button. The new image is pasted onto the Whiteboard, both locally and remotely.

TIP

You can also drag and drop graphics files directly onto the Whiteboard. Simply select a file from anywhere on your hard drive, and hold down your left mouse button while dragging it into the Whiteboard window. When you let go of the mouse button, the crosshairs cursor and outline appear as in step 4 above.

Screen Capture

The Whiteboard also includes a screen capture facility. You can capture a snapshot of a window, your entire desktop, or any region of your screen and then paste it onto the Whiteboard. Think of how useful this capability can be in technical support settings. Instead of trying to describe how that brand new game is spewing unrecognizable garbage all over your screen, why not *show* it to the technical specialist?

Here's how to place a screen capture onto the Whiteboard:

1. Select one of the options from the Capture menu. Selecting Window lets you choose any window currently on your desktop; selecting Desktop captures your entire desktop; and selecting Region lets you choose a screen region to capture.

   ▪ For this example, go ahead and select Window. As soon as you do, the Whiteboard is temporarily minimized, and a crosshairs cursor lets you choose any window currently on your desktop.

2. Position the cross-hairs cursor over the Conference window and click. The Whiteboard pops back up. Your cursor now includes a movable outline indicating the size of the captured image.

3. Move the outline to the location on the Whiteboard where you want to place it; then simply click. An image of the Conference window now appears exactly where you indicated, as you can see in Figure 11-39.

Figure 11-39: A new screen capture on the Whiteboard.

Markup & the Pointer Tool

As a convenience for collaborative work, the Whiteboard distinguishes between static material in what's called the *image layer* (screen captures and images loaded from disk) and *markup* (anything you add to the Whiteboard using the various drawing tools). If these terms are unfamiliar to you, here's an example. Let's say you place a new image on the Whiteboard to get your friend's feedback. Using the drawing tools, he puts a bunch of circles and arrows all over your picture, creating something like Figure 11-40.

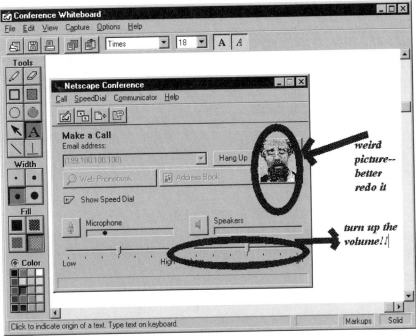

Figure 11-40: A marked-up graphic on the Whiteboard.

And now let's say you think his comments are completely bogus. Wouldn't it be nice to get rid of what your pal added without getting rid of the original picture?

Well, you can! Just select Clear Markups from the Edit menu, and you're back to ground zero, a nice clean screen capture just like the one in Figure 11-39. You can also erase portions of the markup using the Eraser tool, without deleting any of the underlying graphic. You also can clear your own markups just as easily.

Conference's Whiteboard offers another feature that's especially useful for collaborative work: the Pointer tool. You select the Pointer tool by clicking the arrow button in the left-hand tool bar. It then lets you place an arrow pointer anywhere on the Whiteboard. But this highly visible arrow is not fixed in place like the other graphics tools such as lines and circles. If you still have the Pointer tool selected and you click your cursor somewhere else, the arrow moves to the new location. Thus, as you discuss the various elements on your Whiteboard with another Conference user, you can point to them. You can think of the Pointer tool as your virtual index finger.

TIP

If you suspect that you and the person you're conferencing with are not seeing the same stuff on your Whiteboard, you can make sure by selecting Synchronize Page from the Edit menu.

I could say a lot more about the Whiteboard, but you'll have more fun exploring on your own. Let's move on now and take a look at the File Exchange feature.

File Exchange

In the section on Conference's Chat feature, you learned how you can paste text files right into your online conversation. But what if you want to send files that aren't text—for instance, spreadsheets, graphics files, or even entire programs?

The classic way of transferring files across the Internet or an intranet is via FTP, which you learned about in Chapter 8. But FTP is neither immediate nor direct. It requires that you log on to a special FTP server and deposit your file, which can then be retrieved by another individual who has access to the same server. Not only does this procedure add extra time to the process, but the majority of Net users do not have access to FTP servers that they can upload to and use in this way.

Enter Conference's File Exchange facility. It is one of my favorite features in all of Communicator, and what's more, it's so simple that I can demonstrate it in a few paragraphs.

OK, let's assume you're currently connected to another Conference user. In fact, let's pretend it's your editor, and she has just said, "Phil, I can't wait till later for those new chapters—I need them *this instant!*"

"OK," you respond weakly, "I'll send them right now."

And here's what you do next:

1. Click the File Exchange button, the one that shows a page with an arrow.
   The Conference File Exchange window appears, as shown in Figure 11-41.

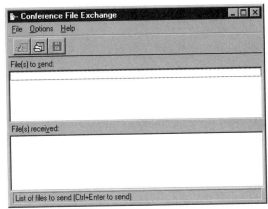

Figure 11-41: The Conference File Exchange window.

2. Click the Open button, which is the middle button on the toolbar. The Add File to Send List dialog box pops up, as shown in Figure 11-42.

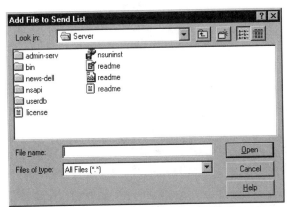

Figure 11-42: The Add File to Send List dialog box.

3. Use the controls in this standard file open dialog box to navigate to the directory that contains the file you want to send. Select it and click Open. You are returned to the File Exchange window. The file you've just selected appears in the top File(s) to send pane, as shown in Figure 11-43.

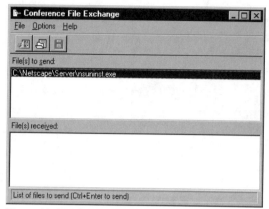

Figure 11-43: The File Conference Exchange window with a file waiting to be sent.

4. Want to send more files? Simply repeat steps 2 and 3, adding as many files as you want. Figure 11-44 shows the Conference File Exchange window with several files.

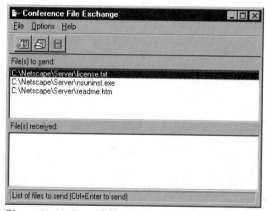

Figure 11-44: Several files in the send list.

TIP

To remove a file from the send list, simply select it and press the Del key. Don't worry, pressing the key doesn't delete the file from your hard drive—it only tells Conference not to send it.

5. Click the Options menu. If you're sending ASCII files, select ASCII; if you're sending binary (non-text) files, select Binary. You should also select Binary if you're sending a mixture of ASCII and binary files.

TIP

A Compress item also appears on the Options menu. Clicking this option tells Conference to compress, or shrink, the files you send; they are automatically decompressed at the other end. If you're sending short files across a relatively fast network connection, you might want to turn compression off to speed up initiating the transfer.

6. When you're ready to send your files, simply click the Send button. The files are sent across the Net or intranet to the remote Conference user. Unless you want to send more files, you can now close the File Exchange window.

And what happens when you *receive* a file from a remote Conference user? No matter what you're currently doing in Conference, the Conference File Exchange window pops up, with the new files listed in the bottom pane, as shown in Figure 11-45.

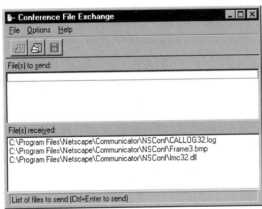

Figure 11-45: The Conference File Exchange window with several new received files.

TIP

If you don't want the Conference File Exchange window to pop up automatically, click Pop Up On Receive in the Options menu to uncheck this feature.

You can now save these files to any folder on your hard drive or on a network drive. Here's how:

1. In the list of received files, select the name of the file you want to save.

2. Click the Save button on the toolbar. The Save Received File dialog box appears, as shown in Figure 11-46.

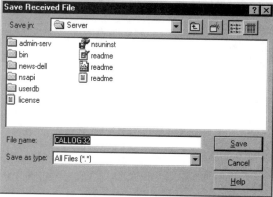

Figure 11-46: The Save Received File dialog box.

3. Navigate to the folder where you want to store the file, type in a new file name if you want, and click the Save button. The file is saved in its new location, and you are returned to the Conference File Exchange window. As you can see in Figure 11-47, the received list no longer contains the file you just saved.

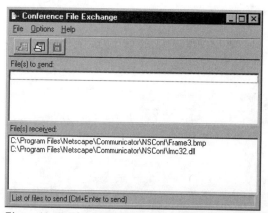

Figure 11-47: The received list after saving one of the files.

4. Repeat steps 1 through 3 for every file you want to save. After you're finished, simply close the Conference File Exchange window.

Collaborative Browsing

OK, here's a short play for your entertainment:

[A man in a room, sitting at computer. Enter co-worker, who stands behind the man's chair, staring over the man's shoulder at the computer screen.]

Co-worker: Whatcha doin?
Man: I'm checking up on the competition.
Co-worker: Looks like you're surfing to me.
Man: No way. Check out this business report.
Co-worker: Wow. Are they really going to merge with ConHugeCo?
Man: Here, check out these stock price comparisons.
Co-worker: Man, I had no idea. . . !

[Man clicks from Web site to Web site. Co-worker continues to look over man's shoulder for next three hours, constantly commenting, as audience slowly exits theater.]

This scene must get repeated thousands of times a day. Once you know a little bit about getting around the Web, you become a tour guide for your friends. And now, thanks to the collaborative browsing feature built right into Conference, you can be a *remote* tour guide.

Collaborative browsing is really a pretty simple concept. Using this feature, you can direct a remote Conference user to a specific Web page. That means you can use the multimedia documents that you both view simultaneously as the basis for your Conference discussion. As soon as you click a link, the remote user is immediately taken to the same site. It's as if you were controlling the remote user's copy of Navigator 4 yourself.

Let's give it a try:

1. Following the steps outlined earlier in this chapter, launch Netscape Conference and establish a connection with a remote user.

2. Click the Collaborative Browsing button, which depicts two windows with pointers in them. The Collaborative Browsing dialog box pops up, as shown in Figure 11-48.

Figure 11-48: The Collaborative Browsing dialog box.

3. Click the Start Browsing button. The remote Conference user is informed that you have requested a collaborative browsing session and is asked to join. Assuming he or she agrees to join by clicking Open Navigator, Navigator 4 is launched on both systems.

4. Simply cruise the Web using any of the techniques discussed in Chapter 3. Wherever you go, your colleague goes as well. Take a moment to savor the feeling of power this feature gives you.

Of course, your power is by no means absolute. *Either* party can cancel collaborative Web browsing at any time. Here's how:

1. Click the Collaborative Browsing button again. You are returned to the Collaborative Browsing dialog box, but it looks a bit different now, as shown in Figure 11-49.

Figure 11-49: The Collaborative Browsing dialog box during an active Collaborative session.

TIP

If your browser and your partner's browser are not currently displaying the same Web page, click the Sync Browsers button. That will assure that you are both viewing the same URL.

2. To end the collaborative browsing session, click the Stop Browsing button. The remote user is informed that you have terminated the session. Remember, though, that you are still connected via Conference and can resume collaborative browsing—as well as any other Conference facility—at any point.

Who's Leading?

Collaborative Web browsing is like ballroom dancing: one of the partners is always leading, and the other follows. But Conference lets you switch these roles very fluidly. Take another look at Figure 11-49 above. If you uncheck the Control the Browsers check box in the middle of a session, your partner becomes the lead. As he or she moves from site to site, you are dragged along.

You can switch back and forth like this as often as you want. But remember that the "follower" cannot assume the lead unless the leader has relinquished it. In other words, you can *uncheck* the Control the Browsers check box when you're in the role of leader, but you cannot check it when you're not.

Moving On

Now that you're familiar with Netscape Conference, I'm sure you'll come up with all kinds of interesting ways to use it. And I think you'll agree that with its flexibility and dazzling combination of features, it is potentially one of the most *fun* Communicator components.

Real-time conferencing is one of the hottest new trends on the Net, as well as on office intranets. But now that you've got an extraordinary way to enhance your meetings, how are you going to keep your schedule from getting overcrowded? How will you make sure you can conference with Marketing in time for that big meeting with PR? For conflict-free time scheduling, you need Netscape Calendar. So, turn the page. . .

CHAPTER 12

Netscape Calendar

The cornerstone of the business world, it seems, is meetings. Whether it's in a 50-story office building or over the intranet of a virtual corporation, meetings are vital places for participants to gather and solve problems, share information, and strategize for the future.

Yet coordinating meetings has in the past been a problem in itself. Any company with more than three people will inevitably have scheduling conflicts, resource conflicts, and time considerations to take into account when planning meetings. Before intranets, it took a squadron of able administrative assistants and several rounds of "telephone tag" to coordinate the meeting needs of a department.

With the advent of intranets, Netscape Communicator offers Calendar to coordinate your event data along with your corporation's intranet data. With the addition of the Netscape Calendar Server to your network, your company can gather all scheduling and resource information into a central place. From there, Netscape Calendar helps you to access, check, and schedule events. Further, you can set up, track, and manage tasks online.

In the course of this chapter, I'll show you how to access Calendar data, manage your own agenda, track tasks, and gather people into groups that can be assigned to meetings and other events. You may not be able to order a better brand of donut for your Monday afternoon sales meetings, but at least you'll be able to make sure that everyone knows about the meetings.

Let's start at the beginning. First, you'll need to sign in to the Calendar Server to access and share calendar information, then you'll need to set your preferences.

Signing In

Netscape Calendar may operate a little differently from what you expect when you first use it. When you first open Navigator or Messenger, the application is launched to a home page or an inbox and proceeds from there. But with Calendar, you must first sign in to the server to access the intranet's Calendar data. Failure to sign in means you can't use Calendar.

You may launch Netscape Calendar by choosing Communicator I Calendar from the Navigator screen or choosing the Calendar icon from the Communicator Professional program group. The sign-in screen is launched, as you can see in Figure 12-1.

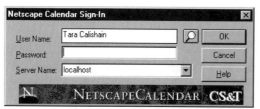

Figure 12-1: Signing in to the Netscape Calendar Server.

TIP

If you try all the steps below and you still can't access the Netscape Calendar Server, check with your network administrator. You may be trying to sign in to the wrong server, or you may be using the wrong password.

There are two states under which you can sign in—offline and online. You sign in offline when you can't reach the server—for example, when you're on the road with your laptop. To sign in using the offline state, enter your user name and password, click on the server pull-down box, and choose Offline. You won't be able to access your server's calendar data, of course, because you won't be connected to the server.

The more common way to sign in is online. The online state connects you to your intranet's online server. Again, enter your name and password. Check and see whether your network's Calendar Server is listed as the server in the pull-down server box. If it isn't, use the pull-down box to find your intranet's Calendar Server.

Now click the OK button. If all goes well, you should be connected to the server. If all doesn't go well, the logon screen may tell you it doesn't recognize your name. That's okay—you can do a search for it.

Searching for a User Name

In Figure 12-1, you may have noticed a small icon of a magnifying glass on the sign-in screen. That's there to help you find your sign-in name if you don't know what it is. Click on it now. You'll get the screen displayed in Figure 12-2.

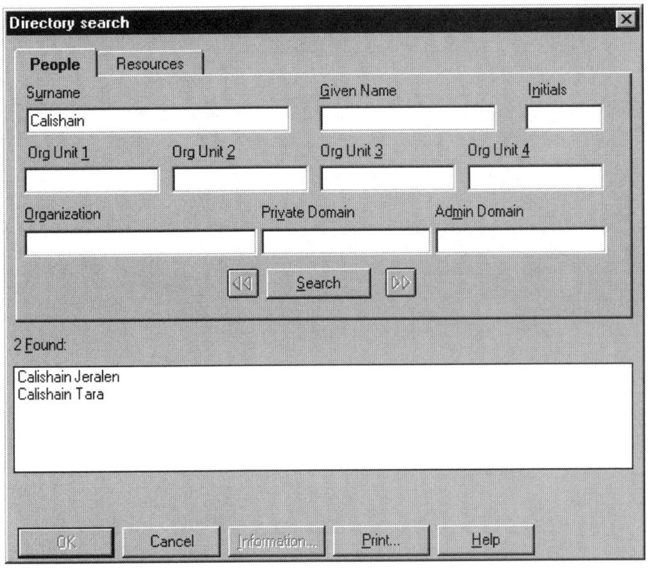

Figure 12-2: Searching for a sign-in name in Netscape Calendar.

Enter the first few letters of your last name at Surname, then click Search. The server will display a list of names, in the Found list box, that match the first few letters of your last name. Double-click on your name under Found, click OK, then proceed to sign in as you did before.

Sometimes you want to sign in as a *resource*, not as a user. (A resource is a location or some other item you use for a meeting, like a meeting room. You can't overschedule them, either.) You can find resource names in this box as well.

Searching for a Resource Name

The procedure is the same as searching for a user name. Click the magnifying glass icon in the sign-in screen. Click the Resources tab to go to the resources. Enter the number or the first few letters of the resource's name and click the Search button. In the Found list box, you'll find a list of possible resource names. Click on the one you're interested in, click OK, and sign in normally.

Okay, you've signed in. Now you want to use Calendar, but before we get into that, let's set your preferences.

Setting Calendar Preferences

When you've signed in to Calendar, you'll get a screen like the one shown in Figure 12-3.

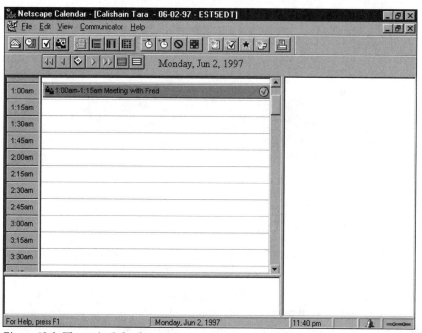

Figure 12-3: The main Calendar screen.

To access Calendar's preferences, choose Edit | Preferences from the main calendar screen. The Preferences settings are divided into several categories: Agenda, In-Tray, Scheduling, Entry Defaults, General, Offline, and Palmtop. We'll cover each one in its own section.

> **TIP**
>
> *With seven separate sections of preferences, you may feel like Calendar is pretty complicated and will only get more complex from here. Fortunately, you'll discover that as you learn some parts of Calendar, a lot of what you learn can be applied to the other areas.*

Agenda Preferences

The "Agenda" is the first screen you see when you start Calendar. It's your main view of your schedule or agenda of the day. When you use Edit I Preferences I Agenda, you'll get a preference screen that looks like the one in Figure 12-4. There are two tabs you must adjust in this screen: the Display tab and the Notification tab.

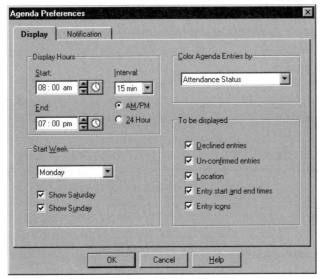

Figure 12-4: The Display tab of the Agenda preferences.

The Display Tab

The Display tab, shown in Figure 12-4, is the tab that determines which hours will be displayed, what day the week will start with, and so forth. Take the following steps:

1. Determine what hours you want displayed on your agenda. These hours are the hours in which you can display and schedule events. The default hours are 8 a.m. to 7 p.m. You can either click on the default time and use the arrows to the right of the time boxes to change the time, or you can click on the default time and enter the new hours. (You can even click the clock icon and set the time that way.)

2. Once you've set the display times, click the pull-down menu beneath the word Interval to choose the intervals that appear on your agenda screen. The default interval is 15 minutes; therefore, the times listed on your agenda screen go as 9:00, 9:15, 9:30, and so on. If you don't anticipate your meetings and tasks running at less than 30-minute or 60-minute intervals, you may want to change the interval to a larger chunk of time.

3. Finally, in the display hour area, you'll need to choose how the time will display. Click the 24-hour button if you want to use the 24-hour clock (where 7 p.m. is 19:00, 9 p.m. is 21:00, etc.) or click the AM/PM button if you want to use the more traditional 12-hour system.

Beneath the Display hours choices are the Start Week choices. Use the pull-down menu to determine on what day of the week you want your agenda to start—the default is Monday. Underneath the Start Day indicator are two check boxes labeled Show Saturday and Show Sunday. Click the boxes to remove the checks if you don't want the weekend displayed on your agenda.

In the upper right-hand corner of this tab is a pull-down box to specify how meetings on your agenda should be colored. Your choices are Attendance Status, Importance Level, or Entry Ownership. We'll discuss these later in the chapter, but for now leave the agenda entry colored by Attendance Status.

Finally, in the Display tab, there are several check boxes that list the type of information that appears in your agenda. All of these are checked as default and will appear in your agenda. If you don't want any of these types of information to appear on your agenda screen, uncheck them.

- **Declined entries**. Events you have declined to attend.
- **Unconfirmed entries**. Entries to which you have been invited but to which you have not yet responded.
- **Location**. The location of your events, if available.
- **Entry start and end times**. The start and end times of your events, if available.
- **Entry icons**. Any icons (reminder or comment icons) that are associated with an event. (We'll cover icons later in the chapter.)

When you've finished setting your display options, click the Notification tab.

The Notification Tab

The Notification tab specifies how you're going to learn about new entries on your agenda, and how you're going to alert the attendees for whom you create events. It looks like Figure 12-5.

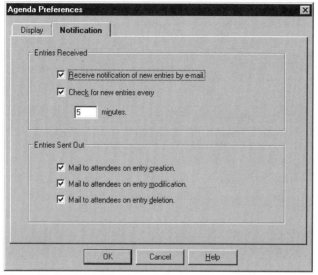

Figure 12-5: The Notification tab for the Agenda Preferences.

This tab is divided into two sections, both of which contain mostly check boxes. The first check box is to confirm the option of receiving notification of new events by e-mail. If you want to find out about new events without constantly checking Calendar, make sure the box for this option is checked. The second check box will check the agenda for new events during time intervals specified by you. (The minimum interval is 15 minutes.) When a new event appears, an icon pops up on your Agenda's status bar.

The second section of this tab is the Entries Sent Out section. There are three check boxes here to indicate how you want to notify other event attendees of a new event. To activate any of these options, make sure their check boxes are marked.

- **Mail to attendees on entry creation**. You'll have the option to send an e-mail to attendees when you invite them to an event.

- **Mail to attendees on entry modification**. You'll have the option to send an e-mail to attendees when you modify an event with which they're involved.

- **Mail to attendees on entry deletion**. You'll have the option to send an e-mail to attendees when you delete an event with which they were involved.

When you're finished with this tab, click the OK button to close this screen and choose Edit | Preferences | In-Tray to move on to the In-Tray preferences.

In-Tray Preferences

Your In-Tray is where new events to which you're invited appear. From the In-Tray you'll have the option of viewing, accepting, and declining invitations to events. (We'll get more in-depth with the In-Tray later in this chapter.) The In-Tray Preferences screen is divided into four tabs: New, Accepted, Sent, and Refused (see Figure 12-6).

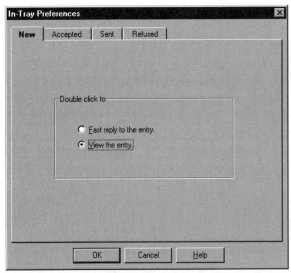

Figure 12-6: The New preferences tab.

New

The New tab, shown in Figure 12-6, has only one option: how you want a double-click to affect a new entry to the In-Tray. Click the appropriate radio button once you've decided which of the following two options you want to use.

■ **Fast reply to the entry**. Respond to the entry without viewing its specifics first. This is recommended as an option only if you're familiar with the types of events to which you might be invited.

■ **View the entry first**. View the prospective event before you respond to it.

When you've made your decision, click on the Accepted tab.

Accepted

You may find yourself a bit confused when you see the first option in this tab—the option to double-click for a fast reply or to view the entry before replying to an invitation. Isn't this the option you just determined in the New tab?

But it isn't! This tab, shown in Figure 12-7, applies only to those In-Tray entries you've accepted—that's why it's called the Accepted tab.

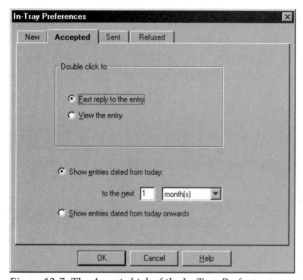

Figure 12-7: The Accepted tab of the In-Tray Preferences.

First make your decision as to what you want to happen to an accepted entry when you double-click on it—whether you want to fast reply to it or you want to view it before responding. I know it seems silly to reply to it again if you had already—specifying that you want to fast reply to it really just removes you from having to look at all the details about it again.

Second, you'll need to decide how many of the accepted entries you want to view. The bottom radio button gives you the option to "Show entries dated from today onwards." That option would list every entry that you've accepted from today onward—and if you have a busy schedule, that could be a lot of entries!

Viewing that many entries could be overwhelming. That's why the next-to-last button gives you the option to show entries dated from today to the next x intervals, where both the number (x) and the intervals are specified by you. Put a number in the blank box and use the pull-down menu to specify the time interval—you can specify days, weeks, months, or years. If you have a moderate number of entries, set this tab to show entries dated from today to the next week. That gives you a good outlook for your schedule without overwhelming you with events.

Once you've finished with this tab, you'll see a familiar sight when you click the Sent tab.

Sent

The Sent tab, shown in Figure 12-8, has only one option: which sent entries that *you* have sent you want to see. As in the Accepted tab, you'll have the option of either viewing all sent entries from today onward, or viewing all entries from today through a certain number of time intervals—three weeks, for example.

Once you've set up this tab, click the Refused tab.

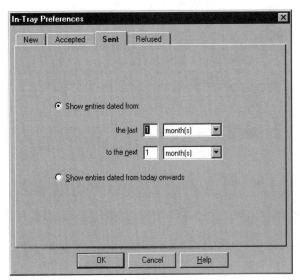

Figure 12-8: The Sent tab.

Refused

The Refused tab, shown in Figure 12-9, is a clone of the Accepted tab, except that the In-Tray entries for which you are determining preferences are those entries you have refused.

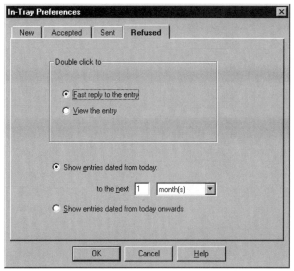

Figure 12-9: The Refused tab.

When you've finished setting up the options for this tab, click on OK to close this screen and choose Edit | Preferences | Scheduling to choose the scheduling preferences.

Scheduling Preferences

The Scheduling Preferences screen is the same screen tab repeated seven times—once for each day of the week. We'll walk through the first screen, and then you can set up the rest of the days of the week by yourself.

If you've chosen to list Saturday and Sunday on your agenda, the first tab on this screen will be Sunday. It looks like Figure 12-10.

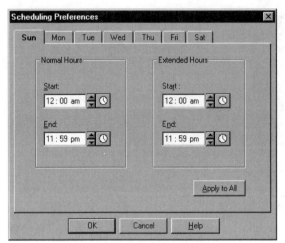

Figure 12-10: The Sunday tab in the Scheduling Preferences.

What you're doing in this screen is setting the hours where Calendar will look to schedule an event when you use its "Suggest a Time/Date" ability.

The first set of hours, on the left, are the regular hours when you're available. Use the arrow keys and the clock to set these hours. The second set of hours, on the right, are your extended hours, "second-choice" hours when Calendar is suggesting a time.

When you're done filling out this first tab, click each day's tab to fill it out.

TIP

Do you have the same hour preferences for every day? Fill out the first tab and click on the Apply to All button. Your hour preferences for the first day will be applied to every day of the week.

When you've set your regular and extended hours, click OK to close the screens and choose Edit | Preferences | Entry Defaults to set the defaults for agenda entries.

Entry Defaults

The Entry Defaults screen affects the events that you add to your agenda—how they appear on the screen, the level of importance they're automatically ascribed, and so on. The screen is divided into four tabs: Agenda Entries, Tasks, Day Events, and Daily Notes.

Agenda Entries

On the Agenda Entries tab, shown in Figure 12-11, your first task is to decide the default importance and access levels of entries as you add them to your agenda. Use the pull-down menus to decide the default Importance level (Highest, High, Normal, Low, and Lowest) and Access level (Personal, Confidential, Normal, and Public).

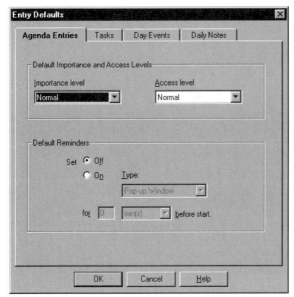

Figure 12-11: The Agenda Entries tab of the Entry Defaults screen.

The second task is to decide whether you want reminders to be automatically activated for the events you add to your agenda. The default state for this option is Off; if you don't want reminders for upcoming events, leave the Off radio button checked.

If you do want reminders for upcoming events, click the On radio button. You'll also have to decide what kind of reminder you want (whether it's a pop-up window or the event marked as upcoming—we'll talk about pop-up windows shortly) and how soon you want the reminder to make itself known in advance of the event. (You set the number of time intervals, and choose from intervals of minutes, hours, days, weeks, months or years. You can be reminded of an event ten minutes, days, weeks, or months before it happens.)

When you're finished with this screen, click the Tasks tab.

Tasks

The Tasks tab, shown in Figure 12-12, lets you set the default states of the tasks that you enter into your agenda.

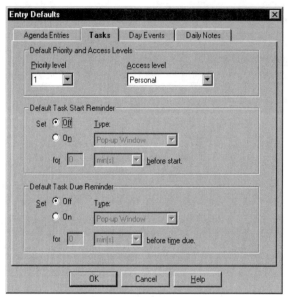

Figure 12-12: The Tasks tab on the Entry Defaults screen.

First, decide what the default Priority and Access level of each task you enter onto your agenda will be. You have the choice of 1-9 and A-Z for your priority; and Personal, Confidential, Normal, and Public for your access level.

Once you've decided that, you'll need to determine whether you want to be reminded about tasks before they start, and also before they're due. This works just like it did on the agenda entries tab: click the On radio button if you want to activate a reminder, choose the time interval before you want the reminder to pop up, and decide how many time intervals in advance you want the reminder.

Bear in mind that you're deciding two options here. The first option is how far in advance of the task start you want the reminder, and the second is how far in advance of the task due date you want to receive the reminder. For example, say I have a task that starts January 11 and is due January 31. I could set my Default Task Start Reminder for 10 days before start, and my Default Task Due Reminder for two days before time due. Thus, I would get one reminder on January 1, and another reminder on January 29.

When you're finished with this tab, click the Day Events tab.

Day Events

Day Events, strangely enough, are events that last an entire day. In this screen you'll need to assign them a default Access level (Personal, Confidential, Normal, or Public) and set up your default reminders.

After the other tabs, this one, shown in Figure 12-13, should be easy to figure out. The next one, Daily Notes, should be even easier.

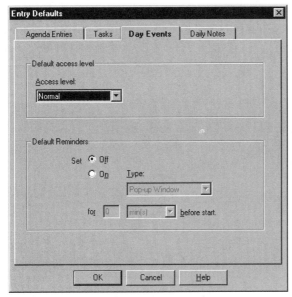

Figure 12-13 Setting the Day Events preferences.

Daily Notes

Daily Notes are things you want to enter on your agenda but which don't fall under the category of events or tasks. The Daily Notes tab, shown in Figure 12-14, is just like the Day Events tab, only it affects the default state of the Daily Notes as you put them into your agenda. For example, you might be expecting a shipment of widgets on Tuesday and put a daily note on your calendar to call WidgetCo if you haven't gotten the shipment by 4 p.m.

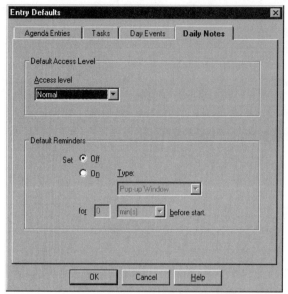

Figure 12-14: Setting the Daily Notes preferences.

Again, decide what you want the default Access level of your daily notes to be and whether you want reminders to be associated with your daily notes. Once you've done that, click OK to close this screen and choose Edit | Preferences | General to edit Netscape Calendar's General Preferences.

General Preferences

The general preferences for Calendar set the "tone" and the look of the whole application. They're the little things that determine how the information you get from the server looks, the format in which the day and time are presented, and so on. The General Preferences screen is divided into three tabs: Names, Date and Time, and Time Zones.

Names

The Names tab, shown in Figure 12-15, determines how name information that you get from the Calendar Server or from doing a name search will appear on your screen. Use the pull-down menu to indicate your choices. You'll have several different options: John Smith, John C. Smith, Smith, John C., and so on. You'll also have the option of showing the organizational field along with the name. (This option may or may not be meaningful to you, depending on how your company uses Calendar. There are many, many, many organizational fields that your network administrator can fill out—and you can use all of them when showing names on your screen, if you click on their check boxes.) At the bottom of this tab you need to indicate how you want to display resource information—as Name Only, Name and Number, or Number and Name.

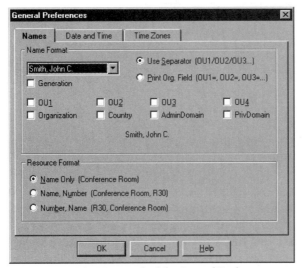

Figure 12-15: The Names tab of the General Preferences screen.

Two more items appear on this screen. The Use Separator button separates organizational information with a forward slash (/) and the Generation check box means you'll show the generation of the person listed, if appropriate. For example, you'll see John Smith III, instead of John Smith.

Made all these decisions? Then click the Date and Time tab.

Date and Time

There are three sections in this screen, shown in Figure 12-16. The first section is for you to determine how a short date should be formatted. Click the appropriate radio button to choose to format the date as Month,Day,Year (MDY), Day,Month,Year (DMY), or Year,Month,Day (YMD). Then click in the separator box and choose what ASCII character you would like to use as a separator between these three elements (a period or a hyphen work nicely). Finally, choose whether or not you want to indicate the century along with the year (1997 vs. 97).

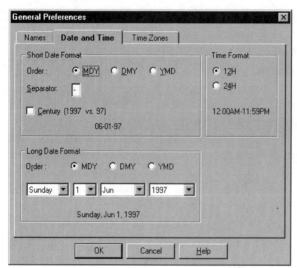

Figure 12-16: The Date and Time tab of the General Preferences screen.

The second section is a radio button choice for time format. Click the appropriate button for either 12-hour or 24-hour format.

The last section in this tab is how you want a long date to look. Click the appropriate button to determine whether you want long dates to be listed in MDY, DMY, or YMD order. When you've determined that, click the pull-down menus to "tweak" how you want the long dates to display (you'll have the choice between Thursday and Thu, February and Feb, and so on). The final indicator of how a long date will look will appear at the bottom of the tab.

Finally, click the Time Zones button to set the time zone for Calendar.

Time Zones

Sometimes when you're working offline or in another area, you'll want to change your time zone. There are two ways you can do it in this tab, shown in Figure 12-17. The first way is to use the pull-down menu and find your time zone that way. If you're not sure what time zone you're in, click the Load regions button at the right side of the tab. Calendar will load a list of countries and country areas. Double-click on your country or region, and Calendar will select the correct time zone.

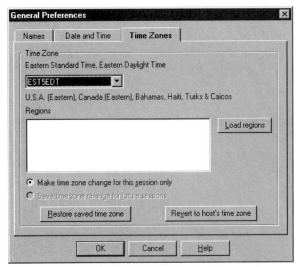

Figure 12-17: The Time Zone tab of General Preferences.

When you're done selecting your time zone, click the radio button to indicate whether you're making the time zone change for this session of using Calendar only, or whether you want to make the change in time zone permanent. If you're confused or you want to restore the original time zone, click the Restore saved time zone button. If you want to set your time zone according to the time zone on your operating system, click the Revert to host's time zone button.

All finished? Okay. Now click OK to close the screen and choose Edit | Preferences | Off-line to choose the offline preferences for Calendar.

Offline Preferences

You're not always going to be at your desk when you're using Calendar. Sometimes you're going to be away from your main computer and sometimes you're going to be away from the Netscape Calendar Server. "Offline," in this case, doesn't mean away from a computer, it means away from the office intranet. The Off-line Preferences screen determines how Calendar will behave when it's not attached to the intranet or to the Netscape Calendar Server. The screen is divided into five tabs: Location, Download, People/Resources, Groups, and Reconciliation.

Location

The only thing indicated in the Location tab, shown in Figure 12-18, is where you want your offline agenda file to be located. Calendar suggests a location for you, but you can choose any directory you like. Use the Browse button to find a directory if you're not sure where you want the offline agenda to go.

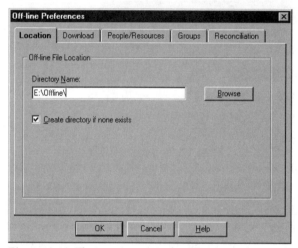

Figure 12-18: The Location tab in the Offline Preferences screen.

If you're indicating a directory that doesn't exist, be sure to click the check box that reads Create directory if none exists. Calendar will create the directory for you.

The second tab on this screen is the Download tab.

Download

The first decision for you to make in this tab, shown in Figure 12-19, is how many entries you want to download to your Offline agenda before you go offline. (We'll discuss Offline agendas later in this chapter.) Creating an Offline agenda is like packing a suitcase before you go on a trip: you want to have enough clothes for the trip, but you don't have to carry lots of suitcases (or one big file) with you. You can choose to download all your agenda entries by clicking on the Download all Entries radio button, or you can choose to download only a range of entries. Use the pull-down menus to determine the time range in which you'd like to download entries.

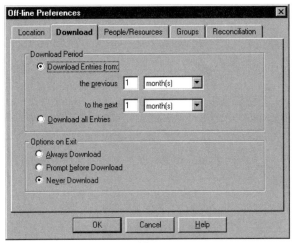

Figure 12-19: The Download tab of the Off-line Preferences screen.

The second section in this tab, Options on Exit, might be confusing. What this section does is let you set how often you want your Offline Agenda file to be updated by your Online Agenda file, the one that's connected to the Netscape Calendar Server. You have three options in this section:

- **Always Download**. Updates your Offline Agenda file every time you exit your Online Agenda file.

- **Prompt before Download**. Asks you every time you exit your Online Agenda file whether you want to update your Offline file.

- **Never Download**. Never updates the Offline file on exit. In order to update the Offline file, you'll have to use the File | Go Offline command.

If you're planning to be absent from the Calendar Server or on the road a lot, I recommend always downloading your Offline agenda. If you're always connected to the server, or don't rely on your calendar, I recommend you prompt before download or never download your Offline agenda.

Once you've settled on these options, click the People/Resources tab.

People/Resources

In this tab, shown in Figure 12-20, you'll set up the list of people and resources whose agendas you want to download. Enter the name of the person whose agenda you want to download in the text box. Then click the check icon to add that person to the list, or click the X icon to remove them. Click the magnifying

594 OFFICIAL NETSCAPE COMMUNICATOR 4 PROFESSIONAL EDITION BOOK

glass if you need to look up a name (it works just the way it did when you signed in earlier in the chapter). If you want to download the agenda of a group, click on the group icon. Finally, if you need assistance, click on the question mark icon.

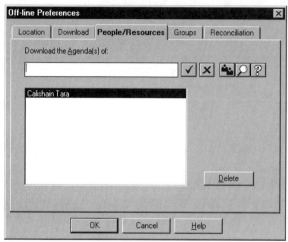

Figure 12-20: The People/Resources tab of the Off-line Preferences section.

A list of people, groups, and resources whose agendas you are download-ing will appear in the box in the center of this tab. If you change your mind and decide you don't want to download the agenda of someone on the list, click on their name and click on the Delete key. They'll vanish from your list.

TIP

You can only download the agenda for those people and resources to whose agendas you have access. If you try to download an agenda that you don't have access to, it won't download.

Click the Groups tab to move on.

Groups

The Groups tab, shown in Figure 12-21, gives you another outlet to indicate which groups you'd like to download agendas for. You may choose to download No Groups, All Groups, or Select Groups. Additionally, you may choose to view lists of private and public groups and select them from there. If you choose to download the agendas of some groups, click the Private Groups and/or the Public Groups check box, then click Load. The groups will list and you'll be able to click on the groups you want. Private groups are available only to certain people, while public groups are accessible and viewable by everyone. (A human resources task force would be a private group, while the refreshment committee might be public.)

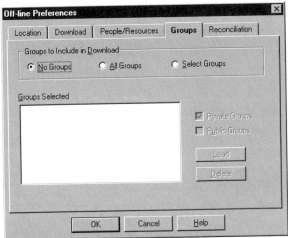

Figure 12-21: The Groups tab of the Off-line Preferences screen

Once you've chosen the groups you want to download, click the Reconciliation tab.

Reconciliation

Reconciliation is what happens when you bring the entries you've added in your Offline agenda to the Online agenda. The Calendar Server will compare the entries in the Offline agenda to those of the Online agenda and help you straighten out any scheduling conflicts.

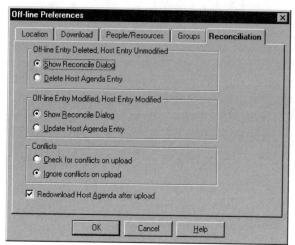

Figure 12-22: The Reconciliation tab in the Off-line Preferences screen.

This tab, shown in Figure 12-22, is divided into three sections. The first section allows you to indicate what you want to do when an entry in the Offline agenda has been deleted but it remains in the Online agenda. (You can choose to show the reconciliation dialog box and fix it, or you can choose to automatically delete the entry in the Online agenda.)

The second section allows you to indicate what you want to do when an entry in the Offline agenda has been modified and an entry in the Online agenda has been modified as well. (You can choose to show the reconciliation dialog box or update the Online agenda based on the Offline agenda.)

The third section allows you to indicate what you want to do if there's a conflict between the Offline agenda and the Online agenda. (You can choose to check for conflicts when uploading the Offline agenda and work through them using the reconciliation dialog, or just ignore the conflicts.)

At the bottom of this tab there's a check box. Click this check box if you want to update your Offline agenda after uploading it and working through all the scheduling conflicts.

Whew! We're almost done. You've got one more preferences section to fill out. Click OK to close this screen and then choose Edit | Preferences | Palmtop to edit your palmtop preferences. (If you don't have a palmtop computer, you can skip this next section, of course.)

Palmtop Reconciliation Preferences

The Palmtop Reconciliation Preferences section, shown in Figure 12-23, works very much like the Offline Preferences. You need to decide how the agenda you've created on your Palmtop behaves when it's uploaded to the agenda that's connected to the Calendar Server.

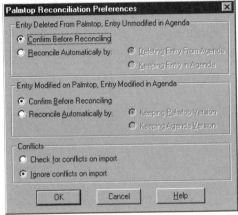

Figure 12-23: The Palmtop Reconciliation Preferences screen.

When you've decided how your Palmtop will work, click OK and you're finished!

Wow! A few dozen pages into this chapter and we've only just covered the preferences for Calendar. Pat yourself on the back; someone of lesser constitution would have thrown this book across the room and gone back to their paper calendar solution. But take heart—when you've learned Calendar you're going to find a lot of your previous scheduling problems have vanished.

Also reflect a minute and consider that you've actually learned quite a bit. You've learned about agendas, Offline and Online states, and In-Trays. So as we go into the next section, you're going to find out that many things look familiar, just because you took the time to set your preferences.

That having been said, let's get into your agenda: what it is, what it looks like, how to add things to it, and how to show your day in five-minute increments (as if it didn't move slowly enough).

The Agenda

When you first launch Calendar and sign in, you get a default Agenda screen, as you saw at the beginning of the chapter. Let's take another look at that in Figure 12-24.

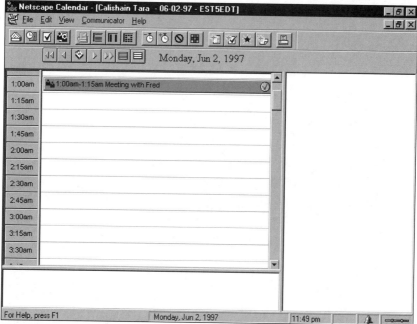

Figure 12-24: The default Agenda screen.

The left side of the screen, with the grid of times and lines, is your agenda—a place for those events in your day that take place within a schedule. (That's the theory, anyway.) The right side of the screen is for your tasks—a list of things that need to be accomplished within the framework of the day but don't have any ties to a particular schedule. And the lower left-hand side of the screen, below the agenda, is for your daily notes—those things that aren't tasks and aren't events, but things that need to be noted.

Directly above the agenda is the day of the week and the date (exactly how it looks depends on how you set your preferences) and also a set of control buttons that looks kind of like a VCR control panel. It's the date control bar for your agenda; it looks like Figure 12-25.

Figure 12-25: Your agenda's date control bar.

From left to right, here's what those buttons do to your agenda.

- **Way back**. Moves you back a certain number of time units, depending on how you're viewing the calendar. (On the daily view, it moves you back a week; on the weekly view, it moves you back a month; on the monthly view, it moves you back six months.)

- **Back**. Moves you back the time unit of the agenda you're viewing. For example, if you're viewing your daily agenda, it moves you back one day.

- **Calendar**. Pops up a calendar so you can zoom to a date. (Handy when you're trying to move from May 1 to February 4 or some other not-easily-navigable date.)

- **Forward**. Moves you forward according to the time unit of the agenda you're viewing. For example, if you're viewing your weekly agenda, it moves you forward one week.

- **Way forward**. Moves you forward a certain number of time units, depending on how you're viewing the calendar. (On the daily view, it moves you forward a week; on the weekly view, it moves you forward a month; on the monthly view, it moves you forward six months.)

- **Decrease**. Decreases the size of the time slots on your agenda (not the actual time allotted to a slot, but the actual physical height of the slot. Click it and you'll see what I mean).

- **Increase**. Increases the size of the time slots on your agenda.

Work with these buttons for a few moments and get used to moving around within the agenda. When you're finished, take a look at the icon bar above the date control bar. It looks like Figure 12-26.

Figure 12-26: The icon control bar.

Let's take a look at these from left to right.

- **In-Tray**. Open the In-Tray.

- **Agenda**. Open an Agenda. This can either be your agenda or someone else's agenda to which you have access.

- **Tasks**. Open your task list.

- **Group**. Open a group's agenda.

- **Go to Entry**. Go to an entry you've highlighted on the agenda.

- **Day View**. View one day of your agenda.

- **Week View**. View one week of your agenda.

- **Month View**. View one month of your agenda.

- **Decrease Time Slot**. This icon decreases the time intervals on the agenda grids. For example, say you've set your agenda to display time in 15-minute intervals. One click on this icon would cause your agenda to display time in 10-minute intervals. Two clicks and your agenda would display time in 5-minute intervals.

- **Increase Time Slot**. This icon increases the time intervals on the agenda grids.

- **No Icons**. Removes the icons from the toolbar (above your agenda) and the status bar (below your agenda). Note that this won't remove the icons that we're discussing in this section, but rather the icons associated with specific agenda entries.

- **Event Colors**. Allows you to specify how you want your agenda entries colored and gives you a color key of what each color means.

- **New Entry**. Creates a new entry on your agenda.

- **New Task**. Creates a new task.

- **New Day Event**. Creates a new event that lasts an entire day.

- **New Daily Note**. Allows you to create a new daily note.

- **Print**. Lets you print your agenda.

Now that we've gotten those icon bars transformed from a bunch of intimidating squares to a couple of simple explanations, let's get down to the real meat of the application: putting entries in your agenda! (You thought you'd never get to this part, didn't you?) We'll break this down into four sections: adding events, adding tasks, adding day events, and adding daily notes.

Adding Events to Your Agenda

Take a look at your agenda. You'll see that there's a scroll bar on the side of the agenda so you can scroll through your day (or week or month, depending on how you've set your view).

To add an event to this agenda, you've got a few choices:

■ You can choose the New Event icon from the icon bar.

■ You can choose File I New I Agenda Entry.

■ You can find the appropriate time slot to which you wish to add an event and double-click on it.

Let's walk through the process of adding an item to your agenda. Scroll through your agenda and pick a time period where you want to add an event. Double-click on the slot next to the time period you've selected. You'll be presented with a screen that looks like the one in Figure 12-27.

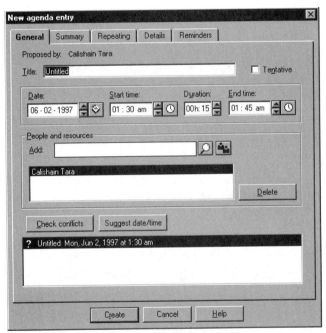

Figure 12-27: Adding an event to your agenda.

You'll see that the process of adding an item to your agenda consists of five screens: General, Summary, Repeating, Details, and Reminders.

TIP

Of course, you don't have to go through all these screens every single time. Just walk through them once to learn what's on them.

Importing & Exporting Information Into Your Agenda

Sometimes you'll want to import information into your agenda from other locations. This is not the same as going online after being offline (we'll cover being offline later on in the chapter). Instead, the import utility allows you to bring information into your agenda from certain file formats and palmtops. (At this writing, the compatible palmtops are the Hewlett-Packard HP-100LX and HP-200LX, and the compatible file formats are the HP-100LX and HP-200LX Appointment Book files, Schedule+ files, and vCalendar files. See the Calendar help file for additional information.)

Importing data takes several steps:

1. Choose File|Import Data from the main Calendar screen.

2. Use the radio buttons to indicate whether you're importing from a file or a palmtop.

3. Use the pull-down menu or the browse box to indicate the name of the file from which you want to import. (If you're importing from a palmtop, you won't have the option of using a browse box.)

4. Use the arrow keys and Calendar button to indicate the date range you wish to import.

5. Click the Import button.

Conversely, you may occasionally want to export data from your agenda to another format. Calendar can export data in the palmtop formats mentioned above as well as in several ASCII formats and a vCalendar format. Exporting data takes several steps:

1. Choose File|Export Data from the main Calendar screen.

2. Use the radio buttons and the pull-down menu to indicate the format you want to export data into.

3. Use the arrow buttons and the calendar icon to set the dates for which you want to export data. (You can also click the All button if you want to export all the information from your agenda.)

4. Use the text box and magnifying glass to list the people for whom you want to export agenda information.

5. Indicate under which file name you'd like Calendar to export the data. (Calendar automatically indicates a file name; you can let that name stand or select another one.)

6. Click Export. Calendar exports the data without giving you any kind of confirmation dialog. Click the Cancel button to close the box.

TIP

If you double-click in an area that already has an agenda entry, you'll get the entry editing screen, which looks different from the new entry screen. If you double-click on your agenda and get a different screen than the one discussed below, find a blank spot on your agenda and double-click on that instead.

General

Here's how to use the General screen:

1. Enter the title of your event into the title box. If the event involves more than a couple of people, be sure to name the event something everyone understands. Instead of "Client Meeting," call it "Client Meeting with CWR," for example. If the meeting is tentative, click the Tentative check box.

2. Now set the date and time. Use the arrow keys to the right of the time and date boxes, or click on the calendar and clock icons to set the date and time directly. After you've set the date and start time, set the length of the event in the duration box.

TIP

As you set the start time and the duration, the time in the End time box will adjust itself automatically—you don't need to set it.

3. When you've determined the date, time, and length of the meeting, you need to decide who will attend. You are automatically added to the attendee list, but you'll have to add anyone else manually. Enter a name in the Add text box and press Enter. The matching name will appear in the list box below the Add text box. If you're unsure about spelling or the user name of the person you want to add, click on the magnifying glass icon and follow the same procedure that you used to find your user name when you signed on. To add a group to your event, click on the group icon next to the magnifying glass icon. If you add a person or a group to your event and you want to delete them, click their name in the list box so it's highlighted, and click the Delete button.

Making a Group

Many times the same group of people will work on the same set of events. There are two ways you can go about adding those people. You can select each individual person and add that person to each individual task. Or you can create a group of people and assign the group, instead of each person, to a task.

To create a group, choose Edit|Manage Groups. You'll get a screen that looks like the one shown in Figure 12-28.

Figure 12-28: The Managing Groups Screen.

If by some chance you've already set up some groups, they'll appear here. But if you haven't, you'll have to start from the beginning. In the Add group: text box, type the name of the group you want to create. Call it TestGroup. Next to the text box is a pull-down menu to indicate who will be able to access the group, assign it to events, and so on. There are four types of access:

- **Public**. It's accessible by everyone on the intranet.

- **Private**. It's accessible only by its creator.

- **Admin**. Accessible only by the network administrators.

- **Members Only**. Accessible only by the members of the group.

Once you've created the group, click the check mark next to the pull-down menu. Now you'll need to add members. On the right side of the screen, you'll see the Add Member text box. Enter the member's name into the text box and click the check mark to add the member to the group. If you're not sure of someone's name, you can use the magnifying glass dialog box to find them and add them to the list, just as you do when you add someone to an event.

If you want to print a listing of groups, delete a group, or print the members of a group, there are handy buttons for this at the bottom of the screen.

Finally, you're going to want to do the most important thing of all: check for conflicts. This is where having all the scheduling information gathered in one place really comes in handy.

The information you've specified thus far is shown in the list box below the Check Conflicts button. A question mark is to the information's left, specifying that you have not yet checked the event for conflicts. To check this meeting against the schedules of other people you want to include, click the Check Conflicts button. Calendar will connect to the Calendar Server and check your schedule and the schedule of the other event invitees. If there's no conflict, the question mark will turn into a green check mark. If there are conflicts, the question mark will turn into a red X. Double-click on the X for more information on the conflicts. You'll get a list of the conflicts and which person invited to the event has the conflict. A sample of this list is shown in Figure 12-29.

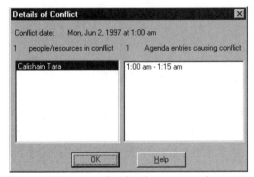

Figure 12-29: A conflict list for a proposed event.

A really easy way to get rid of a conflict is to delete the person who's having the conflict from your event. But, while that's very easy, it might annoy them a bit. Another option you have is to suggest alternative event times.

Click the Suggest Time/Date button. You'll get a screen that looks like the one in Figure 12-30.

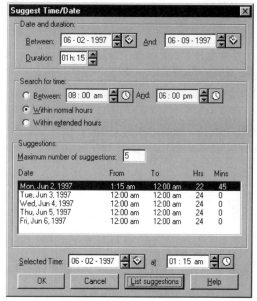

Figure 12-30: Suggesting alternative times for proposed events.

Use the top of the screen to specify the date and time range in which you find alternate scheduling for the event permissible. Then click the List suggestions button. Calendar will list up to five conflict-free alternative meeting times. Highlight the one you want, click OK, and Calendar will reschedule the meeting for the conflict-free time you selected.

Click the Summary tab to move to the next phase of the meeting scheduling.

TIP

You have to click on the tabs to move between these screens—you can't click on OK. If you click on OK, you'll be taken back to the General screen.

Summary

The Summary tab, shown in Figure 12-31, lists the lowdown on who proposed the meeting, where it's located, who's involved, its importance, and the access level. (The access level refers to the other people's ability to access the details of the event.) The only things you need to indicate in this tab are the location, importance, and access level.

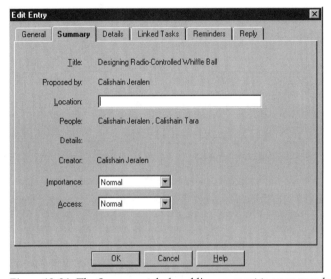

Figure 12-31: The Summary tab, for adding an event to your agenda.

Repeating

Do you have meetings or events that repeat periodically? Use the Repeating tab, shown in Figure 12-32, to set them once and have them reappear on your agenda where necessary.

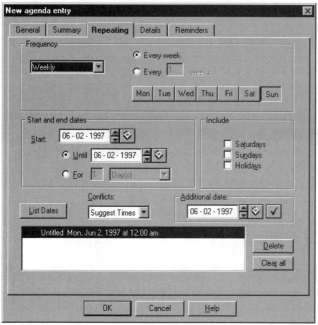

Figure 12-32: The Repeating tab, for use when a meeting is held periodically.

1. Use the pull-down menu to determine how frequently this meeting will repeat (weekly, daily), then choose how the length of time you want it to repeat for (every two weeks, every three days). Depending on the time interval you've chosen, you'll have a couple of additional options for clarifying when you want the event to repeat.

2. The second section indicates the start and end time for the repetition. The start button is the current date. (You can change it to any date you like, however.) The second radio button is the Until button, which lists the end date of the repeated meetings. (If you don't want to repeat the event, make sure that the start date and the end date match.) Below the Until button is another radio button, where instead of specifying the end date you can specify a time span during which the meetings should repeat.

For example, say you're holding a daily meeting for a project that starts on May 1 and lasts 21 days. You'd specify a daily frequency at the top of the page, and under the start and end date sections you could specify either an end date of May 22 or click on the For radio button and specify 21 days.

To the right of the start and end dates section are three check boxes. Here you can specify whether you want the time spans for the meetings to include

Saturdays, Sundays, and holidays. (This is especially important to writers, the less fortunate of whom have no weekends or holidays.)

At the bottom of the screen you're given another opportunity to check for date conflicts and either display them, list alternative dates, or ignore the conflicts. You're also given the opportunity to list an additional date for the event.

Once you've set your event to repeat, move on by clicking the Details tab.

TIP

Eventually, you may want to edit an event on your agenda that's set as a recurring event. When you do this, Calendar will ask whether you want to edit only the selected event, or whether you want the edits to affect all instances of that repeated event.

Details

The Details tab, shown in Figure 12-33, is just what its name implies—it's for adding the details of the event. Bear in mind that other people you've invited to this event might not know as much about it as you do. It's a good idea to include as many details as possible, though you don't have to include any at all.

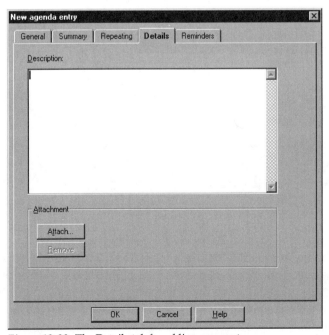

Figure 12-33: The Details tab for adding an event.

If there's another source for information about the event—a document containing the meeting agenda, or a list of speakers—you can include that by clicking on the Attachment button at the bottom of the tab. If you've included an attachment and you want to remove it, click on the name of the attachment in the file list box and then click the Remove button.

Set your details? Then click Reminders to move to the Reminders tab. You don't want to forget this meeting that you've worked so hard to set up, do you?

Reminders

If you're the type who can't remember events until five minutes after they've started, consider setting up a reminder (see Figure 12-34).

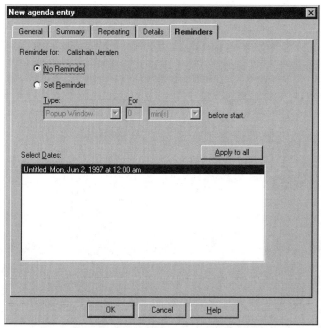

Figure 12-34: The Reminders tab for setting up an event.

If you don't want a reminder, leave the No Reminder radio button clicked. If you do want a reminder, click the Set Reminder button. Use the pull-down menu to determine the type of reminder; you can have either a pop-up box to remind you of an upcoming event or have a note appear in the Daily Notes section of the Calendar screen. After you've set up what kind of reminder you want, use the input box and pull-down menu to specify the time intervals for the reminder. (For a pop-up reminder, you can choose to be reminded anywhere from a few minutes before the event to a few years before the event. For a daily note reminder, you can choose to be reminded days, weeks, months, or years before the event.)

What's a Pop-Up Reminder Box?

When you specify that you want a pop-up reminder box, you have a more active reminder of an event or task—a screen that "pops up" in front of whatever you're doing to remind you about an event or task. It looks like Figure 12-35:

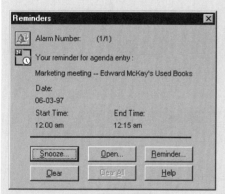

Figure 12-35: The pop-up Reminder box.

The pop-up box tells you what reminder it's referring to, a summary of the event or task information, and the following button options:

- **Snooze**. Temporarily turns off the alarm. Gives you a dialog box with which you can reset the alarm.

- **Open**. Takes you directly to the task or event so you can view it.

- **Reminder**. Takes you to the Reminder tab of the event or task so you can view and alter it.

- **Clear**. Clears all reminders for this task or event.

- **Clear All**. Clears all active pop-up reminders for all tasks and events. (It doesn't affect the Display Note reminders, and is grayed out if you only have one active pop-up reminder.) Use this command with extreme caution!

- **Help**. Takes you to the Netscape Calendar help file.

If you've chosen for this event to repeat, the Select Dates box at the bottom of the screen will contain a list of all the dates for this event. Click the Apply to All button to apply reminders to all the events in the list, or click the events to select them individually.

TIP

To select an individual date, click on it. To select a list of dates, shift+click on the first and last dates in the list. And to select several individual dates, Ctrl+click on each of them.

Let's put this all together. Choose a date in your agenda and add an event to it. Make sure that the event repeats a couple of times and that you have a reminder pop-up.

When you're done filling out the Agenda tab, click OK. You'll be taken back to the General tab on the screen. Click Create Event and the event will appear on your agenda. It'll look like Figure 12-36.

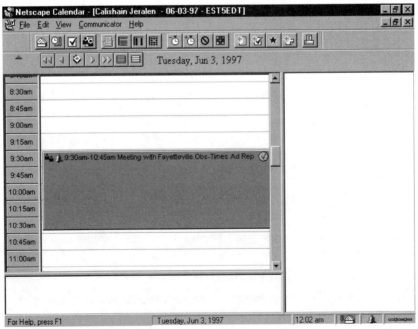

Figure 12-36: A new event on your agenda.

You're probably seeing a few icons on the screen that you haven't seen before. Let's take a look at them:

- **The Bell**. The Bell indicates that this entry has a reminder on it.

- **The Group**. The Group indicates that there are other people invited to your event.

Here are two more items that you'll see attached to agenda listings:

- **Description**. Indicates that there are descriptions associated with the event.

- **Paper Clip**. Indicates that there are file attachments associated with the event.

As you continue to learn about Calendar, you'll become familiar with more icons. The icons come in handy because they show you what kind of information is associated with an event without your having to open or activate the event itself.

Editing an Event

You may wish to edit an event once you've entered it onto your agenda, or you may wish to edit an event that someone else has put on your agenda. To do that, double-click on its listing from the main Calendar screen.

The screen you'll get looks just like the screen you get when you add an event to the agenda, with two differences: the Linked Tasks tab and the Reply tab.

- **Linked Tasks tab**. The Linked Tasks tab gives you the opportunity to link a task to the event. Your tasks will be listed in a text box. Click the ones you want to link to the event, or click on the New button to create a new task.

- **Reply tab**. The Reply tab gives you summary data for the event and the opportunity to respond to the entry with the response "I will attend," "I will not attend," "I will confirm later," or "I would prefer another time." There's also an e-mail button here so you can respond directly to the person with another suggestion.

TIP

To toggle the icon display on the main Calendar screen on and off, choose View | Icons On/Off.

Though sometimes it seems like it, the entirety of your work experience does not consist of meetings. However, in some cases, you'll need to track the progress of tasks. The next section shows you how to add a task to your agenda.

Adding a Task

Not everything you do in your business life has a date attached to it. Some things are events while other things are tasks not associated with dates. For example, going to see an editor and signing a contract is an event. Drafting the actual assignment is a task.

There are several ways you can add a task to your agenda:

■ Choose the New Task icon from the icon bar.

■ Choose File | New | Task.

■ Press the F7 function key.

Creating a new task brings you to a screen with three tabs: General, Reminders, and Details. If the names of these tabs look familiar, it's because they're very similar to the ones that you used when you created a new event for your agenda. (I told you you were learning more than you thought you were!)

General

At the top of this screen, shown in Figure 12-37, you'll see a place to enter a description of your task. Again, keep in mind that other people may see your task, so it's good to give the task as precise a name as possible. A bad task name is "Create human resources department." A good task name is "Draft first employee handbook."

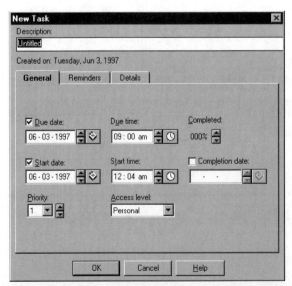

Figure 12-37: Setting general characteristics of a new task.

The tabs are lined up underneath the description so that you can see the description as you set the characteristics of the task.

Though some tasks don't have due dates and start dates, many do. The General tab provides check boxes to specify whether there are due or start dates associated with the task you're adding. There are also calendar and time menus, so you can get very specific about when tasks start and when they're due. You can start a task at 12:01 a.m. on August 10 if you like.

TIP

Bear in mind that the due and start dates are not a "both or none" situation. You can have a due date without a start date and vice-versa. That's why they each have a check box.

To the right of the due date and due time line in the General tab, you'll see a Completed indicator that initially stands at 000%. As you track a task, you can update its completion percentage by clicking on the arrow buttons to the right of the 000% figure. The percentage increases in 5 percent increments.

Below the Completed indicator is another check box to indicate a completion date. When you've finished the task, click this box. It'll indicate the current date and the Completed indicator will jump up to 100%. (Wouldn't it be great if finishing a task at your job was as easy as just clicking the Completion date box?)

There are also pull-down menus for Priority and Access level in this tab. The priorities run from 1-9 and A-Z. These are for your use only, so use the priority numbers that correspond to your own task management system. The access level affects how many people will be able to see this task information. You have the choice of Personal, Confidential, Normal, and Public access levels.

Once you've set these attributes, click the Reminders tab.

Reminders

The reminders for a task work just like the reminders for an event. You can specify a reminder for a start time, and a separate reminder for a due time, as shown in Figure 12-38.

When you're done setting your reminders, click the Details tab.

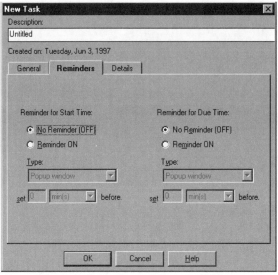

Figure 12-38: The Reminders tab for task adding.

Details

Once again, this Details tab, shown in Figure 12-39, works like the one you saw when you added an event. You can attach files to tasks, just like you can to an event.

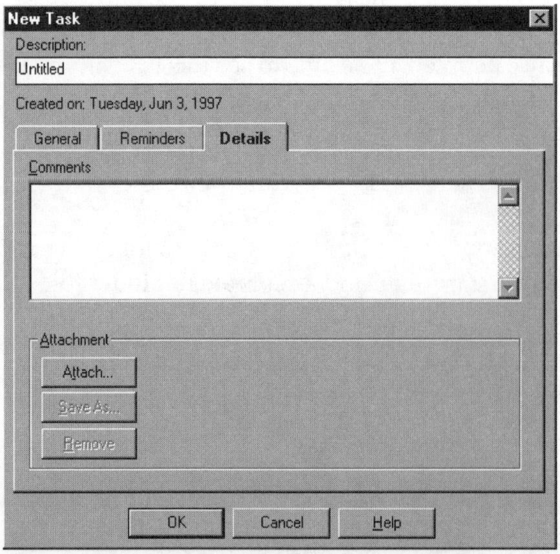

Figure 12-39: The Details tab when adding a task.

When you finish filling out the information for the task, click OK. The task will show up on the right side of the screen on your task list.

Take a few moments now and create a task for yourself. Give it a start and a due date, and have it be 15% completed. When you click the OK button, the listing on your task bar will look like Figure 12-40.

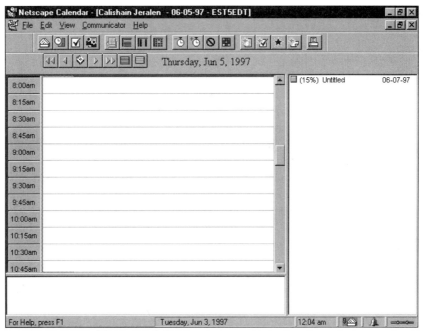

Figure 12-40: A task in your task bar.

You guessed it: I'm going to introduce you to another icon you might see, in addition to others you already recognize.

Note: There is one thing you'll see next to a task name that isn't an icon. That's the (15%) next to the name of the task. That indicates the percentage of the task that's completed, and is taken from the Competed indicator in the General tab of the task.

The icon you'll see that looks unfamiliar is the gray square. The gray square indicates that your task has a due date. If there's a red outline around the gray square, it means that your task is overdue. To indicate that a task is completed, click on the gray square. A blue check mark will appear in the square and any percentage listed next to the task will disappear (since by checking the square you've indicated that the task is 100% complete).

You've added events, and you've added tasks, and by now your agenda is starting to look pretty busy, isn't it? But sometimes you'll want to add an event that takes the entire day. That won't color your whole agenda with an event, however—instead, it'll put a note down in your Daily Notes section. Let's talk Day Events.

Going Offline

When you either log in as an offline user or choose File|Go Offline from the main Calendar screen, Calendar behaves very much as it usually does, with a few notable exceptions.

First of all, an offline Calendar user cannot check meetings for conflicts, because he or she is not connected to the server. For the same reason, the offline Calendar user can't look up names. Anything that requires direct interaction with the server is out. (If you're ever having trouble with Calendar where the server seems to have forgotten your existence, check the status bar in the lower right-hand corner. Is it a broken blue-line? If it is, you're in offline mode and should go back into online mode to communicate with the Calendar Server.)

If one can't connect to the server, why use Netscape Calendar? Because you can still add items to your agenda: events, tasks, and so on. Calendar will store these items in your offline agenda. Once you reconnect to the Calendar Server, Calendar will integrate these entries into the online mode, and help you resolve scheduling conflicts that might have popped up.

Adding a Day Event

There are daily sales seminars, and then there are those seminars that last an entire day. A Day Event is any event that takes an entire working day; if I mapped out my life with Netscape Calendar, then Thursday would have laundry as a day event.

Having a day event color your entire agenda can be confusing and could make you miss some of your other events; for example, you could have a seminar day event but three sales meetings within the day. To alleviate this confusion, Calendar marks a day event down in the Daily Notes section; it's the first thing listed and has a star next to its name.

It's not necessary to walk through adding a day event, because you know a considerable amount about it through adding a regular event. Click on the star icon on the menu bar, or choose File I New I Day Event from the agenda screen. But let's talk about a few differences in the four tabs—General, People/Resources, Repeating, and Reminders—that make up the New Day Event screen.

- **General**. There's no time start, finish, or duration, because the event takes all day.
- **People/Resources**. Works like the People/Resources section of an event's General tab.
- **Repeating**. Works like the Repeating tab of a regular event.
- **Reminders**. Works like the Reminders tab of a regular event.

Create a day event for yourself and click OK to return to the main Calendar screen. You'll find the event in the bottom left-hand part of the screen; the Day Event is listed along with a star icon to indicate that it is a day event.

With the day event appearing at the bottom of the screen in the Daily Notes section, perhaps it's not too surprising that adding a daily note is exactly like adding a day event.

Adding a Daily Note

A Daily Note is something you want to be aware of but which doesn't fit the description of an event or a task. I might have a daily note that I am running low on copier paper and should go to the office supply store to get some more.

Adding a Daily Note is exactly the same as adding a Daily Event. Yes, exactly, except that you click on the star and folded paper icon, or choose File | New | Daily Note from the main agenda screen.

Are you feeling confident? Are you feeling in control of your agenda? Good. Unfortunately, no man is an island, and no computer on an intranet is either. Eventually, someone's going to add a meeting to your agenda, and you're going to have to decide whether you're going to attend that meeting or blow it off and go to the Cubs game. You make those decisions through the Netscape Calendar screen called the In-Tray.

The In-Tray

The In-Tray is where meeting information is sent when other folks on the intranet add you to their events. You can access the In-Tray in two ways: by choosing File | Open In-Tray or by clicking on the In-Tray icon in the toolbar. Once you've accessed it, you'll get a screen that looks like the one in Figure 12-41.

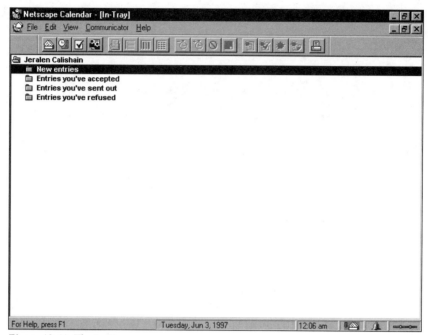

Figure 12-41: The In-Tray.

The In-Tray is divided into four folders: New Entries, Entries You've Accepted, Entries You've Sent Out, and Entries You've Refused. Double-click on the icon next to the name of the folder and you'll see that the icon changes to an opened folder and any listings appear under the folder's name.

Initially, every event to which you're added appears in the New Entries folder. You can see an example of this in Figure 12-42.

Click on the entry's icon and you'll see a list of people who have been invited to the entry. Next to their names will be one of five icons:

- **Check**. The person will attend.

- **X**. The person will not attend.

- **Question mark**. The person has not yet responded to the invitation.

- **Calendar and check mark**. The person will attend but would prefer a different time.

- **Calendar and X**. The person will not attend but might be interested if the event were rescheduled.

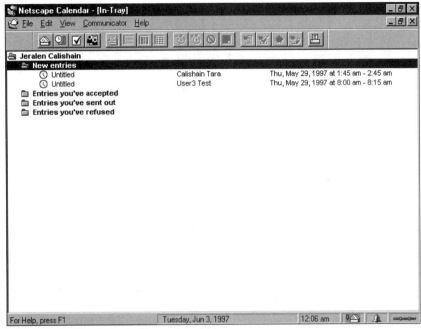

Figure 12-42: Events in the New entries folder.

Now, double-click on the entry and you'll be taken to the View Entry screen, which consists of five tabs: General, Details, Linked Tasks, Reminders, and Reply.

TIP

These tabs refer only to events to which you're invited. Other agenda items look a bit different—for example, Daily Notes have General, People/Resources, Reminders, and Agenda tabs.

These tabs are much like the ones you've seen before while working with agendas. The big difference is the Reply tab, shown in Figure 12-43.

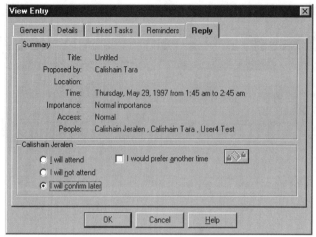

Figure 12-43: The Reply tab in the View Entry screen.

The top of the reply tab gives you the basic information about the event. The bottom of the tab gives you the opportunity to respond. You can reply that you will attend, will not attend, will confirm later, or that you would prefer another time. There's also an e-mail button for you to communicate directly with the person who created the event.

Sending an E-mail

Sending an e-mail is about the first thing you learn when you get on the company intranet. There's an e-mail feature integrated into Calendar so that you can send invitees additional information about events and tasks. Depending on how you set your preferences at the beginning of this chapter, you may be asked if you want to send an e-mail to invitees every time you create, modify, or delete an event. Creating and sending a message is easy.

1. Use the input box to create a list of people to whom you want to send a message. This works just as it does when you're adding people to an event or a task list.

2. Summary information about the event to which you're referring will already appear in the Message to Send box. Scroll past that information and add your details below. (Obviously this little box is not the place to draft a *War and Peace* type of message. If you have extensive additional information, consider adding it to the event as an attachment.)

3. Click Send when you're finished.

That's it!

If you respond to the invitation, the event moves to either the Entries You've Accepted or the Entries You've Refused folder, depending on your response to the invitation. How many of the items in this folder you can view depends on how you set up your In-Box preferences.

TIP

Items like Daily Notes don't have acceptances attached to them. Instead, when you double-click on your name, you're taken to an agenda entry screen that gives you the option of keeping the item in your agenda, removing it from your agenda, or deciding later.

As you can see, the In-Tray makes it a lot easier to keep your event information straight, especially since you're connected to the intranet where information about new events, new tasks, and new daily notes can constantly invade your calendar.

But sometimes you've got to take your show on the road. Sometimes, heaven forbid, you even have to get away from your computer!

In the next section, we're going to talk about printing, and how you can print out your agenda, put it in your organizer, and keep up with your day even when you're nowhere near a computer.

Printing

It seems a little strange to devote a whole section of this chapter to printing, doesn't it? I mean, printing a document or a calendar agenda is pretty straightforward, right?

If Calendar had only basic printing abilities, that would be true and printing would be a pretty straightforward thing. But Calendar's printing abilities are more extensive. Calendar can print in several calendar formats, any range of time you care to specify, using any of the fonts on your system. Thus, printing with Calendar gets a section to itself in this chapter.

Let's talk about setting up a print job, and from there move into setting up a print job for a specific type of organizer layout.

Setting Up a Print Job

The starting point is the File | Print command. That should be familiar if you've used Windows at all. When you choose File | Print, you'll get a screen that looks like Figure 12-44.

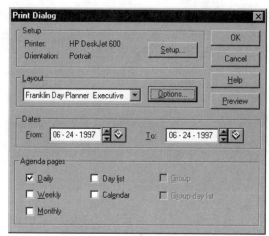

Figure 12-44: Printing in Calendar.

If you've printed from Windows before, the Setup section at the top of the screen is familiar. It lists the name of the printer and the orientation of the paper, and offers the Setup… button to configure your printer. See your network administrator if you need printer setup help.

Below the Setup section is the Layout section, which has a pull-down menu to specify how you want to print the Calendar. Calendar offers a number of types of popular organizers that you can use to print out your appointments. We'll go over setting up a printout for your organizer in a minute. First, though, you'll need to decide what days you want to print, which is what the section underneath the Layout section is for. Use the arrow buttons and the Calendar buttons to specify the date range you want to print.

Below that section is the place where you specify the viewpoint you want to print from. You have the choice of Daily, Weekly, Monthly, Day list, Calendar, Group, or Group day list. (Some of these choices might be "grayed out" and unavailable depending on what you want to print and whether or not you're online.)

TIP

Once you've set up all your options, you can use the Preview button on this screen to see what your agenda will look like—before you print it.

Have you set all that? Okay, now let's work on your layout. We'll walk through setting up a print job for my organizer, the Franklin Day Planner Executive. The other organizer formats work pretty much the same way.

Setting Up a Print Layout

Use the pull-down menu in the Layout section to find the Franklin Day Planner Executive option, then click the Options button beside the pull-down menu. You'll see a screen that looks like the one shown in Figure 12-45.

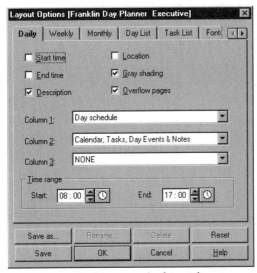

Figure 12-45: Setting up a print layout for your organizer.

There are seven tabs in this screen. You can only see six of them because the screen isn't wide enough for seven. Click the right arrow at the top right of the screen (beside the tabs) and you'll see the extra tab. The tabs are Daily, Weekly, Monthly, Day List, Task List, Fonts, and Margins.

The tabs for Daily, Weekly, Monthly, and Day List are very much alike, containing check boxes with which you can indicate what event and task information appears on your printout. We'll go through one of them, and then the Fonts and Margins tabs. (I want this book to be large enough so that it helps you use Communicator Professional but not so large that you can't flatten the dust bunnies that may roll out from under your desk.)

Lets start with the Daily tab.

Daily

Did you ever try to print out pages for your Organizer using preprinted template pages? First you have to find the template pages. Then you have to make sure your printer margins are set to handle them. Then you have to make sure you feed the paper into the printer properly.

Forget all that. Calendar not only prints out the appointments you have, it prints out the template of your organizer, too. Handy? Yes! Convenient? Yes! Fantastic? Yes!

Let's get started. The Daily tab looks like Figure 12-46.

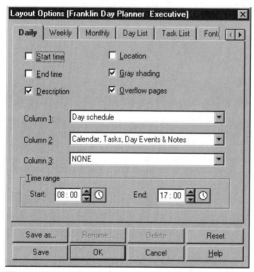

Figure 12-46: The Daily tab for the print layout setup.

The top part of the tab has six check boxes. Click them to specify the inclusion of the following items on your printout:

- **Start time**. The beginning of the event or task.
- **End time**. The end of your event or task.
- **Description**. The description of your event or task.
- **Location**. Where the event or task is located.
- **Gray shading**. This option shades the entries on your printed agenda with gray, to make your available time more visible.
- **Overflow pages**. This option will print extra pages if your agenda information doesn't fit on one page.

Below these check boxes are three pull-down menus with which you can specify how the page is laid out. Initially, the menus are set so the Day Schedule appears in column one of your printout, the Calendar, Tasks, Day Events, and Notes appear in column two, and nothing appears in column three. You can specify a column three if you like (you'll have the option to include your agenda's notepad, calendar, task list, notes, or a combination) but it will make your first two columns narrower. This is okay if you have a full-page organizer, but if you're using one of those vest-pocket size types, three columns will be hard on your eyeballs.

The third section in this tab is the time range, indicating what range of time you want to include in your agenda.

The final part of this tab is a series of eight buttons. They cover all the settings in each of the tabs of this screen. Here's how they work.

■ **Save as**. Saves the changes you make to the layout as a new layout type. The new layout type appears in the print screen on the pull-down menu. For example, I might make changes to this layout and use the Save As button to save the layout as TaraPlan. Later, when I use File | Print to print another agenda page, I could use the pull-down menu in the main print screen to choose the TaraPlan layout.

■ **Rename**. This button will be grayed out unless you've saved the layout. It gives you the option of renaming the layout.

■ **Delete**. This button will be grayed out unless you've saved the layout. It gives you the option of deleting the layout.

■ **Reset**. Resets the layout to its default conditions. Handy to use if you've made too many changes and gotten completely confused.

■ **Save**. Saves the changes to the layout. Bear in mind that if you use the Save button to save the changes to a layout and then click on the Reset button, Calendar will revert the layout to its defaults—not to the changes you've made.

■ **OK**. Approves the changes you've made without saving a layout.

■ **Cancel**. Exits the screen without making changes to the layout.

■ **Help**. Takes you to Calendar's help files.

Take a few moments and go through the Weekly, Monthly, and Day List tabs to see how they compare to the Daily tab. As you can see, they're mostly check boxes that allow you to specify what kind of information you want to print in your agenda.

Once you're finished poking around those tabs, take a look at the Fonts tab.

Fonts

When you click the Fonts tab, you'll get a screen that looks like Figure 12-47.

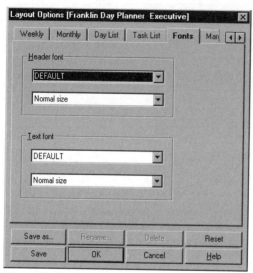

Figure 12-47: The Fonts tab.

This tab consists of four pull-down menus in two sections. The first section allows you to specify which font you want to use in the printed headers. Click the top menu and you'll see that you have the choice of any font on your system. The menu beneath that is to specify what size you want the header font to be. You're not specifying a particular font size, just whether you want the font to be larger or smaller than the regular size.

The second section covers the text that prints the agenda entries, and it works the same way. Choose a font and a font size.

All set? You didn't choose Scrawly RightWeird font to view your agenda entries, did you? Okay. Now click on the Margins tab.

Margins

The Margins tab, shown in Figure 12-48, is self-explanatory. Use the pull-down menu on the tab to choose how you want to measure the margins (inches or centimeters) and then use the Columns and Rows, Margins, and Internal Margins sections to set the margins of each area of the page.

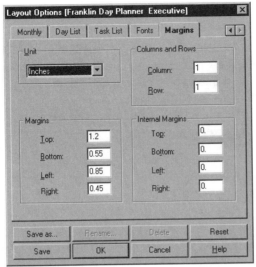

Figure 12-48: The Margins tab.

TIP

Don't mess with these if you don't know what you're doing—they're already set to the appropriate defaults! This is especially important if you're using a formatted template like the Franklin Organizer. If you mess around with the margins too much your agenda may print so strangely that it won't fit in your organizer.

Once you've finished filling out all of these options, you've got four choices:

- Click the Save as button and give a name to your format. This name will show up on the print screen's pull-down menu the next time you want to print something.

- Click the Save button and save these changes for the next time you want to print.

- Click OK to save the changes for this session.

- Click Cancel to abandon your changes.

No matter what choice you make, you'll be returned to the main Print screen. Once there, click Cancel to abandon the print job or click OK to proceed to print.

That's it!

Moving On

This chapter showed you how to add items to your agenda, how to invite other people to your events, how to print out your agenda and take it with you, and even how to import and export your agenda data.

Now that you know how to schedule events and tasks, you probably want to protect the information you use and share during these events and tasks. And that's what the next chapter is about—common-sense security while online.

CHAPTER 13

Commerce & Security

The Internet has had a colorful history. The military started it, the academic world helped to develop and refine it, and thousands of individuals began using it for everything from research to interactive games. Then, as with every other innovation, people figured out ways to make money with it. Online transactions are now commonplace. And as the Net has grown and become more commercialized, security has jumped to the foreground as one of the most important considerations of online interactions. It goes without saying that the administrators and users of office intranets have their own very serious security concerns as well.

Whether you're shopping online or sharing sensitive company information with one of your co-workers, Communicator Professional offers the most powerful and flexible data security of any commercial communications program. In this chapter, you'll learn how to use and configure Communicator's security options for your own specific needs. But first, understanding a little about the underlying issues and technology might help.

Security on the Net & on Intranets

When I was a kid, the mix of technology and commerce was already cause for panic. "Some companies encourage you to order products by telephone," complained the news media. "When you place your order, they'll try to get you to tell them your credit card number instead of mailing a check. Don't do it!" they warned. "Don't give *anyone* your credit card number over the phone!"

Twenty-something years later these fears seem quaint. The American public has become used to home shopping and 800 numbers and has clearly decided that convenience is worth a little risk. Did the nightmare scenarios come true? Did unscrupulous employees at companies all over the country steal thousands of credit card numbers and spend all your money at the track? Of course not. Most employees want to keep their jobs.

Security is about people, not technologies. No matter what methods you use to transfer information, somebody can steal it if he or she wants it badly enough. Germany under Hitler was home to some of the world's cleverest cryptographers and information scientists, and yet the Allied powers were able to crack the secret codes. Right now hundreds or perhaps even thousands of workers—telephone sales agents, customer service representatives, data entry personnel, managers, bank tellers, system administrators—have access to your financial records or your credit card information. The operator could even listen in on your phone calls. And yet how often do you get ripped off?

The people who handle Internet transactions are really no different from the workers who already know or have access to your credit card numbers. Let's dispel a few myths:

- The Internet is *not* a den of hacker-thieves looking for a quick buck. There are easier ways to steal.

- Sending data across the Net does *not* give everyone on the Net access to that data.

- Most businesses set up shop on the Net because it offers a new, cost-effective point of sale, *not* because it enables them to collect more personal information about their customers—although this is an increasing problem.

- The Internet is *not* a leaky old boat full of giant security holes that can never be plugged.

That said, the security of information on the Net is still an important issue. Even though the biggest security hole is people rather than software or hardware, and even though abuses have been exaggerated by weekly magazines and news shows, nothing is wrong with making the Internet as secure a medium as possible for financial transactions. And, of course, if you're on an office intranet, you want to make sure that neither the outside world nor unscrupulous individuals within the company have access to trade secrets or sensitive personnel information.

Netscape, recognizing from its inception as a company that commercial transactions were the Next Big Thing on the Net and that intranets were the Next Big Thing in the business community, has taken a lead in bolstering the security of transmitted data. In this chapter, we'll take a brief look at how Communicator addresses security. After that, we'll get into the nuts and bolts of actually *using* the security features available to you.

Communicator 4 & Security

To understand what Netscape has done to address security issues, you have to understand the issues it is addressing. In other words, in what ways is it even possible to improve Internet and intranet security?

Information traveling between your computer and another machine, such as a Web server, is routed from node to node—or machine to machine—until it finally reaches its destination. It may pass through a handful or even dozens of computer systems. At any one of these sites, a technically proficient but unscrupulous individual can access the stream of data for ulterior motives. Somebody could eavesdrop on you, collecting personal or financial information; somebody could copy your intellectual property, such as a great new idea for a patent; or somebody could even change your data before it reaches its destination, causing all kinds of mayhem. The Internet itself provides no built-in mechanism for preventing such activities, nor do intranets.

Netscape's response to this lack of security was to develop the *Secure Sockets Layer (SSL) protocol*. The SSL protocol enhances Internet security in four ways:

- It provides a mechanism for server authentication. That means you can be sure you're really connected to the site you intended to connect with.

- It provides for user authentication as well. A secure Web site can make sure it's really dealing with you, not some cheap imitation.

- It provides privacy by using a powerful encryption technique on transmitted data.

- It provides data integrity, ensuring that the information you send arrives exactly as you sent it.

If you think about this situation for a moment, you'll realize that for SSL to work, both ends of the link—the client and the server—must run software that supports these features. If your Web browser encrypts your credit card information, for example, the server you're talking to must be able to decrypt it. Currently, SSL is supported by Netscape Communicator and all of Netscape's Web servers, which are rapidly becoming a standard for businesses on the Net.

How does SSL work? The Internet and intranets can be seen as layered sets of protocols. In Chapter 1, you learned that everything rests on TCP/IP, the protocol suite that actually divides your data into packets and ships them out to the right destination. Above this layer are application protocols such as Telnet, FTP, and HTTP. They are the support protocols for the various services available on the Net. SSL actually provides a new protocol layer, situating itself between TCP/IP and the application protocol, HTTP in this case. That way, it is not dependent on any of these other protocols to do its job. Figure 13-1 illustrates how a message you type is processed by the various protocol layers and then travels across the Net to a Web server that "unprocesses" the information.

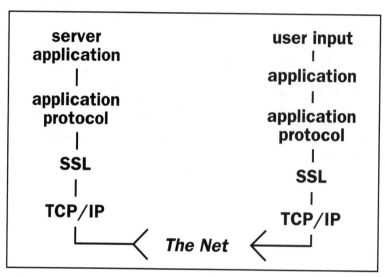

Figure 13-1: A secure message sent to a Web server.

SSL uses a powerful mechanism known as *public key encryption* for protecting data. Each secure Netscape server has its own unique pair of digital keys, which are really just long strings of random bytes. One of these keys is private and kept secret at the server site; the other is made public. When you send a message to a secure server, it is encrypted and automatically includes the public key for that site. The private key at the server end must be the one that "fits" this public key; otherwise, your data will not be decrypted and you will not be able to communicate. Since these pairs of keys are guaranteed to be unique, you can be certain that your information has reached the right destination before it is decrypted.

Can't Some Hacker Crack SSL?

Sure, hackers can break anything. The issue is just a matter of how much work it takes.

SSL uses authentication and encryption technology that was developed by RSA Data Security. The standard "export" version of Netscape Communicator, which is required by the United States government to use a weaker version of encryption than the U.S.-only version, relies on what is known as RSA's "40-bit key RC4 algorithm." Even in this weaker implementation, the security is pretty impressive. Let's say your neighbor knows you are about to transmit your credit card number. He goes outside with a ladder and a bunch of equipment and manages to capture the encrypted data from your phone line. If you're a forgiving sort of person, you should go out and warn him that it takes an average of 64 MIPS-years to break the code. If he gets a 64-MIPS computer to work around the clock on deciphering your information, he'll probably have the answer in about a year. By that time, your credit card will be maxed out anyway.

Of course, this scenario is assuming your neighbor doesn't know much about you and is trying to crack the code by trying millions of random combinations. Using various heuristics—educated guesses—the time can be greatly reduced. If you're concerned and want to use the very strongest security available, get the 128-bit U.S.-only version of Communicator. In fact, some financial services, such as Fidelity, require this stronger version for stock trading and other transactions. You can get more information on obtaining it from the Netscape home page.

Site Certificates

In conjunction with public key encryption, SSL offers another level of security called *site certification*. Here's how it works:

To operate in secure mode and use the features of SSL, anyone who sets up a Netscape server in secure mode must have requested and been sent a special digital certificate, a unique pattern of bytes that "unlocks" these features. Before issuing a certificate (which, of course, is sent encrypted), a special certifying authority makes sure that the requesting organization is "for real."

A secure server may include its site certificate along with any data it sends you, whether it's a Web page, a Netcaster channel, a Java program, or even a simple e-mail message. Data that's sent along with a digital certificate—also known as a digital signature—is called *signed* data. Based on the identity of the sender, you may choose to reject certain features of the information. For example, you may not want to grant an unknown party access to your hard drive via a signed Java applet.

A site certificate also includes the organization's public encryption key so that Communicator can automatically transmit encrypted information back to the site.

Digital certificates, in conjunction with public key encryption, help to protect you from fraud, pranks, and theft of intellectual property.

Personal Certificates

Communicator also supports *personal certificates*. They are just like site certificates, but they positively identify individuals running Communicator rather than organizations running a Netscape server. A personal certificate assures a secure Web site that you are really you. A certificate can make it unnecessary for you to type in a name and password each time you access a secure site— the Web server gets much more complete authentication information automatically from your personal certificate.

A personal certificate also enables others to send you encrypted e-mail, since your certificate includes your unique encryption key. And, of course, you can't send encrypted e-mail to others unless they've already included *their* keys in digital signatures.

Communicator allows you to have several different personal certificates. Within the next year or so, you'll even be able to obtain personal certificates that are specific to particular payment methods. You may have a Visa personal certificate, for example, as well as a MasterCard one.

You learn how to obtain personal certificates later in this chapter, in the section called "Getting a Personal Certificate."

Passwords

OK, let's say you have several personal certificates. That means you might be able to log on to a secure site without typing a special password—the software handles authentication for you. But suppose somebody else can access your machine. Since the authentication process is automatic, hasn't this whole system made online transactions less rather than more secure?

Not really. If you think that somebody else might access your machine, Communicator lets you create a personal password that you must type every time you launch the program. You can change this password as often as you like, and there is no way for another user to discover it. In fact, it is so secure that it may even cause *you* some headaches: if you forget what it is, there is no way to find out, and you have to get all new personal certificates!

Security Alerts

Most of Communicator's security features are set into motion automatically. For example, once you fill in credit card information and click the Submit button in a form from a secure server, your information is automatically encrypted as it makes its way across the Net. Because of this automation, you must know when you are in fact communicating with a secure server and when you're not. Fortunately, Communicator lets you know with special messages called *alerts*. By default, Communicator lets you know when you're in the following situations:

- You're entering an encrypted site.
- You're leaving an encrypted site.
- You're viewing a page that includes a mix of encrypted and unencrypted data.
- You're about to send unencrypted information to a site.

In addition, Communicator warns you when you're about to download a Java applet or JavaScript code that uses your system resources in any way that may compromise your security. You may have already seen one of these warnings, or Java Security alerts, if you've run Communicator's Netcaster component. Communicator can even warn you before you download a signed plug-in or before a server tries to store any information in the form of "cookies" on your machine.

TIP

Cookies are pieces of system or configuration information transmitted between a Web server and the browser software and then stored on the client machine. Cookies enable a Web page to adjust its display or other configuration options for particular clients that connect, but they may also be used to trace exactly what documents a user accesses on the site. In other words, they can be useful in developing a "click profile" of a user, and some people feel this capability is an invasion of privacy. To change your cookie settings—that is, to disable them or activate an alert when they are sent to your machine—select Preferences from the Edit menu of any Communicator component and then click the Advanced category. These options are also covered in Chapter 3, in the section called "Advanced Preferences."

Firewalls & Proxies

You've probably read horror stories about hackers who get online only to sabotage or destroy data. As the new information technologies mature, acts like these probably won't have the same thrill they used to, but cyber-criminals will never disappear completely. For this reason, businesses, universities, government agencies, and other sites that have sensitive data on their networks are forced to think of ways to keep these types of users away. Firewalls are software and hardware solutions that provide a layer or several layers of protection between the Internet and a local network. These layers are designed to keep the bad guys out, but they also restrict users within a network from getting out on the Internet directly. For this reason, *proxy gateways,* or simply *proxies,* were created to enable users to work through firewalls and access the outside world.

Proxies are security features deployed by many businesses. System administrators set up proxy gateways so that users on an intranet or other LAN are not actually connected directly to the Internet. Instead, any Internet data they send or receive is handled by the proxy computer, which passes the information on. The proxy may be completely transparent, allowing all data in and out of the organization and simply monitoring activity, or it may be part of a firewall that restricts both inbound and outbound access in various ways. The proxy settings in Netscape Communicator allow the program to pass on a network request to an outside agent through a firewall, which performs the request for Communicator. The proxy agent then returns any Internet information to Communicator.

When you use a Communicator component through a proxy gateway, you might think you're on the Internet even though you really aren't. Proxy gateways are implemented based on the type of service in use, such as FTP, Gopher, WAIS, news, and HTTP (the World Wide Web). Each URL access method can send its requests to a different proxy.

How does this system work? Typically, when you try to access a particular kind of network server, you specify its address—or click a link that includes the address. Communicator then sends a request to the server using a particular software *port number* associated with that kind of network service. For example, the port usually associated with FTP is 21, so Communicator sends messages to an FTP server specifying port 21. The server then knows that FTP is the service required. With a proxy server in use, though, Communicator does not send its request or a standard port number directly to the actual

Internet server. Instead, it sends its request to the proxy server's address with a special port number that's unique to the proxy server itself. The proxy server then sends the request on to the appropriate Internet server, using the usual port number for that service.

Configuring Proxy Settings

Before configuring proxy settings, your first task is to ask your system administrator whether a proxy is even necessary or available. If you're running Communicator on an internal network from behind a firewall, you need to know the URL of the file your network uses for automatic proxy configuration. Or if your system administrator has not enabled automatic configuration, you need the proxy port numbers for each network service supported by your proxy server. This data is necessary for filling out the Proxies category in Communicator's Preferences. To get to the correct dialog box, click Preferences in the Edit menu of any Communicator component. Then expand the Advanced category by double-clicking it and select Proxies. The Proxies page appears, as shown in Figure 13-2.

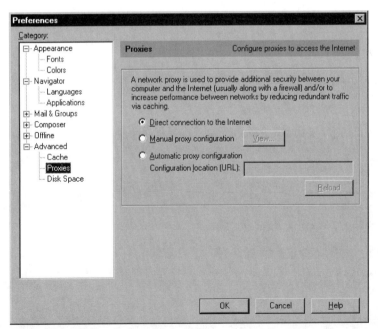

Figure 13-2: The Proxies page.

The Proxies page includes the following items:

- **Direct connection to the Internet**. Configures Netscape Communicator to run without a proxy. This option is the default setting.

- **Manual proxy configuration**. Allows the most flexible configuration of proxy gateways for each type of URL. If you want to configure the proxy settings yourself, use this option, as described in the section "Configuring a Proxy Manually."

- **Automatic proxy configuration**. Instructs Netscape Communicator to configure your proxies automatically based on a configuration file designed expressly for your proxy server. Click the radio button, and then provide the file's URL in the Configuration location (URL) field.

Configuring a Proxy Manually

To set a proxy using the Manual proxy configuration choice, follow these steps:

1. While you're still in the Proxies page, click the Manual proxy configuration radio button.

2. Click the View button to display the Manual Proxy Configuration dialog box, as shown in Figure 13-3.

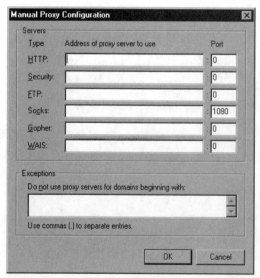

Figure 13-3: The Manual Proxy Configuration dialog box.

- The long list of proxies should be blank unless already configured by your network administrator. The Port settings will all have zeros in them, with the exception of the Socks host port, which should read 1080. If you see some other data already listed, stop and ask someone whether you're using the proper settings. If so, you're done.

3. Fill in each of the proxy fields with the following information:

   - **HTTP**. Enter the Internet address of the system running the proxy software and the port number for HTTP protocol access. When these addresses are set correctly, you'll be able to access Web pages and sites.

   - **Security**. Enter the information for your Secure Sockets Layer (SSL) protocol resource.

   - **FTP**. Enter the Internet address of the system running the proxy software and the port number for FTP protocol access. When these addresses are set correctly, you'll be able to access anonymous FTP sites.

   - **Socks**. If your network uses a Socks Host gateway as part of a firewall, enter its Internet address here.

   - **Gopher**. Enter the Internet address of the system running the proxy software and the port number for Gopher protocol access. When these addresses are set correctly, you'll be able to access Gopher menus.

   - **WAIS**. Enter the Internet address of the system running the proxy software and the port number for WAIS protocol access. When these addresses are set correctly, you'll be able to access WAIS databases.

TIP

You can put the Internet addresses for multiple hosts in each field. If your network administrator provides you with multiple proxy addresses for each protocol, you should separate them with commas. Do not use wildcards for multiple addresses!

4. Your network may be configured to allow you to access certain sites directly, without going through a proxy. If so, enter the addresses for these sites in the Exceptions box. The format of these entries is the Internet address followed by the port number for the allowed protocol. For example, the standard port number for Gopher is 70, so to allow direct access to the Gopher server at pjames.com, you would enter **pjames.com:70**. You can specify multiple sites in the Exceptions box, separating them with commas.

> **TIP**
>
> *Unless you have a photographic memory, take this book or page with you when you talk to your site administrator. Have him or her fill out the correct addresses and ports for each setting. Then enter them yourself in your copy of Netscape Communicator. Why? Because you need to make sure all these settings are perfect before trying to use Communicator. Otherwise, you'll experience problems and won't be able to access anything on the Net. Of course, if your administrator is really on the ball, she'll have already set and locked your proxies using Mission Control so you don't have to worry about it!*

5. Click OK to save your changes.

Once you've got your proxy all set up, you should be able to connect to the Internet via your company's LAN. Give it a try by clicking the Home button. If you can't connect this way, you'll need to talk once more to your network administrator. Every network is configured a little differently, so we can't give you any easy answers here.

Now that you have a broad overview of Communicator's security features, let's see how these features work in some individual Communicator components, starting with Navigator 4.

Security in Navigator 4

The first thing to understand about security in Navigator 4 is the concept of *secure* and *insecure* Web pages. An insecure Web page is one that has not been encrypted and does not include a digital certificate assuring you of the source. A secure page is encrypted and includes a certificate. The vast majority of Web pages are insecure; there is simply no need to ensure the privacy or authenticity of most Web communications, and the security safeguards aren't worth the slight amount of extra time they would add to the transfer of the information.

> **TIP**
>
> *Netscape considers data security of utmost importance, and the Communicator development team was still busy tweaking security features as this book went to press. Consequently, you might find some very slight "holes" or inconsistencies in this chapter where option screens had not been finalized. The differences are mainly cosmetic, however, and you will be able to figure everything out very easily by following the procedures outlined here.*

If you click the Security button or the Security icon on the status line when visiting a typical Web site, you'll get information like that shown in Figure 13-4.

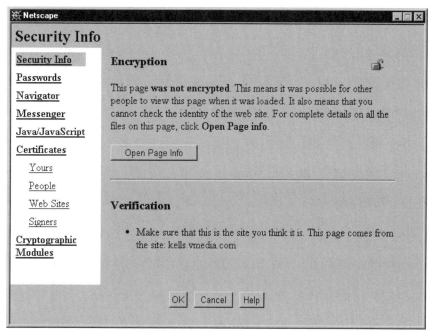

Figure 13-4: Security Info for an insecure Web page.

As you can see, Communicator has correctly identified this page as unencrypted. In addition, the Verification section of this dialog box does not indicate that a digital certificate was included with the page. But you *can* get some more information about the document. Try clicking the Open Page Info button. You will see something like Figure 13-5.

The top frame of the Document info page identifies the actual documents currently displayed in the Navigator 4 window, including the URLs for the HTML file itself and for any inline graphics. The bottom panel is composed of a miscellany of information about the files, including security information. As you select a file in the top frame, the bottom frame gives you information about that specific file.

OFFICIAL NETSCAPE COMMUNICATOR 4 PROFESSIONAL EDITION BOOK

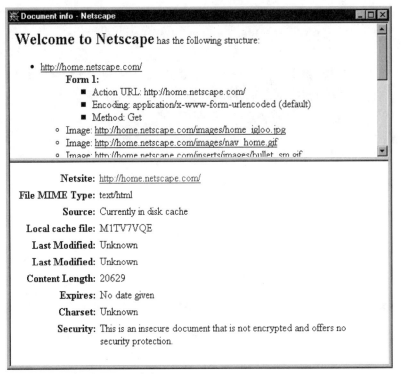

Figure 13-5: The Document info page.

Scroll through the bottom panel to view information about the file you have selected. Not all this information is directly related to security issues, but even the more general items can help you determine the authenticity of a document. Here's a list of the fields and their meanings:

■ **Netsite (or Location).** This field simply provides the URL of the file.

■ **File MIME Type.** For an HTML file, the MIME type is text/html. For graphics, it will depend on the graphic format.

■ **Source.** This field tells you how Netscape Navigator 4 is currently accessing the file. In many cases, it will have been cached to disk, and Communicator will indicate it is reading the cached version.

■ **Local cache file.** This field indicates the name of the file on your local hard drive that contains the source for the cached document.

■ **Content Length.** This field simply indicates the size of the file, if available.

■ **Expires.** This field indicates when the cache file expires, based on your

Preferences settings.

■ **Charset**. This field indicates the character set used by the document. In most cases, the Charset will be iso-8859-1, which is the technical name for ISO-Latin (the character set used for Western European languages). Obviously, if the file is a graphic, the charset will be unspecified or labeled unknown.

■ **Security**. This field indicates the type of security used for this document. In this case, it's an insecure document, so this field reads "This is an insecure document that is not encrypted and offers no security protection."

TIP

For graphics files, several additional fields include specific information about the format and resolution of the image.

And now for a totally different experience, let's visit a secure site:

1. Make sure you are connected to the Internet, either directly or through a SLIP or PPP connection with your access provider.

2. Launch Netscape Navigator 4.

3. Click your mouse inside the Netsite/Location box at the top of the window to select the URL http://home.netscape.com/.

4. Replace this URL with **https://www.att.com/**, the URL for AT&T's secure home page. (No, that's not a typo. To access documents on secure servers, you type **https** instead of **http** in the protocol section of the URL). A Security Information alert appears, as shown in Figure 13-6.

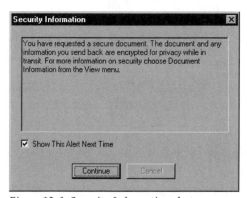

Figure 13-6: Security Information alert.

Whenever you are presented with a notification dialog box like this, you have the option of unchecking the Show This Alert Next Time check box. If you uncheck it, a corresponding check box is unchecked in the Navigator security preferences window, making it a default *not* to show the alert. You can also change this option *directly* in the Navigator security preferences window. You'll learn how to make this change in a few minutes, in the section unsurprisingly called "Navigator Security Preferences."

Note: If the site you are accessing attempts to send you several documents—for example, if it includes multiple frames—you may be presented with several of these Security Information alerts.

Once you've responded to any alerts, the AT&T page itself finally appears in the Navigator 4 window, as shown in Figure 13-7.

Since this site is secure, the Security button—as well as the Security icon in the status line—now depicts a locked padlock. Go ahead and click either the button or the icon. The Security Info page for this site appears, as shown in Figure 13-8.

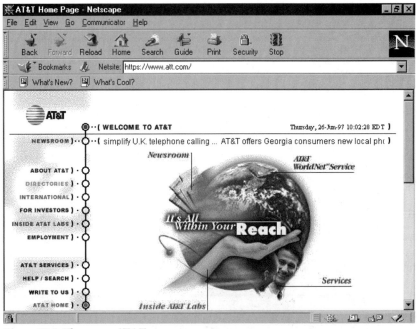

Figure 13-7: The secure AT&T page.

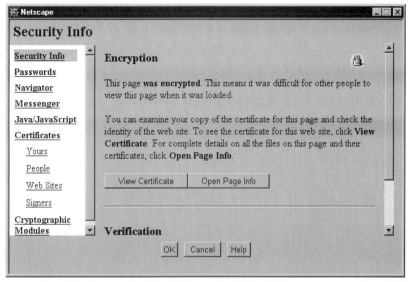

Figure 13-8: Security Info for the AT&T secure Web site.

The top portion of the page informs you that this document is encrypted and that it is "signed" with a digital security certificate. To view the contents of the certificate, click the View Certificate button. The View A Certificate window appears, as shown in Figure 13-9.

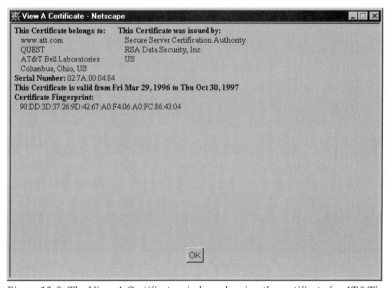

Figure 13-9: The View A Certificate window, showing the certificate for AT&T's secure site.

- **This Certificate belongs to.** The certifying authority RSA requires that each applicant for a certificate submit a registered organization name and a variety of other identifying information. Obviously, if you think you're at an AT&T site, but the owner of the Digital ID is not AT&T, you may have found a security problem.

- **This Certificate was issued by.** For now, this field should indicate that the certificate was issued by RSA. Other organizations might be involved in the certification process in the future, but if this field reads something like "Hacker d00d," you probably should not submit your credit card number.

- **Serial Number.** As you might expect, this field indicates a unique number assigned by the certifying authority.

- **This Certificate is valid from.** As an added protection, digital certificates are issued for set lengths of time. This field indicates when the current certificate expires.

- **Certificate Fingerprint.** This field indicates a special digital signature that helps assure the authority of the certificate.

You shouldn't need to access this information very often, but if you suspect a security problem, the View A Certificate page offers you ample opportunity to play digital detective.

Now click OK to return to the Security Info page, as shown earlier in Figure 13-8. Once you're there, click the Open Page Info button this time. The Document info window appears, as shown in Figure 13-10.

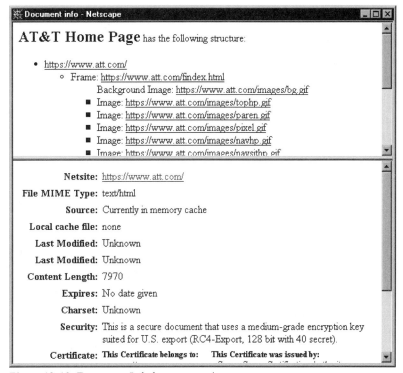

Figure 13-10: Document Info for a secure site.

This window looks pretty much like the Document info we saw earlier for an insecure site, but if you scroll down to the bottom of the bottom frame, you'll see that the Security field now indicates the type of encryption being used. In addition, a new Certificate field includes the same information you saw in the View A Certificate window, as shown in Figure 13-11. Of course, you can view this information for any file listed in the top frame. Simply click the URL to see the specific information.

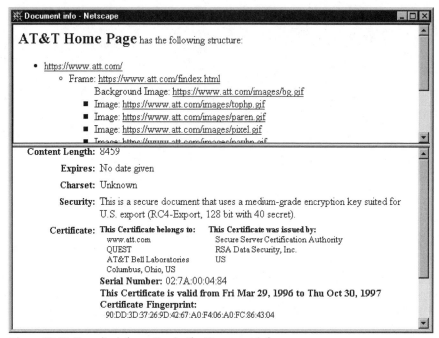

Figure 13-11: Security information in the Document info page.

Now that we've seen how Communicator's security features work at a particular Web site, let's examine some of the configuration options available to you.

Navigator 4 Security Preferences

Communicator provides a number of options that let you tailor Navigator's security features for your particular needs. For example, if you're on a small office intranet and are very familiar with all the material you access with Navigator 4, you may want to turn off some of the alerts.

To configure the Navigator 4 security preferences, follow these steps:

1. Click the Security button in any Communicator component that includes it. Optionally, click the Security icon in the status line. The Security Info page appears.

2. In the list at the left of the window, click Navigator. The Navigator security preferences window appears, as shown in Figure 13-12.

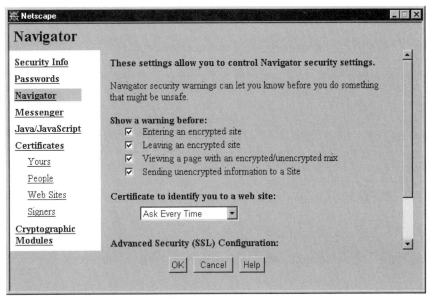

Figure 13-12: Navigator security preferences.

Earlier in the chapter, you saw that Navigator 4 pops up special security alert messages to inform you of changes in the security status of your connection. Leaving these alerts enabled is a good idea, but the top section of this dialog box lets you turn off any that you don't want to see. Here are the results of unchecking each of these boxes:

- **Entering an encrypted site.** Unchecking this box means that you will not receive notification when you are about to access a document on a secure server. If you spend a lot of time on secure servers and know what you are doing, you might want to uncheck this box.

- **Leaving an encrypted site.** Unchecking this box means that you will not be notified when you are about to *leave* a secure server and access a document that is not secure.

- **Viewing a page with an encrypted/unencrypted mix.** Unchecking this box means that you will not receive an alert when you are about to access a document that contains both secure and insecure information.

- **Sending unencrypted information to a site.** Unchecking this box means that you will not receive notification when you are about to submit information insecurely over the Net or your intranet. If you do a lot of online shopping and are concerned about credit card fraud, I would not recommend unchecking this item.

I mentioned earlier that you can obtain a digital security certificate of your own; in the section called "Getting a Personal Certificate," I'll show you how. With your own certificate, you can electronically sign your e-mail messages, assuring your recipients that it's really you. You also can use a certificate to identify yourself to Web sites that require user authentication. In this case, a digital certificate acts like a password, except that it is more secure and completely automatic. You don't need to type anything to identify yourself to the site.

I also mentioned earlier that you can have several different personal certificates, and the next option in the Navigator security preferences dialog box lets you choose how to handle this situation. The drop-down box in the middle of the page contains at least two choices:

- **Ask Every Time.** Select this option if you want Navigator to ask you which certificate to use every time a Web site requests your certificate.

- **Select Automatically.** Select this option if you want Navigator to send a certificate automatically, without asking you which one.

The rest of the drop-down list is composed of any personal certificates you've obtained and installed. You can select any one of them from the list to designate it as the certificate that's sent whenever an identifying certificate is required.

The bottom section of the Navigator security preferences dialog box lets you check which versions of SSL you want to use. It also lets you configure them to use a variety of different encryption algorithms. Unless you know what you're doing and have very specific reasons for disallowing any of the protocols or encryption types, you should *leave these settings alone!*

Note: SSL 3 has several advantages over earlier implementations. Besides being more efficient, it includes an extra encryption mechanism, better digital certificate management, and better support for hardware devices.

Certificates You've Accepted

Once you've accepted a certificate from a Web site, it is saved on your system. Communicator lists all the certificates you've accepted and lets you view their details even when you're not connected to the particular site. You can also tell Navigator what action to take when it encounters another document originating from the holder of any one of the certificates you've collected. For example, you might want to *reject* any pages from the holder of a particular certificate.

Follow these steps to view certificates you've accepted from Web sites:

1. Click the Security button or Security icon in a Communicator component. The Security Info page appears.

2. In the list on the left, click Web Sites, under the Certificates category. The Web Sites' Certificates dialog box appears.

After selecting a particular certificate from the list, you can use the buttons to delete it from your system, verify it (determine whether it is still a valid certificate or whether it has expired), or edit the actions Navigator takes when you are sent a page from the holder of this certificate.

Certificate Signers (Certifying Authorities)

Security certificates are granted to Web sites—as well as to individuals—by special certifying authorities or *signers*. These authorities can be compared to notaries public—they check the identity of the applicant and then assure that the digital certificate they assign is unique. You can instruct Navigator 4, as well as other Communicator components, to react in various ways to digitally signed information based on the identity of the certificate's signer. And guess how you know the identity of these certifying authorities? That's right, they have certificates too!

To view signers' certificates, follow these steps:

1. Click the Security button or Security icon in a Communicator component. The Security Info page appears.

2. In the list on the left, click Signers, under the Certificates category. The Certificate Signers' Certificates dialog box appears, as shown in Figure 13-13.

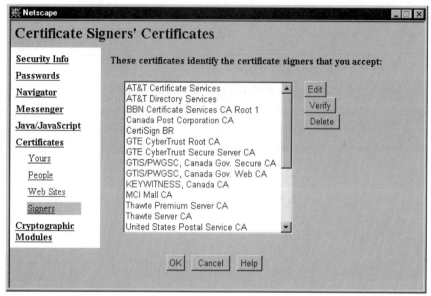

Figure 13-13: The Certificate Signers' Certificates dialog box.

3. Select a certificate from the list.

4. To delete the selected certificate, click Delete. To verify it (determine whether it has expired), click Verify. To edit the action Communicator takes when it encounters a certificate signed by the selected certifying authority, click Edit. The Edit A Certification Authority dialog box appears, as shown in Figure 13-14.

Check boxes in this dialog box let you do the following:

■ **Accept this Certificate Authority for Certifying network sites.** Checking this check box means that you will not automatically reject Web site certificates signed by this certifying authority.

■ **Accept this Certificate Authority for Certifying e-mail users.** Checking this check box means that you will not automatically reject certificates included with e-mail if they are signed by this authority. (See the next section called "E-mail Security (S/MIME).")

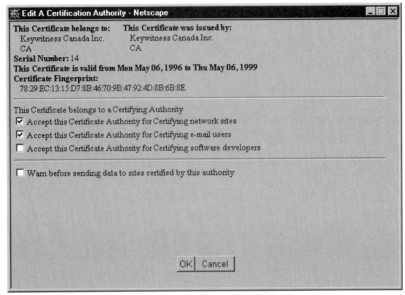

Figure 13-14: The Edit A Certification Authority dialog box.

- ■ **Accept this Certificate Authority for Certifying software developers.**
  Checking this check box means that you will not automatically reject
  certificates included with Java objects, plug-ins, and software upgrades if
  they are signed by this authority. (See the section called "Java &
  JavaScript Security" later in this chapter.)

- ■ **Warn before sending data to sites certified by this authority.** If you
  check this check box, Communicator will pop up an alert before you
  send any data (for example, in a form) to a site whose certificate is signed
  by this certifying authority.

Now that you've seen some of Communicator's security features that are
specific to Web sites, let's move on to an area where just about everybody
cares about privacy: e-mail.

E-mail Security (S/MIME)

As we start using e-mail for financial transactions and other sensitive communications, the privacy of our messages becomes increasingly important.

Communicator's Messenger and Discussion Group components support a
standard known as S/MIME (Secure MIME) for digitally signed and encrypted e-mail messages. S/MIME can assure you that messages you send and

receive are authentic and have not been read anywhere between their point of origin and their final destination. In this section, I'll cover the basic features of S/MIME as implemented in Messenger.

TIP

> *If your incoming e-mail server is an IMAP server (rather than POP3), it may support encrypted connections, automatically encrypting information it sends you. If your network administrator has told you that this is the case, select Preferences from Messenger's Edit menu and then click the Mail Server category. Check the very last check box, "Server supports encrypted connections (SSL)," in the Mail Server dialog box.*

Let's start with sending signed and encrypted messages.

Sending Signed & Encrypted Messages

Messenger lets you send *signed messages* that include a digital security certificate assuring the recipient that the message did in fact come from you, or at least from somebody sitting at your computer. Like site certificates, personal digital security certificates are issued by special certifying organizations. Getting a personal security certificate can be compared with getting a passport from the Post Office, except that it is a "cyber-passport" and you can obtain one electronically, using Netscape Communicator, of course. Later in this chapter, in the section called "Getting a Personal Certificate," I'll show you how to obtain a new personal security certificate, but for now let's assume you already have one. Here's how you attach it to your e-mail:

1. Follow the steps outlined in Chapter 5 for creating a new e-mail message.

2. In the Composition window, click the Sending Options tab, as shown in Figure 13-15.

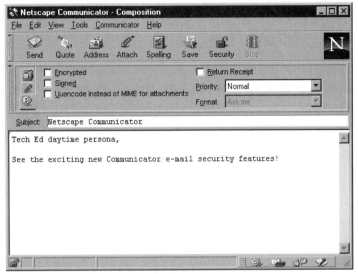

Figure 13-15: The Sending Options tab.

3. Check the check box labeled Signed.

4. Send your message by clicking the Send button.

TIP

After you check the Signed check box, a signature tag appears as part of the icon on the Security button.

That's it! And what does the recipient see when he or she looks at a signed message? I'll cover that information in the section called "Receiving Signed & Encrypted Messages," but for now let's move on to sending encrypted messages.

As you learned earlier, encrypted messages are scrambled using a special *algorithm*, or formula, so that they cannot normally be read at any point between your computer and your recipient's computer. In encrypting your message, Messenger uses a key that's part of your recipient's digital security certificate—that's how your recipient can *de*crypt it at the other end. Yes, you have to have received a signed message from an individual before you can send that individual an encrypted message. You do not necessarily need your *own* digital certificate to send encrypted e-mail, but without one nobody will be able to send *you* encrypted messages.

Getting a Recipients' Certificate from a Directory Server

Your recipient may have added his or her digital certificate to an LDAP directory server on your intranet—or even to a large public directory on the Net. If that is the case, you can obtain the certificate—and send encrypted e-mail—without already having received a message signed by your recipient. Here's how:

1. In Messenger, click the Security button or the Security icon on the status line.

2. On the left side of the Security Info page, select People under the Certificates category. The Other People's Certificates dialog box appears.

3. Click the Search Directory button. In the next dialog box that appears, select a directory server from the drop-down list, type in the e-mail address of the person whose certificate you want, and click the Search button. After a few moments, a Search Results dialog box appears listing any matches.

4. To save any certificates that were found, click OK.
   You can now send encrypted e-mail to your recipient.

To send an encrypted message, follow these steps:

1. Follow the steps outlined in Chapter 5 for creating a new e-mail message.

2. In the Composition window, click the Sending Options tab, as shown earlier in Figure 13-15.

3. Check the check box labeled Encrypted.

4. Send your message by clicking the Send button.

TIP

After you check the Encrypted check box, the padlock icon on the Security button appears locked rather than open.

Receiving Signed & Encrypted Messages

What happens when you receive a signed and/or encrypted message? Check out Figure 13-16:

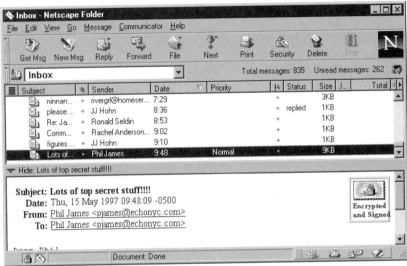

Figure 13-16: A signed and encrypted message selected in Messenger.

The Messenger window looks different in several ways:

- The Security button now depicts a locked padlock (indicating an encrypted message) with a tag hanging from it (indicating that it's also a signed message).
- The status line padlock is now locked, and the "signed" icon appears to its right.
- Just to the right of the usual headers, the message itself contains a special "Encrypted and Signed" icon.

TIP

Remember, signing and encryption are related but independent S/MIME features. You may receive messages that are just encrypted, or just signed. In these cases, the icon will, of course, be slightly different.

The whole idea of signed messages is that you can verify the identity of the sender. Obviously, the mere presence of these new icons doesn't necessarily give you the assurance you need. When Immigration agents ask you to verify your identity, they usually want to see a bit more than your passport's blue and gold cover. Well, go ahead and click the new icon within the message, or the Security button, or the padlock icon on the status line. Any one of these actions has the same result: it opens up the message sender's electronic passport. A new Security Info window appears, providing detailed security information, as shown in Figure 13-17.

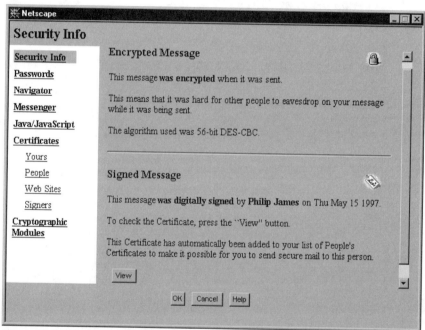

Figure 13 17: The Security Info for a signed and encrypted e-mail message.

To see more identifying information about the message sender, simply click the View button. The details of the individual's security certificate appear in a new window, as shown in Figure 13-18.

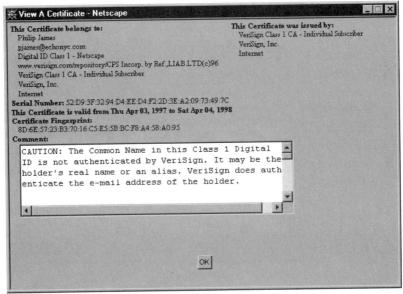

Figure 13-18: The View A Certificate window.

Note: Several classes of personal digital certificates are available, graded (and priced) according to how positively they identify an individual or organization. A Class 1 certificate does not positively identify the individual who holds it—the certifying authority has not done any background work to match the stated name with the person applying for the certificate. In fact, you can even get a Class 1 certificate using an alias or nickname instead of your real name. Class 2 certificates, on the other hand, require positive identification using a real name. The View A Certificate page tells you what class certificate this is.

Click OK after you've finished viewing the sender's security certificate. Now that you've received the security certificate, you can send encrypted e-mail to this individual.

Messenger Security Preferences

Back in the Security Info window, as shown in Figure 13-17, click the Messenger category at the left side. A new dialog box appears, as shown in Figure 13-19.

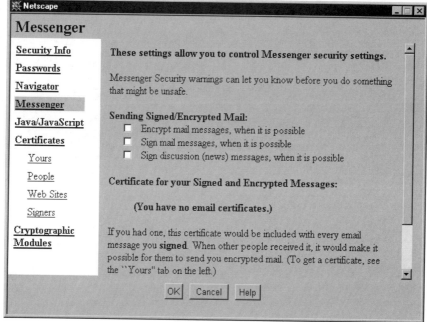

Figure 13-19: Messenger security preferences.

By checking the respective check boxes, you can activate the following options:

- **Encrypt mail messages, when it is possible.** If you check this check box, Messenger will encrypt all outgoing messages as long as you already have a digital security certificate for the recipient.

- **Sign mail messages, when it is possible.** If you check this check box, Messenger will digitally sign all outgoing messages as long as you already have a *personal* (your own) digital security certificate.

- **Sign discussion (news) messages, when it is possible.** If you check this check box, Messenger will digitally sign all outgoing discussion group messages (see Chapter 6) as long as you already have a personal digital security certificate.

In the drop-down list near the center of this window, you can choose which personal digital certificate you want to use for your encrypted mail. (You may have several different digital certificates from different certifying authorities.)

As you already know, other individuals can't send you encrypted mail unless they have already received your personal certificate, which contains the special encryption key that will be used to encrypt messages in a way that only you can decrypt. Typically, your recipients will have your certificate because you've sent them signed messages. But you can also make your certificate available by publishing it as part of your identifying information (e-mail address, and so on) on an LDAP directory server on your intranet or even on the Net itself. To do so, click the Send Certificate to Directory button. Then select a directory from the drop-down list that appears, and click the OK button. Now anyone who accesses you by means of this directory will be able to send you encrypted e-mail.

At the bottom of the page, a button lets you select what S/MIME ciphers (encryption algorithms) to use. Covering the specifics of different ciphers is beyond the scope of this book, but please don't play around with this option unless you really know what you're doing!

Since I keep mentioning personal security certificates, maybe it's time to go get one.

Getting a Personal Certificate

A personal certificate enhances your online experience in various ways:

- It lets you digitally sign e-mail messages so that others can be assured of your identity.

- It lets you receive encrypted messages.

- It can serve as an electronic passport, automatically identifying you to private or secure Web sites. At many of these sites, you won't need to type a username or password as long as you have a personal certificate.

OK, now let's get one!

1. Make sure you're connected to the Net.

2. Launch Communicator, and click the Security button or Security icon. The Security Info page appears.

3. On the left side of the page, click Yours under the Certificates category. The Your Certificates dialog box appears, as shown in Figure 13-20.

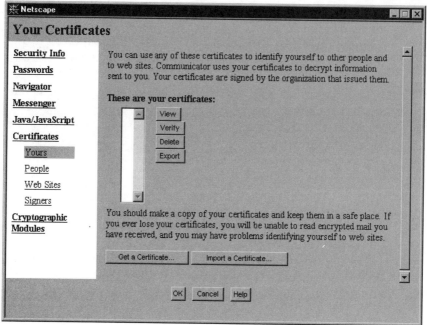

Figure 13-20: Your Certificates.

4. To obtain a new personal security certificate, click the Get a Certificate button. Netscape's Client Certification page appears in a Navigator 4 window, as shown in Figure 13-21.

5. Read the page and then click a link to one of the certifying authorities listed. VeriSign is the best known provider of individual certificates, so you might want to click that link.

Once you've reached the home page of a certifying authority, follow all the directions for obtaining a certificate (sometimes called a digital ID) very carefully. They can be complex! Since the procedure will vary depending on what class certificate you want, I'm not going to go into the details here. Prices for different kinds of certificates vary as well, so you might want to shop around.

Toward the end of the process of obtaining and installing your new certificate, you will be given the opportunity to make a copy of it. This is something you should definitely do! If something goes wrong with your software, and you have to do a complete reinstall, you need to be able to retrieve your certificate.

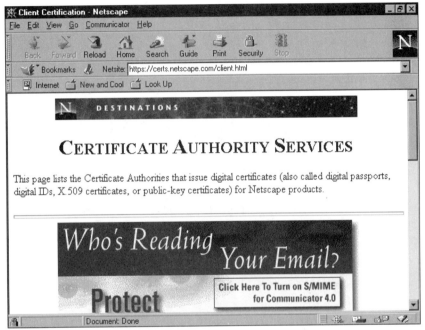

Figure 13-21: The Client Certification page.

Figure 13-22 shows what the Your Certificates dialog box looks like once you've installed a new personal certificate.

OFFICIAL NETSCAPE COMMUNICATOR 4 PROFESSIONAL EDITION BOOK

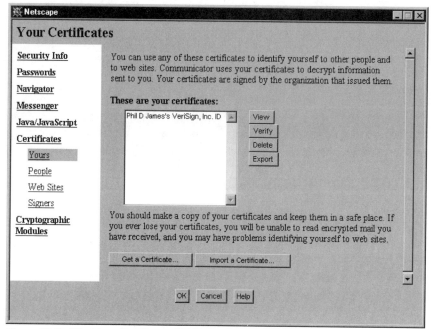

Figure 13-22: The Your Certificates dialog box.

Now you can use the buttons to the right of the certificate list to view your certificate, to verify it (make sure it has not expired), to delete it, or to export it (copy it to a file for safekeeping). Once you've exported a certificate, you can always reinstall it in Communicator using the Import a Certificate button at the bottom of this dialog box.

You've got your own personal certificate now—maybe even a few of them. What's to keep somebody from walking over to your machine and sending all kinds of interesting messages using your certificate? Passwords come in handy at this point.

Passwords

Once you have a personal certificate, you might want to protect it from unauthorized use with a password. To do so, follow these directions:

1. Once again, click the Security button or Security icon.

2. At the left side of the Security Info page, click Passwords. The Passwords dialog box appears, as shown in Figure 13-23.

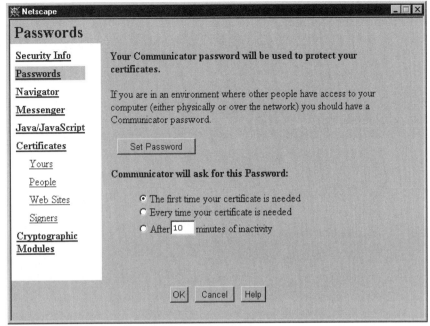

Figure 13-23: The Passwords dialog box.

3. Select one of the Communicator will ask for this Password options:

■ Select "The first time your certificate is needed" if you want Communicator to ask you for your password only once per session, the first time you need to use it for signed e-mail or when it is requested by a Web site.

■ Select "Every time your certificate is needed" if you want Navigator to ask for your password each time it transmits your personal certificate information.

■ Select "After 10 minutes of inactivity" if you want Navigator to ask you for your password after 10 minutes of idle time. You can also change the number of minutes if you want.

4. To actually set your password, click the Set Password button. The Setting Up Your Communicator Password dialog box appears, as shown in Figure 13-24.

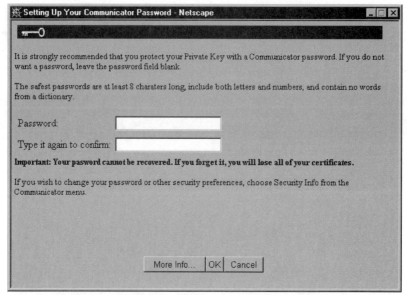

Figure 13-24: The Setting Up Your Communicator Password dialog box.

5. Type in your new password and click OK. You are returned to the Passwords dialog box.

To change your password at any point, return to the Passwords dialog box and click Set Password again. Then fill out the Change Password dialog box that appears. To eliminate your password entirely and work without one, leave the New Password field blank.

We have only a few more security issues left to discuss. By far the most important of these is how Communicator deals with Java and JavaScript.

TIP

You may find that you cannot run Java or JavaScript. That's because your network administrator has the option of turning off Java and JavaScript capabilities in your copy of Communicator as a security precaution.

Java & JavaScript Security

As you have learned in various chapters throughout this book, Java is a programming language that extends Communicator's capabilities and provides new multimedia elements or even entire interfaces. Java programs, or applets, are referenced in Web pages or channels. They may be downloaded automatically by Communicator and then run locally on your machine. Because you are in effect running a new program that you know nothing about, Java may in rare cases create havoc on your system or pose security risks.

JavaScript is a simpler language than Java, and it has more built-in security. It is used for lots of small "special effects" within the browser window, things like scrolling marquees and kiosk mode. In spite of its additional security, you might still have some concerns in highly sensitive situations.

To disable Java or JavaScript in Communicator:

1. Select Preferences from the Edit menu of any Communicator component.

2. From the category list that appears on the left, select Advanced. The Advanced preferences dialog box appears, as shown in Figure 13-25.

3. To disable Java, uncheck the Enable Java check box.

4. To disable JavaScript, uncheck the Enable JavaScript check box.

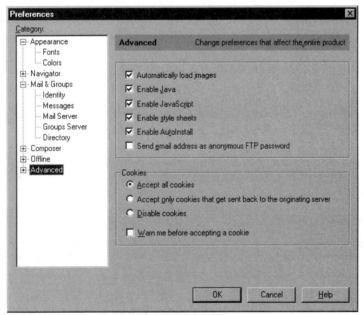

Figure 13-25: Advanced preferences.

TIP

If you disable Java, you will not be able to run Netcaster!

Other Advanced Options

The Advanced preferences dialog box also includes several other options related to security:

- **Enable style sheets.** Style sheets are collections of formatting and layout information that may be stored for reuse by multiple Web pages. In most cases, you should leave this item checked.

- **Enable AutoInstall.** Communicator includes an exciting new feature whereby new plug-ins (see Chapters 7 and 10), upgrades, or other extensions to the program may be installed automatically. You don't need to request or install the software yourself.

Once you've approved an electronic security certificate that appears on your screen identifying the source of the software, the files simply download, unpack their virtual bags, and make themselves at home on your computer. A typical example: Navigator encounters a multimedia file that requires a special plug-in to display properly. You are asked to approve the installation of the new plug-in, which then installs itself automatically on your system. Within minutes or even seconds, the multimedia file is displayed correctly in the browser window. In cases in which using this feature imposes a security risk, you may want to uncheck this check box.

- **Send e-mail address as anonymous FTP password.** When you log on to anonymous FTP sites to browse and download files (see Chapter 8), the convention is to send your e-mail address as the password. But you may not want to spread your e-mail address around. In most cases, you should not check this box; Navigator will generate a password for you.

The bottom section of this window deals with *cookies* and whether you want Navigator to accept them. Cookies, in this case, are bits of information that a Web site stores on your own hard drive. This capability enables the site to "remember," from session to session, information that's specific to your use of the site. For example, you may have chosen a particular color configuration on the site or a category of information that you want to access each time. Cookies enable Web page designers to do things that would be very clumsy otherwise, but not everybody likes the idea of them. They may be used, for example, to provide advertisers and other collectors of demographics with information about the trail of pages at their site you have visited.

This dialog box lets you deal with cookies in one of three ways. You can accept them; you can accept them only if the information they contain is sent back to the originating Web site, not to some other URL; or you can reject them.

Signed Java and JavaScript

Typically, Java applets that are downloaded to your machine are written in a subset of the Java language that includes several security precautions. For instance, applets can't perform most file system access or file I/O routines. And JavaScript, as you learned in Chapter 10, is even more restrictive in terms of security.

There may be times, though, when you want to grant a Java applet more access to your system. You may want a Java applet at work to be able to update certain data files stored on your hard drive, or you may want to use Communicator's Java-based Netcaster component, which needs to store channel information on your system.

For both tightening and loosening security, Communicator supports what are known as *signed Java* applets and *signed JavaScript*. A signed Java applet is one that will not be downloaded to your system until you approve a security certificate that positively identifies the sender. Similarly, signed JavaScript will not be executed without your approval. If the Java applet or JavaScript code performs any unusual function that could compromise security, you will be asked to approve this action as well. A special security alert asks you to approve a digital certificate and to allow a specific kind of access to your system. Let's say an applet needs to read files from your hard drive. In this case, the alert will let you select among the following options:

- To view the details of the digital certificate—in other words to get more information about the organization or individual distributing this Java applet—click the View Certificate button.

- To view more information about the special access this Java applet is requesting, select the action from the list and click the Details button.

- To grant this specific access for this *one Communicator session*, select the Grant button.

- To grant this specific access for any applets from this same distributor, check the "Remember this decision. . ." check box at the bottom of the page before clicking Grant. In this case, the digital certificate is saved to your system.

- To deny the specifically requested privileges, click Deny. The Java applet will not be downloaded to your system.

When you have selected the appropriate choices, click OK. Assuming you have allowed the specific access to your system, the Java applet will now "do its thing."

Let's take a closer look at what you get when you click the Details button. Figure 13-26 shows a typical Java Security's Target Details window that appears.

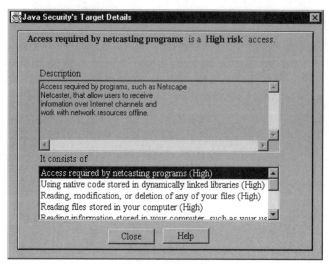

Figure 13-26: A Java Security's Target Details window.

As you can see, this dialog box lists exactly what access privileges the application is requesting. It's a good idea to take a look here before clicking Grant.

What if you want to change these access privileges later? Assuming you've checked the "Remember this decision..." check box before clicking Grant, you can adjust the privileges allowed to Java applets on a certificate-by-certificate basis at any time. To adjust the Java privileges for a particular certificate you've already received:

1. Click the Security button or the Security icon at the left of the status line in any Communicator component.

2. From the list on the left, select Java/JavaScript. The Java/JavaScript dialog box appears, as shown in Figure 13-27.

The scrolling list includes all the security certificates that you've already approved, presumably when launching a new signed Java applet. If you select a certificate from the list, you can then use the buttons on the right to:

- **View Certificate.** Click this button for a detailed view of the certificate.

- **Remove.** Click this button to remove the certificate from the list. Java applets from this point of origin will no longer be downloaded and executed automatically on your computer. Instead, you will be presented again with the option of approving a digital certificate.

- **Edit Privileges.** Select a certificate from the list and then click this button for the Edit Privileges page, as shown in Figure 13-28.

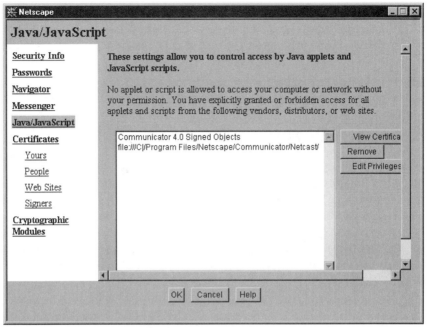

Figure 13-27: Java/JavaScript dialog box.

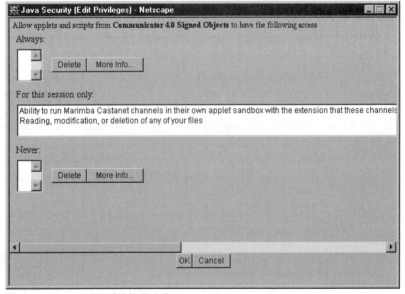

Figure 13-28: A typical Edit Privileges page.

In this dialog box you can choose which specific privileges you want to grant for this session only or for any future sessions. You may also be able to deny specific privileges.

Signed Plug-ins and Upgrades

With Communicator, plug-ins and even upgrades to the program itself may be installed automatically. Simply click a link to start the upgrade process—or, in the case of a Netcaster channel that's dedicated to upgrading your software, you may not even have to do *anything*!

Obviously, this kind of automation is a great convenience, but it imposes certain security risks. When you enhance Communicator with plug-ins or automatically upgrade a piece of software, you want to be sure you're getting the new code from the appropriate vendor or distributor rather than from Hackers 'R Us. For this reason, many automated plug-ins and upgrades are digitally signed, just like Java objects. Prior to allowing any modification of your software, you may be asked to agree to a license and to approve the installation of a particular plug-in or upgrade. Once you approve the installation, the installation proceeds. Or, if you already have a certificate from the vendor or distributor, the plug-in or upgrade may be installed automatically right away.

The Most Powerful Security: Common Sense

There is no question that Netscape Communicator provides very powerful protection from theft, fraud, and abuse of sensitive electronic information. I applaud Netscape for working so diligently towards making online commerce a safe and sensible option. I wouldn't be surprised if electronic transactions become the norm a few years from now. SSL and digital certification are paving the way for this new way of doing business.

But you already possess an even more powerful security tool: your common sense. I hate to get Forrest Gumpish on you, but here are a few things your mama should have always said:

■ If you don't know anything about a company, don't send it your money. If you need more information, what better place for doing the research than the Net?

■ Don't send sensitive information if the document doesn't include an e-mail address or a phone number you can use to get back in touch if you experience problems.

- Expect some sort of acknowledgment of any online transaction. If you don't receive one, get in touch with the company right away.
- Read the fine font.
- Disorganized Web pages could indicate sloppy business practices as well.
- If something looks like a scam, it just may *be* a scam.

Add these truisms to SSL, and you've got *real* security.

Moving On

By this time, we've covered most of the features of Netscape Communicator, and you're well on your way to becoming a savvy veteran of the Net or your office intranet. (With the accelerated sense of history imposed by electronic media, becoming a savvy veteran of anything takes only a week or two.)

Since Communicator Professional is such a full-featured suite, chances are it provides all the communications power you need. But so far all we've really covered are the regular components of Communicator. For the rest of the book we're going to be getting into what makes Professional great—how it can straighten out your schedule and make it easier to keep your Communicator software updated. We'll begin that journey with the next chapter, which explains the scheduling software Communicator.

CHAPTER 14

An Overview of Mission Control

O kay, here's the scenario. You're the network administrator of a medium-sized company. Your intranet is accessed by 200 people, all running Communicator. Most of your technical support hours are spent helping people who accidentally messed up their configurations, can't find the company home page, accidentally renamed their mail and news servers, or need help installing Communicator.

What you need—what would really make your job easier—is a tool that allows you to make configuration changes to Communicator, to lock preferences in Communicator so they can't be changed, and to package additions to Communicator and distribute them without using "sneaker net."

The solution you're looking for is called Mission Control.

TIP

Mission Control is not, strictly speaking, a part of the Communicator suite. Instead, it's purchased separately as a developer tool for network administrators. If you're an end user, you don't have to worry about the problems and solutions outlined in the next three chapters. For more information on acquiring Mission Control, please check out Netscape's home page at http://www.netscape.com.

You might have heard about Mission Control when it was called the Administration Kit. Despite the name change, its purpose is still the same: to give you a way to centrally administer changes and additions to Communicator. It also gives you a way to lock changes to Communicator so that users can't change preferences and render their copies of Communicator inoperable.

In this chapter we'll take a look at the things Mission Control can do for you, the three components that make up Mission Control, and the three questions you should consider before firing up Mission Control.

> **TIP**
>
> *Does your computer have what it takes to run Mission Control? In order to run the program, you'll need an installed version of Communicator Professional, a text editor for editing configuration files (Notepad will work fine), and at least 16MB of RAM on your computer. If you want to use the Install Builder application of Mission Control, you'll have to have Windows 95 or Windows NT.*

How Mission Control Makes Your Job Easier

As a network administrator, a significant portion of your day can be spent doing technical support, voluntary or not. Someone snags you in the hallway and asks you the URL for the company's human resources page. Someone calls you while you're eating lunch at your desk and asks how they can set their signature file. You receive a new plug-in that you want to distribute to all your users—by tomorrow at noon.

And this is on a good day.

Mission Control centralizes these kinds of chores and makes them easier to handle. It gives you more control over the configuration of Communicator, and it gives you the means to distribute and install additions to Communicator without wearing out your shoes or your patience.

Let's take a look at all the things Mission Control can do to make your job easier.

Mission Control Saves Tech Support Time & Effort

Mission Control takes some of the tedium out of your tech support difficulties by making it possible to avoid some of the basic configuration problems and technical issues caused by well-meaning patrons. For example, you can preset server information, cache allowances, and technical information in Communicator's preferences and lock them so they can't be changed.

Mission Control also gives you the opportunity to get your patrons little help desks of their own. You can add items to the help menu and other Communicator menus that can assist your patron with matters specific to your intranet. For example, you could add the departmental intranet pages to the help menu and never have to give that information out again to anyone who forgot it (or wrote it down and lost the paper).

Tired of the "sneaker net" that forces you to go to each individual computer and install a new Communicator plug-in? Maybe instead you e-mailed your patrons about the new software and asked them to install it, and maybe half or two-thirds of them did. With Communicator Professional's AutoAdmin and Mission Control, you can create packages of plug-ins or new applications and distribute them via Communicator automatically.

Mission Control Gives You More Control Over Security

Your concern might be less with tech support and more with security. Mission Control gives you access to the security aspects of Communicator with the ability to set and lock different security preferences. Do you have security concerns with enabling Java or JavaScript? You can disable it through Mission Control. Do you want your patrons to enter their e-mail passwords every time they access Messenger, instead of having Messenger remember the password? You can set that too. You can even set whether or not Communicator will accept "cookies"—the text strings used by some Web servers to track the interests and preferences of users.

Mission Control Lets You Set a Standard of Usage

Perhaps many of the patrons on your intranet use Communicator to interact with the "outside world." It might be for sales, technical support, or something else, but you want to maintain a standard of usage for your patrons— you want all their communications to have the same "look."

This can be done with Mission Control. You can set message headers, the signature for each patron (whether or not they attach address cards to their outgoing correspondence) and how messages and postings are displayed in Messenger and Collabra. Users' outgoing correspondence can have a standard signature file, with standard headers identifying the correspondent.

Now that you've gotten an idea of what Mission Control can do to make your job easier, let's take a look at the three applications that make up Mission Control.

Mission Control's Three Components

Mission Control consists of three components: the Configuration Editor, the JAR Packager, and the Installation Builder. Each of the components perform a specific task of customizing, packaging, or preparation for distribution. Here's how they break down.

TIP

This is an overview chapter, and as such we're not going to get into the "guts" of each application, but we will do that in the next two chapters.

The Configuration Editor

The Configuration Editor is an HTML-based way to set configuration settings for Communicator and its components. Using the Configuration Editor, you can set preferences and lock them so that they cannot be changed by the user. You can also use the editor to set Communicator's preferences to update automatically from a central preferences file.

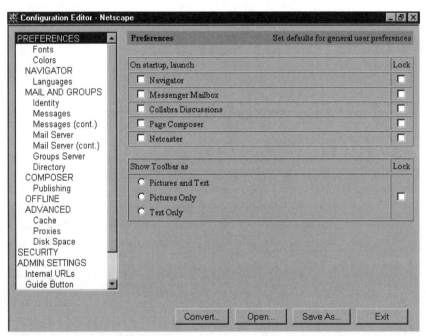

Figure 14-1: The Configuration Editor.

The Configuration Editor is more than the HTML interface to Communicator's preferences, however. You can also edit the text file produced by the Configuration Editor with JavaScript, which gives you even more control over Communicator's customization. Don't sweat it if you're not a JavaScript expert—the Configuration Editor includes sample files with

JavaScript code for the manual changes you're likely to make. There are also pointers available to online resources for learning and using JavaScript.

The Configuration Editor is ideal for creating Communicator configurations for your intranet. But distributing new things for Communicator to use— applications and plug-ins, for example—is the function of the JAR Packager.

JAR Packager

JAR stands for "Java Archive." The JAR Packager is a Java applet that allows you to "package" files—be they plug-ins, Communicator components, or other files—and distribute them automatically to the users of your intranet.

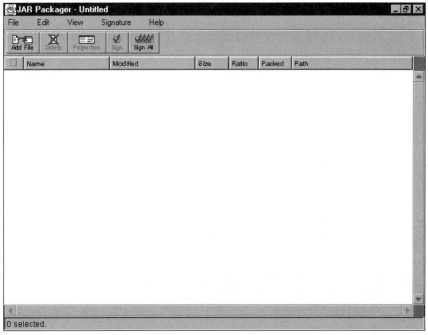

Figure 14-2: The JAR Packager.

There are two ways to send files with the JAR Packager. The first way is through the SmartUpdate feature of Communicator. The other way is using AutoUpdate, which is the scheduled automatic updating feature available only with Communicator Professional Clients.

Also available through the JAR Packager are security options. You have the option of adding digital signatures to the archives you create. You can add signatures to an individual file or to all the files in the archives. By using digital signatures, you can assure the users on your intranet that they're using legitimate files that haven't been tampered with.

We've been discussing how to create configurations and how to create add-on packages to Communicator. But how can you distribute custom versions of Communicator to begin with?

That's where the Install Builder comes in.

The Install Builder

The Install Builder allows you to incorporate both the configuration changes you have made and Communicator itself into one installable package. That package is called an *installer*.

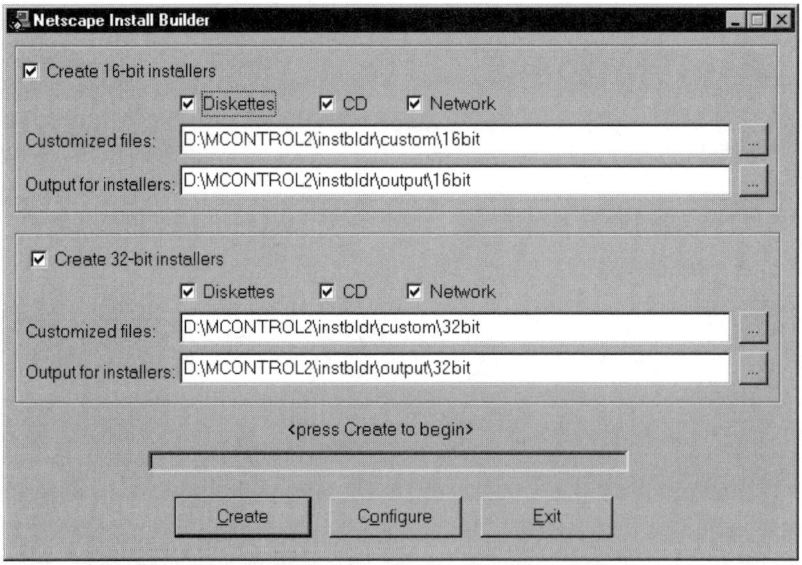

Figure 14-3: The Install Builder.

You can build either 32-bit or 16-bit Windows installers for your intranet users, and include a variety of different files, including:

- Communicator or Communicator Professional
- Plug-ins
- Dial-up modules

Once you've decided what you want to include in your version of Communicator, you can build an installer for floppy disks, CD-ROMs, or network files.

> **TIP**
>
> *The Install Builder works only on Windows 95 or Windows NT. Macintosh and UNIX users can create installers manually.*

Now that you know how Mission Control can help you create a personalized version of Communicator that you can update via your intranet, you may want to jump right into customizing, configuring, and packaging.

But slow down for a minute. Configuring and creating Communicator is a big job. Before you get too far into it, why not take a few moments and ask yourself three questions that will help you define your mission.

Defining the Mission: Three Questions

Each intranet has its own particular users, functions, and needs. Mission Control was designed to cover all the various requirements for configuration and distribution of Communicator software.

But before you can get the most out of Mission Control, take some time to think about your intranet, your users, and your needs. Considering three questions will help you decide how you can best use Mission Control in your company.

How Technically Adept are My Patrons?

Consider first the people who are going to use Communicator. Are they technically adept enough to make simple configuration changes? If not, you might want to set as many configuration options as possible and lock them so that they can't be tampered with. On the other hand, if you have technically astute users who can set their own configurations without requiring assistance, perhaps you should set and lock only those static configuration elements, like the names of the mail and news servers.

Are Security Issues Important?

How concerned are you with security issues? Do you want to make absolutely sure that the copies of Communicator on your intranet can't run Java? Are you suspicious of "cookies"? Does it make you crazy when one of your users allows Communicator to remember his or her e-mail password? You might want to concentrate more on making sure Communicator is secure, and then deal with technical support issues and image issues as secondary concerns.

Do You Have an "Image" You Want to Maintain via Communicator?

If your patrons use Communicator a lot to share and spread information, you might want to maintain an "image" with your preferences. You might want to lock the preferences that deal with organization, signature files, whether messages are sent as HTML by default, and how messages are displayed.

More than likely, the needs and concerns of your intranet are a little of this and a little of that. But by thinking about these three questions, you can begin to formulate in your mind how you want to approach the customization of Communicator.

Moving On

With this short chapter we've taken a look at what makes up Mission Control. It's not as large and powerful as Communicator, but it's certainly large and powerful enough to keep you occupied for quite a while!

Now that you have some ideas about what Mission Control is, the next couple of chapters will show you how to use it. Chapter 15 covers the Configuration Editor, and Chapter 16 covers the JAR Packager and the Install Builder.

CHAPTER 15

Mission Control's Configuration Editor

The Configuration Editor is the heart of Mission Control. It is in the Configuration Editor that you can make adjustments to how Communicator looks, how it runs, and how strong its security is.

In this chapter we'll be discussing how you can change Communicator's configuration and how you can distribute the configuration files to the users on your intranet. But before we get into that, we'll focus briefly on how Communicator handles user preferences. If you understand preferences, it'll make more sense when I explain how some preferences can be altered only with local configuration files, while other preferences can be changed using the AutoConfig file.

TIP

When I say user preferences, *I mean the whole nine yards—all the choices that a user makes in order to have Communicator conform to his or her preferences—how messages are displayed, which mail server is used, what the default home page is. Using the Configuration Editor, you can even change some things that aren't changeable by the user!*

Communicator's Preferences Setup

In addition to the preset defaults built into Communicator, there are three files that contain user preferences for Communicator:

- **User Preferences**. This is a file automatically generated by Communicator when a user sets preferences. It's called prefs.js on Windows and Netscape Preferences on Macintosh.

- **Netscape.cfg**. This is the local configuration file. It's called netscape.cfg on all platforms.

- **AutoConfig File**. The AutoConfig file is unique to Communicator Professional. It's a configuration file that's located remotely on the intranet. Communicator Professional can be set to check this file periodically through AutoAdmin to see if there are changes to its configuration that should be implemented. If any are found, they're implemented automatically. More information on AutoConfig is available in the "What's AutoAdmin" sidebar below.

In this chapter we'll be discussing the creation of AutoConfig and local configuration files.

What's AutoAdmin?

AutoAdmin, available as a feature of Communicator Professional only, was designed to help network administrators distribute files through an intranet. It distributes files in two ways:

- **AutoConfig**. AutoConfig lets the network administrator put a configuration file on the intranet and have users' copies of Communicator "poll" the file periodically for changes. The AutoConfig feature supports LDAP-capable servers, like the Netscape Directory Server, so users can retrieve preferences very specific to them and their systems. LDAP stands for Lightweight Directory Access Protocol.

- **AutoUpdate**. Going beyond mere configuration files, AutoUpdate allows network administrators to install software—plug-ins and new Communicator components, for example—via the intranet. Using the JAR Packager, which will be covered in the next chapter, administrators can package files into downloadable and installable modules.

Let's first talk about using the Configuration Editor's HTML-based editor to make changes to basic Communicator preferences. As the chapter progresses, we'll discuss editing the JavaScript in the configuration files, creating local and AutoConfig files, and distributing these files to your users on the intranet.

Starting the Configuration Editor

Choose the Netscape Configuration Editor from the Mission Control Group on your Windows 95 start menu. You'll be presented with a screen that looks like Figure 15-1.

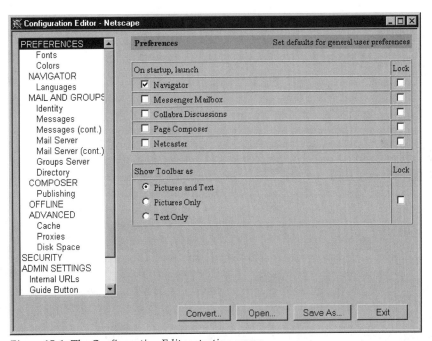

Figure 15-1: The Configuration Editor starting screen.

The Configuration editor is extremely easy to use. There's a column of the different preference lists on the left side of the screen, while on the right side of the screen are the preferences themselves. In this chapter we'll be walking through each configuration screen to explore how it works. Some of these settings you'll remember from the Communicator setup screens, but a lot of

them you won't. This Configuration Editor will set practically every preference with which you're concerned—except how you like your coffee in the
morning.

Let's get started.

TIP

> *Bear in mind that you don't have to go through each and every one of these configu-
> ration screens. It's a good idea to walk through them once, though, to get a good
> idea of what's here.*
>
> *You don't have to open a configuration file to edit; the Configuration Editor
> automatically opens Communicator's default preferences, leaving you to edit those.
> Nor do you have to go through each and every list of preferences in the Configura-
> tion Editor. It's a good idea to go through them at least once to get familiar with
> them, however, just so you know what they are.*
>
> *If you do want to edit an existing configuration file, click Open, and then use
> the browse button to find the file.* Warning! *Don't open files to which you've
> already added JavaScript instructions this way—you will lose the additional infor-
> mation you added!*

Setting Configurations

The first preferences to set are the general preferences, as you can see in Figure
15-1. Many of the Preferences lists will look like this one, with check boxes,
radio buttons, and occasional text boxes. All Preferences lists have the check
boxes to the extreme right of the screen, just under the word Lock.

The "lock boxes" do just what you might expect—they "lock" aspects of the
Netscape configuration so that they can't be changed. When you click on a
lock box next to a preference, you have frozen that preference so that whoever
uses the configuration file you generate cannot change that particular preference. For example, say you set the home page to http://www.
companyexample.com using the Configuration Editor and click on this
preference's lock box. You've just assured that anyone using this configuration
will always see the http://www.companyexample.com page when they sign
on. (This can come in handy when you're trying to assure that the people on
your intranet are reading company announcements in the morning, and not
The Dilbert Zone.)

> **TIP**
>
> *What does the user see when an item is locked? When a preference is locked, it's "grayed out" so that it is not available to the user.*

Let's get started setting configurations. Take a look at the Configuration Editor starting screen again. You've got two settings here. The first setting is which programs should be opened upon starting Communicator. Navigator is set as the default, but you can have any of these five possible programs open, or a few of them, or all of them. (It is recommended that at least one of them opens.)

> **TIP**
>
> *When you're deciding what programs to open, consider the memory on the machines in your intranet. If everyone has MMX machines with 64MB of RAM, then it might be okay to open Navigator, Messenger, and Netcaster upon startup. However, if the machines are mostly 486/66 types with 16MB of RAM, it's best to open only one application at startup.*

The second preference choice in this screen is how the toolbar is displayed. You have the option of setting the toolbar to pictures and text, pictures only, or text only. There's a knowledge/space tradeoff here—if you have your toolbars listed as text only, you'll have a little more space on the screen for text pages. But if your intranet surfers aren't familiar with Netscape, they may find the pictures helpful when using Navigator.

You're done with the first screen! That wasn't so bad, was it? The preferences that you're setting with the Configuration Editor aren't difficult to understand; it's just that there are so many of them you might feel a little overwhelmed.

Next, click on Fonts in the list box on the left to move to the Fonts list. That's how you move between screens in the Configuration Editor—by clicking on the name of the screen in the list box. (Think of it as an HTML page with a frame and you'll be fine.)

> **TIP**
>
> *You may have noticed that each list has four buttons at the bottom: Convert..., Open..., Save As..., and Exit. The Exit button is self-explanatory (it quits the program) but you might not be able to figure out the other three. Don't worry about it; we'll cover them later in the chapter.*

The Fonts List

The Fonts list, shown in Figure 15-2, is even easier to deal with—there's only one item on it. Here you'll specify how you want Communicator to react when an HTML document provides its own fonts. You have three possible options:

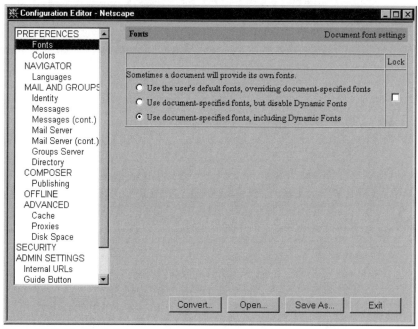

Figure 15-2: The Fonts list.

- **Use the user's default fonts, overriding document-specified fonts**. Web pages will always display using the serif and sans-serif font specified by Netscape. You might miss out on some nice design this way, but everything will be legible.

- **Use document-specified fonts, but disable Dynamic Fonts**. Dynamic Fonts is a new feature that allows Web pages to send fonts to surfers. You can disable this feature but allow the use of document-specified fonts, as long as they're already installed on the surfer's computer. (For example, you may come across a page that uses the Optima font—not one of Netscape's default fonts. However, if it's already installed on your computer, Netscape will use it to display the page.)

- **Use document-specified fonts, including Dynamic Fonts**. Allows the use of Dynamic Fonts in addition to any fonts that the page specifies that are already on the surfer's computer.

Don't forget about the lock box! To lock this preference, click on the check box to the far right of the screen.

The next list covers color choices. This list will look a little alien because it lists colors as hex values, and not names, but once you get past that it's easy to understand.

Colors

As you see in Figure 15-3, the first four things in this list for you to specify are the colors in which the text, backgrounds, and links will appear. But instead of giving you color names or palettes to specify, you're instead supposed to specify the hex value of the color. This is the name of the color as the machine sees it.

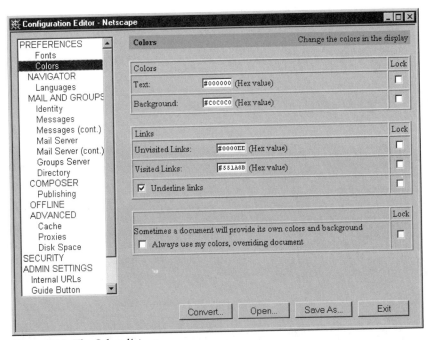

Figure 15-3: The Colors list.

> **TIP**
>
> *Obviously you're not expected to know all the color hex values off the top of your head. If you like, you can leave these values the way they are, or you can check the Web for color/hex resources. http://www.10mb.com/brv/colorama.htm lets you choose colors to see how they look along with their hex values.*

The first two lines of the list are for specifying the colors of Communicator's text and background. The second two are for specifying what color links—for Web pages that you have visited or not visited—should appear.

Beneath the link lines is a check box specifying whether or not links should be underlined. (I recommend you make sure this check box is checked and that its lock box is checked; non-underlined links are more confusing than anything else.)

The final thing on this list is a check box specifying whether Communicator will always use its colors and background, overriding the colors and background specified by Web pages or HTML-enriched e-mail. By checking this box you're assuring that everything will be legible, but you might miss out on some design elements.

Once you're done with this list, click on NAVIGATOR in the scroll box to move on.

Navigator

This list, shown in Figure 15-4, covers some of the basic functionality of Navigator. The first setting in the list is the page with which the browser starts. You can specify a Blank page, the Home page, or the Last page visited. Beneath this you can specify the Home Page. The default home page is Netscape's page, but you can set this to any page you like.

> **TIP**
>
> *If you have a page on your intranet that company employees should check daily, consider setting it as the default home page and locking it. That way they'll have to access it at least once a day, when they first start Navigator.*

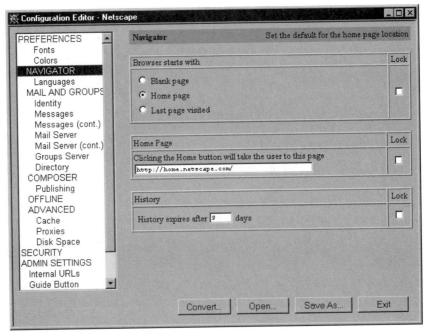

Figure 15-4: The Navigator list.

The final thing on this list is the History setting. The "history" that Communicator refers to is the list of links that you've visited. A link you've visited will stay the color of a visited link for as many days as you specify in this box. For example, your history setting is five days. You visit the Wall Street Journal site at http://www.wsj.com. Any link you encounter that points to the Wall Street Journal's main page will be the color of a visited link for five days. After five days, any link you see that points to the Wall Street Journal's main page will turn the color of an unvisited link.

Click on Languages in the scroll box to move to the Languages list.

Languages

There's only one thing to specify in this list, shown in Figure 15-5: the language in which you want to view Web pages.

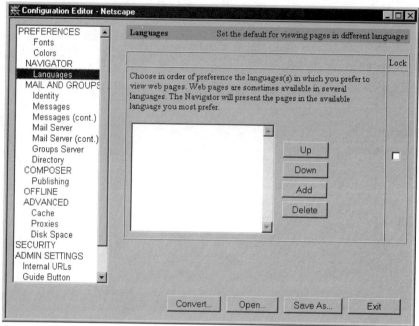

Figure 15-5: The Languages list.

Of course, most Web pages only give you one language, with no other choice, and you're either able to read it or not. However, sometimes Web pages are available in more than one language. Here you can specify a list of languages and the order of your preferences.

To add a language to this list, click on the Add button. You'll get a screen that looks like the one in Figure 15-6.

Figure 15-6: Adding a language to the Languages list.

Scroll through the choices to find the language you want and click on it. Then click on the OK button. You'll be returned to the Languages screen with the language you chose in the list box.

Bear in mind that you can add one language, or several, or none at all. If you add several, the Web page will be displayed in the available language in order of preference. For example, say you've listed English, French, and Japanese as your language preferences. You come to a page that has pages available in English and French. Your Web browser would display them in English, because that's your preferred language. But say your browser had pages available in French, Korean, and Japanese; it would display the pages in French, because that's your second choice and there are no English pages available.

Make sense? Great. Click on MAIL AND GROUPS in the scroll box and let's move on.

Mail & Groups

As shown in Figure 15-7, the first setting in the Mail and Groups list is for specifying how you want quoted text to appear in messages. Use the pull-down menu to specify Style (plain, bold, or italic), Size, or Color (those hex values again).

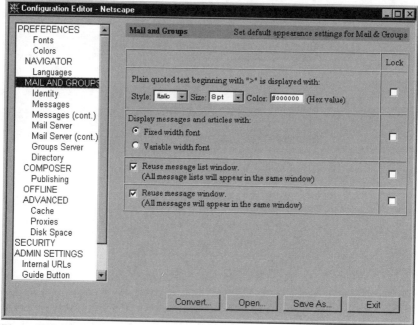

Figure 15-7: The Mail and Groups list.

The second setting is for specifying whether messages and articles will appear in fixed-width font (fixed width looks like this) or in variable-width font. (Unless you're expecting to see a lot of plain-text tables and other formatted items in your e-mail and newsgroup messages, set this to variable-width font; it's easier to read.)

The final two settings on this list have to do with reusing windows. This isn't so much recycling as assuring that Communicator doesn't spawn several different windows to show all the lists of messages in which you're interested. You have the option to show all the message lists in the same window, or to show all the messages in the same window.

What Communicator means by showing all the messages in the same window is not that every message you open will appear in one window at the same time. What it does mean is that instead of spawning a new window every time you want to read a message, it'll erase the previous message from the window (though not from the hard drive) and display a new message.

When you're done with this list, click on Identity to move on to the Identity section.

Identity

When you click on this item, you might say to yourself, "I can't set universal identity settings for my users. Their identity information is too variable for this to work properly."

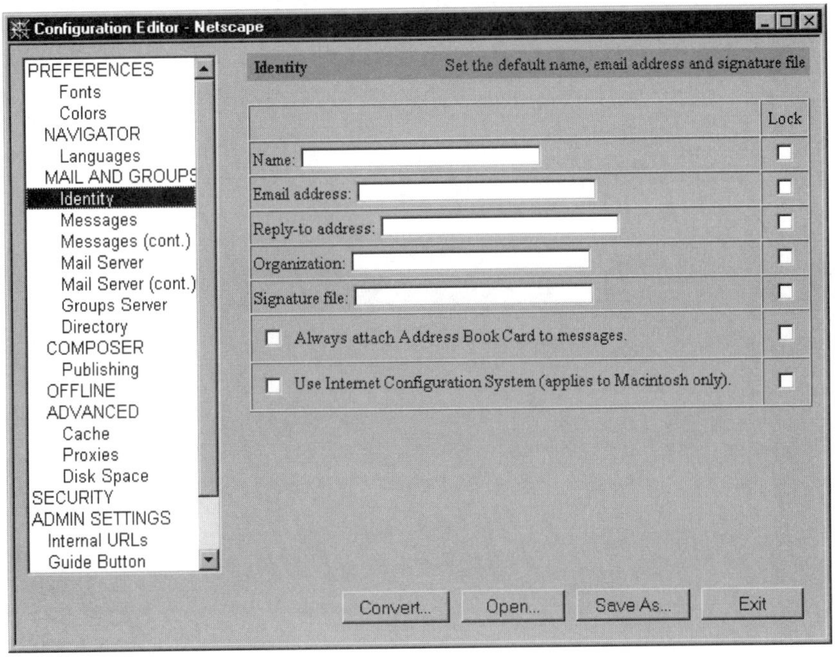

Figure 15-8: The Identity list.

Not the case. Remember, Communicator Professional's AutoAdmin supports LDAP protocols and allows you to tailor configuration files to fit each user on your intranet. We'll be talking about this later in the chapter; right now, let's concentrate on filling out the default settings, shown in Figure 15-8.

Most of these settings are self-explanatory: Name, E-mail address, Reply-to address, and Organization. Bear in mind that the path for the Signature file might not be the same on the user's computer as it is on yours. If there's a standard directory on which Communicator is installed, a good idea might be to include the signature file with Communicator, using the Install Builder (which we'll discuss in the next chapter), and refer to that file.

The last two settings give you the option of always attaching your address book card to messages (recommended) and using the Internet Configuration System (this you don't have to worry about unless you're using Macintosh).

When you're finished here, click on Messages and we'll move on.

Messages

Figure 15-9 shows part one of the Messages settings. Part two is under the section Messages (Continued), but we'll get to that in a moment.

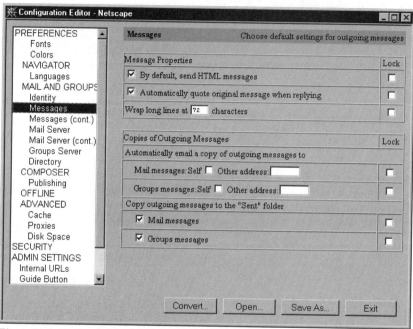

Figure 15-9: Part one of the Messages list.

The first thing on this list is a check box to indicate whether HTML messages should be sent by default. After that, there's a check box to specify that original messages should be automatically quoted in replies. (If you have users that reply to your detailed queries six weeks later with one-word responses and without quoting the original message, I recommend locking this one.)

You're also able to specify here when lines should be wrapped. A good length to set (and lock) is 72 characters; going shorter might mess up text formatting, and going longer can often make the lines harder to read.

The second section of this list deals with what should happen to copies of outgoing messages. You have the option of having copies of mail messages and newsgroup postings sent to the user's e-mail address (activate the Self check box) or to another e-mail address. If you want only the users to get copies of their mail and newsgroup posts, keep these items blank and make sure the items underneath them—the check boxes that specify that outgoing mail and newsgroup postings should be copied into the "Sent" folder—are checked.

TIP

Sending someone else copies of a user's mail could lead to him or her getting a lot of mail. Don't do this unless you keep mail copies for archive purposes.

Click on Messages (cont.) to move on to the remainder of the Messages section.

Messages (Continued)

There are only two items in this list, as shown in Figure 15-10. The first one deals with how Communicator reacts when addressing messages. Usually Communicator can "expand addresses"—fill them in based on information in a user's personal address book—whether the user is inserting the addressee's real name or the nickname. With the Configuration Editor, you can set this preference so that Communicator expands addresses based only on the nickname.

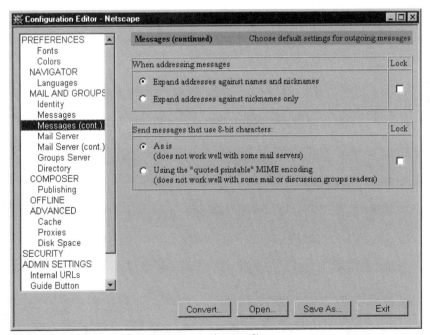

Figure 15-10: Part two of the Messages preferences list.

Let's look at an example. Doug Hall is in your address book, with a nickname of TrainedBrain. With Communicator's default, you could type either TrainedBrain or Doug Hall in a message's To: field to list his address. However, if you choose to expand addresses against nicknames only, you'd have to type "TrainedBrain" in the To: field to obtain Doug Hall's address from your address book. Typing "Doug Hall" wouldn't work.

Also on this list you can specify how Communicator will treat messages with 8-bit characters. You can have Communicator send them as-is, which could cause trouble with some mail servers, or have them sent using the "quoted printable" MIME encoding, which would upset the digestion of some mail or discussion group servers. I recommend leaving this at the default (sending them as-is) unless the default messes up the mail server on your intranet.

From here, click on Mail Server to go to the first part of the Mail Server configuration.

Mail Server

In this list, shown in Figure 15-11, you're first prompted to enter the names of the Outgoing and Incoming mail servers. (If these are the only mail servers on your intranet, you may want to lock these preferences.)

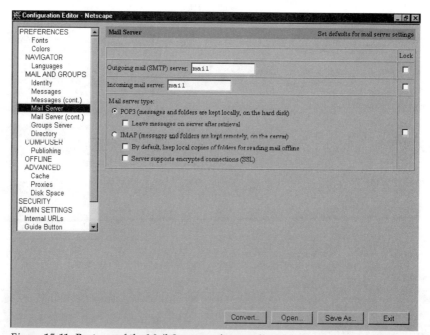

Figure 15-11: Part one of the Mail Server preferences list.

The other item on this list is the type of mail server your users will be using. Click the radio button to specify POP3 or IMAP server. (This is another preference that you may wish to lock to avoid accidental changing of this configuration later.)

Click on Mail Server (cont.) to move on to the second half of the mail server preferences.

Mail Server (Continued)

Every item on this list, shown in Figure 15-12, is a check box. The first check box asks if and how often Communicator should check for mail on the server. (If you leave it unchecked, it doesn't check for mail at all—you have to retrieve mail manually.) The second check box is for indicating that Communicator should sound an audio alert when messages arrive.

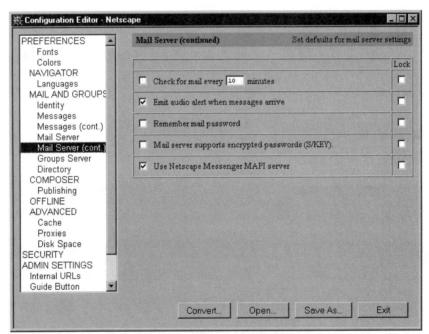

Figure 15-12: The second part of the Mail Server preferences list.

The third check box, when checked, has Communicator remember a user's e-mail password, never prompting for it more than once. If you have security concerns with your intranet, I encourage you to leave this box unchecked and to lock this preference.

Below the Remember mail password check box is the check box for indicating whether your Mail server supports encrypted passwords (if you're in doubt, leave this unchecked). Finally, there's a check box to indicate whether Communicator should use the MAPI protocol to communicate with your intranet's mail server.

Getting tired? Don't worry about it; you're halfway through using the HTML-based Configuration Editor. After this, I'll show you how to edit the JavaScript files you can create with the Editor and modify Communicator even more—you can really get "under the hood" with Mission Control!

Click on Groups Server to move on to the next screen.

Groups Server

There are only two options here, as shown in Figure 15-13. The first one is to specify the name of the news server on your intranet. (Again, consider locking this preference.)

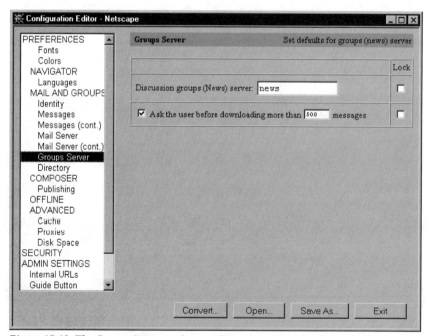

Figure 15-13: The Groups Server preferences list.

The second item is a check box for confirming downloads when a user has more than 500 messages (the 500 can be changed to any number). By having a user confirm the download or choose to download only the most recent newsgroup postings, you're saving time and intranet traffic.

Finished here? Click on Directory to move on to the next list.

Directory

The Directory list, shown in Figure 15-14, is where you can start adding resources to Communicator, making it easier for your users to use.

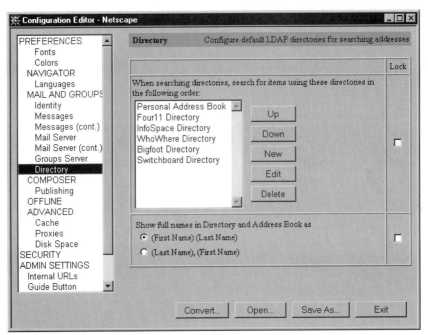

Figure 15-14: The Directory list.

The Directory list is ordinarily a list of LDAP directories where a user can find address information. If the LDAP acronym looks familiar to you, it's because it's the Lightweight Directory Access Protocol that we talked about at the beginning of this chapter.

Inside the list box you'll see a set of resources. These resources, in the order in which they are listed, will be used to find e-mail address information. If you have an LDAP directory on your intranet, this is a perfect place to insert it.

Deleting materials off this list is easy: highlight the resource you want removed and click Delete. Moving a resource is equally easy: highlight it and click on either the Up or the Down button to change its position in the lineup.

To add a resource, click the New button. You'll get a screen that looks like the one in Figure 15-15.

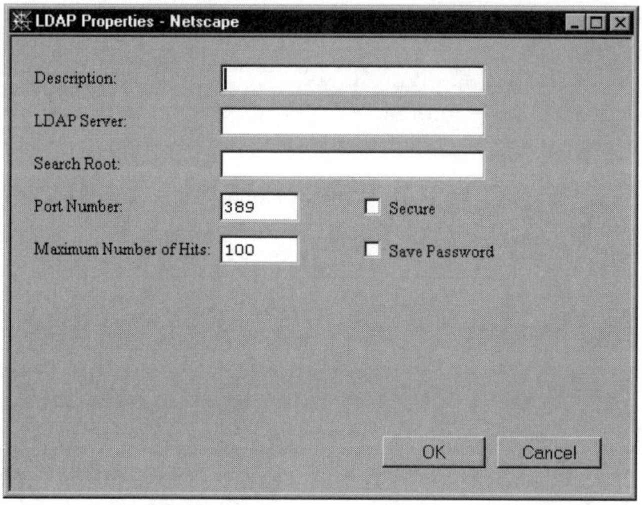

Figure 15-15: Adding a resource to the LDAP directory list.

Fill in the information, click OK, and you'll see that the new resource appears in the list box.

TIP

Want to edit a resource? Highlight it and click Edit. You'll get the same screen shown in Figure 15-15, with information specific to the item you want to edit.

The only other item in Figure 15-14 is for specifying how full names in the Directory and Address Books should be shown: Firstname, Lastname or Lastname, Firstname.

Click on COMPOSER and we'll get into the publishing preferences.

Composer

The first two settings on this list, as shown in Figure 15-16, are fairly straight-forward: the name of the page's author and an option to automatically save the page being created at specified intervals (every certain number of minutes).

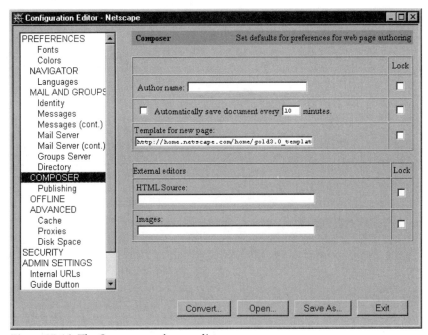

Figure 15-16: The Composer preferences list.

It's with the third option that things can get interesting, especially if you're trying to maintain a standard image. You have the option of setting up a template for a new page. By putting up a page on your intranet and using this preference to point to it, you're establishing a standard image for pages that originate from your intranet.

The last two items on this list are for specifying external "helper applica-tions" for HTML Source editing (the editor could be as simple as Windows Notepad, or something more complex like HoTmeTaL) and image editing (such as Paint Shop Pro or some other graphics illustrator).

Click on Publishing and we'll get into how the pages made with Communi-cator get on sites.

Publishing

Composer makes it easier to handle Web page creation by automatically relocating links and images, if you like. The first two check boxes in this list, shown in Figure 15-17, deal with setting links and images. By clicking on the Maintain links check box, you'll set Composer to automatically adjust the links so that they work from the location where the page is finally published.

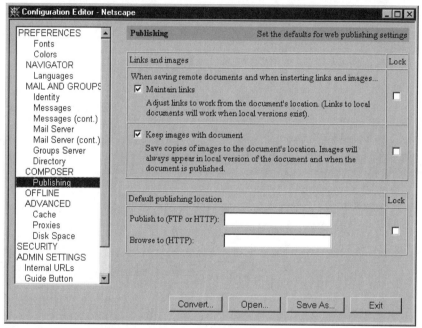

Figure 15-17: The Publishing preferences list.

By clicking on the Keep images with document button, copies of the images you use in Composer pages will automatically be sent to the folder where the page is finally published.

The final two items on this list are for specifying default publishing locations of pages. By entering an FTP site or HTTP (Web site) location, you can specify to what directory created Composer pages should automatically be published. The Browse to: text box is to specify the appropriate http:// equivalent of an FTP address.

For example, you may have Composer set to automatically publish to ftp://www.fictionalexample.com/users/tara/public_html/, which is the FTP site where your Web pages are kept. However, Composer can't use that address to maintain the page's links. Instead, you'll need to specify the Web site address that points to that FTP directory, which in this case would be http://www. fictionalexample.com/~tara/.

Make sense? Click on OFFLINE and we'll move on to the one-item Offline list, where you'll be on your own.

Offline

As shown in Figure 15-18, there's only one item on this list, and it specifies which mode Communicator should start in. You have the choice of Online, Offline, and Ask the User. All these are explained thoroughly in the list, so I'll leave you to make your choice. I'll be over on the Advanced preferences list.

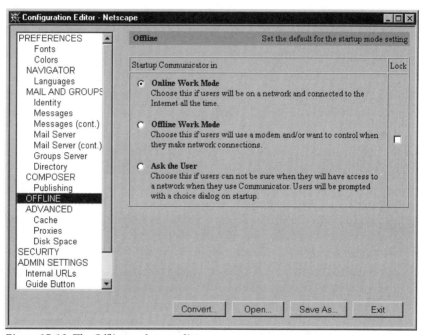

Figure 15-18: The Offline preferences list.

Advanced

Though they're called the Advanced preferences, most of these preferences deal specifically with security. As shown in Figure 15-19, the first item is a check box for turning on the automatic loading of images and other data types. Unchecking this box can save your intranet a lot of traffic.

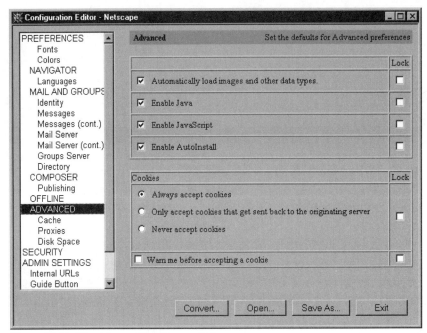

Figure 15-19: The Advanced preferences list.

The next three check boxes are for enabling Java, JavaScript, and AutoInstall. By unclicking these items you'll diminish the capabilities of Communicator somewhat. However, you'll also be protecting Communicator against possible security breaches.

Cookies aren't a real security hazard. However, some people consider them an invasion of privacy, because many times they're used to track the interests and preferences of someone who's perusing a Web site. You can use the last item in the Advanced list to specify how Communicator will treat cookies: Always accepting them, Only accepting the cookies that are sent back to the originating server, or Never accepting cookies at all. There's also a check box at the bottom of this list specifying that the user always be warned before accepting a cookie.

TIP

A cookie is a small string of text that some Web servers place on your hard drive. The cookie is designed to hold information about your surfing habits and preferences, and make it easier for you as a surfer to find online information you're interested in.

When you've got all your cookies in order, click on Cache and we'll arrange your users' hard drive space.

Cache

Caches hold recently visited Web sites so that surfers can "page back" and revisit sites without having to reconnect to the site and reload the pages, as shown in Figure 15-20.

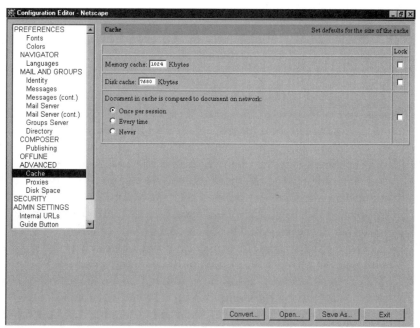

Figure 15-20: The Cache settings.

You have two things to set at the top of the list: the size of the Memory cache (RAM) and the size of the Disk cache (hard drive space). The size of these caches depends a lot on the amount of RAM and the size of the hard drive the target machine has.

The other item on this list is how often a document (Web page or page component) in the cache should be compared to its online counterpart on the intranet or the Internet. The fewer the times a document in the cache is compared to its online counterpart, the less network traffic is generated. These are the options:

- Once per surfing session
- Every time the Web page cached is accessed by the surfer
- Never

In the case of the last option, users will have to force the document to reload (by using the reload button in the browser) before they'll know if there is any new information on the Web page.

Let's move on and set up your network Proxies. If you have a direct connection to the intranet and no firewalls, you can skip this part and go on to the Disk Space section.

Proxies

When you have a security firewall on your intranet, you have to access Internet services through a proxy. If you don't have a firewall and operate through a direct connection to the Internet, click on the first radio button that reads "Direct connection to the Internet," as shown in Figure 15-21. If you'd like to manually configure your proxies, click the "Manual proxy configuration" button and then click View. You'll see a screen that looks like Figure 15-22. Fill in the name of each proxy host and port, then click OK.

If you anticipate that the proxy information will be changing often, you can set up an AutoConfig file (which we'll talk more about later). Click on the "Automatic proxy configuration" radio button and enter the location where the URL containing the configuration is located.

Let's catch up with the other folks and move on to the Disk Space list.

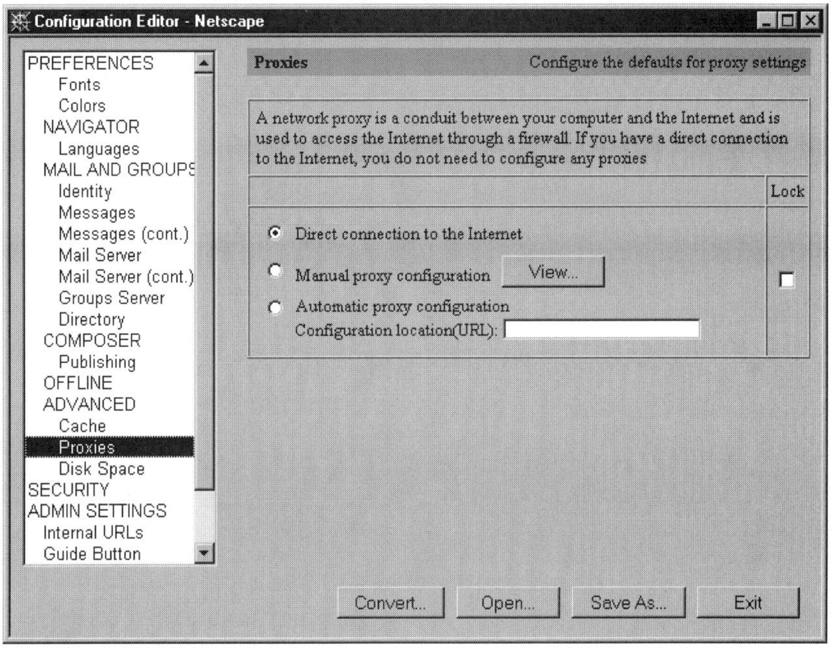

Figure 15-21: The Proxies preferences list.

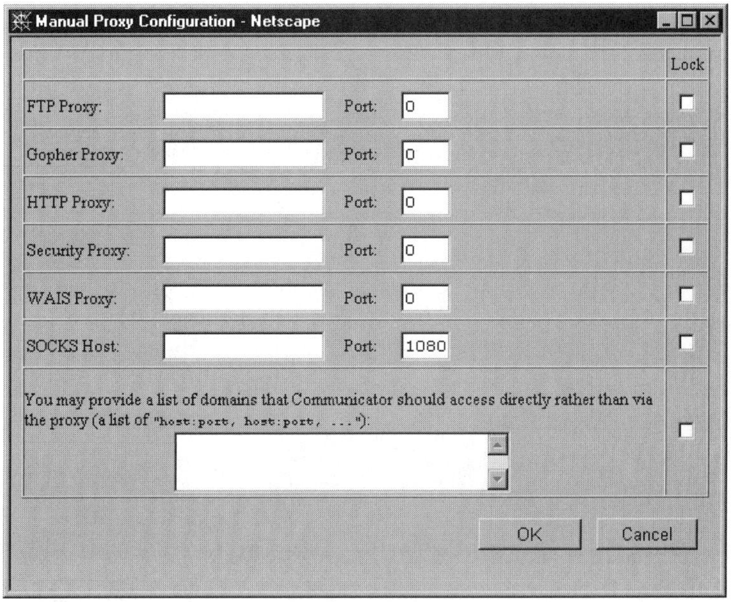

Figure 15-22: Configuring proxies manually.

Disk Space

We've already talked a little bit about disk space with the cache preferences. This disk space list deals with the amount of disk space taken up by messages. As shown in Figure 15-23, for all messages (that is to say, mail and newsgroup postings) you have the check box for not downloading any message larger than 50K and asking about compacting mail and newsgroup folders when the amount of space saved is over 100K. You can change the 50K and 100K to whatever sizes you like.

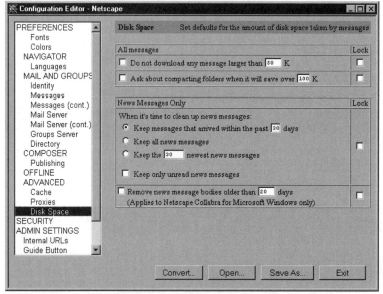

Figure 15-23: The Disk Space preferences list.

The other three items on this list deal with news messages only, even though it might look like more than three, thanks to all the radio buttons and text boxes.) The first item allows you to set Communicator's action in cleaning up news messages. You choose from the following:

- Keep all messages that have arrived in the last 30 days (or change that 30 to whatever number you like).

- Keep all news messages.

- Keep the 30 newest news messages (or any number you choose).

Base your decision on the amount of free space available on the hard drive (text messages don't take up much room, but HTML messages can) and how often the user reads his or her messages. No matter which of these radio buttons you click, there's a check box at the bottom to specify that Communicator should keep only unread messages when cleaning out the newsgroup listings.

The last item on this list applies to the Windows version of Collabra only. You can remove message bodies older than 20 days (or whatever number you choose) when this check box is checked.

Ready to move on to the Security list? You'll be surprised when you see it; there's a lot less to it than you think.

Security

The security list has only two items on it, as shown in Figure 15-24. The first is a checkbox to indicate whether an e-mail address should be sent as the password when logging on to an FTP site as an anonymous user. The second is a set of radio buttons to indicate when the Communicator user should be asked for a password. The options are:

- Once per session (when the user logs on).

- Every time a digital certificate is used.

- After 30 minutes of inactivity (or whatever number you choose).

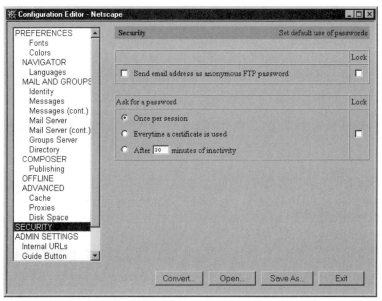

Figure 15-24: The Security list, with two items.

If you're creating a configuration file for a user who uses a dial-up connection and is the only user with access to his or her computer, leaving this setting at "Once per session" is all right. But if you're creating a configuration file for a user in a group setting, then you need to set this to after 30 minutes of inactivity—or even 5 or 10 minutes of inactivity. Otherwise, person X could get up and leave Communicator running, and person Y could sit down 20 minutes later and send e-mail and newsgroup postings in person X's name! Not cool, not professional, and not secure.

You've wrapped up the basics. From now on we get into the really neat stuff—the customizations that change the way Communicator looks, and the customizations that make Communicator easier to use and more relevant to the users on your intranet. Click on ADMIN SETTINGS and let's get started.

Admin

Beginning with the Admin Settings list, shown in Figure 15-25, you're going to customize Communicator. The first customization is not going to appear to the user, however, but to the Web servers with which Communicator interacts.

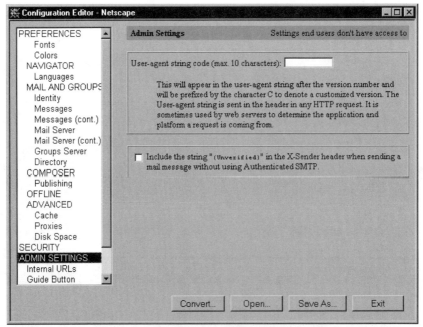

Figure 15-25: The Admin Settings preferences list.

The first thing on this list is the User-agent string code. This will appear in the user-agent string that the Web server sees when it interacts with Communicator. The string is sometimes used by Web servers to keep track of the kind of browsers that are making requests of it.

There's also a check box in this list to include the string "unverified" in the X-Sender when sending a mail message without using Authenticated SMTP. This is good for tracking the status of messages that go in and out.

Click on Internal URLs and let's have some fun resetting the Internal URLs for Communicator.

Internal URLs

There are only three items in this list. They're for replacing URLs that are "hard coded" into Communicator with your own. They are:

- **Animated logo button URL**. Did you ever click on the animated Netscape logo in the upper right-hand corner? It takes you to the Netscape site. In this text box you can enter any URL you like—say, that of your intranet home page—and when a user clicks on the logo they'll be taken to the URL you specify. (you can change the logo, too, but we'll get into that later in the chapter).

- **Search button URL**. This is the URL to which Communicator will go when the user clicks on the Search button in Communicator's toolbar. You can choose to leave it at the URL specified by Communicator, or choose another URL (a search page for your intranet pages, perhaps).

- **Plug-in finder URL**. When Communicator comes across a document type that it doesn't understand embedded in a Web page, it will query this page to see if the type has a plug-in. Unless you've got a really great plug-in page living somewhere on your intranet, I recommend leaving this URL as it is.

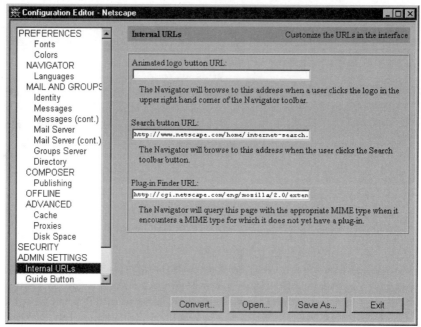

Figure 15-26: Setting the Internal URLs.

TIP

> *You'll notice that there aren't any lock check boxes on this page (or on a few of the other lists in the Configuration Editor). That's because there isn't any way for the user to change the settings that we're getting into now. They can only be accessed like this through Mission Control.*

Let's add some objects to the guide menus now. Click on the Guide Button.

Guide Button

There's a Guide Button on the toolbar, as shown in Figure 15-27. When you click on it, a menu appears under the button with a list of sites for the user to check out.

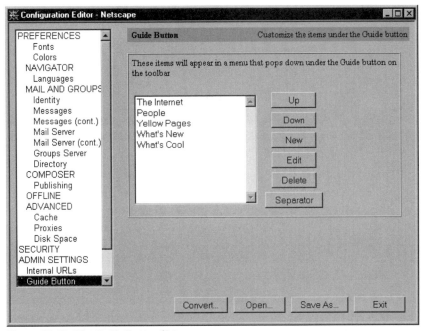

Figure 15-27: The Guide Button list.

You can add your own items to this menu, move 'em up or down, whatever. There are several items already on this list. Click on them to highlight them, and then click on the Up or Down button to move them up or down the list. You can click on Delete to get rid of an item, or click on Separator to put a small horizontal line between one item and the next.

Want to add an item to the list? This is a good place to put pointers to your major intranet sites—human resources, company resources, and other items. Click on the New button and you'll get a screen like the one shown in Figure 15-28.

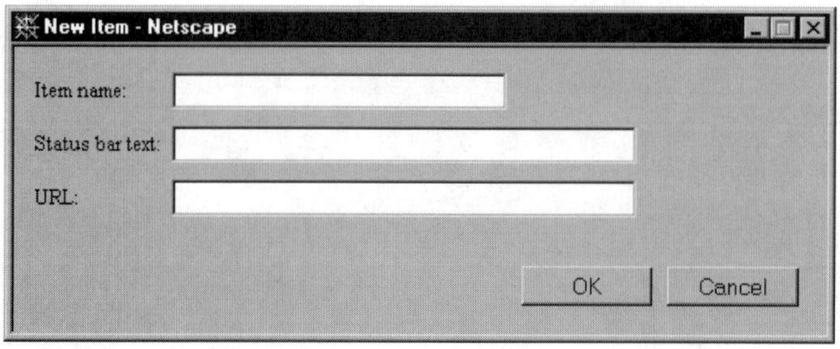

Figure 15-28: Adding an item to the Guide Button.

You'll see that there's a place for the name of the resource, the status bar information (which is generally the URL) and the URL of the resource. Click on OK and you see that the item you've added is now in the list box.

Take a few minutes now and add some resources to the guide button. You'll see that the procedure is very much the same when you go to the Guide Menu, which is up next.

Guide Menu

The first thing you're going to say when you see this list, shown in Figure 15-29, is "What's up with the ampersands?" There are ampersands all over the place in the list of resources that the Guide Menu points to, but you don't see the ampersands on the Communicator menu.

Actually, the ampersands specify key shortcuts. An ampersand before a letter specifies an underlined key shortcut accessible by pressing Alt and the letter. For example, &Human Resources could be reached by the key shortcut Alt+U. Do you want to use an ampersand in your guide menu without specifying a key shortcut? Use a double ampersand (&&).

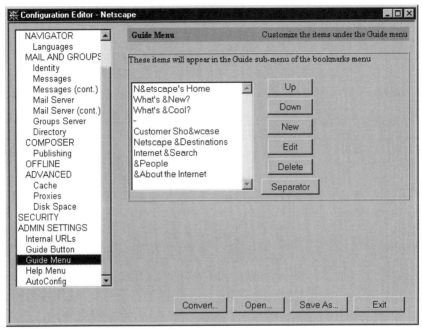

Figure 15-29: The Guide Menu preferences list.

You can move items around just like in the Guide Button settings—moving items up and down, adding new items, and putting in separators.

The Help menu works the same way. Click on Help Menu to continue.

Help Menu

The items of the Help Menu work the same way, right down to the ampersands, as shown in Figure 15-30. You'll see that there's a separator line here, too.

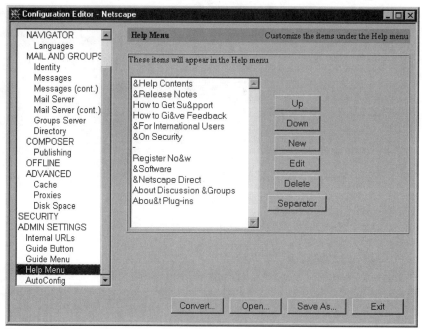

Figure 15-30: The Help Menu preferences list.

Once you're finished with this menu, click on AutoConfig. It's the last list in the Configuration Editor. The last one? You bet! Just click it, and let's finish this up so we can get into the local configuration files and AutoConfig files.

AutoConfig

The first item on this list, as shown in Figure 15-31, is the AutoConfig URL from which Communicator should get its AutoConfig file, using AutoAdmin. Beneath that is a check box to indicate whether or not Communicator should append the user's e-mail address when polling the AutoConfig URL. By appending an e-mail address when polling the AutoConfig URL, very specific configurations can be returned to the user.

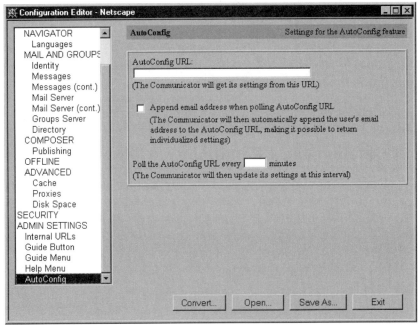

Figure 15-31: The AutoConfig list.

The last item on this list is to specify how often to poll the AutoConfig URL. You can poll the AutoConfig URL as often as you like, but bear in mind that the more frequently Communicator polls the URL, the more network traffic is generated.

You're finished! Well, you're finished but not done. What does it take to be done? We've barely scratched the surface. You know how to use the Configuration Editor to change the preferences of a configuration file. But now we're going to talk about creating a local configuration file and an AutoConfig file, and how you can test your configuration file.

Creating Configuration Files

There are two kinds of configuration files you can create: a local configuration file, which is kept on the user's local hard drive, and an AutoConfig file, which is kept on a Web server.

Let's get into the local configuration file, and from there we'll discuss AutoConfig.

Creating Local Configuration Files

Since we've already gone through how you can use the Configuration Editor to make changes to a configuration file, we're going to build on that as I show you how to save your work as a local configuration file. Here's how to go about doing it:

1. Go through the Configuration Editor and make the changes you want to the Configuration Editor.

2. Click on the Save As... button to save your configuration masterpiece. You'll get a screen like the one shown in Figure 15-32.

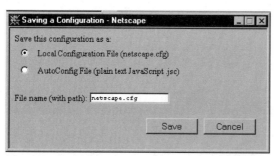

Figure 15-32: Saving a configuration.

3. Decision time! If you do not intend to make any changes to the Configuration Editor, save it as a local configuration file with the extension .cfg. If you do intend to edit the file with a text editor, save it as an AutoConfig file (which is a JavaScript file). (You can make additional configuration changes through editing the text file (we'll talk about that shortly).

4. If you saved your configuration changes as a local configuration file, you're done. If you saved it as an AutoConfig file, you're not finished yet.

5. Edit the AutoConfig file using your favorite text editor (we'll discuss doing that later in the chapter). Save it, and remember where you saved the file.

6. Launch the Configuration Editor. Click on the Convert button. You'll get a screen that looks like the one shown in Figure 15-33.

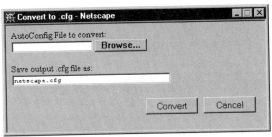

Figure 15-33: Converting a file.

7. In the AutoConfig File to convert text box, enter the name of the AutoConfig file you've just edited. In the lower Save output .cfg file as text box, enter the path where you want the file to be saved and the name of the file, which should be netscape.cfg.

8. Move the file to its proper place. For Windows users, it should be placed in the same directory as the Communicator application. For Mac users, the file should be placed in the Essential Files folder.

You're finished! Now that you know how to make local configuration files, let's talk AutoConfig files.

TIP

You can distribute your customized local configuration files using the Install Builder. We'll take a look at doing that in the next chapter.

Creating AutoConfig Files

Before we get into the steps, you need to know a few things: the limitations of changing your configuration using AutoConfig. The only Admin setting you can change using AutoConfig is the AutoConfig setting itself. All of the other Admin settings—Internal URLs, Guide Button, Help Menu, and so on—have to be changed using a local configuration file.

Now that we've gotten that straight, let's talk AutoConfig.

1. Make the configuration changes you want using the Configuration Editor. Remember that the Admin settings will not work. You can change them but the changes won't take effect.

2. When setting the AutoConfig file, leave the AutoConfig URL blank. You'll need to set that up in the local configuration files. But you can specify how often the local version of Communicator should "poll" the online version of the AutoConfig file.

3. Click the Save As button and save the file as an AutoConfig file.

4. You can edit the AutoConfig file with a plain text editor if you like (we'll talk about that later in this chapter).

5. If you haven't already saved the AutoConfig file to a Web server, do that now. You can do it through Communicator or a stand-alone FTP application.

6. Map the .jsc file extension as a new MIME type on your Web server.

You're done! Remember, you'll have to specify where the AutoConfig file is located through a local configuration file.

TIP

When you use the Save As and Convert buttons in the Configuration Editor, you don't get any kind of indicator to tell you that the file has been saved. You'll have to click Cancel to exit the Save As or Convert screens.

What Happens if a User Has Already Made a Configuration File?

If a Communicator user has already created a configuration file by setting local preferences, then setting another preference in the local configuration or AutoConfig file that you create will not override the previous user's preferences. The only way you can override an existing preference is by setting and locking a preference.

Now that you've created a configuration file, I know you'll want to test it.

Testing the Configuration File

To test the local configuration file isn't that difficult. Close down Communicator, place the local configuration file that you created in the appropriate directory, and restart Communicator. Then, test Communicator to make sure that the new configuration file is being used. I usually like to make a really obvious change—like changing the URL that's accessed when the Navigator button is clicked—so I know the new local configuration file is being used without looking around too much.

To test the AutoConfig file, you'll have to do the following:

1. Make sure you're connected to your intranet.

2. Make sure the AutoConfig file is available at the URL you specified in the local configuration file.

3. Allow the appropriate number of minutes to pass before Communicator polls the specified URL to get the new configuration information.

4. Then test it and see if it works.

You've gone as far as you can by using the HTML-based part of the Configuration Editor. But you can customize Communicator's preferences even more by editing the AutoConfig version of the configuration files and inserting JavaScript. Let's get to it.

Editing AutoConfig Files With a Text Editor

By using JavaScript, you can edit the AutoConfig files with a text editor and add a variety of enhancements to the base configurations.

Unfortunately, it is outside the scope of this book to cover each enhancement you can make using JavaScript and a text editor. Seriously, we'd be here all month! Instead, I'm going to touch on highlights of things you can do without a thorough knowledge of JavaScript. The Configuration Editor's online documentation has extensive information on editing with a text file, as well as sample scripts that cover LDAP support and AutoUpdate issues.

Changing an AutoConfig File With a Text Editor

The typical plain-text configuration file looks like Figure 15-34.

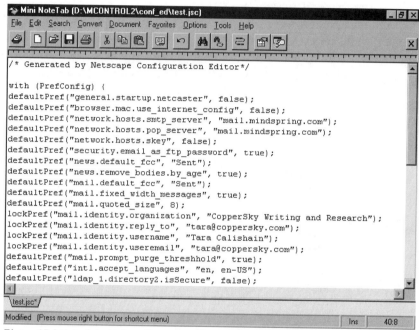

Figure 15-34: A plain-text configuration file opened in the text editor.

As you can see, the file is created in JavaScript. Most of the configurations you'll see here are ones you can alter using the HTML-based Configuration Editor, which you'll agree is a lot easier to use. However, there are some things you cannot do in the HTML-based editor that you can do in the text editor. Let's take a look.

These configuration changes should be inserted into the AutoConfig text file like this:

```
config(preference,value);
```

The first item specifies that it is a user configuration file, the second item is the name of the preference that you're changing, and the third item is the value you're changing the preference to. For example, if there were a configuration called coffee_breaks, and I wanted to change it to four times a day instead of three, it would look like this:

```
config(coffee_breaks,4)
```

See? Okay, let's get into some real configurations:

■ **autoadmin.failover_to_cached**. This parameter specifies what should happen if Communicator fails to load an AutoConfig preference file. The value *true* means that Communicator will load using a cached version of the AutoConfig file. The value *false* means Communicator will fail to run.

■ **Toolbar.logo.win_small_file**. This is the value for a custom logo that you can place in the stead of the Netscape meteor shower logo and animation. The still and animation files should be saved continuously in a 16-color .BMP file and saved to the same directory that the netscape.cfg file is in. The small file size should be 30x30 pixels, or 30x(30* the number of animation frames). For example, if you had 10 frames, the size of the file should be 30x300 pixels, or 30x(30*10).

> **TIP**
>
> *Envision the BMP as a strip of film, being "pulled" through the viewing window of the Communicator toolbar. That might help.*

■ **Toolbar.logo.win_large_file**. The same, for the large version of the logo. The size for a large file should be 48x48 pixels, or 48x(48*the number of animation frames).

■ **Toolbar.logo.frames**. The number of frames in the animation. Its default value is -1, for no animation. For animation, the possible values are any number between 1 and 40.

> **TIP**
>
> *Bear in mind that if you're going to make changes to the customized animation graphics, you must convert this AutoConfig file to a local config file and save it to the local hard drive. You can't make animation graphics changes via the AutoConfig file.*

The above files apply only to the Windows version of Communicator. For Mac users the parameter is mac_animation_file. Mac users should use resource files instead of .BMP files for graphics.

■ **About_text**. This is the text that will go in the Help | About Communicator section. Because its value is a text string, be sure to insert it in quotation marks (""). For example: config(about_text,"This is my example.").

Moving On

Wow! There was a lot more to the configuration files than you ever suspected, wasn't there? You've gotten hip-deep into them and you've come out alive. Congratulate yourself!

In the next chapter we'll work on putting all of this together—figuring out how to create "packages" of files to be installed via Communicator Professional's AutoUpdate feature, as well as using Install Builder to create custom versions of Communicator for you to distribute to your users.

CHAPTER 16

JAR Archive & Install Builder

In the preceding chapter, we discussed customizing files and how to make your intranet's copy of Communicator unique by using the Configuration Editor. In this chapter, we'll focus on how to create "packages" of files that you can distribute over your intranet. You can do this in two ways, using the JAR Packager and the Install Builder. The JAR Packager can contain applications, plug-ins, and additions to Communicator, while the Install Builder was designed to build only custom versions of Communicator.

The JAR Packager (JAR stands for "Java Archive") lets you create a digital "envelope" that houses a collection of files. If you're familiar with PC protocols, this probably sounds like a ZIP file. And you're right, it's a lot like a ZIP file. But it's a little more than that, too. The JAR Packager supports digital signatures, which you learned about in Chapter 13, "Commerce & Security." The digital signatures can be applied to individual files within an archive or to all the files in an archive. The signatures assure that the users on your intranet are getting files from a trusted source—probably you! Further, JAR archives are used by Communicator for SmartUpdates, allowing system and network administrators to update software remotely without relying on the users or "sneakernet" to make sure that software becomes updated.

The Install Builder takes those customized items that we created in the previous chapter—the animated logo, the new Communicator configuration file, and so on—and puts them into a package that you can distribute via your network, CD-ROM, or even disks.

We'll cover the JAR Packager first and then move into the Install Builder. Let's get started.

The JAR Packager

Open your Mission Control group and choose Netscape JAR Packager. That'll get you into the JAR Packager main screen, which looks like Figure 16-1.

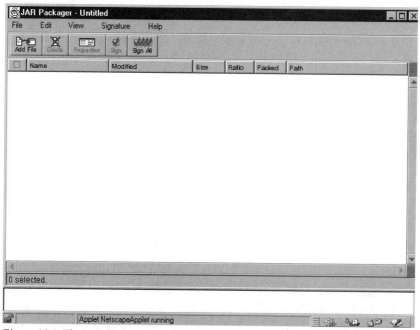

Figure 16-1: The JAR Packager's main screen.

Unlike Netscape Calendar and some of the other Communicator Professional Components, the JAR Packager is a simple application that does a single thing and does it very well. Nowhere is that point brought home more than in the options.

What's that? You don't want to think about setting the options because that always takes 20 pages and a dozen screen shots? Fear not. Just open up Edit I Options. You'll get a screen that looks like the one in Figure 16-2.

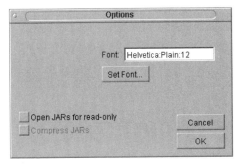

Figure 16-2: Setting up Options in JAR Packager.

Wow! One screen and that's it. Click Set Font and you'll be given a drop-down menu of your available fonts, as well as a chance to set the point size. Aside from that, there are only two other things to set in the options: there's a check box to open JARs for read-only (you can't edit them, but neither can you accidentally dispose of their signatures), and another check box where you can choose to compress JARs. The read-only feature would be used for just looking at a JAR package that you've received, while the compression option compresses the JAR files you create so that they are smaller.

When you're finished with this short option box, click OK, and we'll get back into the business of building JARs. We'll start with opening a JAR file.

Opening JARs

Opening a JAR is easy. Choose File | Open from the main JAR packager screen. You'll be shown a screen that looks like the one in Figure 16-3.

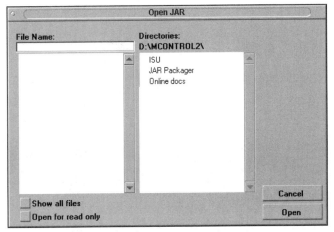

Figure 16-3: Opening a JAR.

Now, you might not know it, but I bet you can open a file using the JAR Packager right now, even if you don't have any .JAR files on your hard drive. That's because the JAR Packager can open ZIP files and automatically convert them to JARs.

On the lower left-hand side of this screen there's a check box that reads "Show all files." Click on that and you'll see all the files in that directory. Use the right list to move through the folders on your hard drive until you find a ZIP file you can open. Click on it to open it. You'll get a screen that looks like the one in Figure 16-4.

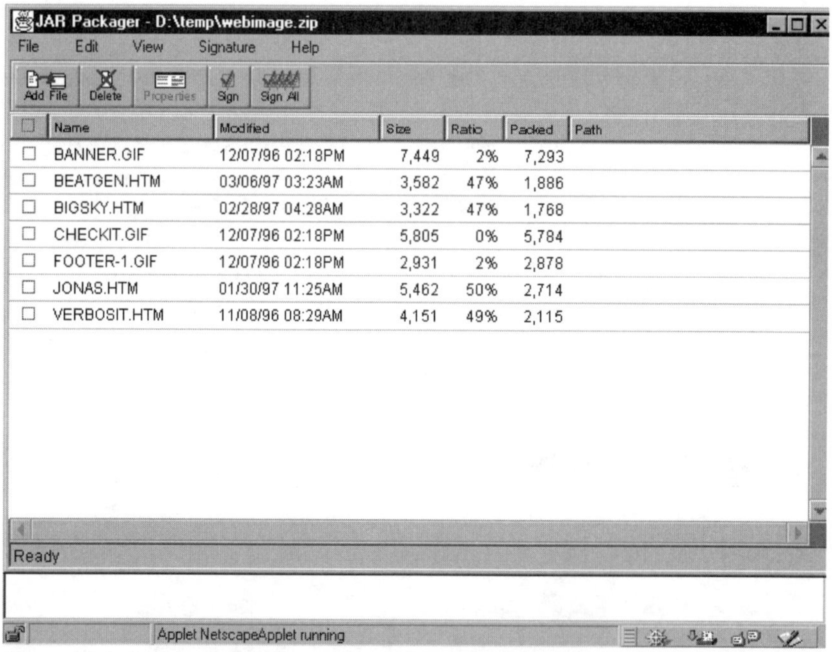

Figure 16-4: Opening a ZIP file.

The screen looks the same if you're opening a JAR: you'll see the name of the file, the date the file was last modified, the size of the file, the compression ratio of the file, the size of the compressed file, and the path of the file. When you see a ZIP file you want to open, click on it to open it up.

> **TIP**
>
> *If you open a file that has signatures that aren't yours, you'll get a screen warning you that the JAR has existing signatures that cannot be saved. You have two options:*
>
> - *Discard the signatures, which will allow you to edit the JAR but will also remove the secure signatures and show that the file has been tampered with.*
>
> - *Open the JAR as read-only, which will keep the security measures intact but will not allow you to edit the JAR.*

But wait a minute. What's that box all the way to the left? That's where a notation for a signature goes. A ZIP file will not have any digital signatures associated with it, but a JAR file can have digital signatures.

Now that you know how to open JAR and ZIP files, let's talk about creating them from scratch.

Creating JARs

Select File | New from the main JAR Packager screen. You'll get a screen that looks like the one in Figure 16-1.

You'll need to add files. There's no fun having an empty archive. Click the Add File icon at the top left of the screen. You'll get the Add Files to JAR dialog box, which looks like Figure 16-5.

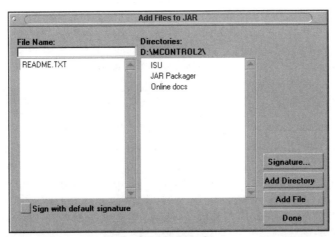

Figure 16-5: Adding a file to the JAR Archive.

It's a lot like the dialog box used for opening a JAR archive, isn't it? Use the left side of the box to move through your file system, and the right side of the box to add items. To add a file, click on the file to highlight it and click Add File. To add a directory, click on the directory to highlight it and click Add Directory.

If you have serious security concerns, at this point you might want to go ahead and sign the files as you're adding them to the archive. Click on the Signature… button. You'll get an additional dialog box that looks like Figure 16-6.

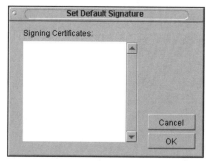

Figure 16-6: Setting a default signature.

All the available digital certificates will be listed in this box. (If you don't have a digital signature certificate and you want one, please refer to Chapter 13, "Commerce & Security.") Choose one and click OK. You have just set your Default Signature.

What does that mean? Well, not much until you click on the "Sign with default signature" check box in the lower left part of the Add Files window. When you've clicked on that, files will automatically be signed with the digital signature you specified as you add them to the JAR.

When you're all done adding files, click OK. Your archive should look like 16-4.

Whoops! Did you add a file you didn't mean to add? That's okay; highlight the file and click the Delete button in the upper left corner. That'll get rid of it.

It's entirely possible that you might want to sign a file after it's been added to the archive. Highlight a file by clicking on it and clicking on either the Sign button or the Sign All button on the menu bar. You'll get a list of available signatures, like you did in Figure 16-6. Choose one, click on it to highlight it, and click OK.

All right. You've added files, you've signed them with your digital signature—now, you need to set an installer. Maybe. If you've created this archive with the idea that it would be automatically installed, you'll have to include an "installer"—a JavaScript script that will install the contents of the JAR on a system.

To set the installer, choose File | Set Installer from the main screen. You'll get a screen that looks like the one in Figure 16-7.

Figure 16-7: Setting the installer.

If there's already an installer associated with the JAR, there will be a file listed in the box. If you want to choose another file, click on Browse and use the browser box to find the file.

What's an Installer?

The installer, strangely enough, is the program used to install the application or updates being packaged. In JAR Packages, the installer comes in one of two flavors: a JavaScript installation script or the installer that comes with the software itself. If you choose to use the installer that comes with the software itself, you'll still have to write a small JavaScript to launch the installer once the JAR package has been downloaded to the user's computer.

This is for the JavaHeads out there: You can of course use any classes you want when creating a JavaScript installation, but Netscape has added netscape.softupdate.VersionInfo and nescape.softupdate.SoftwareUpdate. These classes can allow you to specify a version for your software, specify directories on the user's computer, and extract files from the JAR archive to the user's computer.

Time to save the JAR! All done! Click File | Save or File | Save As and you're finished!

Okay, you've created a JAR, perhaps with a plug-in or some other component to use with Communicator. But before you can update Communicator with a JAR, you need to create an installation of Communicator itself. For that you need to build an installation of Communicator using the Install Builder.

The Install Builder

In the last chapter, we discussed customizing Communicator configuration files, and how you could distribute those files to the users on your intranet. But what if you need to give them the entire Communicator or Communicator Professional application—from scratch?

No big deal. That's what the Install Builder is all about. The Install Builder allows you to combine customized components—like custom bookmark files, address books, and configuration files—with standard elements of Communicator or Communicator Professional into an installation-ready package. You can distribute this package via CD-ROM, network, or even using disks.

Before we get into using the Install Builder, let's do a little more customization. I might have piqued your curiosity there in the last paragraph when I mentioned combining custom bookmarks files and address books. Let me show you how to do that now, so when you're ready to build an installation of Communicator you can add your own customized components.

Creating Customized Components

There are three types of customized components you can create: the bookmarks file, the personal address book, and the corporate address book.

Creating a Customized Bookmarks File

Sure, you could install a vanilla copy of Communicator on a user's computer, and then wait for them to find all the great pages you've put up on the company intranet. Or you could give them a little preemptive nudge by including the best intranet and corporate resources on a set of customized bookmarks.

The easiest way to create a customized bookmarks file for Communicator is simply to use your copy of Communicator and edit your bookmarks file. By doing this you'll be absolutely certain to follow the correct protocols when creating the bookmarks file. Another way you can do it is by using a text editor, like Windows Notepad, to edit the bookmarks file. If you have a list of bookmarks you need to "drop in," this might be the easiest way to do it.

TIP

Don't use an HTML editor to edit your bookmarks file. It might include unnecessary code that renders the bookmarks unusable. When creating a bookmarks file, you want the cleanest HTML code possible.

Once you've created the file, save it and set it aside for the moment. I'll show you where to put it when we get into actually using the Install Builder.

You absolutely have to use Communicator to create your personal address book. There's no other way to edit the file.

Creating a Personal Address Book

Address books are not maintained in an HTML file. They're maintained in a file called abook.nab. You'll have to add items to the address book file manually (as you learned how to do in Chapter 5, "Messenger"), or import items to the address book file.

After you've altered the address book to suit your tastes, save it and set it aside. (You can find the file in Program Files\Netscape\Users\(Username)\, where the user preferences are stored. On Mac systems you can find the address book in System Folder\Preferences\NetscapeUsers\(Username)\ Netscape Preferences.)

Sometimes you're not going to want to create a personal address book. Sometimes you're going to want to create a corporate address book (CAB), which you can swap out and change without disturbing the addresses in a user's personal address book. The CAB works exactly like the personal address book, with two major exceptions:

- You can't automatically expand names while composing a message.

- The user cannot edit the CAB. They can add and delete addresses from the personal address book only.

Create an address book as usual, manually adding names or importing them. When you're done, rename the abook.nab file that you've created to something else. For example, if I were going to create a corporate address book for CopperSky Writing and Research, I might call it abook_csky.nab.

You'll need to make note of the CAB in the configuration file. Open the Configuration Editor and choose the Directory screen. Use the New button to add your new CAB to the directory list. You need to fill in only the name of the CAB; you can leave the other fields blank. Take note of what number the CAB is on your directory list!

Save the configuration file as an AutoConfig file, because you'll need to edit it a little bit.

> **TIP**
>
> *Of course, you can't just randomly edit a configuration file and expect the changes to apply to all the other configuration files that you create from then on. These instructions are meant mostly to be added as a "last step" to your configuration process.*

Open the AutoConfig file with your favorite text editor. Scroll through the file until you find the description label for the directory. Figure 16-8 shows the descriptive label of the CAB in an AutoConfig file.

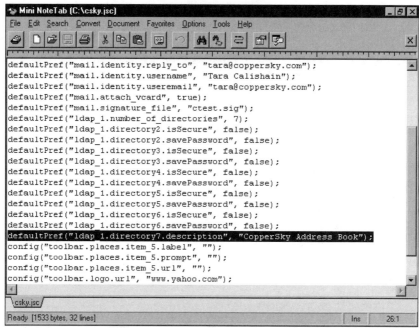

Figure 16-8: The CAB added to an AutoConfig file.

You'll need to add three values to this section, preceded by defaultPref or lockPref. They are:

- **ldap_1.directory#.filename**. The # should be the order number of the CAB as it appears in your Directory list (1, 2, 4, whatever). The value should be the name of the CAB, in my case abook_csky.nab.

- **ldap_1.directory#.dirType**. Again, the # should be the order number of the CAB, and the value should be the directory type of the CAB, which is 2. (It's always 2, no matter in what order your directory appears.)

- **ldap_1.directory#.isOffline**. One more time! The # should be the order number of the CAB, and the value for this item should be true.

Let's put this all together. I've created a file called abook_csky.nab, and have added it to the directory as the first item. So I would add the following after the notation of the directory:

```
lockPref("ldap_1.directory1.filename","abook_csky.nab");
lockPref("ldap_1.directory1.dirtype",2);
lockPref("ldap_1.directory1.isOffline",true);
```

Got it? Remember, these go after the notation of the directory, which will look something like this:

```
defaultPref("ldap_1.directory2.description","CopperSky Address Book");
```

Set the CAB file aside. We'll work with that after a while.

Now that you know how to make customized files, let's talk about how you can build a customized version of Communicator to install across a network. But before we get into that, you need to know where you should put your files.

> **TIP**
>
> *The Windows installation procedure is quite different from the Mac installation procedure. Please see the sidebar "Creating Installers for the Mac," later in this chapter for specific Mac installation instructions.*

Placing Customized Files

The Install Builder comes with four complete sets of installer modules—two each for 32-bit and 16-bit. We'll treat this as if you're using a 32-bit installation. If you're using a 16-bit installation for Windows 3.1 machines, just substitute the directory name 16-bit where I use the directory name 32-bit.

There are two directories for 32-bit installations. From the Mission Control directory, they are Instbldr\Original\32bit\ and Instbldr\Custom\32bit.

Now listen, because this is very important. You want to move your customized items, bookmarks, customized address books, and customized configuration files into the Custom directory. Never move customized files into the Original directory! The Original directory is for keeping "clean" copies of the installer files. You don't want to change those clean copies with your customizations. The next step is to move any configuration files you have created into the appropriate directory.

The first thing you want to move is the customized local configuration file you've created. From the Mission Control directory, the appropriate path to use to move the netscape.cfg file is Instbldr\Custom\32bit\Nav40\Program.

The next thing is the bookmark file, if you've created one. That belongs in Instbldr\Custom\32bit\Nav40\Program\Defaults.

Finally, you should move over your address book and CAB as well if you've created customized ones (be sure if you're including a CAB that you've also added the proper code to the configuration file!). The customized address books also belong in Instbldr\Custom\32bit\Nav40\Program\Defaults.

TIP

Make sure that you're including all appropriate files when you move your local configuration file. For example, if you've customized the configuration file to include a nifty new animation, be sure to move the animation graphic in addition to the configuration file. The animation graphic belongs in the same directory as the configuration file.

Have you moved everything? You did move it into the Custom directory, right? You didn't move it into the Original directory? Good. Now you can get to actually using the Install Builder program.

Using the Install Builder

Open the Mission Control group and choose Netscape Install Builder. You're presented with a screen that looks like the one in Figure 16-9.

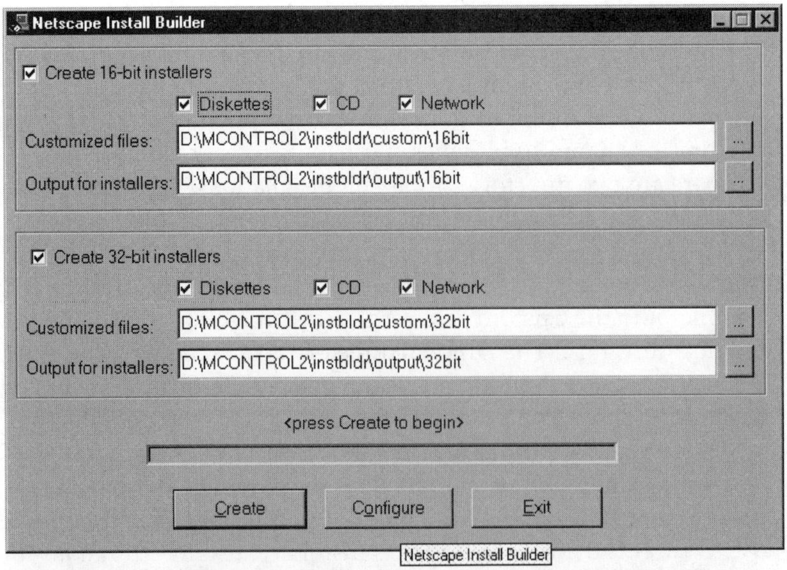

Figure 16-9: The Netscape Install Builder.

Choose which type of file you'd like to create. You can create either 16-bit or 32-bit installations (or both, if you'd like—just be sure that you have moved the customization files to all the appropriate directories).

TIP

When should you choose 16-bit files? When you're creating installations for Windows 3.1. When should you choose 32-bit files? When you're creating installations for Windows95.

Now, choose what kind of installation you want to build: one to be distributed via CD-ROM, disks, or over a network. Uncheck the distribution methods you don't want.

To further customize what kind of modules you want to include with your installation of Communicator, click the Configure button at the bottom of the screen. You'll get something that looks like Figure 16-10.

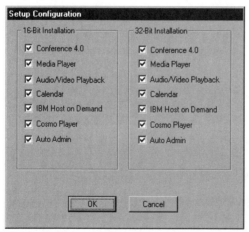

Figure 16-10: Configuring which modules you want to include.

As you can see, this is a series of check boxes. Each check box is a module you can include with the Communicator installation. If you want to create a Communicator Professional installation, leave all the boxes checked. If you want to create a Communicator installation, uncheck the Calendar, IBM Host on Demand, and AutoAdmin check boxes.

When you've decided what modules you want to include, click OK and you'll be taken back to the main Install Builder screen. Now all you have to do is click Create and go get a sandwich. When the Install Builder is finished, you'll get an alert box that reads "Installation creation complete."

But wait a minute! Where are your files?

The installation output is in the directory specified in the "Output for installers" text box on the main Install Builder screen. Most of the time that's something like c:\missioncontrol\instbldr\output\32bit (or c:\missioncontrol\instbldr\output\16bit if you're creating Windows 3.1 installations).

Now, how do you actually handle the files that appear in this directory? It depends on what kind of installation medium you want to use.

- **CD-ROM files**. There'll be a CD-ROM folder in the output directory. Copy the contents of the directory onto a CD-ROM.

- **Network**. There'll be a network folder in the output directory. There's only one file in it. Copy that file to the area on the network from which you want your users to copy it.

- **Disks**. There'll be a disk folder in the output directory. Within that folder there will be several folders, one for each diskette that's required to hold the installation (a typical all-module installation takes 12 disks). Install each directory's contents on a separate diskette and label them appropriately (install directory 1 on a diskette that you then label #1, etc.).

Creating Installers for the Mac

Creating installers for the Mac relies on Installer VISE, from MindVision. To create an installer file, you need:

- A set of VISE archives, one for each module to be installed.

- A Preference file which governs the installation process.

- Customized files, if you plan to use any.

In the Macintosh Install Builder program, there are modules for both Communicator and Communicator Professional. You can't add to these modules, but you can remove modules that you don't want. To remove a module, look at the Installer Preferences file. Find the [Packages] flag group. Find the line that refers to the module you want to remove, and remove the entire line.

At this printing, the Macintosh Install Builder doesn't support disk-based installations. Instead it creates a CD-installer. Copy the contents of the created Installer folder to a CD-ROM. (Don't copy the folder itself.)

To create a network-compatible installer, compress the contents of the Installer folder and place it on your network.

Moving On

You've done it! You've created a custom installation of Communicator! Now your users on the intranet can have a version of Communicator specifically built for their needs and with their interests in mind.

Now, in the interests of creating a nice, circular book, I refer you to Appendix A, which will explain how to install Communicator and create user profiles.

APPENDIX A

Installing Netscape Communicator 4 Professional & Setting Profiles

Netscape Communicator 4 Professional is a large program that performs a variety of tasks, but setting it up isn't complex. In fact, Netscape walks you through installation with several dialog boxes designed to figure out the best way to install Communicator Professional on your computer. Communicator can also maintain several different "profiles," so users can have their own identification and preferences without having to reset them every time after someone else uses Communicator.

In this appendix, we'll go over the process of installing Communicator as well as creating a user profile. Creating a user profile is not required, however; Communicator automatically creates a user profile upon installation. You need to create additional ones only if several users will be accessing Communicator.

TIP

Keep in mind that in order for certain aspects of Communicator Professional to function, the appropriate server programs need to be active on your intranet. If you've installed Communicator and you can't seem to get certain aspects of the program to work, check with your network administrator to make sure all server components are active on the intranet.

Installing Netscape Communicator 4

All of Communicator is contained within one large file, usually called some-thing like *cp32e40.exe*. To begin the installation process, double-click this filename. (Where this file is located depends on whether you're getting Com-municator off of a CD-ROM or downloading it from the Internet or your company intranet.)

TIP

> *Make sure that you've exited all programs before beginning Communicator's installation; the installation process will take a lot of memory. Make especially sure that you've exited any other versions of Communicator that you have on your system. Communicator Professional will not install if there are other active versions of Communicator running.*

A message box will appear, letting you know that you're beginning the process of installing Netscape Communicator Professional and asking if you want to continue. Click the Yes button. Another message box will appear, alerting you that installation has begun and asking you to wait as it prepares to install Communicator. This process generally just takes a moment—exactly how long varies depending on your computer's RAM and processor power. After it's prepared, you'll see the dialog box shown in Figure A-1.

Figure A-1: Welcome to Netscape Communicator Professional Setup.

The next box is a license agreement that you must agree to before you can install Communicator Professional. Read the agreement and click the Yes button if you agree. If you don't agree, click the No button and the installation program will end without installing Communicator Professional.

The third dialog box, as you see in Figure A-2, gives you a choice of installation types.

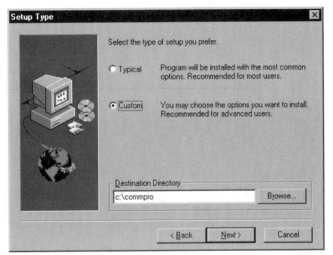

Figure A-2: Choosing the setup type.

On this dialog box, you have a choice between Typical and Custom setup. Typical absolves you of some decision-making; it installs Communicator Professional as it's most commonly installed. If you're not comfortable with software installation, or you don't want to get very involved with the installation, click the radio button next to Typical. Custom gives you far more control over the installation process, letting you choose what components of Communicator you want to install. I recommend this option for everyone who's reasonably comfortable with software installation, as it lets you see what the installation program is putting on your hard drive.

On this dialog box, you can also specify where you want to install Communicator Professional. Generally, you can let it install to the default directory (which will be something like c:\netscape\communicator). If you want to change the directory, click the Browse button, and a browser box will pop up, allowing you to specify another directory.

After you've decided the type of setup you want to use and where you want Communicator to install on your hard drive, click the Next button. Typical takes care of many installation questions for you, so we're going to proceed as if we have decided on a custom setup. The next dialog box after you decide you want a Custom installation looks like the one in Figure A-3.

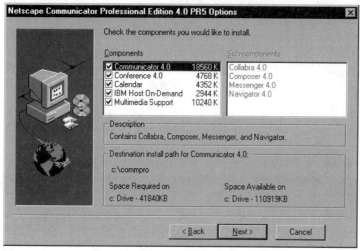

Figure A-3: Customizing—choosing the components you want to install.

Communicator Professional has five possible components to install: Communicator 4.0, Conference 4.0, Calendar, IBM Host On-Demand, and Multimedia Support. For every item that you don't want to install, click the check box next to the item name. An unchecked check box means that the component will not be installed.

One of the components, Multimedia Support, has sub-components that you can choose to install or not install. Click the Multimedia Support item in the Components list, and you'll get a dialog box that looks like Figure A-4.

You can click any of the check boxes under Sub-components to prevent their installation. For the most part, you want to install everything possible; however, you may have a disk space problem you need to consider. For that reason, the Communicator setup program lists the size of every component so that you can determine where you might save on disk space. At the bottom of the dialog box in Figure A-4, you'll see that the space required for the current configuration and the space available on the drive where you're installing Communicator are both listed, so you can keep track of how much space you're using.

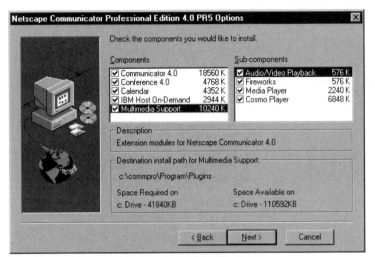

Figure A-4: Sub-components of the Multimedia Support component.

TIP

A full installation of Netscape Communicator Professional takes a little over 40MB on your hard drive.

After you've decided which components you want to install, click Next. (If you want to install everything, just click Next—Netscape will automatically install all components without your having to specify them.)

If you have a previous version of Communicator installed on your hard drive, you'll get an alert box at this point warning you that Communicator Setup has detected a previous installation of Navigator. The alert box will also let you know that you'll have to reinstall any helpers and plug-ins after you've installed Communicator Professional.

The next dialog box, in Figure A-5, gives you the option of setting up associations.

Figure A-5: Setting up associations for Communicator.

With associations, a particular program will open a file on your computer, based on the extension of that particular file. For example, if you have Word on your computer, then your associations are set up so that if you double-click a file called Whatever.doc, it's automatically opened in Word. The file extension *.doc* associates that file with the program Word.

Similarly, Netscape Communicator gives you the option to associate the following file extensions:

- **HTML** (.htm, .html)—HTML is the format in which Web pages are created.

- **JPEG** (.jpe, .jpg, .jpeg)—JPEG is a graphics format.

- **GIF** (.gif)–GIF is a graphics format.

- **JavaScript Source File** (.js)—Java is a programming language used on the Web.

- **Netscape Conference Call** (.nsc)—A source file used by Conference.

This way, if you double-click a filename, the file is automatically opened by Navigator. In this dialog box, you're also given the option to associate files with the extension *.nsc* with the Netscape Conference application.

If you're using a graphics program like Photoshop or Paint Shop Pro, then uncheck the JPEG or GIF boxes, since you've already got associations set up for your JPEG and GIF graphics files. Leave the other ones checked.

After you've finished making your selections on this page, click the Next button. The next dialog box is for selecting where you want the program icon files to appear, as you see in Figure A-6.

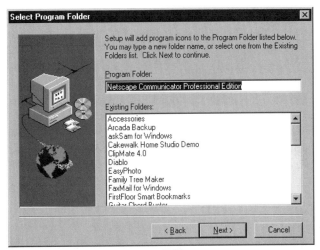

Figure A-6: Selecting a Program Folder.

You can either specify a new folder (the default new folder is called Netscape Communicator Professional) or double-click an existing folder to install Communicator's icons in it.

Netscape Communicator Professional has so many icons that giving it its own folder is a good idea. You don't have to call the folder Netscape Communicator, but you should give the icons their own folder.

Once you click the Next button, you'll be taken to the final dialog box, which you see in Figure A-7.

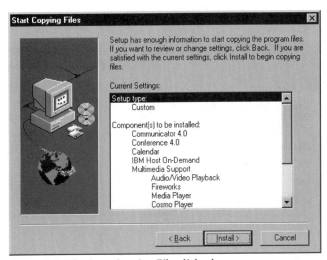

Figure A-7: The Start Copying Files dialog box.

This dialog box lists all the decisions you've made for installation thus far. Go over the list, and if you want to change anything, click the Back button to page back through the previous dialog boxes and change the installation options. If everything looks all right, click Install and the program will install itself to your hard drive.

Once you've installed Communicator Professional, you already have a user profile. However, if you're going to be using Communicator for completely different tasks—for example, for personal use and for business use—you might want to set up two different profiles for yourself. The separate profiles will allow you to keep different bookmarks, mail and newsgroup listings, and preferences.

Creating Additional User Profiles

To begin creating a new user profiles, go to the program group where you put your Netscape Communicator icons. Choose the Setup New User Profile icon to launch the Profile Setup Wizard, the first dialog box of which you see in Figure A-8.

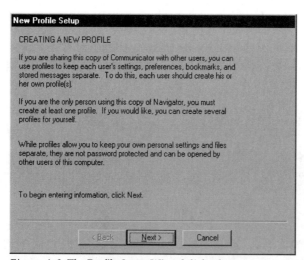

Figure A-8: The Profile Setup Wizard dialog box.

This initial dialog box gives you an overview of the profile setup process and how it will affect your use of Communicator. Clicking Next will take you to the name and address setup dialog box, as you see in Figure A-9.

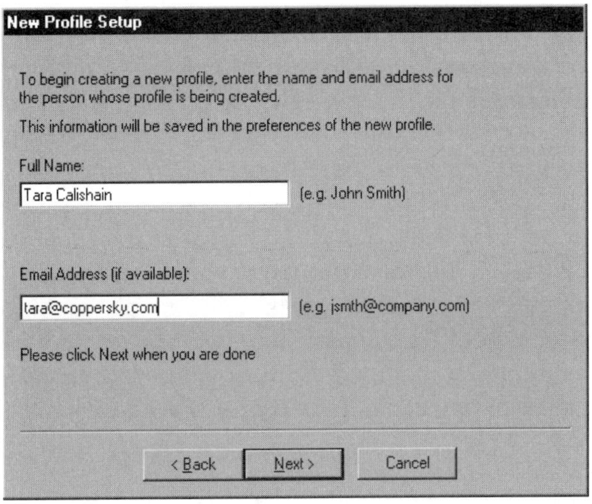

Figure A-9: The name and address setup dialog box.

This dialog box is pretty simple, isn't it? Just enter your name and your e-mail address. Click Next to continue. The next dialog box, shown in Figure A-10, will ask for a profile name and a place to store the profile's data.

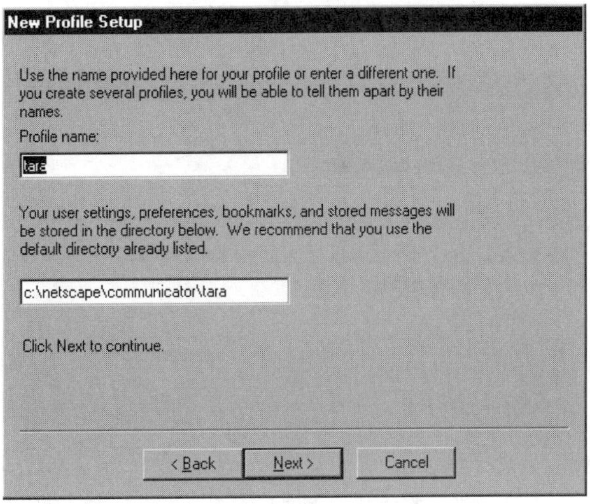

Figure A-10: Naming your profile.

Choose a name for your profile. Make it distinctive, especially if you're creating more than one profile for yourself. For example, if I want to create two business profiles for myself—one for working and one for personal surfing—I might call one TARAWORK and the other TARASURF, or something like that.

The Profile Setup Wizard will give you a default directory to store your user settings, bookmarks, and messages. The directory is based on where you installed Communicator in the first place. My suggestion is that you leave the directory as it is.

After you've decided on a name for your profile, click the Next button. In the next dialog box, shown in Figure A-11, you'll be asked to set up your mail and discussion group identification.

First enter your name, or the identification of your e-mail account. (If you're doing technical support and technical support only on an account, your "name" might be Technical Support.) Then enter your e-mail address, organization or company name, and outgoing mail server. The organization name is optional, but adding it is one more way to build awareness of your company's name.

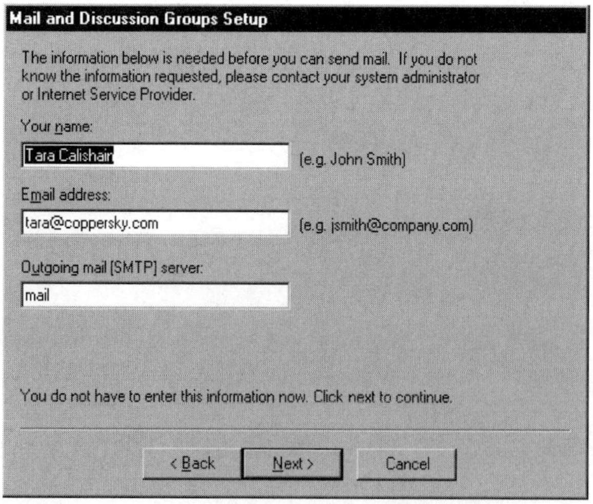

Figure A-11: Setting up mail and news identification.

TIP

If you don't know some of the information this setup wizard is asking for, leave it blank. You can use the Profile Manager icon later on to add information.

Click the Next button to get to the second part of the mail and discussion group setup, as shown in Figure A-12.

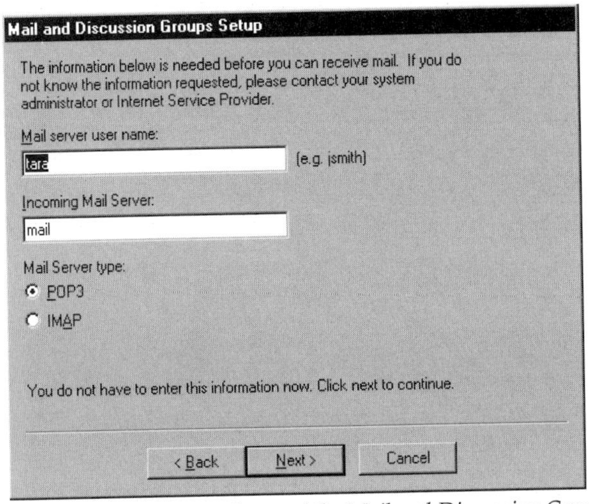

Figure A-12: The second part of the Mail and Discussion Groups Wizard dialog box.

The first box requires you to enter your mail server username. Your mail server username is usually your e-mail name, without the @company.com. For example, if my e-mail address is sky@mindspring.com, then my mail server username would be "sky." The second box requires you to enter the name of your incoming mail server. Your incoming mail server name is usually mail.companyname.com. For example, because my Internet provider is Mindspring, the name of my incoming mail server is mail.mindspring.com. The last choice on this dialog box is determining the type of mail server you have. POP3 is used by accounts that dial into the Internet from a stand-alone machine, whereas IMAP is often used by accounts that dial into the Internet through a LAN. If you don't know which server type you have, ask your Internet provider's technical support people or your company's technical support department. Click Next when you're done setting up the dialog box.

The final dialog box in the Profile Setup Wizard, shown in Figure A-13, is for indicating the news server.

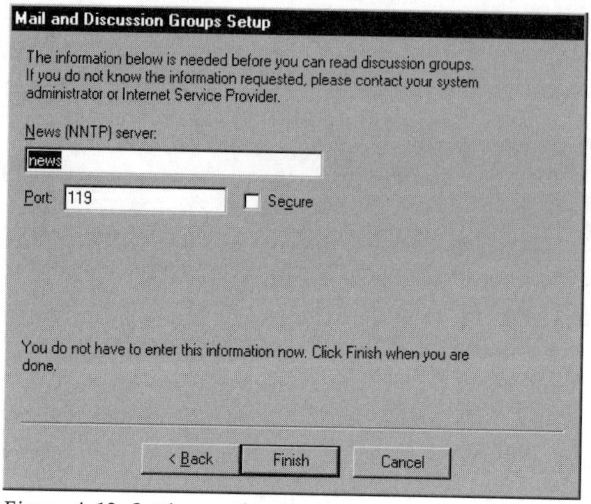

Figure A-13: Setting up the news server.

The news server is usually news.companyname.com—its name is structured like the name of the mail server. Because my Internet provider is Mindspring, the name of my news server is news.mindspring.com.

After you've entered the name of your news server, click Finish, and the Profile Setup Wizard will finish putting together the profile for you. From now on, Netscape Communicator will give you a choice of available profiles every time you begin the program.

Glossary

access privileges   A user's rights on a host. Typically users are allowed to create or edit files only in their home directories and its subdirectories, though they can run programs from public directories.

account   An agreement with an organization allowing you to take advantage of various services. For instance, an account on an e-mail server lets you log on to send and receive e-mail. Accounts are often protected by *authentication*, requiring that you type in a user name and password.

activate   To make a window the active one by clicking on it.

active window   The window with the highlighted title bar, where the user is currently interacting with a program.

ACU   *Automatic Call Unit.* Fancy word for a modem.

address area   The area in Messenger's New Message window where you can edit your list of e-mail addresses.

Address Book   A Communicator feature that lets you store individual e-mail addresses and address lists.

Address Book Card   An electronic record of an individual's name, e-mail address, etc., often used in e-mail. Also known as a vCard.

address list   A list of e-mail addresses. The address list lets you send e-mail to many individuals at once without entering each address.

addressing   The assignment of unique names or numbers to every node on a network so that information doesn't get misdelivered.

agents   Search tool that automatically seeks out online information based on your queries. Also called intelligent agents, knowbots, and droids.

algorithm   The step-by-step process a software program uses to produce its results.

alias   An alternate name used in place of a "real" one. Rather than using your real name to log in to a system, you probably use a shorter alias. Commands can also have aliases. For instance, you can create command files on a UNIX system so that instead of typing **ls -al** to see all the files in your directory, you could just type **dir**.

American Standard Code for Information Interchange   *See* **ASCII**.

anchor   In HTML, the target of a link, usually in the same document. It is sometimes also used to mean any link.

application protocol   A **protocol** that "sits on top of" the underlying transport layer of a communications system. For example, **FTP** and **Telnet** are application protocols that format data in particular ways and use the services of the lower-level **TCP/IP** transport layer.

Archie   A network service used for locating files available at **FTP** sites that accept anonymous logins.

ARP   *Address Resolution Protocol.* Protocol used on a network for mapping Ethernet addresses to IP addresses.

ARPAnet   A wide area network developed in the 1960s by the Advanced Research Projects Agency of the U.S. Department of Defense. It links government and academic networks around the world.

ASCII   *American Standard Code for Information Interchange.* This standard assigns a binary value to common text and control characters. ASCII is used for manipulating text in a program and for transmitting text to other devices or systems.

ASCII file   A human-readable file made up only of letters, numbers, and symbols. An ASCII file contains no formatting except tabs, linefeeds, and carriage returns. Also known as a *text file.*

assigned numbers   The usual port numbers for well-known Internet services such as **Telnet**, **FTP**, and so on. For instance, hosts usually wait for Telnet connections on TCP port 23, for World Wide Web connections on port 80, and for Usenet news connections on port 119. These assigned port numbers are how the host knows what kind of connection is being requested.

asynchronous transmission   The transmission of data without special timing information. Each character you transmit is made up of several bits of information. In asynchronous communications, the characters are "packaged," usually by special start and stop bits, so that the receiving hardware or software knows when it has received an entire character. This way, the interval *between* characters doesn't have to be fixed, and information can arrive at any time. *See also* **synchronous transmission**.

Attachment   A text or binary file included with an e-mail message.

attachment encoding   The method used to encode an attached binary file so that it can be delivered to the recipient via any intermediary systems without being corrupted.

attachments list   The list of attached files that will be sent along with an e-mail message sent.

attribute (text)   The display characteristics of text. Text attributes include bold, italic, underlined, and so on. In **World Wide Web** documents, text may be tagged with a wide variety of attributes using **HTML**.

AU sound   Audio format developed by Sun and used for sound files on the Web. Netscape browsers play AU files using the helper program NAPLAYER.

authentication   The process of identifying a user to determine if he or she should have access to a particular computer system. Name and password prompts are a form of authentication.

authoring software   Any software that lets you create HTML or other multimedia documents.

bandwidth   The range of frequencies that can be transmitted over a network, limited by the hardware. Higher bandwidth allows more information on the network at one time.

baud rate   The number of signal changes per second as data is transmitted from one device to another. For instance, 110 transitions per second from a high frequency to a low frequency on a phone line would be 110 baud. Each signal change may signify one bit of data (for instance, high frequency to low could signify 1, low to high could signify 0); if a signal changes in multiple ways (frequency, amplitude, etc.), it may signify multiple bits of data. In the first case, baud rate would equal **bits per second**; in the second case, bits per second would be higher than the baud rate. The difference between baud rate and bits per second is a common icebreaker at nerd parties.

BBS   *See* **bulletin board system**.

BCC Short for *blind carbon copy*. A copy of an e-mail message that does not include information about who the other recipients are.

binary Numbers composed of combinations of two different digits, specifically 1 and 0. In the context of this book, binary data means information that may contain the full range of combinations of binary digits in a **byte**, as opposed to information that contains only the limited range of information that is displayable as text. Bytes of **ASCII** text contain only seven significant **data bits**, as in 1011001, while programs, graphics, spreadsheet files, and so on, contain eight significant data bits per byte, as in 10011011.

binary file Any file, such as an executable or graphic, that cannot be read as text, usually containing characters that have eight rather than seven significant data bits and are therefore beyond the range of **ASCII**. In some cases binary files need to be encoded as seven-bit files in order to be transmitted across certain systems (*see* **attachment encoding**).

BIND *Berkeley Internet Name Domain* server. This is the DNS server on BSD and related UNIX systems. *See also* **DNS**.

BinHex A file format, used mainly in the Macintosh world, for storing and transmitting binary data as **ASCII** text. This format is useful for transferring 8-bit data over 7-bit networks or data paths, or for including binary files as part of mail messages. Among UNIX and PC users, **UUENCODING** is more common.

bit A *binary dig*it, the smallest piece of information that a computer can hold. A bit is always one of two values, written as 1 or 0 and corresponding to the on/off state of a digital switch or the high/low state of electrical impulses. Combinations of bits are used to represent more complex information, such as **ASCII** text or commands to the computer.

bitmap A representation of an image as an array of bits.

bit rate The rate at which bits are transmitted, usually expressed as a certain number of **bits per second**, or bps. *See also* **baud rate**.

bits per second *See* **bit rate**.

bookmarks In Netscape browsers, a means of permanently storing the **URL**s for sites you want to revisit.

bridge (1) A device or a combination of hardware and software for connecting networks together. *See also* **internet**.

browser A software program, such as Netscape Navigator 4, that is designed for accessing documents on the World Wide Web, or HTML documents on an intranet.

bulk cipher An **encryption** method used to encrypt large quantities of information.

bulletin board system (BBS) An electronic version of the old cork bulletin board—a place to leave and collect messages and files. A modern BBS is really like a whole collection of bulletin boards, with different sections covering different areas of interest. Users can generally exchange public as well as private messages, and many BBSes include extensive areas for distributing shareware or public domain software.

byte A combination of **bits** used to represent a single character. In the world of personal computers, a byte is eight bits long.

cable   A bundle of wires or fiber strands wrapped with insulation and used to connect devices.

cache   An area of memory or a file used to store frequently accessed instructions or data. A memory cache is used to reduce hard disk access time. Memory and file caches are also used by Web browsers and other online programs to store images or data that rarely change; thus, a large home page does not have to be re-sent each time a connection is established.

carrier   A steady background signal on a communication channel used to indicate that the system is ready for the transmission of data. The carrier is then modified to represent the data transmitted.

CC   Short for *carbon copy*. A copy of a message sent to a secondary or additional recipients.

category   In the context of Netsape Collabra discussion groups, a subdirectory used to organize similar groups.

CCITT   *Consultative Committee on International Telegraphy and Telephony.* This is an international standards-setting body that makes recommendations for international communications technologies.

certificate   *See* **digital certificate**.

Certifying Authorities   Organizations that distribute **digital certificates**.

CGI   *Common Gateway Interface.* A standardized technique that lets Web clients pass information to Web servers, and then on to other programs that process the information. When a Web site accepts the information you enter into a form, it is using CGI.

channels   Collections of information, usually including multimedia files, that are downloaded and then stored locally on your system. Subscribed-to channels may be updated on a regular basis so that they contain the latest information available from the provider. In Communicator, the **Netcaster** component is used to subscribe to, view, and configure channels.

Channel Finder   A Netcaster feature that lets you preview selected **channels,** which you may then subscribe to.

character entities   In HTML, special symbols that stand for other characters. Character entities begin with an ampersand (&) and end with a semicolon (;). For example, *>* in an HTML document would appear on your screen as > (greater than).

character set encoding   The encoding methods that enable software to properly interpret characters and symbols from a variety of languages. To view Web pages that use the standard English alphabet, for instance, you choose the Latin1 character set.

check box   A Windows 95 and Windows NT control that lets you choose a particular option by clicking. Once you click, an X or checkmark appears in the check box; click again and it is cleared.

CIX   *Commercial Internet Exchange.* CIX is an agreement among Internet service providers allowing them to make the Internet available to commercial traffic.

Clear To Send   A signal from a **DCE** to a **DTE** indicating that circuits are ready for data transmission. *See also* **DCE; DTE**.

clickable image   In a Web page, an image you can click in order to access a different URL. *See also* **image map**.

client   A computer or a software program that can access particular services on a network. The machine or the software that provides the service for a client is called a **server**. For instance, an e-mail client would request received mail from an e-mail server.

client pull   A method specific to Netscape products whereby a Web client can request the Web server to send it a particular set of data. *See also* **server push**.

client/server architecture   A system in which a **client** program establishes a connection with a **server** and then requests information or services. *See also* **client**; **server**.

client write key   The software key used to encrypt data written or transmitted by the client in a client/server system.

Clipboard or clipboard   An area of memory where objects (data) are placed when a user carries out a Cut or Copy command or chooses a menu option. This data can then be passed to another program.

Collabra   The component of Netscape Communicator that lets you view and respond to intranet discussion groups as well as **Usenet** newsgroups.

column heading   A Windows 95 and Windows NT control that displays data in a multicolumn list.

combo box   A standard Windows 95 and Windows NT control that combines a text box and a list box.

command button   A control used to initiate a command; also known as a push button.

command prompt   A set of characters or a symbol that indicates where you type in commands. The DOS C:\ prompt is an example of a command prompt.

Communicator   The Netscape software suite that currently includes **Navigator** for Web browsing, **Messenger** for e-mail, **Collabra** for reading or participating in discussion groups, **Composer** for creating HTML documents, and **Conference** for interacting in real time with other individuals on the Net or on an intranet. The Communicator Professional version includes Calendar for scheduling events and tasks, and IBM Host on Demand for connecting to mainframes.

Component bar   The Communicator control that lets you access the various components of the program (**Navigator**, **Collabra**, etc.) by clicking on icons. The Component Bar may be anchored to the status line of the various Netscape programs, or it may "float" on your desktop.

Composer   The Communicator component that lets you create and edit HTML files.

Conference   The Communicator component that lets you interact in real time with other individuals across the Net or an intranet. Features include full-duplex voice communication, chat, file transfer, a special graphical whiteboard for collaborative design and planning, and collaborative Web browsing.

computer name   On Microsoft networks, a unique name of up to 15 characters that identifies a particular computer on the network.

configuration registry   In Windows 95 and Windows NT, a database that stores information about a computer's configuration as well as the configuration of various software. The registry may be edited by using the program *regedit* in Windows 95 or *regedt32* in Windows NT.

connect time   The amount of time you're connected to a host or to a service provider.

connection   A link between two computers for the purpose of transferring or sharing information.

container   Any screen object that holds other objects; for instance, a folder.

content-type   The MIME name for particular types of files to be transferred by e-mail or the Web. For instance, the content-type for a GIF file is **image/gif**. *See also* **MIME**.

control   Any window object that lets you interact with a program by selecting an action, inputting data, and so on.

Control menu   The menu that pops up when you click the icon at the top left of a program's main window. It contains commands such as Move, Size, Maximize, Minimize, and Close.

cookie   A piece of system or configuration information transmitted between a Web server and the browser software and then often stored on the client machine. Cookies enable a Web page to adjust its display or other configuration options for particular clients that connect.

crawler   *See* **spider**.

cross-platform   Describes software that can be used on more than one operating system, such as Windows, Macintosh, and UNIX.

CSLIP   A common variant of the SLIP protocol that uses compressed IP headers. *See also* **SLIP**.

cyberspace   A slightly dated term referring to the entire world of online information and services. It was originally coined by the writer William Gibson.

daemon   UNIX-speak for a program that's always running on a server machine, waiting for requests for a particular service. For instance, an FTP server daemon sits and waits for an FTP client to connect and request files.

data   Information used or processed by a software program.

data bits   Bits that carry information as opposed to control information. For example, the bits in the middle of a **byte** might signify a text character and are, therefore, data bits, while the bits at the beginning and end of the byte merely mark the beginning and end of the data.

Data Carrier Detect (DCD or CD)   A signal from a **DCE**, such as a modem, to a **DTE**, such as a PC, indicating that a communication channel has been established with a remote device. *See also* **DCE**; **DTE**.

data-file object   An object representing a data file (spreadsheet, document, image, sound clip, etc.) in the file system.

Data Terminal Ready (DTR)   A signal from a DTE to a DCE indicating that it's ready to receive and transmit data. Usually, a modem keeps DTR high as long as it's turned on. *See also* **DCE**; **DTE**.

DCE   *Data Communication Equipment*. A device used by a **DTE** to transmit and receive information. Your modem is a DCE.

DDE   *See* **dynamic data exchange**.

decode   To translate electronic information back into its original form. Unlike decrypting, decoding does not need any special key. *See* **encoding**.

decrypt   To translate electronic information back to its original form through the use of a special electronic key that insures privacy or security. *See* **encryption**.

default   In software, the "out of the box" value of a configuration option. The software will use this value unless the user explicitly indicates a different one in a setup program, property sheet, or .INI file.

desktop   The visual work area that fills your screen and holds the objects you interact with, such as icons, the task bar, and so on. The desktop is a container (or folder) that can also be used as a convenient place to access files.

destination directory   The directory to which you copy, move, or download a file or files.

device driver   A program used by the system to access devices such as video cards, printers, and mice.

dialog box   In Windows 95 and Windows NT, a box that appears on your screen requesting your input; it engages you in a *dialogue* with the software. It may contain edit fields, check boxes, list boxes, radio buttons, and so on, and it stays on your screen until you click its Cancel or OK button.

dial-up networking   A facility built into Windows 95 that allows users to link to a network or to the Internet using phone lines. Similar to **Remote Access Dialer** in Windows NT.

digital certificate   A unique electronic key that identifies you and authorizes you to access secure Web sites. Also, a digital certificate may be included with an e-mail message, identifying the originator of the message and allowing it to be encrypted. *See also* **personal certificate, site certificate**.

digital signature   The inclusion of a digital certificate (for instance with an e-mail message) that matches a key you hold, allowing decryption.

dimmed   A button, menu item, or other control is dimmed or *grayed* (displayed in light gray instead of black) to indicate it represents an option or command that is not currently available.

direct connection   A permanent connection between a computer and the Internet as opposed to a temporary dial-up or **SLIP/PPP** connection.

directory   1. A structure on a disk that contains files or other subdirectories. Also sometimes referred to as a folder. 2. A collection of names, addresses, and other contact information stored as part of a directory service, useful for looking up individuals for e-mail.

directory service   An Internet or intranet service used for looking up e-mail addresses or other contact information.

directory tree   A hierarchical display of a disk's directories and subdirectories.

DLS server   *Dynamic Lookup Service* server. A server that provides the e-mail addresses of and other information for people who want to be included in the list—in other words, a server that acts as a sort of phonebook.

DNS   *Domain Name Service*, an Internet service that returns the appropriate **IP address** when queried with a **domain-name address**.

dock   To configure a toolbar so that it no longer floats, but lines up with the edge of a window or pane.

document (World Wide Web)   On the **World Wide Web**, a file or set of related files that can be transferred from a **Web server** to a Web **client**. The document may contain text, graphics, sound, or hyperlinks to other documents.

document encoding   *See* **encoding**.

document window   A window that lets you view the contents of a document.

domain   A collection of associated computers on the Internet, given a specific domain name that is used as part of the Internet address. For Windows NT Server, a domain is also a uniquely named collection of computers that share a domain database and security policy.

domain-name address   The "plain English" address of a computer on the Internet, as opposed to its numeric **IP address**. For instance, www.echonyc.com is a domain-name address.

download   To get a file or files from a remote computer; the opposite of **upload**.

draft   A message that you're still working on, that is stored in a special holding area (the drafts folder in Netscape Messenger, for instance) until you're ready to send it.

drag   To move a mouse while pressing and holding one of its buttons. Dragging is used to move or resize objects on the screen. (Also known as "drag-and-drop.")

droids   *See* **agents**.

drop-down combo box   A Windows 95 and Windows NT control that combines a text box with a drop-down list box.

drop-down list box   A Windows 95 and Windows NT control that displays a current text selection, but that can be opened to display the entire list of choices.

drop-down menu   A menu that is displayed from a menu bar.

DSU   *Digital Services Unit.* The piece of equipment that enables transmission of data in synchronous digital connections to the Net.

DTE   *Data Terminal Equipment.* A device that serves as the originating point or the final destination of information. Typically, a computer or a terminal is a DTE.

dynamic data exchange (DDE)   The exchange of data between programs such that any change in the data in one program affects that same data in the other program. For instance, if spreadsheet data are shared via DDE by Word and Excel, any changes made to the data in Excel will also appear in the Word document.

edit field   *See* **text box**.

electronic mail   A network service for transmitting messages from one computer to another. Also called *e-mail*.

ellipsis   The "..." added to a menu item or button label to show that the command needs more information to be completed. When you choose a command with an ellipsis, a dialog box appears so you can enter additional information.

encoding   The technique used for storing or expressing data. For instance, text may be stored via ASCII encoding or some form of encoding that uses compression (such as ZIP). In Web browsers, document encoding refers to the translation of incoming characters into display fonts. For instance, you may set Netscape browsers to Japanese encoding so that information in a Japanese HTML document will be correctly displayed.

encryption   A method of **encoding** information for secure transmission. The data can be read in its original form only after it has been decoded. *See also* **public-key encryption**.

environment variable   A symbolic name associated with a string of characters used by an operating system or programs for its own informational purposes. For instance, the environment variable GIF_DIRECTORY could be set to C:\GIF so that a graphics program knows where to look for GIF files. Typically, you set an environment variable by using the Set command at a command prompt or in a batch file. In Windows NT, you can use the System option in Control Panel to define environment variables.

Ethernet   A hardware system and a protocol that is commonly used to connect computers on a LAN.

external viewer   A separate program used by a **World Wide Web** browser to display graphics or to play sound or video files. After downloading a particular media file, the Web browser launches the external viewer program appropriate to the type of file. In order for this to work, you must configure your Web browser with the names of the external viewer programs you have on your system. Another term for external viewer is **helper application**.

extension   The period and characters at the end of a file or directory name, often used to indicate the type of file or directory. For instance, INDEX.HTML includes the .HTML extension to indicate it is an HTML document.

extranet   A TCP/IP network that links businesses to customers, suppliers, etc.; part of an enterprise intranet that is made available to the outside world for marketing or other specific purposes.

e-zine   A zine, or small non-mass-market magazine in electronic format. Some e-zines are text files distributed via electronic mail or posted on a BBS; others are Web pages with extensive graphics and even sounds.

FAQ   Abbreviation for *frequently asked question*. FAQs are lists of frequently asked questions (and their answers) in a particular topic area. For instance, a Windows NT FAQ would help users understand the basics of using Windows NT by providing answers to common questions. Most mailing lists and network newsgroups regularly provide updated FAQs. It is important to read the FAQ for a particular newsgroup before beginning to post messages.

file   A named collection of **ASCII** or **binary** information stored on a disk or other storage device. Files include text, programs, databases, spreadsheets, graphics, and so on.

file server   A computer that provides storage space for files and applications that may be shared by network users.

file system   In an operating system such as Windows 95 or Windows NT, the structure used for storing, organizing, and naming files.

file transfer protocol   Any **protocol** for transferring files from one computer to another. A file transfer protocol usually includes provisions for making sure the data was transferred without errors and for resending any blocks of information that were corrupt.

filter   A facility for automatically organizing your received e-mail into separate folders. When your e-mail program retrieves messages that match criteria you've specified in a filter (for instance a particular name in the From header), it can automatically store those messages in a particular folder instead of your **inbox**. It can also delete the messages immediately.

finger   A UNIX program that lets you retrieve basic information about an Internet user or host. Finger is available via the Web at various sites.

firewall   Software and/or hardware that places an electronic barrier between an internal network and the Net, allowing only controlled access. This protects the network from access by the outside world and may also be used to monitor or limit the Internet activities of employees in an organization.

flag   A characteristic of a file that may restrict its use in particular ways. A file may be flagged read-only, for instance. Also, a special designation for an e-mail message. Flagged messages may be found quickly in a list of messages.

flame   A public message on any electronic forum, such as a **BBS** or online service, that personally attacks another user. Usually a flame is in response to an earlier message. If the user who has been flamed responds with another flame, or if other users jump into the fray, a "flame war" ensues. Flaming, though common in **Usenet** newsgroups, is generally considered an obnoxious waste of other users' time and of network bandwidth.

folder   A container that holds and organizes objects, typically files or other folders. On the desktop, a folder may represent a directory in the file system; other folders within it are equivalent to subdirectories.

font   A particular style for displayed or printed characters, including the shape, weight, slant, and so on.

font size   The size of a **font**; typically represented in units of measurement called *points*.

FQDN   *Fully Qualified Domain Name.* The full domain name of a computer on the Internet, including both the host name and the domain name. *See also* **domain-name address**.

frame   A portion of a Web browser window that may contain a different document from other frames within the same window.

frameset   An HTML page that contains several **frames**.

FTP   Abbreviation for *File Transfer Protocol*. A particular file transfer protocol that is common on the Internet. It is also used as a verb, as in, "FTP me that file, wouldya?"

full duplex   A communications link in which both ends can transmit data simultaneously, as in a telephone conversation. In situations where you are working interactively online, full duplex communication lets a remote host echo back to you each character you type so that you can see what you're writing as you work. *See also* **half duplex**.

FYI   *For Your Information.* A series of technical documents on various Internet-related topics, available at many public FTP sites. *See also* **RFC**.

gateway   A device or the software that links networks that use different protocols. For instance, a Novell network might have an Internet gateway that "packages" information into the **TCP/IP** packets required for Internet communication. The term *gateway* is also used in a very specialized sense to mean a program on a **World Wide Web** host that accepts and processes information sent by a Web client. For instance, a document on a **Web server** might display a form in which you can type your name; the gateway program would then enter your name in a database.

GIF   (Pronounced "jiff.") Abbreviation for *Graphic Interchange Format*. This is a format for compressed graphic files developed by CompuServe and Unisys.

Gopher   A menu-based client/server system for exploring information resources on the Internet. A Gopher client is seamlessly built into Web browsers, so you don't need a separate Gopher client program.

GopherSpace   All of the information presented by a **Gopher** server, in the form of directory and file menus.

grayed   *See* **dimmed**.

half duplex   A communications link in which both ends can transmit and receive data, but not at the same time. Half duplex communication is like two-way radio or CB, where only one person speaks at a time. In situations where you are working interactively online in half duplex, you will not see characters you type echoed to the screen unless you set your communications program to echo them locally. *See also* **full duplex**.

handle   An interface element added to an object to enable the user to move, resize, or reshape it.

handshaking   The initial negotiation and the exchange of control information between a **DCE** and a **DTE** or between two DTEs in a communications link. Handshaking is necessary to make sure both devices are ready to transfer data and can "understand" each other. *See also* **Data Carrier Detect; Data Terminal Ready; XOFF; XON**.

hardware handshake A protocol whereby a **DTE** tells the connected computer to start or stop sending data. Typically hardware handshaking is implemented by raising and lowering the voltage on the DTR (**Data Terminal Ready**) line in the cable that connects the **DTE** and **DCE**. *See also* **XOFF; XON**.

header Text within a Web page that indicates the main point of the document or of a section within it. Headers often use the specific HTML heading styles. *See also* **message header**.

helper applications Programs that a Web browser such as Netscape Navigator 3.0 uses to perform tasks such as displaying particular types of graphics, playing sounds, or initiating Telnet sessions.

history list In Netscape Navigator 3.0, the list of Web documents you've displayed during the current session.

home page The **HTML** document you choose to display when you open a **Web browser** such as Netscape Navigator 3.0. It may be located on your own hard drive or on a remote **Web server**. Home page can also refer to the top-level document at a particular Web site.

host computer A computer that a user can connect to in order to access information or run programs. A user may log in locally using a **terminal** or remotely using a computer and phone lines or the Internet.

host name The name clients use to access your Web server or other Internet server. For instance, your Web server's host name might be www.acme.com.

hotlist In a **Web browser**, a user-built list of frequently accessed **World Wide Web** sites. Also, an **HTML** document consisting of hotlinks to Web sites or other Internet resources.

HTML Abbreviation for *Hypertext Markup Language*. A "markup language" for indicating attributes and links in a Web document. An HTML **tag** may tell a Web browser program how to display a piece of text or a graphic, or it may direct the browser to another file or document.

HTML message An e-mail message formatted using **HTML** rather than **plain text**. Also sometimes referred to as a **rich text message**.

HTTP *Hypertext Transfer Protocol*. The **protocol** that World Wide Web **clients** and **servers** use to communicate with each other.

HTTPS A variant of HTTP that provides security for transferred documents.

hyperlink *See* **link**.

hypermedia **Hypertext** that also includes nontext information such as graphics, video, or sound.

hypertext Text that is organized by means of links, or jumps, from one piece of information to another. The reader can move among related topics by clicking on tagged words or phrases.

IAB—*Internet Architecture Board*. The organization that decides on Internet standards.

IBM Host on Demand An application of Communicator Professional that allows a Web browser to access mainframe data.

icon An image used to represent an object such as a file or program.

image map A graphic in a Web document that lets you click on certain portions in order to activate particular **URLs**. It has an associated map file that identifies these hot spots. *See also* **clickable image**.

IMAP *Internet Message Access Protocol.* A protocol that lets you access your e-mail messages on a remote server machine instead of retrieving them and viewing them on your own computer. The most common implementation of IMAP is IMAP4. It provides an alternative to **POP3** e-mail servers.

inactive window A window with which you are not currently interacting. Its title bar is not highlighted, and it receives no keyboard or mouse input. *See also* **active window**.

inbox In Netscape Messenger, the folder where new e-mail messages are stored by default after retrieval from a POP3 or IMAP server.

inline images Graphic images contained within **World Wide Web** documents. An inline image displays automatically as part of a document when it is retrieved; a non-inline image must be retrieved by clicking on a **link**.

intelligent agents *See* **agents**.

internet A larger network made up of two or more connected LANs (**local area networks**) or WANs (**wide area networks**).

Internet The huge worldwide Internet made up of cooperative networks and using **TCP/IP** protocols to offer a variety of services.

Internet access provider A business or organization that provides Internet access to consumers, often via dial-up **SLIP** or **PPP** connections. Also known as an **ISP**, or Internet service provider.

Internet address *See* **IP address**.

Internet presence provider—An Internet-connected business that provides equipment and services to customers without equipment or technical expertise.

Intranet A network of connected computers that uses the same protocols and provides many of the same services as the **Internet,** but which cannot be accessed by the public. For instance, a corporation may have an intranet for its employees.

IP address Also called *Internet address.* The unique address for each computer on the Internet. The IP address appears as a set of four numbers separated by periods.

ISDN *Integrated Services Digital Network.* The telecommunications standard that supports digital transmission of voice, video, and data over phone lines.

ISOC *Internet Society.* Organization that was formed to support a worldwide information network. The ISOC sponsors the **IAB**.

ISP *Internet Service Provider.* Another term for an **Internet access provider**.

IPP *See* **Internet Presence Provider**.

Java An object-oriented programming language developed by Sun Microsystems. It allows developers to create applications that may be run from within Web browsers such as Netscape Navigator 3.0.

JavaScript A set of commands that can be added to HTML files to add functionality to Web documents. JavaScript is useful for scrolling text, data validation in forms, etc.

JPEG A format for compressed graphics files. JPEG graphics are commonly used as part of **World Wide Web** documents.

kbyte *See* **kilobyte**.

kilobyte (K) 1024 (2^{10}) **bytes** of data. Thus, a 64K file consists of 65,536 bytes.

knowbot   A software program that can retrieve information from a variety of electronic sources when you give it a set of search parameters. Same as **agent**.

LAN   *See* **local area network**.

LDAP   *Lightweight Directory Access Protocol*. A protocol that lets individuals search directories on the Net or an intranet. *See also* **directory service**.

link   A special hidden **tag** in an HTML document on the Web. It includes the **URL** for another file or document, or for another anchor point within the same document. When you click a word, phrase, or graphic that's tagged as a link, Netscape Navigator 3.0 automatically retrieves the appropriate target.

list box   A control that displays a scrollable list of choices.

Live3D   Netscape's **VRML** technology.

LiveConnect   Netscape technology that allows Navigator plug-ins, Java applets, and JavaScript to communicate with each other.

local area network (LAN)   A group of computers connected together by cable or wireless transceivers so that users can share resources such as database files, programs, printers, and so on. *See also* **wide area network**.

log file   A file that is automatically generated by software, indicating events that occurred such as errors, attempts to access your server, etc.

log in   To identify yourself to a remote system or network by typing in your login name and password.

login name   The name you use for security verification when you call into a remote system.

login prompt   The prompt (usually *login:* or *name:*) a remote host uses to tell you it's ready for you to type in your login name.

logon script   A file containing simple commands that automate the process of logging on to a server, **SLIP** or **PPP** account, or other computer. In Windows NT, the files SWITCH.INF and MODEM.INF are logon scripts that automate the process of logging on to a remote machine using the **Remote Access Dialer**. In Windows 95, logon scripts generally have a .SCP extension and are associated with particular **Dial-Up Networking** connections using Microsoft's Dial-Up Scripting utility.

log off   To tell a remote host system or a network, using the appropriate commands, that you are terminating interaction. In many cases, logging off will also break the communications link to the remote machine.

log on   To tell a remote system or network, using the appropriate commands, that you are initiating a session.

mail headers   The informational fields at the beginning of every e-mail message, indicating sender, recipient, time and date sent, etc. Mail headers may not be visible in an e-mail program, but they are used by the program to organize messages.

mail host   An Internet or intranet server that sends e-mail for you and/or temporarily stores your incoming messages. A client program like Messenger sends e-mail via a mail host and retrieves new e-mail from a mail host.

mailing list   A list of e-mail addresses. Messages sent to the list are actually sent to every member of the list individually. Mailing lists are useful for disseminating information to established groups of individuals, or to subscribers who want ongoing information in a particular area of interest.

mailto link   A special kind of HTML **link** whose URL includes an e-mail address. When you click a mailto link, Communicator pops up a New Message window with the recipient's address already filled in. Mailto links are useful for soliciting response to a Web page.

maximize   To expand a window to its maximum size. *See also* **minimize**.

maximize button   The button used to maximize a window. In Windows 95 and Windows NT 4.0, it is the second button from the right in the title bar.

megabyte (MB)   1024 **kilobytes**, or 1,048,576 bytes.

menu bar   A horizontal bar at the top of a window (between the title bar and the rest of the window) that contains menu choices. *See also* **drop-down menu**.

menu button   A command button that displays a menu.

menu item   A choice on a menu.

message box   A window that appears to inform you of something, for instance that a connection has been established or that an error has occurred.

message area   The part of the main Messenger window that displays the actual contents of the currently selected e-mail message.

message body   The main content portion of an e-mail message, distinguished from the **mail headers**.

Message Center   In Communicator, the window that displays a list of e-mail and discussion group folders.

message flag   *See* **flag**.

Message List window   In Communicator, the window that displays a list of received e-mail and discussion group messages.

message status   How a message has been handled so far by the e-mail software and an individual recipient. For instance, a message's status may be new, unread, read, replied to, or forwarded.

message thread   *See* **thread**.

Message window   In Netscape Messenger and Collabra, the window that displays the actual contents of an e-mail or discussion message.

Messenger   The Communicator component that lets you send, retrieve, and organize e-mail messages.

MIME   *Multipurpose Internet Mail Extensions*. MIME is a convention for identifying different types of **binary** information, such as images or sounds, and thereby indicating the appropriate programs for viewing or playing this information. MIME is used in attaching binary files to e-mail messages so that they can be displayed or played automatically when received.

minimize   To minimize the size of a window; in some cases, this means to hide the window. *See also* **maximize**.

minimize button   The button used to minimize a window.

modem   Short for *modulator/demodulator*. A hardware device that connects your computer to other computers using analog telephone lines.

modem command   An instruction, typed from the keyboard or transmitted automatically by a software program, that tells a modem to perform some action. For instance, the command ATH0 tells a modem to hang up the line.

moderated discussion group   A discussion group that only includes messages that have been seen and approved by a discussion **moderator**.

moderator   An individual responsible for viewing and approving discussion group postings before they are made available to the group as a whole.

Mozilla   This word stands for "Mosaic meets Godzilla." It is the name for the early Netscape products and for the Netscape-specific extensions to the HTML language. It has also become the Netscape mascot. The word and the associated image appear frequently in Netscape products.

MPEG   *Moving Pictures Expert Group.* MPEG is a standard format for compressed video files, sometimes known as "desktop movies." MPEG files may be part of **World Wide Web** documents, but they require a special **helper application** for viewing.

MUDs and MOOs   Text-based multiuser interactive games, accessed using specialized software or via **Telnet**.

multiple selection list box   A special list box that's used for multiple independent selections.

multiuser system   An operating system, such as UNIX, that lets more than one user at a time access services.

My Computer   A Windows 95 and Windows NT 4.0 object (icon) that represents all of your local data storage.

Navigator   The Communicator component that lets you browse the Web or HTML documents on an intranet.

NCSA   *National Center for Supercomputing Applications.* NCSA is the department of the University of Illinois where the Web browser Mosaic was developed. Mosaic was the forerunner of all modern graphically based Web browsers.

Netcaster   The Communicator component that lets you display and configure **channels**.

netiquette   Proper behavior on the Net (derived from etiquette).

Netscape Security Advisor   A Communicator feature that helps you maintain and organize your digital keys and certificates, as well as showing you the security status of documents you access.

Netsite   The label for Navigator's Netsite/Location field when you accessing a Web site that uses one of Netscape's server programs.

network   A collection of interconnected computers. Each attached computer runs its own software processes, whereas in an unnetworked **multiuser system**, users run all processes on the central host computer and use terminals simply to interact. A network lets users share information as well as devices such as printers, disks, and modems.

network administrator   In an organization, the individual who is responsible for configuring and maintaining the network. This is the person to talk to if you have problems with a direct "hard-wired" connection to the Internet.

Network Neighborhood   A Windows 95 and Windows NT 4.0 folder that includes objects stored on a network file system.

New Message window In Messenger, the window that lets you compose, edit, and send e-mail and Collabra discussion group messages.

newsgroup A special forum that allows users to exchange messages (postings) in a particular area of interest. These messages are accessible by all members of the group. Some newsgroups, like the Usenet newsgroups, are accessible to the public; others, like those on Collabra servers, may be private.

news host The computer that stores discussion group messages and makes them available to all memebers of the group.

NFS *Network File System*. NFS is a set of protocols developed by Sun Microsystems for allowing computers running different operating systems to share files and disk storage.

NIC *Network Information Center*. The organization responsible for supplying information about the Internet.

NNTP *Network News Transport Protocol*. The protocol used by news hosts and client programs like Collabra to transfer discussion group messages over the Net or an intranet.

NNTP host *See* **news host**.

NOC *Network Operations Center*. The organization in charge of the day-to-day operations of a network on the Internet.

node Any computer or other device on a network that has its own unique network address.

NTFS A **file system** that can be used under Windows NT. It supports a variety of advanced features including system recovery.

object An entity that you manipulate in some way to perform a task. (Is that vague enough?) Typical objects are **icons** or **folders** on the **desktop**.

offline Not currently connected to a remote computer or a network; not currently on the Internet or office intranet.

online Currently connected to a remote computer or network.

option button A control that allows a user to select one choice from a set of mutually exclusive choices (also known as a *radio button*). *Compare* **check box**.

outbox In Messenger and similar e-mail client programs, the folder that stores outgoing messages before they are actually delivered. For instance, when you work **offline** any messages you compose are stored in the outbox until you go **online**.

packet A block of information that has been "packaged" with address information, error-checking information, and so on, for transmission on a **network** or on the **Internet**.

parameter A variable that affects the results of a command. For instance, in the command *dir /p, /* p is a parameter.

parity A crude system of error-checking used in data communications. For most scenarios these days, your communications software should be set to "no parity."

parsed HTML HTML files that are read and manipulated by separate software on a server machine after the server software has answered a client request for the document. Using parsed HTML, for instance, a program could customize a Web document based on who requested it. Parsed HTML is also known as server-parsed HTML and SHTML. Often HTML files that will be parsed end with the extension .SHTML instead of .HTML.

Perl   *Practical Extraction and Report Language.* A programming language first developed by Larry Wall for UNIX systems. Because of its power in pattern matching and in handling strings, it is often the language of choice for creating **CGI** programs.

personal certificate   A digital **encryption** certificate for which only you hold the decryption key. If you "sign" an e-mail message with your personal certificate, the recipient can then encrypt messages he or she sends you. *See also* **digital certificate**, **site certificate**.

pixel   The smallest unit of graphic information on a computer screen. Graphic images are usually measured in pixels, and a pair of pixel coordinates can indicate an exact point within an image.

plain text   Text that doesn't contain any special formatting such as HTML tags.

plain-text message   In Messenger, an e-mail message that contains HTML tags and that hasn't been encrypted or encoded.

plug-in   Software programs that extends the capabilities of Netscape Navigator. For instance, a plug-in may let you view PostScript files right within the browser window.

PNG   *Portable Network Graphics.* A standard for highly compressed graphics files that may include trillions of colors, multiple layers of transparency, and searchable text information.

POP   *Point of Presence.* The local dial-up node an Internet access provider makes available for its customers.

POP3   *Post Office Protocol, version 3.* The protocol used by Netscape Navigator 3.0 and other e-mail programs to retrieve messages from your e-mail server. *See also* **SMTP, IMAP**.

pop-up menu   A menu that appears right at the location of a selected object (sometimes called a *shortcut menu*). The menu contains items related to the selection.

pop-up window   A window with no title bar that appears next to an object and provides information about that object.

port   (1) A hardware connector on the back panel of a computer where you can plug in a serial, parallel, or network **cable**. (2) A unique number assigned to a particular Internet **service** on a host machine. For instance, most **MUDs** and **MOOs** require that you Telnet to a host using a specific port different from the standard Telnet port number. You can usually specify a port number as part of an Internet address, as in *lambda.parc.xerox.com 8888*.

POTS   *Plain Old Telephone Service.* What it sounds like; the current analog phone system, as distinguished from ISDN and other digital technologies.

PPP   *Point-to-Point Protocol.* This is a protocol that lets a computer link to the **Internet** by calling in to a service provider using a modem and a standard telephone line.

properties   Characteristics of an object defining its state, appearance, or value. Often used to mean a program's settings.

property inspector   A viewer that displays the properties of the current selection.

protocol   A set of rules for interaction between software programs on a network. Protocols may include requirements for formatting data, for passing control information back and forth, and for error checking.

proxy   A server that allows communication with the outside world (for instance the Internet) through a **firewall**. When a client behind a firewall requests a specific Internet service, the request actually goes to the proxy, which then relays it on.

public-key encryption   An **encryption** method that requires two unique software keys (one public and one private) for decrypting the data, making it secure across public networks. Pretty Good Privacy (PGP) is a well-known public-key encryption system.

query string   The word or phrase you pass to a Web search engine.

QuickTime   A multimedia file format developed by Apple. It is often used for video clips or "movies."

quoted-printable   A **MIME** type for binary data that has been specially encoded to seven-bit ASCII text so it can be transmitted across a variety of networks. The recipient's software must then decode it back to binary data.

radio button   *See* **option button**.

random access memory (RAM)   Computer memory that temporarily stores information; for instance, software code that you've loaded by launching a program or data that you're processing. Generally, the more of it, the better!

read-only memory (ROM)   Computer memory containing data that cannot be changed by the user and that remains even when the computer is turned off. ROM is used for storing your computer's BIOS, for instance, which is the code that lets you boot up and that performs a variety of low-level functions.

refresh   In Netscape Web browsers such as Navigator 3.0, the command that reloads a document into the browser window from a disk or memory **cache**.

regedit   A program in Windows 95 for editing the **configuration registry**. In Windows NT this program is called regedt32.

registry   *See* **configuration registry**.

reload   In Netscape Web browsers such as Navigator 3.0, the command that reloads a document into the browser window from its original local or remote source.

remote   Any system that you can connect to by using only communications devices rather than just local wiring.

Remote Access Dialer   A Windows NT program for connecting via ordinary phone lines or **ISDN** to a remote computer, often used for **SLIP** or **PPP** connectivity.

remote computer   A computer you link to via telephone lines, satellite, or other communication links.

resolution   The density of an image, expressed in dots per inch.

restore button   The button that replaces the maximize button once a window has been maximized. It lets you return the window to the size it was before maximizing.

reverse lookup   The process of looking up the domain name of an Internet-connected computer when all that's known is the numeric IP address. For instance, you may have a numeric IP address assigned by a **SLIP** or **PPP** access provider, but no associated domain name. When you try to log in to certain security-conscious FTP sites, the host software looks up your domain name via DNS reverse lookup. If it can't find one, you are not allowed on the system. *See also* **domain-name address**.

RFC   *Request for Comments*. An RFC is a proposal or report electronically distributed via the Internet, usually for the purpose of elucidating or helping to define a new Internet technical standard.

rich text   Text that contains HTML or other special formatting. *See also* **plain text**.

rich-text message   A message that includes encoded, encrypted, or HTML-formatted content. *See also* **plain text message**.

robot   *See* **spider**.

root directory   The top-level **directory** on a disk such as your hard drive. For example, C:\ would be the root directory of your C: drive.

RS-232   The standard used by your serial port. RS-232 lines are the individual pins and wires that make up the hardware interface, such as the send data line, the receive data line, and the various hardware handshaking (or hardware flow control) lines.

RTF   *Rich Text Format*. A file format that can be read by many word processing programs across all platforms.

RTS/CTS   *Ready to Send/Clear to Send*. In an RS-232 serial port, the two lines that allow two devices to signal each other when they are ready to send or receive data. This process is known as **hardware handshaking** or hardware flow control. *See also* **RS-232**.

script   A software program that doesn't need to be compiled. It is run by another program "as is," in human-readable form. *See also* **logon script**.

scroll bar   The control that lets you move the image or text within a window either horizontally or vertically to view data that is not currently visible.

search engine   A program on the Net that lets users search for online information. Typical search engines include Infoseek and Alta Vista, both available from Netscape's Search page.

security key   A special file that is needed in order to access a secure document. *See also* **public key encryption**.

server   A computer or a program that provides a particular service on a network or on the Internet. Typical services include file access, printing, e-mail, **FTP**, and so on. The computers and software that access servers are called **clients**.

server push   A technique specific to Netscape products whereby a Web server can initiate the transmission of data to the Web **client**. Server push is often used for animation or sound. *See also* **client pull**.

server write key   The software key used to encrypt data written or transmitted by the server in a **client/server** system. *See also* **client write key**.

service   A specialized function or utility provided by a **server**.

service provider   An organization, usually commercial, that provides connections to the Internet.

session   A connection between two machines on a network or on the Internet.

SGML   *Standard Generalized Markup Language*. A high-level standard for the electronic publication of information. **HTML** is a subset of SGML.

shell account   An account with an access provider that lets you access a text-based system for performing routine Internet tasks. You connect to a shell account via Telnet or a dial-up terminal emulation program. Some Internet access providers let you put your own Web pages on their server using a shell account.

shortcut   A desktop icon that can be used as a quick way to launch a program or document. Another word for *hotlink* in a WWW document.

SHTML   *See* **parsed HTML**.

signature   A text file that contains any information that you want to attach regularly to your e-mail messages and network news posts. A signature is usually less than five lines long and contains contact information.

single selection list box   A list box that lets you choose only a single item from a list.

site certificate   A **digital certificate** that lets you send an encrypted message to all recipients at a particular site. *See* **digital certificate**, **personal certificate**.

slider   A control that displays a continuous range of values and lets you choose one.

SLIP   *Serial Line Internet Protocol*. Like **PPP**, this is a protocol that lets a computer link to the Internet by calling in to a service provider using a modem and a standard telephone line.

S-MIME   *Secure Multipurpose Internet Mail Extension*. A secure version of **MIME**, useful for insuring e-mail privacy.

SMTP   *Simple Mail Transfer Protocol*. The most common protocol for sending e-mail messages over the Internet. *See also* **POP3**.

snail mail   A form of messaging that utilizes carbon-based materials to create and address human-readable data, which is then transmitted over a complex network of streets and air routes by human entities known as "postal employees."

snews   Part of a domain address indicating a secure news (discussion group) server. For example, snews.whatever.com would be a secure news server, while messages on news.whatever.com would not be automatically encrypted.

sockets   A software mechanism that allows programs to communicate locally or remotely by setting up endpoints for sending and receiving data. The application programmer does not have to worry about the nuts-and-bolts details of how the data travels from one point to the other, as that is taken care of by the operating system or other resident software. The Windows Sockets API (**Winsock**) uses this concept.

SOCKS   A protocol that lets a host server on an internal network access the Web through a **firewall**.

spam   Unsolicited messages that are sent to many e-mail recipients or posted in several discussion groups. Spam is an aggressive electronic version of junk mail and is considered an egregious violation of **netiquette**.

spider   A program that wanders around the Web looking for new content. Links to new sites that it finds may then be added to large directory documents such as Yahoo. Spiders are also known as robots, wanderers, crawlers, and WebCrawlers.

spin box   A control that displays a limited range of values and lets you choose one.

SSL   *Secure Sockets Layer*. A version of the **HTTP** protocol that includes encryption. SSL allows for the secure transfer of sensitive information across the Net, as in financial transactions.

string   Geek-speak for a set of characters. Your name, for instance, is a string.

symbolic link A name that does not refer to an actual object but points to another name. For instance, on an FTP site, a directory list might include the entry WINDOWS, even though there is no WINDOWS directory at this level. The WINDOWS entry could be a symbolic link to a directory buried much deeper in the file system, such as /pub/micro/pc/GUI/windows. Symbolic links provide convenient shortcuts to actual objects.

synchronous transmission A method of transmitting data that uses a special timing signal to ensure a set time interval between any two characters. *See also* **asynchronous transmission**.

tag A special code used in an **HTML** document to indicate how a piece of text or a graphic should be displayed by a Web browser; it may also establish a **link** to another document.

target The reference the browser "jumps to" when a user clicks on a link. The word is usually used for references within the same document.

TCP/IP *Transmission Control Protocol/Internet Protocol.* TCP/IP is a set of protocols that applications use for communicating across networks or over the Internet. These protocols specify how packets of data should be constructed, addressed, checked for errors, and so on.

Telnet A program that lets you log in to a remote **host computer** and access its data and services as if you were using a text-based **terminal** attached locally.

terminal A keyboard and display screen used to access a **host computer**.

terminal emulation A software program that lets you use a personal computer to communicate with a **host computer**. It transmits special commands and interprets incoming data as if it were a terminal directly connected to the host.

text box A control that lets you enter and edit text.

text file *See* **ASCII file**.

text-only Containing no visual information other than human-readable **ASCII** text. When you **Telnet** into a UNIX system, for instance, your user interface is text-only, as distinguished from the graphical user interface of systems like Windows.

thread A software process or task. Operating systems like Windows 95 and Windows NT allow for many threads to occur simultaneously.

title bar The horizontal bar at the top of a window that includes the window name. The title bar also acts as a handle that can be used to drag the window.

title bar icon The small icon at the top-left corner of the title bar. You can use it to display the pop-up menu. Double-clicking this icon closes the program.

TN3270 Protocol and **terminal emulation** used to make a Telnet connection to IBM mainframe systems. Using TN3270, your computer behaves like a 3270 terminal rather than the VT100 usually used in standard Telnet connections.

toolbar A control that provides a defined area for a set of other controls such as icon buttons, drop-down list boxes, and so on.

traffic Data traveling across a network or across the Internet.

tree control A control that lets you display a set of hierarchical objects in an expandable outline format.

upload To send a file to a remote system; the opposite of **download**.

URL   *Uniform Resource Locator.* A URL is a specially formatted address that a Web browser uses to locate, retrieve, and display a document. The URL includes the Internet address of the data, where it is located on the Web server machine, and what kind of transport protocol is required to retrieve it. URLs are contained in the **hotlinks** within **HTML** documents; they may also be specified by the user of a Web browser "on the fly."

Usenet   A large collection of networked users who communicate using the UNIX-to-UNIX Copy Protocol (UUCP) rather than **TCP/IP**. Usenet is connected to the Internet by gateways, and many Internet users are familiar with its broad range of discussion forums known as newsgroups.

UUCP   *UNIX to UNIX copy.* An older set of network commands for sending and receiving data on dial-up networks.

Uuencoding   A standard for encoding binary data that allows it to be transmitted as 7-bit ASCII information; it is then *UUDECODED* into its original binary form.

VCard   *See* **Address Book Card**.

virtual server   A server that appears like a separate server to clients, but which actually runs on the same machine and uses the same server software as other servers. For instance, the Netscape FastTrack server lets you set up www.server1.com, www.server2.com, and www.server3.com all at once. Somebody logging onto www.server2.com would access different information from somebody logging onto www.server1.com.

VRML   *Virtual Reality Modeling Language.* VRML is a specialized language that allows for the creation of three-dimensional user interfaces that can be accessed via Web browsers such as Netscape Navigator 3.0.

WAIS   *Wide-Area Information Server.* WAIS is a specialized Internet client/server system for re-searching information in Internet databases.

WAN   *See* **wide area network**.

wanderer   *See* **spider**.

Web   Short for **World Wide Web**.

Web browser   A program for retrieving and viewing **HTML** documents on the **World Wide Web**. Also known as a Web **client**.

WebCrawler   *See* **spider**.

Web document   Any document available on the **World Wide Web**.

Webmaster   The individual in charge of developing or administering a Web site.

Web server   A computer that stores Web documents and allows **Web browsers** to retrieve them over the Internet using the **HTTP** protocol. Also, the software that makes this possible.

Webtop   A Netcaster **channel** that's anchored to the desktop and often used as a primary user interface. Other channels may appear within the Webtop.

wide area network   A group of computers and/or networks connected to one another by means of long-distance communication devices such as telephone lines and satellites, rather than just through local wiring. *See also* **local area network**.

widget   In HTML geek-speak, an object in a Web document that accepts user input. Examples are check boxes, radio buttons, drop-down lists, and so on.

wildcard character   A character used when you specify a filename; it is a variable that stands for any other valid character or characters. The question mark (?) stands for a single character, while the asterisk (*) stands for any string of characters in the filename. For instance, *.*txt* means "any file that has the .TXT extension"; *??.txt* means "any file that has a two-letter name and the .TXT extension."

Windows NT Server   The version of the Windows NT operating system that provides centralized network management and security as well as additional connectivity options.

Windows NT Workstation   The version of the Windows NT operating system that provides operating and networking functionality, but without centralized management.

Winsock   *Windows Sockets API.* A software "toolkit" that lets Windows programmers access **TCP/IP** services using a standard interface. Any Internet programs that use this standard, such as e-mail clients, Web browsers, and so on, will work under Windows 95 and Windows NT.

workgroup   On Microsoft networks, a collection of grouped computers with a unique name.

workstation   In Windows NT, a computer running the **Windows NT Workstation** software.

World Wide Web (WWW)   An Internet service used for browsing hypermedia documents; the "Internet within the Internet" formed by all the Web servers and **HTML** documents currently online.

WYSIWYG   *What You See Is What You Get.* A description of data that already looks like the final output as you work on it. For instance, a WYSIWYG HTML editor like Composer lets you move graphic elements around the page rather than typing in HTML code.

XOFF   A special character that's used to control the flow of information between a **DCE** and a **DTE**. When one device receives an XOFF character from the other, it stops transmitting until it receives an **XON**.

XON   A special character used to control the flow of data between a **DCE** and a **DTE**. *See also* **XOFF**.

Index

VENTANA

Official Netscape Communicator Book

$39.99, 800 pages
Beginning to Intermediate
Windows Edition: part #: 1-56604-617-3
Macintosh Edition: part #:1-56604-620-3

The sequel to Ventana's blockbuster international bestseller *Official Netscape Navigator Book*! Discover the first suite to integrate key intranet and Internet communications services into a single, smart interface. From simple e-mail to workgroup collaboration, from casual browsing to Web publishing, from reading text to receiving multimedia Netcaster channels—learn to do it all without leaving Communicator! Covers:

- All Communicator components: Navigator, Netcaster, Messenger, Collabra, Composer and Conference.
- Complete, step-by-step instructions for both intranet and Internet task.
- Tips on using plug-ins, JavaScript and Java applets.

The CD-ROM includes a fully-supported version of Netscape Communicator plus hyperlinked listings.

Official Netscape Communicator Professional Edition Book

$39.99, 608 pages, part #:1-56604-739-0

Windows Edition • Intermediate

Your Guide to Business Communications Over the Intranet & the Web! Unlock the immeasurable potential of Web technologies for improving and enhancing day-to-day business tasks. Netscape Communicator and your office intranet provide the tools and the environment. This easy-to-use, step-by-step guide opens the door to each key module—and its most effective use. Covers:

- Navigator 4, Messenger, Collabra, Conference, Composer, Calendar, Netcaster and AutoAdmin.
- Key business tasks: e-mail, workgroups, conferencing and Web publishing.
- Step-by-step instructions, tips and guidelines for working effectively.

VENTANA

Official Online Marketing With Netscape Book

$34.99, 544 pages, illustrated, part #: 1-56604-453-7

The perfect marketing tool for the Internet! Learn how innovative marketers create powerful, effectove electronic newsletters and promotional materials. Step-by-step instructions show you how to plan, deisgn and distribute professional-quality pieces. With this easy-to-follow guide, you'll soon be flexing Netscape Navigator's marketing muscle to eliminate paper and printing costs, automate market research and customer service, and much more.

Official Netscape Guide to Online Investments

$24.99, 528 pages, illustrated, part #: 1-56604-452-9

Gain the Internet investment edge! Here's everything you need to make the Internet a full financial partner. Features an overview of the Net and Navigator; in-depth reviews of stock and bond quote services, analysts, brokerage houses, and mutual fund reports. Plus a full listing of related financial services such as loans, appraisals, low-interest credit cards, venture capital, entrepreneurship, insurance, tax counseling, and more.

Official Netscape Guide to Internet Research

$29.99, 480 pages, illustrated, part #: 1-56604-604-1

Turn the Internet into your primary research tool. More than just a listing of resources, this official guide provides everything you need to know to access, organize, cite and post information on the Net. Includes research strategies, search engines and information management. Plus timesaving techniques for finding the best, most up-to-date data.

VENTANA

Official Netscape Messenger & Collabra Book

$39.99, 408 pages, part #: 1-56604-685-8

Windows, Macintosh • Intermediate to Advanced

The Power of Web-based Communications—Without a Web Site!
Stay in touch with customers; promote products and services visually; share the latest market trends—with simple Internet dial-up access! This step-by-step guide helps you harness Netscape Communicator's e-mail, newsreader, HTML authoring and real-time conference tools to achieve faster, more powerful business communications—without the effort or expense of a Web site. Learn how to:
- Integrate Messenger, Collabra, Conference and Composer for efficient business communications.
- Distribute eye-catching, HTML-based marketing materials without a Web site.
- Use the Net to gather, organize and share information efficiently.

Official Netscape Composer Book

$39.99, 600 pages, part #: 1-56604-674-2

Windows • Beginning to Intermediate

Forget about tedious tags and cumbersome code! Now you can create sophisticated, interactive Web pages using simple, drag-and-drop techniques. Whether you want to create your personal home page, promote your hobby, or launch your business on the Web, here's everything you need to know to get started:
- Step-by-step instructions for designing sophisticated Web sites with no previous experience.
- JavaScript basics and techniques for adding multimedia, including animation and interactivity.
- Tips for businesses on the Web, including creating forms, ensuring security and promoting a Web site.

The CD-ROM features a wide selection of Web tools for designing Web pages, adding multimedia, creating forms and building image maps.

Official Netscape Plug-in Book, Second Edition

$39.99, 700 pages, part #: 1-56604-612-2

Windows, Macintosh • All Users

Your One-Stop Plug-in Resource & Desktop Reference!
Why waste expensive online time searching the Net for the plug-ins you want? This handy one-stop reference includes in-depth reviews, easy-to-understand instructions and step-by-step tutorials. And you avoid costly download time—the hottest plug-ins are included! Includes:
- In-depth reviews & tutorials for most Netscape plug-ins.
- Professional tips on designing pages with plug-ins.
- Fundamentals of developing your own plug-ins.

The CD-ROM includes all the featured plug-ins available at press time.

VENTANA

Microsoft Windows NT 4 Workstation Desktop Companion

$39.99, 1016 pages, illustrated, part #: 1-56604-472-3

Workstation users become masters of their own universe with this step-by-step guide. Covers file management, customizing and optimizing basic multimedia, OLE, printing and networking. Packed with shortcuts, secrets, productivity tips and hands-on tutorials. The CD-ROM features dozens of valuable utilities and demos for Windows NT. Innovative web-site designs, reference information, wallpaper textures, animated cursors, custom utilities and more.

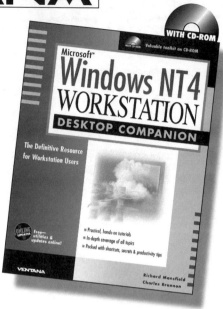

Microsoft Office 95 Companion

$34.95, 1136 pages, illustrated, part #: 1-56604-188-0

The all-in-one reference to Microsoft's red-hot suite is a worthy sequel to Ventana's bestselling *Windows, Word & Excel Office Companion*. Covers basic commands and features, and includes a section on using Windows 95. The companion disk features examples, exercises, software and sample files from the book.

SmartSuite Desktop Companion

$24.95, 784 pages, illustrated, part #: 1-56604-184-8

Here's "Suite success" for newcomers to the critics' choice of business packages. This introduction to the individual tools and features of Lotus' star software packages—1-2-3, Ami Pro, Approach, Freelance Graphics and Organizer—has been updated for the latest versions. Features new enhancements for Windows 95. The companion disk features sample exercises and files that follow the lessons in the book.

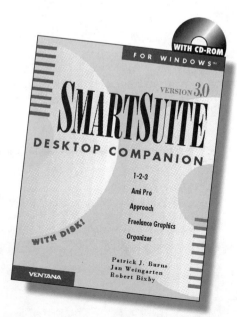

The Comprehensive Guide to SmartSuite 97

James Meade
$34.99, 528 pages, illustrated, part #: 1-56604-651-3

Here's Suite relief for business users at all levels. Step by step, learn to use applications together, work collaboratively, and maximize Internet and intranet connectivity. Packed with tips and shortcuts.

For Windows 95/NT • Beginning to Intermediate

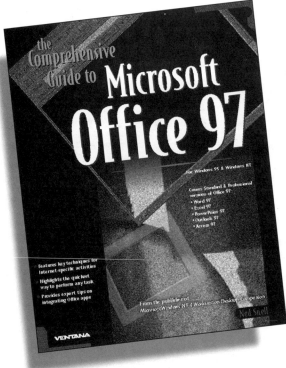

The Comprehensive Guide to Microsoft Office 97

Ned Snell
$39.99, 848 pages, illustrated, part #: 1-56604-646-7

The "right-size" guide to the world's hottest suite! Easy enough for beginners, yet in-depth enough for power users. Covers all five applications, plus tips, shortcuts, Internet techniques and more.

For Windows 95/NT • Beginning to Intermediate

VENTANA

Official HTML Publishing for Netscape, Second Edition

$39.99, 800 pages, part #: 1-56604-650-5

Windows 95/NT, Macintosh • Intermediate

Make the Most of the Latest Netscape Features!
Learn how the latest developments in Netscape Navigator and HTML enhance your ability to deliver eye-catching, interactive Web pages to a broad audience, and how to harness new technologies to create a compelling site. Includes:

• Playing to Navigator's hottest features, including tables, frames, plug-ins and support for Java applets.
• Guidelines for designing great Web pages.
• New material on style sheets, sound, multimedia and databases.

The CD-ROM contains an example Web site on the Net, sample JavaScript, clip objects, backgrounds and more.

Official Netscape JavaScript 1.2 Book, Second Edition

$29.99, 520 pages, part #: 1-56604-675-0

All platforms • Beginning to Intermediate

Brew up instant scripts—even if you're not a programmer!
Learn all the skills you need to perk up your Web pages with multimedia and interactivity. Fully updated for Netscape Communicator, this bestseller now includes:

• Basic programming techniques.
• Tips for using existing scripts and building your own from scratch.
• Nearly 200 script samples and interactive tutorials online.

Official Netscape FastTrack Server Book

$39.99, 600 pages, part #: 1-56604-483-9

Windows NT • Intermediate to Advanced

Turn your PC into an Internet/intranet powerhouse!
This step-by-step guide to the hottest server software on the Net provides all the instructions you need to launch your Internet or intranet site, from technical requirements to content creation and administration. Learn how to exploit FastTrack Server's high-performance server architecture to easily create and manage customized web sites. Plus, enhance your site with FTP and Telnet; ensure security for online transactions; and import and convert documents.

To order any Ventana title, complete this order form and mail or fax it to us, with payment, for quick shipment.

TITLE	PART #	QTY	PRICE	TOTAL

SHIPPING

For orders shipping within the United States, please add $4.95 for the first book, $1.50 for each additional book.
For "two-day air," add $7.95 for the first book, $3.00 for each additional book.
Email: vorders@kdc.com for exact shipping charges.
Note: Please include your local sales tax.

Subtotal = $ _____

Shipping = $ _____

Tax   = $ _____

Total   = $ _____

Mail to: International Thomson Publishing • 7625 Empire Drive • Florence, KY 41042
☎ **US orders 800/332-7450 • fax 606/283-0718**
☎ **International orders 606/282-5786 • Canadian orders 800/268-2222**

Name _____

E-mail _____ Daytime phone _____

Company _____

Address (No PO Box) _____

City _____ State_____ Zip_____

Payment enclosed ____VISA ____MC ____ Acc't # _____ Exp. date_____

Signature _____ Exact name on card _____

Check your local bookstore or software retailer for these and other bestselling titles, or call toll free:

800/332-7450
8:00 am - 6:00 pm EST

Technical support for installation related issues only provided by Ventana.
The Ventana technical support office is open from 8:00 A.M. to 6:00 P.M. (EST)
Monday through Friday and can be reached via the following methods:

World Wide Web: http://www.netscapepress.com/support

E–mail: help@vmedia.com

Phone: (919) 544-9404 extension 81

FAX: (919) 544-9472

America Online: keyword **Ventana**